To Steve —

Best regards, and thank
you again for your encouragement
and assistance.

INTERNATIONAL ENVIRONMENTAL LAW:

Basic Instruments and References

By
Edith Brown Weiss
Daniel Barstow Magraw
Paul C. Szasz

 Transnational Publishers, Inc.

Library of Congress Cataloging-in-Publication Data

Weiss, Edith Brown, 1942-
International environmental law : basic instruments and references
/ by Edith Brown Weiss, Daniel Barstow Magraw, Paul C. Szasz.
p. cm.
Includes index.
ISBN 0-941320-68-5 : $75.00
1. Environmental law, International. I. Magraw, Daniel Barstow.
II. Szasz, Paul C. III. Title.
K3583.W45 1991
341.7'62--dc20

91-718

CIP

This book is dedicated
to our spouses - Chuck, Cindy, and Frances

TABLE OF CONTENTS

ACKNOWLEDGMENTS

The authors wish to express their appreciation to the many individuals and organizations who have assisted in the preparation and publication of this book. These persons are too numerous to allow us to mention them all by name. We would like to offer our thanks expressly to several persons who have been unusually helpful. Mary Brandt, Hugo Caminos, Antônio Cançado Trindade, David Caron, Kevin Chu, Karen Davidson, Barbara J. Lausche, Charlie Lambert, Stephen McCaffrey, Thomas Mensah, Gerald Moore, James Nafziger, Marlene J. O'Dell, W. Paatii Ofuso-Amaah, Richard Reisert, Charles Renfrew, Seymour Rubin, Andrei D. Terekhov, and Michael Walls provided copies of or information about specific instruments. Pravakar Adhikari, Alexandra Andrews, Deborah Dufty, Gwen Fleener, Jeffrey Gordon, Anita Halvorssen, Mary Lee, Valeria Neale, Anna Paiewonsky, Steve Porter, Rebecca Raines, Dana Rose, Mary Scherschel, Paul Schmidt, Joaquin Taesan, and Janet Waidley provided invaluable research assistance in compiling instruments and references. The library personnel and secretarial staffs at the University of California (Berkeley), the University of Colorado, Georgetown University Law Center, the National Center for Atmospheric Research, and the United Nations, as well as the United Nations Treaty Section and the depositaries for the international agreements reproduced herein, assisted us in essential ways. Margaret A. Hanley of the United Nations designed, and Kenneth Mathews of the University of California Law School at Berkeley revised, a most useful computer program to facilitate the preparation of the list of international environmental instruments. We would also like to thank the American Law Institute and the International Law Association for permitting us to reproduce instruments herein. Finally, our families provided support throughout the preparation of this volume, for which we are deeply grateful.

INTRODUCTION

This collection of international environmental instruments and related references is intended to serve as a primary source for those researching or otherwise working in this area. The motivation for preparing a primary source book and reference tool stems from two facts—the difficulty in obtaining the texts of certain types of legal instruments, and the vast amount and variety of materials directly related to international environmental issues. At a time when these issues are increasingly prevalent and important, it is often difficult to know about and locate instruments related to a particular problem. Moreover, in spite of the publication of several specialized collections of environmental instruments,[1] the publication of environmental instruments in law journals and commercial services,[2] and the resumption, in loose-leaf form, of the massive compendium by Mssrs. Rüster, Simma and Bock,[3] there is no convenient, broad-based, up-to-date compilation of basic international environmental instruments. Nor is there any comprehensive reference list of such instruments. Hopefully, this book will fill these lacunae.

Eighty-five instruments are reproduced in whole or in part in the Instruments portion of this book. Those and approximately 800 other instruments (plus amendments) are referenced in the List of International Environmental Instruments. We have been expansive in providing parallel citations, bearing in mind that access to particular sources varies considerably. We have also provided status and other information about the instruments reproduced. Finally, for some instruments, we have cited literature that discusses the specific provisions of those instruments, to facilitate research. We did not attempt to provide general bibliographies; many excellent sources exist that we do not reference.

Instruments and references are organized by subject matter, according to four major categories with thirty-three chapters. The four categories are: General Principles, Protection of Particular Resources, Protection Against Particular Threats, and Techniques of Environmental Protection. Within the larger chapters there are subdivisions, sometimes at several levels, usually arranged from the most general—e.g., in a geographic sense—to the most specific. Thus, documents that relate globally or without geographic restriction are reproduced or referred to before any

---

[1]E.g., P. Sand, *Marine Environmental Law in the United Nations Environment Programme* (Tycooly 1988); P. Sands, *Chernobyl: Law and Communication* (Grotius 1988); S. Lyster, *International Wildlife Law* (Grotius 1985); G. Timagenis, *International Control of Marine Pollution* (Oceana 1980).

[2]E.g., *International Legal Materials* (published by the American Society of International Law); *Environmental Law and Policy* (published by the International Union for the Conservation of Nature and Natural Resources); *International Environment Reporter* (published by the Bureau of National Affairs); UNEP Reference Series 3, *Selected Multilateral Treaties in the Field of the Environment* (A. C. Kiss ed. 1983) (the United Nations Environment Programme plans to publish a second volume of instruments).

[3]*International Protection of the Environment: Treaties and Related Documents* [1754-1981] (Oceana: B. Rüster, B. Simma & M. Bock eds., Vols. I-XXX 1975-82, plus Index Vol. 1983); *International Protection of the Environment: Treaties and Related Documents*—Second Series [1981-1988] (Oceana: B. Rüster & B. Simma eds. 1990) (looseleaf binders).

regional documents on the same topic. Similarly, regional, bilateral, and municipal documents are arranged in that order. Regions are arranged alphabetically (*e.g.*, Africa, Americas, Antarctica, Asia, Europe, Oceana). Oceans (in Chapter 4) are listed alphabetically, followed by various seas. Within the subdivisions, documents and references are presented chronologically, except that dependent instruments (*i.e.*, a treaty and its amendments or protocols) are listed together. If an instrument appropriately belongs in more than one category (*e.g.*, it refers to a particular resource, a particular threat, and a particular means of protection), it may be referred to more than once in the List of International Environmental Instruments; but it has not proven possible to list under each category all instruments with only one or a few provisions relating to that category. However, if the text of an instrument (or a part thereof) is included in the book, it is reproduced only once.

Aside from the above-mentioned logical order in which the instruments are arranged, we included an alphabetical index containing the popular names of instruments, their formal names, and the page numbers (if any) on which they are reproduced. Our experience is that even persons generally familiar with international environmental law are sometimes left adrift by the short popular names of environmental instruments. A chronological list of the instruments reproduced in this book and a subject-matter list of those instruments are included, immediately before the reproductions. No other index is contained because the structure of the List of International Environmental Instruments itself constitutes a subject index (that organizational structure is set forth immediately before the List itself).

In deciding which instruments to include in the List of International Environmental Instruments, we needed, of course, to be selective. A threshold question was how restrictively to define "environmental." We have excluded general health matters, occupational safety, and food and drug labelling and additives; these are important areas, but not at the core of environmental protection. We included military activities that have enduring environmental impacts. We only selectively included other military activities; the presence of flying bullets is not healthy for living things, but that presence does not have long-lasting environmental effects, such as those resulting from nuclear testing or warfare. We excluded most scientific research agreements. We included the treatment of animals. We also included cultural heritage because we consider culture to be an important part of the human environment.

We were still faced with far more instruments than could be published here. With respect to deciding which instruments to reproduce, our first priority was to include universal documents of enduring importance. Beyond those, we selected significant instruments that are constrained geographically, instruments that are important for historical reasons, or instruments that are examples of significant types of regimes. Occasionally, we summarized an instrument because of its importance (*e.g.*, as part of a regime) even though there was not room to reproduce it. We included only the most important multilateral instruments regarding cultural heritage. For human rights, we included only the most important international instruments that are relevant to the environment. Although many national constitutions provide environmental rights,[4] extracts from only the Namibian one are reproduced, because of the international genesis of that instrument. Regarding international rivers and boundaries, we included only those instruments that contain provisions protecting the environment.[5]

The instruments referenced or reproduced herein include many that have, have had, or are intended to have (on entry into force) a binding effect, as well as others that are merely programmatic declarations or non-binding recommendations or guidelines. Except as stated later in this Introduction, we have found it impractical to, and therefore have not attempted to, indicate whether or not a particular instrument has binding force, and for what entities. It should be recognized that States that had (or whose predecessors had) entered into an agreement many years ago may currently differ as to its continued force, and also that some basically non-binding guidelines may be incorporated into binding international agreements or national legislation.

In deciding whether to reproduce all or only part of an instrument, we reproduced an instrument fully only if it deals entirely with environmental protection. Even for such instruments, we frequently deleted the so-called final clauses (which deal with administrative matters), unless they are of particular interest. With respect to instruments that are not focussed on environmental protection, we reproduced only those portions that relate specifically or directly to the environment.

Obviously, these are not crystal-clear guidelines; intuition and judgment often were involved. We welcome suggestions regarding both the contents of the List of International Environmental Instruments and the selection of reproduced instruments.

The citations follow *A Uniform System of Citation* (14th ed.) to the extent possible. Either as required by space constraints or to improve comprehensibility, however, we adopted abbreviations different than those called for in that publication. A list of abbreviations appearing herein is provided immediately following this Introduction.

Regarding the dates in citations, we used the date of an international agreement that is commonly used (if there is one), which normally is the date it was opened for signature. Usually, but not always, that is the same as the date the instrument was concluded (finalized). For instruments (other than agreements) that originated in a conference, we used the last date of a conference.

In addition to the citations, this book contains basic information about each of the instruments that are reproduced herein. This information appears immediately preceding the text of the instrument, in the following sequence:

TITLE: This entry provides an English-language title for each instrument. Most instruments, however, do not have an official title. We selected what we believe to

---

[4]Some national constitutions, such as Chile's, contain provisions that make environmental rights enforceable. For a list of constitutional provisions on environmental rights and duties, *see* E. Brown Weiss, *In Fairness to Future Generations: International Law, Common Patrimony, and Intergenerational Equity* 297 (Appendix B) (Transnational 1988).

[5]For other early international river instruments, *see* United Nations Legislative Series, Legislative Texts and Treaty Provisions Concerning the Utilization of International Rivers for Other Purposes than Navigation, ST/LEG/SER.B12 (1963) (UN Sales No. 63.V.4).

be the most widely accepted (in English) or most informative title. For multilateral instruments, we often included the city where the instrument was finalized or the name (abbreviated according to the List of Abbreviations) of the international organization under whose auspices the instrument was prepared. With respect to bilateral and trilateral agreements, we began the title with the names of the countries (in alphabetical order) that are parties to the agreement. For example, an agreement between Canada and the United States would begin "Canada-United States." Where an original party has been succeeded by another State or entity, we included the name of the successor in parentheses and marked it with an asterisk.

POPULAR NAME: We provided the popular name or names (in English) of instruments. These names are also indexed alphabetically in the Index of Popular Names at the end of this book.

CITATION: A full citation using the approach described above follows the title of the instrument (or any popular name).

EDITORS' NOTES: These notes contain background information on the instrument or instruments in question. For groups of related instruments, we sometimes combined this information into an Editors' Introductory Note that precedes the entire set of related instruments.

ENTRY INTO FORCE: For international agreements, this entry provides either the date the agreement entered into force or a statement that the agreement is not yet in force.

DEPOSITARY: For international agreements, this entry identifies the country, countries, or international organization that is the depositary.

LANGUAGES: This entry identifies the authentic languages of the instrument. Only English-language versions (originals or translations) are reproduced in this book.

PARTIES: This entry lists the parties or prospective parties (*i.e.*, those States or organizations that have taken all steps required to be bound) to international agreements, reflecting the latest information from the depositary or other reliable sources. In listing parties, we usually used the current official name (in English) of the country concerned, even if that is not the name that is commonly used. Thus, we used "Burkina Faso" (for Upper Volta), "Côte d'Ivoire" (for Ivory Coast), "Czech and Slovak Federal Republic" (for Czechoslovakia), and "Myanmar" (for Burma). Countries are listed in alphabetical order, followed (if applicable) by international organizations in alphabetical order. We alphabetized the country names under the name we believe most people would search for first. Thus, the Republic of Korea is listed as "Korea, Republic of." A more substantive complication arises from the fact that a few countries have recently combined, and it is not yet clear what agreements the resulting countries will adhere to. In such cases, we have continued to list the pre-combination parties separately unless the depositary for the instrument indicated otherwise. Thus, the lists contain references to "Democratic Yemen" and "Yemen" (now combined as Yemen) and the "Federal Republic of Germany" and the "German Democratic Republic" (now combined as the Federal Republic of Germany). In the few instances where a depositary has indicated that the post-absorption Federal Republic of Germany is a party, we have listed "Federal Republic of Germany" and indicated that fact with a footnote.[6] (References to "Germany" in the List of International Environmental Instruments are to pre-1945 Germany). The list of parties also indicates if parties have made geographic extensions or limitations, reservations, or declarations. Withdrawals are also indicated.

SIGNING STATES: This entry applies only to instruments that are not intended to be legally binding. It lists States that have signed the instrument in question; it should not be confused with a list of signatories to instruments that are intended to be binding (we do not include lists of such signatories). The comments made above regarding "Parties" otherwise apply here as well.

AMENDMENTS: This entry lists amendments that are not included in the instrument as reproduced.

---

[6]We understand that a list of international agreements that will remain in effect for all or parts of post-absorption Federal Republic of Germany was agreed upon just as this book went to print. Because of the timing, we have not been able to take it into account.

LIST OF ABBREVIATIONS IN CITATIONS

A/xx/yy — UN General Assembly document number yy of the xx session

A/AC.105/C.2/L.yy — Limited distribution document yy of the Legal Sub-Committee of the UN Committee on the Peaceful Uses of Outer Space (COPUOS)

A/C.2/xx/yy — UN General Assembly Second (Economic) Committee document number yy of the xx UNGA session

A/CONF.xx/yy — Document number yy of the xx conference convened by United Nations General Assembly

A/CN.4/274 — Document 274 of the International Law Commission of the United Nations: set out in 1974:II (Pt. Two) *Yearbook of the International Law Commission* 265: "Legal Problems Relating to the Non-navigational Uses of International Watercourses"

A/RES/yy(RN) or A/RES/xx/yy — UN General Assembly (UNGA) resolution number yy of the RN (Roman numeral) or xx (Arabic numeral) session. [All UNGA resolutions for a given session are set out in the final Supplement to the Official Records (*GAOR*) of that session.]

AALCC — Asian-African Legal Consultative Committee

AIDI — *Annuaire de l'Institut de Droit International (Yearbook of the Institute of International Law)*

AJIL — American Journal of International Law

AMR/SCM/xx/yy — Document yy of the session in 19xx of the Special Consultative Meeting on Antarctic Mineral Resources

Arg. — *Argentina Treaty Series*

ATS — *Australian Treaty Series*

xx ATSCM/ — xxth Special Consultative Meeting of Antarctic Treaty Parties

Bevans

Bevans, *Treaties and Other International Agreements of the U.S.A., 1776-1949*

BFSP

British and Foreign State Papers

BGBl

Bundesgesetzblatt (Official Journal) [of Austria or the Federal Republic of Germany]

Brown Weiss

Edith Brown Weiss, *In Fairness to Future Generations: International Law, Common Patrimony, and Intergenerational Equity* (UNU and Transnational Publishers, 1989)

C/E

Council of Europe

C/E Rec.

Recommendation of the C/E Parliamentary Assembly

C/E Res.

Resolution of C/E

CFR

US *Code of Federal Regulations*

CJI

Inter-American Juridical Committee of the OAS

Cmnd

United Kingdom Command Papers

Congress Report

Report of the 1990 World Congress of Local Governments for a Sustainable Future (unnumbered document)

CO-ORDINATION/R.xx

Document xx of the UN's Administrative Committee on Co-ordination (ACC)

CSSR

Czechoslovak Treaty Series

CTS

Consolidated Treaty Series (Parry)

Dir. No.

EEC Directive number

DSB

US *Department of State Bulletin*

E/19xx/yy

Document yy of ECOSOC in year 19xx

E/C.10/19xx/yy

Document yy of the Commission on Transnational Corporations of ECOSOC in the year 19xx

E/CN.4/

Document of the Commission on Human Rights

(UNCHR) of ECOSOC

E/CONF.xx/yy	Document yy of the xx conference convened by ECOSOC
E/ECE/yy	Document yy of ECE
EAS	US *Executive Agreements Series*
EB.AIR/yy	Document yy of the Executive Body of ECE's Convention on Long-Range Transboundary Air Pollution
ECA	UN's Economic Commission for Africa
ECA/CM.xx/yy	Document yy of the xx session of the ECA Council of Ministers
ECE	UN's Economic Commission for Europe
ECE/RES/xx(yy) or ECE/DEC/xx(yy)	Resolution or decision xx of ECE, taken at the yy session. [The resolutions and decisions of each session of ECE are published in its report on the session submitted to ECOSOC; compendia of all the resolutions and decisions of ECE through 1989 have been published in documents E/ECE/836 and /Add.1.]
ECOSOC	UN Economic and Social Council
EEC	European Economic Community
EGDZ	*Dokumente der Zeit: Dokumente zur Aussenpolitik der Regierung der Deutschen Demokratischen Republik (DDR) (East Germany)*
EGND	East German *Neues Deutschland*
EPL	*Journal of Environmental Policy and Law*
ETS	*European Treaty Series*
Euratom	European Atomic Energy Community
EYB	*European Yearbook*
FAO	Food and Agriculture Organization of the United Nations

FAO Conf/Res.	Resolution of the FAO Conference
FAOSB	*FAO Soils Bulletin*
F.R.	US *Federal Register*
xx GAOR Ann a.i. yy	UN General Assembly Official Records of the xx session, Annexes, agenda item yy
IAEA	International Atomic Energy Agency
IAEA LegSer #xx	IAEA *Legal Series* No. xx
IAEA INFCIRC/xx	IAEA *Information Circular* xx
IAEA GC(xx)/RES/yy	IAEA General Conference Resolution yy taken at the xx session
IAEA PR	IAEA Press Release
IELMT	*International Environmental Law: Multilateral Treaties* (Verlag Schmidt, Berlin; W. Burhenne ed. 1974-present-) (looseleaf)
IER	*International Environment Reporter* (BNA)
IIL YB	Institute for International Law *Yearbook* [see AIDI]
IJECL	*International Journal of Estuarine and Coastal Law*
xx ILA	Report on xx session of the International Law Association
ILM	*International Legal Materials* (of the American Society of International Law)
ILO	International Labour Organisation or Office
ILO OB Ser.A	ILO *Official Bulletin* Series A
IMCO	Intergovernmental Maritime Consultative Organization (now IMO)
IMCO/Res	Resolution of the IMCO Assembly
IMO	International Maritime Organization (formerly

IMCO)

IMO:A.xx/Res.yy	Resolution yy of the xxth Assembly of the IMO
IPE	*International Protection of the Environment: Treaties and Related Documents* (Oceana; B. Ruster, B. Simma & M. Bock eds. Vol. I-XXX 1975-82, Index Vol. 1983)
IPE(2)	*International Protection of the Environment: Treaties and Related Documents* (Second Series) (Oceana; B. Ruster & B. Simma eds. 1990-) (looseleaf)
ISBN	International Standard Book Number
ITTO	International Tropical Timber Organization
IUCN	World Conservation Union, formerly named the International Union for Conservation of Nature and Natural Resources
IUCN Proc.	*Proceedings* of the IUCN
LEG/SER.B/12	UN *Legislative Series* (ST/LEG/SER.B/) number 12: ''Legislative Texts and Treaty Provisions concerning the Utilization of International Rivers for other Purposes than Navigation''
LNTS	*League of Nations Treaty Series*
Martens(x)	*Noveau Recueil Général de Traités et autres Actes relatifs aux Rapports de Droit international* x series
Misc	*United Kingdom Command Papers, Miscellaneous Series*
Montreal Protocol	1987 Montreal Protocol on Substances that Deplete the Ozone Layer
NetTract.	Netherlands *Tractatenblad*
Norw.	*Overenskomster Med Fremmede Stater* (Norwegian Treaty Series)
OAS	Organization of American States

OAS Doc. AG/doc	Document of the OAS General Assembly
OAS Doc. CP/doc	Document of the OAS Permanent Council
OAU:CM/yy	Document yy of the Council of Ministers of the Organization of African Unity
OEA	Organizacion de los Estados Americanos (OAS)
OECD	Organisation for Economic Co-operation and Development
OECD C(xx)	OECD Council, year 19xx
OECD p.xx	*OECD and the Environment* (OECD, 1986), page xx
OJEC	*Official Journal of the European Communities*
OJ Gre	*Official Journal* of Greece
Peaslee	A. Peaslee, *International Governmental Organizations: Constitutional Documents* (3rd rev. ed.) (1979)
Reg. No.	EEC Regulation number
RGDIP	*Revue Générale de Droit International Public*
S/yy	Document yy of the UN Security Council
SATS	*South African Treaty Series*
Stat	US *Statutes at Large*
TD/	Document of the Trade and Development Board of the UN Conference on Trade and Development (UNCTAD)
TIAS yyyy	US *Treaties and other International Acts* number yyyy. [A long dash signifies that the US State Department has indicated that the cited treaty would be published in TIAS but has not yet assigned a number.]
TRHG	*Törvényes Rendeletek Hivatalos Gyüteménye* (Hungarian Official Collection of Legislative Decrees)
TS	US *Treaties*

UKTS	*United Kingdom Treaty Series*
UN	United Nations
UN Water Ser. No.13	UN Department of Technical Co-operation for Development, *Natural Resources/Water Series* No. 13: "Treaties Concerning the Utilization of Water Courses for Other Purposes than Navigation, Africa" (UN Document ST/ESA/141)
UN Sales No.	UN Sales Publication number
UNCTC	UN Centre on Transnational Corporations
UNEP	United Nations Environment Programme
UNEP/GC/DEC/xx/yy	Decision number yy of the UNEP Governing Council, taken at the xx session of the Council. [The decisions adopted by the Council at each session are reproduced in an Annex to the Report of the Council to the UN General Assembly on that session, which constitutes Supplement No. 25 to the Official Records of the Assembly for its regular session (e.g., A/zz/25).]
UNEP/GC.xx/yy	Document yy of the UNEP Governing Council taken at its xx regular session
UNEP/GCSS.I/yy	Document yy of the UNEP Governing Council's First Special Session
UNEP/IG.xx/yy	Document yy of the xxth Intergovernmental Group convened by the UNEP Governing Council
UNEP/Oz.L.Pro.x/	Document of the x session of the Parties to the 1987 Montreal Protocol
UNEP/Oz.L.Pro.ExCom.x	Document of the x session of the Executive Committee of the Multilateral Fund under the 1987 Montreal Protocol
UNEP3	UNEP Reference Series 3: *Selected Multilateral Treaties in the Field of the Environment* (Nairobi; A. C. Kiss ed. 1983)
UNEP ELPG	UNEP *Environmental Law Guidelines and Principles*
UNEP EMG #	UNEP *Environmental Management Guidelines*, No.

UNEP Pub.	UNEP Publication
UNEP Reg.	UNEP: *Register of International Treaties and Other Agreements in the Field of the Environment* (UN Document UNEP/GC.15/Inf.2, Nairobi, May 1989). [This document gives the status, in particular the participation of States, as of 13 December 1988, of 140 international environmental treaties; it does not reproduce their texts or give official citations. The texts of many of the treaties are reproduced in UNEP3.]
UNEP/WG.xx	UNEP Working Group xx
UNGA	United Nations General Assembly
UNHRC	[UN] Human Rights Commission of ECOSOC
UNJYB	*United Nations Juridical Yearbook*
UNTS	United Nations *Treaty Series*
UNTS Reg. #	UNTS Registration Number [used when the cited treaty has been registered and assigned a number, but the volume of UNTS in which the treaty is to appear has not yet been published]
UNYB	UN *Yearbook*
US	United States
US Sen. Exec. Print	US Senate Executive Print [of a treaty presented by the President to the Senate for advice and consent to ratification]
US Sen. Tr. Doc.	US Senate Treaty Document
UST	US *Treaties and Other International Agreements*
WCED	World Commission on Environment and Development (the Brundtland Commission)
Weekly Comp. Pres. Doc.	Weekly Compilation of [US] Presidential Documents
WMO	World Meteorological Organization
WB	World Bank (International Bank for Reconstruction

and Development)

WTI World Treaty Index

YBILC *Yearbook* of the UN International Law Commission

LIST OF INTERNATIONAL
ENVIRONMENTAL INSTRUMENTS

Structure of List, by Subject Matter

List of Instruments

Abbreviations are explained in the list of Abbreviations at
page xv.

Name   Citations

Part I.   GENERAL PRINCIPLES

Chapter 1.   General Environment

1.A.   Global or Other Non-Regional
1.A.i.   General

UNGA Resolution: Development and Environment 20 December 1971	A/RES/2849(XXVI) 11 ILM 422 (1972) 1 IPE 107
OECD Council Recommendation: Guiding Principles Concerning International Economic Aspects of Environmental Policies 26 May 1972	OECD C(72)128 OECD p.23 1 IPE 116
Stockholm Declaration on the Human Environment of the United Nations Conference on the Human Environment 16 June 1972	*Infra* p.171 A/CONF.48/14/Rev.1, Ch.I UNEP ELPG #1 1972 UNYB 319 11 ILM 1416 (1972) 67 DSB 116 (1972) 1 IPE 118
Action Plan for the Human Environment of the UN Conference on the Environment 16 June 1972	A/CONF.48/14/Rev.1, Ch.II
UNESCO Convention Concerning the Protection of the World Cultural and Natural Heritage, Paris 16 November 1972	*Infra* p.554 1037 UNTS 151 27 UST 37 TIAS 8226 UNEP3 #55, p.276 1972 UNJYB 89 11 ILM 1358 (1972) 14 IPE 7238 IELMT 972: 86
UNGA Resolution: Institutional and Financial Arrangements for International Environmental Co-operation (UNEP "Statute") 15 December 1972	*Infra* p.719 A/RES/2997(XXVII) 1 IPE 152
UNGA Resolution: Co-operation in the Field of the Environment Concerning Natural Resources Shared by Two or More States 13 December 1973	A/RES/3129(XXVIII) 13 ILM 232 (1974) 18 IPE 9062
Cocoyoc Declaration of the UNEP/UNCTAD Symposium (Cocoyoc, Mexico)	UNEP Executive Ser.No.1, p.107

12 October 1974

OECD Ministerial Declaration: Environmental Policy 14 November 1974	OECD p.15 1 IPE 293
Charter of Economic Rights and Duties of States (CERDS) (Arts. 29, 30) 12 December 1974	Infra p.177 A/RES/3281(XXIX) 1 IPE 326
OECD: Guidelines for Multinational Enterprises, General Policies, para. 2 21 June 1976	OECD C(76)99(Final) 1976 15 ILM 969 (1976)
— Modified 17 May 1984	OECD C/MIN(84)5(Final) OECD C(84)90
Modification Clarified by OECD Committee on International Investment and Multinational Enterprises (CIME) November 1985	OECD p.191 25 ILM 494 (1986)
International Institute for Environment and Development (IIED): Multilateral Aid and the Environment (interim report on the environmental procedures and practices of 9 multilateral development agencies) August 1977	
UNGA Resolution: Institutional Arrangements for Institutional Co-operation in the Field of Human Settlements (HABITAT Statute) 19 December 1977	A/RES/32/162 30 IPE 99
UNEP Governing Council Decision: Principles of Conduct in the Field of the Environment for Guidance of States in the Conservation and Harmonious Utilization of Natural Resources Shared by Two or More States 19 May 1978	Infra p.180 A/RES/3129(XXVIII) UNEP ELPG #2 17 ILM 1097 (1978)
OECD Council Recommendation on Strengthening International Co-operation on Environmental Protection in Transfrontier Regions (with annexed guidelines) 21 September 1978	OECD C(78)77(Final) OECD p.154 18 IPE 9406
UNCHS/UNEP Memorandum of Understanding Regarding Co-operation for Incorporating Environmental Guidelines in Human Settlement Planning 1980	UNEP/GC/ INFORMATION /6/ Add.4
UNGA Resolution: Historical Responsibility of	Infra p.638

States for the Protection of Nature for the Benefit
of Present and Future Generations
30 October 1980

A/RES/35/8
IPE(2) I/C/30-10-80

Summary of the Recommendations of the High-
Level Group of Experts on the Interrelationship
between People, Resources, Environment and Development (UNEP)
17 December 1981

A/36/25, Annex II
IPE(2) I/C/17-12-81.a

UNEP Nairobi Declaration: State of Worldwide
Environment
18 May 1982

A/37/25, Pt. One,
Annex II
IPE(2) I/D/18-05-82.b

UNEP Council: approval of "Programme for the
Development and Periodic Review of Environmental Law", adopted by the Ad Hoc Meeting of Senior Government Officials Expert in Environmental Law (Montevideo, 6 Nov. 1981)
31 May 1982

UNEP/GC.10/5/Add.2
UNEP/GC/DEC/10/21
IPE(2) I/D/31-05-82

UNCTC: Draft Code of Conduct for Transnational
Corporations (paras. 41-43)
5 June 1982

E/C.10/1982/6
22 ILM 199 (1983)
E/1990/94

World Charter for Nature
28 October 1982

Infra p.184
A/RES/37/7
1982 UNYB 1023
22 ILM 455 (1983)
IPE(2) I/C/28-10-82

UNGA Resolution: Protection Against Products
Harmful to Health and the Environment
17 December 1982

A/RES/37/137

Bonn (Summit) Economic Declaration Towards
Sustained Growth and Higher Employment
4 May 1985

21:19 Weekly Comp.
Pres. Doc. 577

OECD Ministerial Declaration on Environment
Resources for the Future
29 June 1985

OECD p.19

"Our Common Future", Report of the World
Commission on Environment and Development
(WCED)
4 August 1987

A/42/427

Experts Group on Environmental Law of the World
Commission on Environment and Development
(WCED): Legal Principles for Environmental Protection and Sustainable Development
4 August 1987

Infra p.188
A/42/427, Annex I

Restatement (Third) of the Foreign Relations Law of the United States, Introduction to Part VI (Law of the Environment) (Secs. 601-02 and Comments) 1987	*Infra* p.195
UNGA Resolution: The Environmental Perspective to the Year 2000 and Beyond 11 December 1987	A/42/25, Annex II A/RES/42/186 UNEP Pub. E.88:111D.6 IPE(2) I/C/11-12-87.b
Goa Guidelines on Intergenerational Equity 15 February 1988	Brown Weiss, Appendix A
United Nations System-Wide Medium-Term Environment Programme 1990-1995 18 March 1988	UNEP/GCSS.I/7/Add.1 UNEP/GC/DEC/SS.I/3 IPE(2) I/D/18-03-88
Paris Economic Summit, Economic Declaration (paras. 33-51) 16 July 1989	28 ILM 1292 (1989)
UNGA Resolution: Implementation of General Assembly Resolutions 42/186 [Environmental Perspective to the Year 2000] and 42/187 [Report of the World Commission on Environment and Development] 22 December 1989	A/RES/44/227
UNGA Resolution: International Co-operation in the Field of the Environment 22 December 1989	A/RES/44/229
UNCTC Criteria for Sustainable Development Management 1990	20 EPL 186 (1990)
Conclusions of the Siena Forum on International Law of the Environment 21 April 1990	A/45/666
UNGA Resolution: International Development Strategy for the Fourth United Nations Development Decade, Part III.B.4 "Environment" (paras. 96-97) 21 December 1990	A/RES/45/199
Beijing Ministerial Declaration on Environment and Development (adopted by ministers from 41 developing countries) 19 June 1991	A/46/293
London Economic Summit, Economic Declaration (paras. 47-57)	A/46/309—S/22807

17 July 1991

1.A.ii. Non-Regional Bilateral

United States of America-Union of Soviet Socialist Republics: Agreement on Co-operation in the Field of Environmental Protection 23 May 1972	846 UNTS 105 23 UST 845 TIAS 7345 11 ILM 761 (1972) 1 IPE 50
United States of America-Federal Republic of Germany: Agreement on Co-operation in Environmental Affairs 9 May 1974	26 UST 840 TIAS 8069 13 ILM 598 (1974) 1 IPE 77
Japan-United States of America: Agreement on Co-operation in the Field of Environmental Protection 5 August 1975	26 UST 2534 TIAS 8172 18 IPE 8992
——— Extension and Amendment 5 August 1980	32 UST 2468 TIAS 9853
——— Extension and Amendment 31 July 1985	TIAS —
United States of America-Union of Soviet Socialist Republics: Agreement on Environmental Co-operation 1 November 1989	
Belgium-United States of America: Arrangement for Exchange of Technical Information on Regulatory Matters and on Co-operation in Safety Research and in Standards Development 6 June 1978	30 UST 1327 TIAS 9255
Nigeria-United States of America: Memorandum of Understanding on Environmental Protection, Lagos 22 September 1980	32 UST 2626 TIAS 9864 29 IPE 271
Canada-Union of Soviet Socialist Republics: Protocol (to the 1971 Agreement on General Exchanges) for Consultation on the Development of a Programme of Scientific and Technical Cooperation in the Arctic and the North 1984	
France-United States of America: Memorandum of Understanding on Environmental Cooperation, Paris 21 June 1984	TIAS — IPE(2) I/A/14-08-83

Netherlands-United States of America: Memorandum of Understanding Concerning Cooperation in the Field of Environmental Protection 17 June 1985	TIAS — IPE(2) I/A/17-06-85
United Kingdom-United States of America: Memorandum of Understanding Concerning Co-operation in the Field of Environmental Affairs, Washington 2 June 1986	TIAS — IPE(2) I/A/02-06-86
Italy-United States of America: Memorandum of Understanding Concerning Cooperation in the Field of Environmental Protection, Rome 3 March 1987	TIAS —

1.B. Africa (see also 5.B, 9.C)
1.B.i. General

OAU Assembly of Heads of State and Government: Declaration on the Denuclearization of Africa 21 July 1964	A/5975 20 GAOR Ann. a.i. 105
UNGA Resolution: Declaration on the Denuclearization of Africa 3 December 1965	A/RES/2033(XX) 16 IPE 7951
African Convention on the Conservation of Nature and Natural Resources, Algiers 15 September 1968	*Infra* p.203 1001 UNTS 3 OAU:CM/232 UNEP3 #37, p.207 5 IPE 2037 IELMT 982: 68
OAU: Declaration on African Co-operation, Development, and Economic Independence (paras. A.40-44) 28 May 1973	12 ILM 1005 (1973)
ECA Council of Ministers Resolution: Environment and Development in Africa 27 June 1984	ECA/CM.10/38

1.B.ii. North Africa
1.B.iii. West & Central Africa

Germany (pre-post-WWII)-United Kingdom: London Agreement respecting the boundary between British and German Territories from Yola to Lake Tchad 19 March 1906	200 CTS 403 3 Martens(3) 691

France-Germany (pre-post-WWII): Berlin Convention to Define the Frontier between the Camerouns and the French Congo
18 April 1908

206 CTS 403
4 AJIL 100
1 Martens (3) 162

Liberia-United Kingdom: London Convention supplementary to the Convention of 21 January 1911, respecting the boundary between Sierra Leone and Liberia
25 June 1917

5 LNTS 39

Ouagadougou Convention Establishing a Permanent Inter-State Drought Control Committee for the Sahel
12 September 1973

13 ILM 537 (1974)
17 IPE 8640

Abidjan Convention for Co-operation in the Protection and Development of the Marine and Coastal Environment of the West and Central African Region
23 March 1981

UN Water Ser. No.13
UNEP/IG/22/7
20 ILM 746 (1981)
IPE(2) II/A/23-03-81.a
IELMT 981 : 23

———— Abidjan Protocol concerning Co-operation in Combating Pollution in Cases of Emergency
23 March 1981

20 ILM 756 (1981)
IPE(2) II/A/23-03-81.b
IELMT 981: 24

1.B.iv.   East Africa

Italy-United Kingdom: London Exchange of Notes regarding boundary between Kenya & Italian Somaliland, together with the Agreement adopted by the Boundary Commission & Appendices
22 November 1933

30 Martens(3) 63

Nairobi Convention for the Protection, Management and Development of the Marine and Coastal Environment of the Eastern African Region
21 June 1985

UNEP Reg. p.226
IPE(2) II/A/21-06-85.a
IELMT 985: 46

———— Nairobi Protocol concerning Protected Areas and Wild Fauna and Flora in the Eastern African Region
21 June 1985

UNEP Reg. p.228
IELMT 985: 47

1.B.v.   South of Sahara

Phyto-sanitary Convention for Africa South of the Sahara, Kinshasa
13 September 1968

UNEP312, p.115

Constitution of the Republic of Namibia (Arts. 91(c), 95(1))

Infra p.210
U.N. Doc. S/20967/Add.2.

21 March 1990

1.C.   Americas (see also 5.C)
1.C.i.   General

Washington Convention on Nature Protection and Wildlife Preservation in the Western Hemisphere 12 October 1940	*Infra* p.211 161 UNTS 193 3 Bevans 630 56 Stat. 1354 TS 981 UNEP3 #2, p.64 4 IPE 1729 IELMT 940: 76
Tlatelolco Treaty for the Prohibition of Nuclear Weapons in Latin America 14 February 1967	634 UNTS 281, 362, 364 22 UST 754, 762 TIAS 7137, 10147 15 IPE 7827 IELMT 967: 13
Panama-United States of America: Washington Agreement Pursuant to Article VI of the Convention on Nature Protection and Wildlife Preservation in the Western Hemisphere 7 September 1977	33 UST 446 TIAS 10035
Panama-United States of America: Panama Agreement Relating to Article VI of the Panama Canal Treaty Concerning Establishment of a Joint Commission on the Environment 1 October 1979	TIAS —
Intergovernmental Regional Meeting on the Environment in Latin America and the Caribbean, Mexico City (Resolutions and Recommendations) 12 March 1982	UNEP/GC.33/5, Annex V UNEP/IG.33/5, Annex V A/37/25, Pt. One, Annex I
OAS Inter-American Juridical Committee: American Declaration on the Environment 1989	CJI/RES.II-10/89 OAS Doc. AG/doc.2416/89
Declaration of San Francisco de Quito, by the Ministers of Foreign Affairs of the States Parties to the Amazonian Co-operation Treaty 1989	OAS Doc. CP/doc.2834/89
Brasilia Declaration on the Environment, by the 6th Ministerial Meeting on the Environment in Latin America and the Caribbean 31 March 1989	A/44/683, Annex 28 ILM 1311 (1989)
OAS General Secretariat: Study on the Creation of an Inter-American System of Nature Conservation	OAS Doc.: OEA/Ser.G CP/doc.2036/89/Re.1

(in compliance with OAS General Assembly Resolution AG/RES.948 (XVIII-0/88))
1 November 1990

1.C.ii.   North America

Canada-United States of America: Washington | *Infra* p.412
Treaty Relating to Boundary Waters and Questions | 12 Bevans 319
Arising Along the Boundary Between the United | 36 Stat. 2448
States and Canada (Art. IV) | TS 548
11 January 1909 | 102 BFSP 137
| LEG/SER.B/12, p.261
| 10 IPE 5158

Canada-Mexico-United States of America: North | 28 UST 6223
American Plant Protection Agreement, Yosemite | TIAS 8680
(California) | 20 IPE 10364
13 October 1976

Mexico-United States of America: Memorandum | 17 ILM 1056 (1978)
of Understanding for Cooperation on Environmen- | 18 IPE 9013
tal Programs and Transboundary Problems, Mex-
ico City
6 June 1978

Canada-United States of America: Free Trade | 27 ILM 281 (1988)
Agreement (Arts. 603, 609)
22 December 1987

Mexico-United States of America: La Paz | TIAS 10827
Agreement for Cooperation on Environmental Pro- | 22 ILM 1025 (1983)
grams and Transboundary Problems | IPE(2) I/A/14-08-83
14 August 1983

————— Annex I, Agreement of Cooperation for | 26 ILM 18 (1987)
the Solution of the Border Sanitation Problem of
San Diego, California-Tijuana, Baja California,
San Diego
18 July 1985

————— Annex II, Agreement for Cooperation re- | 26 ILM 19 (1987)
garding Pollution of the Environment along the
Inland International Boundary by Discharge of
Hazardous Substances, San Diego
18 July 1985

————— Annex III, Transboundary Shipment of | *Infra* p.617
Hazardous Wastes and Hazardous Substances, | 26 ILM 25 (1987)
Washington
12 November 1986

————— Annex IV, Agreement of Cooperation re- | 26 ILM 33 (1987)
garding Transboundary Air Pollution Caused by

Copper Smelters along their Common Border,
Washington
29 January 1987

———— Annex V: Agreement of Cooperation re-   29 ILM 30 (1990)
garding International Transport of Urban Air Pollution
3 October 1989

Mexico-United States of America: Memorandum   TIAS ——
of Understanding on Cooperation in Management
and Protection of Natural Parks and Other Protected Natural and Cultural Heritage Sites
24 January 1989

Mexico-United States of America: Washington   29 ILM 26 (1990)
Agreement on Cooperation for the Protection and
Improvement of the Environment of the Metropoli-
tan Area of Mexico City
3 October 1989

1.C.iii.   Central & South America

El Salvador-Guatemala: San Salvador Treaty of   131 UNTS 132
Free Trade and Economic Integration (Art. 19)   LEG/SER.B/12, p.227
14 December 1951   1 IPE 16

Guatemala-Honduras: Guatemala Treaty of Free   263 UNTS 66
Trade and Economic Integration (Art. 19)   LEG/SER.B/12, p.229
22 August 1956   1 IPE 17

Brasilia Treaty for Amazonian Co-operation   *Infra* p.545
                                                  UNEP3 #75, p.496
                                                  UNEP Reg. p.164
                                                  17 ILM 1045 (1978)
                                                  18 IPE 9017
                                                  IELMT 978: 49

Amazon Declaration, adopted by the Presidents of   *Infra* p.551
the States Parties to the Treaty for Amazonian Co-   A/44/275, Annex
operation, Manaus (Brazil)   E/1989/79, Annex
6 May 1989   28 ILM 1303 (1989)

1.C.iv.   Caribbean (see 4.I)
1.D.   Antarctica (see 9.A)
1.E.   Asia (see also 5.D)

FAO Plant Protection Agreement for the [South-   247 UNTS 400
East] Asia and Pacific Region, Rome, (amended   FAO Council 23rd sess.
1967, 1979, 1983—see 8.D)   UNEP3 #12, p.117
27 February 1956   4 IPE 1822
                                                    IELMT 956: 15

ASEAN Agreement on the Conservation of Nature   *Infra* p.215
and Natural Resources, Kuala Lumpur   15 EPL 64 (1985)
9 July 1985   IELMT 985: 51

UNGA Resolution: Establishment of a Nuclear-   A/RES/45/53
Weapon-Free Zone in South Asia
4 December 1990

1.F.   Europe (see also 5.E)
1.F.i.   General

ECE Decision: Terms of reference of the Senior   ECE/DEC/8(XXIX)
Advisers to ECE Governments on Environmental
Problems
29 April 1974

Helsinki Final Act of the Conference on Security   *Infra* p.228
and Co-operation in Europe (CSCE) (Basket Two: 73 DSB 335 (1975)
"Co-operation in the Fields of Economics, of Sci-   14 ILM 1307 (1975)
ence and Technology and of the Environment",   18 IPE 9139
Sec. 5: "Environment")
1 August 1975

C/E Convention on the Conservation of European   ETS #104
Wildlife and Natural Habitats, Berne   UKTS No.56 (1982)
19 Sepember 1979   Cmnd 8738
                                                      UNEP #77, p.589
                                                      23 IPE 40
                                                      IELMT 979: 70

European Outline Convention on Transfrontier Co-   ETS #106
operation between Territorial Communities or Au-   UNEP Reg. p.187
thorities, C/E, Madrid   IELMT 980: 40
21 May 1980

CSCE: Concluding Document of the Madrid Meet-   22 ILM 1400 (1983)
ing (Co-operation in the Field of Economics, of
Science and Technology and of the Environment)
9 September 1983

ECE Declaration on Conservation of Flora, Fauna   E/ECE/1172
and their Habitats   ECE/DEC/E(43), para. 2
21 April 1988

CSCE: Concluding Document of the Sofia Follow-
up Meeting on the Environment
1989

Agreement Establishing the European Bank for   29 ILM 1083 (1990)
Reconstruction and Development (EBRD) (Arts.
2(1)(vii), 11(1)(v), 35(2))
29 May 1990

CSCE: Charter of Paris for a new Europe (A New Era of Democracy, Peace and Unity: Economic Liberty and Responsibility. Guidelines for the Future: Environment) 21 November 1990

A/45/859, Annex
30 ILM 193 (1991)

1.F.ii. Nordic

Nordic Mutual Emergency Assistance Agreement in Connection with Radiation Accidents 17 October 1963

525 UNTS 75
IAEA LegSer#15, p.487
IAEA INFCIRC/49
7 IPE 6102
IELMT 963: 77

Nordic (Denmark, Finland, Norway, Sweden) Convention on the Protection of the Environment and Protocol, Stockholm 19 February 1974

Infra p.235
1092 UNTS 279
UNEP3 #62, p.403
13 ILM 591 (1974)
1 IPE 70
IELMT 974: 14

Finland-Union of Soviet Socialist Republics: Co-operation Agreement on the Protection of the Environment 5 July 1985

Norway-Union of Soviet Socialist Republics: Co-operation Agreement on the Protection of the Environment, Oslo 1988

Nordic Agreement on Co-operation over National Territorial Borders with the Aim of Preventing or Limiting Damage to Man or Property or the Environment in the Event of Accidents 20 January 1989

1.F.iii. EEC Area

Federal Republic of Germany-Netherlands: Frontier Treaty (Ch. 4, Arts. 56-73) 8 April 1960

508 UNTS 26
11 IPE 5588

EEC Council: Declaration on the Programme of Action on the Environment (First Environmental Action Programme) 22 November 1973

OJEC 1973 C 112
13 ILM 164 (1974)
1 IPE 206

EEC Council: Second Environmental Action Programme (1977-1981) 17 May 1977

OJEC 1977 C 139/1
18 IPE 9297

Benelux Convention on Nature Conservation and Landscape Protection, Brussels 8 June 1982	UNEP Reg. p.207 IELMT 982: 43
EEC Council: Third Environmental Action Programme (1982-1986) 7 October 1983	OJEC 1983 C 46/1
EEC Single European Act (additions to the EEC Treaty: Art. 18—adding Art. 100a, Art. 25—adding Title VII (Arts. 130r-t: "Environment")) 17 February 1986	*Infra* p.232 OJEC 1987 L 169/1 25 ILM 506 (1986) IPE(2) I/H/18-02-86.a IELMT 986: 16
EEC Council: Fourth Environmental Action Programme (1987-1992) 8 October 1986	OJEC 1987 C 328/1
EEC Council Regulation: Action by the Community Relating to the Environment 23 July 1987	Reg. No. 2242/87 OJEC 1987 L 207/8 IPE(2) I/H/23-07-87
EEC Council Regulation: Establishment of the European Environment Agency and the European Environment Information and Observation Network 7 May 1990	Reg. No. 1210/90 OJEC 1990 L 120/1
German Democratic Republic-Federal Republic of Germany: Bonn Treaty Establishing a Monetary, Economic and Social Union (Art. 16 "Protection of the Environment") 18 May 1990	29 ILM 1130 (1990)

1.F.iv.   Other Europe

Poland-Union of Soviet Socialist Republics: Agreement concerning the Regime of the Soviet-Polish State Frontier (Arts. 16, 17, 18(1), 25, 27) 8 July 1948	37 UNTS 66 9 IPE 4475
France-Federal Republic of Germany-Switzerland: Exchange of Notes concerning the Establishment of an Intergovernmental Commission on Neighbourhood Problems in Border Areas 22 October 1975	18 IPE 8998

1.G.   Oceania

Australia-Indonesia: Treaty on the Zone of Co-operation in an Area between the Indonesian Province of East Timor and Northern Australia (Arts. 18-19)	29 ILM 469 (1990)

11 December 1989

Chapter 2. Human Rights and the Environment

European Social Charter (Arts. 3(1), (3), 11) 18 October 1961	529 UNTS 89 ETS #35 9 EYB 71 IELMT 961: 78
International Convenant on Economic, Social and Cultural Rights (Arts. 12(2)(b), 25. See also Arts. 7, 11, 12(1), (2)(c)) 16 December 1966	*Infra* p.240 993 UNTS 3 A/RES/2200A(XXI) 6 ILM 360 (1967) 1 IPE 28 IELMT 966: 94
African Charter on Human and Peoples' Rights (Art. 24), OAU, Nairobi 27 June 1981	*Infra* p.242 21 ILM 59 (1982)
Draft Charter on Human and People's Rights in the Arab World (Art. 18) 1987	
American Convention on Human Rights, San Jose 1969, San Salvador Additional Protocol on Economic, Social and Cultural Rights (Art. 11) 17 November 1988	*Infra* p.242 28 ILM 161 (1989)
Declaration of the Hague 11 March 1989	*Infra* p.247 A/44/340 E/1989/120 28 ILM 1308 (1989)
Convention on the Rights of the Child (Art. 29(1)(e)) 20 November 1989	*Infra* p.241 A/RES/44/25 28 ILM 1456 (1989) 29 ILM 1340 (1990)(correction)
UN Commission on Human Rights Resolution: Movement and Dumping of Toxic and Dangerous Products and Waste 1990	E/CN.4/Sub.2/1990/7 UNHRC Res.1990/43
Constitution of the Republic of Namibia (Arts. 91(c), 95(1)) 21 March 1990	*Infra* p.210 UN Doc. S/20967/Add.2
UNGA Resolution: Need to Ensure a Healthy Environment for the Well-Being of Individuals 14 December 1990	A/RES/45/94

Part II. PROTECTION OF PARTICULAR RESOURCES

Chapter 3. Atmosphere

3.A. General

France-United Kingdom-United States of America: Agreement on Monitoring the Stratosphere 5 May 1976	1037 UNTS 3 27 UST 1437 TIAS 8255 16 IPE 8289 IELMT 976: 35
The Changing Atmosphere: Implications for Global Security (Report of a conference convened by the Canadian Department of External Affairs, Toronto) 30 June 1988	
Conference on the Changing Atmosphere: Statement of the Meeting of Legal and Policy Experts, Ottawa 22 February 1989	A/C.2/44/2
Declaration of the Hague 11 March 1989	*Infra* p.247 A/44/340 E/1989/120 28 ILM 1308 (1989)
Noordwijk Declaration by the Ministerial Conference on Atmospheric Pollution and Climate Change 7 November 1989	A/C.2/44/5, Annex

3.B   Air Quality (including Acid Deposition)

Canada-United States of America: Ottawa Convention for the Establishment of a Tribunal to Decide Questions of Indemnity Arising from the Operation of the Smelter at Trail, British Columbia 15 April 1935	162 LNTS 73 49 Stat. 3245 TS 893 15 IPE 7737
— Supplementary Agreement to Decide Questions of Indemnity and Future Regime 24 January 1950	151 UNTS 171 3 UST 539 TIAS 2412 15 IPE 7813
EEC Council Directive: Approximation of Laws of Member States relating to Measures to be Taken against Air Pollution by Gases from Positive-Ignition Engines of Motor Vehicles 20 March 1970	Dir. No. 70/220 OJEC 1970 L 76/1 15 IPE 7535

C/E Committee of Ministers, Resolution On Air Pollution in Frontier Areas
26 March 1971

C/E Res. 71(5)
19 EYB 263
15 IPE 7580

EEC Council Directive: Emissions from Diesel Engines for Use in Motor Vehicles
2 August 1972

Dir. No. 72/306
OJEC 1972 L 190/1
15 IPE 7604

OECD Council Recommendation: Guidelines for Action to Reduce Emissions of Sulphur Oxides and Particulate Matter from Fuel Combustion in Stationary Sources (with annexed Technical Note)
18 June 1974

OECD C(74)16(Final)
OECD p.34
15 IPE 7627

OECD Council Recommendation: Measures Required for Further Air Pollution Control
14 November 1974

OECD C(74)219
OECD p.38
1 IPE 304

ILO Convention (#148) concerning the Protection of Workers Against Occupational Hazards in the Working Environment Due to Air Pollution, Noise and Vibration, Geneva
20 June 1977

LX:3 ILO OB Ser.A,
    p.136
UNEP3 #73, p.482
28 IPE 335
IELMT 977: 37

ILO Recommendation (#156) concerning the Protection of Workers Against Occupational Hazards in the Working Environment Due to Air Pollution, Noise and Vibration, Geneva
22 June 1977

LX:3 ILO OB Ser.A,
    p.146

ECE Convention on Long-Range Transboundary Air Pollution (with resolution and with Declaration on Low and Non-Waste Technology, and Reutilization and Recycling of Wastes), Geneva
13 November 1979

Infra p.250
TIAS 10541
Cmnd 7885
Misc 10 1980
UNEP3 #78, p.519
E/ECE/1010
18 ILM 1442 (1979)
28 IPE 341
IELMT 979: 84

——— Geneva Protocol on Long-Term Financing of Co-operative Programme for Monitoring and Evaluation of the Long-Range Transmission of Air Pollutants in Europe (EMEP)
28 September 1984

EB.AIR/AC.1/4
IELMT 979: 84/A/1

——— Helsinki Protocol on the Reduction of Sulphur Emissions or their Transboundary Fluxes by at least 30 percent
8 July 1985

Infra p.256
EB.AIR/12
27 ILM 707 (1988)
IELMT 979: 84/B

——— Sofia Protocol concerning the Control of Emissions of Nitrogen Oxides or their Transboundary Fluxes

Infra p.259
EB.AIR/21
28 ILM 214 (1989)

31 October 1988	IELMT 979: 84/C
EEC Council Directive: Air Quality Limit Values and Guide Values for Sulphur Dioxide and Suspended Particulates 15 July 1980	Dir. No. 80/779 OJEC 1980 L 229/30 28 IPE 477
Canada-United States of America: Memorandum of Intent concerning Transboundary Air Pollution 5 August 1980	32 UST 2521 TIAS 9856 20 ILM 690 (1981) 28 IPE 352
New York-Quebec Agreement on Acid Precipitation 26 July 1982	21 ILM 721 (1982)
EEC Council Directive: Air Quality Limit Value for Lead 3 December 1982	Dir. No. 82/884 OJEC 1982 L 378/15
Canada-United States of America: Agreement to Track Air Pollution across Eastern North America (Cross Appalachian Tracer Experiment) 23 August 1983	TIAS 10771 22 ILM 1017 (1983)
C/E Parliamentary Assembly Recommendation: Air Pollution and Acid Rain 1984	C/E Rec. 977 (1984)
EEC Council Directive: Combating Air Pollution from Industrial Plants 28 June 1984	Dir. No. 84/360 OJEC 1984 L 188/20
OECD Council Recommendation: Control of Air Pollution from Fossil Fuel Combustion (with annexed Guiding Principles) 20 June 1985	OECD C(85)101 OECD p.39
EEC Commission Regulation: Protection of Forests against Atmospheric Pollution 17 November 1986	Reg. No. 3528/86 OJEC 1986 L 326/2
EEC Council Directives: Lead Content of Petrol 20 March 1985; 20 December 1985; 21 July 1987	Dir. No. 85/210 OJEC 1985 L 96/25 Dir. No. 85/581 OJEC 1985 L 372/37 Dir. No. 87/416 OJEC 1987 L 225 /33
Mexico-United States of America: La Paz Agreement for Cooperation on Environmental Programs and Transboundary Problems, 1983 (see Sec. 1.C.ii), Annex IV, Agreement of Cooperation	26 ILM 33 (1987)

regarding Transboundary Air Pollution Caused by
Copper Smelters along their Common Border,
Washington
29 January 1987

IIL Cairo Resolution (III) on Transboundary Air   62: II IIL YB, p.296
Pollution
20 September 1987

EEC Council Directive: Gaseous Emissions from   Dir. No. 88/77
Commercial Vehicles (Diesel Engines)   OJEC 1988 L 36/33
3 December 1987

EEC Council Directive: Gaseous Emissions from   Dir. No. 88/76
Passenger Cars   OJEC 1988 L 36/1
3 December 1987

EEC Council Directive: Particulate Pollutant Emis-   Dir. No. 88/436
sions from Diesel Engines (amending Directive   OJEC 1988 L 214/1
No. 70/220)
16 June 1988

EEC Council Directive: Emissions from Large   Dir. No. 88/609
Combustion Plants   OJEC 1988 L 336/1
24 November 1988

ECE Decision: Air Pollution   ECE/DEC/J(44)
21 April 1989

EEC Council Directive: Prevention of Air Pollu-   Dir. No. 89/369
tion from new Municipal Waste-Incineration   OJEC 1989 L 163/32
Plants
8 June 1989

EEC Council Directive: Reduction of Air Pollution   Dir. No. 89/429
from Existing Municipal Waste-Incineration Plants   OJEC 1989 L 203/50
21 June 1989

EEC Council Directive (amending Directive No.   Dir. No. 89/427
80/779): Air Quality Limit Values and Guide Val-   OJEC 1989 L 201/53
ues for Sulphur Dioxide and Suspended Particu-
lates
21 June 1989

Mexico-United States of America: Agreement for   29 ILM 30 (1990)
Cooperation on Environment, 1983 (see 1.C.i),
Annex V: Agreement of Cooperation regarding International Transport of Urban Air Pollution
3 October 1989

Finland-Union of Soviet Socialist Republics: Action Programme on the Restriction and Reduction

of the Fluxes of Air Pollutants and their Adverse
Effects Stemming from Adjacent Boundary Regions
26 October 1989

Canada-United States of America: Ottawa   *Infra* p.263
Agreement on Air Quality   30 ILM (1991)
13 March 1991

3.C.   Ozone Layer

Vienna Convention for the Protection of the Ozone   *Infra* p.276
Layer   26 ILM 1529 (1987)
22 March 1985   IELMT 985: 22

——— Montreal Protocol on Substances that De-   *Infra* p.289
plete the Ozone Layer   26 ILM 1550 (1987)
16 September 1987   IELMT 985: 22/A

——— Helsinki Declaration on the Protection of   28 ILM 1335 (1989)
the Ozone Layer (First Meeting of Parties to the
1985 Vienna Convention and the 1987 Montreal
Protocol)
2 May 1989

——— Decisions of the Second Meeting of Parties   *Infra* p.298
to the Montreal Protocol (MP) (Annexes I (Adjust-   UNEP/Oz.L.Pro.2/3
ments to MP), II (Amendments to MP), III (Non-
Compliance Procedure))
29 June 1990

Reports of the First and Second Meetings of the   UNEP/Oz.L.Pro.ExCom.1/
Executive Committee of the Multilateral Fund un-   . . .
der the Montreal Protocol [on Substances that Deplete the Ozone Layer]
1990

EEC Council Directive: CFCs and Halons which   Dir. No. 3322/88
Deplete the Ozone Layer   OJEC 1988 L 297/1
1988

EEC Council Proposed Regulation: Substances   OJEC 1990 C 86/4
that Deplete the Ozone Layer
25 January 1990

Resolution by the Governments of the European   UNEP/OzL.Pro.2/3,
Communities Represented at the Second Meeting   Annex VII
of the Parties to the Montreal Protocol on Substances that Deplete the Ozone Layer
29 June 1990

3.D. Weather

Canada-United States of America: Agreement on the Exchange of Information on Weather Modification Activities 26 March 1975	977 UNTS 385 26 UST 540 TIAS 8056 14 ILM 589 (1975) 16 IPE 8269
UNEP Governing Council Decision: Provisions for Co-operation between States in Weather Modification Activities 29 April 1980	UNEP/GC/DEC/8/7A UNEP ELGP #3

3.E. Climate

WMO: First World Climate Conference Declaration and Supporting Documents 23 February 1979	WMO Pub. No.537 (1979)
Canada-United States of America: Memorandum of Understanding on Cooperation in the Field of Climate-Related Programs 28 June 1985	TIAS —
UNGA Resolution: Protection of Global Climate for Present and Future Generations of Mankind 6 December 1988	*Infra* p.313 A/RES/43/53 28 ILM 1326 (1989)
UNGA Resolution: Climatic Effects of Nuclear War, Including Nuclear Winter (noting the UN Secretary-General's Report: Study on the Climatic and Other Effects of Nuclear War) 7 December 1988	A/RES/43/78D UN Sales No. E.89.IX.1
Declaration of the Hague 11 March 1989	*Infra* p.247 A/44/340 E/1989/120 28 ILM 1308 (1989)
UNEP Governing Council Decision: Global Climate Change 25 May 1989	UNEP/GC/DEC/15/36
EEC Council Resolution: Greenhouse Effect and the Community 21 June 1989	EEC 89/C 183/4 OJEC 1989 C 183/4 28 ILM 1306 (1989)
Final Communiqué of the 20th South Pacific Forum, Tarawa (Kiribati) July 1989	A/44/463, Annex
Non-Aligned States: 9th Conference of the Heads of State and Government, Belgrade	A/44/551, Annex

September 1989

UNGA Resolution: Protection of Global Climate for Present and Future Generations of Mankind 22 December 1989	A/RES/44/207
UNGA Resolution: Possible adverse effects of sea-level rise on islands and coastal areas, particularly low-lying coastal areas 22 December 1989	A/RES/44/206
Second World Climate Conference: Ministerial Declaration, Geneva 7 November 1990	A/45/696/Add.1, Annex III
UNGA Resolution: Protection of Global Climate for Present and Future Generations of Mankind [establishment of an International Negotiating Committee for a framework convention on climate change] 21 December 1990	A/RES/45/212

Chapter 4.   Oceans

4.A.   General

International Convention for the Prevention of Pollution of the Sea by Oil, London (and 1962, 1969, 1971 (2x) Protocols—see Section 12.A) 12 May 1954	327 UNTS 3 12 UST 2989 TIAS 4900 UNEP3 #11, p.101 1 IPE 332 IELMT 954: 36
———— IMO London Amendments concerning the Protection of the Great Barrier Reef 12 October 1971	IMCO/Res/A.232(VII) 1 IPE 378 IELMT 971: 77
Convention on the Territorial Sea and the Contiguous Zone (Art. 24(a)) 29 April 1958	516 UNTS 205 15 UST 1606 TIAS 5639 1 IPE 387 IELMT 958: 32
Convention on the Continental Shelf, Geneva (Arts. 2(4), 5(1), (2), (7)) 29 April 1958	499 UNTS 311 15 UST 471 TIAS 5578 UNEP3 #15, p.127 6 IPE 2928, 16 IPE 8297 IELMT 958: 30
Convention on the High Seas, Geneva (Arts. 24,	450 UNTS 82

25) 29 April 1958	13 UST 2312 TIAS 5200 UNEP3 #16, p.129 1 IPE 385 IELMT 958: 33
Convention on Fishing and Conservation of the Living Resources of the High Seas 29 April 1958	559 UNTS 285 17 UST 138 TIAS 5969 UNEP3 #17, p.133 6 IPE 2929 IELMT 958: 31
Copenhagen Convention for the International Council for the Exploration of the Sea (amended) 12 September 1964	652 UNTS 237 24 UST 1080 TIAS 7628 UNEP3 #34, p.195 1 IPE 425 IELMT 964: 68
Brussels International Convention relating to Intervention on the High Seas in Cases of Oil Pollution Casualties 29 November 1969	970 UNTS 211 26 UST 765 TIAS 8068 UNEP3 #43, p.230 1969 UNJYB 166 1 IPE 460 IELMT 969: 89
———— London Protocol relating to Intervention on the High Seas in Cases of Marine Pollution by Substances other than Oil 2 November 1973	TIAS 10561 34 UST 3407 UNEP3 #60, p.400 1973 UNJYB 91 13 ILM 605 (1974)
Brussels International Convention on Civil Liability for Oil Pollution Damage 29 November 1969	*Infra* p.671 973 UNTS 3 UNEP3 #44, p.235 UKTS No.106 (1975) UNEP Reg. p.81 1969 UNJYB 174 9 ILM 45 (1970) 1 IPE 470 IELMT 969: 88
———— London Amending Protocol 19 November 1976	16 ILM 617 (1977) 19 IPE 9443
———— Amendment 25 May 1984	IELMT 969: 88/A/1 13 EPL 66
Lima Declaration by Latin American States on the Law of the Sea (Resolution 3: On the Problem of the Contamination of the Marine Environment) 8 August 1970	A/AC.138/28 10 ILM 207 (1971) 2 IPE 801, 8 IPE 4028

Declaration of Principles Governing the Sea-Bed and the Ocean Floor, and the Subsoil Thereof, Beyond the Limits of National Jurisdiction (paras. 1, 4, 9, 11)
17 December 1970

A/RES/2749(XXV)
2 IPE 804

Treaty on the Prohibition of the Emplacement of Nuclear Weapons and Other Weapons of Mass Destruction on the Sea-Bed and the Ocean Floor and in the Subsoil Thereof
11 February 1971

955 UNTS 115
23 UST 701
TIAS 7337
UNEP3 #48, p.249
2 IPE 498
IELMT 971: 12

Brussels International Convention on the Establishment of an International Fund for Compensation for Oil Pollution Damage
18 December 1971

Infra p.678
1110 UNTS 57
UNEP3 #51, p.255
Cmnd 7383
UKTS No.95 (1978)
UNEP Reg. p.98
1971 UNJYB 103
11 ILM 284 (1972)
2 IPE 529
IELMT 971: 94

———— London Amending Protocol (revising Unit of Account provision)
19 November 1976

UNEP Reg. p.98
16 ILM 621 (1977)
19 IPE 9447

———— London Amending Protocol
25 May 1984

IPE(2) II/A/25-05-84.b
IELMT 971: 94/A

ILA New York Rules on Marine Pollution of Continental Origin
26 August 1972

55 ILA XVII & 97
19 IPE 9641

IMO Convention on the Prevention of Marine Pollution by Dumping of Wastes and Other Matter (London Ocean Dumping Convention—LDC) (amended 1978 (2x) [IELMT 972: 96/A, 972: 96/B], 1980, 1989)
29 December 1972

Infra p.318
1046 UNTS 120
26 UST 2403
TIAS 8165
UNEP3 #56, p.283
11 ILM 1294 (1972)
2 IPE 537
IELMT 972: 96

————13th Consultative Meeting of Contracting Parties, Resolution calling for the phasing out of industrial waste dumping by 31 December 1995
2 November 1990

———— 13th Consultative Meeting of Contracting Parties, Resolution placing sub-seabed disposal of radioactive wastes under the current voluntary moratorium on sea disposal of low-level radioactive wastes

2 November 1990

| London International Convention for the Prevention of Pollution from Ships (MARPOL) 2 November 1973 | IMO: MP/CONF/WP.35 UNEP3 #59, p.320 1973 UNJYB 81 12 ILM 1319 (1973) 2 IPE 552 IELMT 973: 84 |

————— Annex V, Regulations for the Prevention of Pollution by Garbage from Ships 2 November 1973

Infra p.327
IMO: MP/CONF/WP.35
TIAS —
12 ILM 1434 (1973)
UNEP3 #59, p.380

————— London Protocol (later amendments to the 1978 Protocol or to the 1973 Convention: 1984, 1985 (2x), 1987, 1989 (3x)) 17 February 1978

TIAS —
Cmnd 5748
21 IELR 2381
UNEP3 #59, p.382
17 ILM 546 (1978)
19 IPE 9451
IELMT 978: 13

UNGA Resolution: Protection of the Marine Environment 13 December 1973

A/RES/3133(XXVIII)
13 ILM 234 (1974)
8 IPE 4042

Convention on the Intergovernmental Maritime Consultative Organization (IMCO—now IMO), 17 March 1948 (289 UNTS 3), as amended by IMO Assembly (Art. 1(a), and Pt. IX, Arts. 38-42) 14 November 1975

IMO: A.IX/Res.358
34 UST 497
TIAS 10374
Peaslee Pt. V
19 IPE 9651

UNEP Governing Council Decision: Conclusions of the Study of Legal Aspects Concerning the Environment Related to Offshore Mining and Drilling Within the Limits of National Jurisdiction 31 May 1982

UNEP/GC/DEC/10/14VI
UNEP ELGP #4
7 EPL 50

Washington Agreement Concerning Interim Arrangements Relating to Polymetallic Nodules of the Deep Sea Bed 2 September 1982

34 UST 3451
TIAS 10562
IELMT 982: 65

UN Convention on the Law of the Sea, Montego Bay (Arts. 19(h), 43, 64-67, 116-120, 145, 192-237, Annex I) 10 December 1982

Infra p.332
Cmnd 8941
Misc 11 (1983)
A/CONF.62/122
21 ILM 1261 (1982)
IPE(2) II/A/10-12-82
IELMT 982: 92

Provisional Understanding Regarding Deep Seabed Matters (with memorandum of implementa-

TIAS —
IELMT 984: 58

tion, joint record and related exchanges of notes),
Geneva
3 August 1984

UNEP Governing Council Decision: Montreal Guidelines for the Protection of the Marine Environment Against Pollution from Land-Based Sources 24 May 1985	UNEP/GC.13/9/Add.3 UNEP/GC/DEC/13/18II UNEP ELPG #7 IPE(2) II/D/24-05-85
EEC Council Decision: Establishment of a Community Information System for the control and reduction of pollution caused by the spillage of hydrocarbons and other harmful substances at sea 6 March 1986	Reg. No. 86/85 OJEC 1986 L 77/33
Restatement (Third) of the Foreign Relations Law of the United States (Secs. 603-04 and Comments) 1987	*Infra* p.354
UNEP Environmental Guidelines for Coastal Protection Measures 1988	UNEP EMG #17
UNEP Council Decision: Precautionary Approach to Marine Pollution, including Waste-Dumping at Sea 25 May 1989	UNEP/GC/DEC/15/27

4.B.   Antarctic Ocean (see 9.A)

4.C.   Arctic Ocean

Oslo Convention for the Prevention of Marine Pollution by Dumping from Ships and Aircraft (and 1978 Protocol) 15 February 1972	932 UNTS 3 UKTS No.119 (1975) UNEP3 #52, p.266 11 ILM 262 (1972) 2 IPE 530 IELMT 972: 12
Paris Convention for the Prevention of Marine Pollution from Land-Based Sources 4 June 1974	*Infra* p.360 UKTS No.64 (1978) UNEP3 #64, p.430 13 ILM 352 (1974) 2 IPE 748 IELMT 974: 43
Canada-Union of Soviet Socialist Republics: Protocol (to the 1971 Agreement on General Exchanges) for Consultation on the Development of a Programme of Scientific and Technical Cooperation in the Arctic and the North 1984	

Canada-United States of America: Ottawa
Agreement on Arctic Cooperation
11 January 1988

TIAS —
IPE(2) II/A/11-01-88

Canada-United States of America: Agreement on
Arctic Cooperation and Exchange of Notes Concerning Transit of Northwest Passage
10 October 1989

28 ILM 141 (1989)

Union of Soviet Socialist Republics-United States
of America: Agreement Concerning Cooperation
in Combatting Pollution in the Bering and Chukchi
Seas in Emergency Situations
17 October 1989

4.D.   Atlantic Ocean
4.D.i.   North Atlantic

Washington International Convention for the
North-West Atlantic Fisheries (Preamble, Art.
VI(1)) (Protocols and Declarations 1956, 1961,
1963, 1965, 1969, superseded by Ottawa Convention of 24 October 1978)
8 February 1949

157 UNTS 157
1 UST 477
TIAS 2089
6 IPE 2760
IELMT 949: 11

North-East Atlantic Fisheries Convention, London
(Preamble, Arts. 1(1), 6(1), 7(1))
24 January 1959

486 UNTS 157
UNEP3 #18, p.136
6 IPE 2938
IELMT 959: 07

Convention for the International Council for the
Exploration of the Sea
12 September 1964

7 ILM 302 (1968)
1 IPE 425
IELMT 964: 68

Rio de Janeiro International Convention for the
Conservation of Atlantic Tunas
14 May 1966

673 UNTS 63
20 UST 2887
TIAS 6767
UNEP3 #36, p.202
6 IPE 3018
IELMT 966: 38

———— Amending Protocol
10 July 1984

IELMT 966: 38/A

Oslo Convention for the Prevention of Marine Pollution by Dumping from Ships and Aircraft (and
1978 Protocol)
15 February 1972

932 UNTS 3
UKTS No.119 (1975)
UNEP3 #52, p.266
11 ILM 262 (1972)
2 IPE 530
IELMT 972: 12

Paris Convention for the Prevention of Marine Pollution from Land-Based Sources

Infra p.360
UKTS No.64 (1978)

4 June 1974

UNEP3 #64, p.430
13 ILM 352 (1974)
2 IPE 748
IELMT 974: 43

Ottawa Convention on Future Multilateral Co-operation in the North-West Atlantic Fisheries
24 October 1978

US Sen. Exec. Print I,
    96: 1 Cong.
Misc 9 (1979)
Cmnd 7569
22 IPE 107
IELMT 978: 79

London Convention on Future Multilateral Co-operation in the North-East Atlantic Fisheries
18 November 1980

Cmnd 8474
Misc 2 (1981)
OJEC 1981 L 227/22
IPE(2) III/A/18-11-80
IELMT 980: 85

Reykjavik Convention for the Conservation of
Salmon in the North Atlantic Ocean
2 March 1982

TIAS 10789
UNEP Reg. p.205
IPE(2) III/A/22-01-82

Canada-Denmark: Agreement for Cooperation relating to the Marine Environment
26 August 1983

IPE(2) II/A/26-08-83

Lisbon Agreement on Cooperation for the Protection of the Shores and Waters of the North-East
Atlantic Against Pollution
17 October 1990

4.D.ii.   South Atlantic

FAO Convention on the Conservation of the Living
Resources of the South-East Atlantic, Rome
23 October 1969

801 UNTS 101
UNEP3 #42, p.225
7 IPE 3290
IELMT 969: 79

———— Amendments to Arts VIII, XVII,
XVIII(1), XIX and XXI (approved at 8th session
of the International Commission for Southeast Atlantic Fisheries, Tarragona (Spain))
12 December 1985

IPE(2) III/A/12-12-85

Abidjan Convention for Co-operation in the Protection and Development of the Marine and Coastal
Environment of the West and Central African
Region
23 March 1981

UNEP/IG.22/7
UN Water Ser. No.13
20 ILM 746 (1981)
IPE(2) II/A/23-03-81.a
IELMT 981: 23

4.E.   Indian Ocean

FAO Agreement for the Establishment of the Indo-

120 UNTS 59

Pacific Fisheries [Council] Commission (IPFC),   62 Stat. 3711
Baguio (amended 1961 (see below) and November   TIAS 1895
1977 (72nd FAO Council))   IELMT 948: 15
26 February 1948

———— Amending (superseding) Agreement   418 UNTS 348
(adopted by IPFC, 20 Jan. 1961, Karachi)   FAO Conf 11th sess.
23 November 1961   13 UST 2511
                                                   TIAS 5218

Nairobi Convention for the Protection, Manage-   UNEP Reg. p.226
ment and Development of the Marine and Coastal   IPE(2) II/A/21-06-85.a
Environment of the Eastern African Region   IELMT 985: 46
21 June 1985

————Nairobi Protocol Concerning Co-operation   UNEP Reg. p.230
in Combating Marine Pollution in Cases of Emer-   IPE(2) II/A/21-06-85.c
gency in the Eastern African Region   IELMT 985: 48
21 June 1985

4.F.   Pacific Ocean

FAO Agreement for the Establishment of the Indo-   120 UNTS 59
Pacific Fisheries [Council] Commission (IPFC),   62 Stat. 3711
Baguio (amended 1961 (see below) and November   TIAS 1895
1977 (72nd FAO Council))   IELMT 948: 15
26 February 1948

———— Amending (superseding) Agreement   418 UNTS 348
(adopted by IPFC, 20 Jan. 1961, Karachi)   FAO Conf. 11th sess.
23 November 1961   13 UST 2511
                                                   TIAS 5218

4.F.i.   North Pacific

Convention for the Preservation of the Halibut   32 LNTS 93
Fishery of the Northern Pacific Ocean   6 IPE 2596
2 March 1923

Canada-United States of America: Convention for   121 LNTS 45
the Preservation of the Halibut Fishery of the   6 IPE 2636
Northern Pacific Ocean and the Bering Sea (revised
1937 and 1953, amended 1979—see 8.C.ii.a)
9 May 1930

Canada-Japan-United States of America: Tokyo   205 UNTS 65
International Convention for the High Seas Fisher- 4 UST 380
ies of the North Pacific Ocean (Preamble, Arts.   TIAS 2786
III(6)(c), IV)   UNEP3 #10, p.96
9 May 1952   6 IPE 2876
                                                   IELMT 952: 35

———— Seattle Amending Protocol (superseding   30 UST 1095

the 1952 Convention and the Seattle Amendments
of 1960 & 1963. The Protocol was amended: 3
times on 9 April 1986, and on 8 June 1987)
25 April 1978

TIAS 9242
IPE(2) III/A/25-04-73
IELMT 978: 34

Washington Interim Convention on the Conservation of North Pacific Fur Seals (amended and extended 1963, 1969, 1976, 1980 and 1984—see
8.C.iii)
9 February 1957

314 UNTS 105
8 UST 2283
TIAS 3948
UNEP Reg. p.29
UNEP3 #3, p.67
8 IPE 3716
IELMT 957: 11

Japan-United States of America: Washington
Agreement Concerning Commercial Sperm Whaling in the Western Division Stock of the North
Pacific (with summary of discussions)
13 November 1984

TIAS —

Canada-Japan-United States of America: Vancouver Memorandum of Understanding concerning
salmonid research and enforcement of the International Convention for the high seas fisheries of the
North Pacific Ocean
9 April 1986

Republic of Korea-United States of America:
Washington Agreement Regarding the High Seas
Squid Driftnet Fisheries in the North Pacific Ocean
(with record of discussions)
26 September 1989

TIAS —

4.F.ii.   South Pacific

International Convention for the Prevention of Pollution of the Sea by Oil, 1954, IMO London
Amendments Concerning the Protection of the
Great Barrier Reef
12 October 1971

IMCO/RES/A.232(VII)
1 IPE 378
IELMT 971: 77

Apia Convention on the Conservation of Nature in
the South Pacific
12 June 1976

UNEP3 #68, p.463
20 IPE 10359
IELMT 976: 45

Lima Convention for the Protection of the Marine
Environment and Coastal Area of the South-East
Pacific
12 November 1981

UNEP/CPPS/IG/32/4
IPE(2) II/A/12-11-81.a
IELMT 981: 84

————— Quito Protocol for the Protection of the
South-East Pacific Against Pollution from Land-
Based Sources
23 July 1983

UNEP Reg. p.199
IPE(2) II/A/22-07-83.a
IELMT 983: 54

Lima Agreement on Regional Co-operation in Combating Pollution of the South-East Pacific by Oil and Other Harmful Substances in Cases of Emergency
12 November 1981

UNEP Reg. p.197
IPE(2) II/A/12-11-81.b
IELMT 981: 85

———— Quito Protocol
22 July 1983

UNEP Reg. p.198
IPE(2) II/A/22-07-83.b
IELMT 983: 55

———— Supplementary Protocol
20 May 1987

South Pacific Nuclear Free Zone Treaty, Raratonga
6 August 1985

UNEP Reg. p.232
24 ILM 1440 (1985)
IELMT 985: 58

Noumea Convention for the Protection of the Natural Resources and Environment of the South Pacific Region
25 November 1986

UNEP Reg. p.241
IPE(2) II/A/24-11-86
IELMT 986: 87

———— Noumea Protocol for the Prevention of Pollution of the South Pacific Region by Dumping
25 November 1986

UNEP Reg. p.243
IPE(2) II/A/24-11-86.b
IELMT 986: 87/A

———— Noumea Protocol Concerning Co-operation in Combating Pollution Emergencies in the South Pacific Region
25 November 1986

UNEP Reg. p.245
IPE(2) II/A/24-11-86.a
IELMT 986: 87/B

Wellington Convention on the Prohibition of Driftnet Fishing in the South Pacific
24 November 1989

A/44/807
29 ILM 1454 (1990)

———— Protocols I and II, Noumea
20 October 1990

29 ILM 1462, 1463 (1990)

4.G.   North & Baltic Seas

Bonn Agreement for Co-operation in Dealing with Pollution of the North Sea by Oil
9 June 1969

704 UNTS 3
UNEP3 #41, p.223
9 ILM 359 (1970)
19 IPE 9439
IELMT 969: 43

Oslo Convention for the Prevention of Marine Pollution by Dumping from Ships and Aircraft (and 1978 Protocol)
15 February 1972

932 UNTS 3
UKTS No.119 (1975)
UNEP3 #52, p.266
11 ILM 262 (1972)
2 IPE 530
IELMT 972: 12

Copenhagen (Nordic) Agreement on Co-operation   2 IPE 502
in Oil Pollution
16 September 1971

Paris Convention for the Prevention of Marine Pol-   *Infra* p.360
lution from Land-Based Sources   UKTS No.64 (1978)
4 June 1974   UNEP3 #64, p.430
                                                      13 ILM 352 (1974)
                                                      2 IPE 748
                                                      IELMT 974: 43

Ministerial Declaration of the First International   IPE(2) II/B/1-11-84
Conference on the Protection of the North Sea,
Bremen
1 November 1984

Gdansk Convention on Fishing and Conservation   UNEP3 #58, p.317
of the Living Resources in the Baltic Sea and the   12 ILM 1291 (1973)
Belts   7 IPE 3367
13 September 1973   IELMT 973: 68

———— Warsaw Protocol to Provide for EEC   22 ILM 704 (1983)
Membership   IPE(2) III/A/11-11-82
11 November 1982   IELMT 973: 68/A

Helsinki Convention for the Protection of the Ma-   UNEP3 #63, p.405
rine Environment of the Baltic Sea Area   13 ILM 546 (1974)
22 March 1974   2 IPE 733
                                                      IELMT 974: 23

Bonn Agreement for Co-operation in Dealing with   UNEP Reg. p.218
Pollution of the North Sea by Oil and Other Harm-   IPE(2) II/A/13-09-83
ful Substances   IELMT 983: 68
13 September 1983

Ministerial Declaration of the Second International   IPE(2) II/B/25-11-87
Conference on the Protection of the North Sea,
London
25 November 1987

Ministerial Declaration of the Third International
Conference on the Protection of the North Sea,
The Hague
8 March 1990

4.H.   Mediterranean Sea (see also 9.B)

Barcelona Convention for the Protection of the   *Infra* p.370
Mediterranean Sea against Pollution   UNTS Reg. #16908
16 February 1976   UNEP3 #66, p.448
                                                      UNEP Reg. p.136
                                                      15 ILM 290 (1976)
                                                      19 IPE 9497

IELMT 976: 13

———— Barcelona Protocol concerning Co-operation in Combating Pollution of the Mediterranean
Sea by Oil and Other Harmful Substances in Cases
of Emergency
16 February 1976

Infra p.381
UNTS Reg. #16908
UNEP Reg. p.140
15 ILM 306 (1976)
19 IPE 9506
IELMT 976: 15

———— Barcelona Protocol for the Prevention of
Pollution of the Mediterranean Sea by Dumping
from Ships and Aircraft
16 February 1976

Infra p.377
UNTS Reg. #16908
UNEP Reg. p.138
15 ILM 300 (1976)
19 IPE 9515
IELMT 967: 14

———— Athens Protocol for the Protection of the
Mediterranean Sea against Pollution from Land-
Based Sources
17 May 1980

Infra p.384
UNTS Reg. #22281
UNEP Reg. p.142
19 ILM 869 (1980)
IELMT 980: 37

———— Geneva Protocol concerning Mediterranean Specially Protected Areas
3 April 1982

Infra p.389
UNTS Reg. #24079
IELMT 982: 26

FAO Agreement for the Establishment of a General
Fisheries Council for the Mediterranean (GFCM),
Rome (amended 1963 (12th FAO Conference) and
December 1976 (70th FAO Council))
24 September 1949

126 UNTS 237
UNEP3 #5, p.88
6 IPE 2857
IELMT 949: 72

4.I.   Caribbean Sea

Santo Domingo de Guzman Declaration of Specialized Conference of Caribbean Countries Concerning the Problems of the Sea (paragraphs on Marine
Pollution)
9 June 1972

11 ILM 893 (1972)
2 IPE 871

Cartagena Convention for the Protection and Development of the Marine Environment of the Wider
Caribbean Region
24 March 1983

TIAS —
Misc 19
Cmnd 9022
22 ILM 221 (1983)
IPE(2) II/A/24-03-83.a
IELMT 983: 23

———— Cartagena Protocol concerning Co-operation in Combating Oil Spills in the Wider Caribbean Region
24 March 1983

UNEP/GC.15/INF/2,
p.204 (1989)
UNEP Reg. p.204
22 ILM 240 (1983)
IPE(2) II/A/24-03-83.b
IELMT 983: 24

————— Kingston Protocol Concerning Specially
Protected Areas and Wildlife
16 January 1990

4.J.   Middle Eastern Seas

Action Plan for the Protection and Development of   19 IPE 9874
the Marine Environment and the Coastal Areas of
Bahrain, Iran, Iraq, Kuwait, Oman, Qatar, Saudi
Arabia, and the United Arab Emirates
23 April 1978

Kuwait Regional Convention for Co-operation on   1140 UNTS 133
the Protection of the Marine Environment from   UNEP3 #74, p.486
Pollution   17 ILM 511 (1978)
24 April 1978   19 IPE 9551
          IELMT 978: 31

————— Kuwait Protocol concerning Regional Co-   17 ILM 526 (1978)
operation in Combating Pollution by Oil and Other   19 IPE 9551
Harmful Substances in Cases of Emergency   IELMT 978: 32
24 April 1978

Jeddah Regional Convention for the Conservation   9 EPL 56 (1982)
of the Red Sea and Gulf of Aden Environment   UNEP Reg. p.201
14 February 1982   IPE(2) II/A/14-02-82.a
          IELMT 982: 13

————— Jeddah Protocol concerning Regional Co-   UNEP Sales No:
operation in Combating Pollution by Oil and other   GE.83-IX-02934
Harmful Substances in Cases of Emergency   IPE(2) II/A/14-02-82.b
14 February 1982   IELMT 982: 14

Chapter 5.   Fresh Waters

5.A.   General

IIL Madrid Resolution on International Regula-   24 AIDI 365
tions regarding the Use of International Water-   11 IPE 5702
courses for Purposes other than Navigation (Pre-
amble)
19 April 1911

Geneva Convention Relating to the Development   36 LNTS 75
of Hydraulic Power Affecting more than one State   LEG/SER.B/12, p.91
(Art. 4)   11 IPE 5506
9 December 1923

ILA Helsinki Rules on the Uses of the Waters of   *Infra* p.395
International Rivers (Arts. IX-XI, XV)   52 ILA 484 (1967)
20 August 1966   11 IPE 5741

AALCC, Draft Propositions on the Law of Interna-   A/CN.4/274, p.226

tional Rivers 7 January 1973	26 IPE 136
OECD Council Recommendation: Control of Eu- trophication of Waters 14 November 1974	OECD C(74)220 OECD p.44
OECD Council Recommendation: Strategies for Specific Water Pollutants Control 14 November 1974	OECD C(74)221 OECD p.45 1 IPE 308
ILA Madrid Resolution on International Water Re- sources Administration (Art. 1, Annex 6(g), (h)) 4 September 1976	57 ILA 248 26 IPE 159
ILA Madrid Resolution on the Protection of Water Resources and Water Installations in Times of Armed Conflict (Arts. IV, V) 4 September 1976	57 ILA 234 26 IPE 159
UN Water Conference, Recommendation on Envi- ronment and Health, Mar del Plata 25 March 1977	E/CONF.70/29 26 IPE 166
OECD Council Recommendation: Water Manage- ment Policies and Instruments (with appended Ex- planatory Notes) 5 April 1978	OECD C(78)4(Final) OECD p.46 26 IPE 239
IIL Athens Resolution on Pollution of Rivers and Lakes and International Law 1979	58: I AIDI 193
ILA Belgrade Articles on the Regulation of the Flow of Water of International Watercourses (Part III, A, B, Art. 1(C)) 23 August 1980	59 ILA 362

WHO/FAO/UNEP Memorandum of Understand-
ing Governing Collaboration in the Prevention and
Control of Water-Borne and Associated Diseases
in Agricultural Water Development Activities
1981
	UNEP/GC/
	    INFORMATION/6/
	    Add.6

UNEP Environmental Guidelines for Watershed Development 1982	UNEP EMG #3
ILA Montreal Rules on Water Pollution in an Inter- national Drainage Basin 4 September 1982	60 ILA 535 (1983)
ILA Seoul Rules on International Groundwaters	*Infra* p.403

30 August 1986   62 ILA 251 (1987)

ILC: Draft Articles on the Law of the Non-Naviga-   *Infra* p.404
tional Uses of International Watercourses (Arts. 7,   A/46/10 (1991), Ch.III
20-25, 29)
19 July 1991

5.B.   Africa (see also 9.C)

Cameroon-Nigeria: London Agreement respecting   218 CTS 23
the settlement of the frontier between Nigeria and   9 Martens(3) 190
the Cameroons, from Yola to the sea, and the regu-
lation of navigation on the Cross River
11 March 1913

Belgium-United Kingdom: London Agreement re-   190 LNTS 104
garding water rights on the boundary between Tan-   139 BFSP 746
ganyika and Ruanda-Urundi (Art.3)   LEG/SER.B/12, p.97
22 November 1934   25 IPE 236

Portugal-United Kingdom: Lisbon Agreement with   210 UNTS 280
regard to certain Angolan and Northern Rhodesian   LEG/SER.B/12, p.141
Natives living on the Kwando River (Art. 1(2)(a))
18 November 1954

Niamey Agreement Concerning the Niger River   587 UNTS 21
Commission and the Navigation and Transport on   11 IPE 5648
the River Niger (Art. 12)   IELMT 964: 87
25 November 1964

Gambia-Guinea-Senegal: Kaolack Convention Re-   UN Water Ser. No.13
lating to the status of the River Gambia   Tr. #10
30 June 1978

Harare Agreement on the Action Plan for the Envi-   27 ILM 1109 (1988)
ronmentally Sound Management of the Common
Zambezi River System
28 May 1987

5.C.   Americas
5.C.i.   General

Montevideo Declaration concerning Industrial and   A/5409 III, Ann.I
Agricultural Use of International Rivers   11 IPE 5707
24 December 1933

OAS/IAJC Draft Convention on Industrial and Ag- OEA/Ser.1/VI.1
ricultural Use of International Rivers and Lakes
1965

Argentina-Chile: Act of Santiago concerning Hy- A/CN.4/274 I 180

drologic Basins (Preamble, Art. 2)   11 IPE 5771
26 June 1971

Argentina-Uruguay: Buenos Aires Declaration on   A/CN.4/274, para.328
Water Resources   11 IPE 5774
9 July 1971

5.C.ii. Great Lakes

Canada-United States of America: Washington   *Infra* p.412
Treaty Relating to Boundary Waters and Questions   12 Bevans 319
Arising Along the Boundary between the United   36 Stat. 2448
States and Canada (Art. IV)   TS 548
11 January 1909   102 BFSP 137
                                              LEG/SER.B/12, p.261
                                              10 IPE 5158

Canada-United States of America: Washington   6 UST 2836
Convention on Great Lakes Fisheries   TIAS 3326
10 September 1954

Canada-United States of America: Report by the   8 ILM 1363 (1969)
International Joint Commission on Risks of Oil
Pollution in Lake Erie
27 October 1969

Cana-United States of America: Great Lakes Water   11 ILM 694 (1972)
Quality Agreement   10 IPE 5292
15 April 1972

———— Washington Agreement Concerning Ap-   TIAS 9257
pendix I: Reduction in Phosphorus Loadings in   10 IPE 5334
Lakes Superior and Huron
21 November 1973

Canada-United States of America: Great Lakes   *Infra* p.419
Water Quality Agreement, Ottawa   30 UST 1383
22 November 1978   TIAS 9257
                                              26 IPE 19

———— Amending Protocol   *Infra* p.419
16 October 1983   TIAS 10798

———— Amending Protocol   *Infra* p.419
18 November 1987

5.C.iii. Other Particular Waters

Mexico-United States of America: Washington   3 UNTS 314
Treaty relating to the Utilization of the Waters of   59 Stat. 1219
the Colorado & Tijuana Rivers, and of the Rio   TS 994
Grande (Rio Bravo) from Fort Quitman (Texas) to   LEG/SER.B/12, p.238

the Gulf of Mexico (Art. 3) 3 February 1944	25 IPE 240
Canada-United States of America: Ottawa Agreement relating to a Study to be made by the International Joint Commission with respect to the Upper Columbia River Basin (para. 2(G)) 3 March 1944	109 UNTS 191 58 Stat. 1236 EAS 399 LEG/SER.B/12, p.192 10 IPE 5181
Argentina-Uruguay: Montevideo Agreement on the Boundary Constituted by the Uruguay River (Art. 7(e), (f)) 7 April 1961	LEG/SER.B/12, p.164 10 IPE 4888
Asuncion Declaration on the Use of International Rivers (Act of Asuncion) adopted by Ministers for Foreign Affairs of countries of La Plata River Basin (Argentina, Bolivia, Brazil, Paraguay & Uruguay) 3 June 1971	A/CN.4/274, para.326 11 IPE 5768
Argentina-Chile: Santiago Act Concerning Hydrologic Basins 26 June 1971	A/CN.4/274, para.327 11 IPE 5771
Argentina-Bolivia: Buenos Aires Act on Hydrological Basins 12 July 1971	Arg. No.99 (1971) 11 IPE 5774
Canada-United States of America: Ottawa Agreement Relating to the Establishment of a Canada-United States Committee on Water Quality in the St. John River and its Tributory Rivers and Streams which cross the Canada-United States Boundary 21 September 1972	23 UST 2813 TIAS 7470 10 IPE 5327
Mexico-United States of America: Agreement concerning the Permanent and Definitive Solution to the International Problem of the Salinity of the Colorado River 30 August 1973	915 UNTS 203 24 UST 1968 TIAS 7708 12 ILM 1105 (1973) 11 IPE 5368
Argentina-Uruguay: Statute of the Uruguay River (Arts. 36-41) 1975	
Brasilia Treaty for Amazonian Co-operation 3 July 1978	*Infra* p.546 UNEP3 #75, p.496 UNEP Reg. p.164 17 ILM 1045 (1978) 18 IPE 9017 IELMT 978: 49

Amazon Declaration, adopted by the Presidents of the States Parties to the Treaty for Amazonian Co-operation, Manaus (Brazil)
6 May 1989

Infra p.551
A/44/275, Annex
E/1989/79, Annex
28 ILM 1303 (1989)

5.D.   Asia

Jordan-Syrian Arab Republic: Damascus Agreement concerning the Utilization of the Yarmuk Waters (Art. 10(h))
4 June 1953

184 UNTS 25
LEG/SER.B/12, p.383

Afghanistan-Union of Soviet Socialist Republics: Moscow Treaty concerning the Regime of the Soviet-Afghan State Frontier (Arts. 9, 12, 13, 22)
18 January 1958

321 UNTS 166
LEG/SER.B/12, p.276
9 IPE 4579

Varna Convention concerning Fishing in the Black Sea (amended 30 June 1965) (Arts. 1, 5)
7 July 1959

377 UNTS 203
UNEP3 #19, p.141
6 IPE 2976
IELMT 959: 51

5.E.   Europe
5.E.i.   General

ECE Declaration of Policy on Water Pollution Control
29 April 1966

ECE/RES/10(XXI)
11 IPE 5740

ECE Decision: Body on Water Resources and Water Pollution Control Problems
2 May 1968

ECE/DEC/E(XXIII)
E/ECE/682, Annex V

EEC Council Directive: Quality of Surface Water Intended for Drinking Water
16 June 1975

Dir. No. 75/440
OJEC 1975 L 194/26
11 IPE 5818

EEC Council Directive: Quality of Bathing Water
8 December 1975

Dir. No. 76/160
OJEC 1976 L 31/1
11 IPE 5826

EEC Council Directive: Pollution Caused by Certain Dangerous Substances Discharged into the Aquatic Environment of the Community
4 May 1976

Dir. No. 76/464
OJEC 1976 L 129/23
15 ILM 1113 (1976)
11 IPE 5835

EEC Council Directive: Quality of Fresh Water Needing Protection in Order to Support Fish Life
18 July 1978

Dir. No. 78/659
OJEC 1978 L 222/1
26 IPE 247

EEC Council Directive: Quality Required of Shell-

Dir. No. 79/923

fish Waters 30 October 1979	OJEC 1979 L 281/47 24 IPE 177
EEC Council Directive: Protection of Groundwater against Pollution Caused by Certain Dangerous Substances 17 December 1979	Dir. No. 80/68 OJEC 1980 L 20/43 26 IPE 274
ECE Decision: Declaration of Policy on Prevention and Control of Water Pollution, Including Transboundary Pollution 23 April 1980	*Infra* p.433 ECE/DEC/B(XXXV) E/1980/28 6 EPL 148 26 IPE 280
EEC Council Directive: Quality of Water Intended for Human Consumption 15 July 1980	Dir. No. 80/778 OJEC 1980 L 229/11 26 IPE 285
ECE Decision: International Co-operation on Shared Water Resources 2 April 1982	ECE/DEC/D(XXXVII)
ECE Decision: Declaration of Policy on the Rational Use of Water 14 April 1984	ECE/DEC/C(XXXIX)
ECE Decision: Co-operation in the Field of Transboundary Waters 26 April 1986	ECE/DEC/B(41)
ECE Decision: Principles on Co-operation in the Field of Transboundary Waters 10 April 1987	ECE/DEC/I(42)
ECE Decision: Charter on Ground-Water Management 21 April 1989	ECE/DEC/E(44), para.1 E/ECE/1197

5.E.ii.   Rhine

Baden (Federal Republic of Germany*)-Switzerland: Berne Convention Establishing Uniform Regulations Concerning Fishing in the Rhine between Constance and Basle 9 December 1869	149 CTS 137 9 IPE 4695
Baden (Federal Republic of Germany*)-France-Switzerland: Basle Convention Establishing Uniform Regulations Concerning Fishing in the Rhine and its Tributaries, Including Lake Constance 25 March 1875	149 CTS 139 9 IPE 4702
Germany (pre-post-WWII)-Netherlands-Switzer-	LEG/SER.B/12, p.393

land: Berlin Convention to Regulate the Fishing for Salmon in the Rhine Basin 12 June 1885	IELMT 885: 48
Baden (Federal Republic of Germany*)-Alsace-Lorraine (France*)-Switzerland: Lucerne Convention Establishing Uniform Rules for Fishing in the Rhine and its Tributaries, including Lake Constance (Art. 10) 18 May 1887	LEG/SER.B/12, p.397 9 IPE 4730
Berne Convention on the International Commission for the Protection of the Rhine against Pollution 29 April 1963	*Infra* p.438 994 UNTS 3 UNEP3 #29, p.176 10 IPE 4820 IELMT 963: 31
——— Bonn Additional Agreement 3 December 1976	OJEC 1977 L 240/35 25 IPE 290
Bonn Convention for the Protection of the Rhine River against Chemical Pollution 3 December 1976	*Infra* p,442 1124 UNTS 375 UNEP3 #70, p.468 16 ILM 242 (1977) 25 IPE 440 IELMT 976: 89
Bonn Convention for the Protection of the Rhine River against Pollution by Chlorides 3 December 1976	*Infra* p.450 16 ILM 265 (1977) 26 IPE 1 IELMT 976: 90

5.E.iii. Other particular waters (see also 8.C.ii.b)

Denmark-Germany (pre-post-WWII): Agreement relating to Watercourses and Dikes on the Danish-German Frontier (Arts. 29, 45, 46) (together with a Final Protocol and Instructions for the Frontier Water Commission and the Supreme Frontier Water Commission) 10 April 1922	10 LNTS 201 LEG/SER.B/12, p.577 11 IPE 5473
Belgium-Germany (pre-post-WWII): Provisions Concerning the Common Frontier of Belgium and Germany Established by a Delimitation Commission in Implementation of the Treaty of Versailles (Arts. III, V) 6 November 1922	14 Martens(3) 834 LEG/SER.B/12, p.411 11 IPE 5495
Finland-Norway: Oslo Convention and Statute Regarding the Floating of Timber on the Pasvik 14 February 1925	49 LNTS 390
Poland-Union of Soviet Socialist Republics: Mos-	37 UNTS 66

cow Agreement Concerning the Regime on the So-
viet-Polish State Frontier (Arts. 16(3), 17)
8 July 1948

LEG/SER.B/12, p.889
9 IPE 4475

Finland-Union of Soviet Socialist Republics: Moscow Agreement Concerning the Regime of the So-
viet-Finnish Frontier
9 December 1948

217 UNTS 135
155 BFSP 382
10 IPE 4973

Belgium-France-Luxembourg: Brussels Protocol
for the Establishment of a Standing Tripartite Commission for Polluted Waters
8 April 1950

66 UNTS 286
LEG/SER.B/12, p.422
11 IPE 5553
IELMT 950: 27

Romania-Yugoslavia: Agreement on Questions of
Water Control, Water Control System and Frontier
Waters (Arts. 1, 3, Commission Statute, Art. 2)
7 April 1955

LEG/SER.B/12, p.928
9 IPE 4531

Hungary-Yugoslavia: Belgrade Agreement, together with the Statute of the Yugoslav-Hungarian
Water Economy Commission (Art. 1(2)(f))
8 August 1955

LEG/SER.B/12, p.831
9 IPE 4538

Austria-Hungary: Vienna Treaty Concerning the
Regulation of Water Economy Questions in the
Frontier Region
9 April 1956

438 UNTS 123
25 IPE 272

Czechoslovakia-Hungary: Prague Treaty Concerning the Regime of the State Frontier
13 October 1956

300 UNTS 125
9 IPE 4545

France-Federal Republic of Germany-Luxembourg: Luxembourg Convention for the Channelling of the Mosel (Art. 7)
27 October 1956

LEG/SER.B/12, p.424
11 IPE 5575

Czechoslovakia-Union of Soviet Socialist Republics: Moscow Agreement Concerning the Regime
of the Soviet-Czechoslovak Frontier and the Procedure for the Settlement of Frontier Incidents (Arts.
14(1), 16(3))
30 November 1956

266 UNTS 302
LEG/SER.B/12, p.576
9 IPE 4558

Italy-Yugoslavia: Nova Gorica Agreement Concerning the Provision of Water to the Commune of
Gorizia in Accordance with Paragraph 5 of Annex
V to the Treaty of Peace with Italy (Art. 7)
18 July 1957

LEG/SER.B/12, p.868

Czechoslovakia-Poland: Prague Agreement Concerning the Use of Water Resources in Frontier

538 UNTS 89
15 IPE 7401

Waters
21 March 1958

Bulgaria-Yugoslavia: Sofia Agreement Concerning Water Economy Questions (Art. 2(e)) 4 April 1958	367 UNTS 104 LEG/SER.B/12, p.558 9 IPE 4600
Federal Republic of Germany-Netherlands: Hague Treaty Concerning the Course of the Common Frontier, the Boundary Waters, Real Property Situated near the Frontier, Traffic Crossing the Frontier on Land and Via Inland Waters, and Other Frontier Questions (Frontier Treaty) (Art. 58(2)(e)) 8 April 1960	1960 NetTract. #68 LEG/SER.B/12, p.757 11 IPE 5588
Belgium-Netherlands: Treaty concerning the Improvement of the Terneuzen and Ghent Canal (Titles VI, VII) 20 June 1960	423 UNTS 19 LEG/SER.B/12, p.555 11 IPE 5591
Finland-Union of Soviet Socialist Republics: Helsinki Agreement Concerning the Regime of the Finnish-Soviet State Frontier and the Procedure for the Settlement of Frontier Incidents (Arts. 15, 21) 23 June 1960	379 UNTS 330 LEG/SER.B/12, p.656 10 IPE 5039
Steckborn Convention on the Protection of Lake Constance against Pollution 27 October 1960	LEG/SER.B/12, p.438 10 IPE 4814 IELMT 960: 80
Paris Protocol concerning the Constitution of an International Commission for the Protection of the Mosel Against Pollution 20 December 1961	940 UNTS 211 UNEP3 #25, p.165 11 IPE 5618 IELMT 961: 94
France-Switzerland: Paris Convention Concerning the Protection of the Waters of Lake Geneva Against Pollution 16 November 1962	922 UNTS 49 10 IPE 4872
Finland-Union of Soviet Socialist Republics: Helsinki Agreement concerning Frontier Watercourses (Arts. 2, 4) 24 April 1964	537 UNTS 231 10 IPE 5076
Poland-Union of Soviet Socialist Republics: Warsaw Agreement Concerning the Use of Water Resources in Frontier Waters (Arts. 3(7), (12), 4(2), 11) 17 July 1964	552 UNTS 175 9 IPE 4641
German Democratic Republic-Poland: Berlin Agreement on Co-operation in Water Economy	52 EGDZ 331 WTI p.1298

Questions in Frontier Waters (on Border Area Water Use) 11 March 1965	25 IPE 294
Austria-Federal Republic of Germany-Switzerland: Agreement regulating the Withdrawal of Water from Lake Constance (Art. 3) 30 April 1966	620 UNTS 191 10 IPE 4825 IELMT 966: 32
Austria-Czechoslovakia: Vienna Treaty Concerning the Regulation of Water Management Questions Relating to Frontier Waters 7 December 1967	728 UNTS 313 9 IPE 4648
Czechoslovakia-Union of Soviet Socialist Republics: Bratislava Convention Concerning Water Economy Questions in Frontier Waters 26 November 1968	266 UNTS 243 1969 CSSR No.63
Finland-Sweden: Stockholm Agreement Concerning Frontier Rivers (Arts. 1-3, 6(3), 7(2), 8, 9, 13) 16 September 1971	825 UNTS 191 10 IPE 5092
Czechoslovakia-German Democratic Republic: Prague Agreement concerning Water Economy Questions in Frontier Waters 27 February 1974	1974 EGND 2802
Czechoslovakia-Hungary: Budapest Convention Concerning the Regulation of Water Economy Questions in Frontier Waters 31 May 1975	1978 TRHG 488
Czechoslovakia-Hungary: Budapest Treaty Concerning the Construction and Operation of the Hydraulic Works of Gabcikovo and Nagymaros 16 September 1977	1978 TRHG 305
Finland-Norway: Agreement concerning a Norwegian-Finnish Commission for Frontier Watercourses 1980	1981 Norw. 236
Czechoslovakia-Federal Republic of Germany (post-absorption)-European Community: Convention creating an international commission to protect the Elbe River 1990	

Chapter 6.   Land and Soil (see also 23.B.iii)

FAO: World Soil Charter 1981	*Infra* p.456 21 FAO Conf

Chapter 7.   Outer Space

2 April 1981

Agreement Governing the Activities of States on the Moon and Other Celestial Bodies (Arts. 4(1), 7) 5 December 1979	A/RES/34/68 IELMT 979: 92

Brazil-United States of America: Brasilia Agreement for Use of the Geostationary Operational Environmental Satellite in the Brazilian National Plan for Data Collection Platforms 14 June 1982	34 UST 1351 TIAS 10419

Netherlands Working Paper submitted to the Legal Sub-Committee of the UN Committee on the Peaceful Uses of Outer Space: Space debris (an explanatory note) 21 March 1989	A/AC.105/C.2/L.171

Draft Principles Relevant to the Use of Nuclear Power Sources in Outer Space [being elaborated by the COPUOS Legal Sub-Committee] 20 April 1990	A/45/20, Annex II

UNGA Resolution: International Co-operation in the Peaceful Uses of Outer Space (references to space debris: preamble and paras. 21-23) 11 December 1990	A/RES/45/72

Chapter 8.   Biological Resources

8.A.   General

London Convention relative to the Preservation of Fauna and Flora in their Natural State 8 November 1933	172 LNTS 241 UKTS No.27 (1930) Cmnd 5280 UNEP3 #1, p.57 4 IPE 1693 IELMT 933: 83

Washington Convention on Nature Protection and Wildlife Preservation in the Western Hemisphere 12 October 1940	Infra p.211 161 UNTS 193 3 Bevans 630 56 Stat. 1354 TS 981 UNEP3 #2, p.64 4 IPE 1729 IELMT 940: 76

Brussels Agreed Measures for the Conservation of Antarctic Fauna and Flora 13 June 1964	17 UST 992 TIAS 6058 8 IPE 4002 5 IPE 2405

IELMT 964: 41

Washington Convention on International Trade in Endangered Species of Wild Fauna and Flora (CITES)
3 March 1973

Infra p.466
993 UNTS 243
27 UST 1087
TIAS 8249
UKTS No.101 (1976)
Cmnd 6647
UNEP3 #57, p.289
12 ILM 1088 (1973)
5 IPE 2228
IELMT 973: 08

———— Bonn Amendment
22 June 1979

22 IPE 389
US Sen. Exec. Print C, 96: 2
    Cong.

———— Gaborone Amendment
30 April 1983

US Sen. Tr. Doc. 98-10

C/E Convention on the Conservation of European Wildlife and Natural Habitats, Berne
19 September 1979

ETS #104
UKTS No.56 (1982)
Cmnd 8738
UNEP3 #77, p.589
23 IPE 40
IELMT 979: 70

Canberra Convention on the Conservation of Antarctic Marine Living Resources (CCAMLR)
20 May 1980

Infra p.520
Cmnd 8714
33 UST 3476
TIAS 10240
UKTS No.48 (1982)
19 ILM 841 (1980)
IPE(2) III/A/20-05-80
IELMT 980: 39

EEC Commission Regulation: Implementation of CITES Treaty
3 December 1982

Reg. No. 3626/82
OJEC 1982 L 384/1

Action Plan for Biosphere Reserves (adopted at the 8th Session of the International Co-ordinating Council of the Programme on Man and the Biosphere)
December 1984

UNEP/GC.13/L.6

Nairobi Convention for the Protection, Management and Development of the Marine and Coastal Environment of the Eastern African Region, 1985, Nairobi Protocol concerning Protected Areas and Wild Fauna and Flora in the Eastern African Region
21 June 1985

UNEP Reg. p.228
IELMT 985: 46

ECE Declaration on Conservation of Flora, Fauna and their Habitats 21 April 1988	E/ECE/1172 ECE/DEC/E(43), para.2
EEC Council Proposed Directive: Protection of Natural and Semi-Natural Habitats of Wild Fauna and Flora 1990	OJEC 1988 C 247/3
Cartagena Convention on the Marine Environment of the Wider Caribbean Region, 1983, Kingston Protocol Concerning Specially Protected Areas and Wildlife 16 January 1990	

8.B.   Diversity

IUCN World Conservation Strategy, Living Resources Conservation for Sustainable Development (in co-operation with UNEP, WWF, FAO and UNESCO), Gland (Switzerland) 1980	UNEP/GC/DEC/8/11 23 IPE 420
IUCN, Draft Articles for Inclusion in a Proposed Convention on the Conservation of Biological Diversity by means of the Preservation in Situ of Wild Genetic Resources 10 February 1988	IPE(2) I/I/10-02-88

8.C.   Fauna
8.C.i.   General

London Convention for the Protection of Wild Animals, Birds and Fish in Africa 19 May 1900	94 BFSP 715 4 IPE 1605
FAO Convention on the Conservation of the Living Resources of the South-East Atlantic, Rome 23 October 1969	801 UNTS 101 UNEP3 #42, p.225 7 IPE 3290 IELMT 969: 79
——— Amendments to Arts VIII, XVII, XVIII(1), XIX and XXI (approved at 8th session of the International Commission for Southeast Atlantic Fisheries, Tarragona (Spain)) 12 December 1985	IPE(2) III/A/12-12-85
Wellington Convention on the Prohibition of Driftnet Fishing in the South Pacific 24 November 1989	A/44/807 29 ILM 1454 (1990)
——— Protocols I and II, Noumea	29 ILM 1462, 1463 (1990)

20 October 1990

Authority of the Organization of Eastern Caribbean States: Castries Declaration on establishment of a regional regime for the regulation and management of the pelagic resources in the Lesser Antilles region that would outlaw use of drift nets
24 November 1989

A/45/64, Annex

UNGA Resolution: Large-scale pelagic driftnet fishing and its impact on the living marine resources of the world's oceans and seas
22 December 1989

A/RES/44/225
29 ILM 1556 (1990)

Antarctic Treaty, Protocol on Environmental Protection (see 9.A), Annex II (Conservation of Antarctic Fauna and Flora)
21 June 1991

XI ATSCM/2

8.C.ii.   Fishes & Crustaceans

Canada-United States of America: Convention for the Preservation of the Halibut Fishery of the Northern Pacific Ocean
2 March 1923

32 LNTS 93
6 IPE 2596

Canada-United States of America: Convention for the Preservation of the Halibut Fishery of the Northern Pacific Ocean and the Bering Sea
9 May 1930

121 LNTS 45
6 IPE 2636

———— Revised Convention
29 January 1937

181 LNTS 209
6 IPE 2639

———— Revised Convention, Ottawa
2 March 1953

222 UNTS 77
5 UST 5
TIAS 2900
6 IPE 2655

———— Amendment
29 March 1979

32 UST 2483
TIAS 9855
22 IPE 121

London Convention for the Regulation of the Meshes of Fishing Nets and the Size Limits of Fish
5 April 1946

231 UNTS 199
6 IPE 2710
IELMT 946: 26

FAO Agreement for the Establishment of the Indo-Pacific Fisheries [Council] Commission (IPFC), Baguio (amended 1961 (see below) and November 1977 (72nd FAO Council))
26 February 1948

120 UNTS 59
62 Stat. 3711
TIAS 1895
IELMT 948: 15

———— Amending (superseding) Agreement
(adopted by IPFC, 20 Jan. 1961, Karachi)
23 November 1961

418 UNTS 348
FAO Conf 11th
sess.
13 UST 2511
TIAS 5218

8.C.ii.a. Salt Water

Washington International Convention for the
North-West Atlantic Fisheries (Preamble, Art.
VI(1))
8 February 1949

157 UNTS 157
1 UST 477
TIAS 2089
6 IPE 2760
IELMT 949: 11

———— Protocol
25 June 1956

10 UST 59
TIAS 4170
6 IPE 2780
IELMT 956: 47

———— Declaration
24 April 1961

14 UST 924
TIAS 5380
6 IPE 2783
IELMT 961: 31

———— Washington Protocol
15 July 1963

590 UNTS 292
17 UST 635
TIAS 6011
6 IPE 2786
IELMT 963: 52

———— Protocols
29 November 1965

21 UST 567, 576
TIAS 6840, 6841
6 IPE 2789, 2793
IELMT 965: 88

———— Protocol
1 October 1969

6 IPE 2796
IELMT 969: 73

Canada-Japan-United States of America: Tokyo
International Convention for the High Seas Fisheries of the North Pacific Ocean (Preamble, Arts
III(6)(c), IV)
9 May 1952

205 UNTS 65
4 UST 380
TIAS 2786
UNEP3 #10, p.96
6 IPE 2876
IELMT 952: 35

———— Amendment
17 November 1962

14 UST 953
TIAS 5385
6 IPE 2894
IELMT 962: 85

———— Seattle Amending Protocol (superseding
the 1952 Convention and the Seattle Amendments
of 1960 & 1963). The Protocol was amended: 3

30 UST 1095
TIAS 9242
IPE(2) III/A/25-04-78

times on 9 April 1986, and on 8 June 1987   IELMT 978: 34
25 April 1978

———— Amendment   IPE(2) III/A/09-04-86
9 April 1986

Washington Convention for the Establishment of   80 UNTS 3
an Inter-American Tropical Tuna Commission   1 UST 230
(Preamble, Art. II)   TIAS 2044
31 May 1949   UNEP3 #4, p.76
                                                    6 IPE 2848
                                                    IELMT 949: 41

FAO Agreement for the Establishment of a General   126 UNTS 237
Fisheries Council for the Mediterranean (GFCM),   UNEP3 #5, p.80
Rome (amended 1963 (12th FAO Conference) and   6 IPE 2857
December 1976 (70th FAO Council))   IELMT 949: 72
24 September 1949

Denmark-Norway-Sweden: Oslo Agreement [on]   175 UNTS 205
Measures for Protection of the Stocks of Deep-sea   UNEP3 #9, p.94
Prawns (Pandalus Borealis), European Lobsters   8 IPE 3769
(Homarus vulgaris), Norway Lobsters (Nephrops   IELMT 952: 18
norvegicus) and Crabs (Cancer Pagurus)
7 March 1952

———— Amendment   8 IPE 3772
14 October 1959   IELMT 959: 76

Convention on Fishing and Conservation of the   559 UNTS 285
Living Resources of the High Seas   17 UST 138
29 April 1958   TIAS 5969
                                                    UNEP3 #17, p.133
                                                    6 IPE 2929
                                                    IELMT 958: 31

London North-East Atlantic Fisheries Convention   486 UNTS 157
(Preamble, Arts. 1(1), 6(1), 7(1))   UNEP3 #18, p.136
24 January 1959   6 IPE 2938
                                                    IELMT 959: 07

Varna Convention concerning Fishing in the Black   377 UNTS 203
Sea (as amended 30 June 1965) (Arts. 1, 5)   UNEP3 #19, p.141
7 July 1959   6 IPE 2976
                                                    IELMT 959: 51

German Democratic Republic-Poland-Union of   460 UNTS 219
Soviet Socialist Republics: Warsaw Agreement   UNEP3 #27, p.170
concerning Co-operation in Marine Fishing (Arts.   6 IPE 2981
1, 3(2))   IELMT 962: 56
28 July 1962

Gdansk Convention on Fishing and Conservation   UNEP3 #58, p.317

of the Living Resources in the Baltic Sea and the Belts
13 September 1973

12 ILM 1291 (1973)
7 IPE 3367
IELMT 973: 68

———— Warsaw Protocol to Provide for EEC Membership
11 November 1982

22 ILM 704 (1983)
IPE(2) III/A/11-11-82

Rio de Janeiro International Convention for the Conservation of Atlantic Tunas
14 May 1966

673 UNTS 63
20 UST 2887
TIAS 6767
UNEP3 #36, p.202
6 IPE 3018
IELMT 966: 38

EEC Commission: Proposed Regulation on a Community System for the Conservation and Management of Fishery Resources
8 October 1976

15 ILM 1376 (1976)
24 IPE 55

EEC Council Directive: Quality of Fresh Water Needing Protection in Order to Support Fish Life
18 July 1978

Dir. No. 78/659
OJEC 1978 L 222/1
26 IPE 247

Ottawa Convention on Future Multilateral Co-operation in the North-West Atlantic Fisheries
24 October 1978

US Sen. Exec. Print I, 96: 1 Cong.
Misc 9 1979
Cmnd 7569
22 IPE 107
IELMT 978: 79

EEC Council Directive: Quality Required of Shellfish Waters
30 October 1979

Dir. No. 79/923
OJEC 1979 L 281/47
24 IPE 177

London Convention on Future Multilateral Co-operation in the North-East Atlantic Fisheries
18 November 1980

Cmnd 8474
Misc 2 (1981)
OJEC 1981 L 227/22
IPE(2) III/A/18-11-80
IELMT 980: 85

Reykjavik Convention for the Conservation of Salmon in the North Atlantic Ocean
2 March 1982

TIAS 10789
UNEP Reg. p.205
IPE(2) III/A/22-01-82

Canada-Japan-United States of America: Vancouver Memorandum of Understanding concerning salmonid research and enforcement of the international convention for the high seas fisheries of the North Pacific Ocean
9 April 1986

Australia-United States of America: Port Moresby

TIAS —

Treaty on Fisheries
2 April 1987

Pacific Islands Regional Fisheries Treaty   26 ILM 1048 (1987)
2 April 1987

Lima Convention for the Establishment of a Latin
American Tuna Organization
1989

Republic of Korea-United States of America: TIAS —
Washington Agreement Regarding the Collection
and Exchange of Data on Fisheries Harvests in the
International Waters of the Bering Sea
14 July 1988

Republic of Korea-United States of America: TIAS —
Washington Agreement Regarding the High Seas
Squid Driftnet Fisheries in the North Pacific Ocean
(with record of discussions)
26 September 1989

8.C.ii.b. Fresh Water

France-Switzerland: Paris Convention Establishing   157 CTS 295
Uniform Regulations Concerning Fishing in   10 IPE 4844
Boundary Waters
28 December 1880

Germany (pre-post-WWII)-Netherlands-Switzer-   LEG/SER.B/12, p.393
land: Berlin Convention to Regulate the Fishing   IELMT 885: 48
for Salmon in the Rhine Basin
12 June 1885

Baden (Federal Republic of Germany*)-Alsace-   LEG/SER.B/12, p.397
Lorraine (France*)-Switzerland: Lucerne Conven-   9 IPE 4730
tion Establishing Uniform Rules for Fishing in the
Rhine and its Tributaries, including Lake Constance
18 May 1887

Luxembourg-Prussia (Federal Republic of Ger-   LEG/SER.B/12, p.716
many*): Luxembourg Convention Concerning the   9 IPE 4750
Regulation of Fisheries in Boundary Waters
5 November 1892

Bregenz Convention concerning Uniform Rules for   LEG/SER.B/12, p.403
Fishing in Lake Constance   9 IPE 4756
5 July 1893

France-Switzerland: Convention for the Regulation   LEG/SER.B/12, p.701
of Fishing in Frontier Waters (Art. 17)
9 March 1904

Italy-Switzerland: Lugano Convention Establish-　LEG/SER.B/12, p.839
ing Uniform Regulations Concerning Fishing in　11 IPE 5440
Frontier Waters
13 June 1906

Romania-Serbia (Yugoslavia*): Bucharest Con-　4 Martens(3) 219
vention Concerning Fishing in the Frontier Section　25 IPE 229
of the Danube Between the two Countries
11 March 1908

Estonia (Union of Soviet Socialist Republics*)-　54 LNTS 231
Latvia (Union of Soviet Socialist Republics*):　122 BFSP 458
Riga Convention for the Protection of Fish and the　6 IPE 2599
Regulation of Fishing
28 October 1925

Czechoslovakia-Poland: Katowice Convention Re-　119 LNTS 385
garding Fishing and the Preservation of Fish in　9 IPE 4421
Frontier Waters and in the Waters of their Basins
18 February 1928

Austria-Czechoslovakia: Prague Treaty Regarding　108 LNTS 10
the Settlement of Legal Questions Connected with　LEG/SER.B/12, p.458
the Frontier Described in Article 27, Paragraph　11 IPE 5543
6 [of the Treaty of Saint-Germain-en-Laye of 10
September 1919] (Section IV)
12 December 1928

Canada-United States of America: Convention for　50 Stat. 1355
the Protection, Preservation and Extension of the　TS 918
Sockeye Salmon Fisheries in Fraser River (amend.　6 IPE 2663
1944 (EAS 479), 1956 (8 UST 1057, TIAS 3867),
1977 (32 UST 2475, TIAS 9854), replaced by
1985 Pacific Salmon Treaty)
26 May 1930

Latvia (Union of Soviet Socialist Republics*)-　118 LNTS 175
Lithuania (Union of Soviet Socialist Republics*):　9 IPE 4431
Riga Convention Relating to Fishing in Boundary
Waters, with Regulations Concerning the Organization and Activity of the Mixed Latvian-Lithua-
nian Fisheries Commission
25 January 1931

Colombia-Venezuela: Caracas Statute Regulating　238 UNTS 97
the Frontier Regime (Art. 23)　144 BFSP 1127
5 August 1942　LEG/SER.B/12, p.225
　10 IPE 5275

Canada-United States of America: Washington　6 UST 2836
Convention on Great Lakes Fisheries　TIAS 3326
10 September 1954

Hungary-Yugoslavia: Belgrade Agreement Con-　LEG/SER.B/12, p.836

cerning Fishing in Frontier Waters 25 May 1957	9 IPE 4572
Afghanistan-Union of Soviet Socialist Republics: Moscow Treaty concerning the Regime of the Soviet-Afghan State Frontier (Art. 22) 18 January 1958	321 UNTS 166 LEG/SER.B/12, p.276 9 IPE 4579
Bucharest Convention concerning Fishing in the Waters of the Danube (with Annex) 29 January 1958	339 UNTS 23 LEG/SER.B/12, p.430 UNEP3 #14, p.123 9 IPE 4582 IELMT 958: 08
France-Spain: Madrid Convention Concerning Fishing in the Bidassoa and the Bay of Figuier 14 July 1959	LEG/SER.B/12, p.694 9 IPE 4365
Finland-Norway: Oslo Agreement Regarding new Fishing Regulations for the Fishing Area of the Tana River (Arts. 18 of the annexed Norwegian and Finnish Fishing Regulations) 15 November 1960	383 UNTS 160 LEG/SER.B/12, p.619 10 IPE 5064
Greece-Yugoslavia: Skopje Agreement Concerning Fishing in Lake Dojran 24 March 1972	1974:I OJ Gre. 741

8.C.iii.   Sea Mammals

Treaty for the Preservation and Protection of Fur Seals 7 July 1911	37 Stat. 1542 TS 564 104 BFSP 175 8 IPE 3678
Convention for the Regulation of Whaling 24 September 1931	155 LNTS 349 49 Stat. 3079 TS 880 7 IPE 3466 IELMT 931: 71
London International Agreement for the Regulation of Whaling 8 June 1937	190 LNTS 79 7 IPE 3475
———— London Amending Protocol 24 June 1938	196 LNTS 131 7 IPE 3482
Washington International Convention for the Regulation of Whaling (with schedule of whaling regulations. Up to 16 June 1989 there have been 43 amendments to the schedule, listed in US Treaties in Force)	*Infra* p.479 *1946* 161 UNTS 72 62 Stat. 1716 TIAS 1849 UKTS No.5 (1949)

| 2 December 1946 | 7 IPE 3498 |
| | IELMT 946: 89 |

—— Amending Protocol	*Infra* p.479
19 November 1956	338 UNTS 366
	10 UST 952
	TIAS 4228
	UKTS No.68 (1959)
	7 IPE 3539
	IELMT 956: 87

Washington Interim Convention on the Conservation of North Pacific Fur Seals	314 UNTS 105
	8 UST 2283
9 February 1957	TIAS 3948
	UNEP Reg. p.29
	UNEP3 #3, p.67
	8 IPE 3716
	IELMT 957: 11

—— Amending Protocol	494 UNTS 303
8 October 1963	15 UST 316
	TIAS 5558
	UNEP Reg. p.29
	8 IPE 3724
	IELMT 963: 75

—— Extending Agreement (exchange of notes)	20 UST 2992
3 September 1969	TIAS 6774
	UNEP Reg. p.29
	8 IPE 3727
	IELMT 969: 64

—— Amending Protocol	27 UST 3371
7 May 1976	TIAS 8368
	UNEP Reg. p.29
	UNEP3 #67, p.460
	22 IPE 311
	IELMT 976: 37

—— Amending Protocol	32 UST 5881
14 October 1980	TIAS 10020
	UNEP Reg. p.29
	IPE(2) III/A/14-10-80
	IELMT 957: 11/D

| —— Amending Protocol | UNEP Reg. p.29 |
| 10 December 1984 | IELMT 957: 11/E |

Norway-Union of Soviet Socialist Republics: Agreement on Measures to Regulate Sealing and to Protect Seal Stocks in the North-Eastern Part of the Atlantic Ocean	309 UNTS 269
	8 IPE 3733
22 November 1957	

London Arrangements for the Regulation of Antarctic Pelagic Whaling 6 June 1962	486 UNTS 263
London Agreement Concerning an International Observer Scheme for Factory Ships Engaged in Pelagic Whaling in the Antarctic 28 October 1963	3 ILM 107 (1964) 7 IPE 3624
Canada-Norway: Agreement on Sealing and Conservation of Seal Stocks in the North-West Atlantic 15 July 1971	LEG/SER.B/16, p.655 8 IPE 3750
London Convention for the Conservation of Antarctic Seals 1 June 1972	29 UST 441 TIAS 8826 UKTS No.45 (1978) Cmnd 7209 UNEP3 #54, p.272 11 ILM 251, 417 (1972) 8 IPE 3753 IELMT 972: 41
EEC Commission Regulation: Imports of Whales and Other Cetacean Products 20 January 1981	Reg. No. 348/81 OJEC 1981 L 39/1
EEC Council Directive: Importation of Skins of Seal Pups 28 March 1983	Dir. No. 83/129 OJEC 1983 L 91/30 IPE(2) III/H/28-03-83
UNEP Global Plan of Action for the Conservation, Management and Utilization of Marine Mammals 28 May 1984	UNEP/GC.12/15, Annex I UNEP/GC/DEC/12/12
Japan-United States of America: Washington Agreement Concerning Commercial Sperm Whaling in the Western Division Stock of the North Pacific (with summary of discussions) 13 November 1984	TIAS —
Iceland-United States of America: Washington Agreement Concerning Icelandic Whaling for Scientific Purposes 15 September 1987	TIAS — IPE(2) III/A/15-09-87

8.C.iv.   Land Animals

Mexico-United States of America: Convention for the Protection of Migratory Birds and Game Mammals 7 February 1936	178 LNTS 309 TS 912 9 Bevans 1017 50 Stat. 1311 4 IPE 1723

———— Supplementary Agreement
10 March 1972

837 UNTS 125
23 UST 260
TIAS 7302
5 IPE 2217

European Convention for the Protection of Animals During International Transport, C/E, Paris
(Preamble, Art. 30)
13 December 1968

ETS #65
UNEP3 #39, p.216
5 IPE 2070
IELMT 968: 92

———— Additional Protocol, Strasbourg
10 May 1979

ETS #103
22 IPE 384
IELMT 979: 35

La Paz Convention for the Conservation of Vicuña
16 August 1969

IELMT 969: 61
22 IPE 387

Oslo Agreement on the Conservation of Polar
Bears
15 November 1973

Infra p.486
27 UST 3918
TIAS 8409
UNEP3 #61, p.401
13 ILM 13 (1973)
5 IPE 2276
IELMT 973: 85

European Convention for the Protection of Animals kept for Farming Purposes, C/E, Strasbourg
10 March 1976

ETS #87
20 IPE 10353

European Convention for the Protection of Animals for Slaughter, C/E, Strasbourg
10 May 1979

ETS #102
22 IPE 384

Bonn Convention on the Conservation of Migratory Species of Wild Animals (plus resolution on
assistance to developing countries)
23 June 1979

Infra p.489
Cmnd 7888
Misc 11 1980
UNEP3 #76, p.500
19 ILM 15 (1980)
23 IPE 1
IELMT 979: 55

Lima Convention for the Conservation and Management of the Vicuña
16 October 1979

UNEP Reg. p.183
IELMT 979: 94

Argentina-Bolivia: Agreement for the Protection
and Conservation of Vicuña
16 February 1981

Canada-United States of America: Arrangement
Prohibiting the Importation of Raccoon Dogs
4 September 1981

33 UST 3764
TIAS 10259

European Convention for the Protection of Verte-

ETS #123

brate Animals Used for Experimental and Other
Scientific Purposes, C/E, Strasbourg
18 March 1986

Canada-United States of America: Ottawa   TIAS —
Agreement on the Conservation of the Porcupine
Caribou Herd
17 July 1987

European Convention for the Protection of Pet Ani-   ETS #125
mals, C/E, Strasbourg
13 November 1987

EEC Commission Regulation: Prohibition of Ivory   Reg. No. 2496/89
Imports   OJEC 1989 L 240/5
2 August 1989

8.C.v. Birds

Convention for the Protection of Birds Useful to   191 CTS 91
Agriculture   102 BFSP 969
19 March 1902   4 IPE 1615
    IELMT 902: 22

Canada-United States of America: Convention for   TS 628
the Protection of Migratory Birds in the United   12 Bevans 375
States and Canada   39 Stat. 1702
16 August 1916   4 IPE 1638

Mexico-United States of America: Convention for   178 LNTS 309
the Protection of Migratory Birds and Game   TS 912
Mammals   9 Bevans 1017
7 February 1936   50 Stat. 1311
    4 IPE 1723

———— Supplementary Agreement   837 UNTS 125
10 March 1972   23 UST 260
    TIAS 7302
    5 IPE 2217

Paris International Convention for the Protection   638 UNTS 185
of Birds   UNEP3 #6, p.84
18 October 1950   4 IPE 1791
    IELMT 950: 77

Benelux Convention on the Hunting and Protection   847 UNTS 255
of Birds, Brussels   UNEP3 #45, p.239
10 June 1970   20 IPE 10323

———— Amending Protocol   IELMT 970: 44
3 May 1977

Ramsar Convention on Wetlands of International   *Infra* p.497

Importance, Especially as Waterfowl Habitat
2 February 1971

996 UNTS 245
UKTS No.34 (1976)
Cmnd 6465
UNEP3 #47, p.246
11 ILM 969 (1972)
5 IPE 2161
IELMT 971: 09

———— Paris Amending Protocol
3 December 1982

22 ILM 698 (1983)
IELMT 971: 09/A

Japan-United States of America: Convention for
the Protection of Migratory Birds and Birds in
Danger of Extinction, and their Environment,
Tokyo
4 March 1972

25 UST 3329
TIAS 7990
5 IPE 2192

Japan-Union of Soviet Socialist Republics: Convention for the Protection of Migratory Birds and
Birds under Threat of Extinction and on the Means
of Protecting them
October 1973

Australia-Japan: Agreement for the Protection of
Migratory Birds and Birds in Danger of Extinction
and their Environment
February 1974

1981 ATS No.6
5 IPE 2301

Union of Soviet Socialist Republics-United States
of America: Convention Concerning the Conservation of Migratory Birds and their Environment
19 November 1976

29 UST 4647
TIAS 9073
22 IPE 453

EEC Directive: Conservation of Wild Birds
2 April 1979

Dir. No. 79/409
OJEC 1979 L 103/1
23 IPE 370

Canada-United States of America: Memorandum
of Understanding (U.S. Fish and Wildlife Service
and Canadian Wildlife Service) on the Conservation of the Whooping Crane
1985

8.D.   Flora
8.D.i.   General

Paris Convention for the Establishment of the European and Mediterranean Plant Protection Organization
18 April 1951

UKTS No.44 (1956)
UNEP3 #7, p.86
4 IPE 1797
IELMT 951: 29

FAO International Plant Protection Convention,
Rome (amended November 1979 (20th FAO Con-

150 UNTS 67
UNEP3 #8, p.90

ference))
6 December 1951

4 IPE 1813
IELMT 951: 90

Constitution of the International Board of Plant
Genetic Resources (IBPGR)
1974

FAO Plant Protection Agreement for the [South-
East] Asia and Pacific Region, Rome (Art. II, establishing the [South-East] Asia and Pacific Plant
Protection Commission)
27 February 1956

247 UNTS 400
FAO Council 23rd sess.
UNEP3 #13, p.117
4 IPE 1822
IELMT 956: 15

———— Amendment to Art. I(a)
November 1967

FAO Council 49th sess.
4 IPE 1831

———— Amendment to Title (deletion of "South-
East")
June 1979

FAO Council 75th sess.

———— Amendments to Arts. I(a), II, III, IV, XIV
November 1983

FAO Council 84th sess.

Sofia Agreement concerning Co-operation in the
Quarantine of Plants and their Protection Against
Pests and Diseases
14 December 1959

422 UNTS 33
UNEP3 #22, p.153
4 IPE 1944
IELMT 959: 95

Paris International Convention on the Protection of
New Varieties of Plants
2 December 1961

815 UNTS 89
UNEP Reg. p.49

———— Additional Act, Geneva
10 November 1972

———— Revised Convention, Geneva
23 October 1978

33 UST 2703
TIAS 10199

Phyto-sanitary Convention for Africa South of the
Sahara, Kinshasa
13 September 1968

UNEP3 #12, p.115

Canada-Mexico-United States of America: North
American Plant Protection Agreement, Yosemite
(California)
13 October 1976

28 UST 6223
TIAS 8680
20 IPE 10364

FAO International Undertaking on Plant Genetic
Resources, Rome
23 November 1983

Infra p.502
22 FAO Conf Res 8/83

———— Agreed Interpretation of the International
Undertaking (adopted by the FAO Conference)

Infra p.507
25 FAO Conf Res 4/89

29 November 1989

—————— Farmers' Rights (adopted by the FAO Con-   25 FAO Conf Res 5/89
ference in relation to the International Under-
taking)
29 November 1989

Antarctic Treaty, Protocol on Environmental Pro-   XI ATSCM/2
tection (see 9.A), Annex II (Conservation of Ant-
arctic Fauna and Flora)
21 June 1991

8.D.ii.   Forests & Trees

Agreement for the Establishment on a Permanent   UNEP3 #20, p.143
Basis of a Latin-American Forest Research and   4 IPE 1932
Training Institute (Art. III)   IELMT 959: 85
18 November 1959

Convention Placing the International Poplar Com-   410 UNTS 155
mission within the Framework of FAO, Rome   21 UST 2060
19 November 1959   TIAS 6952
                                                         4 IPE 1935
                                                         IELMT 959: 86

Argentina-Chile: Agreement on Fire Prevention   4 IPE 1959
and Fire Fighting in Boundary Forests
29 December 1961

Canada-United States of America: Washington   753 UNTS 43
Agreement Relating to the Participation of the   21 UST 415
Provinces of New Brunswick and Quebec in the   TIAS 6825
Northeastern Interstate Forest Fire Protection   5 IPE 2123
Compact
29 January 1970

Canada-United States of America: Washington   793 UNTS 77
Agreement Concerning Cooperation in the Detec-   22 UST 721
tion and Suppresion of Forest Fires Along the   TIAS 7132
Boundary Between the Yukon Territory and   5 IPE 2174
Alaska
1 June 1971

Convention on Prohibitions or Restrictions on the   A/CONF. 95/15
Use of Certain Conventional Weapons which may   19 ILM 1534 (1980)
be Deemed to be Excessively Injurious or to have
Indiscriminate Effects, Protocol III On the Use of
Incendiary Weapons (Art. II.4)
10 October 1980

Canada-United States of America: Ottawa Ar-   34 UST 1557
rangement on Mutual Assistance in Fighting Forest   TIAS 10436
Fires

7 May 1982

International Tropical Timber Agreement, Geneva   *Infra* p.
(Preamble, Arts. 1(f), (h), 23(5), 25(2)(f))   TD/TIMBER/11/Rev.1
25 November 1983   IELMT 983: 85

UNEP Environmental Guidelines for Afforestation   UNEP EMG #9
Projects
1985

FAO Committee on Forest Development in the   FAO Publ. M-30,
Tropics: Tropical Forest Action Plan   ISBN 92-5-102315-8
July 1985

EEC Commission Regulation: Protection of Com-   Reg. No. 3529/86
munity Forests against Fire   OJEC 1986 L 326/5
17 November 1986

EEC Commission Regulation: Protection of For-   Reg. No. 3528/86
ests against Atmospheric Pollution   OJEC 1986 L 326/2
17 November 1986

ITTO decision to achieve sustainable tropical forestry management by the year 2000
May 1990

Chapter 9.   Specific Ecosystems

9.A.   Antarctica

Antarctic Treaty, Washington (Arts V(1), IX(f))   *Infra* p.515
1 December 1959   402 UNTS 71
   12 UST 794
   TIAS 4780
   UKTS No.97 (1982)
   UNEP3 #21, p.150
   Cmnd 1535
   1 IPE 18
   IELMT 959: 91

—— Protocol on Environmental Protection   *Infra*. p.536
(with Schedule on Arbitration and four An-   XI ATSCM/2
nexes—Environmental Impact Assessment, Conservation of Antarctic Fauna and Flora, Waste Disposal and Waste Management, and Prevention of
Marine Pollution)
21 June 1991

London Arrangements for the Regulation of Ant-   486 UNTS 263
arctic Pelagic Whaling
6 June 1962

London Agreement Concerning an International Observer Scheme for Factory Ships Engaged in Pelagic Whaling in the Antarctic 28 October 1963	3 ILM 107 (1964) 7 IPE 3624
Brussels Agreed Measures for the Conservation of Antarctic Fauna and Flora 13 June 1964	17 UST 992 TIAS 6058 8 IPE 4002 5 IPE 2405 IELMT 964: 41
Canberra Convention on the Conservation of Antarctic Marine Living Resources (CCAMLR) 20 May 1980	*Infra* p.520 33 UST 3476 TIAS 10240 UKTS No.48 (1982) Cmnd 8714 19 ILM 841 (1980) IPE(2) III/A/20-05-80 IELMT 980: 39
Antarctic Treaty Consultative Meeting Recommendation XI-1 on Antarctic Mineral Resources 7 July 1981	20 ILM 1265 (1981)
Wellington Convention on the Regulation of Antarctic Mineral Resources Activities (Preamble, Arts. 1(4), (15), 2(1)(a), 4(2-4), 8, 10, 13(2), (6), 15, 21(1), (9)(C)) 2 June 1988	*Infra* p.529 AMR/SCM/88/78 (1988) 27 ILM 868 (1988) IELMT 988: 42
UNGA Resolution: Question of Antarctica (Preamble, paras. 3-5, 7) 12 December 1990	A/RES/45/78A

9.B.   Mediterranean (see also 4.H)

EEC Council Proposed Regulation: Action for the Protection of the Environment in the Mediterranean Region 1990	OJEC 1990 C 80/9

9.C.   Particular River Basins (see also 5)

Egypt-United Kingdom: Agreement regarding Cooperation in Meteorological and Hydrological Surveys in Certain Areas of the Nile Basin 20 March 1950	226 UNTS 287
Niamey Act regarding Navigation and Economic Co-operation between the States of the Niger Basin (Preamble, Art. 4) 26 October 1963	587 UNTS 11 UNEP3 #32, p.186 11 IPE 5629 IELMT 963: 80

Fort Lamy (N'Djamena) Convention and Statute relating to the Development of the Lake Chad Basin (amended 22 October 1972 in Yaounde and 1977 in Enugu)
22 May 1964

A/CN.4/274, para. 53
FAO Conf 12th sess.
11 IPE 5633

Portugal-South Africa: Lisbon Agreement in regard to the first phase of development of the water resources of the Cunene River Basin
21 January 1969

1969 SATS 1

Brasilia Treaty of the River Plate Basin
23 April 1969

875 UNTS 3
8 ILM 905 (1969)
10 IPE 4889

Brazil-Peru: Agreement on the Conservation of Flora and Fauna in the Amazon Basin
1975

Rusumo Agreement for the Establishent of an Organization to Manage and Develop the Kagera River Basin
24 August 1977

Kaolack Convention relating to the creation of the Gambia River Basin Development Organization
30 June 1978

Brasilia Treaty for Amazonian Co-operation
3 July 1978

Infra p.545
UNEP3 #75, p.496
UNEP Reg. p.164
17 ILM 1045 (1978)
18 IPE 9017
IELMT 978: 49

Faranah Convention Creating the Niger Basin Authority
21 November 1980

IELMT 980: 86

——— Protocol Relating to the Development Fund of the Niger Basin
21 November 1980

IELMT 980: 87

Amazon Declaration, adopted by the Presidents of the States Parties to the Treaty for Amazonian Co-operation, Manaus (Brazil)
6 May 1989

Infra p.551
A/44/275, Annex
E/1989/79, Annex
28 ILM 1303 (1989)

9.D.   Great Lakes (see also 5.C.ii)

Canada-United States of America: Great Lakes Water Quality Agreement, Ottawa

Infra p.419
30 UST 1383

22 November 1978	TIAS 9257 26 IPE 19
—— Amending Protocol 16 October 1983	*Infra*, p.420
—— Amending Protocol 18 November 1987	*Infra* p.420 TIAS 10798

Chapter 10.   Cultural Heritage

Constitution of the United Nations Educational, Scientific and Cultural Organization (UNESCO) (Art. I.2(c)) 16 November 1945	4 UNTS 275 14 IPE 7130 IELMT 945: 86
Hague Convention for the Protection of Cultural Property in the Event of Armed Conflict 14 May 1954	249 UNTS 215 14 IPE 7132
European Convention on the Protection of the Archeological Heritage, London 6 May 1969	788 UNTS 227 UNEP3 #40, p.221 14 IPE 7203 IELMT 969: 34
UNESCO Convention concerning the Protection of the World Cultural and Natural Heritage, Paris 16 November 1972	*Infra* p.554 1037 UNTS 151 27 UST 37 TIAS 8226 UNEP3 #55, p.276 1972 UNJYB 89 11 ILM 1358 (1972) 14 IPE 7238 IELMT 972: 86
Santiago Convention on the Protection of the Archeological, Historical, and Artistic Heritage of the American Nations (Convention of San Salvador) 16 June 1976	UNEP3 #69, p.466 28 IPE 243
Additional Protocol I to the 1949 Geneva Conventions Relating to the Protection of Victims of International Armed Conflict (Art. 53) 8 June 1977	1125 UNTS Reg. No. 17512 16 ILM 1391 (1977)
Additional Protocol II to the 1949 Geneva Conventions Relating to the Protection of Victims of International Armed Conflict (Art. 16) 1977	1125 UNTS Reg. No. 17513 16 ILM 1442 (1977)
ILA Draft Convention on the Protection of the Underwater Cultural Heritage 1990	64 ILA ——

Part III. PROTECTION AGAINST PARTICULAR THREATS

Chapter 11. Pollution Generally (see also 3.A-B, 17)

11.A. General Principles

African Convention on the Conservation of Nature and Natural Resources (Art. 5), Algiers
15 September 1968

Infra p.202
1001 UNTS 3
OAU:CM/232
UNEP3 #37, p.207
5 IPE 2037
IELMT 968: 68

UNGA Resolution: Promoting Effective Measures for the Prevention and Control of Marine Pollution
13 December 1969

A/RES/2566(XXIV)
2 IPE 799

Asuncion Declaration on the Use of International Rivers (Act of Asuncion) adopted by Ministers for Foreign Affairs of countries of La Plata River Basin (Argentina, Bolivia, Brazil, Paraguay & Uruguay)
3 June 1971

A/CN.4/274, para.326
11 IPE 5768

Oslo Convention for the Prevention of Marine Pollution by Dumping from Ships and Aircraft (and 1978 Protocol)
15 February 1972

932 UNTS 3
UKTS No.119 (1975)
UNEP3 #52, p.266
11 ILM 262 (1972)
2 IPE 530
IELMT 972: 12

Action Plan for the Human Environment of the UN Conference on the Human Environment, "Identification and Control of Pollutants of Broad International Significance" (Recommendations 70-94)
16 June 1972

A/CONF.48/14/Rev.1,
Ch.II

ILA New York Rules on Marine Pollution of Continental Origin
26 August 1972

55 ILA XVII & 97
19 IPE 9641

London International Convention for the Prevention of Pollution from Ships (MARPOL)
2 November 1973

IMO: MP/CONF/WP.35
UNEP3 #59, p.320
1973 UNJYB 81
12 ILM 1319 (1973)
2 IPE 552
IELMT 973: 84

———— London Protocol (later amendments to the 1978 Protocol or to the 1973 Convention: 1984,

TIAS —
Cmnd 5748

1985 (2x), 1987, 1989 (3x))

21 IELR 2381

17 February 1978

UNEP3 #59, p.382
17 ILM 546 (1978)
19 IPE 9451
IELMT 978: 13

Nordic (Denmark, Finland, Norway, Sweden) Convention on the Protection of the Environment, Stockholm (Arts. 2, 3)
19 February 1974

Infra p.235
1092 UNTS 279
UNEP3 #62, p.403
13 ILM 591 (1974)
1 IPE 70
IELMT 974: 14

Draft European Convention for the Protection of International Watercourses Against Pollution
4 April 1974

A/CN.4/274, para.376
11 IPE 5785

Paris Convention for the Prevention of Marine Pollution from Land-Based Sources
4 June 1974

Infra p.360
UKTS No.64 (1978)
UNEP3 #64, p.430
13 ILM 352 (1974)
2 IPE 748
IELMT 974: 43

OECD Council Recommendation on Principles Concerning Transfrontier Pollution (with annexed "Some Principles")
14 November 1974

Infra p.573
OECD C(74)224
OECD p.142
14 ILM 242 (1975)
1 IPE 316

Convention on the Intergovernmental Maritime Consultative Organization (IMCO—now IMO), 17 March 1948 (289 UNTS 3), as amended by IMO Assembly (Art. 1(a), and Pt. IX, Arts. 38-42)
14 November 1975

IMO: A.IX/Res.358
34 UST 497
TIAS 10374
Peaslee Pt. V
19 IPE 9651

OECD Council Recommendation: Equal Right of Access in Relation to Transfrontier Pollution (with annexed "Constituent elements of a system of equal right of access")
11 May 1976

OECD C(76)55(Final)
OECD p.148
15 ILM 1218 (1976)
18 IPE 9235

OECD Council Recommendation: Implementation of a Regime of Equal Right of Access and Non-Discrimination in Relation to Transfrontier Pollution (with annexed principles)
17 May 1977

OECD C(77)28(Final)
OECD p.150
16 ILM 977 (1977)
18 IPE 9344

IIL Athens Resolution on Pollution of Rivers and Lakes and International Law
1979

58: I AIDI 193

ECE Declaration of Policy: Prevention and Control of Water Pollution, Including Transboundary Pol-

ECE/DEC/B(XXXV)
E/1980/28

lution
23 September 1980

6 EPL 148
26 IPE 280

ILA Montreal Rules of International Law Applicable to Transfrontier Pollution
4 September 1982

Infra p.577
60 ILA 158 (1983)

ILA Montreal Rules on Water Pollution in an International Drainage Basin
4 September 1982

60 ILA 535 (1983)

UN Convention on the Law of the Sea, Montego Bay (Arts. 19(h), 43, 192-237)
10 December 1982

Infra p.332
Cmnd 8941
Misc 11 (1983)
A/CONF.62/122
21 ILM 1261 (1982)
IPE(2) II/A/10-12-82
IELMT 982: 92

UNEP Governing Council Decision: Montreal Guidelines for the Protection of the Marine Environment Against Pollution from Land-Based Sources
24 May 1985

UNEP/GC.13/9/Add.3
UNEP/GC/DEC/13/18II
UNEP ELPG #7
IPE(2) II/D/14-05-85

Noordwijk Declaration by the Ministerial Conference on Atmospheric Pollution and Climate Change
7 November 1989

A/C.2/44/5, Annex

11.B.   Particular Areas or Waters

France-Spain: Bayone Final Act of Delimitation of the International Frontier of the Pyrennes between France and Spain (Sec. I, Art. 6 of the Regulations adopted under Second Part of Treaty)
11 July 1868

59 BFSP 430
LEG/SER.B/12, p.674

Baden (Federal Republic of Germany*)-Switzerland: Berne Convention Establishing Uniform Regulations Concerning Fishing in the Rhine between Constance and Basle (Art. 10)
9 December 1869

149 CTS 139
9 IPE 4695

Baden (Federal Republic of Germany*)-France-Switzerland: Basle Convention Establishing Uniform Regulations Concerning Fishing in the Rhine and its Tributaries, Including Lake Constance (Art. 10)
25 March 1875

149 CTS 139
9 IPE 4702

France-Switzerland: Paris Convention Establishing Uniform Regulations Concerning Fishing in

157 CTS 295
10 IPE 4844

Boundary Waters (Arts. 6, 17)
28 December 1880

Baden (Federal Republic of Germany*)-Alsace-   LEG/SER.B/12, p.397
Lorraine (France*)-Switzerland: Lucerne Conven-   9 IPE 4730
tion Establishing Uniform Rules for Fishing in the
Rhine and its Tributaries, including Lake Constance (Art. 10)
18 May 1887

Luxembourg-Prussia (Federal Republic of Ger-   LEG/SER.B/12, p.716
many*): Luxembourg Convention Concerning the   9 IPE 4750
Regulation of Fisheries in Boundary Waters (Art.
2(10), (12))
5 November 1892

Bregenz Convention concerning Uniform Rules for   LEG/SER.B/12, p.403
Fishing in Lake Constance (Arts. 12, 13)   9 IPE 4756
5 July 1893

France-Switzerland: Convention for the Regulation LEG/SER.B/12, p.701
of Fishing in Frontier Waters (Arts. 6, 11, 17, 29)
9 March 1904

Italy-Switzerland: Lugano Convention Establish-   LEG/SER.B/12, p.839
ing Uniform Regulations Concerning Fishing in   11 IPE 5440
Frontier Waters (Art. 12(5))
13 June 1906

Romania-Serbia (Yugoslavia*): Bucharest Con-   4 Martens(3) 219
vention Concerning Fishing in the Frontier Section 25 IPE 229
of the Danube between the two Countries (Art. 11)
11 March 1908

Denmark-Germany (pre-post-WWII): Agreement   10 LNTS 201
relating to Watercourses and Dikes on the Danish- LEG/SER.B/12, p.577
German Frontier (Arts. 29, 45, 46) (together with 11 IPE 5473
a Final Protocol and Instructions for the Frontier
Water Commission and the Supreme Frontier Water Commission)
10 April 1922

Finland-Norway: Oslo Convention and Statute Re-   49 LNTS 390
garding the Floating of Timber on the Pasvik (Statute, Art. III)
14 February 1925

France-Germany (pre-post-WWII): Paris Treaty   75 LNTS 103
Regarding the Delimitation of the Frontier (Art.   LEG/SER.B/12, p.657
44)   11 IPE 5513
14 August 1925

Estonia (Union of Soviet Socialist Republics*)-   54 LNTS 231

Latvia (Union of Soviet Socialist Republics*):   122 BFSP 458
Riga Convention for the Protection of Fish and the   6 IPE 2599
Regulation of Fishing (Art. 6)
28 October 1925

Germany (pre-post-WWII)-Poland: Poznan Treaty   64 LNTS 113
for the Settlement of Frontier Questions (Arts. 30,
34)
27 January 1926

Germany (pre-post-WWII)-Lithuania (Union of   89 LNTS 337
Soviet Socialist Republics*): Berlin Convention   11 IPE 5528
Regarding the Maintenance and Administration of
Frontier Waterways (Arts. 15, 17)
29 January 1928

Czechoslovakia-Poland: Katowice Convention Re-   119 LNTS 385
garding Fishing and the Preservation of Fish in   9 IPE 4421
Frontier Waters and in the Waters of their Basins
(Art. 5)
18 February 1928

Austria-Czechoslovakia: Prague Treaty Regarding   108 LNTS 10
the Settlement of Legal Questions Connected with   LEG/SER.B/12, p.458
the Frontier Described in Article 27, Paragraph   11 IPE 5543
6 [of the Treaty of Saint-Germain-en-Laye of 10
September 1919] (Art. 45)
12 December 1928

Belgium-Germany (pre-post-WWII): Aix-la-Chap-   121 LNTS 327
elle Agreement Concerning the Common Frontier   LEG/SER.B/12, p.529
(Arts. 60-62)   11 IPE 5550
7 November 1929

Latvia (Union of Soviet Socialist Republics*) -   118 LNTS 175
Lithuania (Union of Soviet Socialist Republics*):   9 IPE 4431
Riga Convention Relating to Fishing in Boundary
Waters, with Regulations Concerning the Organization and Activity of the Mixed Latvian-Lithua-
nian Fisheries Commission (Art. 9)
25 January 1931

Romania-Yugoslavia: Belgrade General Conven-   135 LNTS 31
tion Regarding the Hydraulic System (Art. 32)   9 IPE 4435
14 December 1931

Poland-Union of Soviet Socialist Republics: Mos-   141 LNTS 349
cow Convention Concerning Judicial Relations on   135 BFSP 699
the State Frontier (Art. 7(3))   9 IPE 4454
10 April 1932

Poland-Union of Soviet Socialist Republics: Mos-   37 UNTS 66
cow Agreement Concerning the Regime on the So-   LEG/SER.B/12, p.889
viet-Polish State Frontier (Art. 17)   9 IPE 4475

8 July 1948

Finland-Union of Soviet Socialist Republics: Moscow Agreement Concerning the Regime of the Soviet-Finnish Frontier (Art. 13) 9 December 1948	217 UNTS 135 155 BFSP 382 10 IPE 4973
Romania-Union of Soviet Socialist Republics: Moscow Treaty Concerning the Regime of the Soviet-Romanian State Frontier (Arts. 17, 22(2)) 25 November 1949	LEG/SER.B/12, p.919 9 IPE 4488
Norway-Union of Soviet Socialist Republics: Oslo Agreement Concerning the Regime of the Norwegian-Soviet State Frontier (Art. 14(1)) 29 December 1949	83 UNTS 342 155 BFSP 782 LEG/SER.B/12, p.880 10 IPE 4985
Hungary-Union of Soviet Socialist Republics: Moscow Treaty Concerning the Regime of the Soviet-Hungarian State Frontier (Art. 17) 24 February 1950	LEG/SER.B/12, p.823 9 IPE 4493
Belgium-France-Luxembourg: Brussels Protocol for the Establishment of a Standing Tripartite Commission for Polluted Waters 8 April 1950	66 UNTS 286 LEG/SER.B/12, p.422 9 IPE 4730 IELMT 950: 27
German Democratic Republic-Poland: Berlin Agreement Concerning Navigation in Frontier Waters and the Use and Maintenance of Frontier Waters (Art. 17(4)) 6 February 1952	304 UNTS 160 LEG/SER.B/12, p.769 9 IPE 4498
Austria-Hungary: Vienna Treaty Concerning the Regulation of Water Economy Questions in the Frontier Region (Art. 2(7)) 9 April 1956	438 UNTS 123 25 IPE 272
Belgium-Federal Republic of Germany: Brussels Treaty Concerning the Rectification of the Belgian-German Frontier and the Settlement of Various Problems Concerning the Two Countries (Arts. 7, 8) 24 September 1956	314 UNTS 196 LEG/SER.B/12, p.533 11 IPE 5569
Czechoslovakia-Hungary: Prague Treaty Concerning the Regime of the State Frontier (Art. 18(2)) 13 October 1956	300 UNTS 125 9 IPE 4545
France-Federal Republic of Germany: Luxembourg Treaty on the Settlement of the Saar Question (Annex 8, Art. 8) 27 October 1956	LEG/SER.B/12, p.658 11 IPE 5572

France-Federal Republic of Germany-Luxembourg: Luxembourg Convention for the Channelling of the Mosel (Art. 7)
27 October 1956

LEG/SER.B/12, p.424
11 IPE 5575
IELMT 956: 80

Czechoslovakia-Union of Soviet Socialist Republics: Moscow Agreement Concerning the Regime of the Soviet-Czechoslovak Frontier and the Procedure for the Settlement of Frontier Incidents (Art. 14(1))
30 November 1956

266 UNTS 302
LEG/SER.B/12, p.576
9 IPE 4558

Iran-Union of Soviet Socialist Republics: Moscow Treaty Concerning the Regime of the Soviet-Iranian State Frontier (Art. 10(1))
14 May 1957

457 UNTS 161
9 IPE 4570

Hungary-Yugoslavia: Belgrade Agreement Concerning Fishing in Frontier Waters (Art. 5)
25 May 1957

LEG/SER.B/12, p.836
9 IPE 4572

Afghanistan-Union of Soviet Socialist Republics: Moscow Treaty Concerning the Regime of the Soviet-Afghan State Frontier (Art. 13)
18 January 1958

LEG/SER.B/12, p.276
9 IPE 4579

Czechoslovakia-Poland: Prague Agreement Concerning the Use of Water Resources in Frontier Waters (Art. 3)
21 March 1958

538 UNTS 89
15 IPE 7401

France-Spain: Madrid Convention Concerning Fishing in the Bidassoa and the Bay of Figuier (Art. 20(10))
14 July 1959

LEG/SER.B/12, p.694
9 IPE 4365

Belgium-Netherlands: Treaty concerning the Improvement of the Terneuzen and Ghent Canal (Arts. 27 et seq.)
20 June 1960

423 UNTS 19
LEG/SER.B/12, p.555
11 IPE 5591

Finland-Union of Soviet Socialist Republics: Helsinki Agreement Concerning the Regime of the Finnish-Soviet State Frontier and the Procedure for the Settlement of Frontier Incidents (Art. 15)
23 June 1960

379 UNTS 330
LEG/SER.B/12, p.656
10 IPE 5039

India-Pakistan-World Bank (International Bank for Reconstruction and Development): The Indus Water Treaty (Art. IV(10)), Karachi
19 September 1960

419 UNTS 125
55 AJIL 797 (1961)
11 IPE 5609
IELMT 960: 69

Steckborn Convention on the Protection of Lake

LEG/SER.B/12, p.438

Constance against Pollution   10 IPE 4814
27 October 1960   IELMT 960: 80

Finland-Norway: Oslo Agreement Regarding New   383 UNTS 160
Fishing Regulations for the Fishing Area of the   LEG/SER.B/12, p.619
Tana River (Arts. 18 of the annexed Norwegian   10 IPE 5064
and Finnish Fishing Regulations)
15 November 1960

Poland-Union of Soviet Socialist Republics: Mos-   420 UNTS 161
cow Treaty Concerning the Regime of the Soviet-   9 IPE 4602
Polish State Frontier and Co-operation and Mutual
Assistance in Frontier Matters (Arts. 19, 24(2))
15 Feburary 1961

Hungary-Union of Soviet Socialist Republics: Bu-   1962 TRHG 128
dapest Treaty Concerning the Regime of the Sovi-
et-Hungarian State Frontier, Mutual Assistance
and Co-operation in Frontier Questions (Art. 19)
3 October 1961

Paris Protocol concerning the Constitution of an   940 UNTS 211
International Commission for the Protection of the   UNEP3 #25, p.165
Mosel Against Pollution   11 IPE 5618
20 December 1961   IELMT 961: 94

Berne Convention on the International Commis-   *Infra* p.438
sion for the Protection of the Rhine against Pollu-   994 UNTS 3
tion (and 1976 Bonn Additional Agreement—see   UNEP3 #29, p.176
5.E.ii)   10 IPE 4820
29 April 1963   IELMT 963: 31

Belgium-Netherlands: The Hague Treaty Concern-   540 UNTS 3
ing the Connection Between the Scheldt and the   11 IPE 5623
Rhine (Art. 17)
13 May 1963

Hungary-Romania: Budapest Treaty Concerning   576 UNTS 275
the Regime of the Hungarian-Romanian State   9 IPE 4638
Frontier and Co-operation in Frontier Matters (Art.
23(2))
13 June 1963

Finland-Union of Soviet Socialist Republics: Hel-   537 UNTS 231
sinki Agreement concerning Frontier Watercourses   10 IPE 5076
(Art. 2)
24 April 1964

Bulgaria-Greece: Athens Agreement Concerning   69 RGDIP 591
Co-operation in the Use of the Waters of Rivers
Flowing through the Territory of Both Countries
(Art. 2)
9 July 1964

Poland-Union of Soviet Socialist Republics: Warsaw Agreement Concerning the Use of Water Resources in Frontier Waters (Art. 11)
17 July 1964

552 UNTS 175
9 IPE 4641

German Democratic Republic-Poland: Berlin Agreement on Co-operation in Water Economy Questions in Frontier Waters (Art. 8)
11 March 1965

52 EGDZ 331
WTI p.1298
25 IPE 294

Austria-Czechoslovakia: Vienna Treaty Concerning the Regulation of Water Management Questions Relating to Frontier Waters (Art. 3(4))
7 December 1967

438 UNTS 123
9 IPE 4648

Bulgaria-Turkey: Istanbul Agreement concerning Co-operation in the Use of the Waters of Rivers Flowing through the Territory of Both Countries (Art. 2)
23 October 1968

807 UNTS 117
25 IPE 306

Czechoslovakia-Union of Soviet Socialist Republics: Bratislava Convention Concerning Water Economy Questions in Frontier Waters (Art. 7(1))
26 November 1968

1969 CSSR No.63

Hungary-Romania: Bucharest Convention Concerning the Regulation of Water Economy Questions in Contiguous and Successive Water Courses (Art. 7)
3 November 1969

Argentina-Chile: Santiago Act Concerning Hydrologic Basins (para. 2)
26 June 1971

A/CN.4/274, para.327
11 IPE 5771

Argentina-Uruguay: Buenos Aires Declaration on Water Resources (para. 2)
9 July 1971

A/CN.4/274, para.328
11 IPE 5774

Argentina-Bolivia: Buenos Aires Act on Hydrological Basins
12 July 1971

Arg. No. 99 (1971)
11 IPE 5774

Finland-Sweden: Stockholm Agreement Concerning Frontier Rivers (Arts. 1-3, 6(3), 7(2), 8, 9, 13)
16 September 1971

825 UNTS 191
10 IPE 5092

Greece-Yugoslavia: Skopje Agreement Concerning Fishing in Lake Dojran (Art. 6)
24 March 1972

1974: I OJ Gre. 741

Mexico-United States of America: El Paso

23 UST 1286

Agreement Effected by Minute No. 241 of the International Boundary and Water Commission to Improve Immediately the Quality of Colorado River Waters Going to Mexico 14 July 1972	TIAS 7404 11 IPE 5352
Federal Republic of Germany-German Democratic Republic: Bonn Agreement concerning Prevention and Abatement of Injurious Incidents in the Frontier Area (Arts. 2(f), 4) 20 September 1973	1974II BGB1 1238
Argentina-Uruguay: Treaty concerning the La Plata River and its Maritime Limits (Arts. 47-49) 19 November 1973	13 ILM 251 (1974)
Czechoslovakia-German Democratic Republic: Prague Agreement concerning Water Economy Questions in Frontier Waters (Art. 11) 27 February 1974	1974 EGND 2802
Czechoslovakia-Hungary: Budapest Convention Concerning the Regulation of Water Economy Questions in Frontier Waters (Art. 11(1)) 31 May 1975	1978 TRHG 488
Barcelona Convention for the Protection of the Mediterranean Sea against Pollution (and 1976 (2x), 1980, 1982 Protocols—see 4.H) 16 February 1976	*Infra* p.370 UNTS Reg. #16908 UNEP3 #66, p.448 UNEP Reg. p.136 15 ILM 290 (1976) 19 IPE 9497 IELMT 976: 13
Czechoslovakia-Hungary: Budapest Treaty Concerning the Construction and Operation of the Hydraulic Works of Gabcikovo and Nagymaros (Art. 15) 16 September 1977	1978 TRHG 305
Kuwait Regional Convention for Co-operation on the Protection of the Marine Environment from Pollution 24 April 1978	1140 UNTS 133 UNEP3 #74, p.486 17 ILM 511 (1978) 19 IPE 9551 IELMT 978: 31
Brasilia Treaty for Amazonian Co-operation (Art. 4) 3 July 1978	*Infra* p.545 UNEP3 #75, p.496 UNEP Reg. p.164 17 ILM 1045 (1978) 18 IPE 9017 IELMT 978: 49
Hungary-Yugoslavia: Budapest Convention Con-	1979 TRHG 736

cerning the Prevention and Settlement of Violations of the Regime of the Hungarian-Yugoslav Frontier (Art. 2(2)(i))
4 October 1978

Argentina-Brazil-Paraguay: Pres. Stroessner City Agreement on Parana River Projects (Art. 5(j))
19 October 1979

19 ILM 615 (1980)
26 IPE 74

Hungary-Union of Soviet Socialist Republics: Moscow Convention concerning Water Economy Questions in Frontier Waters (Art. 5(1))
22 June 1981

1981 TRHG 996

Lima Convention for the Protection of the Marine Environment and Coastal Area of the South-East Pacific, 1981 (see 4.F.ii), Quito Protocol for the Protection of the South-East Pacific Against Pollution from Land-Based Sources
23 July 1983

UNEP Reg. p.199
IPE(2) II/A/22-07-83.a
IELMT 983: 54

Mexico-United States of America: La Paz Agreement for Cooperation on Environmental Programs and Transboundary Problems, 1983 (see 1.C.ii), Annex I, Agreement of Cooperation for the Solution of the Border Sanitation Problem of San Diego, California-Tijuana, Baja California, San Diego
18 July 1985

26 ILM 18 (1987)

Canada-United States of America: Ottawa Memorandum of Understanding Regarding Accidental and Unauthorized Discharges of Pollutants Along the Inland Boundary
17 October 1985

TIAS —

Noumea Convention for the Protection of the Natural Resources and Environment of the South Pacific Region, 1986 (see 4.F.ii), Noumea Protocol for the Prevention of Pollution of the South Pacific Region by Dumping
25 November 1986

UNEP Reg. p.243
IPE(2) II/A/24-11-86.b
IELMT 986: 87
IELMT 986: 87/A

Lisbon Agreement on Cooperation for the Protection of the Shores and Waters of the North-East Atlantic Against Pollution.
17 October 1990

11.C.   Particular Substances

ILO Convention (#13) concerning the Use of White Lead in Painting, Geneva
25 October 1921

38 UNTS 184
12 Bevans 375
TS 628

UNEP Reg. p.1
29 IPE 137

Mexico-United States of America: Ciudad Juarez
Agreement Approving Minute No. 218 of the International Boundary and Water Commission Concerning the Colorado River Salinity Problem
22 March 1965

776 UNTS 116
11 IPE 5347

European Agreement on the Restriction of the Use
of Certain Detergents in Washing and Cleaning
Products, Strasbourg
13 December 1968

788 UNTS 181
ETS #64
UNEP3 #38, p.214

OECD Council Recommendation: Determination
of the Biodegradability of Anionic Synthetic Surface Active Agents
13 July 1971

OECD C(71)83(Final)
OECD p.43
26 IPE 109

Mexico-United States of America: Agreement concerning the Permanent and Definitive Solution to
the International Problem of the Salinity of the
Colorado River
30 August 1973

915 UNTS 203
24 UST 1968
TIAS 7708
12 ILM 1105 (1973)
11 IPE 5368

OECD Council Recommendation: Measures to Reduce all Man-Made Emissions of Mercury to the
Environment
18 September 1973

OECD C(73)172(Final)
OECD p.99
17 IPE 8755

Brussels International Convention relating to Intervention on the High Seas in Cases of Oil Pollution
Casualties, 1969 (see 4.A), London Protocol relating to Intervention on the High Seas in Cases of
Marine Pollution by Substances other than Oil
2 November 1973

34 UST 3407
TIAS 10561
UNEP3 #6, p.400
1973 UNJYB 91
13 ILM 605 (1974)
IELMT 973: 83

Canada-United States of America: Great Lakes
Water Quality Agreement (1972), Washington
Agreement Concerning Appendix I: Reduction in
Phosphorus Loadings in Lakes Superior and Huron
21 November 1973

30 UST 1383
TIAS 9257
10 IPE 5334

EEC Council Directive: Approximation of the
Laws of the Member States relating to Detergents
22 November 1973

Dir. No. 73/404
OJEC 1973 L 347/51
26 IPE 138

ILO Convention (#139) concerning Prevention
and Control of Occupational Hazards Caused by
Carcinogenic Substances and Agents, Geneva
24 June 1974

LVII ILO OB Ser.A
17 IPE 8682
IELMT 974: 48

ILO Recommendation (#147) concerning Preven-

LVII ILO OB Ser.A

tion and Control of Occupational Hazards Caused by Carcinogenic Substances and Agents 24 June 1974	29 IPE 297
OECD Council Recommendation on Strategies for Specific Water Pollutants Control 14 November 1974	OECD C(74)221 OECD p.45 1 IPE 308
Bonn Convention for the Protection of the Rhine River against Chemical Pollution 3 December 1976	*Infra* p.442 1124 UNTS 375 UNEP3 #70, p.468 16 ILM 242 (1977) 25 IPE 440 IELMT 976: 89
Bonn Convention for the Protection of the Rhine River against Pollution by Chlorides 3 December 1976	*Infra* p.450 16 ILM 265 (1977) 26 IPE 1 IELMT 976: 90
EEC Council Directive On the Protection of Groundwater against Pollution Caused by Certain Dangerous Substances 7 September 1979	Dir. No. 80/68 OJEC 1980 L 20/43 264 IPE 274
EEC Council Directive: Surveillance and Monitoring of Environments Contaminated by Waste from the Titanium-Dioxide Industry 3 December 1982	Dir. No. 82/883 OJEC 1982 L 378/1
ILO Convention (#162) Concerning Safety in the Use of Asbestos, Geneva 24 June 1986	72 ILO Conf. xviii
EEC Council Directive: Prevention and Reduction of Pollution by Asbestos 19 March 1987	Dir. No. 87/217 OJEC 1987 L 85/40

11.D. Emergencies

Barcelona Convention for the Protection of the Mediterrean Sea Against Polution, 1976 (see 4.H), Barcelona Protocol concerning Co-operation in Combatting Pollution of the Mediterranean Sea by Oil and Other Harmful Substances in Cases of Emergency 16 February 1976	*Infra* p.381 UNTS Reg. #16908 UNEP Reg. p.140 15 ILM 306 (1976) 19 IPE 9506 IEMLT 976: 15
Kuwait Regional Convention for Co-operation on the Protection of the Marine Environment from Pollution, 1978 (see 4.J), Kuwait Protocol con-	17 ILM 526 (1978) 19 IPE 9551 IELMT 978: 32

cerning Regional Co-operation in Combating Pollution by Oil and Other Harmful Substances in
Cases of Emergency
24 April 1978

Abidjan Convention for Co-operation in the Pro-tection and Development of the Marine and Coastal Environment of West and Central African Region, 1981 (see 1.B.iii), Abidjan Protocol concerning Co-operation in Combating Pollution in Cases of Emergency 23 March 1981	20 ILM 756 (1981) IPE(2) II/A/23-03-81.b IELMT 981: 23 IELMT 981: 24
Nairobi Convention for Protection, Management and Development of Marine and Coastal Environ-ment of the Eastern African Region, 1985 (see 4.E), Nairobi Protocol concerning Co-operation in Combating Marine Pollution in Cases of Emer-gency in the Eastern African Region 21 June 1985	UNEP Reg. p.230 IPE(2) II/A/21-06-85.c IELMT 985: 46 IELMT 985: 48
IAEA Convention on Early Notification of a Nu-clear Accident, Vienna 26 September 1986	*Infra* p.583 IAEA INFCIRC/335 IAEA LegSer#14 25 ILM 1370 (1986) IELMT 986: 71
IAEA Convention on Assitance in the Case of a Nuclear Accident or Radiological Emergency, Vienna 26 September 1986	*Infra* p.587 UNTS Reg. #24643 IAEA INFCIRC/336 IAEA LegSer#14 25 ILM 1370 (1986) IELMT 986: 71
Noumea Convention for Protection of the Natural Resources and Environment of the South Pacific Region, 1986 (see 4.F.ii), Noumea Protocol con-cerning Co-operation in Combating Pollution Emergencies in the South Pacific Region 25 November 1986	UNEP Reg. p.245 IPE(2) II/A/24-11-86.a IELMT 986: 87 IELMT 986: 87/B
Union of Soviet Socialist Republics-United States of America: Agreement Concerning Cooperation in Combatting Pollution in the Bering and Chukchi Seas in Emergency Situations 17 October 1989	

Chapter 12.   Oil and Other Hydrocarbons

12.A.   General

International Convention for the Prevention of Pol-lution of the Sea by Oil, London	327 UNTS 3 12 UST 2989

12 May 1954	TIAS 4900 UNEP3 #11, p.101 1 IPE 332 IELMT 954: 36
—— IMO London Amendments 11 April 1962	17 UST 1523 TIAS 6109 1 IPE 346 IELMT 962: 27
—— IMO London Amendments 21 October 1969	28 UST 1205 TIAS 8505 1 IPE 366 IELMT 969: 77
—— IMO London Amendments concerning the Protection of the Great Barrier Reef 12 October 1971	IMCO/RES/A.232(VII) 1 IPE 378 IELMT 971: 77
——IMO London Amendments concerning Tank Arrangements and Limitation of Tank Size 15 October 1971	1 IPE 379 IELMT 971: 78
Tanker Owners Voluntary Agreement Concerning Liability for Oil Pollution, "TOVALOP" (amended several times, most recently on 20 February 1987) 7 January 1969	*Infra* p.687 8 ILM 497 (1969)
——Tanker Owners Voluntary Agreement Concerning Liability for Oil Pollution, "TOVALOP," Supplement 20 February 1987	*Infra* p.692
Bonn Agreement for Co-operation in Dealing with Pollution of the North Sea by Oil 9 June 1969	704 UNTS 3 UNEP3 #41, p.223 9 ILM 359 (1970) 19 IPE 9439 IELMT 969: 43
Canada-United States of America: Report by the International Joint Commission on Risks of Oil Pollution in Lake Erie 27 October 1969	8 ILM 1363 (1969)
Brussels International Convention on Civil Liability for Oil Pollution Damage 29 November 1969	*Infra* p.671 973 UNTS 3 UNEP3 #44, p.235 UKTS No.106 (1975) UNEP Reg. p.81 1969 UNJYB 174 9 ILM 45 (1970) 1 IPE 460

Oil Companies: Contract Regarding an Interim Supplement to Tanker Liability for Oil Pollution, "CRISTAL" (amended several times, most recently on 23 October 1989)
14 January 1971

Infra p.696
10 ILM 137 (1971)
20 IPE 490

Copenhagen (Nordic) Agreement on Co-operation in Oil Pollution
16 September 1971

2 IPE 502
IELMT 971: 69

Brussels International Convention on the Establishment of an International Fund for Compensation for Oil Pollution Damage
18 December 1971

Infra p.678
1110 UNTS 57
UNEP3 #51, p.225
Cmnd 7383
UNEP Reg. p.98
1971 UNJYB 103
11 ILM 284 (1972)
2 IPE 529
IELMT 971: 94

Oil Companies Offshore Pollution Liability Agreement ("OPOL")
4 September 1974

13 ILM 1409 (1974)
2 IPE 772

——— Rules of the Offshore Pollution Liability Association (interpreting "OPOL")
2 October 1974

14 ILM 147 (1975)
2 IPE 783

London Convention on Civil Liability for Oil Pollution Damage from Offshore Operations [Resulting from Exploration for and Exploitation of Sea Bed Mineral Resources]
1 May 1977

Misc 8 (1977)
UNEP3 #71, p.474
16 ILM 1450 (1977)
1 IPE 313
IELMT 977: 33

OECD Council Recommendation: Coal and the Environment (with annexed Guidelines to Ensure an Environmentally Successful Development of the Coal Sector)
8 May 1979

OECD C(79)117
OECD p.59

Mexico-United States of America: Agreement of Co-operation regarding Pollution of the Marine Environment by Discharges of Hydrocarbons and other Hazardous Substances
24 July 1980

32 UST 5899
TIAS 10021

Bonn Agreement for Co-operation in Dealing with Pollution of the North Sea by Oil and Other Harmful Substances
13 September 1983

UNEP Reg. p.218
IPE(2) II/A/13-09-83
IELMT 983: 68

12.B.   Emergencies (see also 25.B)

Liberia Board of Investigation Report on the Stranding of the Torrey Canyon 2 May 1967	6 ILM 480 (1967)
Canada-United States of America: Ottawa Agreement Relating to the Establishment of Joint Pollution Contingency Plans for Spills of Oil and Other Noxious Substances 19 June 1974	25 UST 1280 TIAS 7861 19 IPE 9490
Brussels International Convention relating to Intervention on the High Seas in Cases of Oil Pollution Casualties 29 November 1969	970 UNTS 211 26 UST 765 TIAS 8068 UNEP3 #43, p.230 1969 UNJYB 166 1 IPE 460 IELMT 969: 89
Canada-United States of America: Ottawa Agreement on Contingency Plans for Spills of Oil and other Noxious Substances 19 June 1974	951 UNTS 287 25 UST 1280 TIAS 7861 19 IPE 9490
———— Annex IV on the Beaufort Sea 30 August 1977	29 UST 2569 TIAS 8957
———— Annex V on the Waters of Dixon Entrance 17 March 1982	IPE(2) II/A/17-03-82
Barcelona Convention for the Protection of the Mediterranean Against Pollution, 1976 (see 4.H), Barcelona Protocol concerning Co-operation in Combating Pollution of the Mediterranean Sea by Oil and Other Harmful Substances in Cases of Emergency 16 February 1976	*Infra* p.381 UNTS Reg. #16908 UNEP Reg. p.140 15 ILM 306 (1976) 19 IPE 9506 IELMT 976: 15
Bermuda-United States of America: Hamilton Agreement Concerning Assistance to be Rendered on a Reimbursable Basis by the United States Coast Guard in the Event of Major Oil Spills 13 July 1976	27 UST 3788 TIAS 8396 19 IPE 9521
Kuwait Regional Convention for Co-operation on the Protection of the Marine Environment from Pollution, 1978 (see 4.J), Kuwait Protocol concerning Regional Co-operation in Combating Pollution by Oil and Other Harmful Substances in Cases of Emergency 24 April 1978	17 ILM 526 (1978) 19 IPE 9551 IELMT 978: 31 IELMT 978: 32
Lima Agreement on Regional Co-operation in	UNEP Reg. p.197

Combating Pollution of the South-East Pacific by Oil and Other Harmful Substances in Cases of Emergency 12 November 1981	IPE(2) II/A/12-11-81.b IELMT 981: 85
——— Quito Protocol 22 July 1983	UNEP Reg. p.198 IPE(2) II/A/22-07-83.b IELMT 983: 55
——— Supplementary Protocol 20 May 1987	
Jeddah Regional Convention on Red Sea & Gulf of Aden, 1982 (see 4.J), Jeddah Protocol concerning Regional Co-operation in Combating Pollution by Oil and other Harmful Substances in Cases of Emergency 14 February 1982	UNEP Sales No.: GE.83-IX-02934 IPE(2) II/A/14-02-82.b IELMT 982: 13 IELMT 982: 14
OECD Council Recommendation: Certain Financial Aspects of Action by Public Authorities to Prevent and Control Oil Spills (with annexed Certain International Financial Aspects) 28 April 1982	OECD C(81)32(Final) OECD p.159
Cartagena Convention for the Protection & Development of the Marine Environment of the Wider Caribbean Region, 1983 (see 4.I), Cartagena Protocol concerning Co-operation in Combating Oil Spills in the Wider Caribbean Region 24 March 1983	UNEP/GC.15/INF.2, p.214 (1989) UNEP Reg. p.204 22 ILM 240 (1983) IPE(2) II/A/24-03-83.b IELMT 983: 23 IELMT 983: 24
EEC Council Decision: Establishing a Community Information System for the Control and Reduction of Pollution Caused by the Spillage of Hydrocarbons and Other Harmful Substances at Sea 6 March 1986	Dec. No. 86/85 OJEC 1986 L 77/33
London International Convention on Oil Pollution Preparedness, Response and Co-operation, IMO 30 November 1990	30 ILM 735 (1991)

Chapter 13.   Peaceful Nuclear Activities (see also 17.D)

13.A.   General

UNGA Resolution: Establishment of the Scientific Committee on the Effects of Atomic Radiation (UNSCEAR) 3 December 1955	A/RES/913(X) 13 IPE 6517
Statute of the International Atomic Energy Agency	276 UNTS 3

(IAEA) (Arts. III.A.6, XI.E.3, XII.A.1, 5, 6)
23 October 1956

Peaslee Pt. IV
7 IPE 5854
IELMT 956: 78

Rome Treaty Establishing the European Atomic
Energy Community (Preamble, Arts. 30, 34-37,
Annex I(6), (7))
27 March 1957

298 UNTS 167
LEG/SER.B/12, p.426
28 IPE 242
IELMT 957: 23

ILO Convention (#115) concerning the Protection
of Workers Against Ionizing Radiation, Geneva
22 June 1960

431 UNTS 41
XLIII ILO OB Ser.A
UNEP3 #23, p.156
12 IPE 5966
IELMT 960: 48

ILO Recommendation (#114) concerning the Protection of Workers Against Ionizing Radiation
22 June 1960

XLIII ILO OB Ser.A
28 IPE 1

France-Belgium: Agreement on Radiologic Protection concerning the Installations of the Nuclear
Power Station of the Ardennes
7 March 1967

588 UNTS 227

Agreement Concerning a Joint Project for Planning, Design, Experiment Preparation, Performance and Reporting of Reactor Safety Experi-
ments Concerning Containment Response
24 January 1975

28 UST 629
TIAS 8479
27 IPE 64

EURATOM Council Directives: Basic Safety
Standards for Protection against Dangers of Ionizing Radiation (updated 15 July 1980)
1 June 1976; 15 July 1980

Dir. EUR/76/579
OJEC 1976 L 187/1
Dir. EUR/80/836
OJEC 1980 L 246/1
28 IPE 163

Guidelines for Nordic Co-operation Concerning
Nuclear Installations in the Border Areas
15 November 1976

Agreement Concerning a Joint Project for Planning, Design, Experiment Preparation, Performance and Reporting of Reactor Safety Experi-
ments Concerning Critical Flow
14 April 1977

30 UST 129
TIAS 9184
27 IPE 245

Denmark-Federal Republic of Germany: Agreement relating to Exchange of Information on Construction of Nuclear Installations Along the Border
(Preamble)
4 July 1977

IAEA LegSer#15, p.127
17 ILM 274 (1978)
27 IPE 272

United Kingdom-United States of America: Ar-

1095 UNTS 259

rangement in the Field of Nuclear Safety Research
and Development
3 August 1977

IAEA LegSer#15, p.419
28 UST 6755
TIAS 8688

Federal Republic of Germany-Netherlands: Memorandum on the Exchange of Information and Consultation on Nuclear Installations Near Borders
27 September 1977

IAEA LegSer#15, p.293,
  296
27 IPE 275

IAEA Convention on the Physical Protection of
Nuclear Material
3 March 1980

UNTS Reg. #24631
IAEA INFCIRC/274
27 IPE 406
IELMT 980: 18

Arrangement on Research Participation and Tech-
nical exchange between the Federal Minister for
Research and Technology of the Federal Republic
of Germany (BMFT) and the Japan Atomic Energy
Research Institute (JAERI) and the United States
Nuclear Regulatory Commission (USNRC) in a
Coordinated Analytical & Experimental Study of
the Thermo-Hydraulic Behavior of Emergency
Core Coolant during Refill & Reflood Phase of
a Loss-of-Coolant Accident in Pressurized Water
Reactor
18 April 1980

32 UST 2275
TIAS 9835
27 IPE 396

Federal Republic of Germany-United States of
America: Technical Exchange and Cooperative Arrangement in the Field of Reactor Safety Research
and Development, Washington
30 April 1981

IAEA LegSer#15, p.452
TIAS 10654

United Kingdom-United States of America: Arrangement for the Exchange of Technical Information and Cooperation in Nuclear Safety Matters,
Washington
15 May 1981

IAEA LegSer#15, p.419
33 UST 1903
TIAS 10152

Federal Republic of Germany-United States of
America: Arrangement for the Exchange of Technical Information and Cooperation in Nuclear
Safety Matters (with Patent Addendum), Washington
6 July 1981

IAEA LegSer#15, p.330
TIAS —

China-United States of America: Washington Protocol on Cooperation in Nuclear Safety Matters
17 October 1981

IAEA LegSer#15, p.83
33 UST 4110
TIAS 10287

IMO Code of Safety for Nuclear Merchant Ships
19 November 1981

IMO/RES/A.491(XII)
  Part.A

Israel-United States of America: Arrangement for

IAEA LegSer#15, p.419

the Exchange of Technical Information and Cooperation in Nuclear Safety Matters, Washington
11 April 1983

TIAS 10689

France-United States of America: Technical Exchange and Cooperation Arrangement in the Field of Fast Breeder Reactor Safety Research
21 June 1983

IAEA LegSer#15, p.445
TIAS 10741

France-United States of America: Fontenay-aux-Roses Arrangement for the Exchange of Technical Information and Cooperation in the Regulation of Nuclear Safety
17 September 1984

IAEA LegSer#15, p.420
TIAS —

Euratom (European Atomic Community) (European Community*)-United States of America: Arrangement in the Field of Nuclear Safety Research, Brussels
20 September 1984

TIAS —

Greece-United States of America: Arrangement for the Exchange of Technical Information and Cooperation in Nuclear Safety Matters
24 October 1984

TIAS 10950

Philippines-United States of America: Arrangement for the Exchange of Technical Information and Cooperation in Nuclear Safety Matters
18 June 1985

IAEA LegSer#15, p.431
TIAS —

China-United States of America: Agreement for Co-operation Concerning Peaceful Uses of Nuclear Energy (Art. 9)
23 July 1985

24 ILM 1393 (1985)

Yugoslavia-United States of America: Arrangement for the Exchange of Technical Information and Cooperation in Nuclear Safety Matters, Belgrade
19 September 1985

IAEA LegSer#15, p.431
TIAS —

Japan-United States of America: Technical Exchange Arrangement in the Field of Nuclear Regulatory Matters and Nuclear Safety Research
31 December 1985

TIAS —

Euratom (European Community*)-United States of America: Memorandum of Understanding Concerning Research on the Health and Environmental Effects of Radiation, Brussels
7 July 1986

TIAS —

Denmark-Sweden: Agreement on the Exchange of

IAEA LegSer#15, p.155

Information and Reporting relative to Nuclear
Plants and Nuclear Events, Oslo
21 October 1986

France-United States of America: Technical Exchange and Cooperation Arrangement in the Field of Light Water Reactor Safety Research 31 December 1986	IAEA LegSer#15, p.445 TIAS —
Finland-Sweden: Agreement on the Exchange of Information and Reporting relative to Nuclear Plants and Nuclear Events 25 February 1987	IAEA LegSer#15, p.180
Denmark-Finland: Agreement on the Exchange of Information and Reporting relative to Nuclear Plants and Nuclear Events 25 February 1987	IAEA LegSer#15, p.97
Finland-Norway: Agreement on the Exchange of Information and Reporting relative to Nuclear Plants and Nuclear Events 25 February 1987	IAEA LegSer#15, p.177
Mexico-United States of America: Agreement in the Area of Nuclear Reactor Safety Research 2 June 1987	IAEA LegSer#15, p.452 TIAS —
Netherlands-United States of America: Agreement in the Area of Nuclear Reactor Safety Research 1 September 1987	IAEA LegSer#15, p.445 TIAS —
Netherlands-United States of America: Arrangement for the Exchange of Technical Information and Cooperation in Regulatory and Safety Research Matters (with appendices and patent addendum), Vienna 23 September 1987	IAEA LegSer#15, p.385 TIAS —
Switzerland-United States of America: Arrangement for the Exchange of Technical Information and Cooperation in Nuclear Safety Matters (with patent addendum), Vienna 23 September 1987	TIAS —
IAEA General Conference: Prohibition of All Armed Attack Against Nuclear Installations Devoted to Peaceful Purposes September 1987	IAEA GC(XXXI)/RES/475

Norway-Union of Soviet Socialist Republics:
Agreement on the Exchange of Information and
Reporting relative to Nuclear Plants and Nuclear
Events, Oslo

1988

Union of Soviet Socialist Republics-United States   TIAS —
of America: Memorandum of Cooperation in the
Field of Civilian Nuclear Reactor Safety, Washington
26 April 1988

Belgium-United States of America: Arrangement   TIAS —
for the Exchange of Technical Information and Co-
operation in Nuclear Safety Matters, Washington
2 May 1988

UNGA Resolution: Prohibition of Attacks on Nu-   A/RES/45/58J
clear Facilities
4 December 1990

13.B.   Emergencies

Nordic Mutual Emergency Assistance Agreement   525 UNTS 75
in Connection with Radiation Accidents   IAEA LegSer#15, p.487
17 October 1963   IAEA INFCIRC/49
　　　　　　　　　　　　　　　　　　　　　　　　　　7 IPE 6102
　　　　　　　　　　　　　　　　　　　　　　　　　　IELMT 963: 77

Federal   Republic   of   Germany-Luxembourg: IAEA LegSer#15, p.274
Agreement on the Exchange of Information in Case   29 IPE 251
of Accident which Could Have Radiological Consequences
2 March 1978

Federal   Republic   of   Germany-Switzerland: IAEA LegSer#15, p.312
Agreement on Radiation Protection in Case of   27 IPE 337
Emergency
31 May 1978

France-Switzerland: Agreement on the Exchange   IAEA LegSer#15, p.230
of Information in Case of Accident which Could   27 IPE 382
Have Radiological Consequences
18 October 1979

Belgium-United States of America: Agreement Re-   IAEA LegSer#15, p.469
lating to Severe Nuclear Accident Research   TIAS 10692
18 April 1983

IAEA Guidelines for Mutual Emergency Assis-   IAEA Doc. INFCIRC/310
tance Arrangements in Connection with a Nuclear
Accident or Radiological Emergency
29 April 1983

CMEA Criteria for the Levels of Radioactive Re-   IAEA LegSer#15, p.482

leases from Nuclear Power Plants into the Environment at which it is Necessary to Inform the Other
CMEA Member Countries
1984

IAEA Guidelines on Reportable Events, Integrated   IAEA Doc. INFCIRC/321
Planning and Inforamtion Exchange in a Trans-
boundary Release of Radioactive Materials
May 1984

Japan-United States of America: Agreement Con-   IAEA LegSer#15, p.469
cerning Severe Nuclear Accident Research   TIAS —
1 October 1984

IAEA Convention on Early Notification of a Nu-   *Infra* p.583
clear Accident, Vienna   IAEA INFCIRC/335
26 September 1986   IAEA LegSer#14, p.1
        25 ILM 1370 (1986)
        IELMT 986: 71

IAEA Convention on Assistance in the Case of   *Infra* p.587
a Nuclear Accident or Radiological Emergency,   UNTS Reg. #24643
Vienna   IAEA INFCIRC/336
26 September 1986   IAEA LegSer#14, p.9
        25 ILM 1377 (1986)
        IELMT 986: 72

Finland-Union of Soviet Socialist Republics: IAEA LegSer#15, p.187
Agreement on Early Notification of a Nuclear Ac-
cident and on Exchange of Information relating to
Nuclear Facilities
7 January 1987

EEC Council Decision: Community Arrangements   IAEA LegSer#15, p.479
for the Early Exchange of Information in the Event
of a Radiological Emergency
14 December 1987

Republic of Korea-United States of America: IAEA LegSer#15, p.469
Agreement Relating to Participation in the Pro-   TIAS —
gram of Severe (Nuclear) Accident Research
28 December 1987

Sweden-Union of Soviet Socialist Republics: IAEA LegSer#15, p.407
Agreement on Early Notification of a Nuclear Ac-
cident and on Exchange of Information relating to
Nuclear Facilities
1 January 1988

IAEA/OECD-NEA: The International Nuclear   GOV/INF/600,Attach.
Event Scale   IAEA PR 90/11
April 1990   13 IER 257

13.C. Liability

Paris Convention on Third Party Liability in the Field of Nuclear Energy (1964, 1968, 1982 Amending Protocols) 29 July 1960	956 UNTS 251 UNEP3 #24, p.159 55 AJIL 1082 7 IPE 5972 IELMT 960: 57
—— Brussels Supplementary Convention, (1964, 1982 Amending Protocols) 31 January 1963	UNEP3 #28, p.171 2 ILM 685 (1963) 7 IPE 5990 IELMT 963: 10
—— Additional Protocol 28 January 1964	956 UNTS 335 7 IPE 6005 IELMT 964: 10
Brussels Convention on the Liability of Operators of Nuclear Ships 25 May 1962	IAEA LegSer#4, p.34 57 AJIL 268 IELMT 962: 40
Vienna Convention on Civil Liability for Nuclear Damage 21 May 1963	1063 UNTS 265 IAEA LegSer#4, p.7 2 ILM 727 (1963) UNEP3 #30, p.179 IELMT 963: 40
—— IAEA Board of Governors Decision setting maximum limits for the exclusion by States of small quantities of nuclear materials from coverage by the Vienna Convention 11 September 1964	IAEA LegSer#4, p.18 8 IPE 6642
Brussels Convention relating to Civil Liability in the Field of Maritime Carriage of Nuclear Material (Arts. 1-3) 17 December 1971	974 UNTS 255 IAEA LegSer#4, p.55 UNEP Reg. p.97 UNEP3 #50, p.253 IELMT 971: 93
Vienna Joint Protocol relating to the Application of the Vienna Convention and the Paris Convention on Civil Liability for Nuclear Damage 21 September 1988	UNEP Reg. p.249 IAEA Doc. GOV/2326, Annex 1

Chapter 14. Energy Production (non-nuclear)

14.A. General

OECD Council Recommendation: Energy and the Environment 14 November 1974	OECD C(74)222 OECD p.52 1 IPE 310
Paris Agreement on an International Energy Pro-	27 UST 1685

gram, including Establishment of the International
Energy Agency
18 November 1974

TIAS 8278
UNEP3 #65, p.435
16 IPE 8376
IELMT 974: 85

OECD Council Recommendation: Reduction of
Environmental Impacts from Energy Production
and Use
12 October 1976

OECD C(76)162(Final)
OECD p.53
30 IPE 44

OECD Council Recommendation: Reduction of
Environmental Impacts from Energy Use in the
Household and Commercial Sectors (with attached
General Conclusions)
21 September 1977

OECD C(77)109(Final)
OECD p.56

Australia-United States of America: Memorandum
of Understanding Relating to Coal Information Exchange in the Areas of Health, Safety and Environment
25 October 1978

30 UST 2208
TIAS 9328
29 IPE 87

Nairobi Programme of Action for the Development
of New and Renewable Sources of Energy: Report
of the UN Conference on New and Renewable
Sources of Energy
21 August 1981

UN Sales No.
    E.81.I.24,
    Ch.I, Sec.A

Republic of Korea-United States of America:
Memorandum of Understanding Providing for a
Cooperative Laboratory Relationship in Areas of
Energy Conservation, Washington
6 November 1981

TIAS —

UNGA Resolution: Immediate Implementation of
the Nairobi Programme of Action for the Development and Utilization of New and Renewable
Sources of Energy
21 December 1982

A/RES/37/250, Secs.
    II, III

OECD Council Recommendation: Environmentally Favourable Energy Options and their Implementation (with annexed list of elements)
20 June 1985

OECD C(85)102
OECD p.64

OECD Council Recommendation: Control of Air
Pollution from Fossil Fuel Combustion (with annexed Guiding Principles)
20 June 1985

OECD C(85)101
OECD p.39

EEC Council Directive: Emissions from Large
Combustion Plants
24 November 1988

Dir. No. 88/609
OJEC 1988 L 336/1

14.B. Vehicles

EEC Directive: Approximation of Laws of Member States relating to Measures to be Taken against Air Pollution by Gases from Positive-Ignition Engines of Motor Vehicles
20 March 1970

Dir. No. 70/220
OJEC 1970 L 76/1
15 IPE 7535

EEC Council Directive: Emissions from Diesel Engines for Use in Motor Vehicles
2 August 1972

Dir. No. 72/306
OJEC 1972 L 190/1
15 IPE 7604

OECD Council Recommendation: Traffic Limitation and Low-Cost Improvement of the Urban Environment
14 November 1974

OECD C(74)218
OECD p.164
1 IPE 302

EEC Council Directives: Lead Content of Petrol
20 March 1985; 20 December 1985; 21 July 1987

Dir. No. 85/210
OJEC 1985 L 96/25
Dir. No. 85/581
OJEC 1985 L 372/37
Dir. No. 87/416
OJEC 1987 L 225/33

EEC Council Directive: Gaseous Emissions from Commercial Vehicles (Diesel Engines)
3 December 1987

Dir. No. 88/77
OJEC 1988 L 36/33

EEC Council Directive: Gaseous Emissions from Passenger Cars
3 December 1987

Dir. No. 88/76
OJEC 1988 L 36/1

EEC Directive: Particulate Pollutant Emissions from Diesel Engines (amending Directive No. 70/220)
16 June 1988

Dir. No. 88/436
OJEC 1988 L 214/1

EEC Council Directive: Exhaust Systems and Noise Level of Motor Cycles
13 March 1989

Dir. No. 89/235
OJEC 1989 L 98/1

EEC Council Directive: Emission Standards for Cars below 1.4 litres
18 July 1989

Dir. No. 89/458
OJEC 1989 L 226/1

14.C. Industry

OECD Council Recommendation: Guidelines for Action to Reduce Emissions of Sulphur Oxides and Particulate Matter from Fuel Combustion in Stationary Sources (with annexed Technical Note)
18 June 1974

OECD C(74)16(Final)
OECD p.34
15 IPE 7627

EEC Council Directive: Combating Air Pollution from Industrial Plants
28 June 1984

Dir. No. 84/360
OJEC 1984 L 188/20

Chapter 15. Industrial Activities

15.A. General

Montevideo Declaration concerning Industrial and Agricultural Use of International Rivers
24 December 1933

A/5409 III, Annex I
11 IPE 5707

OAS/IAJC Draft Convention on Industrial and Agricultural Use of International Rivers and Lakes
1965

OEA/Ser.1/VI.1

15.B. Chemical

ILO Convention (#136) concerning Protection Against Hazards of Poisoning Arising from Benzene, Geneva
23 June 1971

885 UNTS 45
LIV ILO OB Ser.A
UNEP3 #49, p.251
15 IPE 7503
IELMT 971: 47

ILO Recommendation (#144) concerning Protection against Hazards of Poisoning Arising from Benzene
23 June 1971

LIV ILO OB Ser.A
28 IPE 374

OECD Council Decision: Protection of the Environment by Control of Polychlorinated Biphenyls (with appended Technical Note)
13 February 1973

OECD C(73)1(Final)
OECD p.93
17 IPE 8739

OECD Council Recommendation: Assessment of Potential Environmental Effects of Chemicals (with Explanatory Note)
14 November 1974

OECD C(74)215
OECD p.100
1 IPE 296

OECD Council Recommendation: Guidelines in Respect of Procedures and Requirements for Anticipating the Effects of Chemicals on Man and in the Environment (with annexed Guidelines)
7 July 1977

OECD C(77)97(Final)
OECD p.102

OECD Council Decision: Mutual Acceptance of Data in the Assessment of Chemicals (with annexed OECD Test Guidelines and OECD Principles of Good Laboratory Practice)
12 May 1981

OECD C(81)30(Final)
OECD p.109

OECD Council Recommendation: Mutual Recog-

OECD C(83)95(Final)

nition of Compliance with Good Laboratory　　OECD p.126
Practice
26 July 1983

OECD Council Recommendation: Exchange of　　OECD C(93)97(Final)
Confidential Data on Chemicals (with appended　　OECD p.129
Suggested Principles)
26 July 1983

OECD Council Recommendation: OECD List of　　OECD C(83)98(Final)
Non-Confidential Data on Chemicals (with ap-　　OECD p.135
pended OECD List)
26 July 1983

OECD Council Recommendation: Protection of　　OECD C(83)96(Final)
Proprietary Rights to Data Submitted in Notifica-　　OECD p.128
tion of New Chemicals
26 July 1983

OECD Council Recommendation: Information Ex-　　OECD C(84)37(Final)
change Related to Export of Banned or Severely　　OECD p.137
Restricted Chemicals (with appended Guiding
Principles)
4 April 1984

UNEP Governing Council Decision: Provisional　　UNEP/GC/12/12/Add.1
Notification Scheme for Banned and Severely Re-　　UNEP/GC/DEC/12/14
stricted Chemicals　　UNEP ELGP #6
28 May 1984　　IPE(2) I/D/28-05-84

UNEP Governing Council Decision: London　　*Infra* p.644
Guidelines for the Exchange of Information on　　UNEP/PIC/WG.2/2, p.9
Chemicals in International Trade　　UNEP/GC.14/17,
19 June 1987　　　　Annex IV
　　UNEP/GC/DEC/14/27
　　UNEP ELGP #10
　　IPE(2) I/D/19-06-87

———— Amended London Guidelines　　UNEP/GC/DEC/15/30
25 May 1989

UNEP Governing Council Decision: Revised Ob-　　UNEP/GC/DEC/15/28,
jectives and Strategies of the International Register　　Annex
of Potentially Toxic Chemicals
25 May 1989

15.C.　Mining

UNEP Governing Council Decision: Conclusions　　UNEP/GC/DEC/10/14VI
of the Study of Legal Aspects Concerning the En-　　UNEP ELGP #4
vironment Related to Offshore Mining and Drilling　　7 EPL 50
Within the Limits of National Jurisdiction
31 May 1982

Washington Agreement Concerning Interim Arrangements Relating to Polymetallic Nodules of the Deep Sea Bed 2 September 1982	34 UST 3451 TIAS 10562 IELMT 982: 65
UNEP Environmental Guidelines: Restoration and Rehabilitation of Land and Soils After Mining Activities 1983	UNEP EMG #8
Provisional Understanding Regarding Deep Seabed Matters (with memorandum of implementation, joint record and related exchanges of notes), Geneva 3 August 1984	TIAS — IELMT 984: 58
Wellington Convention on the Regulation of Antarctic Mineral Resources Activities (Preamble, Arts. 1(4), (15), 2(1)(a), 4(2-4), 8, 10, 13(2), (6), 15, 21(1), (9)(C)) 2 June 1988	*Infra* p.529 AMR/SCM/88/78 (1988) 27 ILM 868 (1988) IELMT 988: 42

15.D.   Other

UNEP Environmental Guidelines for Pulp and Paper Industry 1982	UNEP EMG #4
UNEP Environmental Guidelines for Hides and Skin Industry 1982	UNEP EMG #5
Mexico-United States of America: La Paz Agreement for Cooperation on Environmental Programmes and Transboundary Problems, 1983 (see 1.C.ii), Annex IV, Agreement of Cooperation regarding Transboundary Air Pollution Caused by Copper Smelters along their Common Border, Washington 29 January 1987	26 ILM 33 (1987)

Chapter 16.   Agricultural Activities

16.A.   General

Montevideo Declaration concerning Industrial and Agricultural Use of International Rivers 24 December 1933	A/5409 III, Ann.I 11 IPE 5707
Constitution of the Food and Agriculture Organization of the United Nations (FAO) (Art. I.2(c)) 3 June 1943	FAO Basic Texts Peaslee, Pt. II 1 IPE 85

OAS/IAJC Draft Convention on Industrial and Agricultural Use of International Rivers and Lakes 1965 — OEA/Ser.1/VI.1

WHO/FAO/UNEP Memorandum of Understanding Governing Collaboration in the Prevention and Control of Water-Borne and Associated Diseases in Agricultural Water Development Activities 1981 — UNEP/GC/INFORMATION/6/Add.6

European Convention for the Protection of Animals During International Transport, C/E, Paris (Preamble, Art. 30) 13 December 1968 — ETS #65 / UNEP3 #39, p.216 / 5 IPE 2070 / IELMT 968: 92

———— Additional Protocol, Strasbourg 10 May 1979 — ETS #103 / 22 IPE 384 / IELMT 979: 35

European Convention for the Protection of Animals kept for Farming Purposes, C/E, Strasbourg 10 March 1976 — ETS #87 / 20 IPE 10353

European Convention for the Protection of Animals for Slaughter, C/E, Strasbourg 10 May 1979 — ETS #102 / 22 IPE 384

OECD Council Recommendation: Role of Agriculture in the Planning and Management of Peri-Urban Areas 14 May 1979 — OECD C(79)18(Final) / OECD p.179

FAO: Comparative Legal Study on Environmental Impact Assessment and Agricultural Development 1982 — FAO Environmental Paper 2

UNEP Environmental Guidelines for the Formulation of National Soil Policies 1983 — UNEP EMG #7

UNEP Environmental Guidelines for Afforestation Projects 1985 — UNEP EMG #9

UNEP Environmental Guidelines for Agricultural Mechanization 1986 — UNEP EMG #10

UNEP Environmental Guidelines for Agroforestry Projects 1986 — UNEP EMG #11

UNEP Environmental Guidelines for Farming Sys- — UNEP EMG #12

tems Research
1986

EEC Council Directive: Protection of the Environ- ment, and in Particular of the Soil, when Sewage Sludge is Used in Agriculture 12 June 1986	Dir. No. 86/278 OJEC 1986 L 181/6
UNEP Environmental Guidelines for Rural Roads 1987	UNEP EMG #13
UNEP Environmental Guidelines for Rural Work- camps 1988	UNEP EMG #15
UNEP Environmental Guidelines for Flood Plain Management 1988	UNEP EMG #16

16.B.   Pesticides

UNEP Environmental Guidelines for Pesticide Use on Industrial Crops 1982	UNEP EMG #1
FAO: Guidelines on Environmental Criteria for the Registration of Pesticides 1985	
FAO: Guidelines for the Packaging and Storage of Pesticides 1985	
FAO: Guidelines on Good Labelling Practices for Pesticides 1985	
FAO: Guidelines for the Registration and Control of Pesticides (including a model scheme for the establishment of national organizations) 1985	
——— Addenda 1988	
FAO: International Code of Conduct on the Distri- bution and Use of Pesticides 28 November 1985	23 FAO Conf Res 10/85
——— Amended (to include Prior Informed Con- sent in Art. 9) December 1989	FAO Conf 25th sess. FAO Doc: M/U0610E/I/9.90

FAO: Guidelines for Retail Distribution of Pesticides with particular reference to Storage and Handling at the Point of Supply to Users in Developing Countries
1988

FAO: Guidelines for Legislation on the Control of Pesticides
1989

FAO: Guidelines on the Operation of Prior Informed Consent (PIC) (in respect of the distribution and use of pesticides)
1990

Chapter 17.   Waste Disposal

17.A.   General

EEC Council Directive: A Framework for Waste Management 15 July 1975	Dir. No. 75/442 OJEC 1975 L 194/39 17 IPE 8855
OECD Council Recommendation: A Comprehensive Waste Management Policy (with annexed Principles) 28 September 1976	OECD C(76)155(Final) OECD p.68 30 IPE 40
OAU Council of Ministers Resolution: Dumping of Nuclear and Industrial Waste in Africa 23 May 1988	28 ILM 567 (1989)
EEC Council Proposed Directive: Civil Liability for Damage Caused by Waste 1 September 1989	OJEC 1989 C 251/3
Antarctic Treaty, Protocol on Environmental Protection (see 9.A), Annex III (Waste Disposal and Waste Management) 21 June 1991	XI ATSCM/2

17.B.   Incineration

EEC Council Directive: Prevention of Air Pollution from new Municipal Waste-Incineration Plants 8 June 1989	Dir. No. 89/369 OJEC 1989 L 163/32
EEC Council Directive: Reduction of Air Pollution from Existing Municipal Waste-Incineration Plants 21 June 1989	Dir. No. 89/429 OJEC 1989 L 203/50

17.C.   Waste Water & Sewage

Brussels Agreement on the Implementation of a European Project on Pollution, on the Topic "Sewage Sludge Processing"
23 November 1971

12 ILM 9 (1973)
11 IPE 5664
IELMT 971: 87

IMO Convention on the Prevention of Marine Pollution by Dumping of Wastes and Other Matter (London Ocean Dumping Convention—LDC) (amended 1978 (2x), 1980, 1989)
29 December 1972

Infra p.318
1046 UNTS 120
26 UST 2403
TIAS 8165
UNEP3 #56, p.283
11 ILM 1294 (1972)
2 IPE 537
IELMT 972: 96

———— London Amendments on Incineration of Wastes and other Matter at Sea
12 October 1978

IELMT 972: 96/A

UNEP Environmental Guidelines for Domestic Wastewater Management
1988

UNEP EMG #14

UNEP Council Decision: Precautionary Approach to Marine Pollution, including Waste-Dumping at Sea
25 May 1989

UNEP/GC/DEC/15/27

EEC Council Proposed Directive: Municipal Waste Water Treatment
9 November 1989

OJEC 1989 C 300/8
OJEC 1990 C 1/20

17.D.   Radioactive Wastes

Federal Republic of Germany-United States of America: Technical Exchange and Cooperative Arrangement in the Field of Management of Radioactive Wastes (with Patent Addendum and Appendix), Bonn
20 December 1974

1148 UNTS 91
29 UST 4544
TIAS 9067
8 IPE 6447

———— Extension and Amendments
19 March 1980

33 UST 509
TIAS 10040
27 IPE 5

———— Extension and Amendments (17 & 19 April 1985)
19 April 1985

TIAS —

OECD Council Recommendation: Multilateral Consultation and Surveillance Mechanism for Sea

OECD C(77)115(Final)
OECD p.181

Dumping of Radioactive Waste (with appended Interpretations)
22 July 1977 — 19 IPE 9743

Belgium-United States of America: Agreement in the Field of Radioactive Waste Management
19 January 1981 — 32 UST 4569 / TIAS 9970

Canada-United States of America: Ottawa Agreement Respecting Cooperation in Radioactive Waste Management
25 August 1982 — 34 UST 1773 / TIAS 10456

Euratom (European Community*)-United States of America: Brussels Agreement for Exchange of Information Concerning a Cooperative Program in the Field of Management of Radioactive Wastes
6 October 1982 — 34 UST 2751 / TIAS 10521

France-United States of America: Paris Agreement for Cooperation in the Field of Radioactive Waste Management
26 July 1983 — TIAS 10753

France-United States of America: Technical Exchange and Cooperation Arrangement in the Field of Safety of Radioactive Waste Management
10 January 1984 — TIAS 10918

Switzerland-United States of America: Agreement on Cooperation in Radioactive Waste Management Safety Research
26 September 1986 — TIAS —

United Kingdom-United States of America: London Agreement in the Field of Radioactive Waste Management Technology
30 October 1986 — TIAS —

Japan-United States of America: Washington Agreement in the Area of Radioactive Waste Management
3 December 1986 — TIAS —

OAU Council of Ministers Resolution on Dumping of Nuclear and Industrial Waste in Africa
23 May 1988 — 28 ILM 567 (1989)

UNGA Resolution: Prohibition of the Dumping of Radioactive Wastes for Hostile Purposes
7 December 1988 — A/RES/43/75Q

UNGA Resolution: Dumping of Radioactive — A/RES/43/75T

Wastes
7 December 1988

EEC Council Proposed Directive: Basic safety standards for the health protection of the general public and workers against the dangers of ionizing radiation as to shipments of radioactive waste 1 December 1989	OJEC 1990 C 5/7
African, Caribbean and Pacific States-European Economic Community (European Community*): Fourth Lomé Convention (Art. 39 and Annexes VIII, IX, X) 15 December 1989	29 ILM 783 (1990)
Union of Soviet Socialist Republics-United States of America: Vienna Co-operation Agreement in the Area of Environmental Restoration and Nuclear Waste Management 18 September 1990	
IAEA Code of Practice on the International Transboundary Movement of Radioactive Waste 21 September 1990	*Infra* p.597 IAEA Doc GC(34)/920 IAEA GC(XXXIV)/RES/530
IMO Convention on the Prevention of Marine Pollution by Dumping of Wastes and Other Matter, 13th Consultative Meeting of Contracting Parties Resolution placing sub-seabed disposal of radioactive wastes under the current voluntary moratorium on sea disposal of low-level radioactive waste 2 November 1990	
UNGA Resolution: Prohibition of the Dumping of Radioactive wastes 4 December 1990	A/RES/45/58K

17.E.   Other Hazardous Wastes

EEC Council Directive: Toxic and Dangerous Waste (as amended) 20 March 1978	Dir. No. 78/319 OJEC 1978 L 84/43 18 IPE 9355
OECD Council Decision/Recommendation: Transfrontier Movements of Hazardous Waste (with Principles Concerning Transfrontier Movements of Hazardous Wastes and appended Definitions) 1 February 1984	OECD C(83)180(Final) OECD p.78 32 EYB OECD 19
EEC Council Directive: Transboundary Shipment of Hazardous Waste 6 December 1984	Dir. No. 84/631 OJEC 1984 L 326/31

OECD Council Resolution: International Co-operation Concerning Transfrontier Movements of Hazardous Wastes (with appended Conclusions and Recommendations of 1985 Basel Conference and List of Issues) 20 June 1985	OECD C(85)100 OECD p.82
OECD Council Decision/Recommendation: Exports of Hazardous Wastes from the OECD Area (with Measures Concerning the Control of Exports of Hazardous Wastes and appended Definitions) 5 June 1986	OECD C(86)64(Final) OECD p.86
Canada-United States of America: Agreement Concerning the Transboundary Movement of Hazardous Waste, Ottawa 28 October 1986	*Infra* p.616 TIAS —
Mexico-United States of America: La Paz Agreement for Cooperation on Environmental Programs and Transboundary Problems, 1983 (see 1.C.ii), Annex III, Transboundary Shipment of Hazardous Wastes and Hazardous Substances, Washington 12 November 1986	*Infra* p.621 26 ILM 25 (1987)
UNEP Governing Council Decision: Cairo Guidelines and Principles for the Environmentally Sound Management of Hazardous Wastes 17 June 1987	UNEP/GC.14/17, Annex II UNEP/GC/DEC/14/30 UNEP ELPG #8
OECD Council Decision: Transfrontier Movements of Hazardous Wastes 27 May 1988	28 ILM 257 (1989)
Basel Convention on the Control of Transboundary Movements of Hazardous Wastes and their Disposal 22 March 1989	*Infra* p.601 UNEP/WG.190/4 UNEP: IG.80/3 28 ILM 657 (1989) IELMT 989: 22
UNGA Resolution: Traffic in toxic and dangerous products and wastes. Control of transboundary movements of hazardous wastes and their disposal 22 December 1989	A/RES/44/226, parts I & III
UN Commission on Human Rights Resolution: Movement and Dumping of Toxic and Dangerous Products and Waste 1990	E/CN.4/Sub.2/1990/7 UNHRC Res.1990/43
Bamako Convention on the Ban of Import into Africa and the Control of Transboundary Movement and Management of Hazardous Wastes	OAU Doc. 30 ILM 775 (1991) (draft: 20 EPL 173 (1990))

within Africa, OAU (plus Annexes I-V)
30 January 1991

17.F.   Other Wastes

OECD Council Recommendation: Re-Use and Re- OECD C(78)8(Final)
cycling of Beverage Containers (with appended OECD p.72
Brief Review of Measures)   30 IPE 111
3 February 1978

OECD Council Recommendation: Waste Paper OECD C(79)218(Final)
Recovery   OECD p.76
30 January 1980

Chapter 18.   Hazardous Substances (see also 12 and 16.B, 17.D, 17.E)

18.A.   General

EEC Council Directive on Marketing and Use of Dir. No. 76/769
Dangerous Substances   OJEC 1976 L 262/201
27 July 1976   17 IPE 8900

Mexico-United States of America: Agreement of 32 UST 5899
Co-operation regarding Pollution of the Marine En- TIAS 10021
vironment by Discharges of Hydrocarbons and
other Hazardous Substances
24 July 1980

Mexico-United States of America: La Paz 26 ILM 19 (1987)
Agreement for Cooperation on Environmental Programs and Transboundary Problems, 1983 (see
1.C.ii), Annex II, Agreement for Cooperation regarding Pollution of the Environment along the
Inland International Boundary by Discharge of
Hazardous Substances, San Diego
18 July 1985

EEC Council Directive: Limit Values and Quality Dir. No. 86/280
Objectives for Discharges of Dangerous Sub- OJEC 1986 L 181/16
stances included in List 1 of the Annex to Directive
No. 76/464
12 June 1986

OECD Council Decision/Recommendation: Provi- OECD C(88)85
sion of Information to Public and Public Participa- 28 ILM 277 (1989)
tion in Decision-Making Processes Related to Pre-
vention of, and Responses to, Accidents Involving
Hazardous Substances
8 July 1988

UNGA Resolution: Protection against products harmful to health and the environment
22 December 1989

A/RES/44/226,
Part II

18.B. Transport

Fort Lamy (N'Djamena) Convention and Statute relating to the Development of the Lake Chad Basin (Statute, Art. 5) (amended 22 October 1972 in Yaounde and 1977 in Enugu)
22 May 1964

A/CN.4/274, para.53
FAO Conf 12th sess.
11 IPE 5633

OECD Council Decision/Recommendation: Transfrontier Movements of Hazardous Waste (with Principles Concerning Transfrontier Movements of Hazardous Wastes and appended Definitions)
1 February 1984

OECD C(83)180(Final)
OECD p.78
32 EYB OECD 19

EEC Council Directive: Transboundary Shipment of Hazardous Waste
6 December 1984

Dir. No. 84/631
OJEC 1984 L 326/31

OECD Council Resolution: International Co-operation Concerning Transfrontier Movements of Hazardous Wastes (with appended Conclusions and Recommendations of 1985 Basel Conference and List of Issues)
20 June 1985

OECD C(85)100
OECD p.82

OECD Council Decision/Recommendation: Exports of Hazardous Wastes from the OECD Area (with Measures Concerning the Control of Exports of Hazardous Wastes and appended Definitions)
5 June 1986

OECD C(86)64(Final)
OECD p.86

Canada-United States of America: Agreement Concerning the Transboundary Movement of Hazardous Waste, Ottawa
28 October 1986

Infra p.616
TIAS ———

Mexico-United States of America: La Paz Agreement for Cooperation on Environmental Programs and Transboundary Problems, 1983 (see 1.C.ii), Annex III, Transboundary Shipment of Hazardous Wastes and Hazardous Substances, Washington
12 November 1986

Infra p.621
26 ILM 25 (1987)

UNEP Governing Council Decision: London Guidelines for the Exchange of Information on Chemicals in International Trade
19 June 1987

Infra p.644
UNEP/PIC/WG.2/2, p.9
UNEP/GC.14/17,
        Annex IV
UNEP/GC/DEC/14/27
UNEP ELGP #10

IPE(2) I/D/19-06-87

OECD Council Decision: Transfrontier Movements of Hazardous Wastes 27 May 1988	28 ILM 257 (1989)

Basel Convention on the Control of Transboundary Movements of Hazardous Wastes and their Disposal
22 March 1989

Infra p.601
UNEP/WG.190/4
UNEP/IG.80/3
28 ILM 657 (1989)
IELMT 989: 22

Geneva Convention on Civil Liability for Damage Caused during Carriage of Dangerous Goods by Road, Rail and Inland Navigation Vessels
10 October 1989

EEC Council Proposed Directive: Basic safety standards for the health protection of the general public and workers against the dangers of ionizing radiation as to shipments of radioactive waste
1 December 1989

OJEC 1990 C 5/7

IAEA Code of Practice on the International Transboundary Movement of Radioactive Waste
21 September 1990

Infra p.597
IAEA Doc GC(34)/920
IAEA GC(XXXIV)/RES/530

Bamako Convention on the Ban of Import into Africa and the Control of Transboundary Movement and Management of Hazardous Wastes within Africa, OAU (plus Annexes I-V)
30 January 1991

OAU Doc.
30 ILM 775 (1991)
(draft: 20 EPL 173 (1990))

Chapter 19.   Noise

OECD Council Recommendation: Noise Prevention and Abatement
14 November 1974

OECD C(74)217
OECD p.166
1 IPE 299

ILO Convention (#148) concerning the Protection of Workers Against Occupational Hazards in the Working Environment Due to Air Pollution, Noise and Vibration, Geneva
20 June 1977

LX:3 ILO OB Ser.A,
p.136
UNEP3 #73, p.482
28 IPE 335
IELMT 977: 46

OECD Council Recommendation: Noise Abatement Policies
3 July 1978

OECD C(78)73(Final)
OECD p.167

OECD Council Recommendation: Strengthening Noise Abatement Policies
20 June 1985

OECD C(85)103
OECD p.169
28 IPE 403

EEC Council Directive: Noise Generated by Heavy
Excavators and Dozers
22 December 1986

Dir. No. 86/662
OJEC 1986 L 384/1

EEC Council Directive: Exhaust Systems and
Noise Level of Motor Cycles
13 March 1989

Dir. No. 89/235
OJEC 1989 L 98/1

Chapter 20. Biotechnical Activities

EEC Council Directive: Contained Use of Genetically Modified Micro-organisms
23 April 1990

Dir. No. 90/219
OJEC 1990 L 117/1

EEC Council Directive: Deliberate Release into the
Environment of Genetically Modified Organisms
23 April 1990

OJEC 1990 L 117/15

Chapter 21. Tourism

OECD Council Recommendation: Environment
and Tourism (with annexed Guidelines)
8 May 1979

OECD C(79)115
OECD p.174

UNEP Environmental Guidelines for Coastal
Tourism
1982

UNEP EMG #6

Chapter 22. Military Activities

Geneva Protocol for the Prohibition of the Use in
War of Asphyxiating, Poisonous or Other Gases,
and of Biological Methods of Warfare
17 June 1925

26 UST 583
TIAS 8061
94 LNTS 65
IELMT 925: 45

Hague Convention for the Protection of Cultural
Property in the Event of Armed Conflict
14 May 1954

249 UNTS 215
14 IPE 7132

Treaty Banning Nuclear Weapons Tests in the Atmosphere, in Outer Space and Under Water
(PTBT), Moscow
5 August 1963

Infra p.632
480 UNTS 43
14 UST 1313
TIAS 5433
UNEP3 #31, p.185
1 IPE 422
IELMT 963: 59

OAU Assembly of Heads of State and Government: Declaration on the Denuclearization of
Africa
21 July 1964

A/5975
20 GAOR Ann. a.i.105

UNGA Resolution: Declaration on the Denuclearization of Africa
3 December 1965

A/RES/2033(XX)
16 IPE 7951

Tlatelolco Treaty for the Prohibition of Nuclear
Weapons in Latin America
14 February 1967

634 UNTS 281, 362, 364
22 UST 762, 754
TIAS 7137, 10147
15 IPE 7827
IELMT 967: 13

Treaty on the Non-Proliferation of Nuclear Weapons (NPT)
1 July 1968

729 UNTS 161
21 UST 483
TIAS 6839
15 IPE 7848
IELMT 968: 51

Treaty on the Prohibition of the Emplacement of
Nuclear Weapons and Other Weapons of Mass Destruction on the Sea-bed and the Ocean Floor and
in the Subsoil Thereof
11 February 1971

955 UNTS 115
23 UST 701
TIAS 7337
UNEP3 #48, p.249
2 IPE 498
IELMT 971: 12

Convention on the Prohibition of the Development, Production and Stockpiling of Bacteriologi-
cal (Biological) and Toxin Weapons, and on their
Destruction
10 April 1972

1015 UNTS 163
26 UST 583
TIAS 8062
UNEP3 #53, p.269
15 IPE 7858
IELMT 972: 28

France-Union of Soviet Socialist Republics:
Agreement Concerning the Prevention of the Accidental or Unauthorized Use of Nuclear Weapons
16 July 1976

1036 UNTS 299
15 IPE 7903

ILA Madrid Resolution on the Protection of Water
Resources and Water Installations in Times of
Armed Conflict (Arts. IV, V)
4 September 1976

57 ILA 234
26 IPE 159

Convention on the Prohibition of Military or Any
Other Hostile Use of Environmental Modification
Techniques (ENMOD)
18 May 1977

Infra p.634
1108 UNTS 151
31 UST 333
TIAS 9614
A/RES/31/72
UNEP3 #72, p.479
1976 UNJYB 125
16 ILM 88 (1977)
16 IPE 8058
IELMT 977: 37

UNEP Governing Council Decision: Material
Remnants of War
25 May 1977

UNEP/GC/103
UNEP/GC/DEC/101(V)
A/32/137

18 IPE 9259

Additional Protocol I to the 1949 Geneva Conventions Relating to the Protection of Victims of International Armed Conflict (Arts. 35(3), 36, 53, 55, 56)
8 June 1977

1125 UNTS Reg. #17512
16 ILM 1391 (1977)

Additional Protocol II to the 1949 Geneva Conventions Relating to the Protection of Victims of International Armed Conflict (Arts. 14-16)
8 June 1977

1125 UNTS Reg. No. 17513
16 ILM 1442 (1977)

UN Conference on Desertification: Resolution on Effect of Weapons of Mass Destruction on Ecosystems
9 September 1977

A/CONF.74/36, Ch.II,
    Resol.4
30 IPE 82

Convention on Prohibitions or Restrictions of the Use of Certain Conventional Weapons which may be Deemed to be Excessively Injurious or to have Indiscriminate Effects, Protocol II On the Use of Mines, etc.
10 October 1980

A/CONF.95/15
28 IPE 520
19 ILM 1529 (1980)

———— Protocol III On the Use of Incendiary Weapons (Art. II.4)
10 October 1980

A/CONF.95/15
19 ILM 1534 (1980)

UNGA Resolution: Historical Responsibility of States for the Protection of Nature for the Benefit of Present and Future Generations
30 October 1980

Infra p.638
A/RES/35/8
1980 UNJYB 726
IPE(2) I/C/30-10-80

World Charter for Nature (paras. 5, 20)
28 October 1982

Infra p.184
A/RES/37/7
1982 UNYB 1023
22 ILM 455 (1983)
IPE(2) I/C/28-10-82

UNGA Resolution: Provisional Procedures to Uphold the Authority of the 1925 Geneva Protocol
13 December 1982

A/RES/37/98D

UNGA Resolution: Remnants of War (noting UN Secretary-General's report)
20 December 1982

UNEP/GC/DEC/10/8
A/37/25, Pt.Two, Annex
A/RES/37/215

South Pacific Nuclear Free Zone Treaty, Raratonga
6 August 1985

UNEP Reg. p.232
24 ILM 1440 (1985)
IELMT 985: 58

IAEA General Conference: Prohibition of All

IAEA GC(XXXI)/RES/475

Armed Attack Against Nuclear Installations Devoted to Peaceful Purposes
September 1987

UNGA Resolution: Climatic Effects of Nuclear War, Including Nuclear Winter (noting the UN Secretary-General's Report: Study on the Climatic and Other Effects of Nuclear War) 7 December 1988	A/RES/43/78D UN Sales No. E.89.IX.1
UNGA Resolution: Prohibition of the Dumping of Radioactive Wastes for Hostile Purposes 7 December 1988	A/RES/43/75Q
UNGA Resolution: Convention on the Prohibition of Nuclear Weapons 7 December 1988	A/RES/43/76E
UNGA Resolution: Establishment of a Nuclear-Weapon-Free Zone in South Asia 4 December 1990	A/RES/45/53
UNGA Resolution: Prohibition of Attacks on Nuclear Facilities 4 December 1990	A/RES/45/58J
UNGA Resolution: Prohibition of the Dumping of Radioactive Wastes 4 December 1990	A./RES/45/58K
Security Council Resolution relating to a permanent cease-fire in the Gulf War (paragraph relating to Iraq's liability) 3 April 1991	S/RES/687 (1991), para.16 30 ILM 847 (1991)
ILC, Draft Articles on the Law of the Non-Navigational Uses of International Watercourses (Art.29) 19 July 1991	*Infra* p.404 A/46/10 (1991), Ch.III
ILC, Draft Articles on the Draft Code of Crimes Against the Peace and Security of Mankind (Art. 22 (2)(d)) 19 July 1991	A/46/10 (1991), Ch.IV

Chapter 23.   Disasters

23.A.   General

Federal Republic of Germany-Luxembourg: Agreement on Mutual Assistance in Case of Disasters or Major Accidents
18 October 1979

IAEA Guidelines for Mutual Emregency Assistance Arrangements in Connection with a Nuclear Accident or Radiological Emergency
29 April 1983

IAEA Doc. INFCIRC/310

IAEA Guidelines on Reportable Events, Integrated Planning and Information Exchange in a Transboundary Release of Radioactive Materials
May 1984

IAEA Doc. INFCIRC/321

IAEA Convention on Early Notification of a Nuclear Accident, Vienna
26 September 1986

Infra p.583
IAEA INFCIRC/335
IAEA LegSer#14
25 ILM 1370 (1986)
IELMT 986: 71

IAEA Convention on Assistance in the Case of a Nuclear Accident or Radiological Emergency, Vienna
26 September 1986

Infra p.587
UNTS Reg. #24643
IAEA INFCIRC/336
IAEA LegSer#14
25 ILM 1377 (1986)
IELMT 986: 72

UNGA Resolution: International co-operation in the monitoring, assessment and anticipation of environmental threats and in assistance in cases of environmental emergencies
22 December 1989

A/RES/44/224

23.B. Natural
23.B.i. General

UNEP/UNDRO/WFC/UNIDO/ILO/UNESCO/ WHO/WMO Memorandum of Understanding on the Environmental Aspects of Natural Disasters
1979

UNEP/GC/
  INFORMATION/6/
  Add.2

23.B.ii. Locust

FAO Agreement for the Establishment of a Commission for Controlling the Desert Locust in the Eastern Region of its Distribution Area in South-West Asia, Rome (amended November 1977 (72nd FAO Council))
3 December 1963

529 UNTS 217
FAO Conf 12th sess.
UNEP3 #33, p.188
4 IPE 1973
IELMT 963: 91

FAO Agreement for the Establishment of a Commission for Controlling the Desert Locust in the Near East, Rome (amended November 1977 (72nd FAO Council))
2 July 1965

592 UNTS 215
FAO Council 44th sess.
UNEP3 #39, p.198
4 IPE 1994
IELMT 965: 49

FAO Agreement for the Establishment of a Com-

797 UNTS 97

mission for Controlling the Desert Locust in North-West Africa, Rome (amended November 1977 (72nd FAO Conference)) 1 December 1970

FAO Council 55th sess. UNEP3 #46, p.242 5 IPE 2142

23.B.iii.   Drought (Desertification)

UN Conference on Desertification: Plan of Action to Combat Desertification 9 September 1977

A/CONF.74/36, Ch.I 30 IPE 50

Mexico-United States of America: Agreement on Co-operation to Improve Management of Arid and Semi-Arid Lands and Control Desertification 16 February 1979

1168 UNTS #18587 29 IPE 258

Implementation of the Plan of Action to Combat Desertification (UNEP) 26 May 1981

UNEP/GC.9/8 & Add.1

UNEP Environmental Guidelines for Irrigation in Arid and Semi-Arid Areas 1982

UNEP EMG #2

UNEP Environmental Guidelines for Irrigation in Arid and Semi-Arid Lands and Control of Desertification 1982

UNEP EMG #2

UNEP Plan of Action to Combat Desertification, 1978-84 28 May 1984

UNEP/GC.12/9 UNEP/GC/DEC/12/10

African, Caribbean and Pacific States-European Economic Community (European Community*): Third Lomé Convention (Art. 11 and Pt. Two, Title I (Agricultural and rural development and conservation of natural resources), Ch. 2 (Drought and desertification control), Arts. 38-43) 8 December 1984

24 ILM 571 (1985) IELMT 984: 93

23.C.   Anthropogenic (see also 11.D, 12.B, 13.B)

EEC Council Directive: Major Accident Hazards of Certain Industrial Activities ("Seveso Directive") (latest update 14 March 1987) 24 June 1982; 19 March 1987; 24 November 1988

Dir. No. 82/501 OJEC 1982 L 230/1 Dir. No. 87/21 OJEC 1987 L 85/36 Dir. No. 88/610 OJEC 1988 L 336/14

Nordic Agreement on Co-operation over National Territorial Borders with the Aim of Preventing or

Limiting Damage to Man or Property or the Environment in the Event of Accidents
20 January 1989

OECD Council Decision: Exchange of Information   28 ILM 247 (1989)
concerning Accidents Capable of Causing Transfrontier Damage (Preamble, App. I-III)
8 July 1988

OECD Council Decision/Recommendation: Provision of Information to Public & Public Participation in Decision-Making Processes Related to Prevention of, and Response to, Accidents Involving Hazardous Substances
8 July 1988

OECD C(88)85
28 ILM 277 (1989)

120 INTERNATIONAL ENVIRONMENTAL LAW

Part IV. TECHNIQUES OF ENVIRONMENTAL PROTECTION

Chapter 24. Environmental Decisionmaking

24.A. Environmental Impact Statements
24.A.i. General

OECD Council Recommendation: Analysis of the Environmental Consequences of Significant Public and Private Projects 14 November 1974	OECD C(74)216 OECD p.28 1 IPE 297
OECD Council Recommendation: Assessment of Potential Environmental Effects of Chemicals (with Explanatory Note) 14 November 1974	OECD C(74)215 OECD p.100 1 IPE 296
US Agency for International Development (USAID): Environmental Procedures 30 June 1976	41 F.R. 26913 22 CFR Sec.216
OECD Council Recommendation: Assessment of Projects with Significant Impact on the Environment 8 May 1979	OECD C(79)116 OECD p.29
FAO: Comparative Legal Study on Environmental Impact Assessment and Agricultural Development 1982	FAO Environmental Paper 2
OECD Council Recommendation: Environmental Assessment of Development Assistance Projects and Programmes (with appended list of criteria of Projects and Programmes most in Need of Environmental Assessment) 20 June 1985	OECD C(85)104 OECD p.30 IPE(2) I/F/20-06-85.b
EEC Council Directive: Assessment of the Effects of Certain Public and Private Projects on the Environment 27 June 1985	Dir. No. 85/337 OJEC 1985 L 175/40
UNEP Governing Council Decision: Goals and Principles of Environmental Impact Assessment 17 June 1987	UNEP/GC.14/17, Annex III UNEP/GC/DEC/14/25 UNEP ELGP #9 17 EPL 36 (1987) IPE(2) I/D/19-06-87
Wellington Convention on the Regulation of Antarctic Mineral Resources Activities (Arts. 4,	*Infra* p.529 AMR/SCM/88/78 (1988)

37(7)(d)-(e), 39(2)(c), 54(3)(b))	27 ILM 868 (1988)
2 June 1988	IELMT 988: 42

World Bank: Operational Directive "Environmental Assessment"	WB Operational Manual, OD 4.00
November 1989	Annexes A, A1, A2

Espoo (Finland) Convention on Environmental Impact Assessment in a Transboundary Context, ECE	30 ILM 802 (1991)
25 February 1991	

Antarctic Treaty, Protocol on Environmental Protection (see 9.A), Art. 8 and Annex I—Environmental Impact Assessment Procedures	*Infra*, p.536 XI ATSCM/2
21 June 1991	

24.A.ii. Precautionary Principle

Ministerial Declaration of the Second International Conference on the Protection of the North Sea, London	IPE(2) II/B/25-11-87
25 November 1987	

Ministerial Declaration of the Third International Conference on the Protection of the North Sea, The Hague	
8 March 1990	

Vienna Convention on the Protection of the Ozone Layer, 1985, Decisions of the Second Meeting of Parties to the Montreal Protocol (MP) (Annex II, Art. I.A.1 (amendment to 6th preambular para.))	*Infra* p.276 UNEP/OzL.Pro.2/3
29 June 1990	

Second World Climate Conference: Ministerial Declaration, Geneva (para.7)	A/45/696/Add.1, Annex III
7 November 1990	

Bamko Convention on the Ban of Import into Africa and the Control of Transboundary Movement and Management of Hazardous Wastes within Africa, OAU (Art. 4.3(f))	OAU Doc. 30 ILM 775 (1991) (draft: 20 EPL 173 (1990))
30 January 1991	

24.B. Exchange of and Access to Information

OECD Council Resolution: Procedures for Notification and Consultation on Measures for Control of Substances Affecting Man and his Environment (with annexed Procedures)	OECD C(71)73(Final) OECD p.90 18 IPE 9042
18 May 1971	

OECD Council Recommendation: Reporting on the State of the Environment
8 May 1979

OECD C(79)114
OECD p.162
IPE(2) I/F/08-05-79.b

OECD Council Decision: Minimum Pre-Marketing Set of Data in the Assessment of Chemicals (with annexed Data Components and Provisions for Flexible Application)
8 December 1982

OECD C(82)196(Final)
OECD p.122
22 ILM 910 (1983)

OECD Council Recommendation: Protection of Proprietary Rights to Data Submitted in Notification of New Chemicals
26 July 1983

OECD C(83)96(Final)
OECD p.128

OECD Council Recommendation: Exchange of Confidential Data on Chemicals (with appended Suggested Principles)
26 July 1983

OECD C(93)97(Final)
OECD p.129

OECD Council Recommendation: OECD List of Non-Confidential Data on Chemicals (with appended OECD List)
26 July 1983

OECD C(83)98(Final)
OECD p.135

OECD Council Recommendation: Information Exchange Related to Export of Banned or Severely Restricted Chemicals (with appended Guiding Principles)
4 April 1984

OECD C(84)37(Final)
OECD p.137

UNEP Governing Council Decision: A Provisional Notification Scheme for Banned and Severely Restricted Chemicals
28 May 1984

UNEP/GC/12/12/Add.1
UNEP/GC/DEC/12/14
UNEP ELPG #6
IPE(2) I/D/28-05-84

EEC Council Decision: Establishment of a Community Information System for the Control and Reduction of Pollution Caused by the Spillage of Hydrocarbons and Other Harmful Substances at Sea.
6 March 1986

Reg. No. 86/85
OJEC 1986 L 77/33

Canada-United States of America: Agreement Concerning the Transboundary Movement of Hazardous Waste (Art. 3), Ottawa
28 October 1986

Infra p.616
TIAS —

Mexico-United States of America: La Paz Agreement for Cooperation on Environmental Programs and Transboundary Problems, 1983 (see 1.C.ii), Annex III, Transboundary Shipment of Hazardous Wastes and Hazardous Substances (Arts. V, XII), Washington

Infra p.621
26 ILM 25 (1987)

12 November 1986

UNEP Governing Council Decision: London Guidelines for the Exchange of Information on Chemicals in International Trade 17 June 1987	UNEP/PIC/WG.2/2, p.9 UNEP/GC.14/17, Annex IV UNEP/GC/DEC/14/27 UNEP ELGP #10 IPE(2) I/D/19-06-87
—— Amended London Guidelines 25 May 1989	*Infra* p.644 UNEP/GC/DEC/15/30
OECD Council Decision: Exchange of Information concerning Accidents Capable of Causing Transfrontier Damage (Preamble, App. I-III) 8 July 1988	28 ILM 247
OECD Council Decision/Recommendation: Provision of Information to Public & Public Participation in Decision-Making Processes Related to Prevention of, and Response to, Accidents Involving Hazardous Substances 8 July 1988	OECD C(88)85 28 ILM 277 (1989)
FAO: Guidelines on the Registration of Biological Pest Control Agents 1988	
Basel Convention on the Control of Transboundary Movements of Hazardous Wastes and their Disposal (Arts. 4.2(f), (h), 4.7, 6, 10.2) 22 March 1989	*Infra* p.601 UNEP/WG.190/4 UNEP/IG.80/3 28 ILM 657 (1989) IELMT 989: 22
EEC Council Directive: Freedom of Access to Information on the Environment 7 June 1990	*Infra* p.659 Dir. No. 90/313 OJEC 1990 L 158/56 131 IER 7001

24.C   Requirement to Interact (Consult, Negotiate, Agree) (see also 5.A, 11.D, 12.B, 13.A & B, 18 and 23)

African Convention on the Conservation of Nature and Natural Resources, Algiers (Art. XIV) 15 September 1968	*Infra* p.202 1001 UNTS 3 OAU:CM/232 UNEP3 #37, p.207 5 IPE 2037 IELMT 982: 68
Bamako Convention on the Ban of Import into Africa and the Control of Transboundary Movement and Management of Hazardous Wastes within Africa, OAU (Art. 4.3(b))	OAU Doc. 30 ILM 775 (1991) (draft: 20 EPL 173 (1990))

30 January 1991

Canada-United States of America: Ottawa   *Infra* p.263
Agreement on Air Quality
13 March 1991

Chapter 25.   Accountability (Liability)

25.A.   States

Hague Agreement on Public Liability for Damage Caused by the N.S. Savannah 6 February 1963	487 UNTS 113
Convention on International Liability for Damage Caused by Space Objects 29 March 1972	*Infra* p.462 961 UNTS 187 24 UST 2389 TIAS 7762 A/RES/2777(XXXVI) 17 IPE 8629 IELMT 972: 24
Canada-United States of America: Agreement Concerning Liability for Loss or Damage from Certain Rocket Launches 31 December 1974	992 UNTS 97 17 IPE 8691
Canada-Union of Soviet Socialist Republics: Claim for Damage Caused by Soviet Cosmos 954 January 1979	18 ILM 899 (1979) 29 IPE 267
——— Moscow Protocol on Settlement of the Claim 2 April 1981	20 ILM 689 (1981)
Restatement (Third) of the Foreign Relations Law of the United States (Secs. 601-04) 1987	*Infra* pp.194, 354
ILC, Special Rapporteur's Schematic Outline on International Liability for Injurious Consequences Arising out of Acts not Prohibitied by International Law June 1990	*Infra* p.664 2 YBILC 1983, p.223 A/CN.4/373, Annex A/37/10 (1982), p.83
——— Report on the consideration of the 6th report of the Special Rapporteur (Chapters B.2(d), Art. 24, and B.3) 20 July 1990	A/45/10, paras.515-516, 526-530
Draft Principles Relevant to the Use of Nuclear Power Sources in Outer Space [being elaborated	A/45/20, Annex II Principles 8, 9

by the Legal Sub-Committee of the UN Committee
on the Peaceful Uses of Outer Space]
20 April 1990

ILC, Draft Articles on State Responsibility (prov.   *Infra* p.669
draft Art. 19(3)(d), and Commentary paras. 30-32) 2 YBILC 1976, pp.96,
June 1990   108-09
                                           A/44/10 (1989), pp.
                                           190, 218

25.B.   Private Persons (see also 13.C)

Tanker Owners Voluntary Agreement Concerning *Infra* p.687
Liability for Oil Pollution, "TOVALOP" 8 ILM 497 (1969)
(amended several times, most recently on 20 Feb- 1 IPE 448
ruary 1987)
7 January 1969

————— Tanker Owners Voluntary Agreement *Infra* p.692
Concerning Liability for Oil Pollution, "TOVA-
LOP," Supplement
20 February 1987

Brussels International Convention on Civil Liabil- *Infra* p.671
ity for Oil Pollution Damage 973 UNTS 3
29 November 1969   UNEP3 #44, p.235
                                          UKTS No.106 (1975)
                                          UNEP Reg. p.81
                                          1969 UNJYB 174
                                          9 ILM 45 (1970)
                                          1 IPE 460
                                          IELMT 969: 88

————— London Amending Protocol   16 ILM 617 (1977)
19 November 1976   19 IPE 9443

————— Amendment
1984

Oil Companies: Contract Regarding an Interim *Infra* p.696
Supplement to Tanker Liability for Oil Pollution, 10 ILM 137 (1971)
"CRISTAL" (amended several times, most re- 20 IPE 490
cently on 23 October 1989)
14 January 1971

Brussels International Convention on the Estab- *Infra* p.678
lishment of an International Fund for Compensa- 1110 UNTS 57
tion for Oil Pollution Damage   UNEP3 #51, p.255
18 December 1971   Cmnd 7383
                                          UKTS No. 95 (1978)
                                          UNEP Reg. p.98
                                          1971 UNJYB 103
                                          11 ILM 284 (1972)

2 IPE 529
IELMT 971: 94

———— London Amending Protocol (revising Unit
of Account provision)
19 November 1976

UNEP Reg. p.98
16 ILM 621 (1977)
19 IPE 9447

Oil Companies Offshore Pollution Liability
Agreement ("OPOL")
4 September 1974

13 ILM 1409 (1974)
2 IPE 772

———— Rules of the Offshore Pollution Liability
Association (interpreting "OPOL")
2 October 1974

14 ILM 147 (1975)
2 IPE 783

EEC Council: Recommendation on the Application
of the Polluter-Pays Principle
7 November 1974

14 ILM 138 (1975)
18 IPE 9083

OECD Council Recommendation on the Implementation of the Polluter-Pays Principle
14 November 1974

Infra p.706
OECD C(74)223
OECD p.26
14 ILM 234 (1975)

London Convention on Civil Liability for Oil Pollution Damage from Offshore Operations [Result-
ing from Exploration for and Exploitation of Sea-
Bed Mineral Resources]
1 May 1977

Misc 8 (1977)
UNEP3 #71, p.474
16 ILM 1450 (1977)
1 IPE 313
IELMT 977: 33

OECD Council Recommendation: Certain Financial Aspects of Action by Public Authorities to
Prevent and Control Oil Spills (with annexed Certain International Financial Aspects)
28 April 1982

OECD C(81)32(Final)
OECD p.159

Wellington Convention on the Regulation of Antarctic Mineral Resources Actvities (Preamble,
Arts. 1(4), (15), 2(1)(a), 4(2-4), 8, 10, 13(2), (6),
15, 21(1), (9)(c))
2 June 1988

Infra p.529
AMR/SCM/88/78 (1988)
27 ILM 868 (1988)
IELMT 988: 42

IMO International Convention on Salvage, London
28 April 1989

1989 IJECL 300

OECD Council Recommendation on the Application of the Polluter-Pays Principle to Accidental
Pollution
7 July 1989

Infra p.708
OECD C(89)88
28 ILM 1320 (1989)

EEC Council Proposed Directive: Civil Liability
for Damage Caused by Waste
1 September 1989

OJEC 1989 C 251/3

Geneva Convention on Civil Liability for Damage
Caused during Carriage of Dangerous Goods by
Road, Rail and Inland Navigation Vessels
10 October 1989

Australia-Indonesia: Treaty on the Zone of Co-op-   29 ILM 469 (1990)
eration in an Area between the Indonesian Province
of East Timor and Northern Australia (Art. 19)
11 December 1989

IAEA Code of Practice on the International Trans-   *Infra* p.597
boundary Movement of Radioactive Waste   IAEA Doc GC(34)/920
21 September 1990   IAEA GC(XXXIV)/RES/530

IMO Draft International Convention on Liability   IMO LEG 64/4
and Compensation for Damage in connection with
the Carriage of Dangerous Goods by Sea
25 January 1991

Chapter 26.   Surveillance and Monitoring

Egypt-United Kingdom: Agreement regarding Co-   226 UNTS 288
operation in Meteorological and Hydrological Sur-
veys in Certain Areas of the Nile Basin
20 March 1950

Global   Environmental   Monitoring   System   UNEP/GC/
(GEMS)   INFORMATION/2
1974

France-United Kingdom-United States of America: 1037 UNTS 3
Agreement on Monitoring the Stratosphere   27 UST 1437
1976   TIAS 8255
                                                         16 IPE 8289

OECD Council Recommendation: Multilateral   OECD C(77)115(Final)
Consultation and Surveillance Mechanism for Sea   OECD p.181
Dumping of Radioactive Waste (with appended In-   19 IPE 9743
terpretations)
22 July 1977

Brazil-United States of America: Brasilia   34 UST 1351
Agreement for Use of the Geostationary Opera-   TIAS 10419
tional Environmental Satellite in the Brazilian National Plan for Data Collection Platforms
14 June 1982

EEC Council Directive: Surveillance and Monitor-   Dir. No. 82/883
ing of Environments Contaminated by Waste from   OJEC 1982 L 378/1
the Titanium-Dioxide Industry
3 December 1982

Canada-United States of America: Agreement to   TIAS 10771

Track Air Pollution across Eastern North America   22 ILM 1017 (1983)
(Cross Appalachian Tracer Experiment)
23 August 1983

Canada-United States of America: Ottawa Memo-   TIAS —
randum of Understanding Concerning Research
and Development Cooperation in Pollution Measurement and Control
17 October 1985

Republic of Korea-United States of America: TIAS —
Washington Agreement Regarding the Collection
and Exchange of Data on Fisheries Harvests in the
International Waters of the Bering Sea
14 July 1988

UNGA Resolution: International co-operation in   A/RES/44/224
the monitoring, assessment and anticipation of environmental threats and in assistance in cases of
environmental emergencies
22 December 1989

EEC Council Regulation: Establishment of the Eu-   Reg. No. 1210/90
ropean Environment Agency and the European En-   OJEC 1990 L 120/1
vironment Information and Observation Network
7 May 1990

Antarctic Treaty, Protocol on Environmental Pro-   *Infra*, p.536
tection (See 9.A)   IX ATSCM/2
21 June 1991

Chapter 27.   Trade (Import & Export) Restrictions (see also 18.B)

Washington Convention on Nature Protection and   *Infra* p.211
Wildlife Preservation in the Western Hemisphere   161 UNTS 193
12 October 1940   3 Bevans 630
     56 Stat. 1354
     TS 981
     UNEP3 #2, p.64
     4 IPE 1729
     IELMT 940: 76

General Agreement on Tariffs and Trade (GATT)   *Infra* p.714
(Art. XX(b), (f), (g)) (frequently amended)   55 UNTS 187
30 October 1947   1 IPE 7
     IELMT 947: 82

Washington Convention on International Trade in   *Infra* p.466
Endangered Species of Wild Fauna and Flora   993 UNTS 243
(CITES)   27 UST 1087
3 March 1973   TIAS 8249
     UKTS No.101 (1976)

Cmnd 6647
UNEP3 #57, p.289
12 ILM 1088 (1973)
5 IPE 2228
IELMT 973: 18

——— Bonn Amendment
22 June 1979

US Sen. Exec. Print C, 96:2
    Cong.
22 IPE 389

——— Gaborone Amendment
30 April 1983

US Sen. Tr. Doc. 98-10

EEC Commission Regulation: Imports of Whales
and Other Cetacean Products
20 January 1981

Reg. No. 348/81
OJEC 1981 L 39/1

Canada-United States of America: Arrangement
Prohibiting the Importation of Raccoon Dogs
4 September 1981

33 UST 3764
TIAS 10259

EEC Commission Regulation: Implementation of
CITES Treaty
3 December 1982

Reg. No. 3626/82
OJEC 1982 L 384/1

EEC Council Directive: Importation of Skins of
Seal Pups
28 March 1983

Dir. No. 83/129
OJEC 1983 L 91/30
IPE(2) III/H/28-03-83

Canada-United States of America: Free Trade
Agreement (Arts. 603, 609, 1201)
22 December 1987

Infra p.715
27 ILM 281 (1988)

EEC Council Directive On the Export and Import
of Certain Dangerous Chemicals
16 June 1988

Dir. No. 1734/88
OJEC 1988 L 155/2

EEC Council Directive: Export of Certain Chemical Products
20 February 1989

Dir. No. 428/89
OJEC 1989 L 50/1

Canada-United States of America: Agreement
Concerning the Transboundary Movement of Hazardous Waste, Ottawa
28 October 1986

Infra p.616
TIAS ———

Mexico-United States of America: La Paz
Agreement for Cooperation on Environmental Programs and Transboundary Problems, 1983 (see
1.C.ii), Annex III, Transboundary Shipment of
Hazardous Wastes and Hazardous Substances,
Washington
12 November 1986

Infra p.621
26 ILM 25 (1987)

UNEP Governing Council Decision: London Guidelines for the Exchange of Information on Chemicals in International Trade 17 June 1987	*Infra* p.644 UNEP/PIC/WG.2/2, p.9 UNEP/GC.14/17, Annex IV UNEP/ GC/DEC/14/27 UNEP ELGP #10 IPE(2) I/D/19-06-87
Basel Convention on the Control of Transboundary Movements of Hazardous Wastes and Their Disposal 22 March 1989	*Infra* p.601 UNEP/WG.190/4 UNEP/IG.80/3 28 ILM 657 (1989) IELMT 989: 22
EEC Commission Regulation: Prohibition of Ivory Imports 2 August 1989	Reg. No. 2496/89 OJEC 1989 L 240/5
IAEA Code of Practice on the International Transboundary Movement of Radioactive Waste 21 September 1990	*Infra*, p.597 IAEA Doc GC(34)/920 IAEA GC(XXXIV)/RES/530
UNGA Resolution: Environment and International Trade 21 December 1990	A/RES/45/210

Chapter 28. Establishment of an Organization or Organ

28.A. Specifically Environmental

Fontainbleau Agreement Establishing the International Union for Conservation of Nature and Natural Resources (IUCN Statutes) 5 October 1948	1 IPE 8 IELMT 948: 75
——— Revised Statutes (at VIth IUCN General Assembly), Athens August 1958	1 IPE 8
——— Revised Statutes (adopted at XIIIth IUCN General Assembly), Morges (Geneva) 22 April 1977	13 IUCN Proc. 155 18 IPE 8960
Belgium-France-Luxembourg: Brussels Protocol for the Establishment of a Standing Tripartite Commission for Polluted Waters 8 April 1950	66 UNTS 286 LEG/SER.B/12, p.422 11 IPE 5553 IELMT 950: 27
Paris Convention for the Establishment of the European and Mediterranean Plant Protection Organization 18 April 1951	UKTS No.44 (1956) UNEP3 #7, p.86 4 IPE 1797 IELMT 951: 29
UNGA Resolution: Establishment of the Scientific	A/RES/913(X)

Committee on the Effects of Atomic Radiation (UNSCEAR) 3 December 1955	13 IPE 6517
FAO Plant Protection Agreement for the [South-East] Asia and Pacific Region, Rome (Art. II, establishing the [South-East] Asia and Pacific Plant Protection Commission) (amended 1967, 1979, 1983—see 8.D) 27 February 1956	247 UNTS 400 FAO Council 23rd sess. UNEP3 #13, p.117 4 IPE 1822 IELMT 956: 15
Paris Protocol concerning the Constitution of an International Commission for the Protection of the Mosel Against Pollution 20 December 1961	940 UNTS 221 UNEP3 #25, p.165 11 IPE 5618 IELMT 961: 94
Kano Convention on the African Migratory Locust Organization (Preamble, Arts. 3, 4(2), (9)) 25 May 1962	486 UNTS 103 UNEP Reg. p.51 UNEP3 #26, p.167 IELMT 962: 39
Berne Convention on the International Commission for the Protection of the Rhine against Pollution (and 1976 Bonn Additional Agreement—see 5.E.ii) 29 April 1963	*Infra* p.438 994 UNTS 3 UNEP3 #29, p.176 10 IPE 4820 IELMT 963: 31
FAO Agreement for the Establishment of a Commission for Controlling the Desert Locust in the Eastern Region of its Distribution Area in South-West Asia, Rome (amended November 1977 (72nd FAO Council)) 3 December 1963	529 UNTS 217 FAO Conf 12th sess. UNEP3 #33, p.188 4 IPE 1973 IELMT 963: 91
FAO Agreement for the Establishment of a Commission for Controlling the Desert Locust in the Near East, Rome (amended November 1977 (72nd FAO Council)) 2 July 1965	592 UNTS 215 FAO Council 44th sess. UNEP3 #35, p.198 4 IPE 1994 IELMT 965: 49
ECE Decision: Body on Water Resources and Water Pollution Control Problems 2 May 1968	ECE/DEC/E(XXIII) E/ECE/682, Annex V
Phyto-sanitary Convention for Africa South of the Sahara (establishment of the Inter-African Phyto-Sanitary Commission) 13 September 1968	UNEP3 #12, p.115
UN Administrative Committee on Co-ordination (ACC) Decision: Establishment of the Joint Group of Experts on the Scientific Aspects of Marine Pollution (GESAMP) 1969	

FAO Agreement for the Establishment of a Commission for Controlling the Desert Locust in North-West Africa, Rome (amended November 1977 (72nd FAO Council))
1 December 1970

797 UNTS 97
FAO Council 55th sess.
UNEP3 #46, p.242
5 IPE 2142

Canada-United States of America: Ottawa Agreement Relating to the Establishment of a Canada-United States Committee on Water Quality in the St. John River and its Tributary Rivers and Streams which cross the Canada-United States Boundary
21 September 1972

23 UST 2813
TIAS 7470
10 IPE 5327

UNESCO World Heritage Convention (see 8.A), Pt. III (Arts. 8-14, Intergovernmental Committee for the Protection of the World Cultural and Natural Heritage)
16 November 1972

Infra p.554
1037 UNTS 151
27 UST 37
TIAS 8226
UNEP3 #55, p.276
1972 UNJYB 89
11 ILM 1358 (1972)
14 IPE 7238

UNGA Resolution: Institutional and Financial Arrangements for International Environmental Cooperation (UNEP ''Statute'')
15 December 1972

Infra p.719
A/RES/2997 (XXVII)
1 IPE 152

Ouagadougou Convention Establishing a Permanent Inter-State Drought Control Committee for the Sahel
12 September 1973

13 ILM 537 (1974)
17 IPE 8640

IMCO Assembly: Establishment of a Marine Environment Protection Committee
23 November 1973

IMO: A.VIII/Res.297
13 ILM 476 (1974)
2 IPE 882

Constitution of the International Board of Plant Genetic Resources (IBPGR)
1974

ECE Decision: Terms of reference of the Senior Advisers to ECE Governments on Environmental Problems
29 April 1974

ECE/DEC/8(XXIX)

Establishment of UNEP Working Group of Experts on Environmental Law
25 May 1977

UNEP/GC/DEC/91(V)

Panama-United States of America: Panama Agreement Relating to Article VI of the Panama Canal Treaty Concerning Establishment of a Joint Commission on the Environment

TIAS —

1 October 1979

UNGA Resolution: Establishment of an Intergovernmental Committee on New and Renewable Sources of Energy (ICNRSE) 21 December 1982	A/RES/37/250, Secs. II, III
EEC Task Force on Accidental Pollution at Sea (Drawn from the Community Information System Inventory of Resources for Combating Pollution of the Sea by Hydrocarbons) 6 March 1986	Dir. No. 86/85 OJEC 1986 L 77/33, Annex I
Reports of the First and Second Meetings of the Executive Committee of the Multilateral Fund under the Montreal Protocol [on Substances that Deplete the Ozone Layer] 1990	UNEP/OzL.Pro.ExCom.1/ . . .
EEC Council Regulation: Establishment of the European Environment Agency and the European Environment Information and Observation Network 7 May 1990	Reg. No. 1210/90 OJEC 1990 L 120/1
Constitution of the International Council for Local Environmental Initiatives, established by the World Congress of Local Governments for a Sustainable Future, New York City 8 September 1990	Congress Report, p.16 (1990)
Antarctic Treaty, Protocol on Environmental Protection (see 9.A), Arts. 11 and 12 21 June 1991	*Infra,* p.536 XI ATSOM/2

28.B.   With Some Environmental Functions

Denmark-Germany (pre-post-WWII): Agreement relating to Watercourses and Dikes on the Danish-German Frontier (Arts. 29, 45, 46) (together with a Final Protocol and Instructions for the Frontier Water Commission and the Supreme Frontier Water Commission) 10 April 1922	10 LNTS 201 LEG/SER.B/12, p.577 11 IPE 5473
Latvia (Union of Soviet Socialist Republics*)-Lithuania (Union of Soviet Socialist Republics*): Riga Convention Relating to Fishing in Boundary Waters, with Regulations Concerning the Organization and Activity of the Mixed Latvian-Lithuanian Fisheries Commission 25 January 1931	118 LNTS 175 9 IPE 4431
Constitution of the Food and Agriculture Organiza-	FAO Basic Texts

tion of the United Nations (FAO) (Art. I.2(c))   Peaslee, Pt. II
3 June 1943   1 IPE 85

Constitution of the United Nations Educational,   4 UNTS 275
Scientific and Cultural Organization (UNESCO)   14 IPE 7130
(Art. I.2(c))   IELMT 945: 86
16 November 1945

General Agreement on Tariffs and Trade (GATT)   *Infra*, p.714
(Art. XX(b), (f), (g)) (frequently amended)   55 UNTS 187
Infra, p.   1 IPE 7
30 October 1947   IELMT 947: 82

FAO Agreement for the Establishment of the Indo-   120 UNTS 59
Pacific Fisheries [Council] Commission (IPFC),   62 Stat. 3711
Baguio (amended 1961 (see below) and November   TIAS 1895
1977 (72nd FAO Council))
26 February 1948

———— Amending (superseding) Agreement   418 UNTS 348
(adopted by IPFC, 20 Jan. 1961, Karachi)   FAO Conf 11th sess.
23 November 1961   13 UST 2511
    TIAS 5218

Washington Convention for the Establishment of   80 UNTS 3
an Inter-American Tropical Tuna Commission   1 UST 230
(Preamble, Art. II)   TIAS 2044
30 May 1949   UNEP3 #4, p.76
    6 IPE 2848
    IELMT 949: 41

FAO Agreement for the Establishment of a General   126 UNTS 237
Fisheries Council for the Mediterranean (GFCM),   UNEP3 #5, p.80
Rome (amended 1963 (12th FAO Conference) and   6 IPE 2857
December 1976 (70th FAO Council))   IELMT 949: 72
24 September 1949

Romania-Yugoslavia: Agreement on Questions of   LEG/SER.B/12, p.928
Water Control, Water Control System and Frontier   9 IPE 4531
Waters (Commission Statute)
7 April 1955

Hungary-Yugoslavia: Belgrade Agreement, to-   LEG/SER.B/12, p.831
gether with the Statute of the Yugoslav-Hungarian   9 IPE 4538
Water Economy Commission (Art. 1(2)(f))
8 August 1955

Statute of the International Atomic Energy Agency   276 UNTS 3
(IAEA) (Arts. III.A.6, XI.E.3, XII.A.1, 5, 6)   Peaslee Pt. IV
23 October 1956   7 IPE 5854
    IELMT 956: 78

Rome Treaty Establishing the European Atomic   298 UNTS 167

Energy Community (Euratom) (Preamble, Arts. 30, 34-37, Annex I(6), (7))
27 March 1957

28 IPE 242
IELMT 957: 23

Convention Placing the International Poplar Commission within the Framework of FAO, Rome
19 November 1959

410 UNTS 155
21 UST 2060
TIAS 6952
4 IPE 1935
IELMT 959: 86

Fort Lamy (N'Djamena) Convention and Statutes relating to the Development of the Lake Chad Basin (amended 22 October 1972 in Yaounde and 1977 in Enugu)
22 May 1964

A/CN.4/274, para.53
FAO Conf 12th Sess.
11 IPE 5633

Convention for the International Council for the Exploration of the Sea
12 September 1964

7 ILM 302 (1968)
1 IPE 425
IELMT 964: 68

Niamey Agreement Concerning the Niger River Commission and the Navigation and Transport on the River Niger (Art. 12)
25 November 1964

587 UNTS 21
11 IPE 5648
IELMT 964: 87

Nouakchott Convention concerning the Status of the Senegal River, and Convention Establishing the Senegal River Development Organization (amended)
11 March 1972

UN Water Ser. No.13, pp.16&21

Paris Agreement on an International Energy Program, including Establishment of the International Energy Agency
18 November 1974

27 UST 1685
TIAS 8278
UNEP3 #65, p.435
16 IPE 8376
IELMT 974: 85

France-Federal Republic of Germany-Switzerland: Exchange of Notes concerning the Establishment of an Intergovernmental Commission on Neighbourhood Problems in Border Areas
27 October 1975

18 IPE 8998

Convention on the Intergovernmental Maritime Consultative Organization (IMCO—now IMO), 17 March 1948 (289 UNTS 3), as amended by IMO Assembly (Art. 1(a), and Pt. IX, Arts. 38-42))
14 November 1975

IMO: A.IX/Res.358
34 UST 497
TIAS 10374
Peaslee Pt. V
19 IPE 9651

Rusumo Agreement for the Establishment of an Organization to Manage and Develop the Kagera River Basin
24 August 1977

UNGA Resolution: Institutional Arrangements for
Institutional Co-operation in the Field of Human
Settlements (HABITAT Statute)
19 December 1977

A/RES/32/162
30 IPE 99

Kaolack Convention relating to the creation of the
Gambia River Basin Development Organization
30 June 1978

Finland-Norway: Agreement concerning a Norwe-
gian-Finnish Commission for Frontier Watercourses
1980

1981 Norw. 236

Faranah Convention Creating the Niger Basin Authority and Protocol Relating to the Development
Fund of the Niger Basin
21 November 1980

IELMT 980: 86
IELMT 980: 87

EEC Single European Act (additions to the EEC
Treaty: Art. 18—adding Art. 100a, Art. 25—adding Title VII (Arts. 130r-t: "Environment"))
17 February 1986

Infra p.232
OJEC 1987 L 169/1
25 ILM 506 (1986)
IPE(2) I/H/18-02-86.a
IELMT 986: 16

Chapter 29.   Special Area Management

Washington Convention on Nature Protection and
Wildlife Preservation in the Western Hemisphere
12 October 1940

Infra p.211
161 UNTS 193
3 Bevans 630
56 Stat. 1354
TS 981
UNEP3 #2, p.64
4 IPE 1729
IELMT 940: 76

Ramsar Convention on Wetlands of International
Importance, Especially as Waterfowl Habitat
2 February 1971

Infra p.497
996 UNTS 245
UKTS No.34 (1976)
Cmnd 6465
UNEP3 #47, p.246
11 ILM 969 (1972)
5 IPE 2161
IELMT 971: 09

London Convention for the Conservation of Antarctic Seals (Art. 3(1)(d))
1 June 1972

29 UST 441
TIAS 8826
UKTS No.45 (1978)
Cmnd 7209
UNEP3 #54, p.272
11 ILM 251, 417 (1972)
8 IPE 3753
IELMT 972: 41

UNESCO Convention concerning the Protection of the World Cultural and Natural Heritage (Art. 11), Paris
16 November 1972

Infra p.554
27 UST 37
TIAS 8226
UNEP3 #55, p.276
1972 UNJYB 89
11 ILM 1358 (1972)
14 IPE 7238
IELMT 972: 86

MARPOL, 1973 (see 4.A), Annex V, Regulations for the Prevention of Pollution by Garbage from Ships (Regs. 1 and 5)
2 November 1973

Infra p.327
IMO: MP/CONF/WP.35
TIAS —
12 ILM 1434 (1973)
UNEP3 #58, p.380

London International Convention for the Prevention of Pollution from Ships (MARPOL) (Annex I, Regs. 1(10) and 10, Annex II, Regs. 1(7) and 5)
2 November 1973

IMO: MP/CONF/WP.35
UNEP3 #59, p.320
1973 UNJYB 81
12 ILM 1319 (1973)
2 IPE 552
IELMT 973: 84

Agreement Governing the Activities of States on the Moon and Other Celestial Bodies (Art. 7(3))
5 December 1979

A/RES/34/68
IELMT 979: 92

Canberra Convention on the Conservation of Antarctic Marine Living Resources (CCAMLR) (Art. IX(2)(g))
20 May 1980

Infra p.520
33 UST 3476
TIAS 10240
UKTS No.48 (1982)
Cmnd 8714
19 ILM 841 (1980)
IPE(2) III/A/20-05-80

Barcelona Convention for the Protection of the Mediterranean Sea against Pollution, Geneva Protocol concerning Mediterranean Specially Protected Areas
3 April 1982

Infra p.389
UNTS Reg. #24079
IELMT 982: 26

UN Convention on the Law of the Sea, Montego Bay (Art. 211)
10 December 1982

Infra p.332
Cmnd 8941
Misc 11 (1983)
A/CONF.62/122
21 ILM 1261 (1982)
IPE(2) II/A/10-12-82
IELMT 982: 92

Cartegena Convention for the Protection and Development of the Marine Environment of the Wider Caribbean Region, Kingston Protocol Concerning Specially Protected Areas and Wildlife
16 January 1990

IMO Marine Environment Protection Committee,
Approval of the Great Barrier Reef as a particularly
sensitive sea area
16 November 1990

IMO: Draft Guidelines for Designation of Special
Areas (approved by IMO's Marine Environment
Protection Committee)
December 1990

Chapter 30.   Development Assistance

Action Plan for the Human Environment of the UN
Conference on the Human Environment, "Development and Environment" (Recommendations
102-109)
16 June 1972

A/CONF.48/14/Rev.1,
Ch.II

US Agency for International Development
(USAID): Environmental Procedures
30 June 1976

41 F.R. 26913
22 CFR Sec.216

Multilateral Development Institutions: Declaration
of Environmental Policies & Procedures relating to
Economic Development, adopted by ADB, Arab
Bank for Economic Development in Africa, AfDB,
World Bank, EEC (Commission), OAS, UNDP &
UNEP
1 February 1980

Infra p.727
19 ILM 524 (1980)

African, Caribbean and Pacific States-European
Economic Community (European Community*):
Third Lomé Convention (Art. 11 and Pt. Two,
Title I (Agricultural and rural development and
conservation of natural resources), Ch. 2 (Drought
and desertification control), Arts. 38-43)
8 December 1984

24 ILM 571 (1985)
IELMT 984: 93

OECD Council Recommendation: Environmental
Assessment of Development Assistance Projects
and Programmes (with appended list of criteria of
Projects and Programmes most in Need of Environmental Assessment)
20 June 1985

OECD C(85)104
OECD p.30
IPE(2) I/F/20-06-85.b

World Bank: Operational Directive "Environmental Assessment"
November 1989

WB Operational Manual,
OD 4.00
Annexes A, A1, A2

African, Caribbean and Pacific States-European
Economic Community (European Community*):
Fourth Lomé Convention (Arts. 6(2), 14-17, 33-
41, 55, 69, Annexes VIII, IX, X, XXIII)

29 ILM 783 (1990)

15 December 1989

Agreement Establishing the European Bank for   29 ILM 1083 (1990)
Reconstruction and Development (EBRD) (Arts.
2(1)(vii), 11(1)(v), 35(2))
29 May 1990

UNDP-UNEP-World Bank: Directors' call for the
creation of a Global Environment Facility
September 1990

Chapter 31.   Pollution Restrictions
31.A. Prohibitions

Canada-United States of America: Washington   *Infra* p.412
Treaty Relating to Boundary Waters and Questions   12 Bevans 319
Arising Along the Boundary Between the United   36 Stat. 2448
States and Canada   TS 548
11 January 1909   102 BFSP 137
                                                 LEG/SER.B/12, p.261
                                                 10 IPE 5158

Restatement (Third) of the Foreign Relations Law   *Infra* p.354
of the United States (Sec. 603 and Comments)
1987

Treaty Banning Nuclear Weapons Tests in the At-   *Infra* p.632
mosphere, in Outer Space and Under Water   480 UNTS 43
(PTBT), Moscow   14 UST 1313
5 August 1963   TIAS 5433
                                                 UNEP3 #31, p.185
                                                 1 IPE 422
                                                 IELMT 963: 59

Decisions of the Second Meeting of Parties to the   *Infra* p.298
Montreal Protocol (MP) (Annex I (Adjustments to   UNEP/Oz.p.L.Pro.2/3
MP))
29 June 1990

IMO Convention on the Prevention of Marine Pol-   *Infra* p.318
lution by Dumping of Wastes and Other Matter   1046 UNTS 120
(London Ocean Dumping Convention—LDC)   26 UST 2403
(amended 1978 (2x) [IELMT 972: 96/A, 972 :   TIAS 8165
96/B], 1980, 1989)   UNEP3 #56, p.283
29 December 1972   11 ILM 1294 (1972)
                                                 2 IPE 537
                                                 IELMT 972: 96

———— 13th Consultative Meeting of Contracting
Parties, Resolution calling for the phasing out of
industrial waste dumping by 31 December 1995
2 November 1990

——— 13th Consultative Meeting of Contracting Parties, Resolution placing sub-seabed disposal of radioactive wastes under the current voluntary moratorium on sea disposal of low-level radioactive wastes
2 November 1990

London International Convention for the Prevention of Pollution from Ships (MARPOL) 2 November 1973	IMO: MP/CONF/WP.35 UNEP3 #59, p.320 1973 UNJYB 81 12 ILM 1319 (1973) 2 IPE 552 IELMT 973: 84
——— Annex V, Regulations for the Prevention of Pollution by Garbage from Ships 2 November 1973	*Infra* p.327 IMO: MP/CONF/WP.35 TIAS— 12 ILM 1434 (1973) UNEP3 #59, p.380
UN Convention on the Law of the Sea, Montego Bay 10 December 1982	*Infra* p.332 Cmnd 8941 Misc 11 (1983) A/CONF.62/122 21 ILM 1261 (1982) IPE(2) II/A10-12-82 IELMT 982: 92
Paris Convention for the Prevention of Marine Pollution from Land-Based Sources 4 June 1974	*Infra* p.360 UKTS No.64 (1978) UNEP3 #64, p.430 13 ILM 352 (1974) 2 IPE 748 IELMT 974: 43
Barcelona Convention for the Protection of the Mediterranean Sea against Pollution 16 February 1976	*Infra* p.370 UNTS Reg. #16908 UNEP3 #66, p.448 UNEP Reg. p.136 15 ILM 290 (1976) 19 IPE 497 IELMT 976: 13
——— Barcelona Protocol for the Prevention of Pollution of the Mediterranean Sea by Dumping from Ships and Aircraft 16 February 1976	*Infra* p.377 UNTS Reg. #16908 UNEP Reg. p.138 15 ILM 300 (1976) 19 IPE 9515 IELMT 967: 14
——— Athens Protocol for the Protection of the Mediterranean Sea against Pollution from Land-Based Sources 17 May 1980	*Infra* p.384 UNTS Reg. #22281 UNEP Reg. p.142 19 ILM 869 (1980)

IELMT 980: 37

ILA Helsinki Rules on the Uses of the Waters of International Rivers (Arts. IX-XI, XV) 20 August 1966

Infra p.395
52 ILA 484 (1967)
11 IPE 5741

ILA Seoul Rules on International Groundwaters 30 August 1986

Infra p.403
62 ILA 251 (1987)

ILC: Draft Articles on the Law of the Non-Navigational Uses of International Watercourses (draft Arts. 7, 20-25, 29) 19 July 1991

Infra p.404
A/45/10 (1991), CH.III

ECE Decision: Declaration of Policy on Prevention and Control of Water Pollution, Including Transboundary Pollution 23 April 1980

Infra p.433
ECE/DEC/B(XXXV)
E/1980/28
6 EPL 148
26 IPE 280

Bonn Convention for the Protection of the Rhine River against Chemical Pollution 3 December 1976

Infra p.442
1124 UNTS 375
UNEP3 #70, p.468
16 ILM 242 (1977)
25 IPE 440
IELMT 976: 89

Canada-United States of America: Great Lakes Water Quality Agreement, Ottawa 22 November 1978

Infra p.419
20 UST 1383
TIAS 9257
26 IPE 19

31.B. Limitations
31.B.i. General

ECE Convention on Long-Range Transboundary Air Pollution (with resolution and with Declaration on Low and Non-Waste Technology, and Reutilization and Recycling of Wastes), Geneva 13 November 1979

Infra p.250
TIAS 10541
CMND 7885
Misc 10 1980
UNEP3 #78, p.519
E/ECE/1010
18 ILM 1442 (1979)
28 IPE 341
IELMT 979: 84

———— Helsinki Protocol on the Reduction of Sulphur Emissions or their Transboundary Fluxes by at least 30 percent 8 July 1985

Infra p.256
EB.AIR/12
27 ILM 707 (1988)
IELMT 979: 84/B

———— Sofia Protocol concerning the Control of Emissions of Nitrogen Oxides or their Transboundary Fluxes

Infra p.259
EB.AIR/21
28 ILM 214 (1989)

31 October 1988	IELMT 979: 84/C

Vienna Convention for the Protection of the Ozone Layer
22 March 1985

Infra p.276
26 ILM 1529 (1987)
IELMT 985: 22

———— Montreal Protocol on Substances that Deplete the Ozone Layer
16 September 1987

Infra p.288
26 ILM 1550 (1987)
IELMT 985: 22/A

———— Decisions of the Second Meeting of Parties to the Montreal Protocol (MP) (Annex II (Amendments to MP))
29 June 1990

Infra p.298
UNEP/Oz.L.Pro.2/3

Annex V (to London International Convention for the Prevention of Pollution from Ships (MARPOL)), Regulations for the Prevention of Pollution by Garbage from Ships
2 November 1973

Infra p.327
IMO: MP/CONF/WP.35
TIAS —
12 ILM 1434 (1973)
UNEP3 #59, p.380

Paris Convention for the Prevention of Marine Pollution from Land-Based Sources
4 June 1974

Infra p.360
UKTS No.64 (1978)
UNEP3 #64, p.430
13 ILM 352 (1974)
2 IPE 748
IELMT 974: 43

Bonn Convention for the Protection of the Rhine River against Chemical Pollution
3 December 1976

Infra p.442
1124 UNTS 375
UNEP3 #70, p.468
16 ILM 242 (1977)
25 IPE 440
IELMT 976: 89

Bonn Convention for the Protection of the Rhine River against Pollution by Chlorides
3 December 1976

Infra p.450
16 ILM 265 (1977)
26 IPE 1
IELMT 976: 90

Canada-United States of America: Great Lakes Water Quality Agreement, Ottawa
22 November 1978

Infra p.419
30 UST 1383
TIAS 9257
26 IPE 19

Canada-United States of America: Ottawa Agreement on Air Quality
13 March 1991

Infra p.263

31.B.ii.   Tradeable Limits

Montreal Protocol on Substances that Deplete the Ozone Layer

Infra p.289
26 ILM 1550 (1987)

16 September 1987   IELMT 985: 22/A

Bamako Convention on the Ban of Import into   OAU DOC.
Africa and the Control of Transboundary Move-   30 ILM 775 (1991)
ment and Management of Hazardous Wastes   (draft: 20 EPL 173 (1990))
within Africa, OAU (Art. 4.3(c))
30 January 1991

Chapter 32   Penalties

32.A.   Civil & Administrative

Paris Convention for the Prevention of Marine Pol-   *Infra* p.358
lution from Land-Based Sources   UKTS No.64 (1978)
4 June 1974   UNEP #64, p.430
                                                     13 ILM 352 (1974)
                                                     2 IPE 748
                                                     IELMT 974: 43

32.B.   Criminal

Paris Convention for the Prevention of Marine Pol-   *Infra* p.358
lution from Land-Based Sources   UKTS No.64 (1978)
4 June 1974   UNEP3 #64, p.430
                                                     13 ILM 352 (1974)
                                                     2 IPE 748
                                                     IELMT 974: 43

ILC, Draft Articles on State Responsibility (prov.   *Infra* p.669
draft Art. 19(3)(d), and Commentary paras. 30-32)   2 YBILC 1976, pp.96,
July 1989   108-09
                                                     A/44/10 (1989), pp.
                                                         190, 218

8th UN Congress on the Prevention of Crime and   A/CONF.144/7, paras.
the Treatment of Offenders (Havana, 27 Aug.—7   49-62
Sep. 1990) resolution: The Role of Criminal Law   A/CONF.144/28,
in the Protection of Nature and the Environment   Ch.I.C.2
7 September 1990

Bamako Convention on the Ban of Import into   OAU doc.
Africa and the Control of Transboundary Move-   30 ILM 775 (1991)
ment and Management of Hazardous Wastes   (draft: 20 EPL 173
within Africa, OAU (Art. 4.1)   1990))
30 January 1991

ILC, Draft Articles on the Draft Code of Crimes   A/46/10 (1991),
Against the Peace and Security of Mankind (Arts.   Ch.IV
22(2)(d), 26)
19 July 1991

Chapter 33   Education

African Convention on the Conservation of Nature
and Nautural Resources, Algiers (Art. XIII)
15 September 1968

Infra p.203
1001 UNTS 3
OAU:CM/232
UNEP3 #37, p.207
5 IPE 2037
IELMT 982: 68

UNESCO Convention Concerning the Protection
of the World Cultural and Natural Heritage, Paris
(Ch. VI)
16 November 1972

Infra p.554
27 UST 37
TIAS 8226
UNEP3 #55, p.276
1972 UNJYB 89
11 ILM 1358 (1972)
14 IPE 7238

EEC Council Directive: Coordination of Certain
Provisions Laid down by Law, Regulation or Administrative Action in Member States Concerning
the Pursuit of Television Broadcasting Activities
(Art. 12(e))
3 October 1989

Dir. No. 89/552
OJEC 1989 L 298/23

Convention on the Rights of the Child (Art.
29(1)(e))
20 November 1989

Infra p.241
A/RES/44/25
28 ILM 1456 (1989)
29 ILM 1340
(1990) (correct.)

*Successor country or entity

INTERNATIONAL
ENVIRONMENTAL INSTRUMENTS

TITLES OF INSTRUMENTS REPRODUCED, BY SUBJECT MATTER

CHRONOLOGICAL LIST OF INSTRUMENTS REPRODUCED

INSTRUMENTS

PART I:
GENERAL PRINCIPLES

CHAPTER 1
GENERAL ENVIRONMENT

A. GLOBAL OR OTHER NON-REGIONAL

STOCKHOLM DECLARATION OF THE UNITED NATIONS CONFERENCE ON THE HUMAN ENVIRONMENT

Popular Name: Stockholm Declaration, Declaration on the Human Environment
Done at Stockholm on 16 June 1972, *in* Report of the United Nations Conference
on the Human Environment, U.N. Doc. A/CONF.48/14/Rev.1, at 3 (1973), U.N.
Doc. A/CONF.48/14, at 2-65, and Corr.1 (1972), *reprinted in* UNEP ELGP #1,
1972 UNYB 319, 67 DSB 116 (1972), 11 ILM 1416 (1972), 1 IPE 118.

Languages: Arabic, Chinese, English, French, Russian, Spanish

Literature: Sohn, *The Stockholm Declaration on the Human Environment*, 14 Harv. J. Int'l L. 423 (1973)

Editors' Note

  The United Nations Conference on the Human Environment, held 5-16 June
1972 in Stockholm, marked the emergence of international environmental law as a
separate branch of international law. Much preparatory work preceded the Stockholm Conference, in which 113 States participated (the Soviet Union and other
Eastern European States boycotted the Conference because of the exclusion of
the German Democratic Republic), together with 13 specialized agencies, several
intergovernmental organizations, and numerous non-governmental organizations.
The Stockholm Conference adopted the basic Declaration on the Human Environment, an Action Plan (which contains 109 specific recommendations, focussing on
environmental assessment through establishing an Earthwatch, plus related educational and other activities), and a detailed resolution on institutional and financial
arrangements (which led, *inter alia*, to the formation of the United Nations Environment Programme (UNEP)).

  The Declaration on the Human Environment, which was adopted by acclamation, contains a preamble (''proclaiming'' seven points) and 26 principles covering
many international environmental issues, including human rights, natural resource
management, pollution prevention, the relation between environment and development, institutional arrangements, education, the obligation to prevent pollution (the
famous principle 21), whether standards should be the same for developed and
developing countries, and nuclear weapons. The Declaration does not cover some
important topics, however. For example, a draft principle requiring notification of
the risk of adverse transboundary effects was deleted from the Declaration.

The Stockholm Declaration was subsequently endorsed by the General Assembly on 15 December 1972 (UNGA Res. 2994), by 112 to none, with ten abstentions. Although the language of the Declaration often is normative (''shall'') rather than precatory (''should''), the Declaration was intended not to be legally binding. However, at least one portion of the Declaration—principle 21—is now generally viewed as customary international law (though there is disagreement about its precise meaning). More generally, the Stockholm Declaration has had great and widespread influence.

DECLARATION OF THE UNITED NATIONS CONFERENCE ON THE HUMAN ENVIRONMENT

The United Nations Conference on the Human Environment,
Having met at Stockholm from 5 to 16 June 1972,
Having considered the need for a common outlook and for common principles to inspire and guide the peoples of the world in the preservation and enhancement of the human environment,

I

Proclaims that:

1. Man is both creature and moulder of his environment, which gives him physical sustenance and affords him the opportunity for intellectual, moral, social and spiritual growth. In the long and tortuous evolution of the human race on this planet a stage has been reached when, through the rapid acceleration of science and technology, man has acquired the power to transform his environment in countless ways and on an unprecedented scale. Both aspects of man's environment, the natural and the man-made, are essential to his well-being and to the enjoyment of basic human rights—even the right to life itself.

2. The protection and improvement of the human environment is a major issue which affects the well-being of peoples and economic development throughout the world; it is the urgent desire of the peoples of the whole world and the duty of all Governments.

3. Man has constantly to sum up experience and go on discovering, inventing, creating and advancing. In our time, man's capability to transform his surroundings, if used wisely, can bring to all peoples the benefits of development and the opportunity to enhance the quality of life. Wrongly or heedlessly applied, the same power can do incalculable harm to human beings and the human environment. We see around us growing evidence of man-made harm in many regions of the earth: dangerous levels of pollution in water, air, earth and living beings; major and undesirable disturbances to the ecological balance of the biosphere; destruction and depletion of irreplaceable resources; and gross deficiencies, harmful to the physical, mental and social health of man, in the man-made environment, particularly in the living and working environment.

4. In the developing countries most of the environmental problems are caused by under-development. Millions continue to live far below the minimum levels required for a decent human existence, deprived of adequate food and clothing, shelter and education, health and sanitation. Therefore, the developing countries must direct their efforts to development, bearing in mind their priorities and the need to safeguard and improve the environment. For the same purpose, the industrialized

countries should make efforts to reduce the gap themselves and the developing countries. In the industrialized countries, environmental problems are generally related to industrialization and technological development.

5. The natural growth of population continuously presents problems for the preservation of the environment, and adequate policies and measures should be adopted, as appropriate, to face these problems. Of all things in the world, people are the most precious. It is the people that propel social progress, create social wealth, develop science and technology and, through their hard work, continuously transform the human environment. Along with social progress and the advance of production, science and technology, the capability of man to improve the environment increases with each passing day.

6. A point has been reached in history when we must shape our actions throughout the world with a more prudent care for their environmental consequences. Through ignorance or indifference we can do massive and irreversible harm to the earthly environment on which our life and well-being depend. Conversely, through fuller knowledge and wiser action, we can achieve for ourselves and our posterity a better life in an environment more in keeping with human needs and hopes. There are broad vistas for the enhancement of environmental quality and the creation of a good life. What is needed is an enthusiastic but calm state of mind and intense but orderly work. For the purpose of attaining freedom in the world of nature, man must use knowledge to build, in collaboration with nature, a better environment. To defend and improve the human environment for present and future generations has become an imperative goal for mankind—a goal to be pursued together with, and in harmony with, the established and fundamental goals of peace and of worldwide economic and social development.

7. To achieve this environmental goal will demand the acceptance of responsibility by citizens and communities and by enterprises and institutions at every level, all sharing equitably in common efforts. Individuals in all walks of life as well as organizations in many fields, by their values and the sum of their actions, will shape the world environment of the future. Local and national governments will bear the greatest burden for large-scale environmental policy and action within their jurisdictions. International co-operation is also needed in order to raise resources to support the developing countries in carrying out their responsibilities in this field. A growing class of environmental problems, because they are regional or global in extent or because they affect the common international realm, will require extensive co-operation among nations and action by international organizations in the common interest. The Conference calls upon Governments and peoples to exert common efforts for the preservation and improvement of the human environment, for the benefit of all the people and for their posterity.

II

Principles

States the common conviction that:

Principle 1

Man has the fundamental right to freedom, equality and adequate conditions of life, in an environment of a quality that permits a life of dignity and well-being, and he bears a solemn responsibility to protect and improve the environment for present and future generations. In this respect, policies promoting or perpetuating *apartheid*, racial segregation, discrimination, colonial and other forms of oppression and foreign domination stand condemned and must be eliminated.

Principle 2

The natural resources of the earth, including the air, water, land, flora and fauna and especially representative samples of natural ecosystems, must be safeguarded for the benefit of present and future generations through careful planning or management, as appropriate.

Principle 3

The capacity of the earth to produce vital renewable resources must be maintained and, wherever practicable, restored or improved.

Principle 4

Man has a special responsibility to safeguard and wisely manage the heritage of wildlife and its habitat, which are now gravely imperilled by a combination of adverse factors. Nature conservation, including wildlife, must therefore receive importance in planning for economic development.

Principle 5

The non-renewable resources of the earth must be employed in such a way as to guard against the danger of their future exhaustion and to ensure that benefits from such employment are shared by all mankind.

Principle 6

The discharge of toxic substances or of other substances and the release of heat, in such quantities or concentrations as to exceed the capacity of the environment to render them harmless, must be halted in order to ensure that serious or irreversible damage is not inflicted upon ecosystems. The just struggle of the peoples of all countries against pollution should be supported.

Principle 7

States shall take all possible steps to prevent pollution of the seas by substances that are liable to create hazards to human health, to harm living resources and marine life, to damage amenities or to interfere with other legitimate uses of the sea.

Principle 8

Economic and social development is essential for ensuring a favourable living and working environment for man and for creating conditions on earth that are necessary for the improvement of the quality of life.

Principle 9

Environmental deficiencies generated by the conditions of under-development and natural disasterspose [sic] grave problems and can best be remedied by accelerated developent through the transfer of substantial quantities of financial and technological assistance as a supplement to the domestic effort of the developing countries and such timely assistance as may be required.

Principle 10

For the developing countries, stability of prices and adequate earnings for primary commodities and raw materials are essential to environmental management since economic factors as well as ecological processes must be taken into account.

Principle 11

The environmental policies of all States should enhance and not adversely affect the present or future development potential of developing countries, nor should they hamper the attainment of better living conditions for all, and appropriate steps should be taken by States and international organizations with a view to reaching agreement on meeting the possible national and international economic consequences resulting from the application of environmental measures.

Principle 12

Resources should be made available to preserve and improve the environment, taking into account the circumstances and particular requirements of developing countries and any costs which may emanate from their incorporating environmental safeguards into their development planning and the need for making available to them, upon their request, additional international technical and financial assistance for this purpose.

Principle 13

In order to achieve a more rational management of resources and thus to improve the environment, States should adopt an integrated and co-ordinated approach to their development planning so as to ensure that development is compatible with the need to protect and improve environment for the benefit of their population.

Principle 14

Rational planning constitutes an essential tool for reconciling any conflict between the needs of development and the need to protect and improve the environment.

Principle 15

Planning must be applied to human settlements and urbanization with a view to avoiding adverse effects on the environment and obtaining maximum social, economic and environmental benefits for all. In this respect, projects which are designed for colonialist and racist domination must be abandoned.

Principle 16

Demographic policies which are without prejudice to basic human rights and which are deemed appropriate by Governments concerned should be applied in those regions where the rate of population growth or excessive population concentrations are likely to have adverse effects on the environment of the human environment and impede development.

Principle 17

Appropriate national institutions must be entrusted with the task of planning, managing or controlling the environmental resources of States with a view to enhancing environmental quality.

Principle 18

Science and technology, as part of their contribution to economic and social development, must be applied to the identification, avoidance and control of environmental risks and the solution of environmental problems and for the common good of mankind.

Principle 19 *

Education in environmental matters, for the younger generation as well as adults, giving due consideration to the underprivileged, is essential in order to broaden the basis for an enlightened opinion and responsible conduct by individuals, enterprises and communities in protecting and improving the environment in its full human dimension. It is also essential that mass media of communications avoid contributing to the deterioration of the environment, but, on the contrary, disseminate information of an educational nature on the need to protect and improve the environment in order to enable man to develop in every respect.

Principle 20

Scientific research and development in the context of environmental problems, both national and multinational, must be promoted in all countries, especially the developing countries. In this connexion, the free flow of up-to-date scientific information and transfer of experience must be supported and assisted, to facilitate the solution of environmental problems; environmental technologies should be made available to developing countries on terms which would encourage their wide dissemination without constituting an economic burden on the developing countries.

Principle 21

States have, in accordance with the Charter of the United Nations and the principles of international law, the sovereign right to exploit their own resources pursuant to their own environmental policies, and the responsibility to ensure that activities within their jurisdiction or control do not cause damage to the environment of other States or of areas beyond the limits of national jurisdiction.

Principle 22

States shall co-operate to develop further the international law regarding liability and compensation for the victims of pollution and other environmental damage caused by activities within the jurisdiction or control of such States to areas beyond their jurisdiction.

Principle 23

Without prejudice to such criteria as may be agreed upon by the international community, or to standards which will have to be determined nationally, it will be essential in all cases to consider the systems of values prevailing in each country, and the extent of the applicability of standards which are valid for the most advanced countries but which may be inappropriate and of unwarranted social cost for the developing countries.

Principle 24

International matters concerning the protection and improvement of the environment should be handled in a co-operative spirit by all countries, big and small, on an equal footing. Co-operation through multilateral or bilateral arrangements or other appropriate means is essential to effectively control, prevent, reduce and eliminate adverse environmental effects resulting from activities conducted in all spheres, in such a way that due account is taken of the sovereignty and interests of all States.

Principle 25

States shall ensure that international organizations play a co-ordinated, efficient and dynamic role for the protection and improvement of the environment.

Principle 26

Man and his environment must be spared the effects of nuclear weapons and all other means of mass destruction. States must strive to reach prompt agreement, in the relevant international organs, on the elimination and complete destruction of such weapons.

21st plenary meeting
16 June 1972

UNGA RESOLUTION: INSTITUTIONAL AND FINANCIAL ARRANGEMENTS FOR INTERNATIONAL ENVIRONMENTAL COOPERATION *Infra,* p. 719

CHARTER OF ECONOMIC RIGHTS AND DUTIES OF STATES

Popular Name: CERDS

Adopted by the United Nations General Assembly on 12 December 1974, G.A. Res. 3281(XXIX), 29 U.N. GAOR Supp. (No. 31) at 51, U.N. Doc. A/9946 (1974), *reprinted in* 1 IPE 326.

Languages: Arabic, Chinese, English, French, Russian, Spanish

Editors' Note

Concern about economic development increased following World War II, as evidenced by references to improved standards of living in the U.N. Charter and by the creation of the International Bank for Reconstruction and Development (the World Bank). At the same time, the process of decolonization began, resulting in the creation of the majority of the States now in existence. Almost all the new States are or were relatively poor economically.

This situation led to a formal call in 1974 for a New International Economic Order (NIEO). That call was contained in three instruments, the most important of which was the Charter of Economic Rights and Duties of States (CERDS). CERDS was adopted by the U.N. General Assembly by a vote of 120 in favor, six (including the United States) opposed, and ten abstentions. The basic thrust of NIEO is that the developing States must develop economically, that the standard-of-living gap between developed and developing States must narrow, and that there must be a transfer of resources from developed to developing States to accomplish those ends. Although NIEO has been strongly criticized, and although proponents of NIEO have been somewhat muted in recent years, it nevertheless remains relevant because the economic conditions (abject poverty and large wealth disparities) underlying it remain unalleviated. Indeed, two of the most difficult issues concerning the environment—how to achieve sustainable development (*see infra* this Chapter) and how to involve and treat developing States in international environmental protection efforts—raise issues at the heart of NIEO, as is evident from the excerpts from CERDS reproduced below.

CHARTER OF ECONOMIC RIGHTS
AND DUTIES OF STATES

PREAMBLE

The General Assembly,

Reaffirming the fundamental purposes of the United Nations, in particular the maintenance of international peace and security, the development of friendly relations among nations and the achievement of international co-operation in solving international problems in the economic and social fields,

Affirming the need for strengthening international co-operation in these fields,

Reaffirming further the need for strengthening international co-operation for development,

Declaring that it is a fundamental purpose of the present Charter to promote the establishment of the new international economic order, based on equity, sovereign equality, interdependence, common interest and co-operation among all States, irrespective of their economic and social systems,

Desirous of contributing to the creation of conditions for:

(*a*) The attainment of wider prosperity among all countries and of higher standards of living for all peoples,

(*b*) The promotion by the entire international community of the economic and social progress of all countries, especially developing countries,

(*c*) The encouragement of co-operation, on the basis of mutual advantage and equitable benefits for all peace-loving States which are willing to carry out the provisions of the present Charter, in the economic, trade, scientific and technical fields, regardless of political, economic or social systems,

(*d*) The overcoming of main obstacles in the way of the economic development of the developing countries,

(*e*) The acceleration of the economic growth of developing countries with a view to bridging the economic gap between developing and developed countries,

(*f*) The protection, preservation and enhancement of the environment,

Mindful of the need to establish and maintain a just and equitable economic and social order through:

(*a*) The achievement of more rational and equitable international economic relations and the encouragement of structural changes in the world economy,

(*b*) The creation of conditions which permit the further expansion of trade and intensification of economic co-operation among all nations,

(*c*) The strengthening of the economic independence of developing countries, (*d*) The establishment and promotion of international economic relations, taking into account the agreed differences in development of the developing countries and their specific needs,

Determined to promote collective economic security for development, in particular of the developing countries, with strict respect for the sovereign equality of each State and through the co-operation of the entire international community,

Considering that genuine co-operation among States, based on joint consideration of and concerted action regarding international economic problems, is essential for fulfilling the international community's common desire to achieve a just and rational development of all parts of the world,

Stressing the importance of ensuring appropriate conditions for the conduct of normal economic relations among all States, irrespective of differences in social and economic systems, and for the full respect of the rights of all peoples, as well as strengthening instruments of international economic co-operation as a means for the consolidation of peace for the benefit of all,

Convinced of the need to develop a system of international economic relations on the basis of sovereign equality, mutual and equitable benefit and the close interrelationship of the interests of all States,

Reiterating that the responsibility for the development of every country rests primarily upon itself but that concomitant and effective international co-operation is an essential factor for the full achievement of its own development goals,

Firmly convinced of the urgent need to evolve a substantially improved system of international economic relations,

Solemnly adopts the present Charter of Economic Rights and Duties of States.

* * *

Article 29

The sea-bed and ocean floor and the subsoil thereof, beyond the limits of national jurisdiction, as well as the resources of the area, are the common heritage of mankind. On the basis of the principles adopted by the General Assembly in resolution 2749 (XXV) of 17 December 1970, all States shall ensure that exploration of the area and exploitation of its resources are carried out exclusively for peaceful purposes and that the benefits derived therefrom are shared equitably by all States, taking into account the particular interests and needs of developing countries; an international régime applying to the area and its resources and including appropriate international machinery to give effect to its provisions shall be established by an international treaty of a universal character, generally agreed upon.

Article 30

The protection, preservation and enhancement of the environment for the present and future generations is the responsibility of all States. All States shall endeavour to establish their own environmental and developmental policies in conformity with such responsibility. The environmental policies of all States should enhance and not adversely affect the present and future development potential of developing countries. All States have the responsibility to ensure that activities within their jurisdiction or control do not cause damage to the environment of other

States or of areas beyond the limits of national jurisdiction. All States should co-operate in evolving international norms and regulations in the field of the environment.

* * *

UNITED NATIONS ENVIRONMENT PROGRAMME GOVERNING COUNCIL DECISION: PRINCIPLES OF CONDUCT IN THE FIELD OF THE ENVIRONMENT FOR THE GUIDANCE OF STATES IN THE CONSERVATION AND HARMONIOUS UTILIZATION OF NATURAL RESOURCES SHARED BY TWO OR MORE STATES

Popular Name: UNEP Guidelines on Shared Natural Resources

Done at Nairobi on 19 May 1978, G.A. Res. 3129 (XXVIII), UNEP ELGP #2, *reprinted in* 17 ILM 1097 (1978).

Languages: Arabic, Chinese, English, French, Russian, Spanish

Editors' Note

This resolution responded to a decision by the UNEP Governing Council. It led to an effort in the UNEP Governing Council to draft a code of conduct, but that effort did not reach fruition. The resolution has never been considered by the United Nations General Assembly, although it has been widely acclaimed internationally.

DRAFT PRINCIPLES OF CONDUCT IN THE FIELD OF THE ENVIRONMENT FOR THE GUIDANCE OF STATES IN THE CONSERVATION AND HARMONIOUS UTILIZATION OF NATURAL RESOURCES SHARED BY TWO OR MORE STATES

EXPLANATORY NOTE

The draft principles of conduct, in this note have been drawn up for the guidance of States in the field of the environment with respect to the conservation and harmonious utilization of natural resources shared by two or more States. The principles refer to such conduct of individual States as is considered conducive to the attainment of the said objective in a manner which does not adversely affect the environment. Moreover, the principles aim to encourage States sharing a natural resource, to co-operate in the field of the environment.

An attempt has been made to avoid language which might create the impression of intending to refer to, as the case may be, either a specific legal obligation under international law, or to the absence of such obligation.

The language used throughout does not seek to prejudice whether or to what extent the conduct envisaged in the principles is already prescribed by existing rules of general international law. Neither does the formulation intend to express an opinion as to whether or to what extent and in what manner the principles—as far as they do not reflect already existing rules of general international law—should be incorporated in the body of general international law.

DRAFT

Principle 1

It is necessary for States to co-operate in the field of the environment concerning the conservation and harmonious utilization of natural resources shared by two or more States. Accordingly, it is necessary that consistent with the concept of equitable utilization of shared natural resources, States co-operate with a view to controlling, preventing, reducing or eliminating adverse environmental effects which may result from the utilization of such resources. Such co-operation is to take place on an equal footing and taking into account the sovereignty, rights and interests of the States concerned.

Principle 2

In order to ensure effective international co-operation in the field of the environment concerning the conservation and harmonious utilization of natural resources shared by two or more States, States sharing such natural resources should endeavor to conclude bilateral or multilateral agreements between or among themselves in order to secure specific regulation of their conduct in this respect, applying as necessary the present principles in a legally binding manner or should endeavor to enter into other arrangements, as appropriate, for this purpose. In entering into such agreements or arrangements, States should consider the establishment of institutional structures, such as joint international commissions, for consultations on environmental problems relating to the protection and use of shared natural resources.

Principle 3

1. States have, in accordance with the Charter of the United Nations and the principles of international law, the sovereign right to exploit their own resources pursuant to their own environmental policies, and the responsibility to ensure that activities within their jurisdiction or control do not cause damage to the environment of other States or of areas beyond the limits of national jurisdiction.
2. The principles set forth in paragraph 1, as well as the other principles contained in this document, apply to shared natural resources. _to_
3. Accordingly, it is necessary for each State to avoid the maximum extent possible and to reduce to the minimum extent possible the adverse environmental effects beyond its jurisdiction of the utilization of a shared natural resource so as to protect the environment, in particular when such utilization might:
   (a) cause damage to the environment which could have repercussions on the utilization of the resource by another sharing State;
   (b) threaten the conservation of a shared renewable resource;
   (c) endanger the health of the population of another State.

Without prejudice to the generality of the above principle, it should be interpreted, taking into account, where appropriate, the practical capabilities of States sharing the natural resource.

Principle 4

States should make environmental assessments before engaging in any activity with respect to a shared natural resource which may create a risk of significantly[8] affecting the environment of another State or States sharing that resource.

---

[8]See definition.

Principle 5
    States sharing a natural resource should, to the extent practicable, exchange information and engage in consultations on a regular basis on its environmental aspects.

Principle 6
    1. It is necessary for every State sharing a natural resource with one or more other States:
        (*a*) to notify in advance the other State or States of the pertinent details of plans to initiate, or make a change in, the conservation or utilization of the resource which can reasonably be expected to affect significantly[8] the environment in the territory of the other State or States; and
        (*b*) upon request of the other State or States, to enter into consultations concerning the above-mentioned plans; and
        (*c*) to provide, upon request to that effect by the other State or States, specific additional pertinent information concerning such plans; and
        (*d*) if there has been no advance notification as envisaged in sub-paragraph (a) above, to enter into consultations about such plans upon request of the other State or States.
    2. In cases where the transmission of certain information is prevented by national legislation or international conventions, the State of States withholding such information shall nevertheless, on the basis, in particular, of the principle of good faith and in the spirit of good neighbourliness, co-operate with the other interested State or States with the aim of finding a satisfactory solution.

Principle 7
    Exchange of information, notification, consultations and other forms of co-operation regarding shared natural resources are carried out on the basis of the principle of good faith and in the spirit of good neighbourliness and in such a way as to avoid any unreasonable delays either in the forms of co-operation or in carrying out development or conservation projects.

Principle 8
    When it would be useful to clarify environmental problems relating to a shared natural resource, States should engage in joint scientific studies and assessments, with a view to facilitating the finding of appropriate and satisfactory solutions to such problems on the basis of agreed data.

Principle 9
    1. States have a duty urgently to inform other States which may be affected:
        (*a*) Of any emergency situation arising from the utilization of a shared natural resource which might cause sudden harmful effects on their environment;
        (*b*) Of any sudden grave natural events retaled [sic] to a shared natural resource which may affect the environment of such States.
    2. States should also, when appropriate, inform the competent international organizations of any such situation or event.
    3. States concerned should co-operate, in particular by means of agreed contingency plans, when appropriate, and mutual assistance, in order to avert grave situations, and to eliminate, reduce or correct, as far as possible, the effects of such situations or events.

Principle 10
    States sharing a natural resource should, when appropriate, consider the possibility of jointly seeking the services of any competent international organization in

clarifying the environmental problems realting [sic] to the conservation or utilization of such natural resource.

Principle 11
1. The relevant provisions of the Charter of the United Nations and of the Declaration of Principles of International Law concerning Friendly Relations and Co-operation among States in accordance with the Charter of the United Nations apply to the settlement of environmental disputes arising out of the conservation or utilization of shared natural resources.
2. In case negotiations or other non-binding means have failed to settle a dispute within a reasonable time, it is necessary for States to submit the dispute to an appropriate settlement procedure which is mutually agreed by them, preferably in advance. The procedure should be speedy, effective and binding.
3. It is necessary for the States parties to such a dispute to refrain from any action which may aggravate the situation with respect to the environment to the extent of creating an obstacle to the amicable settlement of the dispute.

Principle 12
1. States are responsible for the fulfillment of their international obligations in the field of the environment concerning the conservation and utilization of shared natural resources. They are subject to liability in accordance with applicable international law for environmental damage resulting from violations of these obligations caused to areas beyond their jurisdiction.
2. States should co-operate to develop further international law regarding liability and compensation for the victims of environmental damage arising out of utilization of a shared natural resource and caused to areas beyond their jurisdiction.

Principle 13
It is necessary for States, when considering, under their domesic [sic] environmental policy, the permissibility of domestic activities, to take into account the potential adverse environmental effects arising out of the utilization of shared natural resources, without discrimination as to whether the effects would occur within their jurisdiction or outside it.

Principle 14
States should endeavour, in accordance with their legal systems and, where appropriate, on a basis agreed by them, to provide persons in other States who have been or may be adversely affected by environmental damage resulting from the utilization of shared natural resources with equivalent access to and treatment in the same administrative and judicial proceedings, and make available to them the same remedies as are available to persons within their own jurisdictions who have been or may be similarly affected.

Principle 15
The present principles should be interpreted and applied in such a way as to enhance and not to affect adversely development and the interests of all countries, and in particular of the developing countries.

DEFINITION

In the present text, the expression "significantly affect" refers to any appreciable effects on a shared natural resource and excludes "*de minimis*" effects.

UNGA RESOLUTION: HISTORICAL RESPONSIBILITY OF STATES FOR THE PROTECTION OF NATURE FOR THE BENEFIT OF PRESENT AND FUTURE GENERATIONS.
Infra, p. 638.

WORLD CHARTER FOR NATURE

Adopted by the United Nations General Assembly on 28 October 1982, G.A. Res. 37/7, 37 U.N. GAOR Supp. (No. 51) at 17, U.N. Doc. A/37/51 (1983), 1982 UNYB 1023, *reprinted in* 22 ILM 455 (1983), IPE(2) I/C/28-10-82.

Languages: Arabic, Chinese, English, French, Russian, Spanish

Literature: W.E. Burhenne & W.A. Irwin, World Charter for Nature (Erich Schmidt Verlag, Berlin 1986)

' Editors' Note

The World Charter for Nature was adopted by the United Nations Assembly by a vote of 111 to 1 (United States of America), with 18 abstentions (including Mexico, which later advised the Secretariat it had intended to vote in favor). It restates many of the principles in the Stockholm Declaration of the Human Environment (*supra*, p. 171). It also reflects basic principles contained in the 1980 World Conservation Strategy prepared jointly by the International Union for the Conservation of Nature and Natural Resources, the United Nations Environment Programme, and the World Wildlife Fund. Among other significant features, the Charter proclaims duties not only for States, but also for "all human conduct," thus including individuals and associations.

The World Charter for Nature is not a binding international law *per se*, although some of its provisions may express customary international law (for example, principle 21(d), which restates the second half of the Stockholm Declaration's principle 21). Moreover, it contains normative language ("shall" instead of "should") and it was "solemnly proclaim[ed]" (rather than just declared) by the General Assembly, thus enhancing its force.

WORLD CHARTER FOR NATURE

The General Assembly,
Reaffirming the fundamental purposes of the United Nations, in particular the maintenance of international peace and security, the development of friendly relations among nations and the achievement of international co-operation in solving international problems of an economic, social, cultural, technical, intellectual or humanitarian character,
Aware that:
(*a*) Mankind is a part of nature and life depends on the uninterrupted functioning of natural systems which ensure the supply of energy and nutrients,
(*b*) Civilization is rooted in nature, which has shaped human culture and influenced all artistic and scientific achievement, and living in harmony with nature gives man the best opportunities for the development of his creativity, and for rest and recreation,

Convinced that:

(*a*) Every form of life is unique, warranting respect regardless of its worth to man, and, to accord other organisms such recognition, man must be guided by a moral code of action,

(*b*) Man can alter nature and exhaust natural resources by his action or its consequences and, therefore, must fully recognize the urgency of maintaining the stability and quality of nature and of conserving natural resources,

Persuaded that:

(*a*) Lasting benefits from nature depend upon the maintenance of essential ecological processes and life support systems, and upon the diversity of life forms, which are jeopardized through excessive exploitation and habitat destruction by man,

(*b*) The degradation of natural systems owing to excessive consumption and misuse of natural resources, as well as to failure to establish an appropriate economic order among peoples and among States, leads to the breakdown of the economic, social and political framework of civilization,

(*c*) Competition for scarce resources creates conflicts, whereas the conservation of nature and natural resources contributes to justice and the maintenance of peace and cannot be achieved until mankind learns to live in peace and to forsake war and armaments,

Reaffirming that man must acquire the knowledge to maintain and enhance his ability to use natural resources in a manner which ensures the preservation of the species and ecosystems for the benefit of present and future generations,

Firmly convinced of the need for appropriate measures, at the national and international, individual and collective, and private and public levels, to protect nature and promote international co-operation in this field,

Adopts, to these ends, the present World Charter for Nature, which proclaims the following principles of conservation by which all human conduct affecting nature is to be guided and judged.

I. General Principles

1. Nature shall be respected and its essential processes shall not be impaired.

2. The genetic viability on the earth shall not be compromised; the population levels of all life forms, wild and domesticated, must be at least sufficient for their survival, and to this end necessary habitats shall be safeguarded.

3. All areas of the earth, both land and sea, shall be subject to these principles of conservation; special protection shall be given to unique areas, to representative samples of all the different types of ecosystems and to the habitats of rare or endangered species.

4. Ecosystems and organisms, as well as the land, marine and atmospheric resources that are utilized by man, shall be managed to achieve and maintain optimum sustainable productivity, but not in such a way as to endanger the integrity of those other ecosystems or species with which they coexist.

5. Nature shall be secured against degradation caused by warfare or other hostile activities.

II. Functions

6. In the decision-making process it shall be recognized that man's needs can be met only by ensuring the proper functioning of natural systems and by respecting the principles set forth in the present Charter.

7. In the planning and implementation of social and economic development activities, due account shall be taken of the fact that the conservation of nature is an integral part of those activities.

8. In formulating long-term plans for economic development, population growth and the improvement of standards of living, due account shall be taken of the long-term capacity of natural systems to ensure the subsistence and settlement of the populations concerned, recognizing that this capacity may be enhanced through science and technology.

9. The allocation of areas of the earth to various uses shall be planned and due account shall be taken of the physical constraints, the biological productivity and diversity and the natural beauty of the areas concerned.

10. Natural resources shall not be wasted, but used with a restraint appropriate to the principles set forth in the present Charter, in accordance with the following rules:

(*a*) Living resources shall not be utilized in excess of their natural capacity for regeneration;

(*b*) The productivity of soils shall be maintained or enhanced through measures which safeguard their long-term fertility and the process of organic decomposition, and prevent erosion and all other forms of degradation;

(*c*) Resources, including water, which are not consumed as they are used shall be reused or recycled;

(*d*) Non-renewable resources which are consumed as they are used shall be exploited with restraint, taking into account their abundance, the rational possibilities of converting them for consumption, and the compatibility of their exploitation with the functioning of natural systems.

11. Activities which might have an impact on nature shall be controlled, and the best available technologies that minimize significant risks to nature or other adverse effects shall be used; in particular:

(*a*) Activities which are likely to cause irreversible damage to nature shall be avoided;

(*b*) Activities which are likely to pose a significant risk to nature shall be preceded by an exhaustive examination; their proponents shall demonstrate that expected benefits outweigh potential damage to nature, and where potential adverse effects are not fully understood, the activities should not proceed;

(*c*) Activities which may disturb nature shall be preceded by assessment of their consequences, and environmental impact studies of development projects shall be conducted sufficiently in advance, and if they are to be undertaken, such activities shall be planned and carried out so as to minimize potential adverse effects;

(*d*) Agriculture, grazing, forestry and fisheries practices shall be adapted to the natural characteristics and constraints of given areas;

(*e*) Areas degraded by human activities shall be rehabilitated for purposes in accord with their natural potential and compatible with the well-being of affected populations.

12. Discharge of pollutants into natural systems shall be avoided and:

(*a*) Where this is not feasible, such pollutants shall be treated at the source, using the best praticable means available;

(*b*) Special precautions shall be taken to prevent discharge of radioactive or toxic wastes.

13. Measures intended to prevent, control or limit natural disasters, infestations and diseases shall be specifically directed to the causes of these scourges and shall avoid adverse side-effects on nature.

III. Implementation

14. The principles set forth in the present Charter shall be reflected in the law and practice of each State, as well as at the international level.

15. Knowledge of nature shall be broadly disseminated by all possible means, particularly by ecological education as an integral part of general education.

16. All planning shall include, among its essential elements, the formulation of strategies for the conservation of nature, the establishment of inventories of ecosystems and assessments of the effects on nature of proposed policies and activities; all of these elements shall be disclosed to the public by appropriate means in time to permit effective consultation and participation.

17. Funds, programmes and administrative structures necessary to achieve the objective of the conservation of nature shall be provided.

18. Constant efforts shall be made to increase knowledge of nature by scientific research and to disseminate such knowledge unimpeded by restrictions of any kind.

19. The status of natural processes, ecosystems and species shall be closely monitored to enable early detection of degradation or threat, ensure timely intervention and facilitate the evaluation of conservation policies and methods.

20. Military activities damaging to nature shall be avoided.

21. States and, to the extent they are able, other public authorities, international organizations, individuals, groups and corporations shall:

(a) Co-operate in the task of conserving nature through common activities and other relevant actions, including information exchange and consultations;

(b) Establish standards for products and manufacturing processes that may have adverse effects on nature, as well as agreed methodologies for assessing these effects;

(c) Implement the applicable international legal provisions for the conservation of nature and the protection of the environment;

(d) Ensure that activities within their jurisdictions or control do not cause damage to the natural systems located within other States or in the areas beyond the limits of national jurisdiction;

(e) Safeguard and conserve nature in areas beyond national jurisdiction.

22. Taking fully into account the sovereignty of States over their natural resources, each State shall give effect to the provisions of the present Charter through its competent organs and in co-operation with other States.

23. All persons, in accordance with their national legislation, shall have the opportunity to participate, individually or with others, in the formulation of decisions of direct concern to their environment, and shall have access to means of redress when their environment has suffered damage or degradation.

24. Each person has a duty to act in accordance with the provisions of the present Charter; acting individually, in association with others or through participation in the political process, each person shall strive to ensure that the objectives and requirements of the present Charter are met.

EXPERTS GROUP ON ENVIRONMENTAL LAW OF THE WORLD COMMISSION ON ENVIRONMENT AND DEVELOPMENT, LEGAL PRINCIPLES FOR ENVIRONMENTAL PROTECTION AND SUSTAINABLE DEVELOPMENT

U.N. Doc. WCED/86/23/Add.1 (1986), A/42/427, Annex I, *reprinted in* Experts Group on Environmental Law of the World Commission on Environment and Development, Environmental Protection and Sustainable Development: Legal Principles and Recommendations 37-133 (1987).
Languages: Arabic, Chinese, English, French, Russian, Spanish

Editors' Note

The United Nations established in 1984 the World Commission on Environment and Development (WCED), a small independent body, to formulate "a global agenda for change." The Commission, after several years of hearings and deliberations, published its report, *Our Common Future* (1987).

As part of the WCED effort, the Commission appointed an international group of 13 legal experts to develop legal principles which should be adopted before the year 2000 to support environmental protection and sustainable development. The legal experts group formulated 22 legal principles and 13 proposals for strengthening the legal and institutional framework.

The publication of the experts' report contains commentary for each of the principles, which sets forth the international agreements supporting the principle. Several of the principles in the section on general principles, in particular, go beyond normally accepted rules of customary international law.

LEGAL PRINCIPLES FOR ENVIRONMENTAL PROTECTION AND SUSTAINABLE DEVELOPMENT

adopted by the
WCED EXPERTS GROUP ON ENVIRONMENTAL LAW

USE OF TERMS

For the purposes of the present text:

(a) "use of a natural resource" means any human conduct, which, directly or indirectly, takes advantage of the benefits of a natural resource in the form of preservation, exploitation, consumption or otherwise of the natural resource, in so far as it does not result in an environmental interference as defined in Paragraph (f);

(b) "interference with the use of a natural resource" means any impairment, directly or indirectly, by man of the use of a natural resource in so far as it does not constitute an environmental interference as defined in Paragraph (f);

(c) "transboundary natural resource" means a natural resource which physically crosses the boundary between an area under the national jurisdiction of a State and an area under the national jurisdiction of another State or an area beyond the limits of national jurisdiction to the extent that its use in an area under the national jurisdiction of one State may affect its use in an area under the national jurisdiction of another State or in an area beyond the limits of national jurisdiction or vice versa;

(d) "transboundary interference with the use of a transboundary natural resource" means an interference with the use of a natural resource of which the physical origin is wholly or in part located outside the area under national jurisdiction of a State or outside the area beyond the limits of national jurisdiction in which the use takes place;

(e) "international natural resource" means a natural resource physically within an area beyond the limits of national jurisdiction to the extent that the origin and effects of any impairment of the use of the natural resource remain within the area beyond the limits of national jurisdiction;

(f) "environmental interference" means any impairment of human health, living resources, ecosystems, material property, amenities or other legitimate uses of a natural resource or the environment caused, directly or indirectly, by man through polluting substances, ionizing radiation, noise, explosions, vibration or other forms of energy, plants, animals, diseases, flooding, sand-drift or other similar means;

(g) "transboundary environmental interference" means an environmental interference of which the physical origin is wholly or in part located either outside the area under national jurisdiction of a State in which the effects caused by the interference occur, or outside the area beyond the limits of national jurisdiction in which the effects caused by the interference occur;

(h) "international environmental interference" means an environmental interference of which the physical origin and the effects are located within an area beyond the limits of national jurisdiction;

(i) "conservation" means the management of human use of a natural resource or the environment in such a manner that it may yield the greatest sustainable benefit to present generations while maintaining its potential to meet the needs and aspirations of future generations. It embraces preservation, maintenance, sustainable utilization, restoration and enhancement of a natural resource or the environment.

GENERAL PRINCIPLES CONCERNING NATURAL RESOURCES AND ENVIRONMENTAL INTERFERENCES

Article 1
Fundamental human right

All human beings have the fundamental right to an environment adequate for their health and well-being.

Article 2
Conservation for present and future generations

States shall ensure that the environment and natural resources are conserved and used for the benefit of present and future generations.

Article 3
Ecosystems, related ecological processes, biological diversity, and sustainability

States shall:

(a) maintain ecosystems and related ecological processes essential for the functioning of the biosphere in all its diversity, in particular those important for food production, health and other aspects of human survival and sustainable development;

(b) maintain maximum biological diversity by ensuring the survival and promoting the conservation in their natural habitat of all species of fauna and flora, in particular those which are rare, endemic or endangered;

(c) observe in the exploitation of living natural resources and ecosystems, the principle of optimum sustainable yield.

Article 4
Environmental standards and monitoring

States shall:

(a) establish specific environmental standards, in particular environmental quality standards, emission standards, technological standards and product standards aimed at preventing or abating interferences with natural resources or the environment;

(b) establish systems for the collection and dissemination of data and regular observation of natural resources and the environment in order to permit adequate planning of the use of natural resources and the environment, to permit early detection of interferences with natural resources or the environment and ensure timely intervention, and to facilitate the evaluation of conservation policies and methods.

Article 5
Assessment of planned activities

States planning to carry out or permit activities which may significantly affect a natural resource or the environment shall make or require an assessment of their effects before carrying out or permitting the planned activities.

Article 6
Timely information, access and due process

States shall inform all persons in a timely manner of activities which may significantly affect their use of a natural resource or their environment and shall grant the concerned persons access to and due process in administrative and judicial proceedings.

Article 7
Planning and implementation of development activities

1. States shall ensure that the conservation of natural resources and the environment is treated as an integral part of the planning and implementation of development activities. Particular attention shall be paid to environmental problems arising in developing countries and to the need to incorporate environmental considerations in all development assistance programmes.

2. States shall make available to other States, and especially to developing countries, upon their request and under agreed terms scientific and technical information and expertise, results of research programmes, training opportunities and specialized equipment and facilities which are needed by such other States to promote rational use of natural resources, and the environment or to prevent or abate interference with natural resources or the environment, in particular in cases of environmental emergencies.

Article 8
General obligation to co-operate

States shall co-operate in good faith with other States or through competent international organizations in the implementation of the provisions of the preceding articles.

PRINCIPLES SPECIFICALLY CONCERNING TRANSBOUNDARY NATURAL RESOURCES AND ENVIRONMENTAL INTERFERENCES

Article 9
Reasonable and equitable use of transboundary natural resources

States shall use transboundary natural resources in a reasonable and equitable manner.

Article 10
Prevention and abatement of a transboundary environmental interference

States shall, without prejudice to the principles laid down in Articles 11 and 12, prevent or abate any transboundary environmental interference or a significant risk thereof which causes substantial harm—i.e. harm which is not minor or insignificant.

Article 11
Liability for transboundary environmental interferences resulting from lawful activities

1. If one or more activities create a significant risk of substantial harm as a result of a transboundary environmental interference, and if the overall technical and socio-economic cost or loss of benefits involved in preventing or reducing such risk far exceeds in the long run the advantage which such prevention or reduction would entail, the State which carried out or permitted the activities shall ensure that compensation is provided should substantial harm occur in an area under national jurisdiction of another State or in an area beyond the limits of national jurisdiction.

2. A State shall ensure that compensation is provided for substantial harm caused by transboundary environmental interferences resulting from activities carried out or permitted by that State notwithstanding that the activities were not initially known to cause such interferences.

Article 12
Transboundary environmental interferences involving substantial harm far less than cost of prevention

1. If a State is planning to carry out or permit an activity which will entail a transboundary environmental interference causing harm which is substantial but far less than the overall technical and socio-economic cost or loss of benefits involved in preventing or reducing such interference, such State shall enter into negotiations with the affected State on the equitable conditions, both technical and financial, under which the activity could be carried out.

2. In the event of a failure to reach a solution on the basis of equitable principles within a period of 18 months after the beginning of the negotiations or within any other period of time agreed upon by the States concerned, the dispute shall at the request of any of the States concerned, and under the conditions set forth in Paragraphs 3 and 4 of Article 22, be submitted to conciliation or thereafter to arbitration or judicial settlement in order to reach a solution on the basis of equitable principles.

Article 13
Non-discrimination between domestic and transboundary environmental interferences

Without prejudice to the principles laid down in Articles 10, 11 and 12 when calling for a more stringent approach, States shall, when considering under their domestic policy or law the permissibility of an environmental interference or a significant risk thereof, take into account the detrimental effects which are or may be caused by the environmental interference without discrimination as to whether the effects would occur inside or outside the area under their national jurisdiction.

Article 14
General obligation to co-operate on transboundary environmental problems

1. States shall co-operate in good faith with the other States concerned in maintaining or attaining for each of them a reasonable and equitable use of a transboundary natural resource or in preventing or abating a transboundary environmental interference or significant risk thereof.

2. The co-operation shall, as much as possible, be aimed at arriving at an optimal use of the transboundary natural resource or at maximizing the effectiveness of measures to prevent or abate a transboundary environmental interference.

Article 15
Exchange of information

States shall provide the other States concerned upon their request and in a timely manner with all relevant and reasonably available data concerning a transboundary natural resource, including the uses made of such a resource and transboundary interferences with them, or concerning a transboundary environmental interference.

Article 16
Prior notice of planned activities, environmental impact assessments

1. States planning to carry out or permit activities which may entail a transboundary interference or a significant risk thereof with the reasonable and equitable use of a transboundary natural resource or which may entail a transboundary environmental interference or a significant risk thereof causing substantial harm in an area under national jurisdiction of another State or in an area beyond the limits of national jurisdiction shall give timely notice to the States concerned. In particular, they shall on their own initiative or upon request of the other States concerned provide such relevant information as will permit those other States to make an assessment of the probable effects of the planned activities.

2. When a State has reasonable grounds for believing that planned activities may have the effects referred to in Paragraph 1, it shall make an assessment of those effects before carrying out or permitting the planned activities.

Article 17
Consultations

Consultations shall be held in good faith, upon request, at an early stage between, on the one hand, States whose reasonable and equitable use of a transboundary natural resource is or may be affected by a transboundary interference or whose environmental interests are or may be affected by a transboundary environmental interference and, on the other hand, States in whose area under national jurisdiction or under whose jurisdiction such a transboundary interference originates or may originate in connection with activities carried on or contemplated therein or thereunder.

Article 18
Co-operative arrangements for environmental assessment and protection

In order to maintain or attain a reasonable and equitable use of a transboundary natural resource or to prevent or abate transboundary environmental interferences or significant risks thereof the States concerned shall, inter alia:

(a) establish co-ordinated or unified systems for the collection and dissemination of data relating to the transboundary natural resource or for regular observation of transboundary environmental interferences;

(b) co-ordinate and, where appropriate, jointly undertake scientific or technical studies to that effect;

(c) establish by common agreement specific environmental standards, in particular environmental quality standards and emission standards;

(d) jointly establish or resort to an institutional mechanism or other appropriate arrangement.

Article 19
Emergency situations

1. In the case of an emergency situation or other change of circumstances suddenly giving rise to a transboundary interference or a significant risk thereof with the reasonable and equitable use of a transboundary natural resource or to a transboundary environmental interference or a signfificant risk thereof, causing substantial harm in an area under national jurisdiction of another State or in an area beyond the limits of national jurisdiction, the State in whose area under national jurisdiction or under whose jurisdiction the interference originates shall promptly warn the other States concerned, provide them with such pertinent information as will enable them to minimize the transboundary environmental interference, inform them of steps taken to abate the cause of the transboundary environmental interference, and co-operate with those States in order to prevent or minimize the harmful effects of such an emergency situation or other change of circumstances.

2. States shall develop contingency plans in order to prevent or minimize the harmful effects of an emergency situation or other change of circumstances referred to in Paragraph 1.

Article 20
Non-intergovernmental proceedings

States shall provide remedies for persons who have been or may be detrimentally affected by a transboundary interference with their use of a transboundary natural resource or by a transboundary environmental interference. In particular, States of origin shall grant those persons equal access as well as due process and equal treatment in the same administrative and judicial proceedings as are available to persons within their own jurisdiction who have been or may be similarly affected.

Article 21

1. A State is responsible under international law for a breach of an international obligation relating to the use of a natural resource or the prevention or abatement of an environmental interference.

2. In particular, it shall:

(a) cease the internationally wrongful act;

(b) as far as possible, re-establish the situation which would have existed if the internationally wrongful act had not taken place;

(c) provide compensation for the harm which results from the internationally wrongful act;

(d) where appropriate, give satisfaction for the internationally wrongful act.

PEACEFUL SETTLEMENT OF DISPUTES

Article 22

1. States, when they cannot avoid international disputes concerning the use of a natural resource or concerning an environmental interference in accordance with the preceding articles, shall settle such disputes by peaceful means in such a manner that international peace and security, and justice, are not endangered.

2. States shall accordingly seek a settlement of such disputes by negotiation, good offices, enquiry, mediation, conciliation, arbitration, judicial settlement, resort to appropriate bodies or arrangements, whether global or regional, or by any other peaceful means of their own choice.

3. In the event of a failure to reach a solution by another non-binding peaceful means within a period of 18 months after the dispute has arisen or within any other period of time agreed upon by the States concerned, the dispute shall be submitted to conciliation at the request of any of the States concerned, unless it is agreed to proceed with an already agreed peaceful means or to submit the dispute to another binding or non-binding means of peaceful settlement.

4. In the event that the conciliation envisaged in Paragraph 3, or any other non-binding means of peaceful settlement resorted to in lieu thereof, does not lead to a solution of the dispute, the dispute shall be submitted to arbitration or judicial settlement at the request of any of the States concerned, unless it is agreed to submit the dispute to another means of peaceful settlement.

RESTATEMENT (THIRD) OF THE FOREIGN RELATIONS LAW OF THE UNITED STATES, Introduction to Part VI (Law of the Environment), §§ 601-602 and Comments

Language: English

Editors' Note

The Restatement (Third) of the Foreign Relations Law of the United States was prepared by the American Law Institute (ALI). The ALI is a nonprofit membership association whose approximately 2,000 members are selected on the basis of professional standing. They include judges, legal academicians, and lawyers in private practice, in government, and in law departments of business enterprises. The ALI, which was founded in 1923, is not affiliated with the United States Government.

The Restatement (Third) consists of four parts: Introductory Notes, rules of law presented in numbered sections, Comments, and Reporters' Notes. The Introductory Notes, rules of law, and Comments express the views of the ALI. The Reporters' Notes represent the views of the reporters only. According to the Introduction to the Restatement (Third), the Foreign Relations Law of the United States contained in the Restatement "consists of (a) international law as it applies to the United States and (b) domestic law that has substantial significance for the foreign relations of the United States or has substantial international consequences. . . . Unless otherwise indicated, normative statements . . . set forth rules or principles of international law that apply to states generally, including the United States." The Introduction also explains that "this Restatement represents the opinion of [the ALI] as to the rules that an impartial tribunal would apply if charged with deciding a controversy in accordance with international law." Restatement (Third), at 3, 4.

The Restatement (Third) contains a part on Law of the Environment—the first time there has been such a part. The Introduction and two sections from that part are reproduced immediately below. The remaining two sections (603 & 604) are reproduced *infra* at 354.

Copyright 1987 by The American Law Institute. Reprinted with permission of The American Law Institute.

RESTATEMENT (THIRD) OF THE FOREIGN RELATIONS LAW OF THE UNITED STATES

PART VI THE LAW OF THE ENVIRONMENT

Introductory Note
Section

Introductory Note:
Since the Second World War, the growth of population, the spread of industrialization, and the increase in automobile, air, and maritime traffic have led to a great increase in pollution of land, air, and water. It soon became obvious that unilateral action by states to control pollution was not sufficient, and that international co-operation and regulation to protect the environment were necessary. Strong impetus to the development of international environmental law was given by the Conference on the Human Environment, held in Stockholm in 1972. That Conference adopted the Stockholm Declaration on the Human Environment and an Action Plan. It also made proposals that led the General Assembly of the United Nations to establish a United Nations Environment Program. See § 601, Reporters' Note 1 and § 602, Reporters' Note 1.

This Part addresses primarily transfrontier and marine pollution. Transfrontier pollution occurs when activities in one state cause significant injury in another (usually neighboring) state, by deleterious effect on that state's ecosystem, its air, land, or water, on the health of its inhabitants, or on its living resources. Marine pollution is the introduction into the marine environment of substances that have or are likely to have deleterious effect on the coasts and coastal waters of states or on marine areas beyond the jurisdiction of any state. International environmental law addresses also pollution of the "global commons," *i.e.*, areas over which no state has jurisdiction or control but which are of common interest to all states—outer space, Antarctica, ice floes, and unoccupied islands.

Environmental harm may be caused by activities other than pollution: a dam may cause erosion, or irrigation may increase the salinity of a river. Other environmental problems of international concern include the need to improve habitat and human settlements; to protect archeologic treasures, cultural monuments, nature sanctuaries, endangered fauna and flora, and migratory birds; to lessen the consequences of deforestation, overfishing, and weather modification. Where activities in one state cause environmental injuries in another state, the principles of this Part generally apply.

Sources of environmental law. The principles discussed in this Part are rooted in customary international law. They originated in rules relating to the responsibility of a state for injuries caused to another state or to its property, or to persons within another state's territory or their property. The International Court of Justice has noted that one of the "general and well-recognized principles" of international law is "every State's obligation not to allow knowingly its territory to be used for acts contrary to the rights of other States."[1] The United Nations Survey of International Law concluded that "[t]here has been general recognition of the rule that a State must not permit the use of its territory for purposes injurious to the interests of other States in a manner contrary to international law."[2]

Judge Lauterpacht has said that "[a] State is bound to prevent such use of its territory as, having regard to the circumstances, is unduly injurious to the inhabitants of the neighboring State."[3] He added that the maxim *sic utere tuo ut alienum non laedas* (use your own property so as not to injure the property of another) is applicable to relations of states not less than those of individuals; it is one of those general principles of law applicable under Article 38(1)(c) of the Statute of the International Court of Justice.[4]

This general principle has been applied, in particular, to international rivers. As early as 1911, the Institute of International Law expressed the opinion that where a river forms the boundary of two states, neither state may, "on its own territory, utilize or allow the utilization of the water in such a way as seriously to interfere with its utilization by the other State or by individuals, corporations, etc., thereof."[5] The United States stated similarly that "no State might claim to use the waters of an international river in such a way as to cause material injury to the interests of other States."[6]

In a decision applying the general principle to transfrontier air pollution, which has been frequently quoted by other courts and tribunals, a United States-Canadian tribunal, in the *Trail Smelter Arbitration*, concluded that, "under the principles of international law, as well as of the law of the United States, no State has the right to use or permit the use of its territory in such a manner as to cause injury by fumes in or to the territory of another or the properties or persons therein, when the case is of serious consequence and the injury is established by clear and convincing evidence."[7]

---

[1]Corfu Channel Case (Merits) (United Kingdom/Albania), [1949] I.C.J. Rep. 4, 22.

[2]U.N. Doc. A/CN.4/1/Rev.1 (U.N. Pub. 1948. V.1(1)), at 34 (1949).

[3]1 Oppenheim, International Law 291 (8th ed. by H. Lauterpacht, 1955).

[4]*Id.*, at 346-47.

[5]J. B. Scott, Resolutions of the Institute of International Law Dealing with the Law of Nations 169 (1916). Judge Lauterpacht also pointed out that a state is forbidden to make such use of a river that causes danger to a neighboring state or prevents it from making proper use of the flow of the river. *Supra*, n. 3, at 475.

[6]17 U.N. GAOR C. 6 (764th mtg.) at 158 (1962). See also United States notes to Canada and Mexico, [1978] Digest of U.S. Practice in Int'l L. 1116-17, 1121-22.

[7]Trail Smelter Case, 1941, 3 R. Int'l Arb. Awards 1905, 1965 (1949); 35 Am. J. Int'l L. 684, 716 (1941). See also § 601, Reporters' Note 1.

In recent years many international agreements have dealt with regional transfrontier pollution. Important guidelines on several aspects of such problems have been adopted, by consensus, by the Organization for Economic Co-operation and Development (OECD).[8]

Marine pollution. International law has established a special regime for marine pollution because of the interdependent character of ocean waters (and air) and the cumulative effect of acts of pollution. Any significant pollution of the marine environment, therefore, is of concern to all states. Any state may complain to the offending state or to an appropriate international agency against violation of generally accepted international rules and standards for the protection of the marine environment by another state or its nationals or ships. Remedies are available to a particular state when the pollution of the marine environment has caused injury to that state or to its nationals. See §§ 604 and 902.

With the rapid growth of maritime traffic after the Second World War, pollution from ships and harm to the marine environment from maritime accidents, particularly those involving large oil tankers, reached alarming proportions. Waste dumped into the sea by ever-growing coastal cities, release of toxic substances including radioactive materials, and spills from oil wells on the continental shelf added greatly to marine pollution.

The 1958 Convention on the High Seas requires states to "draw up regulations to prevent pollution of the seas by the discharge of oil from ships or pipelines or resulting from the exploitation and exploration of the seabed and its subsoil" (Article 24). Every state was also obligated to "take measures to prevent pollution of the seas by the dumping of radioactive waste," and to co-operate with the competent international organizations in preventing pollution of the seas and air space above by "any activities with radioactive materials or other harmful agents" (Article 25).[9]

The 1982 Convention on the Law of the Sea (discussed in Part V) includes provisions for the protection of the marine environment against pollution not only by ships or other activities in the sea, but also from land-based sources or from or through the atmosphere. LOS Convention, Part XII, Articles 192-237. Disputes relating to these provisions are made subject to a compulsory dispute settlement procedure. See, in particular, Article 297(1)(c). The Convention also increases the powers of coastal states, particularly port states, to enforce pollution rules and standards against vessels of foreign states. See § 604. Most of the provisions of the Convention concerning the protection of the marine environment reflect customary international law. See Introductory Note to Part V. The dispute settlement provisions, however, are not customary law and will not bind the United States nor will the United States be able to invoke them unless it becoms a party to the Convention.

---

[8]See, *e.g.,* OECD, Non-Discrimination in Relation to Transfrontier Pollution: Leading OECD Documents 8, 32, 49 (1978). See also the Canada-United States joint statement on transboundary air quality. [1979] Digest of U.S. Practice in Int'l L. 1612-15; the Canada-United States Memorandum of Intent Concerning Transboundary Air Pollution, 1980, 32 U.S.T. 2521, T.I.A.S. No. 9856 (expressing "common determination to combat transboundary air pollution in keeping with their existing international rights, obligations, commitments and co-operative practices, including those set forth in the 1909 Boundary Waters Treaty, the 1972 Stockholm Declaration on Human Environment," and in other agreements); and the Mexico-United States Agreement to Co-operate in the Solution of Environmental Problems in the Border Area, 1983, 22 Int'l Leg. Mat. 1025 (1983) (undertaking, "to the fullest extent practical, to adopt the appropriate measures to prevent, reduce and eliminate sources of pollution in their respective territory which affect the border area of the other," the border area being defined for this purpose as "the area situated 100 kilometers on either side of the inland and maritime boundaries" between the parties).

[9]13 U.S.T. 2312, T.I.A.S. No. 5200, 450 U.N.T.S. 82. (As of 1987, this convention was in force for 57 states, including the United States.)

In addition to the provisions in the Law of the Sea Convention, there are numerous international conventions on the protection of the marine environment, both global and regional (see § 603, Reporters' Notes 2-5, and § 604, Reporters' Note 1), and several bilateral agreements (see § 604, Reporters' Note 1).

United States law. International aspects of environmental problems, especially of marine pollution, have been the subject of United States legislation. See, *e.g.*, the Acts relating, respectively, to National Environmental Policy, Clean Air, Federal Water Pollution Control, Toxic Substances Control, Oil Pollution, Ocean Dumping, Deepwater Ports, Rivers and Harbors, Coastal Zone Management, Outer Continental Shelf Lands, Submerged Lands, Fishery Conservation and Management, Deep Seabed Hard Mineral Resources, Resources Conservation and Recovery, Marine Mammals, Endangered Species, and Marine Sanctuaries. See § 601, Reporters' Note 8, and § 603, Reporters' Note 7.

§ 601. State Obligations with Respect to Environment of Other States and the Common Environment

(1) A state is obligated to take such measures as may be necessary, to the extent practicable under the circumstances, to ensure that activities within its jurisdiction or control

    (a) conform to generally accepted international rules and standards for the prevention, reduction, and control of injury to the environment of another state or of areas beyond the limits of national jurisdiction; and

    (b) are conducted so as not to cause significant injury to the environment of another state or of areas beyond the limits of national jurisdiction.

(2) A state is responsible to all other states

    (a) for any violation of its obligations under Subsection (1)(a), and

    (b) for any significant injury, resulting from such violation, to the environment of areas beyond the limits of national jurisdiction.

(3) A state is responsible for any significant injury, resulting from a violation of its obligations under Subsection (1), to the environment of another state or to its property, or to persons or property within that state's territory or under its jurisdiction or control.

Comment:

a. Application of general principles of state responsibility. This Part applies to environmental questions the general principles of international law relating to the responsibility of states for injury to another state or its property or to persons within its territory or their property, or for injury to interests common to all states. A state is responsible under Subsections (2) and (3) for breach of any of its obligations under Subsection (1). It is responsible under Subsection (2) to all states, and any state may request that it abate a threat of pollution and make arrangements to prevent future violations. Under Subsection (3), it is responsible to an injured state for any significant injury and is required to make reparation for the injury. The conditions of responsibility and the remedies available may differ with the circumstances and with the interests affected. See Comment *d* and § 602; see also the general principles in § 711 and §§ 901-902.

b. "Generally accepted international rules and standards." This phrase is adopted from the law of the sea; see § 502, Comment *c*. The obligation under Subsection (1)(a) refers to both general rules of customary international law (see, *e.g.*, the *Trail Smelter* case, Reporters' Note 1) and those derived from international conventions, and from standards adopted by international organizations pursuant to such conventions, that deal with a specific subject, such as oil pollution or radioactive wastes. See Reporters' Notes 3-7 and § 603, Reporters' Notes 4 and 5; see also § 102, Comments *f* and *g*, and § 103, Comment *c*. A state is also obligated to comply with an environmental rule or standard that has been accepted by both it and an injured state, even if that rule or standard has not been generally accepted.

Where an international rule or standard has been violated, any state can object to the violation; where a state has been injured in consequence of such violation, it is entitled to damages or other appropriate relief from the responsible state; where there is a threat of injury, the threatened state, or any state acting on behalf of threatened common interests, is entitled to have the dangerous activity terminated. See § 602.

c. *"Activities within its jurisdiction" and "significant injury."* An activity is considered to be within a state's jurisdiction under this section if the state may exercise jurisdiction to prescribe law with respect to that activity under §§ 402-403. The phrase "activities within its jurisdiction or control" includes activities in a state's territory, on the coastal waters that are under its jurisdiction, Part V, as well as activities on ships flying its flag or on installations on the high seas operating under its authority. See § 502(1)(b) and Comment *c* thereto, § 514, Comment *i* and § 521, Comment *c*. International law does not address internal pollution, but a state is responsible under this section if pollution within its jurisdiction causes significant injuries beyond its borders. "Significant injury" is not defined but references to "significant" impact on the environment are common in both international law and United States law. The word "significant" excludes minor incidents causing minimal damage. In special circumstances, the significance of injury to another state is balanced against the importance of the activity to the state causing the injury. See Reporters' Note 3.

d. *Conditions of responsibility.* A state is responsible under Subsections (2) and (3) for both its own activities and those of individuals or private or public corporations under its jurisdiction. The state may be responsible, for instance, for not enacting necessary legislation, for not enforcing its laws against persons acting in its territory or against its vessels, or for not preventing or terminating an illegal activity, or for not punishing the person responsible for it. In the case of ships flying its flags, a state is responsible for injury due to the state's own defaults under Subsection (1) but is not responsible for injury due to fault of the operators of the ship. In both cases, a state is responsible only if it has not taken "such measures as may be necessary" to comply with applicable international standards and to avoid causing injury outside its territory, as required by Subsection (1). In general, the applicable international rules and standards do not hold a state responsible when it has taken the necessary and practicable measures; some international agreements provide also for responsibility regardless of fault in case of a discharge of highly dangerous (radioactive, toxic, etc.) substances, or an abnormally dangerous activity (*e.g.*, launching of space satellites). See also the principles applicable to weather modification, Comment *f*. In all cases, however, some defenses may be available to the state; *e.g.*, that it had acted pursuant to a binding decision of the Security Council of the United Nations, or that injury was due to the failure of the injured state to exercise reasonable care to avoid the threatened harm. Compare Restatement, Second, Torts §§ 519, 520, and 524. A state is not responsible for injury due to a natural disaster such as an eruption of a volcano, unless such disaster was triggered or aggravated by a human act, such as nuclear explosion in a volcano's vicinity. But a state is responsible if after a natural disaster has occurred it does not take necessary and practicable steps to prevent or reduce injury to other states.

Under Subsections (2)(b) and (3), responsibility of a state for a significant injury entails payment of appropriate damages if the complaining state proves the existence of a causal link between an activity within the jurisdiction of the responsible state and the injury to the complaining state. Determination of responsibility raises special difficulties in cases of long-range pollution where the link between multiple activities in some distant states and the pollution in the injured state might be difficult to prove. Where more than one state contributes to the pollution causing significant injury, the liability will be apportioned among the states, taking into account, where appropriate, the contribution to the injury of the injured state itself.

A state is responsible under this section for environmental harm proximately caused by activity under its own jurisdiction, not for activity by another state. For instance, a state is not responsible under this section merely because it encourages activities in another state, such as plant eradication programs, that inflict environmental injury in that state or in a third state. Similarly, if a group of states imposes economic sanctions on state A depriving it of oil supplies and requiring state A to use coal, which results in an increase in air pollution in state B, the boycotting states are not responsible under principles of international environmental law for injury resulting to state B.

Although there has been no authoritative consideration of the issue, international environmental law has apparently not extended responsibility beyond the state directly responsible for the activities causing injury, under principles analogous to "product liability" which apply in some national legal systems. Thus, under this section, state A is responsible for a radioactive emission from a nuclear reactor operated in its territory that causes injury to state B, but there is no recognized responsibility to B by state C in which the defective reactor was manufactured or from which it was sold to state A. There may, however, be such responsibility pursuant to an international agreement between state A and state C, and in special circumstances under general principles of state responsibility. See, e.g., §§ 207, 711, and 901. Also, there may be liability by the manufacturer or seller of the defective reactor, whether it is a state or a private person, under principles of national law applicable to the transaction. Compare, for example, Restatement, Second, Torts §§ 388-408.

Under this section, a state is obligated to take all necessary precautionary measures where an activity is contemplated that poses a substantial risk of a significant transfrontier environmental injury; if the activity has already taken place, the state is obligated to take all necessary measures to prevent or reduce pollution beyond its borders. Similarly, where a violation of international environmental rules and standards has already occurred, the violating state is obligated to take promptly all necessary preventive or remedial measures, even if no injury has yet taken place.

For the remedies for breach of obligations under this section, see § 602.

e. Obligation to notify and consult. Under Subsection 1(a), a state has an obligation to warn another state promptly of any situation that may cause significant pollution damage in that state. A state has also an obligation to consult with another state if a proposed activity within its jurisdiction or control poses a substantial risk of significant injury to the environment of the other state, but it need not permit such consultations to delay the proposed activity unduly.

f. Weather modification. Weather modification programs are normally used either to prevent injuries to the environment (*e.g.*, by a storm) or to obtain some benefit (*e.g.*, by causing rain during a drought). A state's weather modification programs have sometimes caused injury to another state, *e.g.*, by bringing it excessive rain or by depriving it of rain, or, by changing the direction of a storm, causing injury to that state's ships at sea, to its shore, or to the marine environment. Under international law, a state engaged in weather modification activities is responsible for any significant injuries if causation can be proved, even if the injury was neither intended nor due to negligence, and even if the state took all necessary measures to prevent or reduce injury. Compare the rule as to abnormally dangerous activities. Comment *d*.

§ 602. Remedies for Violation of Environmental Obligations

(1) A state responsible to another state for violation of § 601 is subject to general interstate remedies (§ 902) to prevent, reduce, or terminate the activity threatening or causing the violation, and to pay reparation for injury caused.

(2) Where pollution originating in a state has caused significant injury to persons outside that state, or has created a significant risk of such injury, the state of origin is obligated to accord to the person injured or exposed to such risk access to the same judicial or administrative remedies as are available in similar circumstances to persons within the state.

Comment:

a. International law remedies. The remedies referred to in Subsection (1) usually begin with a protest against the violation, accompanied by a demand that the offending state terminate the violation, desist from further violations, and make reparation for past violations. If the matter is not resolved by diplomatic negotiations, the aggrieved state may resort to agreed third-party procedures, such as conciliation, mediation, arbitration, or adjudication. Some neighboring states have established international joint commissions to deal with transboundary problems, including pollution, but usually such commissions can only make recommendations. Strictly limited and reasonable measures of ''self help'' may be permitted in special circumstances. See § 905. Remedies under international law are to the injured state; whether that state is obligated to pay any reparation received over to any injured person in its territory is a matter of its domestic law. See § 902, Comments *i* and *l*.

Remedies under this section are available for injury to a state's environmental interests within its territory as well as to interests beyond its territory, such as injury to its fishing interests on the high seas; it may pursue remedies, not only for injury to state interests but also to those of its political subdivisions or of its inhabitants or nationals. A state may also pursue appropriate remedies for injury to the common interest in the global commons, such as the high seas.

Even where reparations for past injuries are not appropriate or feasible, a state may demand that violations be discontinued.

b. Local remedies. A state responsible for transfrontier pollution can fulfill its obligation to inhabitants of other states who suffered injuries by giving them access to its tribunals for adjudication of their claims. If such local remedies are available, the person who suffered injuries must exhaust these remedies before the state of which he is a national can bring an international claim on his behalf under Subsection (1). See § 703, Comment *d*; § 713, Comments *b* and *f*; § 902, Comment *k*. The two states, however, may agree at any time to settle the claim or include it in a lump-sum settlement. See § 902, Comment *i*.

Subsection (2) applies the principle of non-discrimination against foreign nationals (§ 711, Comment *f*). This principle requires that a state in which pollution originates avoid discrimination in the enforcement of applicable international rules and standards, as well as give to foreign victims the benefit of its own rules and standards for the protection of the environment, even if they are stricter than the international rules or standards. Subsection (2) applies the principle of nondiscrimination also to remedies. A state must provide the same procedures, and apply the same substantive law and the same measures of compensation, to persons outside its territory as are available to persons injured within its territory. Thus, a state applying the "polluter-pays" principle should apply it to all pollution originating within the state, whether it causes injury at home or abroad. If a state applies the principle of strict liability, a victim of transfrontier pollution will be entitled to the benefit of that principle. On the other hand, if the state makes liability conditional on fault or negligence, the foreign victim can be required to meet that condition even if in the place of injury fault or negligence is not a necessary element for liability. Similarly, if a state's law imposes an obligation to reduce pollution to the lowest level that is attainable by the application of the most advanced technology that is economically feasible, this requirement applies equally to pollution at home and abroad.

When environmental injury in one state results from private activity in another state, a remedy may sometimes be available in the courts of the victim state, or even of a third state, and if the victim has received satisfaction by such a remedy the interstate remedy would abate.

c. Availability of private remedies under state law. Under the law of many states, pollution damage is considered a local tort; suit for damages lies only in the state where the injury occurred, not in the state where the pollution originated. If personal jurisdiction over the person responsible for the pollution can be obtained in the state where the injury occurred, a suit for compensation or for an injunction would lie, but such suit might not be possible if the alleged polluter has no business or property in that state. Even if a suit there is brought under a long-arm statute and results in a default judgment, the judgment might not be enforceable in the polluter's home state. See § 421(2)(j) and § 481, Reporters' Note 4.

UNITED NATIONS EDUCATIONAL, SCIENTIFIC AND CULTURAL ORGANIZATION CONVENTION FOR THE PROTECTION OF THE WORLD CULTURAL AND NATURAL HERITAGE.
Infra, p. 554.

B. AFRICA

AFRICAN CONVENTION ON THE CONSERVATION OF NATURE AND NATURAL RESOURCES

Popular Name: African Conservation Convention

Done at Algiers on 15 September 1968, 1001 UNTS 3, OAU CM/232, *reprinted in* UNEP3 #37, p.207, 5 IPE 2037, IELMT 968: 68.
Entry into Force: 16 June 1969

Depositary: Organization of African Unity

Languages: English, French

Parties as of October 1990: Algeria; Burkina Faso; Cameroon; Central African
    Republic; Congo; Côte d'Ivoire; Djibouti; Egypt; Gabon; Ghana; Kenya; Liberia;
    Madagascar; Malawi; Mali; Morocco; Mozambique; Niger; Nigeria; Rwanda;
    Senegal; Seychelles; Sudan; Swaziland; Tanzania, United Republic of; Togo;
    Tunisia; Uganda; Zaire; Zambia
Literature: S. Lyster, *International Wildlife Law* 112 (1985)

Editors' Note

Africa's wildlife has been the subject of conservation agreements since 1900.
In that year, African colonial powers—France, Germany, Great Britain, Italy,
Portugal, and Spain—signed the Convention for the Preservation of Wild Animals,
Birds and Fish in Africa, 19 May 1900, 94 *Brit. and Foreign St. Papers* 715. That
treaty was superseded in 1936 by the 1933 Convention Relative to the Preservation
of Fauna and Flora in Their Natural State, 18 November 1933, 172 LNTS 241.
The latter treaty emphasized creating protected areas; it continued the basic thrust
of the 1900 treaty, i.e., to protect species of economic or trophy value, but it did
not contain the 1900 treaty's directive to reduce populations of certain species
considered harmful.

The 1933 treaty in turn was superseded by the African Conservation Convention, which contains a more comprehensive conservation approach that includes
soil and water. This Convention obligates member States to adopt "the measures
necessary to ensure the conservation, utilization and development of soil, water,
flora and faunal resources in accordance with scientific principles and with due
regard to the best interests of the people" (art. II), to give "special protection" to
endangered species (listed in an Annex) and to their habitat (art. VII(1)), and to
ensure that ecological factors are given full consideration in formulating development plans (art. XIV). Exceptions are allowed (art. XVII), and various qualifiers,
e.g., "the best interests of the people" (art. II) and "national interest" (art. X)
may affect the strictness of the obligations. An unusual feature is that any party
may submit a dispute regarding the interpretation or application of the Convention
to the Organization of African Unity (OAU) (art. XVIII).

AFRICAN CONVENTION ON THE CONSERVATION OF NATURE AND NATURAL RESOURCES

PREAMBLE

We, the Heads of State and Government of Independent African States,

Fully conscious that soil, water, flora and faunal resources constitute a capital
of vital importance to mankind;

Confirming, as we accepted upon declaring our adherence to the Charter of
the Organization of African Unity, that we know that it is our duty "to harness the
natural and human resources of our continent for the total advancement of our
peoples in spheres of human endeavour";

Fully conscious of the ever-growing importance of natural resources from an economic, nutritional, scientific, educational, cultural and aesthetic point of view;

Conscious of the dangers which threaten some of these irreplaceable assets;

Accepting that the utilization of the natural resources must aim at satisfying the needs of man according to the carrying capacity of the environment;

Desirous of undertaking individual and joint action for the conservation, utilization and development of these assets by establishing and maintaining their rational utilization for the present and future welfare of mankind;

Convinced that one of the most appropriate means of achieving this end is to bring into force a convention;

Have agreed as follows:

Article 1

The Contracting States hereby establish an African Convention on the Conservation of nature and natural resources.

Article II. FUNDAMENTAL PRINCIPLE

The Contracting States shall undertake to adopt the measures necessary to ensure conservation, utilization and development of soil, water, flora and faunal resources in accordance with scientific principles and with due regard to the best interests of the people.

Article III. DEFINITIONS

For purposes of the present Convention, the meaning of the following expressions shall be as defined below:

1. "Natural Resources" means renewable resources, that is soil, water, flora and fauna.

2. "Specimen" means an individual example of a species of wild animal or wild plant or part of a wild plant.

3. "Trophy" means any dead animal specimen or part thereof whether included in a manufactured or processed object or otherwise dealt with, unless it has lost its original identity; also nests eggs and eggshells.

4. "Conservation area" means any protected natural resource area, whether it be a strict natural reserve, a national park or a special reserve;

a) "strict nature reserve" means an area:

    1) under State control and the boundaries of which may not be altered nor any portion alienated except by the competent legislative authority,

    2) throughout which any form of hunting or fishing, any undertaking connected with forestry, agriculture or mining, any grazing, any excavation or prospecting, drilling, levelling of the ground or construction, any work tending to alter the configuration of the soil or the character of the vegetation, any water pollution and, generally, any act likely to harm or disturb the fauna or flora, including introduction of zoological or botanical species, whether indigenous or imported, wild or domesticated, are strictly forbidden,

    3) where it shall be forbidden to reside, enter, traverse or camp, and where it shall be forbidden to fly over at low altitude, without a special written permit from the competent authority, and in which scientific investigations (including removal of animals and plants in order to maintain an ecosystem) may only be undertaken by permission of the competent authority;

b) "national park" means an area:
   1) under State control and the boundaries of which may not be altered or any portion alienated except by the competent legislative authority,
   2) exclusively set aside for the propagation, protection, conservation and management of vegetation and wild animals as well as for the protection of sites, land-scapes or geological formations of particular scientific or aesthetic value, for the benefit and enjoyment of the general public, and
   3) in which the killing, hunting and capture of animals and the destruction or collection of plants are prohibited except for scientific and management purposes and on the condition that such measures are taken under the direction or control of the competent authority,
   4) covering any aquatic environment to which all of the provisions of section (*b*) (1-3) above are applicable.

The activities prohibited in strict nature reserve under the provisions of section (*a*) (2) of paragraph (4) of this article are equally prohibited in national parks except in so far as they are necessary to enable the park authorities to implement the provisions of section (2) of this paragraph, by applying, for example, appropriate management practices, and to enable the public to visit these parks; however, sport fishing may be practiced with the authorization and under the control of the competent authority.

c) "special reserve" means other protected areas such as:
   1) "game reserve" which shall denote an area
      a)   set aside for the conservation, management and propagation of wild animal life and the protection and management of its habitat,
      b)   within which the hunting, killing or capture of fauna shall be prohibited except by or under the direction or control of the reserve authorities,
      c)   where settlement and other human activities shall be controlled or prohibited;
   2) "partial reserve" or "sanctuary" which shall denote an area
      a)   set aside to protect characteristic wildlife and especially bird communities, or to protect particularly threatened animal or plant species and especially those listed in the Annex to this Convention, together with the biotopes essential for their survival,
      b)   in which all other interests and activities shall be subordinated to this end;
   3) "soil", "water" or "forest" reserve shall denote areas set aside to protect such resources.

Article IV. Soil

The Contracting States shall take effective measures for conservation and improvement of the soil and shall in particular combat erosion and misuse of the soil. To this end:
a)   they shall establish land-use plans based on scientific investigations (ecological, pedological, economic, and sociological) and, in particular, classification of land-use capability;
b)   they shall, when implementing agricultural practices and agrarian reforms,
   1) improve soil-conservation and introduce improved farming methods, which ensure long-term productivity of the land,
   2) control erosion caused by various forms of land-use which may lead to loss of vegetation cover.

Article V. WATER

1. The Contracting States shall establish policies for conservation, utilization and development of underground and surface water, and shall endeavour to guarantee for their populations a sufficient and continuous supply of suitable water, taking appropriate measures with due regard to
1) the study of water cycles and the investigation of each catchment area,
2) the co-ordination and planning of water resources development projects,
3) the administration and control of all water utilization, and
4) prevention and control of water pollution.

2. Where surface or underground water resources are shared by two or more of the Contracting States, the latter shall act in consultation, and if the need arises, set up inter-State Commissions to study and resolve problems arising from the joint use of these resources, and for the joint development and conservation thereof.

Article VI. FLORA

1. The Contracting States shall take all necessary measures for the protection of flora and to ensure its best utilization and development. To this end the Contracting States shall:

a) adopt scientifically-based conservation, utilization and management plans of forests and rangeland, taking into account the social and economic needs of the States concerned, the importance of the vegetation cover for the maintenance of the water balance of an area, the productivity of soils and the habitat requirements of the fauna;

b) observe section (*a*) above by paying particular attention to controlling bush fires, forest exploitation, land clearing for cultivation, and over-grazing by domestic and wild animals;

c) set aside areas for forest reserves and carry out afforestation programmes where necessary;

d) limitation of forest grazing to season and intensities that will not prevent forest regeneration; and

e) establish botanical gardens to perpetuate plant species of particular interest.

2. The Contracting States also shall undertake the conservation of plant species or communities, which are threatened and/or of special scientific or aesthetic value by ensuring that they are included in conservation areas.

Article VII. FAUNAL RESOURCES

1. The Contracting States shall ensure conservation, wise use and development of faunal resources and their environment, within the framework of land-use planning and of economic and social development. Management shall be carried out in accordance with plans based on scientific principles, and to that end the Contracting States shall:

a) manage wildlife populations inside designated areas according to the objectives of such areas and also manage exploitable wildlife populations outside such areas for an optimum sustained yield, compatible with and complementary to other land uses; and

b) manage aquatic environments, whether in fresh, brackish or coastal water, with a view to minimize deleterious effects of any water and land use practice which might adversely affect aquatic habitats.

2. The Contracting States shall adopt adequate legislation on hunting, capture and fishing, under which:

a) the issue of permits is properly regulated;

b) unauthorized methods are prohibited;

c) The following methods of hunting, capture and fishing are prohibited:
1) any methods liable to cause a mass destruction of wild animals,
2) the use of drugs, poisons, poisoned weapons or poisoned baits,
3) the use of explosives,
4) the following methods of hunting and capture are particularly prohibited:
   1. the use of mechanically propelled vehicles,
   2. the use of fire,
   3. the use of fire arms capable of firing more than one round at each pull of the trigger,
   4. hunting or capture at night,
   5. the use of missiles containing detonators;
d) the following methods of hunting or capture are as far as possible prohibited:
1) the use of nets and stockades,
2) the use of concealed traps, pits, snares, set-gun traps, deadfalls, and hunting from a blind or hide;
e) with a view to as rational use as possible of game meat the abandonment by hunters of carcasses of animals, which represent a food resource, is prohibited.

Capture of animals with the aid of drugs or mechanically-propelled vehicles, or hunting or capture by night if carried out by, or under the control of, the competent authority shall nevertheless be exempted from the prohibitions under (*c*) above.

Article VIII. PROTECTED SPECIES

1. The Contracting States recognize that it is important and urgent to accord a special protection to those animal and plant species that are threatened with extinction, or which may become so, and to the habitat necessary to their survival. Where such a species is represented only in the territory of one Contracting State, that State has a particular responsibility for its protection. These species which are, or may be listed, according to the degree of protection that shall be given to them are placed in Class A or B of the annex to this Convention, and shall be protected by Contracting States as follows:

1) species in Class A shall be totally protected throughout the entire territory of the Contracting States; the hunting, killing, capture or collection of specimens shall be permitted only on the authorization in each case of the highest competent authority and only if required in the national interest or for scientific purposes; and

2) species in Class B shall be totally protected, but may be hunted, killed, captured or collected under special authorization granted by the competent authority.

2. The competent authority of each Contracting State shall examine the necessity of applying the provisions of this article to species not listed in the annex, in order to conserve the indigenous flora and fauna of their respective countries. Such additional species shall be placed in Class A or B by the State concerned, according to its specific requirements.

Article IX. TRAFFIC IN SPECIMENS AND TROPHIES

1. In the case of animal species to which Article VIII does not apply the Contracting States shall:
a) regulate trade in and transport of specimens and trophies;
b) control the application of these regulations in such a way as to prevent trade in specimens and trophies which have been illegally captured or killed or obtained.

2. In the case of plant and animal species to which Article VIII, paragraph (1), applies, the Contracting States shall:

a) take all measures similar to those in paragraph (1);

b) make the export of such specimens and trophies subject to an authorization:
  1) additional to that required for their capture, killing or collection by Article VIII
  2) which indicates their destination,
  3) which shall not be given unless the specimens or trophies have been obtained legally,
  4) which shall be examined prior to exportation;
  5) which shall be on a standard form, as may be arranged under Article XVI;

c) make the import and transit of such specimens and trophies subject to the presentation of the authorization required under section (*b*) above, with due provision for the confiscation of specimens and trophies exported illegally, without prejudice to the application of other penalties.

Article X. CONSERVATION AREAS

1. The Contracting States shall maintain and extend where appropriate, within their territory and where applicable in their territorial waters, the conservation areas existing at the time of entry into force of the present Convention and, preferably within the framework of land-use planning programmes, assess the necessity of establishing additional conservation areas in order to:

1) protect those ecosystems which are most representative of and particularly those which are in any respect peculiar to their territories;
2) ensure conservation of all species and more particularly of those listed or may be listed in the annex to this Convention;

2. The Contracting States shall establish where necessary, around the borders of conservation areas, zones within which the competent authorities shall control activities detrimental to the protected natural resources.

Article XI. CUSTOMARY RIGHTS

The Contracting States shall take all necessary legislative measures to reconcile customary rights with the provisions of this Convention.

Article XII. RESEARCH

The Contracting States shall encourage and promote research in conservation, utilization and management of natural resources and shall pay particular attention to ecological and sociological factors.

Article XIII. CONSERVATION EDUCATION

1. *a)* The Contracting States shall ensure that their peoples appreciate their close dependence on natural resources and that they understand the need, and rules for, the rational utilization of these resources.

b) For this purpose they shall ensure that the principles indicated in paragraph (1):

1) are included in educational programmes at all levels,
2) form the object of information campaigns capable of acquainting the public with, and winning it over to, the idea of conservation.

2. In order to put into effect paragraph (1) above, the Contracting States shall make maximum use of the educational value of conservation areas.

Article XIV. DEVOLOPMENT PLANS

1. The Contracting States shall ensure that conservation and management of natural resources are treated as an integral part of national and/or regional development plans.

2. In the formulation of all development plans, full consideration shall be given to ecological, as well as to economic and social factors.

3. Where any development plan is likely to affect the natural resources of another State, the latter shall be consulted.

Article XV. ORGANIZATION OF NATIONAL CONSERVATION SERVICES

Each Contracting State shall establish, if it has not already done so, a single agency empowered to deal with all matters covered by this Convention, but, where this is not possible a co-ordinating machinery shall be established for this purpose.

Article XVI. INTER-STATE CO-OPERATION

1. The Contracting States shall co-operate:
a)   whenever such co-operation is necessary to give effect to the provisions of this Convention, and
b)   whenever any national measure is likely to affect the natural resources of any other State.

2. The Contracting States shall supply the Organization of African Unity with:
a)   the text of laws, decrees, regulations and instructions in force in their territories, which are intended to ensure the implementation of this Convention,
b)   reports on the results achieved in applying the provisions of this Convention, and
c)   all the information necessary for the complete documentation of matters dealt with by this Convention if requested.

3. If so requested by Contracting States, the Organization of African Unity shall organize any meeting which may be necessary to dispose of any matters covered by this Convention. Requests for such meetings must be made by at least three of the Contracting States and be approved by two thirds of the States which it is proposed should participate in such meetings.

4. Any expenditure arising from this Convention, which devolves upon the Organization of African Unity shall be included in its regular budget, unless shared by the Contracting States or otherwise defrayed.

Article XVII. PROVISIONS FOR EXCEPTIONS

1. The provisions of this Convention shall not affect the responsibilities of Contracting States concerning:
1) the paramount interest of the State,
2) "force majeure",
3) defence of human life.

2. The provisions of this Convention shall not prevent Contracting States:
1) in time of famine,
2) for the protection of public health,
3) in defence of property,
to enact measures contrary to the provisions of the Convention, provided their application is precisely defined in respect of aim, time and place.

Article XVIII. SETTLEMENT OF DISPUTES

Any dispute between the Contracting States relating to the interpretation or application of this Convention, which cannot be settled by negotiation, shall at the request of any party be submitted to the Commission of Mediation, Conciliation and Arbitration of the Organization of African Unity.

CONSTITUTION OF THE REPUBLIC OF NAMIBIA

Popular Name: Namibian Constitution

Namibia Constitution, 21 March 1990, U.N. Doc. S/20967/Add.2.

Language: English (because this is a U.N. Security Council document, unofficial versions exist in Arabic, Chinese, French, Russian, and Spanish).

Editors' Note

The Constitution of the Republic of Namibia was formulated by a Constituent Assembly elected in November 1989 in UN-supervised elections conducted in South West Africa/Namibia. Working on the basis of a draft submitted by the majority party, the South West Africa People's Organization (SWAPO), the Constitution was adopted on 9 February 1990, was signed by all members of the Assembly on 16 March, and entered into force on the Day of Independence, 21 March 1990.

The environmental provisions of the Constitution (which are reproduced below) had their origin in the SWAPO draft. They were considerably strengthened, however, first in closed-door negotiations in the Standing Committee on Standing Rules and Orders and Internal Arrangements and then in the course of a public debate in the Assembly, acting there on the proposal of the Minister-Designate for Wildlife, Conservation and Tourism.

CONSTITUTION OF THE REPUBLIC OF NAMIBIA

* * *

CHAPTER 10
The Ombudsman

Article 91 Functions
The functions of the Ombudsman shall be defined and prescribed by an Act of Parliament and shall include the following:

. . .
(c) the duty to investigate complaints concerning the over-utilization of living natural resources, the irrational exploitation of non-renewable resources, the degradation and destruction of ecosystems and failure to protect the beauty and character of Namibia;

CHAPTER 11
Principles of State Policy

Article 95 Promotion of the Welfare of the People
The State shall actively promote and maintain the welfare of the people by adopting, *inter alia*, policies aimed at the following:

. . .

(1) maintenance of ecosystems, essential ecological processes and biological diversity of Namibia and utilization of living natural resources on a sustainable basis for the benefit of all Namibians, both present and future; in particular, the Government shall provide measures against the dumping or recycling of foreign nuclear and toxic waste on Namibian territory.

* * *

C. AMERICAS

WASHINGTON CONVENTION ON NATURE PROTECTION AND WILDLIFE PRESERVATION IN THE WESTERN HEMISPHERE

Popular Name: Western Hemisphere Conservation Convention

Done at Washington on 12 October 1940, 161 UNTS 193, 56 Stat. 1354, TS 981,

3 Bevans 630, *reprinted in* UNEP3 #2, p.64, 4 IPE 1729, IELMT 940: 76.
Entry into Force: 30 April 1942

Depositary: Organization of American States (OAS)

Languages: English, French, Portuguese, Spanish

Parties as of 1 January 1990: Argentina*; Brazil; Chile; Costa Rica; Dominican Republic; Ecuador; El Salvador; Guatemala; Haiti; Mexico; Nicaragua; Panama; Paraguay; Peru; Suriname; Trinidad and Tobago; United States of America; Uruguay; Venezuela
Literature: S. Lyster, *International Wildlife Law* 97 (1985)

Editors' Note

This Convention represents the earliest example of a convention that is designed to provide comprehensive protection of biological resources. It was negotiated under the auspices of the Pan American Union, the predecessor to the Organization of American States.

The Convention provides for regulating the international trade in wildlife, for establishing protected areas as a means to conserve habitats, for protecting migratory birds, and for international cooperation, particularly in scientific research. The controls on international trade in endangered species are comparable to those of the Convention on International Trade in Endangered Species (CITES); however, some countries that are parties to the Western Hemisphere Convention do not belong to CITES. While the approaches in the Convention were visionary for their time, they

---

*With reservation

have had limited effect because the Convention does not provide for a secretariat or for a means to review parties' implementation of the Convention or to enforce it.

In the late 1980s the Organization of American States expressed renewed interest in the Convention and in exploring ways to enhance its usefulness.

CONVENTION ON NATURE PROTECTION AND WILD LIFE PRESERVATION IN THE WESTERN HEMISPHERE

PREAMBLE

The Governments of the American Republics, wishing to protect and preserve in their natural habitat representatives of all species and genera of their native flora and fauna, including migratory birds, in sufficient numbers and over areas extensive enough to assure them from becoming extinct through any agency within man's control; and

Wishing to protect and preserve scenery of extraordinary beauty, unusual and striking geologic formations, regions and natural objects of aesthetic, historic or scientific value, and areas characterized by primitive conditions in those cases covered by this Convention; and

Wishing to conclude a convention on the protection of nature and the preservation of flora and fauna to effectuate the foregoing purposes, have agreed upon the following Articles:

Article I

DESCRIPTION OF TERMS USED IN THE WORDING OF THIS CONVENTION

1. The expression NATIONAL PARKS shall denote:

Areas established for the protection and preservation of superlative scenery, flora and fauna of national significance which the general public may enjoy and from which it may benefit when placed under public control.

2. The expression NATIONAL RESERVES shall denote:

Regions established for conservation and utilization of natural resources under government control, on which protection of animal and plant life will be afforded in so far as this may be consistent with the primary purpose of such reserves.

3. The expression NATURE MONUMENTS shall denote:

Regions, objects, or living species of flora or fauna of aesthetic, historic or scientific interest to which strict protection is given. The purpose of nature monuments is the protection of a specific object, or a species of flora or fauna, by setting aside an area, an object, or a single species, as an inviolate nature monument, except for duly authorized scientific investigations or government inspection.

4. The expression STRICT WILDERNESS RESERVES shall denote:

A region under public control characterized by primitive conditions of flora, fauna, transportation and habitation wherein there is no provision for the passage of motorized transportation and all commercial developments are excluded.

5. The expression MIGRATORY BIRDS shall denote:

Birds of those species, all or some of whose individual members, may at any season cross any of the boundaries between the American countries. Some of the species of the following families are examples of birds characterized as migratory: Charadriidae, Scolopacidae, Caprimulgidae, Hirundinidae.

Article II

1. The Contracting Governments will explore at once the possibility of establishing in their territories national parks, national reserves, nature monuments, and

strict wilderness reserves as defined in the preceding article. In all cases where such establishment is feasible, the creation thereof shall be begun as soon as possible after the effective date of the present Convention.

2. If in any country the establishment of national parks, national reserves, nature monuments, or strict wilderness reserves is found to be impractical at present, suitable areas, objects or living species of fauna or flora, as the case may be, shall be selected as early as possible to be transformed into national parks, national reserves, nature monuments or strict wilderness reserves as soon as, in the opinion of the authorities concerned, circumstances will permit.

3. The Contracting Governments shall notify the Pan American Union of the establishment of any national parks, national reserves, nature monuments, or strict wilderness reserves, and of the legislation, including the methods of administrative control, adopted in connection therewith.

Article III

The Contracting Governments agree that the boundaries of national parks shall not be altered, or any portion thereof be capable of alienation, except by the competent legislative authority. The resources of these reserves shall not be subject to exploitation for commercial profit.

The Contracting Governments agree to prohibit hunting, killing and capturing of members of the fauna and destruction or collection of representatives of the flora in national parks except by or under the direction or control of the park authorities, or for duly authorized scientific investigations.

The Contracting Governments further agree to provide facilities for public recreation and education in national parks consistent with the purposes of this Convention.

Article IV

The Contracting Governments agree to maintain the strict wilderness reserves inviolate, as far as practicable, except for duly authorized scientific investigations or government inspection, or such uses as are consistent with the purposes for which the area was established.

Article V

1. The Contracting Governments agree to adopt, or to propose such adoption to their respective appropriate law-making bodies, suitable laws and regulations for the protection and preservation of flora and fauna within their national boundaries, but not included in the national parks, national reserves, nature monuments, or strict wilderness reserves referred to in Article II hereof. Such regulations shall contain proper provisions for the taking of specimens of flora and fauna for scientific study and investigation by properly accredited individuals and agencies.

2. The Contracting Governments agree to adopt, or to recommend that their respective legislatures adopt, laws which will assure the protection and preservation of the natural scenery, striking geological formations, and regions and natural objects of aesthetic interest or historic or scientific value.

Article VI

The Contracting Governments agree to cooperate among themselves in promoting the objectives of the present Convention. To this end they will lend proper assistance, consistent with national laws, to scientists of the American Republics engaged in research and field study; they may, when circumstances warrant, enter into agreements with one another or with scientific institutions of the Americas in order to increase the effectiveness of this collaboration; and they shall make available to all the American Republics equally through publication or otherwise the scientific knowledge resulting from such cooperative effort.

Article VII

The Contracting Governments shall adopt appropriate measures for the protection of migratory birds of economic or aesthetic value or to prevent the threatened extinction of any given species. Adequate measures shall be adopted which will permit, in so far as the respective governments may see fit, a rational utilization of migratory birds for the purpose of sports as well as for food, commerce, and industry, and for scientific study and investigation.

Article VIII

The protection of the species mentioned in the Annex to the present Convention is declared to be of special urgency and importance. Species included therein shall be protected as completely as possible, and their hunting, killing, capturing, or taking, shall be allowed only with the permission of the appropriate government authorities in the country. Such permission shall be granted only under special circumstances, in order to further scientific purposes, or when essential for the administration of the area in which the animal or plant is found.

Article IX

Each Contracting Government shall take the necessary measures to control and regulate the importation, exportation and transit of protected fauna or flora or any part thereof by the following means:
1. The issuing of certificates authorizing the exportation or transit of protected species of flora or fauna, or parts thereof.
2. The prohibition of the importation of any species of fauna or flora or any part thereof protected by the country of origin unless accompanied by a certificate of lawful exportation as provided for in Paragraph 1 of this Article.

MEXICO-UNITED STATES OF AMERICA: AGREEMENT FOR COOPERATION ON ENVIRONMENTAL PROGRAMS AND TRANSBOUNDARY PROBLEMS, ANNEX III, TRANSBOUNDARY SHIPMENT OF HAZARDOUS WASTES AND HAZARDOUS SUBSTANCES. *Infra*, p. 621.

CANADA-UNITED STATES OF AMERICA: WASHINGTON TREATY RELATING TO BOUNDARY WATERS AND QUESTIONS ARISING ALONG THE BOUNDARY BETWEEN THE UNITED STATES AND CANADA. *Infra*, p. 412.

Editors' Introductory Note Regarding the Amazon Basin. *Infra*, p. 545.

BRASILIA TREATY FOR AMAZONIAN CO-OPERATION. *Infra*, p. 546.

AMAZON DECLARATION. *Infra*, p. 551.

D. ANTARCTICA

Editors' Introductory Note Regarding the Antarctic Treaty Regime. *Infra*, p. 514.

ANTARCTIC TREATY. *Infra*, p. 515.

CANBERRA CONVENTION ON THE CONSERVATION OF ANTARCTIC MARINE LIVING RESOURES. *Infra*, p. 520.

WELLINGTON CONVENTION ON THE REGULATION OF ANTARCTIC MINERAL RESOURCE ACTIVITIES. *Infra*, p. 529.

PROTOCOL ON ENVIRONMENTAL PROTECTION TO THE ANTARCTIC TREATY. *Infra, p. 536.*

E. ASIA

ASSOCIATION OF SOUTH EAST ASIAN NATIONS (ASEAN) AGREEMENT ON THE CONSERVATION OF NATURE AND NATURAL RESOURCES

Popular Name: ASEAN Agreement

Done at Kuala Lumpur on 9 July 1985, *reprinted in* 15 EPL 64 (1985).
Entry into Force: Not yet in force

Depositary: Association of South East Asian Nations

Language: English

Parties as of 11 December 1990: Indonesia; Philippines; Thailand

Editors' Note

The 1985 ASEAN Agreement on the Conservation of Nature and Natural Resources illustrates the evolution of regional natural resource protection agreements into instruments that focus on comprehensive ecosystem protection. The Agreement reflects the approach developed in the 1980 World Conservation Strategy, which was jointly prepared by the International Union for the Conservation of Nature and Natural Resources, the United Nations Environment Programme, and the World Wildlife Fund.

The Agreement covers conservation of species and ecosystems, including issues related to genetic diversity, conservation of ecological processes, control of pollution, land use planning, establishment of protected areas, impact assessment, scientific research, and public participation in the planning and implementation of the conservation measures.

Implementation of the Agreement requires rather comprehensive national legislation to make the obligations precise within each country.

AGREEMENT ON THE CONSERVATION OF NATURE AND NATURAL RESOURCES

The Government of Brunei Darussalam, The Government of the Republic of Indonesia, The Government of Malaysia, The Government of the Republic of the Philippines, The Government of the Republic of Singapore and The Government of the Kingdom of Thailand, Member States of the Association of South East Asian Nations (ASEAN)

RECOGNIZING the importance of natural resources for present and future generations;
CONSCIOUS of their ever-growing value from a scientific, cultural, social and economic point of view;
CONSCIOUS also that the inter-relationship between conservation and socio-economic development implies both that conservation is necessary to ensure sustainability of development, and that socio economic [sic] development is necessary for the achievement of conservation on a lasting basis;
RECOGNIZING the interdependence of living resources, between them and with other natural resources, within ecosystems of which they are part;
WISHING TO UNDERTAKE individual and joint action for the conservation and management of their living resources and the other natural elements on which they depend;
RECOGNIZING that international co-operation is essential to attain many of these goals;
CONVINCED that an essential means to achieve such concerted action is the conclusion and implementation of an Agreement;
Have agreed as follows;

CHAPTER 1
Conservation and Development

ARTICLE 1
Fundamental Principle

(1) The Contracting Parties, within the framework of their respective national laws, undertake to adopt singly, or where necessary and appropriate through

concerted action, the measures necessary to maintain essential ecological process and life-support systems, to preserve genetic diversity, and to ensure the sustainable utilization of harvested natural resources under their jurisdiction in accordance with scientific principles and with a view to attaining the goal of sustainable development.

(2) To this end they shall develop national conservation strategies, and shall co-ordinate such strategies within the framework of a conservation strategy for the Region.

ARTICLE 2
Development Planning

(1) The Contracting Parties shall take all necessary measures, within the framework of their respective national laws, to ensure that conservation and management of natural resources are treated as an integral part of development planning at all stages and at all levels.

(2) To that effect they shall, in the formulation of all development plans, give as full consideration to ecological factors as to economic and social ones.

(3) The Contracting Parties shall, where necessary, take appropriate action with a view to conserving and managing natural resources of significant importance for two or several Contracting Parties.

CHAPTER II
Conservation of Species and Ecosystems

ARTICLE 3
Species—genetic diversity

(1) The Contracting Parties shall, wherever possible, maintain maximum genetic diversity by taking action aimed at ensuring the survival and promoting the conservation of all species under their jurisdiction and control.

(2) To that end, they shall adopt appropriate measures to conserve animal and plant species whether terrestrial, marine and freshwater, and more specifically
   (a)   conserve natural, terrestrial, freshwater and coastal or marine habitats;
   (b)   ensure sustainable use of harvested species;
   (c)   protect endangered species;
   (d)   conserve endemic species; and
   (e)   take all measures in their power to prevent the extinction of any species or sub-species.

(3) In order to fulfil the aims of the preceding paragraphs of this Article the Contracting Parties shall in particular endeavour to
   (a)   create and maintain protected areas;
   (b)   regulate the taking of species and prohibit unselective taking methods;
   (c)   regulate and, where necessary, prohibit the introduction of exotic species;
   (d)   promote and establish gene banks and other documented collections of animal and plant genetic resources.

ARTICLE 4
Species—sustainable use

The Contracting Parties shall pay special attention to harvested species, and, to that effect, shall endeavour to

(1) develop, adopt and implement management plans for those species, based on scientific studies and aiming at

(a)   preventing decrease in the size of any harvested population to levels below those which ensure its stable recruitment and the stable recruitment of those species which are dependent upon, or related to them;

(b)   maintaining the ecological relationship between harvested, dependent and related populations of living resources of the ecosystem considered

(c)   restoring depleted populations to at least the levels referred to in sub-paragraph (a) of this paragraph;

(d)   preventing changes or minimizing risk of changes in the ecosystem considered which are not reversible over a reasonable period of time.

(2) Take the appropriate and necessary legislative and administrative measures on harvesting activities in the light of their national interests whereby

(a)   such activities must conform to the management plans referred to above;

(b)   the conduct of such activities is controlled by a permit system;

(c)   all indiscriminate means of taking and the use of all means capable of causing local extinction of, or serious disturbance to, populations of a species of related species are prohibited;

(d)   such activities are prohibited or strictly regulated at certain periods, seasons or places of importance in the life cycle of the species;

(e)   such activities may be regulated more strictly, temporarily or locally in order to assist restoration of population levels or counterbalance any threat caused by special circumstances;

(f)   special measures, such as restocking, are provided for whenever the conservation status of species so warrants;

(g)   trade and possession of specimens or products of specimens are regulated whenever such regulations meaningfully contribute to the implementation of the harvesting regulations;

ARTICLE 5
Species—endangered and endemic

(1) Appendix I to this Agreement shall list endangered species recognized by the Contracting Parties as of prime importance to the Region and deserving special attention. The Appendix shall be adopted by a meeting of the Contracting Parties;
Accordingly, Contracting Parties shall, wherever possible,

(a)   prohibit the taking of these species, except for exceptional circumstances by special allowance from the designated authorities of the Contracting Parties;

(b)   regulate the trade in and possession of specimens and products of those species accordingly;

(c)   especially protect habitat of those species by ensuring that sufficient portions are included in protected areas;

(d)   take all other necessary measures to improve their conservation status, and restore their populations to the highest possible level.

(2) Each Contracting Party shall, wherever possible, apply the above measures to species endangered at national level.

(3) The Contracting Parties recognize their special responsibility in respect of species that are endemic to areas under their jurisdiction and shall undertake accordingly to take, wherever possible, all the necessary measures to maintain the population of such species at the highest possible level.

ARTICLE 6
Vegetation Cover and Forest Resources

(1) The Contracting Parties shall, in view of the role of vegetation and forest cover in the functioning of natural ecosystems, take all necessary measures to ensure

the conservation of the vegetation cover and in particular of the forest cover on lands under their jurisdiction.

(2) They shall, in particular, endeavour to
- (a)   — control clearance of vegetation;
  - — endeavour to prevent bush and forest fires;
  - — prevent overgrazing by, inter alia, limiting grazing activities to periods and intensities that will not prevent regeneration of the vegetation;
- (b) regulate mining and mineral exploration operations with a view to minimizing disturbance of vegetation and to requiring the rehabilitation of vegetation after such operations;
- (c) set aside areas as forest reserves, inter alia, with a view to conserve the natural forest genetic resources;
- (d) in reforestation and afforestation planning avoid as far as possible monoculture causing ecological imbalance;
- (e) designate areas whose primary function shall be the maintenance of soil quality in the catchment considered and the regulation of the quantity and quality of the water delivered from it;
- (f) ensure to the maximum extent possible the conservation of their natural forests, particularly mangroves with a view, inter alia, to maintaining maximum forest species diversity;
- (g) develop their forestry management plans on the basis of ecological principles with a view to maintaining potential for optimum sustained yield and avoiding depletion of the resource capital.

ARTICLE 7
Soil

(1) The Contracting Parties shall, in view of the role of soil in the functioning of natural ecosystems, take measures, wherever possible towards soil conservation, improvement and rehabilitation; they shall, in particular, endeavour to take teps [sic] to prevent soil erosion and other forms of degradation, and promote measures which safeguard the processes of organic decomposition and thereby its continuing fertility.

(2) To that effect, they shall, in particular, endeavour to
- (a) establish land use policies aimed at avoing [sic] losses of vegetation cover, substantial soil losses, and damages to the structure of the soil;
- (b) take all necessary measures to control erosion, especially as it may affect coastal or freshwater ecosystems leading to silation, of downstream areas such as lakes or vulnerable ecosystems such as coral reefs, or damage critical habitats, in particular that of endangered or endemic species;
- (c) take appropriate measures to rehabilitate eroded or degraded soils including rehabilitation of soil affected by mineral exploitation.

ARTICLE 8
Water

(1) The Contracting Parties shall, in view of the role of water in the functioning of natural ecosystems, take all appropriate measures towards the conservation of their underground and surface water resources.

(2) They shall to that effect, in particular, endeavour to
- (a) undertake and promote the necessary hydrological research especially with a view to ascertaining the characteristics of each watershed;
- (b) regulate and control water utilization with a view to achieving sufficient and continuous supply of water for, inter alia, the maintenance of natural life supporting systems and aquatic fauna and flora;

(c)   when planning and carrying out water resource development projects take fully into account possible effects of such projects on natural processes or on other renewable natural resources and prevent or minimize such effects.

ARTICLE 9
Air

The Contracting Parties shall, in view of the role of air in the functioning of natural ecosystems, endeavour to take all appropriate measures towards air quality management compatible with sustainable development.

CHAPTER III
Conservation of Ecological Processes

ARTICLE 10
Environmental Degradation

The Contracting Parties, with a view to maintaining the proper functioning of ecological processes, undertake, wherever possible, to prevent, reduce and control degradation of the natural environment and, to this end, shall endeavour to undertake, in addition to specific measures referred to in the following article;

(a)   to promote environmentally sound agricultural practices by inter alia, controlling the application of pesticides, fertilizers and other chemical products for agricultural use, and by ensuring that agricultural development schemes, in particular for wetland drainage or forest clearance, pay due regard to the need to protect critical habitats as well as endangered and economically important species;

(b)   to promote pollution control and the development of environmentally sound industrial processes and products;

(c)   to promote adequate economic or fiscal incentives for the purposes of sub-paragraphs (a) and (b) above;

(d)   as far as possible to consider the originator of the activity which may lead to environmental degradation responsible for its prevention, reduction and control as well as, wherever possible, for rehabilitation and remedial measures required;

(e)   to take into consideration, when authorizing activities likely to affect the natural environment, the foreseeable interactions between the new activities proposed and those already taking place in the same area, and the result of such interactions on the air, waters and soils of the area;

(f)   to pay particular attention to the regulation of activities which may have adverse effects on processes which are ecologically essential or on areas which are particularly important or sensitive from an ecological point of view, such as the breeding and feeding grounds of harvested species.

ARTICLE 11
Pollution

The Contracting Parties, recognizing the adverse effect that polluting discharges or emissions may have on natural processes and the functioning of natural ecosystems as well as on each of the individual ecosystem components, especially animal and plants species, shall endeavour to prevent, reduce and control such discharges, emissions or applications in particular by

(a)   submitting activities likely to cause pollution of the air, soil, freshwater, or the marine environment, to control which shall take into consideration both the cumulative effects of the pollutants concerned and the self-purificating aptitude of the recipient natural environment;

(b) making such controls conditional on, inter alia, appropriate treatment of polluting emissions; and

(c) establishing national environmental quality monitoring programmes, particular attention being paid to the effects of pollution on natural ecosystems, and co-operation in such programmes for the Region as a whole.

CHAPTER IV
Environmental Planning Measures

ARTICLE 12
Land use Planning

(1) The Contracting Parties shall, wherever possible in the implementation of their development planning, give particular attention to the national allocation of land usage. They shall endeavour to take the necessary measures to ensure the integration of natural resource conservation into the land use planning process and shall, in the preparation and implementation of specific land use plans at all levels, give as full consideration as possible to ecological factors as to economic and social ones. In order to achieve optimum sustainable land use, they undertake to base their land use plans as far as possible on the ecological capacity of the land.

(2) The Contracting Parties shall in carrying out the provisions of paragraph (1) above, particularly consider the importance of retaining the naturally high productivity of areas such as coastal zones and wetlands.

(3) They shall, where appropriate, co-ordinate their land use planning with a view to conserving and managing natural resources of significant importance for two or several Contracting Parties.

ARTICLE 13
Protected Areas

(1) The Contracting Parties shall as appropriate establish, in areas under their jurisdiction, terrestrial, freshwater, coastal or marine protected areas for the purpose of safeguarding

(a) the ecological and biological processes essential to the functioning of the ecosystems of the Region;

(b) representative samples of all types of ecosystems of the Region;

(c) satisfactory population levels for the largest possible number of species of fauna and flora belonging to those ecosystems;

(d) areas of particular importance because of their scientific, educational, aesthetic, or cultural interests; and taking into account their importance in particular as:

(a) the natural habitat of species of fauna and flora; particularly rare or endangered or endemic species;

(b) zones necessary for the maintenance of exploitable stocks of economically important species;

(c) pools of genetic material and said refuge for species, especially endangered ones;

(d) sites of ecological, aesthetic or cultural interest;

(e) reference sources for scientific research;

(f) areas for environmental education.

They shall, in particular, take all measures possible in their power to preserve those areas which are of an exceptional character and are peculiar to their country or the Region as well as those which constitute the critical habitats of endangered or rare species, of species that are endemic to a small area and of species that migrate between countries of Contracting Parties.

(2) Protected areas established pursuant to this Agreement shall be regulated and managed in such a way as to further the objectives for the purpose of which they have been created. Contracting Parties shall, wherever possible, prohibit within such protected areas activities which are inconsistent with such objectives.

(3) Protected areas shall include
    (a)   National Parks
        (i)   This expression denotes natural areas that are sufficiently large to allow for ecological self-regulation of one or several ecosystems, and which have not been substantially altered by human occupation or exploitation.
        (ii) National Parks shall be placed under public ontrol [sic], their boundaries shall not be altered nor shall any portion of any National Park be alienated except by the highest competent authority.
        (iii) National Parks shall be dedicated to conservation and to scientific, educational and recreational uses and the common welfare of the people.
    (b)   Reserves
        (i)   This expression denotes areas set aside for the purpose of preserving a specific ecosystem, the critical habitat of certain species of fauna or flora, a water catchment area or for any other specific purpose relating to the conservation of natural resources or objects or areas of scientific, aesthetic, cultural, educational or recreational interest.
        (ii) After reserves have been established their boundaries shall not be altered nor shall any portion of such reserves be alienated except by the authority establishing them or by higher authority.
        (iii) Reserves shall be dedicated to the purposes for which they have been created and, in the light of the national interests of the Contracting Parties any activity inconsistent with such purposes shall be prohibited.

(4) Contracting Parties shall, in respect of any protected area established pursuant to this Agreement
    (a)   prepare a management plan and manage the area on the basis of this plan;
    (b)   establish, wherever appropriate, terrestrial or aquatic buffer zones that shall be located around protected areas and which, in the case of marine areas, may include coastal land areas or watersheds of rivers flowing into the protected area; in such buffer zones all activities that may have harmful consequences on the ecosystems that such areas purport to protect shall be prohibited or regulated and activities which are consistent with the purpose of the protected area shall be promoted.

(5) Contracting Parties shall, in respect of any protected area established pursuant to this Agreement, endeavour to
    (a)   prohibit the introduction of exotic animal or plant species;
    (b)   prohibit the use or release of toxic substances or pollutants which could cause disturbance or damage to protected ecosystems or to the species they contain;
    (c)   to the maximum extent possible, prohibit or control any activity exercised outside protected areas when such an activity is likely to cause disturbance or damage to the ecosystems or species that such protected areas purport to protect.

(6) Contracting Parties shall co-operate in the development of principles, objectives, criteria and guidelines for the selection establishment and management

of protected areas in the Region with a view to establishing a co-ordinated network of protected areas throughout the Region, giving particular attention to those of regional importance. An Appendix containing such principles, objectives, criteria and guidelines shall be drawn up in the light of the best scientific evidence as adapted to the conservation requirements of the Region and shall be adopted by a meeting of Contracting Parties.

(7) In addition to the establishment of the protected areas referred to in paragraph 3 of this Article, Contracting Parties shall promote, through the adoption of appropriate measures the conservation of natural areas by private owners, community or local authorities.

ARTICLE 14
Impact Assessment

(1) The Contracting Parties undertake that proposals for any activity which may significantly affect the natural environment shall as far as possible be subjected to an assessment of their consequences before they are adopted, and they shall take into consideration the results of this assessment in their decision-making process.

(2) In those cases where any such activities are undertaken, the Contracting Parties shall plan and carry them out so as to overcome or minimize any assessed adverse effects and shall monitor such effects with a view to taking remedial action as appropriate.

CHAPTER V
National Supporting Measures

ARTICLE 15
Scientific Research

The Contracting Parties shall individually or in co-operation with other Contracting Parties or appropriate international organizations, promote and, whenever possible, support scientific and technical programmes of relevance to the conservation and management of natural resources, including monitoring, research, the exchange of technical information and the evaluation of results.

ARTICLE 16
Education, Information and Participation of the Public, Training

(1) The Contracting Parties shall endeavour to promote adequate coverage of conservation and management of natural resources in education programmes at all levels.

(2) They shall circulate as widely as possible information on the significance of conservation measures and their relationship with sustainable development objectives, and shall, as far as possible, organize participation of the public in the planning and implementation of conservation measures.

(3) Contracting Parties shall endeavour to, individually or in cooperation with other Contracting Parties or appropriate international organizations, develop the programmes and facilities necessary to train adequate and sufficient scientific and technical personnel to fulfil the aims of this Agreement.

ARTICLE 17
Administrative Machinery

(1) The Contracting Parties shall identify or maintain the administrative machinery necessary to implement the provisions of this Agreement, and, where several

governmental institutions are involved, create the necessary co-ordinating mechanism for the authorities dealing with designated aspects of the environment.

(2) They shall endeavour to allocate sufficient funds to the task necessary for the implementation of this Agreement, as well as sufficient qualified personnel with adequate enforcement powers.

CHAPTER VI
International Cooperation

ARTICLE 18
Cooperative Activities

(1) The Contracting Parties shall cooperate together and with the competent international organizations, with a view to coordinating their activities in the field of conservation of nature and management of natural resources and assisting each other in fulfilling the obligations under this Agreement.

(2) To that effect, they shall endeavour
   (a)   to collaborate in monitoring activities;
   (b)   to the greatest extent possible, coordinate their research activities;
   (c)   to use comparable or standardized research techniques and procedures with a view to obtaining comparable data;
   (d)   to exchange appropriate scientific and technical data, information and experience, on a regular basis;
   (e)   whenever appropriate, to consult and assist each other with regard to measures for the implementation of this Agreement.

(3) In applying the principles of cooperation and coordination set forth above, the Contracting Parties shall forward to the Secretariat
   (a)   Information of assistance in the monitoring of the biological status of the natural living resources of the Region;
   (b)   Information, including reports and publications of a scientific, administrative or legal nature and, in particular information on
   — measures taken by the Parties in pursuance of the provisions of this Agreement;
   — the status of species included in Appendix 1;
   — any other matter to which the Conference of the Parties may give special priority.

ARTICLE 19
Shared Resources

(1) Contracting Parties that share natural resources shall cooperate concerning their conservation and harmonious utilization, taking into account the sovereignty, rights and interests of the Contracting Parties concerned in accordance with generally accepted principles of international law.

(2) To that end, they shall, in particular
   (a)   cooperate with a view to controlling, preventing reducing or eliminating adverse environmental effects which may result in one Contracting Party from the utilization of such resources in another Party;
   (b)   endeavour to conclude bilateral or multilateral agreements in order to secure specific regulations of their conduct in respect of the resources concerned;
   (c)   as far as possible, make environmental assessments prior to engaging in activities with respect to shared natural resources which may create a risk

of significantly affecting the environment of another sharing Contracting Party or other sharing Contracting Parties;

(d) notify in advance the other sharing Contracting Party or the other sharing Contracting Parties of pertinent details of plans to initiate, or make a change in, the conservation or utilization of the resource which can reasonably be expected to affect significantly the environment in the territory of the other Contracting Party or Contracting Parties;

(e) upon request of the other sharing Contracting Party or sharing Contracting Parties, enter into consultation concerning the above-mentioned plans;

(f) inform the other sharing Contracting Party or other sharing Contracting Parties of emergency situations or sudden grave natural events which may have repercussions on their environment;

(g) whenever appropriate, engage in joint scientific studies and assessments, with a view to facilitating cooperation with regard to environmental problems related to a shared resource, on the basis of agreed data.

(3) Contracting Parties shall especially cooperate together and, where appropriate, shall endeavour to cooperate with other Contracting Parties, with a view to

(a) the conservation and management of
— border or contiguous protected areas;
— shared habitats of species listed in Appendix 1;
— shared habitats of any other species of common concern;

(b) the conservation, management and, where applicable regulation of the harvesting of species which constitute shared resources
— by virtue of their migratory character, or
— because they inhabit shared habitats.

ARTICLE 20
Transfrontier Environmental Effects

(1) Contracting Parties have in accordance with generally accepted principles of international law the responsibility of ensuring that activities under their jurisdiction or control do not cause damage to the environment or the natural resources under the jurisdiction of other Contracting Parties or of areas beyond the limits of national jurisdiction.

(2) In order to fulfil this responsibility, Contracting Parties shall avoid to the maximum extent possible and reduce to the minimum extent possible adverse environmental effects of activities under their jurisdiction or control, including effects on natural resources, beyond the limits of their national jurisdiction.

(3) To that effect, they shall endeavour

(a) to make environmental impact assessment before engaging in any activity that may create a risk of significantly affecting the environment or the natural resources of another Contracting Party or the environment or natural resources beyond national jurisdiction;

(b) to notify in advance the other Contracting Party or Contracting Parties concerned of pertinent details of plans to initiate, or make a change in, activities which can reasonably be expected to have significant effects beyond the limits of national jurisdiction;

(c) to enter into consultation concerning the above-mentioned plans upon request of the Contracting Party or Contracting Parties in question;

(d) to inform the Contracting Party or Contracting Parties in question of emergency situations or sudden grave natural events which may have repercussion beyond national jurisdiction.

(4) Contracting Parties shall, in particular, endeavour to refrain from actions which might directly or indirectly adversely affect wildlife habitats situated beyond the limits of national jurisdiction, especially habitats of species listed in Appendix I or habitats included in protected areas.

CHAPTER VII
International Supporting Measures

ARTICLE 21
Meeting of the Contracting Parties

(1) Ordinary meetings of the Contracting Parties shall be held at least once in three years, in as far as possible in conjunction with appropriate meetings of ASEAN, and extraordinary meetings shall be held at any other time upon the request of one Contracting Party provided that such request is supported by at least one other Party.
(2) It shall be the function of the meetings of the Contracting Parties, in particular
    (a)   to keep under review the implementation of this Agreement and the need for other measures, in particular the Appendices;
    (b)   to adopt, review and amend as required any Apendix to this Agreement;
    (c)   to consider reports submitted by the Contracting Parties in accordance with Article 28 or any other information which may be submitted by a Party, directly or through the Secretariat;
    (d)   to make recommendations regarding the adoption of any Protocol or any amendment to this Agreement;
    (e)   to establish working groups or any other subsidiary body as required to consider any matter related to this Agreement;
    (f)   to consider and undertake any additional action including the adoption of financial rules, that may be required for the achievement of the purposes of this Agreement.

ARTICLE 22
Secretariat

On the coming into force of this Agreement the Contracting Parties shall designate the Secretariat responsible for carrying out the following functions:
    (a)   to convene and prepare the meetings of Contracting Parties;
    (b)   to convene diplomatic conferences for the purpose of adopting Protocols;
    (c)   to transmit to the Contracting Parties notifications, reports and other information received in accordance with this Agreement;
    (d)   to consider inquiries by, and information from, the Contracting Parties, and to consult with them on questions relating to this Agreement.
    (e)   to perform such other functions as may be assigned to it by the Contracting Parties;
    (f)   to ensure the necessary coordination with other competent international bodies and in particular to enter into the such administrative arrangements as may be required for the effective discharge of the secretariat functions.

ARTICLE 23
National Focal Points

In order to facilitate communications with other Parties and the Secretariat, the Contracting Parties shall designate an appropriate national agency or institution responsible for coordinating matters arising from consultations and channeling communications between Contracting Parties or with the Secretariat.

CHAPTER VIII
Final Clauses

ARTICLE 24
Adoption of Protocols

(1) The Contracting Parties shall cooperate in the formulation and adoption of Protocols to this Agreement, prescribing agreed measures, procedures and standards for the implementation of ths Agreement.

(2) The Contracting Parties at a diplomatic conference, may adopt Protocols to this Agreement.

(3) The Protocols of this Agreement shall be subject to acceptance and shall enter into force on the thirtieth day after the deposit with the Depositary of the Instruments of Acceptance of all the Contracting Parties.

ARTICLE 25
Amendment of the Agreement

(1) Any Contracting Parties to this Agreement may propose amendments to the Agreement. Amendments shall be adopted by a diplomatic conference which shall be convened at the request of the majority of the Contracting Parties.

(2) Amendments to this Agreement shall be adopted by a consensus of the Contracting Parties.

(3) Acceptance of amendments shall be notified to the Depositary in writing and shall enter into force on the thirtieth day following the receipt by the Depositary of notification of the acceptance by all the Contracting Parties.

(4) After the entry into force of an amendment to this Agreement any new Contracting Party to this Agreement shall become a Contracting Party to this Agreement as amended.

ARTICLE 26
Appendices and Amendments to Appendices

(1) Appendices to this Agreement shall form an integral part of the Agreement;

(2) Amendments to an Appendix;

    (a) Any Contracting Party may propose amendments to an appendix at a meeting of the Contracting Parties;

    (b) Such amendments shall be adopted by a consensus of the Contracting Parties;

    (c) The Depositary shall without delay communicate the amendment so adopted to all Contracting Parties.

(3) the adoption and entry into force of a new Appendix to this Agreement shall be subject to the same procedure as for the adoption and entry into force of an amendment to an Appendix as provided for in paragraph (2) of this Article provided that, the new Appendix shall not enter into force until such time as the amendment to the Agreement enters into force.

ARTICLE 27
Rules of Procedure

The Contracting Parties shall adopt rules of procedure for their meetings.

ARTICLE 28
Reports

The Contracting Parties shall transmit to the Secretariat reports on the measures adopted in implementation of this Agreement in such form and at such intervals as the meetings of Contracting Parties may determine.

ARTICLE 29
Relationships with Other Agreements

The provisions of this Agreement shall in no way affect the rights and obligations of any Contracting Party with regard to any existing treaty, convention or agreement.

ARTICLE 30
Settlement of Disputes

Any dispute between the Contracting Parties arising out of the interpretation of implementation of this Agreement shall be settled amicably by consultation or negotiation.

F. EUROPE

HELSINKI FINAL ACT OF THE CONFERENCE ON SECURITY AND CO-OPERATION IN EUROPE (CSCE) (BASKET TWO: "CO-OPERATION IN THE FIELD OF ECONOMICS, OF SCIENCE AND TECHNOLOGY AND OF THE ENVIRONMENT," § 5—"ENVIRONMENT")

Popular Name:　　　　　　Helsinki Final Act

Done at Helsinki on 1 August 1975, 73 DSB 335-36 (1975), *reprinted in* 14 ILM 1307 (1975), 18 IPE 9139.
Depositary:　　　　　　　Finland

Languages:　　　　　　　English, French, German, Italian, Russian, Spanish

Signatories: Austria; Belgium; Bulgaria; Canada; Cypress; Czechoslovakia; Denmark; Finland; France; German Democratic Republic; Germany, Federal Republic of; Greece; Holy See; Hungary; Iceland; Ireland; Italy; Liechtenstein; Luxembourg; Malta; Netherlands; Norway; Poland; Portugal; Rumania; San Marino; Spain; Sweden; Switzerland; Turkey; Union of Soviet Socialist Republics; United Kingdom of Great Britain and Northern Ireland; United States of America; Yugoslavia

Editors' Note

The first meeting of the Conference on Security and Cooperation in Europe (CSCE), consisting of Canada, United States, and all European States except Albania (a total of 34 countries), was in Helsinki in August 1975. The Final Act (also known as the Helsinki Accords) signed at that meeting was not intended to be legally binding. It is best known because it included pledges on the inviolability of post-World War II European boundaries, respect for human rights and fundamental freedoms, and freer travel, association, and dissemination of information. The Final Act also contained agreements regarding environmental protection and cooperation (reproduced below). Among other things, those provisions helped lead to the 1979 Convention on Long-Range Transboundary Air Pollution (LRTAP), *infra*, p. 250.

The CSCE has met several times since 1975. The 1989 Sofia meeting issued a Report on Protection of the Environment, CSCE/SEM.36/Rev. 1 (3 Nov. 1989). On 12 December 1990, the CSCE adopted the Charter of Paris for a New Europe. The Charter provides, in the section on Economic Liberty and Responsibility, that "Economic liberty, social justice and environmental responsibility are indispensable for prosperity. . . . Preservation of the environment is a shared responsibility of all our nations. While supporting national and regional efforts in this field, we must also look to the pressing need for joint action on a wider scale." A/45/859, Annex. The Charter's Guidelines for the Future, in the section on Environment, states: "We pledge to intensify our efforts to protect and improve our environment in order to restore and maintain a sound ecological balance in air, water and soil." The Guidelines also emphasize the importance of notification and exchange of information, public awareness, education, clean and low-waste technology, and efficient coordination among international organizations engaged in protecting the environment.

HELSINKI FINAL ACT, BASKET TWO

5. Environment

The participating States,

Affirming that the protection and improvement of the environment, as well as the protection of nature and the rational utilization of its resources in the interests of present and future generations, is one of the tasks of major importance to the well-being of peoples and the economic development of all countries and that many environmental problems, particularly in Europe, can be solved effectively only through close international co-operation,

Acknowledging that each of the participating States, in accordance with the principles of international law, ought to ensure, in a spirit of co-operation, that activities carried out on its territory do not cause degradation of the environment in another State or in areas lying beyond the limits of national jurisdiction,

Considering that the success of any environmental policy presupposes that all population groups and social forces, aware of their responsibilities, help to protect and improve the environment, which necessitates continued and thorough educative action, particularly with regard to youth,

Affirming that experience has shown that economic development and techno-logical progress must be compatible with the protection of the environment and the preservation of historical and cultural values; that damage to the environment is best avoided by preventive measures; and that the ecological balance must be preserved in the exploitation and management of natural resources,

Aims of co-operation

Agree to the following aims of co-operation, in particular:

—to study, with a view to their solution, those environmental problems which, by their nature, are of a multilateral, bilateral, regional or sub-regional dimension;

as well as to encourage the development of an interdisciplinary approach to environmental problems;

—to increase the effectiveness of national and international measures for the protection of the environment, by the comparison and, if appropriate, the harmonization of methods of gathering and analyzing facts, by improving the knowledge of pollution phenomena and rational utilization of natural resources, by the exchange of information, by the harmonization of definitions and the adoption, as far as possible, of a common terminology in the field of the environment;

—to take the necessary measures to bring environmental policies closer together and, where appropriate and possible, to harmonize them;

—to encourage, where possible and appropriate, national and international efforts by their interested organizations, enterprises and firms in the development, production and improvement of equipment designed for monitoring, protecting and enhancing the environment.

Fields of co-operation

To attain these aims, the participating States will make use of every suitable opportunity to co-operate in the field of environment and, in particular, within the areas described below as examples:

Control of air pollution

Desulphurization of fossil fuels and exhaust gases; pollution control of heavy metals, particles, aerosols, nitrogen oxides, in particular those emitted by transport, power stations, and other industrial plants; systems and methods of observation and control of air pollution and its effects, including long-range transport of air pollutants;

Water pollution control and fresh water utilization

Prevention and control of water pollution, in particular of transboundary rivers and international lakes; techniques for the improvement of the quality of water and further development of ways and means for industrial and municipal sewage effluent purification; methods of assessment of fresh water resources and the improvement of their utilization, in particular by developing methods of production which are less polluting and lead to less consumption of fresh water;

Protection of the marine environment

Protection of the marine environment of participating States, and especially the Mediterranean Sea, from pollutants emanating from land-based sources and those from ships and other vessels, notably the harmful substances listed in Annexes I and II to the London Convention on the Prevention of Marine Pollution by the Dumping of Wastes and Other Matters; problems of maintaining marine ecological balances and food chains, in particular such problems as may arise from the exploration and exploitation of biological and mineral resources of the seas and the sea-bed;

Land utilization and soils

Problems associated with more effective use of lands, including land amelioration, reclamation and recultivation; control of soil pollution, water and air erosion, as well as other forms of soil degradation; maintaining and increasing the productivity of soils with due regard for the possible negative effects of the application of chemical fertilizers and pesticides;

Nature conservation and nature reserves

Protection of nature and nature reserves; conservation and maintenance of existing genetic resources, especially rare animal and plant species; conservation of natural ecological systems; establishment of nature reserves and other protected landscapes and areas, including their use for research, tourism, recreation and other purposes;

Improvement of environmental conditions in areas of human settlement

Environmental conditions associated with transport, housing, working areas, urban development and planning, water supply and sewage disposal systems; assessment of harmful effects of noise, and noise control methods; collection, treatment and utilization of wastes, including the recovery and recycling of materials; research on substitutes for non-biodegradable substances;

Fundamental research, monitoring, forecasting and assessment of environmental changes

Study of changes in climate, landscapes and ecological balances under the impact of both natural factors and human activities; forecasting of possible genetic changes in flora and fauna as a result of environmental pollution; harmonization of statistical data, development of scientific concepts and systems of monitoring networks, standardized methods of observation, measurement and assessment of changes in the biosphere; assessment of the effects of environmental pollution levels and degradation of the environment upon human health; study and development of criteria and standards for various environmental pollutants and regulation regarding production and use of various products;

Legal and administrative measures

Legal and administrative measures for the protection of the environment including procedures for establishing environmental impact assessments.

Forms and methods of co-operation

The participating States declare that problems relating to the protection and improvement of the environment will be solved on both a bilateral and a multilateral, including regional and sub-regional, basis, making full use of existing patterns and forms of co-operation. They will develop co-operation in the field of the environment in particular by taking into consideration the Stockholm Declaration on the Human Environment, relevant resolutions of the United Nations General Assembly and the United Nations Economic Commission for Europe Prague symposium on environmental problems.

The participating States are resolved that co-operation in the field of the environment will be implemented in particular through:

—exchanges of scientific and technical information, documentation and research results, including information on the means of determining the possible effects on the environment of technical and economic activities;

—organization of conferences, symposia and meetings of experts;

—exchanges of scientists, specialists and trainees;

—joint preparation and implementation of programmes and projects for the study and solution of various problems of environmental protection;

—harmonization, where appropriate and necessary, of environmental protection standards and norms, in particular with the object of avoiding possible difficulties in trade which may arise from efforts to resolve ecological problems of production processes and which relate to the achievement of certain environmental qualities in manufactured products;

—consultations on various aspects of environmental protection, as agreed upon among countries concerned, especially in connexion with problems which could have international consequences.

The participating States will further develop such co-operation by:

—promoting the progressive development, codification and implementation of international law as one means of preserving and enhancing the human environment, including principles and practices, as accepted by them, relating to pollution and other environmental damage caused by activities within the jurisdiction or control of their States affecting other countries and regions;

—supporting and promoting the implementation of relevant international Conventions to which they are parties, in particular those designed to prevent and combat marine and fresh water pollution, recommending States to ratify Conventions which have already been signed, as well as considering possibilities of accepting other appropriate Conventions to which they are not parties at present;

—advocating the inclusion, where appropriate and possible, of the various areas of co-operation into the programmes of work of the United Nations Economic Commission for Europe, supporting such co-operation within the framework of the Commission and of the United Nations Environment Programme, and taking into account the work of other competent international organizations of which they are members;

—making wider use, in all types of co-operation, of information already available from national and international sources, including internationally agreed criteria, and utilizing the possibilities and capabilities of various competent international organizations.

The participating States agree on the following recommendations on specific measures:

—to develop through international co-operation an extensive programme for the monitoring and evaluation of the long-range transport of air pollutants, starting with sulphur dioxide and with possible extension to other pollutants, and to this end to take into account basic elements of a co-operation programme which were identified by the experts who met in Oslo in December 1974 at the invitation of the Norwegian Institute of Air Research;

—to advocate that within the framework of the United Nations Economic Commission for Europe a study be carried out of procedures and relevant experience relating to the activities of Governments in developing the capabilities of their countries to predict adequately environmental consequences of economic activities and technological development.

EUROPEAN ECONOMIC COMMUNITY SINGLE EUROPEAN ACT, ARTICLES 18 (ADDING ARTICLe 100A TO THE EEC TREATY) AND 25 (ADDING TITLE VII: "ENVIRONMENT," ARTICLES 130R-130T TO PART THREE OF THE EEC TREATY)

Done at Luxembourg on 17 February 1986, and at The Hague on 28 February 1986, 30 OJEC (No. L 169) 8, 11-12 (1987), *reprinted in* 25 ILM 506 (1986), IPE(2) I/ H/18-02-86-a.

Entry into Force: 1 July 1987

Depositary: Italy

Languages: Danish, Dutch, English, French, German, Greek, Irish, Italian, Portuguese, Spanish

Parties as of 1 September 1990: Belgium; Denmark;* France; Germany, Federal
Republic of; Greece; Ireland; Italy; Luxembourg; Netherlands; Portugal; Spain;
United Kingdom of Great Britain and Northern Ireland

Editors' Note

The European Economic Community (EEC) is a customs union composed of
the twelve European countries listed above. It was formed in 1957 by the Treaty
of Rome (also referred to as the Rome Treaty or the EEC Treaty), 25 March
1957, 298 UNTS 3. Although the Treaty of Rome did not specifically mention
environmental controls, the EEC instituted many environmental regulations dealing
with a multitude of areas, pursuant to articles 100 (authorizing the EEC Council to
harmonize laws to remove trade barriers and distortions of competition) and 235
(authorizing the Council to take appropriate action to achieve EEC objectives).
One of the EEC's earliest consciously environmental actions was a 1967 directive
regarding classifying, packaging, and labeling dangerous substances. The Council
(beginning in 1973) has adopted four Action Programmes on the Environment.

The Single European Act of 1986 amended the Treaty of Rome to provide an
explicit basis for environmental actions by the EEC (Title 7, arts. 130r-130t).
Pursuant to the Amendment, the EEC has approved the establishment of a European
Environment Agency.

Environmental actions by the EEC may take three forms: a directive, regulation, or decision. An EEC directive is not binding directly in the member States,
but requires them to take national action to conform with the directive which is
binding within their respective State. A regulation applies directly to the States
throughout the Community. A decision binds those to whom it is addressed. The
European Court of Justice has considered several cases regarding environmental
directives and can be expected to play an increasingly important role. The EEC
appears to be moving toward greater use of environmental regulations.

EEC environmental actions are referenced in the List of International Environmental Instruments. Pursuant to the 1986 Amendment, the EEC issued a directive
on access to environmental information, the text of which is reproduced *infra*, p.
659.

SINGLE EUROPEAN ACT

* * *

Article 18
The EEC Treaty shall be supplemented by the following provisions:

'Article 100a

1. By way of derogation from Article 100 and save where otherwise provided in this
Treaty, the following provisions shall apply for the achievement of the objectives set
out in Article 8a. The Council shall, acting by a qualified majority on a proposal

---

*With a declaration

from the Commission in co-operation with the European Parliament and after consulting the Economic and Social Committee, adopt the measures for the approximation of the provisions laid down by law, regulation or administrative action in Member States which have as their object the establishment and functioning of the internal market.

2. Paragraph 1 shall not apply to fiscal provisions, to those relating to the free movement of persons nor to those relating to the rights and interests of employed persons.

3. The Commission, in its proposals envisaged in paragraph 1 concerning health, safety, environmental protection and consumer protection, will take as a base a high level of protection.

4. If, after the adoption of a harmonization measure by the Council acting by a qualified majority, a Member State deems it necessary to apply national provisions on grounds of major needs referred to in Article 36, or relating to protection of the environment or the working environment, it shall notify the Commission of these provisions.

The Commission shall confirm the provisions involved after having verified that they are not a means of arbitrary discrimination or a disguised restriction on trade between Member States.

By way of derogation from the procedure laid down in Articles 169 and 170, the Commission or any Member State may bring the matter directly before the Court of Justice if it considers that another Member State is making improper use of the powers provided for in this Article.

5. The harmonization measures referred to above shall, in appropriate cases, include a safeguard clause authorizing the Member States to take, for one or more of the non-economic reasons referred to in Article 36, provisional measures subject to a Community control procedure.'.

Article 19
The EEC Treaty shall be supplemented by the following provisions:

'Article 100b

1. During 1992, the Commission shall, together with each Member State, draw up an inventory of national laws, regulations and administrative provisions which fall under Article 100a and which have not been harmonized pursuant to that Article.

The Council, acting in accordance with the provisions of Article 100a, may decide that the provisions in force in a Member State must be recognized as being equivalent to those applied by another Member State.

2. The provisions of Article 100a(4) shall apply by analogy.

3. The Commission shall draw up the inventory referred to in the first subparagraph of paragraph 1 and shall submit appropriate proposals in good time to allow the Council to act before the end of 1992.'.

* * *

Sub-section VI—Environment
Article 25

A Title VII shall be added to Part Three of the EEC Treaty reading as follows:

'TITLE VII
ENVIRONMENT

Article 130r

1. Action by the Community relating to the environment shall have the following objectives:
—to preserve, protect and improve the quality of the environment,
—to contribute towards protecting human health,
—to ensure a prudent and rational utilization of natural resources.
2. Action by the Community relating to the environment shall be based on the principles that preventive action should be taken, that environmental damage should as a priority be rectified at source, and that the polluter should pay. Environmental protection requirements shall be a component of the Community's other policies.
3. In preparing its action relating to the environment, the Community shall take account of:
—available scientific and technical data,
—environmental conditions in the various regions of the Community,
—the potential benefits and costs of action or of lack of action,
—the economic and social development of the Community as a whole and the balanced development of its regions.
4. The Community shall take action relating to the environment to the extent to which the objectives referred to in paragraph 1 can be attained better at Community level than at the level of the individual Member States. Without prejudice to certain measures of a Community nature, the Member States shall finance and implement the other measures.
5. Within their respective spheres of competence, the Community and the Member States shall co-operate with third countries and with the relevant international organizations. The arrangements for Community co-operation may be the subject of agreements between the Community and the third parties concerned, which shall be negotiated and concluded in accordance with Article 228.
    The previous paragraph shall be without prejudice to Member States' competence to negotiate in international bodies and to conclude international agreements.

Article 130s

    The Council, acting unanimously on a proposal from the Commission and after consulting the European Parliament and the Economic and Social Committee, shall decide what action is to be taken by the Community.
    The Council shall, under the conditions laid down in the preceding subparagraph, define those matters on which decisions are to be taken by a qualified majority.

Article 130t

    The protective measures adopted in common pursuant to Article 130s shall not prevent any Member State from maintaining or introducing more stringent protective measures compatible with this Treaty.'

* * *

NORDIC CONVENTION ON THE PROTECTION OF THE ENVIRONMENT BETWEEN DENMARK, FINLAND, NORWAY, SWEDEN, AND ACCOMPANYING PROTOCOL

Popular Names: Nordic Convention, Nordic Environment Convention

Done at Stockholm on 19 February 1974, 1092 UNTS 279, *reprinted in* UNEP3 #62, p. 403, 13 ILM 591 (1974), 1 IPE 70, IELMT 947: 14.
Entry into Force: 5 October 1976

Depositary: Sweden

Languages: Danish, Finnish, Norwegian, Swedish

Parties as of 1 October 1990: Denmark; Finland; Norway; Sweden

Editors' Note

The Nordic Convention addresses a wide variety of transboundary environmentally harmful activities. The Convention provides that each State shall appoint a supervisory authority to safeguard general environmental interests against environmentally harmful activities in other member States. A person who is affected or who may be affected by an environmentally harmful activity in another member State shall have the right to institute proceedings regarding the permissibility of an activity located in another State or regarding compensation, not only in the courts of that State but also before administrative authorities of that State. The supervisory authority also may bring such actions regarding permissibility. In determining permissibility, the nuisance in a member State shall be equated with a nuisance in the State where the activities are carried out. An opinion by a Commission may be demanded under some circumstances.

[Translation[1]]

CONVENTION ON THE PROTECTION OF THE ENVIRONMENT BETWEEN DENMARK, FINLAND, NORWAY AND SWEDEN

The Governments of Denmark, Finland, Norway and Sweden, considering it extremely important to protect and improve the environment, have agreed as follows:

Article 1.

For the purpose of this Convention, environmentally harmful activities shall mean the discharge from the soil or from buildings or installations of solid or liquid waste, gas or any other substance into watercourses, lakes or the sea and the use of land, the sea-bed, buildings or installations in any other way which entails, or may entail environmental nuisance by water pollution or any other effect on water conditions, sand drift, air pollution, noise, vibration, changes in temperature, ionizing radiation, light, etc.

The Convention shall not apply in so far as environmentally harmful activities are regulated by a special agreement between two or more of the Contracting States.

---

[1]Translation provided by the Government of Sweden.

Article 2.

In considering the permissibility of environmentally harmful activities, the nuisance which such activities entail or may entail in another Contracting State shall be equated with a nuisance in the State where the activities are carried out.

Article 3.

Any person who is affected or may be affected by a nuisance caused by environmentally harmful activities in another Contracting State shall have the right to bring before the appropriate Court or Administrative Authority of that State the question of the permissibility of such activities, including the question of measures to prevent damage, and to appeal against the decision of the Court or the Administrative Authority to the same extent and on the same terms as a legal entity of the State in which the activities are being carried out.

The provisions of the first paragraph of this article shall be equally applicable in the case of proceedings concerning compensation for damage caused by environmentally harmful activities. The question of compensation shall not be judged by rules which are less favourable to the injured Party than the rules of compensation of the State in which the activities are being carried out.

Article 4.

Each State shall appoint a special authority (supervisory authority) to be entrusted with the task of safeguarding general environmental interests in so far as regards nuisances arising out of environmentally harmful activities in another Contracting State.

For the purpose or safeguarding such interests, the supervisory authority shall have the right to institute proceedings before or be heard by the competent Court or Administrative Authority of another Contracting State regarding the permissibility of the environmentally harmful activities if an authority or other representative of general environmental interests in that State can institute proceedings or be heard in matters of this kind, as well as the right to appeal against the decision of the Court or the Administrative Authority in accordance with the procedures and rules of appeal applicable to such cases in the State concerned.

Article 5.

If the Court or the Administrative Authority examining the permissibility of environmentally harmful activities (examining authority) finds that the activities entail or may entail nuisance of significance in another Contracting State, the examining authority shall, if proclamation or publication is required in cases of that nature, send as soon as possible a copy of the documents of the case to the supervisory authority of the other State, and afford it the opportunity of giving its opinion. Notification of the date and place of a meeting or inspection shall, where appropriate, be given well in advance to the supervisory authority which, moreover, shall be kept informed of any developments that may be of interest to it.

Article 6.

Upon the request of the supervisory authority, the examining authority shall, in so far as compatible with the procedural rules of the State in which the activities are being carried out, require the applicant for a permit to carry out environmentally harmful activities to submit such additional particulars, drawings and technical specifications as the examining authority deems necessary for evaluating the effects in the other State.

Article 7.

The supervisory authority, if it finds it necessary on account of public or private interests, shall publish communications from the examining authority in the local newspaper or in some other suitable manner. The supervisory authority shall also institute such investigations of the effects in its own State as it deems necessary.

Article 8.

Each State shall defray the cost of the activities of its supervisory authority.

Article 9.

If, in a particular case, the supervisory authority has informed the appropriate Court of Administrative authority of the State in which the activities are being carried out that in the case concerned the duties of the supervisory authority shall be discharged by another authority, the provisions of this Convention relating to supervisory activities shall, where appropriate, apply to that authority.

Article 10.

If necessary for determining the damage caused in another State by environmentally harmful activities, the supervisory authority of that other State shall upon request of the examining authority of the State in which the activities are being carried out make arrangements for on-site inspection. The examining authority or an expert appointed by it may be present at such an inspection.

Where necessary, more detailed instructions concerning inspections such as referred to in the preceding paragraph shall be drawn up in consultation between the countries concerned.

Article 11.

Where the permissibility of environmentally harmful activities which entail or may entail considerable nuisance in another Contracting State is being examined by the Government or by the appropriate Minister or Ministry of the State in which the activities are being carried out, consultations shall take place between the States concerned if the Government of the former State so requests.

Article 12.

In cases such as those referred to in article 11, the Government of each State concerned may demand that an opinion be given by a Commission which, unless otherwise agreed, shall consist of a chairman from another Contracting State to be appointed jointly by the Parties and three members from each of the States concerned. Where such a Commission has been appointed, the case cannot be decided upon until the Commission has given its opinion.

Each State shall remunerate the members it has appointed. Fees or other remuneration of the Chairman as well as any other costs incidental to the activities of the Commission which are not manifestly the responsibility of one or the other State shall be equally shared by the States concerned.

Article 13.

This Convention shall also apply to the continental shelf areas of the Contracting States.

Article 14.

This Convention shall enter into force six months from the date on which all the Contracting States have notified the Swedish Ministry for Foreign Affairs that the constitutional measures necessary for the entry into force of the Convention have been implemented. The Swedish Ministry for Foreign Affairs shall notify the other Contracting States of the receipt of such communications.

Article 15.

Actions or cases relevant to this Convention, which are pending before a Court or an Administrative Authority on the date when this Convention enters into force, shall be dealt with and judged according to provisions previously in force.

Article 16.

Any Contracting State wishing to denounce this Convention shall give notice of its intention in writing to the Swedish Government, which shall forthwith inform the other Contracting States of the denunciation and of the date on which notice was received.

The denunciation shall take effect 12 months from the date on which the Swedish Government received such notification or on such later date as may be indicated in the notice of denunciation.

This Convention shall be deposited with the Swedish Ministry for Foreign Affairs, which shall send certified copies thereof to the Government of each Contracting State.

IN WITNESS WHEREOF the undersigned, representatives of the Contracting States, being duly authorized thereto by their respective Governments, have signed this Convention.

DONE at Stockholm, this 19th day of February 1974 in a single copy in the Danish, Finnish, Norwegian and Swedish languages, all texts being equally authoritative.

[Signatures]

PROTOCOL

In connection with the signing today of the Nordic Environmental Protection Convention the duly authorized signatories agreed that the following comments on its application shall be appended to the Convention.

In the applications of article 1 discharge from the soil, or from buildings or installations of solid or liquid waste, gases or other substances into watercourses, lakes or the sea shall be regarded as environmentally harmful activities only if the discharge entails or may entail a nuisance to the surroundings.

The right established in article 3 for anyone who suffers injury as a result of environmentally harmful activities in a neighbouring State to institute proceedings for compensation before a court or administrative authority of that State shall, in principle, be regarded as including the right to demand the purchase of his real property.

Article 5 shall be regarded as applying also to application for permits where such applications are referred to certain authorities and organizations for their opinion but not in conjunction with proclamation or publication procedures.

The Contracting States shall require officials of the supervisory authority to observe professional secrecy as regards trade secrets, operational devices or business conditions of which they have become cognizant in dealing with cases concerning environmentally harmful activities in another State.

CHAPTER 2
HUMAN RIGHTS AND THE ENVIRONMENT

Editors' Introductory Note
Since World War II, a number of international human rights instruments have been negotiated and entered into by various countries. Several of those instruments include provisions relating to the environment. A selection follows.

INTERNATIONAL COVENANT ON ECONOMIC, SOCIAL AND CULTURAL RIGHTS, ARTS. 12(2)(b) & 25.

Popular Name: Economic and Social Covenant, ICESCR

Adopted by the U.N. General Assembly on 16 December 1966, G.A. Res. 2200A(XXI), 993 UNTS 3, *reprinted in* 6 ILM 360 (1967), 1 IPE 28, IELMT 966: 94.

Entry into Force: 3 January 1976

Depositary: United Nations

Languages: Arabic, Chinese, English, French, Russian, Spanish

Parties as of 31 December 1989: Afghanistan;* Algeria;* Argentina; Australia; Austria; Barbados;* Belgium;* Bolivia; Bulgaria;* Byelorussian Soviet Socialist Republic;* Cameroon; Canada; Central African Republic; Chile; Colombia; Congo;* Costa Rica; Cyprus; Czech and Slovak Federal Republic;* Denmark;* Dominican Republic; Ecuador; Egypt; El Salvador; Equatorial Guinea; Finland; France;* Gabon; Gambia; German Democratic Republic;* Germany, Federal Republic of;**** Greece; Guatemala; Guinea;* Guyana; Honduras; Hungary;* Iceland; India;* Iran, Islamic Republic of; Iraq;* Ireland;* Italy; Jamaica; Japan;* Jordan; Kenya;* Korea, Democratic People's Republic of; Lebanon; Libyan Arab Jamahiriya;* Luxembourg; Madagascar;* Mali; Mauritius; Mexico;* Mongolia;* Morocco; Netherlnds;** New Zealand;* Nicaragua; Niger; Norway;* Panama; Peru; Philippines; Poland; Portugal; Romania;* Rwanda;* Saint Vincent and the Grenadines; San Marino; Senegal; Solomon Islands; Spain; Sri Lanka; Sudan; Suriname; Sweden;* Syrian Arab Republic;* Tanzania, United Republic of; Togo; Trinidad and Tobago;* Tunisia; Uganda; Ukrainian Soviet Socialist Republic;* Union of Soviet Socialist Republics;* United Kingdom of Great Britain and Northern Ireland;*** Uruguay; Venezuela; Yemen, Democratic*

---

*   With a reservation or statement
**   With a reservation and geographic extension
***   With a reservation, declarations, and a geographic extension and limitation
****   With a declaration and a geographic extension

INTERNATIONAL COVENANT ON ECONOMIC, SOCIAL AND CULTURAL RIGHTS

* * *

Article 12

1. The States Parties to the present Covenant recognize the right of everyone to the enjoyment of the highest attainable standard of physical and mental health.
2. The steps to be taken by the States Parties to the present Covenant to achieve the full realization of this right shall include those necessary for:

* * *

(b) The improvement of all aspects of environmental and industrial hygiene;

* * *

Article 25

Nothing in the present Covenant shall be interpreted as impairing the inherent right of all peoples to enjoy and utilize fully and freely their natural wealth and resources.

* * *

CONVENTION ON THE RIGHTS OF THE CHILD, ART. 29(1)(e)

ADOPTED BY THE U.N. GENERAL ASSEMBLY ON 28 NOVEMBER 1989, A/RES/44/25, *REPRINTED IN* 28 ILM 1448 (1989) AND 29 ILM 1340 (1990) (CORRECTIONS).

Entry into Force: 2 September 1990

Depositary: United Nations

Languages: Arabic, Chinese, English, French, Russian, Spanish
Parties as of 15 November 1990: Bangladesh;* Barbados; Belize; Benin; Bhutan; Bolivia; Brazil; Burkina Faso; Burundi; Byelorussian Soviet Socialist Republic; Chad; Chile; Costa Rica; Ecuador; Eqypt;* El Savlador; France;* Gambia; German Democratic Republic; Ghana; Grenada; Guatemala; Guinea; Guinea-Bissau; Holy See;* Honduras; Indonesia;* Kenya; Korea, People's Democratic Republic of; Mali;* Malta;* Mauritius;* Mexico; Mongolia; Namibia; Nepal; Nicaragua; Niger; Pakistan;* Paraguay; Peru; Philippines; Portugal; Romania; Saint Kitts and Nevis; Senegal; Seychelles; Sierra Leone; Sudan; Sweden; Togo; Uganda; Union of Soviet Socialist Republics; Venezuela;* Viet Nam; Zaire; Zimbabwe

CONVENTION ON THE RIGHTS OF THE CHILD

* * *

---

*With a reservation or declaration

Article 29

1. States Parties agree that the education of the child shall be directed to:

* * *

(e) The development of respect for the natural environment.

* * *

AFRICAN CHARTER ON HUMAN AND PEOPLES' RIGHTS

Popular Names: Banjul Charter on Human Rights, African Charter on Human Rights

Done at Banjul on 27 June 1981, *reprinted in* 21 ILM 59 (1982).

Entry into Force: 21 October 1986

Depositary: Organization of African Unity

Parties as of 20 March 1991: Algeria; Angola; Benin; Botswana; Burundi; Burkina Faso; Cameroon; Cape Verde; Central African Republic; Chad; Comoros; Congo; Egypt; Equatorial Guinea; Gabon; Gambia; Ghana; Guinea; Guinea-Bissau; Liberia; Libyan Arab Jamahiriya; Malawi; Mali; Mauritania; Mozambique; Niger; Nigeria; Rwanda; Sahrawi; Democratic Arab Republic; Sao Tome and Principe; Senegal; Sierra Leone; Somalia; Sudan; Tanzania; Togo; Tunisia; Uganda; Zaire; Zambia; Zimbabwe

AFRICAN CHARTER ON HUMAN AND PEOPLES' RIGHTS

* * *

Article 24

All peoples shall have the right to a general satisfactory environment favorable to their development.

* * *

SAN SALVADOR ADDITIONAL PROTOCOL [TO THE AMERICAN CONVENTION ON HUMAN RIGHTS] ON ECONOMIC, SOCIAL AND CULTURAL RIGHTS, Art. 11

Popular Name: Protocol of San Salvador, San Salvador Protocol

Done at San Salvador on 17 November 1988, *reprinted in* 28 ILM 161 (1989).
Entry into Force: Not yet in force as of 1 November 1990

Depositary: Organization of American States

Languages: English, French, Portuguese, Spanish

Parties as of 1 November 1990: Suriname

**ADDITIONAL PROTOCOL TO THE AMERICAN CONVENTION ON
HUMAN RIGHTS IN THE AREA OF ECONOMIC, SOCIAL AND
CULTURAL RIGHTS "PROTOCOL OF SAN SALVADOR"**

* * *

Article 11
Right to a healthy environment

1. Everyone shall have the right to live in a healthy environment and to have access to basic public services.

2. The States Parties shall promote the protection, preservation and improvement of the environment.

* * *

CONSTITUTION OF THE REPUBLIC OF NAMIBIA.
Supra, p. 211.

DECLARATION OF THE HAGUE. *Infra,* p.247

PART II:
PROTECTION OF PARTICULAR RESOURCES

CHAPTER 3
ATMOSPHERE

A. GENERAL

DECLARATION OF THE HAGUE

Popular Name: Hague Declaration

Done at The Hague on 11 March 1989, U.N. Doc. A/44/340, E/1989/120, *reprinted in* 28 ILM 1308 (1989).

Depositary: Netherlands

Languages: English, French

Signatories: Australia; Brazil; Canada; Côte d'Ivoire; Egypt; France; Germany, Federal Republic of; Hungary; India; Indonesia; Italy; Japan; Jordan; Kenya; Malta; Netherlands; New Zealand; Norway; Senegal; Spain

Editors' Note

The Hague Declaration is noteworthy in several respects, including that it ties environmental protection to the human right to life and calls for new international institutional authority empowered to collect information and make effective decisions regarding preserving the earth's atmosphere, even if all States do not agree.

DECLARATION OF THE HAGUE

The right to live is the right from which all other rights stem. Guaranteeing this right is the paramount duty of those in charge of all States throughout the world.

Today, the very conditions of life on our planet are threatened by the severe attacks to which the earth's atmosphere is subjected.

Authoritative scientific studies have shown the existence and scope of considerable dangers linked in particular to the warming of the atmosphere and to the deterioration of the ozone layer. The latter has already led to action, under the 1985 Vienna Convention for the Protection of the Ozone Layer and the 1987 Montreal Protocol, while the former is being addressed by the Intergovernmental Panel on Climatic Change established by UNEP and WMO, which has just begun its work. In addition the UN General Assembly adopted Resolution 43/53 on the Protection of the Global Climate in 1988, recognizing climate change as a common concern of mankind.

According to present scientific knowledge, the consequences of these phenomena may well jeopardize ecological systems as well as the most vital interests of mankind at large.

Because the problem is planet-wide in scope, solutions can only be devised on a global level. Because of the nature of the dangers involved, remedies to be sought involve not only the fundamental duty to preserve the ecosystem, but also the right to live in dignity in a viable global environment, and the consequent duty of the community of nations vis-à-vis present and future generations to do all that can be done to preserve the quality of the atmosphere.

Therefore we consider that, faced with a problem the solution to which has three salient features, namely that it is vital, urgent and global, we are in a situation that calls not only for implementation of existing principles but also for a new approach, through the development of new principles of international law including new and more effective decision-making and enforcement mechanisms.

What is needed here are regulatory, supportive and adjustment measures that take into account the participation and potential contribution of countries which have reached different levels of development. Most of the emissions that affect the atmosphere at present originate in the industrialized nations. And it is in these same nations that the room for change is greatest, and these nations are also those which have the greatest resources to deal with this problem effectively.

The international community and especially the industrialized nations have special obligations to assist developing countries which will be very negatively affected by changes in the atmosphere although the responsibility of many of them for the process may only be marginal today.

Financial institutions and development agencies, be they international or domestic, must coordinate their activities in order to promote sustainable development.

Without prejudice to the international obligations of each State, the signatories acknowledge and will promote the following principles:

(a) The principle of developing, within the framework of the United Nations, new institutional authority, either by strengthening existing institutions or by creating a new institution, which, in the context of the preservation of the earth's atmosphere, shall be responsible for combating any further global warming of the atmosphere and shall involve such decision-making procedures as may be effective even if, on occasion, unanimous agreement has not been achieved;

(b) The principle that this institutional authority undertake or commission the necessary studies, be granted appropriate information upon request, ensure the circulation and exchange of scientific and technological information—including facilitation of access to the technology needed—develop instruments and define standards to enhance or guarantee the protection of the atmosphere and monitor compliance herewith;

(c) The principle of appropriate measures to promote the effective implementation of and compliance with the decisions of the new institutional authority, decisions which will be subject to control by the International Court of Justice;

(d) The principle that countries to which decisions taken to protect the atmosphere shall prove to be an abnormal or special burden, in view, inter alia, of the level of their development and actual responsibility for the deterioration of the atmosphere, shall receive fair and equitable assistance to compensate them for bearing such burden. To this end mechanisms will have to be developed;

(e) The negotiation of the necessary legal instruments to provide an effective and coherent foundation, institutionally and financially, for the aforementioned principles.

The Heads of State and Government or their representatives, who have expressed their endorsement of this Declaration by placing their signatures under it, stress their resolve to promote the principles thus defined by:

—furthering the development of their initiative within the United Nations and in close coordination and collaboration with existing agencies set up under the auspices of the United Nations;

—inviting all States of the world and the international organisations competent in this field to join in developing, taking into account studies by the IPCC, the framework conventions and other legal instruments necessary to establish institutional authority and to implement the other principles stated above to protect the atmosphere and to counter climate change, particularly global warming;

—urging all States of the world and the international organisations competent in this field to sign and ratify conventions relating to the protection of nature and the environment;

—calling upon all States of the world to endorse the present declaration.

The original of this Declaration, drawn up in French and English, will be transmitted to the Government of the Kingdom of the Netherlands, which will retain it in its archives. Each of the participating States will receive from the Government of the Kingdom of the Netherlands a true copy of this Declaration.

The Prime Minister of the Netherlands is requested to transmit the text of this Declaration, which is not eligible for registration under Article 102 of the Charter of the United Nations, to all members of the United Nations.

The Hague, 11 March 1989

B. AIR QUALITY (Including Acid Deposition)

Editors' Introductory Note Regarding
the 1979 Convention on Long-Range Transboundary
Air Pollution and Related Instruments

The 1975 Helsinki Final Act of the Conference on Security and Co-operation in Europe (described *supra*, p. 228) called for "promoting the progressive development, codification and implementation of international law as one means of preserving and enhancing the human environment," including with respect to long-range air pollution. That call was taken up in the context of the U.N. Economic Commission for Europe (ECE), which consists of Canada, the United States, and all European countries except Albania (a total of 34 countries). In 1979, the ECE finalized the 1979 Convention on Long-Range Transboundary Air Pollution (LRTAP), which is a framework convention containing general principles intended to be elaborated by subsequent protocols embodying specific limits and procedures.

The LRTAP Convention was prompted primarily by the desire to deal with long-range acid deposition (also referred to as acid rain), but its scope is broader, extending to other forms of long-range transboundary pollution and to short-range pollution. Contracting Parties are obliged, inter alia, to "endeavour to limit, and, as far as possible, gradually reduce and prevent air pollution, including long-range transboundary air pollution" and to "develop without undue delay policies and strategies which shall serve as a means of combating the discharge of air pollutants." As is evident, these obligations typically require countries to develop appropriate policies rather than to take specific steps to limit or reduce pollution. Moreover, LRTAP's obligations are qualified by difficult-to-interpret and -enforce terms, such as "endeavour" (art. 2), "as far as possible" (art. 2), and compatibility with "balanced development" (art. 6). LRTAP also called for further development of the already existing "Co-operative programme for the monitoring and evaluation of the long-range transmission of air pollutants in Europe" (EMEP), but did not provide for financing EMEP. LRTAP is a major step in the on-going process of improving air quality in Europe.

LRTAP has been implemented by three protocols—regarding finance mechanisms and emissions of sulphur and nitrogen, which are the main pollutants causing acid deposition. The 1984 Geneva Protocol on Long-Term Financing of Co-operative Programme for Monitoring and Evaluation of the Long-Range Transmission of Air Pollutants in Europe (EMEP) establishes a mechanism for financing EMEP, which previously had been supported by funds from the United Nations Environment Programme (UNEP) and voluntary contributions from LRTAP member States. The financing mechanism consists of mandatory and voluntary contributions and is administered at the highest level by the LRTAP Executive Committee and at a subsidiary level by the Steering Body of EMEP.

The 1985 Helsinki Protocol on the Reduction of Sulphur Emissions or Their Transboundary Fluxes by at Least 30 Per Cent requires, as its basic substantive obligation, parties to "reduce their national annual sulphur emissions or their transboundary fluxes by at least 30 per cent as soon as possible and at the latest by 1993," from 1980 levels (art. 2). The Sulphur Protocol is thus definite in its requirements, in contrast to LRTAP.

The 1988 Sofia Protocol Concerning the Control of Emissions of Nitrogen Oxides or Their Transboundary Fluxes prescribes a two-step process. During the first stage, parties are required, inter alia, to stabilize, by 31 December 1994, their nitrogen oxide (NO_x) emissions or transboundary NO_x fluxes at the level of 1987 or any previous year to be specified by the State upon signing the Protocol, subject to certain conditions. Programmatic and co-operative measures are required during the second stage.

Work is now underway on another protocol, on volatile organic compounds (VOCs). VOCs, which enter the food chain, are emitted by automobiles, trucks, ships, and industrial plants, among other sources.

ECONOMIC COMMISSION FOR EUROPE CONVENTION ON LONG-RANGE TRANSBOUNDARY AIR POLLUTION (LRTAP) (WITH ACCOMPANYING RESOLUTION ON LONG-RANGE TRANSBOUNDARY AIR POLLUTION AND DECLARATION ON LOW AND NON-WASTE TECHNOLOGY AND RE-UTILIZATION AND RECYCLING OF WASTES)

Popular Name: LRTAP, LRTAP Convention

Done at Geneva on 13 November 1979, TIAS 10541, Cmnd 7885, Misc. 10 (1980), E/ECE/1010, *reprinted in* 18 ILM 1442 (1979), UNEP3 #78, p. 519, 28 IPE 341.

Entry into Force: 16 March 1983 (LRTAP Convention only; the Resolution and Declaration are not legally binding instruments)

Depositary: United Nations

Languages: English, French, Russian

Parties as of 1 January 1990: Austria; Belgium; Bulgaria; Byelorussian Soviet Socialist Republic; Canada; Czech and Slovak Federal Republic; Denmark; Finland; France; German Democratic Republic; Germany, Federal Republic of;* Greece; Iceland; Ireland; Italy; Liechtenstein; Luxembourg; Netherlands; Norway; Poland; Portugal; Spain; Sweden; Switzerland; Turkey; Ukrainian Soviet Socialist Republic; Union of Soviet Socialist Republics;* United Kingdom of Great Britain and Northern Ireland;** United States of America; Yugoslavia; European Economic Community

CONVENTION ON LONG-RANGE TRANSBOUNDARY AIR POLLUTION

The Parties to the present Convention,
  Determined to promote relations and co-operation in the field of environmental protection,
  Aware of the significance of the activities of the United Nations Economic Commission for Europe in strengthening such relations and co-operation, particularly in the field of air pollution including long-range transport of air pollutants,
  Recognizing the contribution of the Economic Commission for Europe to the multilateral implementation of the pertinent provisions of the Final Act of the Conference on Security and Co-operation in Europe,
  Cognizant of the references in the chapter on environment of the Final Act of the Conference on Security and Co-operation in Europe calling for co-operation to control air pollution and its effects, including long-range transport of air pollutants, and to the development through international co-operation of an extensive programme for the monitoring and evaluation of long-range transport of air pollutants, starting with sulphur dioxide and with possible extension to other pollutants,
  Considering the pertinent provisions of the Declaration of the United Nations Conference on the Human Environment, and in particular principle 21, which expresses the common conviction that States have, in accordance with the Charter of the United Nations[2] and the principles of international law, the sovereign right to exploit their own resources pursuant to their own environmental policies, and the responsibility to ensure that activities within their jurisdiction or control do not cause damage to the environment of other States or of areas beyond the limits of national jurisdiction,
  Recognizing the existence of possible adverse effects, in the short and long term, of air pollution including transboundary air pollution,
  Concerned that a rise in the level of emissions of air pollutants within the region as forecast may increase such adverse effects,
  Recognizing the need to study the implications of the long-range transport of air pollutants and the need to seek solutions for the problems identified,
  Affirming their willingness to reinforce active international co-operation to develop appropriate national policies and by means of exchange of information, consultation, research and monitoring, to co-ordinate national action for combating air pollution including long-range transboundary air pollution,
  Have agreed as follows:

DEFINITIONS
Article 1

For the purposes of the present Convention:
  (a) *"air pollution"* means the introduction by man, directly or indirectly, of substances or energy into the air resulting in deleterious effects of such a nature as

---

* With a declaration
** With a geographic extension

to endanger human health, harm living resources and ecosystems and material property and impair or interfere with amenities and other legitimate uses of the environment, and "air pollutants" shall be construed accordingly;

(b) "*long-range transboundary air pollution*" means air pollution whose physical origin is situated wholly or in part within the area under the national jurisdiction of one State and which has adverse effects in the area under the jurisdiction of another State at such a distance that it is not generally possible to distinguish the contribution of individual emission sources or groups of sources.

FUNDAMENTAL PRINCIPLES
Article 2

The Contracting Parties, taking due account of the facts and problems involved, are determined to protect man and his environment against air pollution and shall endeavour to limit and, as far as possible, gradually reduce and prevent air pollution including long-range transboundary air pollution.

Article 3

The Contracting Parties, within the framework of the present Convention, shall by means of exchanges of information, consultation, research and monitoring, develop without undue delay policies and strategies which shall serve as a means of combating the discharge of air pollutants, taking into account efforts already made at national and international levels.

Article 4

The Contracting Parties shall exchange information on and review their policies, scientific activities and technical measures aimed at combating, as far as possible, the discharge of air pollutants which may have adverse effects, thereby contributing to the reduction of air pollution including long-range transboundary air pollution.

Article 5

Consultations shall be held, upon request, at an early stage between, on the one hand, Contracting Parties which are actually affected by or exposed to a significant risk of long-range transboundary air pollution and, on the other hand, Contracting Parties within which and subject to whose jurisdiction a significant contribution to long-range transboundary air pollution originates, or could originate, in connexion with activities carried on or contemplated therein.

AIR QUALITY MANAGEMENT
Article 6

Taking into account articles 2 to 5, the ongoing research, exchange of information and monitoring and the results thereof, the cost and effectiveness of local and other remedies and, in order to combat air pollution, in particular that originating from new or rebuilt installations, each Contracting Party undertakes to develop the best policies and strategies including air quality management systems and, as part of them, control measures compatible with balanced development, in particular by using the best available technology which is economically feasible and low- and non-waste technology.

RESEARCH AND DEVELOPMENT
Article 7

The Contracting Parties, as appropriate to their needs, shall initiate and co-operate in the conduct of research into and/or development of:

(a) existing and proposed technologies for reducing emissions of sulphur compounds and other major air pollutants, including technical and economic feasibility, and environmental consequences;

(b) instrumentation and other techniques for monitoring and measuring emission rates and ambient concentration of air pollutants;

(c) improved models for a better understanding of the transmission of long-range transboundary air pollutants;

(d) the effects of sulphur compounds and other major air pollutants on human health and the environment, including agriculture, forestry, materials, aquatic and other natural ecosystems and visibility, with a view to establishing a scientific basis for dose/effect relationships designed to protect the environment;

(e) the economic, social and environmental assessment of alternative measures for attaining environmental objectives including the reduction of long-range transboundary air pollution;

(f) education and training programmes related to the environmental aspects of pollution by sulphur compounds and other major air pollutants.

EXCHANGE OF INFORMATION
Article 8

The Contracting Parties, within the framework of the Executive Body referred to in article 10 and bilaterally, shall, in their common interests, exchange available information on:

(a) data on emissions at periods of time to be agreed upon, of agreed air pollutants, starting with sulphur dioxide, coming from grid-units of agreed size; or on the fluxes of agreed air pollutants, starting with sulphur dioxide, across national borders, at distances and at periods of time to be agreed upon;

(b) major changes in national policies and in general industrial development, and their potential impact, which would be likely to cause significant changes in long-range transboundary air pollution;

(c) control technologies for reducing air pollution relevant to long-range transboundary air pollution;

(d) the projected cost of the emission control of sulphur compounds and other major air pollutants on a national scale;

(e) meteorological and physico-chemical data relating to the processes during transmission;

(f) physico-chemical and biological data relating to the effects of long-range transboundary air pollution and the extent of the damage [1] which these data indicate can be attributed to long-range transboundary air pollution;

(g) national, subregional and regional policies and strategies for the control of sulphur compounds and other major air pollutants.

IMPLEMENTATION AND FURTHER DEVELOPMENT OF THE CO-OPERATIVE PROGRAMME FOR THE MONITORING AND EVALUATION OF THE LONG-RANGE TRANSMISSION OF AIR POLLUTANTS IN EUROPE
Article 9

The Contracting Parties stress the need for the implementation of the existing "Co-operative programme for the monitoring and evaluation of the long-range

---

[1]The present Convention does not contain a rule on State liability as to damage.

transmission of air pollutants in Europe'' (hereinafter referred to as EMEP) and, with regard to the further development of this programme, agree to emphasize:

(a) the desirability of Contracting Parties joining in and fully implementing EMEP which, as a first step, is based on the monitoring of sulphur dioxide and related substances;

(b) the need to use comparable or standardized procedures for monitoring whenever possible;

(c) the desirability of basing the monitoring programme on the framework of both national and international programmes. The establishment of monitoring stations and the collection of data shall be carried out under the national jurisdiction of the country in which the monitoring stations are located;

(d) the desirability of establishing a framework for a co-operative environmental monitoring programme, based on and taking into account present and future national, subregional, regional and other international programmes;

(e) the need to exchange data on emissions at periods of time to be agreed upon, of agreed air pollutants, starting with sulphur dioxide, coming from grid-units of agreed size; or on the fluxes of agreed air pollutants, starting with sulphur dioxide, across national borders, at distances and at periods of time to be agreed upon. The method, including the model, used to determine the fluxes, as well as the method, including the model, used to determine the transmission of air pollutants based on the emissions per grid-unit, shall be made available and periodically reviewed, in order to improve the methods and the models;

(f) their willingness to continue the exchange and periodic updating of national data on total emissions of agreed air pollutants, starting with sulphur dioxide;

(g) the need to provide meteorological and physico-chemical data relating to processes during transmission;

(h) the need to monitor chemical components in other media such as water, soil and vegetation, as well as a similar monitoring programme to record effects on health and environment;

(i) the desirability of extending the national EMEP networks to make them operational for control and surveillance purposes.

EXECUTIVE BODY
Article 10

1. The representatives of the Contracting Parties shall, within the framework of the Senior Advisers to ECE Governments on Environmental Problems, constitute the Executive Body of the present Convention, and shall meet at least annually in that capacity.

2. The Executive Body shall:

(a) review the implementation of the present Convention;

(b) establish, as appropriate, working groups to consider matters related to the implementation and development of the present Convention and to this end to prepare appropriate studies and other documentation and to submit recommendations to be considered by the Executive Body;

(c) fulfil such other functions as may be appropriate under the provisions of the present Convention.

3. The Executive Body shall utilize the Steering Body for the EMEP to play an integral part in the operation of the present Convention, in particular with regard to data collection and scientific co-operation.

4. The Executive Body, in discharging its functions, shall, when it deems appropriate, also make use of information from other relevant international organizations.

SECRETARIAT
Article 11

The Executive Secretary of the Economic Commission for Europe shall carry out, for the Executive Body, the following secretariat functions:

(a) to convene and prepare the meetings of the Executive Body;

(b) to transmit to the Contracting Parties reports and other information received in accordance with the provisions of the present Convention;

(c) to discharge the functions assigned by the Executive Body.

AMENDMENTS TO THE CONVENTION
Article 12

1. Any Contracting Party may propose amendments to the present Convention.

2. The text of proposed amendments shall be submitted in writing to the Executive Secretary of the Economic Commission for Europe, who shall communicate them to all Contracting Parties. The Executive Body shall discuss proposed amendments at its next annual meeting provided that such proposals have been circulated by the Executive Secretary of the Economic Commission for Europe to the Contracting Parties at least ninety days in advance.

3. An amendment to the present Convention shall be adopted by consensus of the representatives of the Contracting Parties, and shall enter into force for the Contracting Parties which have accepted it on the ninetieth day after the date on which two-thirds of the Contracting Parties have deposited their instruments of acceptance with the depositary. Thereafter, the amendment shall enter into force for any other Contracting Party on the ninetieth day after the date on which that Contracting Party deposits its instrument of acceptance of the amendment.

SETTLEMENT OF DISPUTES
Article 13

If a dispute arises between two or more Contracting Parties to the present Convention as to the interpretation or application of the Convention, they shall seek a solution by negotiation or by any other method of dispute settlement acceptable to the parties to the dispute.

SIGNATURE
Article 14

1. The present Convention shall be open for signature at the United Nations Office at Geneva from 13 to 16 November 1979 on the occasion of the High-level Meeting within the framework of the Economic Commission for Europe on the Protection of the Environment, by the member States of the Economic Commission for Europe as well as States having consultative status with the Economic Commission for Europe, pursuant to paragraph 8 of Economic and Social Council resolution 36 (IV) of 28 March 1947, and by regional economic integration organizations, constituted by sovereign States members of the Economic Commission for Europe, which have competence in respect of the negotiation, conclusion and application of international agreements in matters covered by the present Convention.

2. In matters within their competence, such regional economic integration organizations shall, on their own behalf, exercise the rights and fulfil the responsibilities which the present Convention attributes to their member States. In such cases, the member States of these organizations shall not be entitled to exercise such rights individually.

RATIFICATION, ACCEPTANCE, APPROVAL AND ACCESSION
Article 15

1. The present Convention shall be subject to ratification, acceptance or approval.

2. The present Convention shall be open for accession as from 17 November 1979 by the States and organizations referred to in article 14, paragraph 1.

3. The instruments of ratification, acceptance, approval or accession shall be deposited with the Secretary-General of the United Nations, who will perform the functions of the depositary.

ENTRY INTO FORCE
Article 16

1. The present Convention shall enter into force on the nineteenth day after the date of deposit of the twenty-fourth instrument of ratification, acceptance, approval or accession.

2. For each Contracting Party which ratifies, accepts or approves the present Convention or accedes thereto after the deposit of the twenty-fourth instrument of ratification, acceptance, approval or accession, the Convention shall enter into force on the nineteenth day after the date of deposit by such Contracting Party of its instrument of ratification, acceptance, approval or accession.

WITHDRAWAL
Article 17

At any time after five years from the date on which the present Convention has come into force with respect to a Contracting Party, that Contracting Party may withdraw from the Convention by giving written notification to the depositary. Any such withdrawal shall take effect on the nineteenth day after the date of its receipt by the depositary.

AUTHENTIC TEXTS
Article 18

The original of the present Convention, of which the English, French and Russian texts are equally authentic, shall be deposited with the Secretary-General of the United Nations.

IN WITNESS WHEREOF the undersigned, being duly authorized thereto, have signed the present Convention.

DONE at Geneva, this thirteenth day of November, one thousand nine hundred and seventy-nine.

HELSINKI PROTOCOL TO THE 1979 CONVENTION ON LONG-RANGE TRANSBOUNDARY AIR POLLUTION ON THE REDUCTION OF SULPHUR EMISSIONS OR tHEIR TRANSBOUNDARY FLUXES BY AT LEAST 30 PER CENT

Popular Name: Sulphur Protocol

Done at Helsinki on 8 July 1985, U.N. Doc. EB.AIR/12, *reprinted in* 27 ILM 707 (1988).

Entry into Force: 2 September 1987

Depositary: United Nations

Languages: English, French, Russian

Parties as of September 1990: Austria; Belgium; Bulgaria; Byelorussian Soviet Socialist Republic; Canada; Czech and Slovak Federal Republic; Denmark; Finland; France; Germany, Federal Republic of; Hungary; Italy; Liechtenstein; Luxembourg; Netherlands; Norway; Sweden; Switzerland; Ukrainian Soviet Socialist Republic; Union of Soviet Socialist Republics

PROTOCOL TO THE 1979 CONVENTION ON LONG-RANGE TRANSBOUNDARY AIR POLLUTION ON THE REDUCTION OF SULPHUR EMISSIONS OR THEIR TRANSBOUNDARY FLUXES BY AT LEAST 30 PER CENT

The Parties,

Determined to implement the Convention on Long-range Transboundary Air Pollution,

Concerned that the present emissions of air pollutants are causing widespread damage, in exposed parts of Europe and North America, to natural resources of vital environmental and economic importance, such as forests, soils and waters, and to materials (including historical monuments) and, under certain circumstances, have harmful effects on human health,

Aware of the fact that the predominant sources of air pollution contributing to the acidification of the environment are the combustion of fossil fuels for energy production, and the main technological processes in various industrial sectors, as well as transport, which lead to emissions of sulphur dioxide, nitrogen oxides, and other pollutants,

Considering that high priority should be given to reducing sulphur emissions, which will have positive results environmentally, on the overall economic situation and on human health,

Recalling the decision of the United Nations Economic Commission for Europe (ECE) at its thirty-ninth session, which stresses the urgency of intensifying efforts to arrive at co-ordinated national strategies and policies in the ECE region to reduce sulphur emissions effectively at national levels,

Recalling the recognition by the Executive Body for the Convention at its first session of the need to decrease effectively the total annual emissions of sulphur compounds or their transboundary fluxes by 1993-1995, using 1980 levels as the basis for calculations of reductions,

Recalling that the Multilateral Conference on the Causes and Prevention of Damage to Forests and Water by Air Pollution in Europe (Munich, 24-27 June 1984) had requested that the Executive Body for the Convention, as a matter of highest priority, adopt a proposal for a specific agreement on the reduction of annual national sulphur emissions or their transboundary fluxes by 1993 at the latest,

Noting that a number of Contracting Parties to the Convention have decided to implement reductions of their national annual sulphur emissions or their transboundary fluxes by at least 30 per cent as soon as possible and at the latest by 1993, using 1980 levels as the basis for calculation of reductions,

Recognizing, on the other hand, that some Contracting Parties to the Convention, while not signing the present Protocol at the time of its opening for signature, will nevertheless contribute significantly to the reduction of transboundary air pollution, or will continue to make efforts to control sulphur emissions, as stated in the document annexed to the report of the Executive Body at its third session,

Have agreed as follows:

Article 1
Definitions

For the purposes of the present protocol,

1. "Convention" means the Convention on Long-range Transboundary Air Pollution, adopted in Geneva on 13 November 1979,

2. "EMEP" means the Co-operative Programme for Monitoring and Evaluation of the Long-range Transmission of Air Pollutants in Europe,

3. "Executive Body" means the Executive Body for the Convention constituted under article 10, paragraph 1 of the Convention,

4. "Geographical scope of EMEP" means the area defined in article 1, paragraph 4 of the Protocol to the 1979 Convention on Long-range Transboundary Air Pollution on Long-term Financing of the Co-operative Programme for Monitoring and Evaluation of the Long-range Transmission of Air Pollutants in Europe (EMEP), adopted in Geneva on 28 September 1984,

5. "Parties" means, unless the context otherwise requires, the Parties to the present Protocol.

Article 2
Basic provisions

The Parties shall reduce their national annual sulphur emissions or their transboundary fluxes by at least 30 per cent as soon as possible and at the latest by 1993, using 1980 levels as the basis for calculation of reductions.

Article 3
Further reductions

The Parties recognize the need for each of them to study at the national level the necessity for further reductions, beyond those referred to in article 2, of sulphur emissions or their transboundary fluxes when environmental conditions warrant.

Article 4
Reporting of annual emissions

Each Party shall provide annually to the Executive Body its levels of national annual sulphur emissions, and the basis upon which they have been calculated.

Article 5
Calculations of transboundary fluxes

EMEP shall in good time before the annual meetings of the Executive Body provide to the Executive Body calculations of sulphur budgets and also of transboundary fluxes and depositions of sulphur compounds for each previous year within the geographical scope of EMEP, utilizing appropriate models. In areas outside the geographical scope of EMEP, models appropriate to the particular circumstances of Parties therein shall be used.

Article 6
National programmes, policies and strategies

The Parties shall, within the framework of the Convention, develop without undue delay national programmes, policies and strategies which shall serve as a means of reducing sulphur emissions or their transboundary fluxes, by at least 30 per cent as soon as possible and at the latest by 1993, and shall report thereon as well as on progress towards achieving the goal to the Executive Body.

* * *

SOFIA PROTOCOL TO THE 1979 CONVENTION ON LONG-RANGE TRANSBOUNDARY AIR POLLUTION CONCERNING THE CONTROL OF EMISSIONS OF NITROGEN OXIDES OR THEIR TRANSBOUNDARY FLUXES

Popular Names: NOx Protocol, NO_x Protocol

Done at Sofia on 31 October 1988, U.N. Doc. EB.AIR/21, *reprinted in* 28 ILM 214 (1989).

Entry into Force: 1 January 1991

Depositary: United Nations

Languages: English, French, Russian

Parties as of December 1990: Austria; Bulgaria; Byelorussian Soviet Socialist Republic; Czech and Slovak Federal Republic; Finland; France; Germany, Federal Republic of;* Netherlands; Norway; Sweden; Switzerland; Ukrainian Soviet Socialist Republic; Union of Soviet Socialist Republic; United States of America

PROTOCOL TO THE 1979 CONVENTION ON LONG-RANGE TRANSBOUNDARY AIR POLLUTION CONCERNING THE CONTROL OF EMISSIONS OF NITROGEN OXIDES OR THEIR TRANSBOUNDARY FLUXES

* * *

Article 1
Definitions

For the purposes of the present Protocol,
1. ''Convention'' means the Convention on Long-range Transboundary Air Pollution, adopted in Geneva on 13 November 1979;

---

* Post-absorption Germany

2. "EMEP" means the Co-operative Programme for Monitoring and Evaluation of the Long-range Transmission of Air Pollutants in Europe;

3. "Executive Body" means the Executive Body for the Convention constituted under article 10, paragraph 1 of the Convention;

4. "Geographical scope of EMEP" means the area defined in article 1, paragraph 4 of the Protocol to the 1979 Convention on Long-range Transboundary Air Pollution on Long-term Financing of the Co-operative Programme for Monitoring and Evaluation of the Long-range Transmission of Air Pollutants in Europe (EMEP), adopted in Geneva on 28 September 1984;

5. "Parties" means, unless the context otherwise requires, the Parties to the present Protocol;

6. "Commission" means the United Nations Economic Commission for Europe;

7. "Critical load" means a quantitative estimate of the exposure to one or more pollutants below which significant harmful effects on specified sensitive elements of the environment do not occur according to present knowledge;

8. "Major existing stationary source" means any existing stationary source the thermal input of which is at least 100 MW;

9. "Major new stationary source" means any new stationary source the thermal input of which is at least 50 MW;

10. "Major source category" means any category of sources which emit or may emit air pollutants in the form of nitrogen oxides, including the categories described in the Technical Annex, and which contribute at least 10 per cent of the total national emissions of nitrogen oxides on an annual basis as measured or calculated in the first calendar year after the date of entry into force of the present Protocol, and every fourth year thereafter;

11. "New stationary source" means any stationary source the construction or substantial modification of which is commenced after the expiration of two years from the date of entry into force of this Protocol;

12. "New mobile source" means a motor vehicle or other mobile source which is manufactured after the expiration of two years from the date of entry into force of the present Protocol.

Article 2
Basic obligations

1. The Parties shall, as soon as possible and as a first step, take effective measures to control and/or reduce their national annual emissions of nitrogen oxides or their transboundary fluxes so that these, at the latest by 31 December 1994, do not exceed their national annual emissions of nitrogen oxides or transboundary fluxes of such emissions for the calendar year 1987 or any previous year to be specified upon signature of, or accession to, the Protocol, provided that in addition, with respect to any Party specifying such a previous year, its national average annual transboundary fluxes or national average annual emissions of nitrogen oxides for the period from 1 January 1987 to 1 January 1996 do not exceed its transboundary fluxes or national emissions for the calendar year 1987.

2. Furthermore, the Parties shall in particular, and no later than two years after the date of entry into force of the present Protocol:

(a) Apply national emissions standards to major new stationary sources and/ or source categories, and to substantially modified stationary sources in major source categories, based on the best available technologies which are economically feasible, taking into consideration the Technical Annex;

(b) Apply national emission standards to new mobile sources in all major source categories based on the best available technologies which are economically feasible, taking into consideration the Technical Annex and the relevant decisions taken within the framework of the Inland Transport Committee of the Commission; and

(c) Introduce pollution control measures for major existing stationary sources, taking into consideration the Technical Annex and the characteristics of the plant, its age and its rate of utilization and the need to avoid undue operational disruption.

3. (a) The Parties shall, as a second step, commence negotiations, no later than six months after the date of entry into force of the present Protocol, on further steps to reduce national annual emissions of nitrogen oxides or transboundary fluxes of such emissions, taking into account the best available scientific and technological developments, internationally accepted critical loads and other elements resulting from the work programme undertaken under article 6.

(b) To this end, the Parties shall co-operate in order to establish:
  (i) Critical loads;
  (ii) Reductions in national annual emissions of nitrogen oxides or transboundary fluxes of such emissions as required to achieve agreed objectives based on critical loads; and
  (iii) Measures and a time-table commencing no later than 1 January 1996 for achieving such reductions.

4. Parties may take more stringent measures than those required by the present article.

Article 3
Exchange of technology

1. The Parties shall, consistent with their national laws, regulations and practices, facilitate the exchange of technology to reduce emissions of nitrogen oxides, particularly through the promotion of:
  (a) Commercial exchange of available technology;
  (b) Direct industrial contacts and co-operation, including joint ventures;
  (c) Exchange of information and experience; and
  (d) Provision of technical assistance.

2. In promoting the activities specified in subparagraphs (a) to (d) above, the Parties shall create favourable conditions by facilitating contacts and co-operation among appropriate organizations and individuals in the private and public sectors that are capable of providing technology, design and engineering services, equipment or finance.

3. The Parties shall, no later than six months after the date of entry into force of the present Protocol, commence consideration of procedures to create more favourable conditions for the exchange of technology to reduce emissions of nitrogen oxides.

Article 4
Unleaded fuel

The Parties shall, as soon as possible and no later than two years after the date of entry into force of the present Protocol, make unleaded fuel sufficiently available, in particular cases as a minimum along main international transit routes, to facilitate the circulation of vehicles equipped with catalytic converters.

Article 5
Review process

1. The Parties shall regularly review the present Protocol, taking into account the best available scientific substantiation and technological development.

2. The first review shall take place no later than one year after the date of entry into force of the present Protocol.

Article 6
Work to be undertaken

The Parties shall give high priority to research and monitoring related to the development and application of an approach based on critical loads to determine, on a scientific basis, necessary reductions in emissions of nitrogen oxides. The Parties shall, in particular, through national research programmes, in the work plan of the Executive Body and through other co-operative programmes within the framework of the Convention, seek to:

(a) Identify and quantify effects of emissions of nitrogen oxides on humans, plant and animal life, waters, soils and materials, taking into account the impact on these of nitrogen oxides from sources other than atmospheric deposition;

(b) Determine the geographical distribution of sensitive areas;

(c) Develop measurements and model calculations including harmonized methodologies for the calculation of emissions, to quantify the long-range transport of nitrogen oxides and related pollutants;

(d) Improve estimates of the performance and costs of technologies for control of emissions of nitrogen oxides and record the development of improved and new technologies; and

(e) Develop, in the context of an approach based on critical loads, methods to integrate scientific, technical and economic data in order to determine appropriate control strategies.

Article 7
National programmes, policies and strategies

The Parties shall develop without undue delay national programmes, policies and strategies to implement the obligations under the present Protocol that shall serve as a means of controlling and reducing emissions of nitrogen oxides or their transboundary fluxes.

Article 8
Information exchange and annual reporting

1. The Parties shall exchange information by notifying the Executive Body of the national programmes, policies and strategies that they develop in accordance with article 7 and by reporting to it annually on progress achieved under, and any changes to, those programmes, policies and strategies, and in particular on:

(a) The levels of national annual emissions of nitrogen oxides and the basis upon which they have been calculated;

(b) Progress in applying national emission standards required under article 2, subparagraphs 2 (a) and 2 (b), and the national emission standards applied or to be applied, and the sources and/or source categories concerned;

(c) Progress in introducing the pollution control measures required under article 2, subparagraph 2 (c), the sources concerned and the measures introduced or to be introduced;

(d) Progress in making unleaded fuel available;

(e) Measures taken to facilitate the exchange of technology; and

(f) Progress in establishing critical loads.

2. Such information shall, as far as possible, be submitted in accordance with a uniform reporting framework.

Article 9
Calculations

EMEP shall, utilizing appropriate models and in good time before the annual meetings of the Executive Body, provide to the Executive Body calculations of nitrogen budgets and also of transboundary fluxes and deposition of nitrogen oxides within the geographical scope of EMEP. In areas outside the geographical scope of EMEP, models appropriate to the particular circumstances of Parties to the Convention therein shall be used.

Article 10
Technical Annex

The Technical Annex to the present Protocol is recommendatory in character. It shall form an integral part of the Protocol.

Article 11
Amendments to the Protocol

1. Any Party may propose amendments to the present Protocol.
2. Proposed amendments shall be submitted in writing to the Executive Secretary of the Commission who shall communicate them to all Parties. The Executive Body shall discuss the proposed amendments at its next annual meeting provided that these proposals have been circulated by the Executive Secretary to the Parties at least ninety days in advance.
3. Amendments to the Protocol, other than amendments to its Technical Annex, shall be adopted by consensus of the Parties present at a meeting of the Executive Body, and shall enter into force for the Parties which have accepted them on the ninetieth day after the date on which two-thirds of the Parties have deposited their instruments of acceptance thereof. Amendments shall enter into force for any Party which has accepted them after two-thirds of the Parties have deposited their instruments of acceptance of the amendment, on the ninetieth day after the date on which that Party deposited its instrument of acceptance of the amendments.
4. Amendments to the Technical Annex shall be adopted by consensus of the Parties present at a meeting of the Executive Body and shall become effective thirty days after the date on which they have been communicated in accordance with paragraph 5 below.
5. Amendments under paragraphs 3 and 4 above shall, as soon as possible after their adoption, be communicated by the Executive Secretary to all Parties.

AGREEMENT BETWEEN THE GOVERNMENT OF THE UNITED STATES OF AMERICA AND THE GOVERNMENT OF CANADA ON AIR QUALITY

Popular Names: Air Quality Accord, Air Quality Agreement Done at Ottawa on 13 March 1991.

Entry into Force: 13 March 1991

Languages: English and French

Editors' Note

The Air Quality Accord is a major step in resolving a longstanding dispute between Canada and the United States over transboundary air pollution generally and acid deposition more particularly. That dispute, which stemmed from the realization that emissions in each of the countries were causing damage in the other, has persisted for more than 20 years. Among other important steps in settling the dispute were: a 1980 Memorandum of Intent Between the Government of Canada and the Government of the United States Concerning Transboundary Air Pollution, 5 August 1980, 80 U.S. Dep't St. Bull. 21 (1980); the appointment of a Special Envoy on Acid Rain by each country and the issuance of a joint report by those envoys, D. Lewis & W. Davis, *Joint Report of the Special Envoys on Acid Rain,* U.S. Dep't of State, Washington, D.C. (Jan. 1986); steps by Canada to reduce the transboundary flux of sulphur dioxide from Canada to the United States by 50%; joint fact-finding programs (necessitated in large part by United States claims that there needed to be more information before the United States would commit to reduce the transboundary flux); and passage of the Clean Air Act Amendments of 1990, Pub. L. No. 101-549, that will accomplish the 50% reduction in the flow of sulphur dioxide from the United States to Canada demanded by Canada. For further discussion of this process, see *International Law and Pollution* 247-64, 310-54 (D. Magraw ed. 1991).

The Air Quality Accord consists of a preamble, 16 articles, and two annexes. It is an executive agreement and went into effect upon signing, including the annexes. Future annexes are contemplated. The Accord requires notification and consultation in a variety of circumstances and makes use of the International Joint Commission, established pursuant to the 1909 Boundary Waters Treaty between the two countries *(supra* page 412), to settle disputes. The first annex concerns acid deposition. The second annex addresses co-operative research and monitoring activities.

AGREEMENT BETWEEN THE GOVERNMENT OF THE UNITED STATES OF AMERICA AND THE GOVERNMENT OF CANADA ON AIR QUALITY

The Government of the United States of America and the Government of Canada, hereinafter referred to as ''the Parties'',

Convinced that transboundary air pollution can cause significant harm to natural resources of vital environmental, cultural and economic importance, and to human health in both countries;

Desiring that emissions of air pollutants from sources within their countries not result in significant transboundary air pollution;

Convinced that transboundary air pollution can effectively be reduced through cooperative or coordinated action providing for controlling emissions of air pollutants in both countries;

Recalling the efforts they have made to control air pollution and the improved air quality that has resulted from such efforts in both countries;

Intending to address air-related issues of a global nature, such as climate change and stratospheric ozone depletion, in other fora;

Reaffirming Principle 21 of the Stockholm Declaration, which provides that ''States have, in accordance with the Charter of the United Nations and the principles of international law, the sovereign right to exploit their own resources pursuant to their own environmental policies, and the responsibility to ensure that activities within their jurisdiction or control do not cause damage to the environment of other States or of areas beyond the limits of national jurisdiction'';

Noting their tradition of environmental cooperation as reflected in the Boundary Waters Treaty of 1909, the Trail Smelter Arbitration of 1941, the Great Lakes Water Quality Agreement of 1978, as amended, the Memorandum of Intent Concerning Transboundary Air Pollution of 1980, the 1986 Joint Report of the Special

Envoys on Acid Rain, as well as the ECE Convention on Long-Range Transboundary Air Pollution of 1979;

Convinced that a healthy environment is essential to assure the well-being of present and future generations in the United States and Canada, as well as of the global community;

Have agreed as follows:

Article I
Definitions

For the purposes of this Agreement:

1. *"Air pollution"* means the introduction by man, directly or indirectly, of substances into the air resulting in deleterious effects of such a nature as to endanger human health, harm living resources and ecosystems and material property and impair or interfere with amenities and other legitimate uses of the environment, and "air pollutants" shall be construed accordingly;

2. *"Transboundary air pollution"* means air pollution whose physical origin is situated wholly or in part within the area under the jurisdiction of one Party and which has adverse effects, other than effects of a global nature, in the area under the jurisdiction of the other Party;

3. *"Boundary Waters Treaty"* means the Treaty Relating to Boundary Waters and Questions Arising along the Boundary between the United States and Canada, signed at Washington on January 11, 1909;

4. *"International Joint Commission"* means the International Joint Commission established by the Boundary Waters Treaty.

Article II
Purpose

The purpose of the Parties is to establish, by this Agreement, a practical and effective instrument to address shared concerns regarding transboundary air pollution.

Article III
General Air Quality Objective

1. The general objective of the Parties is to control transboundary air pollution between the two countries.

2. To this end, the Parties shall:

(a)   in accordance with Article IV, establish specific objectives for emissions limitations or reductions of air pollutants and adopt the necessary programs and other measures to implement such specific objectives;

(b)   in accordance with Article V, undertake environmental impact assessment, prior notification, and, as appropriate, mitigation measures;

(c)   carry out coordinated or cooperative scientific and technical activities, and economic research, in accordance with Article VI, and exchange information, in accordance with Article VII;

(d)   establish institutional arrangements, in accordance with Articles VIII and IX; and

(e)   review and assess progress, consult, address issues of concern, and settle disputes, in accordance with Articles X, XI, XII and XIII.

Article IV
Specific Air Quality Objectives

1. Each Party shall establish specific objectives, which it undertakes to achieve, for emissions limitations or reductions of such air pollutants as the Parties agree to address. Such specific objectives will be set forth in annexes to this Agreement.
2. Each Party's specific objectives for emissions limitations or reductions of sulphur dioxide and nitrogen oxides, which will reduce transboundary flows of these acidic deposition precursors, are set forth in Annex 1. Specific objectives for such other air pollutants as the Parties agree to address should take into account, as appropriate, the activities undertaken pursuant to Article VI.
3. Each Party shall adopt the programs and other measures necessary to implement its specific objectives set forth in any annexes.
4. If either Party has concerns about the programs or other measures of the other Party referred to in paragraph 3, it may request consultations in accordance with Article XI.

Article V
Assessment, Notification, and Mitigation

1. Each Party shall, as appropriate and as required by its laws, regulations and policies, assess those proposed actions, activities and projects within the area under its jurisdiction that, if carried out, would be likely to cause significant transboundary air pollution, including consideration of appropriate mitigation measures.
2. Each Party shall notify the other Party concerning a proposed action, activity or project subject to assessment under paragraph 1 as early as practicable in advance of a decision concerning such action, activity or project and shall consult with the other Party at its request in accordance with Article XI.
3. In addition, each Party shall, at the request of the other Party, consult in accordance with Article XI concerning any continuing actions, activities or projects that may be causing significant transboundary air pollution, as well as concerning changes to its laws, regulations or policies that, if carried out, would be likely to affect significantly transboundary air pollution.
4. Consultations pursuant to paragraphs 2 and 3 concerning actions, activities or projects that would be likely to cause or may be causing significant transboundary air pollution shall include consideration of appropriate mitigation measures.
5. Each Party shall, as appropriate, take measures to avoid or mitigate the potential risk posed by actions, activities or projects that would be likely to cause or may be causing significant transboundary air pollution.
6. If either Party becomes aware of an air pollution problem that is of joint concern and requires an immediate response, it shall notify and consult the other Party forthwith.

Article VI
Scientific and Technical Activities and Economic Research

1. The Parties shall carry out scientific and technical activities, and economic research, as set forth in Annex 2, in order to improve their understanding of transboundary air pollution concerns and to increase their capability to control such pollution.
2. In implementing this Article, the Parties may seek the advice of the International Joint Commission regarding the conduct of monitoring activities.

Article VII
Exchange of Information

1. The Parties agree to exchange, on a regular basis and through the Air Quality Committee established under Article VIII, information on:

(a) monitoring;
(b) emissions;
(c) technologies, measures and mechanisms for controlling emissions;
(d) atmospheric processes; and
(e) effects of air pollutants,
as provided in Annex 2.

2. Notwithstanding any other provisions of this Agreement, the Air Quality Committee and the International Joint Commission shall not release, without the consent of the owner, any information identified to them as proprietary information under the laws of the place where such information has been acquired.

Article VIII
The Air Quality Committee

1. The Parties agree to establish and maintain a bilateral Air Quality Committee to assist in the implementation of this Agreement. The Committee shall be composed of an equal number of members representing each Party. It may be supported by subcommittees, as appropriate.

2. The Committee's responsibilities shall include:
(a) reviewing progress made in the implementation of this Agreement, including its general and specific objectives;
(b) preparing and submitting to the Parties a progress report within a year after entry into force of this Agreement and at least every two years thereafter;
(c) referring each progress report to the International Joint Commission for action in accordance with Article IX of this Agreement; and
(d) releasing each progress report to the public after its submission to the Parties.

3. The Committee shall meet at least once a year and additionally at the request of either Party.

Article IX
Responsibilities of the International Joint Commission

1. The International Joint Commission is hereby given, by a Reference pursuant to Article IX of the Boundary Waters Treaty, the following responsibilities for the sole purpose of assisting the Parties in the implementation of this Agreement:
(a) to invite comments, including through public hearings as appropriate, on each progress report prepared by the Air Quality Committee pursuant to Article VIII;
(b) to submit to the Parties a synthesis of the views presented pursuant to sub-paragraph (a), as well as the record of such views if either Party so requests; and
(c) to release the synthesis of views to the public after its submission to the Parties.

2. In addition, the Parties shall consider such other joint references to the International Joint Commission as may be appropriate for the effective implementation of this Agreement.

Article X
Review and Assessment

1. Following the receipt of each progress report submitted to them by the Air Quality Committee in accordance with Article VIII and the views presented to the International Joint Commission on that report in accordance with Article IX, the

Parties shall consult on the contents of the progress report, including any recommendations therein.

2. The Parties shall conduct a comprehensive review and assessment of this Agreement, and its implementation, during the fifth year after its entry into force and every five years thereafter, unless otherwise agreed.

3. Following the consultations referred to in paragraph 1, as well as the review and assessment referred to in paragraph 2, the Parties shall consider such action as may be appropriate, including:

(a)   the modification of this Agreement;
(b)   the modification of existing policies, programs or measures.

Article XI
Consultations

The Parties shall consult, at the request of either Party, on any matter within the scope of this Agreement. Such consultations shall commence as soon as practicable, but in any event not later than thirty days from the date of receipt of the request for consultations, unless otherwise agreed by the Parties.

Article XII
Referrals

With respect to cases other than those subject to Article XIII, if, after consultations in accordance with Article XI, an issue remains concerning a proposed or continuing action, activity, or project that is causing or would be likely to cause significant transboundary air pollution, the Parties shall refer the matter to an appropriate third party in accordance with agreed terms of reference.

Article XIII
Settlement of Disputes

1. If, after consultations in accordance with Article XI, a dispute remains between the Parties over the interpretation or the implementation of this Agreement, they shall seek to resolve such dispute by negotiations between them. Such negotiations shall commence as soon as practicable, but in any event not later than ninety days from the date of receipt of the request for negotiation, unless otherwise agreed by the Parties.

2. If a dispute is not resolved through negotiation, the Parties shall consider whether to submit that dispute to the International Joint Commission in accordance with either Article IX or Article X of the Boundary Waters Treaty. If, after such consideration, the Parties do not elect either of those options, they shall, at the request of either Party, submit the dispute to another agreed form of dispute resolution.

Article XIV
Implementation

1. The obligations undertaken under this Agreement shall be subject to the availability of appropriated funds in accordance with the respective constitutional procedures of the Parties.

2. The Parties shall seek:

(a)   the appropriation of funds required to implement this Agreement;
(b)   the enactment of any additional legislation that may be necessary to implement this Agreement;
(c)   the cooperation of State and Provincial Governments as necessary to implement this Agreement.

3. In implementing this Agreement, the Parties shall, as appropriate, consult with State or Provincial Governments, interested organizations, and the public.

Article XV
Existing Rights and Obligations

Nothing in this Agreement shall be deemed to diminish the rights and obligations of the Parties in other international agreements between them, including those contained in the Boundary Waters Treaty and the Great Lakes Water Quality Agreement of 1978, as amended.

Article XVI
Entry into Force, Amendment, Termination

1. This Agreement, including Annexes 1 and 2, shall enter into force upon signature by the Parties.
2. This Agreement may be amended at any time by agreement of the Parties in writing.
3. Either Party may terminate this Agreement upon one year's written notice to the other Party, in which case any annexes will also terminate.
4. Annexes constitute an integral part of this Agreement, except that, if an annex so provides, either Party may terminate such annex in accordance with the terms of that annex.

IN WITNESS WHEREOF, the undersigned have signed this Agreement. DONE in duplicate, at OTTAWA, this 13th day of MARCH 1991, in the English and French languages, each version being equally authentic.

*   *   *

Annex 1
SPECIFIC OBJECTIVES CONCERNING SULPHUR DIOXIDE AND NITROGEN OXIDES

1. *Sulphur Dioxide*
   A.   *For the United States:*[1]
   1. Reduction of annual sulphur dioxide emissions by approximately 10 million tons[2] from 1980 levels in accordance with Title IV of the Clean Air Act[3] i.e., reduction of annual sulphur dioxide emissions to approximately 10 million tons below 1980 levels by 2000 (with the exception of sources repowering with qualifying clean coal technology in accordance with section 409 of the Clean Air Act, and sources receiving bonus allowances in accordance with section 405(a) (2) and (3) of the Clean Air Act).
   2. Achievement of a permanent national emission cap of 8.95 million tons of sulphur dioxide per year for electric utilities by 2010, to the extent required by Title IV of the Clean Air Act.
   3. Promulgation of new or revised standards or such other action under the Clean Air Act as the Administrator of the U.S. Environmental Protection Agency (EPA) deems appropriate, to the extent required by section 406 of the Clean Air Act Amendments of 1990 (P. L. 101-549), aimed at limiting sulphur

---

[1]Applies only to reductions in emissions in the forty-eight contiguous States and the District of Columbia.
[2]1 ton = 0.91 tonnes (metric tons).
[3]All references to the Clean Air Act refer to the Act as amended November 15, 1990.

dioxide emissions from industrial sources in the event that the Administrator of EPA determines that annual sulphur dioxide emissions from industrial sources may reasonably be expected to exceed 5.6 million tons.

B.   *For Canada:*

1. Reduction of sulphur dioxide emissions in the seven easternmost Provinces to 2.3 million tonnes per year by 1994 and the achievement of a cap on sulphur dioxide emissions in the seven easternmost Provinces at 2.3 million tonnes per year from 1995 through December 31, 1999.

2. Achievement of a permanent national emissions cap of 3.2 million tonnes per year by 2000.

2. *Nitrogen Oxides*

A. *For the United States:*[4]

With a view to a reduction of total annual emissions of nitrogen oxides by approximately 2 million tons from 1980 emission levels by 2000:

1. *Stationary Sources*

Implementation of the following nitrogen oxides control program for electric utility boilers to the extent required by Title IV of the Clean Air Act:

(a) By January 1, 1995, tangentially fired boilers must meet an allowable emission rate of 0.45 lb/mmBtu and dry bottom wall-fired boilers must meet an allowable emission rate of 0.50 lb/mmBtu (unless the Administrator of EPA determines that these rates cannot be achieved using low NOx burner technology).

(b) By January 1, 1997, EPA must set allowable emission limitations for:

—wet bottom wall-fired boilers;

—cyclones;

—units applying cell burner technology; and

—all other types of utility boilers.

2. *Mobile Sources*

Implementation of the following mobile source nitrogen oxides control program to the extent required by Title II of the Clean Air Act:

(a) Light Duty Trucks (LDT) (up to 6000 lbs gross vehicle weight rating (GVWR)) and Light Duty Vehicles (LDV)—standards for model years after 1993:

	5 yrs/50,000 miles (useful life)	10 years/100,000 miles
LDTs (0 to 3750 lbs Loaded Vehicle Weight (LVW)) and LDVs	0.4 grams per mile (gpm)	0.6 gpm
Diesel LDTs (0 to 3750 lbs LVW) and LDVs (before 2004)	1.0 gpm	1.25 gpm
LDTs (3751 to 5750 lbs LVW)	0.7 gpm[5]	0.97 gpm

In model year 1994, 40% of each manufacturer's sales volume must meet the above standards. In 1995, the percentage shall increase to 80% and, after 1995, to 100%.

(b) Light Duty Trucks more than 6000 lbs GVWR (after model year 1995):

---

[4]Applies only to reductions in emissions in the forty-eight contiguous States and the District of Columbia.
[5]This standard does not apply to diesel-fueled LDTs (3751 to 5750 lbs LVW).

	Gasoline 5 yrs/50,000 miles	Gasoline and Diesel 11 yrs/120,000 miles
LDTs (3751 to 5750 lbs Test Weight (TW))	0.7 gpm	0.98 gpm
LDTs (over 5750 lbs TW)	1.1 gpm	1.53 gpm

In model year 1996, 50% of each manufacturer's sales volume must meet the above standards. Thereafter, 100% of each manufacturer's sales volume must meet the standard.

> (c) Heavy Duty Trucks (HDT) of more than 8500 lbs GVWR (after model year 1990):

	Gasoline and Diesel Engines
HDT (effective model year 1991[6])	5.0 grams per brake horsepower-hour[6] (gbhp-hr)
HDT (model year 1998 and later) Useful life[6]:	4.0 gbhp-hr
gasoline engines	8 years/110,000 miles
diesel engines light heavy-duty:	8yrs/110,000 miles
medium heavy-duty:	8yrs/185,000 miles
heavy heavy-duty:	8yrs/290,000miles

> B. *For Canada:*
>> 1. *Stationary Sources*
>>> (a) As an interim requirement, reduction, by 2000, of annual national emissions of nitrogen oxides from stationary sources by 100,000 tonnes below the year 2000 forecast level of 970,000 tonnes.
>>> (b) By January 1, 1995, development of further annual national emission reduction requirements from stationary sources to be achieved by 2000 and/or 2005.
>> 2. *Mobile Sources*
>>> (a) Implementation of a more stringent mobile source nitrogen oxides control program for gasoline powered vehicles with standards no less stringent than the following:
>>> Light Duty Vehicles (up to 6000 lbs GVWR) (By model year 1996 for passenger cars) (By model year 1996 for light duty trucks[7])

---

[6]As set forth in EPA regulations in effect as of the entry into force of this Agreement.

[7]The Government of Canada will propose this effective date; the final effective date is subject to the procedures and outcome of the regulation development process.

5 yrs/80,000 kilometres
(useful life)

Cars and Light Duty Trucks   0.4 gpm
(0 to 3750 lbs LVW)

Light Duty Trucks   0.7 gpm
(3751 to 5750 lbs LVW)

Medium Duty Vehicles (6001 to 8500 lbs GVWR)
(By model year 1997[7])

5 yrs/80,000 kilometres
(useful life)
0 to 3750 lbs LVW   0.4 gpm
3751 to 5750 lbs LVW   0.7 gpm
Over 5750 lbs LVW   1.1 gpm

Heavy Duty Vehicles (over 8500 lbs GVWR)
(By model year 1998[7])

8 years/110,000 miles
(useful life)
Over 8500 lbs GVWR   4.0 gbhp-hr

(b) Implementation of a more stringent mobile source nitrogen oxides control program for diesel powered vehicles and engines with standards, to the extent possible, no less stringent than the standards for the respective duty classes of gasoline powered vehicles and engines.

3. *Compliance Monitoring*
  A. *Utility Units*
     1. *For the United States:*
     Requirement that, by January 1, 1995, each new electric utility unit and each electric utility unit greater than 25 MWe existing on the date of enactment of the Clean Air Act Amendments of 1990 (November 15, 1990) emitting sulphur dioxide or nitrogen oxides install and operate continuous emission monitoring systems or alternative systems approved by the Administrator of EPA, to the extent required by section 412 of the Clean Air Act.
     2. *For Canada:*
     Requirement that, by January 1, 1995, Canada estimate sulphur dioxide and nitrogen oxides emissions from each new electric utility unit and each existing electric utility unit greater than 25 MWe using a method of comparable effectiveness to continuous emission monitoring, as well as investigate the feasibility of using and implement, where appropriate, continuous emission monitoring systems.
     3. *For Both Parties:*
     The Parties shall consult, as appropriate, concerning the implementation of the above.
  B. *Other Major Stationary Sources*
  Requirement that the Parties work towards utilizing comparably effective methods of emission estimation for sulphur dioxide and nitrogen oxides emissions from all major industrial boilers and process sources, including smelters.

4. *Prevention of Air Quality Deterioration and Visibility Protection*
  Recognizing the importance of preventing significant air quality deterioration and protecting visibility, particularly for international parks, national, state, and provincial parks, and designated wilderness areas:

A. *For the United States:*

Requirement that the United States maintain means for preventing significant air quality deterioration and protecting visibility, to the extent required by Part C of Title I of the Clean Air Act, with respect to sources that could cause significant transboundary air pollution.

B. *For Canada:*

Requirement that Canada, by January 1, 1995, develop and implement means affording levels of prevention of significant air quality deterioration and protection of visibility comparable to those in paragraph A above, with respect to sources that could cause significant transboundary air pollution.

C. *For Both Parties:*

The Parties shall consult, as appropriate, concerning the implementation of the above.

ANNEX 2
SCIENTIFIC AND TECHNICAL ACTIVITIES AND ECONOMIC RESEARCH

1. For the purpose of determining and reporting on air pollutant concentrations and deposition, the Parties agree to coordinate their air pollutant monitoring activities through:

   (a) coordination of existing networks;
   (b) additions to monitoring tasks of existing networks of those air pollutants that the Parties agree should be monitored for the purposes of this Agreement;
   (c) addition of stations or networks where no existing monitoring facility can perform a necessary function for purposes of this Agreement;
   (d) the use of compatible data management procedures, formats, and methods; and
   (e) the exchange of monitoring data.

2. For the purpose of determining and reporting air emissions levels, historical trends, and projections with respect to the achievement of the general and specific objectives set forth in this Agreement, the Parties agree to coordinate their activities through:

   (a) identification of such air emissions information that the Parties agree should be exchanged for the purposes of this Agreement;
   (b) the use of measurement and estimation procedures of comparable effectiveness;
   (c) the use of compatible data management procedures, formats, and methods; and
   (d) the exchange of air emission information.

3. The Parties agree to cooperate and exchange information with respect to:

   (a) their monitoring of the effects of changes in air pollutant concentrations and deposition with respect to changes in various effects categories, e.g., aquatic ecosystems, visibility, and forests;
   (b) their determination of any effects of atmospheric pollution on human health and ecosystems, e.g. research on health effects of acid aerosols, research on the long-term effects of low concentrations of air pollutants on ecosystems, possibly in a critical loads framework;
   (c) their development and refinement of atmospheric models for purposes of determining source receptor relationships and transboundary transport and deposition of air pollutants;
   (d) their development and demonstration of technologies and measures for controlling emissions of air pollutants, in particular acidic deposition precursors, subject to their respective laws, regulations and policies;

(e)   their analysis of market-based mechanisms, including emissions trading; and

(f)   any other scientific and technical activities or economic research that the Parties may agree upon for purposes of supporting the general and specific objectives of this Agreement.

4. The Parties further agree to consult on approaches to, and share information and results of research on, methods to mitigate the impacts of acidic deposition, including the environmental effects and economic aspects of such methods.

C. OZONE LAYER

Editors' Introductory Note Regarding Protection of the Ozone Layer

It has become clear over the past two decades that anthropogenic emissions of gases are depleting the stratospheric ozone layer, which shields the earth by absorbing ultraviolet radiation emanating from outer space. A decrease in stratospheric ozone thus could have serious effects on earth, including an increased incidence of skin cancer and cataracts, crop damage, and harm to phytoplankton, which are the basis of the marine food chain. Concern about depletion of the ozone layer grew as it became evident that an ozone "hole," i.e., a region of severe ozone loss, develops annually over Antarctica.

The gases causing the greatest damage to the ozone layer are chlorofluorocarbons (CFCs), first synthesized around 1930, which are widely used for refrigerants, solvents, insulation foam, aerosol propellant, and other products. CFCs are also implicated in climate change because they are a "greenhouse gas."

In 1978, the United States, which produced about one-half of the world's CFCs, unilaterally banned most CFC use for aerosol propellants (which then constituted over 50 percent of total U.S. consumption of CFCs). Canada (1978), Sweden (1979), and Norway (1981) took similar actions, but most countries did not.

In 1985, the Vienna Convention for the Protection of the Ozone Layer was finalized. The Vienna Convention is a framework convention that provides a general obligation to cooperate in protecting the ozone layer but no precise limits. It was given specific substance in the 1987 Montreal Protocol on Substances that Deplete the Ozone Layer—an innovative and comprehensive instrument that itself was modified in June 1990 by the London Adjustments and Amendments to the Protocol.

As finalized in 1987, the Montreal Protocol generally requires parties (other than developing countries, discussed below) to freeze their consumption and production of CFCs at 1986 levels, to reduce them by 20 percent by 1994, and to reduce them a further 30 percent by 1999 (a total reduction of 50 percent). The consumption and production of halons (the other major group of ozone-depleting substances covered by the Protocol) are to be frozen at 1986 levels. In order to take account of new scientific evidence, adjustments in the amount and timing of reductions in the consumption and production of controlled substances are permitted by consensus of the parties or, failing that, by two-thirds of the parties present and voting representing at least 50 percent of the total consumption of the controlled substances of the parties. (For an earlier—but less forceful—version of the same type of approach, see the 1946 Whaling Convention, *infra*, p. 479.) Other provisions discourage or prohibit trade in controlled substances with nonparty States.

The Montreal Protocol contains several exceptions to the foregoing rules. The most interesting exception concerns developing countries, which are defined as those countries whose annual per capita consumption of specified ozone-depleting substances is less than 0.3 kilograms (approximately two-thirds of a pound). The Protocol allows a developing country to delay compliance with the reduction standards by ten years, as long as it does so to meet domestic needs and does not exceed the 0.3 kilogram threshold. Flexible measurement methods are also allowed to developing countries; and the Protocol requires cooperation in promoting technical assistance to allow countries, especially developing countries, to switch to non-ozone-depleting substances.

A consensus quickly formed that the 1987 Protocol did not go far enough in restricting ozone-depleting substances. In May 1989, several countries declared in the Helsinki Declaration that they would phase out all CFCs by the year 2000 (or sooner, if possible) and halons and other significant ozone-depleting chemicals as soon as feasible.

In June 1990, the Montreal Protocol's reduction requirements were formally adjusted and the Protocol was formally amended in other ways by the London Adjustments and Amendments. Generally speaking, the adjustments (which do not require a separate acceptance) mandate that consumption and production of CFCs and halons (the substances controlled by the Montreal Protocol) be completely phased-out by 2000, except to the extent the parties decide to permit production or consumption of halons necessary to satisfy essential purposes.

The amendments require a phase-out of consumption and production of two additional substances (carbon tetrachloride by the year 2000 and methyl chloroform by the year 2005), and reductions in consumption and production of other fully halogenated CFCs (HCFCs). The amendments also: specify that the amount of controlled substances recycled and reused is not "production;" change in some ways the treatment of developing countries (although the ten-year delay is retained); and establish a financial mechanism—including a multilateral fund financed by contributions from parties based on the United Nations scale of assessments—to provide financial and technical cooperation, including transferring technologies, to developing countries.

Although the Protocol (as adjusted) is in force among countries that account for most of the world's current consumption and production of the substances covered by the Protocol, it has not yet been joined by many of the major developing countries. China and India, for example, have refused to become parties unless they are assured that CFC alternatives will be available at little or no additional cost. It is widely agreed that the participation of those countries, whose consumption of CFCs for uses such as refrigeration and air conditioning is expected to increase dramatically unless current patterns change, is essential to success. Their claim, basically, is that the developed countries enjoyed the benefits of CFCs and other ozone-depleting substances in improving their standards of living and, in the process, caused the ozone-depletion problem, and thus that it would be unfair to deny developing countries the advantages that these substances offer.

The London Conference also adopted an Interim Financial Mechanism to operate for three years or until the Financial Mechanism contained in the Amendments becomes operative. This mechanism is expected to help gain adherence by developing countries. The Conference further adopted interim procedures and institutional mechanisms for determining noncompliance with the Protocol and for the treatment of parties found to be in noncompliance.

VIENNA CONVENTION FOR THE PROTECTION OF THE OZONE LAYER

Popular Names: Ozone Convention, Vienna Ozone Convention

Done at Vienna on 22 March 1985, *reprinted in* 26 ILM 1529 (1987).
Entry into Force: 22 September 1988

Depositary: United Nations

Languages: Arabic, Chinese, English, French, Russian, Spanish

Parties as of 15 November 1990: Argentina;** Australia; Austria; Bahrain;** Bangladesh; Belgium; Brazil; Brunei Darussalam; Burkina Faso; Byelorussian Soviet Socialist Republic; Cameroon; Canada; Chad; Chile;** China; Columbia; Czech and Slovak Federal Republic; Denmark;* Ecuador; Egypt; Equatorial Guinea; Fiji; Finland;** France; Gambia; German Democratic Republic; Germany, Federal Republic of;* Ghana; Greece; Guatemala; Hungary; Iceland; Iran, Islamic Republic of; Ireland; Italy; Japan; Jordan; Kenya; Libyan Arab Jamahiriya; Liechtenstein; Luxembourg; Malaysia; Maldives; Malta; Mexico; Netherlands;*/ ** New Zealand;* Nigeria; Norway;** Panama; Peru; Poland; Portugal; Singapore; South Africa; Spain; Sri Lanka; Sweden;** Switzerland; Syrian Arab Republic; Thailand; Trinidad and Tobago; Tunisia; Uganda; Ukrainian Soviet Socialist Republic; Union of Soviet Socialist Republics; United Arab Emirates; United Kingdom of Great Britain and Northern Ireland;*/** United States of America; Uruguay; Venezuela; Yugoslavia; Zambia; European Economic Community**

VIENNA CONVENTION FOR THE PROTECTION OF THE OZONE LAYER

Preamble

The Parties to this Convention,
Aware of the potentially harmful impact on human health and the environment through modification of the ozone layer,

---

* With varying geographic extensions and limitations
** With a declaration or objection

Recalling the pertinent provisions of the Declaration of the United Nations Conference on the Human Environment, and in particular principle 21, which provides that "States have, in accordance with the Charter of the United Nations and the principles of international law, the sovereign right to exploit their own resources pursuant to their own environmental policies, and the responsibility to ensure that activities within their jurisdiction or control do not cause damage to the environment of other States or of areas beyond the limits of national jurisdiction",

Taking into account the circumstances and particular requirements of developing countries,

Mindful of the work and studies proceeding within both international and national organizations and, in particular, of the World Plan of Action on the Ozone Layer of the United Nations Environment Programme,

Mindful also of the precautionary measures for the protection of the ozone layer which have already been taken at the national and international levels,

Aware that measures to protect the ozone layer from modifications due to human activities require international co-operation and action, and should be based on relevant scientific and technical considerations,

Aware also of the need for further research and systematic observations to further develop scientific knowledge of the ozone layer and possible adverse effects resulting from its modification,

Determined to protect human health and the environment against adverse effects resulting from modifications of the ozone layer,

HAVE AGREED AS FOLLOWS:

Article 1
DEFINITIONS

For the purposes of this Convention:

1. "The ozone layer" means the layer of atmospheric ozone above the planetary boundary layer.

2. "Adverse effects" means changes in the physical environment or biota, including changes in climate, which have significant deleterious effects on human health or on the composition, resilience and productivity of natural and managed ecosystems, or on materials useful to mankind.

3. "Alternative technologies or equipment" means technologies or equipment the use of which makes it possible to reduce or effectively eliminate emissions of substances which have or are likely to have adverse effects on the ozone layer.

4. "Alternative substances" means substances which reduce, eliminate or avoid adverse effects on the ozone layer.

5. "Parties" means, unless the text otherwise indicates, Parties to this Convention.

6. "Regional economic integration organization" means an organization constituted by sovereign States of a given region which has competence in respect of matters governed by this Convention or its protocols and has been duly authorized, in accordance with its internal procedures, to sign, ratify, accept, approve or accede to the instruments concerned.

7. "Protocols" means protocols to this Convention.

Article 2
GENERAL OBLIGATIONS

1. The Parties shall take appropriate measures in accordance with the provisions of this Convention and of those protocols in force to which they are party to protect human health and the environment against adverse effects resulting or likely to result from human activities which modify or are likely to modify the ozone layer.

2. To this end the Parties shall, in accordance with the means at their disposal and their capabilities:

(a)   Co-operate by means of systematic observations, research and informa-
       tion exchange in order to better understand and assess the effects of
       human activities on the ozone layer and the effects on human health and
       the environment from modification of the ozone layer;
(b)   Adopt appropriate legislative or administrative measures and co-operate
       in harmonizing appropriate policies to control, limit, reduce or prevent
       human activities under their jurisdiction or control should it be found that
       these activities have or are likely to have adverse effects resulting from
       modification or likely modification of the ozone layer;
(c)   Co-operate in the formulation of agreed measures, procedures and stan-
       dards for the implementation of this Convention, with a view to the
       adoption of protocols and annexes;
(d)   Co-operate with competent international bodies to implement effectively
       this Convention and protocols to which they are party.

3. The provisions of this Convention shall in no way affect the right of Parties to
adopt, in accordance with international law, domestic measures additional to those
referred to in paragraphs 1 and 2 above, nor shall they affect additional domestic
measures already taken by a Party, provided that these measures are not incompatible with their obligations under this Convention.

4. The application of this article shall be based on relevant scientific and technical
considerations.

Article 3
RESEARCH AND SYSTEMATIC OBSERVATIONS

1. The Parties undertake, as appropriate, to initiate and co-operate in, directly
or through competent international bodies, the conduct of research and scientific
assessments on:
(a)   The physical and chemical processes that may affect the ozone layer;
(b)   The human health and other biological effects deriving from any modifi-
       cations of the ozone layer, particularly those resulting from changes in
       ultra-violet solar radiation having biological effects (UV-B);
(c)   Climatic effects deriving from any modifications of the ozone layer;
(d)   Effects deriving from any modifications of the ozone layer and any conse-
       quent change in UV-B radiation on natural and synthetic materials useful
       to mankind;
(e)   Substances, practices, processes and activities that may affect the ozone
       layer, and their cumulative effects;
(f)   Alternative substances and technologies;
(g)   Related socio-economic matters;
and as further elaborated in annexes I and II.

2. The Parties undertake to promote or establish, as appropriate, directly or through
competent international bodies and taking fully into account national legislation and
relevant ongoing activities at both the national and international levels, joint or
complementary programmes for systematic observation of the state of the ozone
layer and other relevant parameters, as elaborated in annex I.

3. The Parties undertake to co-operate, directly or through competent international
bodies, in ensuring the collection, validation and transmission of research and
observational data through appropriate world data centres in a regular and timely
fashion.

Article 4
CO-OPERATION IN THE LEGAL, SCIENTIFIC AND TECHNICAL
FIELDS

1. The Parties shall facilitate and encourage the exchange of scientific, technical,
socio-economic, commercial and legal information relevant to this Convention as

further elaborated in annex II. Such information shall be supplied to bodies agreed upon by the Parties. Any such body receiving information regarded as confidential by the supplying Party shall ensure that such information is not disclosed and shall aggregate it to protect its confidentiality before it is made available to all Parties.
2. The Parties shall co-operate, consistent with their national laws, regulations and practices and taking into account in particular the needs of the developing countries, in promoting, directly or through competent international bodies, the development and transfer of technology and knowledge. Such co-operation shall be carried out particularly through:
  (a) Facilitation of the acquisition of alternative technologies by other Parties;
  (b) Provision of information on alternative technologies and equipment, and supply of special manuals or guides to them;
  (c) The supply of necessary equipment and facilities for research and systematic observations;
  (d) Appropriate training of scientific and technical personnel.

Article 5
TRANSMISSION OF INFORMATION

The Parties shall transmit, through the secretariat, to the Conference of the Parties established under article 6 information on the measures adopted by them in implementation of this Convention and of protocols to which they are party in such form and at such intervals as the meetings of the parties to the relevant instruments may determine.

Article 6
CONFERENCE OF THE PARTIES

1. A Conference of the Parties is hereby established. The first meeting of the Conference of the Parties shall be convened by the secretariat designated on an interim basis under article 7 not later than one year after entry into force of this Convention. Thereafter, ordinary meetings of the Conference of the Parties shall be held at regular intervals to be determined by the Conference at its first meeting.
2. Extraordinary meetings of the Conference of the Parties shall be held at such other times as may be deemed necessary by the Conference, or at the written request of any Party, provided that, within six months of the request being communicated to them by the secretariat, it is supported by at least one third of the Parties.
3. The Conference of the Parties shall by consensus agree upon and adopt rules of procedure and financial rules for itself and for any subsidiary bodies it may establish, as well as financial provisions governing the functioning of the secretariat.
4. The Conference of the Parties shall keep under continuous review the implementation of this Convention, and, in addition, shall:
  (a) Establish the form and the intervals for transmitting the information to be submitted in accordance with article 5 and consider such information as well as reports submitted by any subsidiary body;
  (b) Review the scientific information on the ozone layer, on its possible modification and on possible effects of any such modification;
  (c) Promote, in accordance with article 2, the harmonization of appropriate policies, strategies and measures for minimizing the release of substances causing or likely to cause modification of the ozone layer, and make recommendations on any other measures relating to this Convention;
  (d) Adopt, in accordance with articles 3 and 4, programmes for research, systematic observations, scientific and technological co-operation, the exchange of information and the transfer of technology and knowledge;
  (e) Consider and adopt, as required, in accordance with articles 9 and 10, amendments to this Convention and its annexes;

(f) Consider amendments to any protocol, as well as to any annexes thereto, and, if so decided, recommend their adoption to the parties to the protocol concerned;

(g) Consider and adopt, as required, in accordance with article 10, additional annexes to this Convention;

(h) Consider and adopt, as required, protocols in accordance with article 8;

(i) Establish such subsidiary bodies as are deemed necessary for the implementation of this Convention;

(j) Seek, where appropriate, the services of competent international bodies and scientific committees, in particular the World Meteorological Organization and the World Health Organization, as well as the Co-ordinating Committee on the Ozone Layer, in scientific research, systematic observations and other activities pertinent to the objectives of this Convention, and make use as appropriate of information from these bodies and committees;

(k) Consider and undertake any additional action that may be required for the achievement of the purposes of this Convention.

5. The United Nations, its specialized agencies and the International Atomic Energy Agency, as well as any State not party to this Convention, may be represented at meetings of the Conference of the Parties by observers. Any body or agency, whether national or international, governmental or non-governmental, qualified in fields relating to the protection of the ozone layer which has informed the secretariat of its wish to be represented at a meeting of the Conference of the Parties as an observer may be admitted unless at least one-third of the Parties present object. The admission and participation of observers shall be subject to the rules of procedure adopted by the Conference of the Parties.

Article 7
SECRETARIAT

1. The functions of the secretariat shall be:

(a) To arrange for and service meetings provided for in articles 6, 8, 9 and 10;

(b) To prepare and transmit reports based upon information received in accordance with articles 4 and 5, as well as upon information derived from meetings of subsidiary bodies established under article 6;

(c) To perform the functions assigned to it by any protocol;

(d) To prepare reports on its activities carried out in implementation of its functions under this Convention and present them to the Conference of the Parties;

(e) To ensure the necessary co-ordination with other relevant international bodies, and in particular to enter into such administrative and contractual arrangements as may be required for the effective discharge of its functions;

(f) To perform such other functions as may be determined by the Conference of the Parties.

2. The secretariat functions will be carried out on an interim basis by the United Nations Environment Programme until the completion of the first ordinary meeting of the Conference of the Parties held pursuant to article 6. At its first ordinary meeting, the Conference of the Parties shall designate the secrtariat from amongst those existing competent international organizations which have signified their willingness to carry out the secretariat functions under this Convention.

Article 8
ADOPTION OF PROTOCOLS

1. The Conference of the Parties may at a meeting adopt protocols pursuant to article 2.

2. The text of any proposed protocol shall be communicated to the Parties by the secretariat at least six months before such a meeting.

Article 9
AMENDMENT OF THE CONVENTION OR PROTOCOLS

1. Any Party may propose amendments to this Convention or to any protocol. Such amendments shall take due account, *inter alia*, of relevant scientific and technical considerations.

2. Amendments to this Convention shall be adopted at a meeting of the Conference of the Parties. Amendments to any protocol shall be adopted at a meeting of the Parties to the protocol in question. The text of any proposed amendment to this Convention or to any protocol, except as may otherwise be provided in such protocol, shall be communicated to the Parties by the secretariat at least six months before the meeting at which it is proposed for adoption. The secretariat shall also communicate proposed amendments to the signatories to this Convention for information.

3. The Parties shall make every effort to reach agreement on any proposed amendment to this Convention by consensus. If all efforts at consensus have been exhausted, and no agreement reached, the amendment shall as a last resort be adopted by a three-fourths majority vote of the Parties present and voting at the meeting, and shall be submitted by the Depositary to all Parties for ratification, approval or acceptance.

4. The procedure mentioned in paragraph 3 above shall apply to amendments to any protocol, except that a two-thirds majority of the parties to that protocol present and voting at the meeting shall suffice for their adoption.

5. Ratification, approval or acceptance of amendments shall be notified to the Depositary in writing. Amendments adopted in accordance with paragraphs 3 or 4 above shall enter into force between parties having accepted them on the ninetieth day after the receipt by the Depositary of notification of their ratification, approval or acceptance by at least three-fourths of the Parties to this Convention or by at least two-thirds of the parties to the protocol concerned, except as may otherwise be provided in such protocol. Thereafter the amendments shall enter into force for any other Party on the ninetieth day after that Party deposits its instrument of ratification, approval or acceptance of the amendments.

6. For the purposes of this article, ''Parties present and voting'' means Parties present and casting an affirmative or negative vote.

Article 10
ADOPTION AND AMENDMENT OF ANNEXES

1. The annexes to this Convention or to any protocol shall form an integral part of this Convention or of such protocol, as the case may be, and, unless expressly provided otherwise, a reference to this Convention or its protocols constitutes at the same time a reference to any annexes thereto. Such annexes shall be restricted to scientific, technical and administrative matters.

2. Except as may be otherwise provided in any protocol with respect to its annexes, the following procedure shall apply to the proposal, adoption and entry into force of additional annexes to this Convention or of annexes to a protocol:

    (a)   Annexes to this Convention shall be proposed and adopted according to the procedure laid down in article 9, paragraphs 2 and 3, while annexes to any protocol shall be proposed and adopted according to the procedure laid down in article 9, paragraphs 2 and 4;

    (b)   Any party that is unable to approve an additional annex to this Convention or an annex to any protocol to which it is party shall so notify the

Depositary, in writing, within six months from the date of the communication of the adoption by the Depositary. The Depositary shall without delay notify all Parties of any such notification received. A Party may at any time substitute an acceptance for a previous declaration of objection and the annexes shall thereupon enter into force for that Party;

(c) On the expiry of six months from the date of the circulation of the communication by the Depositary, the annex shall become effective for all Parties to this Convention or to any protocol concerned which have not submitted a notification in accordance with the provision of subparagraph (b) above.

3. The proposal, adoption and entry into force of amendments to annexes to this Convention or to any protocol shall be subject to the same procedure as for the proposal, adoption and entry into force of annexes to the Convention or annexes to a protocol. Annexes and amendments thereto shall take due account, *intra alia*, of relevant scientific and technical considerations.

4. If an additional annex or an amendment to an annex involves an amendment to this Convention or to any protocol, the additional annex or amended annex shall not enter into force until such time as the amendment to this Convention or to the protocol concerned enters into force.

Article 11
SETTLEMENT OF DISPUTES

1. In the event of a dispute between Parties concerning the interpretation or application of this Convention, the parties concerned shall seek solution by negotiation.

2. If the parties concerned cannot reach agreement by negotiation, they may jointly seek the good offices of, or request mediation by, a third party.

3. When ratifying, accepting, approving or acceding to this Convention, or at any time thereafter, a State or regional economic integration organization may declare in writing to the Depositary that for a dispute not resolved in accordance with paragraph 1 or paragraph 2 above, it accepts one or both of the following means of dispute settlement as compulsory:

(a) Arbitration in accordance with procedures to be adopted by the Conference of the Parties at its first ordinary meeting;

(b) Submission of the dispute to the International Court of Justice.

4. If the parties have not, in accordance with paragraph 3 above, accepted the same or any procedure, the dispute shall be submitted to conciliation in accordance with paragraph 5 below unless the parties otherwise agree.

5. A conciliation commission shall be created upon the request of one of the parties to the dispute. The commission shall be composed of an equal number of members appointed by each party concerned and a chairman chosen jointly by the members appointed by each party. The commission shall render a final and recommendatory award, which the parties shall consider in good faith.

6. The provisions of this article shall apply with respect to any protocol except as otherwise provided in the protocol concerned.

Article 12
SIGNATURE

This Convention shall be open for signature by States and by regional economic integration organizations at the Federal Ministry for Foreign Affairs of the Republic of Austria in Vienna from 22 March 1985 to 21 September 1985, and at United Nations Headquarters in New York from 22 September 1985 to 21 March 1986.

Article 13
RATIFICATION, ACCEPTANCE OR APPROVAL

1. This Convention and any protocol shall be subject to ratification, acceptance or approval by States and by regional economic integration organizations. Instruments of ratification, acceptance or approval shall be deposited with the Depositary.
2. Any organization referred to in paragraph 1 above which becomes a Party to this Convention or any protocol without any of its member States being a Party shall be bound by all the obligations under the Convention or the protocol, as the case may be. In the case of such organizations, one or more of whose member States is a Party to the Convention or relevant protocol, the organization and its member States shall decide on their respective responsibilities for the performance of their obligation under the Convention or protocol, as the case may be. In such cases, the organization and the member States shall not be entitled to exerise rights under the Convention or relevant protocol concurrently.
3. In their instruments of ratification, acceptance or approval, the organizations referred to in paragraph 1 above shall declare the extent of their competence with respect to the matters governed by the Convention or the relevant protocol. These organizations shall also inform the Depositary of any substantial modification in the extent of their competence.

Article 14
ACCESSION

1. This Convention and any protocol shall be open for accession by States and by regional economic integration organizations from the date on which the Convention or the protocol concerned is closed for signature. The instruments of accession shall be deposited with the Depositary.
2. In their instruments of accession, the organizations referred to in paragraph 1 above shall declare the extent of their competence with respect to the matters governed by the Convention or the relevant protocol. These organizations shall also inform the Depositary of any substantial modification in the extent of their competence.
3. The provisions of article 13, paragraph 2, shall apply to regional economic integration organizations which accede to this Convention or any protocol.

Article 15
RIGHT TO VOTE

1. Each Party to this Convention or to any protocol shall have one vote.
2. Except as provided for in paragraph 1 above, regional economic integration organizations, in matters within their competence, shall exercise their right to vote with a number of votes equal to the number of their member States which are Parties to the Convention or the relevant protocol. Such organizations shall not exercise their right to vote if their member States exercise theirs, and vice versa.

Article 16
RELATIONSHIP BETWEEN THE CONVENTION AND ITS PROTOCOLS

1. A State or a regional economic integration organization may not become a party to a protocol unless it is, or becomes at the same time, a Party to the Convention.
2. Decisions concerning any protocol shall be taken only by the parties to the protocol concerned.

Article 17
ENTRY INTO FORCE

1. This Convention shall enter into force on the ninetieth day after the date of deposit of the twentieth instrument of ratification, acceptance, approval or accession.

2. Any protocol, except as otherwise provided in such protocol, shall enter into force on the ninetieth day after the date of deposit of the eleventh instrument of ratification, acceptance or approval of such protocol or accession thereto.

3. For each Party which ratifies, accepts or approves this Convention or accedes thereto after the deposit of the twentieth instrument of ratification, acceptance, approval or accession, it shall enter into force on the ninetieth day after the date of deposit by such Party of its instrument of ratification, acceptance, approval or accession.

4. Any protocol, except as otherwise provided in such protocol, shall enter into force for a party that ratifies, accepts or approves that protocol or accedes thereto after its entry into force pursuant to paragraph 2 above, on the ninetieth day after the date on which that party deposits its instrument of ratification, acceptance, approval or accession, or on the date on which the Convention enters into force for that Party, whichever shall be the later.

5. For the purposes of paragraphs 1 and 2 above, any instrument deposited by a regional economic integration organization shall not be counted as additional to those deposited by member States of such organization.

Article 18
RESERVATIONS

No reservations may be made to this Convention.

Article 19
WITHDRAWAL

1. At any time after four years from the date on which this Convention has entered into force for a Party, that Party may withdraw from the Convention by giving written notification to the Depositary.

2. Except as may be provided in any protocol, at any time after four years from the date on which such protocol has entered into force for a party, that party may withdraw from the protocol by giving written notification to the Depositary.

3. Any such withdrawal shall take effect upon expiry of one year after the date of its receipt by the Depositary, or on such later date as may be specified in the notification of the withdrawal.

4. Any Party which withdraws from this Convention shall be considered as also having withdrawn from any protocol to which it is party.

Article 20
DEPOSITARY

1. The Secretary-General of the United Nations shall assume the functions of depositary of this Convention and any protocols.

2. The Depositary shall inform the Parties, in particular, of:
   (a)   The signature of this Convention and of any protocol, and the deposit of instruments of ratification, acceptance, approval or accession in accordance with articles 13 and 14;
   (b)   The date on which the Convention and any protocol will come into force in accordance with article 17;

(c)   Notifications of withdrawal made in accordance with article 19;
(d)   Amendments adopted with respect to the Convention and any protocol, their acceptance by the parties and their date of entry into force in accordance with article 9;
(e)   All communications relating to the adoption and approval of annexes and to the amendment of annexes in accordance with article 10;
(f)   Notifications by regional economic integration organizations of the extent of their competence with respect to matters governed by this Convention and any protocols, and of any modifications thereof.
(g)   Declarations made in accordance with article 11, paragraph 3.

Article 21
AUTHENTIC TEXTS

The original of this Convention, of which the Arabic, Chinese, English, French, Russian and Spanish texts are equally authentic, shall be deposited with the Secretary-General of the United Nations.

IN WITNESS WHEREOF the undersigned, being duly authorized to that effect, have signed this Convention.

Done at Vienna   on the 22nd day of March 1985

Annex I
RESEARCH AND SYSTEMATIC OBSERVATIONS

1. The Parties to the Convention recognize that the major scientific issues are:
   (a) Modification of the ozone layer which would result in a change in the amount of solar ultra-violet radiation having biological effects (UV-B) that reaches the Earth's surface and the potential consequences for human health, for organisms, ecosystems and materials useful to mankind;
   (b) Modification of the vertical distribution of ozone, which could change the temperature structure of the atmosphere and the potential consequences for weather and climate.

2. The Parties to the Convention, in accordance with article 3, shall co-operate in conducting research and systematic observations and in formulating recommendations for future research and observation in such areas as:
   (a) *Research into the physics and chemistry of the atmosphere*
       (i)   Comprehensive theoretical models: further development of models which consider the interaction between radiative, dynamic and chemical processes; studies of the simultaneous effects of various man-made and naturally occurring species upon atmospheric ozone; interpretation of satellite and non-satellite measurement data sets; evaluation of trends in atmospheric and geophysical parameters, and the development of methods for attributing changes in these parameters to specific causes;
       (ii) Laboratory studies of: rate coefficients, absorption cross-sections and mechanisms of tropospheric and stratospheric chemical and photochemical processes; spectroscopic data to support field measurements in all relevant spectral regions;
       (iii) Field measurements: the concentration and fluxes of key source gases of both natural and anthropogenic origin; atmospheric dynamics studies; simultaneous measurements of photochemically-related species down to the planetary boundary layer, using *in situ* and remote sensing instruments; intercomparison of different sensors, including co-ordinated correlative measurements for satellite instrumentation; three-dimensional fields of key atmospheric trace constituents, solar spectral flux and meteorological parameters;

       (iv) Instrument development, including satellite and non-satellite sensors for atmospheric trace constituents, solar flux and meteorological parameters;

(b)   *Research into health, biological and photodegradation effects*

       (i)   The relationship between human exposure to visible and ultra-violet solar radiation and (a) the development of both non-melanoma and melanoma skin cancer and (b) the effects on the immunological system;

       (ii) Effects of UV-B radiation, including the wavelength dependence, upon (a) agricultural crops, forests and other terrestial ecosystems and (b) the aquatic food web and fisheries, as well as possible inhibition of oxygen production by marine phytoplankton;

       (iii) The mechanisms by which UV-B radiation acts on biological materials, species and ecosystems, including: the relationship between dose, dose rate, and response; photorepair, adaptation, and protection;

       (iv) Studies of biological action spectra and the spectral response using polychromatic radiation in order to include possible interactions of the various wavelength regions;

       (v) The influence of UV-B radiation on: the sensitivities and activities of biological species important to the biospheric balance; primary processes such as photosynthesis and biosynthesis;

       (vi) The influence of UV-B radiation on the photodegradation of pollutants, agricultural chemicals and other materials;

(c)   *Research on effects on climate*

       (i)   Theoretical and observational studies of the radiative effects of ozone and other trace species and the impact on climate parameters, such as land and ocean surface temperatures, precipitation patterns, the exchange between the troposphere and stratosphere;

       (ii) The investigation of the effects of such climate impacts on various aspects of human activity;

(d)   *Systematic observations on*:

       (i)   The status of the ozone layer (i.e. the spatial and temporal variability of the total column content and vertical distribution) by making the Global Ozone Observing System, based on the integration of satellite and ground-based systems, fully operational;

       (ii) The tropospheric and statospheric concentrations of source gases for the NO_x, NO_x, ClO_x and carbon families;

       (iii) The temperature from the ground to the mesosphere, utilizing both ground-based and satellite systems;

       (iv) Wavelength-resolved solar flux reaching, and thermal radiation leaving, the Earth's atmosphere, utilizing satellite measurements;

       (v) Wavelength-resolved solar flux reaching the Earth's surface in the ultra-violet range having biological effects (UV-B);

       (vi) Aerosol properties and distribution from the ground to the mesosphere, utilizing ground-based, airborne and satellite systems;

       (vii)Climatically important variables by the maintenance of programmes of high-quality meteorological surface measurements;

       (viii)Trace species, temperatures, solar flux and aerosols utilizing improved methods for analysing global data.

3. The Parties to the Convention shall co-operate, taking into account the particular needs of the developing countries, in promoting the appropriate scientific and technical training required to participate in the research and systematic observations outlined in this annex. Particular emphasis should be given to the intercalibration of observational instrumentation and methods with a view to generating comparable or standardized scientific data sets.

4. The following chemical substances of natural and anthropogenic origin, not listed in order of priority, are thought to have the potential to modify the chemical and physical properties of the ozone layer.

(a)   Carbon substances

(i) *Carbon monoxide (CO)*

Carbon monoxide has significant natural and anthropogenic sources, and is thought to play a major direct role in tropospheric photochemistry, and an indirect role in stratospheric photochemistry.

(ii) *Carbon dioxide (CO_2)*

Carbon dioxide has significant natural and anthropogenic sources, and affects stratospheric ozone by influencing the thermal structure of the atmosphere.

(iii) *Methane (CH_4)*

Methane has both natural and anthropogenic sources, and affects both tropospheric and stratospheric ozone.

(iv) *Non-methane hydrocarbon species*

Non-methane hydrocarbon species, which consist of a large number of chemical substances, have both natural and anthropogenic sources, and play a direct role in tropospheric photochemistry and an indirect role in stratospheric photochemistry.

(b)   Nitrogen substances

(i) *Nitrous oxide (N_2O)*

The dominant sources of N_2O are natural, but anthropogenic contributions are becoming increasingly important. Nitrous oxide is the primary source of stratospheric NO_x, which play a vital role in controlling the abundance of stratospheric ozone.

(ii) *Nitrogen oxides (NO_x)*

Ground-level sources of NO_x play a major direct role only in tropospheric photochemical processes and an indirect role in stratosphere photochemistry, whereas injection of NO_x close to the tropopause may lead directly to a change in upper tropospheric and stratospheric ozone.

(c)   Chlorine substances

(i) *Fully halogenated alkanes, e.g. CCl_4, $CFCl_3$ (CFC-11), CF_2Cl_2 (CFC-12), $C_2F_3Cl_3$ (CFC-113), $C_2F_4Cl_2$ (CFC-114)*

Fully halogenated alkanes are anthropogenic and act as a source of ClO_x, which plays a vital role in ozone photochemistry, especially in the 30-50 km altitude region.

(ii) *Partially halogenated alkanes, e.g. CH_3Cl, CHF_2Cl (CFC-22), CH_3CCl_3, $CHFCl_2$ (CFC-21)*

The sources of CH_3Cl are natural, whereas the other partially halogenated alkanes mentioned above are anthropogenic in origin. These gases also act as a source of stratospheric ClO_x.

(d)   Bromine substances

Fully halogenated alkanes, e.g. CF_3Br

These gases are anthropogenic and act as a source of BrO_x, which behaves in a manner similar to ClO_x.

(e)   Hydrogen substances

(i) *Hydrogen (H_2)*

Hydrogen, the source of which is natural and anthropogenic, plays a minor role in stratospheric photochemistry.

(ii) *Water (H_2O)*

Water, the source of which is natural, plays a vital role in both tropospheric and stratospheric photochemistry. Local sources of water vapour in the stratosphere include the oxidation of methane and, to a lesser extent, of hydrogen.

Annex II
INFORMATION EXCHANGE

1. The Parties to the Convention recognize that the collection and sharing of information is an important means of implementing the objectives of this Convention and of assuring that any actions that may be taken are appropriate and equitable. Therefore, Parties shall exchange scientific, technical, socio-economic, business, commercial and legal information.

2. The Parties to the Convention, in deciding what information is to be collected and exchanged, should take into account the usefulness of the information and the costs of obtaining it. The Parties further recognize that co-operation under this annex has to be consistent with national laws, regulations and practices regarding patents, trade secrets, and protection of confidential and proprietary information.

3. *Scientific information*

   This includes information on:

   (a)   Planned and ongoing research, both governmental and private, to facilitate the co-ordination of research programmes so as to make the most effective use of available national and international resources;

   (b)   The emission data needed for research;

   (c)   Scientific results published in peer-reviewed literature on the understanding of the physics and chemistry of the Earth's atmosphere and of its susceptibility to change, in particular on the state of the ozone layer and effects on human health, environment and climate which would result from changes on all time-scales in either the total column content or the vertical distribution of ozone;

   (d)   The assessment of research results and the recommendations for future research.

4. *Technical information*

   This includes information on:

   (a)   The availability and cost of chemical substitutes and of alternative technologies to reduce the emissions of ozone-modifying substances and related planned and ongoing research:

   (b)   The limitations and any risks involved in using chemical or other substitutes and alternative technologies.

5. *Socio-economic and commercial information on the substances referred to in annex I*

   This includes information on:

   (a)   Production and production capacity;

   (b)   Use and use patterns;

   (c)   Imports/exports;

   (d)   The costs, risks and benefits of human activities which may indirectly modify the ozone layer and of the impacts of regulatory actions taken or being considered to control these activities.

6. *Legal information*

   This includes information on:

   (a)   National laws, administrative measures and legal research relevant to the protection of the ozone layer;

   (b)   International agreements, including bilateral agreements, relevant to the protection of the ozone layer;

   (c)   Methods and terms of licensing and availability of patents relevant to the protection of the ozone layer.

* * *

MONTREAL PROTOCOL ON SUBSTANCES THAT DEPLETE THE OZONE LAYER

Popular Names: Montreal Ozone Protocol, Montreal Protocol, Ozone Protocol

Done at Montreal on 16 September 1987, *reprinted in* 26 ILM 1550 (1987).

Entry into Force: 1 January 1989 for those States for which the Vienna Convention for the Protection of the Ozone Layer was in force when it deposited its instrument of ratification, acceptance, approval, or accession to the Protocol; for other States and Organizations, on the later date of when the Convention enters into force for that State or Organization or the ninetieth day after the State or Organization deposits its instrument of ratification, acceptance, approval or accession to the Protocol

Depositary: United Nations

Languages: Arabic, Chinese, English, French, Russian, Spanish

Parties as of 20 November 1990: Australia; Austria; Bahrain;** Bangladesh; Belgium; Brazil; Bulgaria; Burkina Faso; Byelorussian Soviet Socialist Republic; Cameroon; Canada; Chile;** Czech and Slovak Federal Republic; Denmark;* Ecuador; Eqypt; Fiji; Finland; France; Gambia; German Democratic Republic; Germany, Federal Republic of;* Ghana; Greece; Guatemala; Hungary; Iceland; Iran, Islamic Republic of; Ireland; Italy; Japan; Jordan; Kenya; Libyan Arab Jamahiriya; Liechtenstein; Luxembourg; Malaysia; Maldives; Malta; Mexico; Netherlands;* New Zealand;* Nigeria; Norway; Panama; Poland; Portugal; Singapore; South Africa;** Spain; Sri Lanka; Sweden; Switzerland; Syrian Arab Republic; Thailand; Trinidad and Tobago; Tunisia; Uganda; Ukrainian Soviet Socialist Republic; Union of Soviet Socialist Republics; United Arab Emirates; United Kingdom of Great Britain and Northern Ireland;*/** United States of America; Venezuela; Zambia; European Economic Community**

Amendments: London Adjustments and Amendments, done 27 June 1990, *infra* p. 298.

MONTREAL PROTOCOL ON SUBSTANCES THAT DEPLETE THE OZONE LAYER

The Parties to this Protocol,
Being Parties to the Vienna Convention for the Protection of the Ozone Layer,
Mindful of their obligation under that Convention to take appropriate measures to protect human health and the environment against adverse effects resulting or

---

* With varying geographic extensions and limitations
** With declaration or objection

likely to result from human activities which modify or are likely to modify the ozone layer,

Recognizing the world-wide emissions of certain substances can significantly deplete and otherwise modify the ozone layer in a manner that is likely to result in adverse effects on human health and the environment,

Conscious of the potential climatic effects of emissions of these substances,

Aware that measures taken to protect the ozone layer from depletion should be based on relevant scientific knowledge, taking into account technical and economic considerations,

Determined to protect the ozone layer by taking precautionary measures to control equitably total global emissions of substances that deplete it, with the ultimate objective of their elimination on the basis of developments in scientific knowledge, taking into account technical and economic considerations,

Acknowledging that special provision is required to meet the needs of developing countries for these substances,

Noting the precautionary measures for controlling emissions of certain chlorofluorocarbons that have already been taken at national and regional levels,

Considering the importance of promoting international co-operation in the research and development of science and technology relating to the control and reduction of emissions of substances that deplete the ozone layer, bearing in mind in particular the needs of developing countries,

HAVE AGREED AS FOLLOWS:

ARTICLE 1: DEFINITIONS

For the purposes of this Protocol:

1. "Convention" means the Vienna Convention for the Protection of the Ozone Layer, adopted on 22 March 1985.
2. "Parties" means, unless the text otherwise indicates, Parties to this Protocol.
3. "Secretariat" means the secretariat of the Convention.
4. "Controlled substance" means a substance listed in Annex A to this Protocol, whether existing alone or in a mixture. It excludes, however, any such substance or mixture which is in a manufactured product other than a container used for the transportation or storage of the substance listed.
5. "Production" means the amount of controlled substances produced minus the amount destroyed by technologies to be approved by the Parties.
6. "Consumption" means production plus imports minus exports of controlled substances.
7. "Calculated levels" of production, imports, exports and consumption means levels determined in accordance with Article 3.
8. "Industrial rationalization" means the transfer of all or a portion of the calculated level of production of one Party to another, for the purpose of achieving economic efficiencies or responding to anticipated shortfalls in supply as a result of plant closures.

ARTICLE 2: CONTROL MEASURES

1. Each Party shall ensure that for the twelve-month period commencing on the first day of the seventh month following the date of the entry into force of this Protocol, and in each twelve-month period thereafter, its calculated level of consumption of the controlled substances in Group I of Annex A does not exceed its calculated level of consumption in 1986. By the end of the same period, each Party producing one or more of these substances shall ensure that its calculated level of production of the substances does not exceed its calculated level of production in 1986, except that such level may have increased by no more than ten per cent based

on the 1986 level. Such increase shall be permitted only so as to satisfy the basic domestic needs of the Parties operating under Article 5 and for the purposes of industrial rationalization between Parties.

2. Each Party shall ensure that for the twelve-month period commencing on the first day of the thirty-seventh month following the date of the entry into force of this Protocol, and in each twelve month period thereafter, its calculated level of consumption of the controlled substances listed in Group II of Annex A does not exceed its calculated level of consumption in 1986. Each Party producing one or more of these substances shall ensure that its calculated level of production of the substances does not exceed its calculated level of production in 1986, except that such level may have increased by no more than ten per cent based on the 1986 level. Such increase shall be permitted only so as to satisfy the basic domestic needs of the Parties operating under Article 5 and for the purposes of industrial rationalization between Parties. The mechanisms for implementing these measures shall be decided by the Parties at their first meeting following the first scientific review.

3. Each Party shall ensure that for the period 1 July 1993 to 30 June 1994 and in each twelve-month period thereafter, its calculated level of consumption of the controlled substances in Group I of Annex A does not exceed, annually, eighty per cent of its calculated level of consumption in 1986. Each Party producing one or more of these substances shall, for the same periods, ensure that its calculated level of production of the substances does not exceed, annually, eighty per cent of its calculated level of production in 1986. However, in order to satisfy the basic domestic needs of the Parties operating under Article 5 and for the purposes of industrial rationalization between Parties, its calculated level of production may exceed that limit by up to ten per cent of its calculated level of production in 1986.

4. Each Party shall ensure that for the period 1 July 1998 to 30 June 1999, and in each twelve-month period thereafter, its calculated level of consumption of the controlled substances in Group I of Annex A does not exceed, annually, fifty per cent of its calculated level of consumption in 1986. Each Party producing one or more of these substances shall, for the same periods, ensure that its calculated level of production of the substances does not exceed, annually, fifty per cent of its calculated level of production in 1986. However, in order to satisfy the basic domestic needs of the Parties operating under Article 5 and for the purposes of industrial rationalization between Parties, its calculated level of production may exceed that limit by up to fifteen per cent of its calculated level of production in 1986. This paragraph will apply unless the Parties decide otherwise at a meeting by a two-thirds majority of Parties present and voting, representing at least two-thirds of the total calculated level of consumption of these substances of the Parties. This decision shall be considered and made in the light of the assessments referred to in Article 6.

5. Any Party whose calculated level of production in 1986 of the controlled substances in Group I of Annex A was less than twenty-five kilotonnes may, for the purposes of industrial rationalization, transfer to or receive from any other Party, production in excess of the limits set out in paragraphs 1, 3 and 4 provided that the total combined calculated levels of production of the Parties concerned does not exceed the production limits set out in this Article. Any transfer of such production shall be notified to the secretariat, no later than the time of the transfer.

6. Any Party not operating under Article 5, that has facilities for the production of controlled substances under construction, or contracted for, prior to 16 September 1987, and provided for in national legislation prior to 1 January 1987, may add the production from such facilities to its 1986 production of such substances for the purposes of determining its calculated level of production for 1986, provided that such facilities are completed by 31 December 1990 and that such production does not raise that Party's annual calculated level of consumption of the controlled substances above 0.5 kilograms per capita.

7. Any transfer of production pursuant to paragraph 5 or any addition of production pursuant to paragraph 6 shall be notified to the secretariat, no later than the time of the transfer or addition.

8. (a)   Any Parties which are Member States of a regional economic integration organization as defined in Article 1(6) of the Convention may agree that they shall jointly fulfil their obligations respecting consumption under this Article provided that their total combined calculated level of consumption does not exceed the levels required by this Article.

     (b)   The Parties to any such agreement shall inform the secretariat of the terms of the agreement before the date of the reduction in consumption with which the agreement is concerned.

     (c)   Such agreement will become operative only if all Member States of the regional economic integration organization and the organization concerned are Parties to the Protocol and have notified the secretariat of their manner of implementation.

9. (a)   Based on the assessments made pursuant to Article 6, the Parties may decide whether:

        (i) adjustments to the ozone depleting potentials specified in Annex A should be made and, if so, what the adjustments should be; and

       (ii) further adjustments and reductions of production or consumption of the controlled substances from 1986 levels should be undertaken and, if so, what the scope, amount and timing of any such adjustments and reductions should be.

     (b)   Proposals for such adjustments shall be communicated to the Parties by the secretariat at least six months before the meeting of the Parties at which they are proposed for adoption.

     (c)   In taking such decisions, the Parties shall make every effort to reach agreement by consensus. If all efforts at consensus have been exhausted, and no agreement reached, such decisions shall, as a last resort, be adopted by a two-thirds majority vote of the Parties present and voting representing at least fifty per cent of the total consumption of the controlled substances of the Parties.

     (d)   The decisions, which shall be binding on all Parties, shall forthwith be communicated to the Parties by the Depositary. Unless otherwise provided in the decisions, they shall enter into force on the expiry of six months from the date of the circulation of the communication by the Depositary.

10. (a)   Based on the assessments made pursuant to Article 6 of this Protocol and in accordance with the procedure set out in Article 9 of the Convention, the Parties may decide:

        (i) whether any substances, and if so which, should be added to or removed from any annex to this Protocol; and

       (ii) the mechanism, scope and timing of the control measures that should apply to those substances;

     (b)   Any such decision shall become effective, provided that it has been accepted by a two-thirds majority vote of the Parties present and voting.

11. Notwithstanding the provisions contained in this Article, Parties may take more stringent measures than those required by this Article.

ARTICLE 3: CALCULATION OF CONTROL LEVELS

For the purposes of Articles 2 and 5, each Party shall, for each Group of substances in Annex A, determine its calculated levels of:

     (a)   production by:

  (i)   multiplying its annual production of each controlled substance by
        the ozone depleting potential specified in respect of it in Annex A;
        and
  (ii) adding together, for each such Group, the resulting figures;
(b)   imports and exports, respectively, by following, *mutatis mutandis*, the
      procedure set out in subparagraph (a); and
(c)   consumption by adding together its calculated levels of production and
      imports and subtracting its calculated level of exports as determined in
      accordance with subparagraphs (a) and (b). However, beginning on 1
      January 1993, any export of controlled substances to non-Parties shall
      not be subtracted in calculating the consumption level of the exporting
      Party.

ARTICLE 4: CONTROL OF TRADE WITH NON-PARTIES

1. Within one year of the entry into force of this Protocol, each Party shall ban the
import of controlled substances from any State not party to this Protocol.
2. Beginning on 1 January 1993, no Party operating under paragraph 1 of Article
5 may export any controlled substance to any State not party to this Protocol.
3. Within three years of the date of the entry into force of this Protocol, the Parties
shall, following the procedures in Article 10 of the Convention, elaborate in an
annex a list of products containing controlled substances. Parties that have not
objected to the annex in accordance with those procedures shall ban, within one
year of the annex having become effective, the import of those products from any
State not party to this Protocol.
4. Within five years of the entry into force of this Protocol, the Parties shall
determine the feasibility of banning or restricting, from States not party to this
Protocol, the import of products produced with, but not containing, controlled
substances. If determined feasible, the Parties shall, following the procedures in
Article 10 of the Convention, elaborate in an annex a list of such products. Parties
that have not objected to it in accordance with those procedures shall ban or restrict,
within one year of the annex having become effective, the import of those products
from any State not party to this Protocol.
5. Each Party shall discourage the export, to any State not party to this Protocol,
of technology for producing and for utilizing controlled substances.
6. Each Party shall refrain from providing new subsidies, aid, credits, guarantees
or insurance programmes for the export to States not party to this Protocol of
products, equipment, plants or technology that would facilitate the production of
controlled substances.
7. Paragraphs 5 and 6 shall not apply to products, equipment, plants or technology
that improve the containment, recovery, recycling or destruction of controlled substances, promote the development of alternative substances, or otherwise contribute
to the reduction of emissions of controlled substances.
8. Notwithstanding the provisions of this Article, imports referred to in paragraphs
1, 3 and 4 may be permitted from any State not party to this Protocol if that State
is determined, by a meeting of the Parties, to be in full compliance with Article 2
and this Article, and has submitted data to that effect as specified in Article 7.

ARTICLE 5: SPECIAL SITUATION OF DEVELOPING COUNTRIES

1. Any Party that is a developing country and whose annual calculated level of
consumption of the controlled substances is less than 0.3 kilograms per capita on
the date of the entry into force of the Protocol for it, or any time thereafter within
ten years of the date of entry into force of the Protocol shall, in order to meet its
basic domestic needs, be entitled to delay its compliance with the control measures

set out in paragraphs 1 to 4 of Article 2 by ten years after that specified in those paragraphs. However, such Party shall not exceed an annual calculated level of consumption of 0.3 kilograms per capita. Any such Party shall be entitled to use either the average of its annual calculated level of consumption for the period 1995 to 1997 inclusive or a calculated level of consumption of 0.3 kilograms per capita, whichever is the lower, as the basis for its compliance with the control measures.
2. The Parties undertake to facilitate access to environmentally safe alternative substances and technology for Parties that are developing countries and assist them to make expeditious use of such alternatives.
3. The Parties undertake to facilitate bilaterally or multilaterally the provision of subsidies, aid, credits, guarantees or insurance programmes to Parties that are developing countries for the use of alternative technology and for substitute products.

ARTICLE 6: ASSESSMENT AND REVIEW OF CONTROL MEASURES

Beginning in 1990, and at least every four years thereafter, the Parties shall assess the control measures provided for in Article 2 on the basis of available scientific, environmental, technical and economic information. At least one year before each assessment, the Parties shall convene appropriate panels of experts qualified in the fields mentioned and determine the composition and terms of reference of any such panels. Within one year of being convened, the panels will report their conclusions, through the secretariat, to the Parties.

ARTICLE 7: REPORTING OF DATA

1. Each Party shall provide to the secretariat, within three months of becoming a Party, statistical data on its production, imports and exports of each of the controlled substances for the year 1986, or the best possible estimates of such data where actual data are not available.
2. Each Party shall provide statistical data to the secretariat on its annual production (with separate data on amounts destroyed by technologies to be approved by the Parties), imports, and exports to Parties and non-Parties, respectively, of such substances for the year during which it becomes a Party and for each year thereafter. It shall forward the data no later than nine months after the end of the year to which the data relate.

ARTICLE 8: NON-COMPLIANCE

The Parties, at their first meeting, shall consider and approve procedures and institutional mechanisms for determining non-compliance with the provisions of this Protocol and for treatment of Parties found to be in non-compliance.

ARTICLE 9: RESEARCH, DEVELOPMENT, PUBLIC AWARENESS AND EXCHANGE OF INFORMATION

1. The Parties shall co-operate, consistent with their national laws, regulations and practices and taking into account in particular the needs of developing countries, in promoting, directly or through competent international bodies, research, development and exchange of information on:
   (a)   best technologies for improving the containment, recovery, recycling or destruction of controlled substances or otherwise reducing their emissions;
   (b)   possible alternatives to controlled substances, to products containing such substances, and to products manufactured with them; and

(c)   costs and benefits of relevant control strategies.

2. The Parties, individually, jointly or through competent international bodies, shall co-operate in promoting public awareness of the environmental effects of the emissions of controlled substances and other substances that deplete the ozone layer.

3. Within two years of the entry into force of this Protocol and every two years thereafter, each Party shall submit to the secretariat a summary of the activities it has conducted pursuant to this Article.

ARTICLE 10: TECHNICAL ASSISTANCE

1. The Parties shall, in the context of the provisions of Article 4 of the Convention, and taking into account in particular the needs of developing countries, co-operate in promoting technical assistance to facilitate participation in and implementation of this Protocol.

2. Any Party or Signatory to this Protocol may submit a request to the secretariat for technical assistance for the purposes of implementing or participating in the Protocol.

3. The Parties, at their first meeting, shall begin deliberations on the means of fulfilling the obligations set out in Article 9, and paragraphs 1 and 2 of this Article, including the preparation of workplans. Such workplans shall pay special attention to the needs and circumstances of the developing countries. States and regional economic integration organizations not party to the Protocol should be encouraged to participate in activities specified in such workplans.

ARTICLE 11: MEETINGS OF THE PARTIES

1. The Parties shall hold meetings at regular intervals. The secretariat shall convene the first meeting of the Parties not later than one year after the date of the entry into force of this Protocol and in conjunction with a meeting of the Conference of the Parties to the Convention, if a meeting of the latter is scheduled within that period.

2. Subsequent ordinary meetings of the Parties shall be held, unless the Parties otherwise decide, in conjunction with meetings of the Conference of the Parties to the Convention. Extraordinary meetings of the Parties shall be held at such other times as may be deemed necessary by a meeting of the Parties, or at the written request of any Party, provided that, within six months of such a request being communicated to them by the secretariat, it is supported by at least one third of the Parties.

3. The Parties, at their first meeting, shall:
    (a)   adopt by consensus rules of procedure for their meetings;
    (b)   adopt by consensus the financial rules referred to in paragraph 2 of Article 13;
    (c)   establish the panels and determine the terms of reference referred to in Article 6;
    (d)   consider and approve the procedures and institutional mechanisms specified in Article 8; and
    (e)   begin preparation of workplans pursuant to paragraph 3 of Article 10.

4. The functions of the meetings of the Parties shall be to:
    (a)   review the implementation of this Protocol;
    (b)   decide on any adjustments or reductions referred to in paragraph 9 of Article 2;
    (c)   decide on any addition to, insertion in or removal from any annex of substances and on related control measures in accordance with paragraph 10 of Article 2;

(d)   establish, where necessary, guidelines or procedures for reporting of information as provided for in Article 7 and paragraph 3 of Article 9;

(e)   review requests for technical assistance submitted pursuant to paragraph 2 of Article 10;

(f)   review reports prepared by the secretariat pursuant to subparagraph (c) of Article 12;

(g)   assess, in accordance with Article 6, the control measures provided for in Article 2;

(h)   consider and adopt, as required, proposals for amendment of this Protocol or any annex and for any new annex;

(i)   consider and adopt the budget for implementing this Protocol; and

(j)   consider and undertake any additional action that may be required for the achievement of the purposes of this Protocol.

5. The United Nations, its specialized agencies and the International Atomic Energy Agency, as well as any State not party to this Protocol, may be represented at meetings of the Parties as observers. Any body or agency, whether national or international, governmental or non-governmental, qualified in fields relating to the protection of the ozone layer which has informed the secretariat of its wish to be represented at a meeting of the Parties as an observer may be admitted unless at least one third of the Parties present object. The admission and participation of observers shall be subject to the rules of procedure adopted by the Parties.

ARTICLE 12: SECRETARIAT

For the purposes of this Protocol, the secretariat shall:

(a)   arrange for and service meetings of the Parties as provided for in Article 11;

(b)   receive and make available, upon request by a Party, data provided pursuant to Article 7;

(c)   prepare and distribute regularly to the Parties reports based on information received pursuant to Articles 7 and 9;

(d)   notify the Parties of any request for technical assistance received pursuant to Article 10 so as to facilitate the provision of such assistance;

(e)   encourage non-Parties to attend the meetings of the Parties as observers and to act in accordance with the provisions of this Protocol;

(f)   provide, as appropriate, the information and requests referred to in subparagraphs (c) and (d) to such non-party observers; and

(g)   perform such other functions for the achievement of the purposes of this Protocol as may be assigned to it by the Parties.

ARTICLE 13: FINANCIAL PROVISIONS

1. The funds required for the operation of this Protocol, including those for the functioning of the secretariat related to this Protocol, shall be charged exclusively against contributions from the Parties.

2. The Parties, at their first meeting, shall adopt by consensus financial rules for the operation of this Protocol.

ARTICLE 14: RELATIONSHIP OF THIS PROTOCOL TO THE CONVENTION

Except as otherwise provided in this Protocol, the provisions of the Convention relating to its protocols shall apply to this Protocol.

ARTICLE 15: SIGNATURE

This Protocol shall be open for signature by States and by regional economic integration organizations in Montreal on 16 September 1987, in Ottawa from 17

September 1987 to 16 January 1988, and at United Nations Headquarters in New York from 17 January 1988 to 15 September 1988.

ARTICLE 16: ENTRY INTO FORCE

1. This Protocol shall enter into force on 1 January 1989, provided that at least eleven instruments of ratification, acceptance, approval of the Protocol or accession thereto have been deposited by States or regional economic integration organizations representing at least two-thirds of 1986 estimated global consumption of the controlled substances, and the provisions of paragraph 1 of Article 17 of the Convention have been fulfilled. In the event that these conditions have not been fulfilled by that date, the Protocol shall enter into force on the ninetieth day following the date on which the conditions have been fulfilled.
2. For the purposes of paragraph 1, any such instrument deposited by a regional economic integration organization shall not be counted as additional to those deposited by member States of such organization.
3. After the entry force of this Protocol, any State or regional economic integration organization shall become a Party to it on the ninetieth day following the date of deposit of its instrument of ratification, acceptance, approval or accession.

ARTICLE 17: PARTIES JOINING AFTER ENTRY INTO FORCE

Subject to Article 5, any State or regional economic integration organization which becomes a Party to this Protocol after the date of its entry into force, shall fulfil forthwith the sum of the obligations under Article 2, as well as under Article 4, that apply at that date to the States and regional economic integration organizations that become Parties on the date the Protocol entered into force.

ARTICLE 18: RESERVATIONS

No reservations may be made to this Protocol.

ARTICLE 19: WITHDRAWAL

For the purposes of this Protocol, the provisions of Article 19 of the Convention relating to withdrawal shall apply, except with respect to Parties referred to in paragraph 1 of Article 5. Any such Party may withdraw from this Protocol by giving written notification to the Depositary at any time after four years of assuming the obligations specified in paragraphs 1 to 4 of Article 2. Any such withdrawal shall take effect upon expiry of one year after the date of its receipt by the Depositary, or on such later date as may be specified in the notification of the withdrawal.

ARTICLE 20: AUTHENTIC TEXTS

The original of this Protocol, of which the Arabic, Chinese, English, French, Russian and Spanish texts are equally authentic, shall be deposited with the Secretary-General of the United Nations.

IN WITNESS WHEREOF THE UNDERSIGNED, BEING DULY AUTHORIZED TO THAT EFFECT, HAVE SIGNED THIS PROTOCOL. DONE AT MONTREAL THIS SIXTEENTH DAY OF SEPTEMBER, ONE THOUSAND NINE HUNDRED AND EIGHTY SEVEN

Annex A
Controlled Substances

Group	Substance	Ozone Depleting Potential*
Group I		
	$CFCl_3$ (CFC-11)	1.0
	CF_2Cl_2 (CFC-12)	1.0
	$C_2F_3Cl_3$ (CFC-113)	0.8
	$C_2F_4Cl_2$ (CFC-114)	1.0
	C_2F_5Cl (CFC-115)	0.6
Group II		
	CF_2BrCl (halon-1211)	3.0
	CF_3Br (halon-1301)	10.0
	$C_2F_4Br_2$ (halon-2402)	(to be determined)

*These ozone depleting potentials are estimates based on existing knowledge and will be reviewed and revised periodically.

* * *

LONDON ADJUSTMENTS AND AMENDMENTS TO THE MONTREAL PROTOCOL ON SUBSTANCES THAT DEPLETE THE OZONE LAYER; AND NON-COMPLIANCE PROCEDURE

Popular Names: London Adjustments and Amendments, London Ozone Agreement, London Ozone Layer Protocol

Done in London on 29 June 1990, UNEP/OzL.Pro.2/3.
Entry into Force: The Adjustments are effective as of 7 March 1991; the Amendments are not yet in force as of 1 November 1990.

Depositary: United Nations

Languages: Arabic, Chinese, English, French, Russian, Spanish

Parties to the Amendments as of 1 November 1990: Canada, New Zealand

ADJUSTMENTS TO THE MONTREAL PROTOCOL ON SUBSTANCES THAT DEPLETE THE OZONE LAYER

The Second Meeting of the Parties to the Montreal Protocol on Substances that Deplete the Ozone Layer decides, on the basis of assessments made pursuant to Article 6 of the Protocol, to adopt adjustments and reductions of production and consumption of the controlled substances in Annex A to the Protocol, as follows, with the understanding that:

(a) References in Article 2 to "this Article" and throughout the Protocol to "Article 2" shall be interpreted as references to Articles 2, 2A and 2B;

(b) References throughout the Protocol to "paragraphs 1 to 4 of Article 2" shall be interpreted as references to Articles 2A and 2B; and

(c) The reference in paragraph 5 of Article 2 to "paragraphs 1, 3 and 4" shall be interpreted as a reference to Article 2A.

A. Article 2A: CFCs

Paragraph 1 of Article 2 of the Protocol shall become paragraph 1 of Article 2A, which shall be entitled "Article 2A: CFCs". Paragraphs 3 and 4 of Article 2 shall be replaced by the following paragraphs, which shall be numbered paragraphs 2 to 6 of Article 2A:

2. Each Party shall ensure that for the period from 1 July 1991 to 31 December 1992 its calculated levels of consumption and production of the controlled substances in Group I of Annex A do not exceed 150 per cent of its calculated levels of production and consumption of those substances in 1986; with effect from 1 January 1993, the twelve-month control period for these controlled substances shall run from 1 January to 31 December each year.

3. Each Party shall ensure that for the twelve-month period commencing on 1 January 1995, and in each twelve-month period thereafter, its calculated level of consumption of the controlled substances in Group I of Annex A does not exceed, annually, fifty per cent of its calculated level of consumption in 1986. Each Party producing one or more of these substances shall, for the same periods, ensure that its calculated level of production of the substances does not exceed, annually, fifty per cent of its calculated level of production in 1986. However, in order to satisfy the basic domestic needs of the Parties operating under paragraph 1 of Article 5, its calculated level of production may exceed that limit by up to ten per cent of its calculated level of production in 1986.

4. Each Party shall ensure that for the twelve-month period commencing on 1 January 1997, and in each twelve-month period thereafter, its calculated level of consumption of the controlled substances in Group I of Annex A does not exceed, annually, fifteen per cent of its calculated level of consumption in 1986. Each Party producing one or more of these substances shall, for the same periods, ensure that its calculated level of production of the substances does not exceed, annually, fifteen per cent of its calculated level of production in 1986. However, in order to satisfy the basic domestic needs of the Parties operating under paragraph 1 of Article 5, its calculated level of production may exceed that limit by up to ten per cent of its calculated level of production in 1986.

5. Each Party shall ensure that for the twelve-month period commencing on 1 January 2000, and in each twelve-month period thereafter, its calculated level of consumption of the controlled substances in Group I of Annex A does not exceed zero. Each Party producing one or more of these substances shall, for the same periods, ensure that its calculated level of production of the substances does not exceed zero. However, in order to satisfy the basic domestic needs of the Parties operating under paragraph 1 of Article 5, its calculated level of production may exceed that limit by up to fifteen per cent of its calculated level of production in 1986.

6. In 1992, the Parties will review the situation with the objective of accelerating the reduction schedule.

B. Article 2B: Halons

Paragraph 2 of Article 2 of the Protocol shall be replaced by the following paragraphs, which shall be numbered paragraphs 1 to 4 of Article 2B:

Article 2B: Halons

1. Each Party shall ensure that for the twelve-month period commencing on 1 January 1992, and in each twelve-month period thereafter, its calculated level of consumption of the controlled substances in Group II Of Annex A does not exceed, annually, its calculated level of consumption in 1986. Each Party producing one or more of these substances shall, for the same periods, ensure that its calculated level of production of the substances does not exceed, annually, its calculated level of production in 1986. However, in order to satisfy the basic domestic needs of the Parties operating under paragraph 1 of Article 5, its calculated level of production may exceed that limit by up to ten per cent of its calculated level of production in 1986.

2. Each Party shall ensure that for the twelve-month period commencing on 1 January 1995, and in each twelve-month period thereafter, its calculated level of consumption of the controlled substances in Group II of Annex A does not exceed, annually, fifty per cent of its calculated level of consumption in 1986. Each Party producing one or more of these substances shall, for the same periods, ensure that its calculated level of production of the substances does not exceed, annually, fifty per cent of its calculated level of production in 1986. However, in order to satisfy the basic domestic needs of the Parties operating under paragraph 1 of Article 5, its calculated level of production may exceed that limit by up to ten per cent of its calculated level of production in 1986.

This paragraph will apply save to the extent that the Parties decide to permit the level of production or consumption that is necessary to satisfy essential uses for which no adequate alternatives are available.

3. Each Party shall ensure that for the twelve-month period commencing on 1 January 2000, and in each twelve-month period thereafter, its calculated level of consumption of the controlled substances in Group II of Annex A does not exceed zero. Each Party producing one or more of these substances shall, for the same periods, ensure that its calculated level of production of the substances does not exceed zero. However, in order to satisfy the basic domestic needs of the Parties operating under paragraph 1 of Article 5, its calculated level of production may exceed that limit by up to fifteen per cent of its calculated level of production in 1986. This paragraph will apply save to the extent that the Parties decide to permit the level of production or consumption that is necessary to satisfy essential uses for which no adequate alternatives are available.

4. By 1 January 1993, the Parties shall adopt a decision identifying essential uses, if any, for the purposes of paragraphs 2 and 3 of this Article. Such decision shall be reviewed by the Parties at their subsequent meetings.

AMENDMENT TO THE MONTREAL PROTOCOL ON SUBSTANCES THAT DEPLETE THE OZONE LAYER

ARTICLE 1: AMENDMENT

A. *Preambular paragraphs*

1. The 6th preambular paragraph of the Protocol shall be replaced by the following:
   Determined to protect the ozone layer by taking precautionary measures to control equitably total global emissions of substances that deplete it, with the ultimate objective of their elimination on the basis of developments in scientific knowledge, taking into account technical and economic considerations and bearing in mind the developmental needs of developing countries,
2. The 7th preambular paragraph of the Protocol shall be replaced by the following:
   Acknowledging that special provision is required to meet the needs of developing countries, including the provision of additional financial resources and access to relevant technologies, bearing in mind that the magnitude of funds necessary is predictable, and the funds can be expected to make a substantial difference in the world's ability to address the scientifically established problem of ozone depletion and its harmful effects,
3. The 9th preambular paragraph of the Protocol shall be replaced by the following:
   Considering the importance of promoting international co-operation in the research, development and transfer of alternative technologies relating to the control and reduction of emissions of substances that deplete the ozone layer, bearing in mind in particular the needs of developing countries,

B. Article 1: Definitions

1. Paragraph 4 of Article 1 of the Protocol shall be replaced by the following paragraph:
   4. "Controlled substance" means a substance in Annex A or in Annex B to this Protocol, whether existing alone or in a mixture. It includes the isomers of any such substance, except as specified in the relevant Annex, but excludes any controlled substance or mixture which is in a manufactured product other than a container used for the transportation or storage of that substance.
2. Paragraph 5 of Article 1 of the Protocol shall be replaced by the following paragraph:
   5. "Production" means the amount of controlled substances produced, minus the amount destroyed by technologies to be approved by the Parties and minus the amount entirely used as feedstock in the manufacture of other chemicals. The amount recycled and reused is not to be considered as "production".
3. The following paragraph shall be added to Article 1 of the Protocol:
   9. "Transitional substance" means a substance in Annex C to this Protocol, whether existing alone or in a mixture. It includes the isomers of any such substance, except as may be specified in Annex C, but excludes any transitional substance or mixture which is in a manufactured product other than a container used for the transportation or storage of that substance.

C. Article 2, paragraph 5

Paragraph 5 of Article 2 of the Protocol shall be replaced by the following paragraph:

5. Any Party may, for any one or more control periods, transfer to another Party any portion of its calculated level of production set out in Articles 2A to 2E, provided that the total combined calculated levels of production of the Parties concerned for any group of controlled substances do not exceed the production limits set out in those Articles for that group. Such transfer of production shall be notified to the Secretariat by each of the Parties concerned, stating the terms of such transfer and the period for which it is to apply.

D. Article 2, paragraph 6

The following words shall be inserted in paragraph 6 of Article 2 before the words "controlled substances" the first time they occur:
Annex A or Annex B

E. Article 2, paragraph 8(a)

The following words shall be added after the words "this Article" wherever they appear in paragraph 8(a) of Article 2 of the Protocol:
and Articles 2A to 2E

F. Article 2, paragraph 9(a)(i)

The following words shall be added after "Annex A" in paragraph 9(a)(i) of Article 2 of the Protocol:
and/or Annex B

G. Article 2, paragraph 9(a)(ii)

The following words shall be deleted from paragraph 9(a)(ii) of Article 2 of the Protocol:
from 1986 levels

H. Article 2, paragraph 9(c)

The following words shall be deleted from paragraph 9(c) of Article 2 of the Protocol:
representing at least fifty per cent of the total consumption of the controlled substances of the Parties
and replaced by:
representing a majority of the Parties operating under paragraph 1 of Article 5 present and voting and a majority of the Parties not so operating present and voting

I. Article 2, paragraph 10(b)

Paragraph 10(b) of Article 2 of the Protocol shall be deleted, and paragraph 10(a) of Article 2 shall become paragraph 10.

J. Article 2, paragraph 11

The following words shall be added after the words "this Article" wherever they occur in paragraph 11 of Article 2 of the Protocol:
and Articles 2A to 2E

K. Article 2C: Other fully halogenated CFCs

The following paragraphs shall be added to the Protocol as Article 2C:

Article 2C: Other fully halogenated CFCs

1. Each Party shall ensure that for the twelve-month period commencing on 1 January 1993, and in each twelve-month period thereafter, its calculated level of consumption of the controlled substances in Group I of Annex B does not exceed, annually, eighty per cent of its calculated level of consumption in 1989. Each Party producing one or more of these substances shall, for the same periods, ensure that its calculated level of production of the substances does not exceed, annually, eighty per cent of its calculated level of production in 1989. However, in order to satisfy the basic domestic needs of the Parties operating under paragraph 1 of Article 5, its calculated level of production may exceed that limit by up to ten per cent of its calculated level of production in 1989.

2. Each Party shall ensure that for the twelve-month period commencing on 1 January 1997, and in each twelve-month period thereafter, its calculated level of consumption of the controlled substances in Group I of Annex B does not exceed, annually, fifteen per cent of its calculated level of consumption in 1989. Each Party producing one or more of these substances shall, for the same periods, ensure that its calculated level of production of the substances does not exceed, annually, fifteen per cent of its calculated level of production in 1989. However, in order to satisfy the basic domestic needs of the Parties operating under paragraph 1 of Article 5, its calculated level of production may exceed that limit by up to ten per cent of its calculated level of production in 1989.

3. Each Party shall ensure that for the twelve-month period commencing on 1 January 2000, and in each twelve-month period thereafter, its calculated level of consumption of the controlled substances in Group I of Annex B does not exceed zero. Each Party producing one or more of these substances shall, for the same periods, ensure that its calculated level of production of the substances does not exceed zero. However, in order to satisfy the basic domestic needs of the Parties operating under paragraph 1 of Article 5, its calculated level of production may exceed that limit by up to fifteen per cent of its calculated level of production in 1989.

L. Article 2D: Carbon tetrachloride

The following paragraphs shall be added to the Protocol as Article 2D:

Article 2D: Carbon tetrachloride

1. Each Party shall ensure that for the twelve-month period commencing on 1 January 1995, and in each twelve-month period thereafter, its calculated level of consumption of the controlled substance in Group II of Annex B does not exceed, annually, fifteen per cent of its calculated level of consumption in 1989. Each Party producing the substance shall, for the same periods, ensure that its calculated level of production of the substance does not exceed, annually, fifteen per cent of its calculated level of production in 1989. However, in order to satisfy the basic domestic needs of the Parties operating under paragraph 1 of Article 5, its calculated level of production may exceed that limit by up to ten per cent of its calculated level of production in 1989.

2. Each Party shall ensure that for the twelve-month period commencing on 1 January 2000, and in each twelve-month period thereafter, its calculated level of consumption of the controlled substance in Group II of Annex B does not exceed zero. Each Party producing the substance shall, for the same periods, ensure that its calculated level of production of the substance does not

exceed zero. However, in order to satisfy the basic domestic needs of the Parties operating under paragraph 1 of Article 5, its calculated level of production may exceed that limit by up to fifteen per cent of its calculated level of production in 1989.

M. Article 2E: 1,1,1-trichloroethane (methyl chloroform)

The following paragraphs shall be added to the Protocol as Article 2E:

Article 2E: 1,1,1,-trichloroethane (methyl chloroform)

1. Each Party shall ensure that for the twelve-month period commencing on 1 January 1993, and in each twelve-month period thereafter, its calculated level of consumption of the controlled substance in Group III of Annex B does not exceed, annually, its calculated level of consumption in 1989. Each Party producing the substance shall, for the same periods, ensure that its calculated level of production of the substance does not exceed, annually, its calculated level of production in 1989. However, in order to satisfy the basic domestic needs of the Parties operating under paragraph 1 of Article 5, its calculated level of production may exceed that limit by up to ten per cent of its calculated level of production in 1989.

2. Each party shall ensure that for the twelve-month period commencing on 1 January 1995, and in each twelve-month period thereafter, its calculated level of consumption of the controlled substance in Group III of Annex B does not exceed, annually, seventy per cent of its calculated level of consumption in 1989. Each Party producing the substance shall, for the same periods, ensure that its calculated level of production of the substance does not exceed, annually, seventy per cent of its calculated level of consumption in 1989. However, in order to satisfy the basic domestic needs of the Parties operating under paragraph 1 of Article 5, its calculated level of production may exceed that limit by up to ten per cent of its calculated level of production in 1989.

3. Each Party shall ensure that for the twelve-month period commencing on 1 January 2000, and in each twelve-month period thereafter, its calculated level of consumption of the controlled substance in Group III of Annex B does not exceed, annually, thirty per cent of its calculated level of consumption in 1989. Each Party producing the substance shall, for the same periods, ensure that its calculated level of production of the substance does not exceed, annually, thirty per cent of its calculated level of production in 1989. However, in order to satisfy the basic domestic needs of Parties operating under paragraph 1 of Article 5, its calculated level of production may exceed that limit by up to ten per cent of its calculated level of production in 1989.

4. Each Party shall ensure that for the twelve-month period commencing on 1 January 2005, and in each twelve-month period thereafter, its calculated level of consumption of the controlled substance in Group III of Annex B does not exceed zero. Each Party producing the substance shall, for the same periods, ensure that its calculated level of production of the substance does not exceed zero. However, in order to satisfy the basic domestic needs of the Parties operating under paragraph 1 of Article 5, its calculated level of production may exceed that limit by up to fifteen per cent of its calculated level of production in 1989.

5. The Parties shall review, in 1992, the feasibility of a more rapid schedule of reductions than that set out in this Article.

N. Article 3: Calculation of control levels

1. The following shall be added after "Articles 2" in Article 3 of the Protocol:
   , 2A to 2E,

2. The following words shall be added after ''Annex A'' each time it appears in Article 3 of the Protocol:
> or Annex B

O. Article 4: Control of trade with non-Parties

1. Paragraphs 1 to 5 of Article 4 shall be replaced by the following paragraphs:
1. As of 1 January 1990, each Party shall ban the import of the controlled substances in Annex A from any State not party to this Protocol.

1 *bis*. Within one year of the date of the entry into force of this paragraph, each Party shall ban the import of the controlled substances in Annex B from any State not party to this Protocol.

2. As of 1 January 1993, each Party shall ban the export of any controlled substances in Annex A to any State not party to this Protocol.

2 *bis*. Commencing one year after the date of entry into force of this paragraph, each Party shall ban the export of any controlled substances in Annex B to any State not party to this Protocol.

3. By 1 January 1992, the Parties shall, following the procedures in Article 10 of the Convention, elaborate in an annex a list of products containing controlled substances in Annex A. Parties that have not objected to the annex in accordance with those procedures shall ban, within one year of the annex having become effective, the import of those products from any State not party to this Protocol.

3 *bis*. Within three years of the date of the entry into force of this paragraph, the Parties shall, following the procedures in Article 10 of the Convention, elaborate in an annex a list of products containing controlled substances in Annex B. Parties that have not objected to the annex in accordance with those procedures shall ban, within one year of the annex having become effective, the import of those products from any State not party to this Protocol.

4. By 1 January 1994, the Parties shall determine the feasibility of banning or restricting, from States not party to this Protocol, the import of products produced with, but not containing, controlled substances in Annex A. If determined feasible, the Parties shall, following the procedures in Article 10 of the Convention, elaborate in an annex a list of such products. Parties that have not objected to the annex in accordance with those procedures shall ban, within one year of the annex having become effective, the import of those products from any State not party to this Protocol.

4 *bis*. Within five years of the date of the entry into force of this paragraph, the Parties shall determine the feasibility of banning or restricting, from States not party to this Protocol, the import of products produced with, but not containing, controlled substances in Annex B. If determined feasible, the Parties shall, following the procedures in Article 10 of the Convention, elaborate in an annex a list of such products. Parties that have not objected to the annex in accordance with those procedures shall ban or restrict, within one year of the annex having become effective, the import of those products from any State not party to this Protocol.

5. Each Party undertakes to the fullest practicable extent to discourage the export to any State not party to this Protocol of technology for producing and for utilizing controlled substances.

3. Paragraph 8 of Article 4 of the Protocol shall be replaced by the following paragraph:
8. Notwithstanding the provisions of this Article, imports referred to in paragraphs 1, 1 *bis*, 3, 3 *bis*, 4 and 4 *bis*, and exports referred to in paragraphs 2 and 2 *bis*, may be permitted from, or to, any State not party to this Protocol, if that State is determined by a meeting of the Parties to be in full compliance

with Article 2, Articles 2A to 2E, and this Article and have submitted data to that effect as specified in Article 7.

4. The following paragraph shall be added to Article 4 of the Protocol as paragraph 9:

9. For the purposes of this Article, the term "State not party to this Protocol" shall include, with respect to a particular controlled substance, a State or regional economic integration organization that has not agreed to be bound by the control measures in effect for that substance.

P. Article 5: Special situation of developing countries

Article 5 of the Protocol shall be replaced by the following paragraphs:

1. Any Party that is a developing country and whose annual calculated level of consumption of the controlled substances in Annex A is less than 0.3 kilograms per capita on the date of the entry into force of the Protocol for it, or any time thereafter until 1 January 1999, shall in order to meet its basic domestic needs, be entitled to delay for ten years its compliance with the control measures set out in Articles 2A to 2E.

2. However, any Party operating under paragraph 1 of this Article shall exceed neither an annual calculated level of consumption of the controlled substances in Annex A of 0.3 kilograms per capita nor an annual calculated level of consumption of the controlled substances of Annex B of 0.2 kilograms per capita.

3. When implementing the control measures set out in Articles 2A to 2E, any Party operating under paragraph 1 of this Article shall be entitled to use:

(a) For controlled substances under Annex A, either the average of its annual calculated level of consumption for the period 1995 to 1997 inclusive or a calculated level of consumption of 0.3 kilograms per capita, whichever is the lower, as the basis for determining its compliance with the control measures;

(b) For controlled substances under Annex B, the average of its annual calculated level of consumption for the period 1998 to 2000 inclusive or a calculated level of consumption of 0.2 kilograms per capita, whichever is the lower, as the basis for determining its compliance with the control measures.

4. If a Party operating under paragraph 1 of this Article, at any time before the control measures obligations in Articles 2A to 2E become applicable to it, finds itself unable to obtain an adequate supply of controlled substances, it may notify this to the Secretariat. The Secretariat shall forthwith transmit a copy of such notification to the Parties, which shall consider the matter at their next Meeting, and decide upon appropriate action to be taken.

5. Developing the capacity to fulfil the obligations of the Parties operating under paragraph 1 of this Article to comply with the control measures set out in Articles 2A to 2E and their implementation by those same Parties will depend upon the effective implementation of the financial co-operation as provided by Article 10 and transfer of technology as provided by Article 10 A.

6. Any Party operating under paragraph 1 of this Article may, at any time, notify the Secretariat in writing that, having taken all practicable steps it is unable to implement any or all of the obligations laid down in Articles 2A to 2E due to the inadequate implementation of Articles 10 and 10A. The Secretariat shall forthwith trasmit a copy of the notification to the Parties, which shall consider the matter at their next Meeting, giving due recognition to paragraph 5 of this Article and shall decide upon appropriate action to be taken.

7. During the period between notification and the Meeting of the Parties at which the appropriate action referred to in paragraph 6 above is to be decided,

or for a further period if the Meeting of the Parties so decides, the non-compliance procedures referred to in Article 8 shall not be invoked against the notifying Party.

8. A Meeting of the Parties shall review, not later than 1995, the situation of the Parties operating under paragraph 1 of this Article, including the effective implementation of financial co-operation and transfer of technology to them, and adopt such revisions that may be deemed necessary regarding the schedule of control measures applicable to those Parties.

9. Decisions of the Parties referred to in paragraphs 4, 6 and 7 of this Article shall be taken according to the same procedure applied to decision-making under Article 10.

Q. Article 6: Assessment and review of control measures

The following words shall be added after ''Article 2'' in Article 6 of the Protocol:

Articles 2A to 2E, and the situation regarding production, imports and exports of the transitional substances in Group I of Annex C

R. Article 7: Reporting of data

1. [sic] Article 7 of the Protocol shall be replaced by the following paragraphs:

1. Each Party shall provide to the Secretariat, within three months of becoming a Party, statistical data on its production, imports and exports of each of the controlled substances in Annex A for the year 1986, or the best possible estimates of such data where actual data are not available.

2. Each Party shall provide to the Secretariat statistical data on its production, imports and exports of each of the controlled substances in Annex B and each of the transitional substances in Group I of Annex C, for the year 1989, or the best possible estimates of such data where actual data are not available, not later than three months after the date when the provisions set out in the Protocol with regard to the substances in Annex B enter into force for that Party.

3. Each Party shall provide statistical data to the Secretariat on its annual production (as defined in paragraph 5 of Article 1), and, separately,

—amounts used for feedstocks,

—amounts destroyed by technologies approved by the Parties,

—imports and exports to Parties and non-Parties respectively,

of each of the controlled substances listed in Annexes A and B as well as of the transitional substances in Group I of Annex C, for the year during which provisions concerning the substances in Annex B entered into force for that Party and for each year thereafter. Data shall be forwarded not later than nine months after the end of the year to which the data relate.

4. For Parties operating under the provisions of paragraph 8(a) of Article 2, the requirements in paragraphs 1, 2 and 3 of this Article in respect of statistical data on imports and exports shall be satisfied if the regional economic integration organization concerned provides data on imports and exports between the organization and States that are not members of that organization.

S. Article 9: Research, development, public awareness and exchange of information

Paragraph 1(a) of Article 9 of the Protocol shall be replaced by the following:

(a) Best technologies for improving the containment, recovery, recycling, or destruction of controlled and transitional substances or otherwise reducing their emissions;

T. Article 10: Financial mechanism

Article 10 of the Protocol shall be replaced by the following:

Article 10: Financial mechanism

1. The Parties shall establish a mechanism for the purposes of providing financial and technical co-operation, including the transfer of technologies, to Parties operating under paragraph 1 of Article 5 of this Protocol to enable their compliance with the control measures set out in Articles 2A to 2E of the Protocol. The mechanism, contributions to which shall be additional to other financial transfers to Parties operating under that paragraph, shall meet all agreed incremental costs of such Parties in order to enable their compliance with the control measures of the Protocol. An indicative list of the categories of incremental costs shall be decided by the meeting of the Parties.

2. The mechanism established under paragraph 1 shall include a Multilateral Fund. It may also include other means of multilateral, regional and bilateral co-operation.

3. The Multilateral Fund shall:

(a) Meet, on a grant or concessional basis as appropriate, and according to criteria to be decided upon by the Parties, the agreed incremental costs;

(b) Finance clearing-house functions to:

(i) Assist Parties operating under paragraph 1 of Article 5, through country specific studies and other technical co-operation, to identify their needs for co-operation;

(ii) Facilitate technical co-operation to meet these identified needs;

(iii) Distribute, as provided for in Article 9, information and relevant materials, and hold workshops, training sessions, and other related activities, for the benefit of Parties that are developing countries; and

(iv) Facilitate and monitor other multilateral, regional and bilateral co-operation available to Parties that are developing countries;

(c) Finance the secretarial services of the Multilateral Fund and related support costs.

4. The Multilateral Fund shall operate under the authority of the Parties who shall decide on its overall policies.

5. The Parties shall establish an Executive Committee to develop and monitor the implementation of specific operational policies, guidelines and administrative arrangements, including the disbursement of resources, for the purpose of achieving the objectives of the Multilateral Fund.

The Executive Committee shall discharge its tasks and responsibilities, specified in its terms of reference as agreed by the Parties, with the co-operation and assistance of the International Bank for Reconstruction and Development (World Bank), the United Nations Environment Programme, the United Nations Development Programme or other appropriate agencies depending on their respective areas of expertise. The members of the Executive Committee, which shall be selected on the basis of a balanced representation of the Parties operating under paragraph 1 of Article 5 and of the Parties not so operating, shall be endorsed by the Parties.

6. The Multilateral Fund shall be financed by contributions from Parties not operating under paragraph 1 of Article 5 in convertible currency or, in certain circumstances, in kind and/or in national currency, on the basis of the United Nations scale of assessments. Contributions by other Parties shall be encouraged. Bilateral and, in particular cases agreed by a decision of the Parties, regional co-operation may, up to a percentage and consistent with any criteria to be specified by decision of the Parties, be considered as a contribution to the Multilateral Fund, provided that such co-operation, as a minimum:

(a) Strictly relates to compliance with the provisions of this Protocol;
(b) Provides additional resources; and
(c) Meets agreed incremental costs.

7. The Parties shall decide upon the programme budget of the Multilateral Fund for each fiscal period and upon the percentage of contributions of the individual Parties thereto.

8. Resources under the Multilateral Fund shall be disbursed with the concurrence of the beneficiary Party.

9. Decisions by the Parties under this Article shall be taken by consensus whenever possible. If all efforts at consensus have been exhausted and no agreement reached, decisions shall be adopted by a two-thirds majority vote of the Parties present and voting, representing a majority of the Parties operating under paragraph 1 of Article 5 present and voting and a majority of the Parties not so operating present and voting.

10. The financial mechanism set out in this Article is without prejudice to any future arrangements that may be developed with respect to other environmental issues.

U. Article 10A: Transfer of technology

The following Article shall be added to the Protocol as Article 10A:

Article 10A: Transfer of technology

Each Party shall take every practicable step, consistent with the programmes supported by the financial mechanism, to ensure:
(a) That the best available, environmentally safe substitutes and related technologies are expeditiously transferred to Parties operating under paragraph 1 of Article 5; and
(b) That the transfers referred to in subparagraph (a) occur under fair and most favourable conditions.

V. Article 11: Meetings of the Parties

Paragraph 4(g) of Article 11 of the Protocol shall be replaced by the following:
(g) Assess, in accordance with Article 6, the control measures and the situation regarding transitional substances;

W. Article 17: Parties joining after entry into force

The following words shall be added after "as well as under" in Article 17:
Articles 2A to 2E, and

X. Article 19: Withdrawal

Article 19 of the Protocol shall be replaced by the following paragraph:
Any Party may withdraw from this Protocol by giving written notification to the Depositary at any time after four years of assuming the obligations specified in paragraph 1 of Article 2A. Any such withdrawal shall take effect upon expiry of one year after the date of its receipt by the Depositary, or on such later date as may be specified in the notification of the withdrawal.

Y. ANNEXES

The following annexes shall be added to the Protocol:

Annex B
Controlled substances

Group	Substance	Ozone-depleting potential
Group I		
CF_3Cl	(CFC-13)	1.0
C_2FCl_5	(CFC-111)	1.0
$C_2F_2Cl_4$	(CFC-112)	1.0
C_3FCl_7	(CFC-211)	1.0
$C_3F_2Cl_6$	(CFC-212)	1.0
$C_3F_3Cl_5$	(CFC-213)	1.0
$C_3F_4Cl_4$	(CFC-214)	1.0
$C_3F_5Cl_3$	(CFC-215)	1.0
$C_3F_6Cl_2$	(CFC-216)	1.0
C_3F_7Cl	(CFC-217)	1.0
Group II		
CCl_4	carbon tetrachloride	1.1
Group III		
$C_2H_3Cl_3$*	1,1,1-trichloroethane	0.1
		(methyl chloroform)

* This formula does not refer to 1,1,2-trichloroethane.

Annex C
Transitional substances

Group	Substance
Group I	
$CHFCl_2$	(HCFC-21)
CHF_2Cl	(HCFC-22)
CH_2FCl	(HCFC-31)
C_2HFCl_4	(HCFC-121)
$C_2HF_2Cl_3$	(HCFC-122)
$C_2HF_3Cl_2$	(HCFC-123)
C_2HF_4Cl	(HCFC-124)
$C_2H_2FCl_3$	(HCFC-131)
$C_2H_2F_2Cl_2$	(HCFC-132)
$C_2H_2F_3Cl$	(HCFC-133)
$C_2H_3FCl_2$	(HCFC-141)
$C_2H_3F_2Cl$	(HCFC-142)
C_2H_4FCl	(HCFC-151)
C_3HFCl_6	(HCFC-221)
$C_3HF_2Cl_5$	(HCFC-222)
$C_3HF_3Cl_4$	(HCFC-223)
$C_3HF_4Cl_3$	(HCFC-224)
$C_3HF_5Cl_2$	(HCFC-225)
C_3HF_6Cl	(HCFC-226)
$C_3H_2FCl_5$	(HCFC-231)
$C_3H_2F_2Cl_4$	(HCFC-232)
$C_3H_2F_3Cl_3$	(HCFC-233)
$C_3H_2F_4Cl_2$	(HCFC-234)
$C_3H_2F_5Cl$	(HCFC-235)
$C_3H_3FCl_4$	(HCFC-241)
$C_3H_3F_2Cl_3$	(HCFC-242)
$C_3H_3F_3Cl_2$	(HCFC-243)
$C_3H_3F_4Cl$	(HCFC-244)
$C_3H_4FCl_3$	(HCFC-251)
$C_3H_4F_2Cl_2$	(HCFC-252)
$C_3H_4F_3Cl$	(HCFC-253)
$C_3H_5FCl_2$	(HCFC-261)
$C_3H_5F_2Cl$	(HCFC-262)
C_3H_6FCl	(HCFC-271)

ARTICLE 2: ENTRY INTO FORCE

1. This Amendment shall enter into force on 1 January 1992, provided that at least twenty instruments of ratification, acceptance or approval of the Amendment have been deposited by States or regional economic integration organizations that are Parties to the Montreal Protocol on Substances that Deplete the Ozone Layer. In the event that this condition has not been fulfilled by that date, the Amendment shall enter into force on the ninetieth day following the date on which it has been fulfilled.

2. For the purposes of paragraph 1, any such instrument deposited by a regional economic integration organization shall not be counted as additional to those deposited by member States of such organization.

3. After the entry into force of this Amendment as provided under paragraph 1, it shall enter into force for any other Party to the Protocol on the ninetieth day following the date of deposit of its instrument of ratification, acceptance or approval.

NON-COMPLIANCE PROCEDURE

1. If one or more Parties have reservations regarding another Party's implementation of its obligations under the Protocol, those concerns may be addressed in writing to the Secretariat. Such a submission shall be supported by corroborating information.

2. The Party whose implementation is at issue is to be given the submission and a reasonable opportunity to reply. Such reply and information in support thereof is to be submitted to the Secretariat and to the Parties involved. The Secretariat shall then transmit the submission, the reply and the information provided by the Parties, to the Implementation Committee referred to in paragraph 3, which shall consider the matter as soon as practicable.

3. An Implementation Committee is hereby established. It shall consist of five Parties elected by the Meeting of the Parties for two years, based on equitable geographical distribution. Outgoing Parties may also be re-elected for one immediate consecutive term. At the first election, two Parties shall be elected for a one-year term.

4. The Committee shall meet as necessary to perform its functions.

5. The functions of the Committee shall be to receive, consider and report on:

   (a) Any submission made by one or more Parties in accordance with paragraphs 1 and 2;

   (b) Any information or observations forwarded by the Secretariat in connection with the preparation of the report referred to in Article 12 (c) of the Protocol.

6. The Committee shall consider the submissions, information and observations referred to in paragraph 5 with a view to securing an amicable resolution of the matter on the basis of respect for the provisions of the Protocol.

7. The Committee shall report to the Meeting of the Parties. After receiving a report by the Committee the Parties may, taking into consideration the circumstances of the case, decide upon and call for steps to bring about full compliance with the Protocol, including measures to assist the Party's compliance with the Protocol, and to further the Protocol's objectives.

8. The Parties involved in a matter referred to in paragraph 5 shall inform, through the Secretariat, the Meeting of the Parties of the results of proceedings taken under Article 11 of the Convention regarding possible non-compliance, about implementation of those results and about implementation of any decision of the Parties pursuant to paragraph 7.

9. The Meeting of the Parties may pending completion of proceedings initiated under Article 11 of the Convention, issue an interim call and/or recommendations.

10. The Meeting of the Parties may request the Committee to make recommendations to assist the Meeting's consideration of cases of possible non-compliance.

11. The members of the Committee and any Party involved in its deliberations shall protect the confidentiality of information they receive in confidence. Decisions of the Second Meeting of Parties to the Montreal Protocol.

E. CLIMATE

UNITED NATIONS GENERAL ASSEMBLY RESOLUTION ON PROTECTION OF GLOBAL CLIMATE FOR PRESENT AND FUTURE GENERATIONS OF MANKIND

Popular Name: General Assembly Resolution on Climate Change

Adopted by the United Nations General Assembly on 6 December 1988, U.N. Doc. A/RES/43/53 (1988), *reprinted in* 28 ILM 1326 (1989).

Languages: Arabic, Chinese, English, French, Russian, Spanish

Editors' Note

So-called greenhouse gases (e.g., principally carbon dioxide, methane, nitrous oxides, and chlorofluorocarbons) trap heat emanating from Earth towards outer space. Scientists and policymakers have become more and more concerned that increased concentrations of greenhouse gases in the Earth's atmosphere might cause the Earth's temperature to rise, with resulting rises in sea level and changes in temperature, rainfall, and wind patterns. Anthropogenic activities such as fossil fuels consumption, deforestation, cattle raising, waste disposal in landfills, and rice cultivation contribute to the increase in greenhouse gas emissions.

Although the issue of climate change (or global warming) is beset with uncertainty, the seriousness of the potential consequences and the perceived likelihood that warming will occur are sufficiently great that a concerted international effort is underway to take steps to reduce greenhouse gas emissions and enhance capabilities to respond to climate changes. Some of the most difficult questions in that process involve equity: how to treat future generations equitably and how to treat developing States (and the individuals in them) equitably.

The U.N. General Assembly Resolution on Protection of Global Climate for Present and Future Generations of Mankind addresses those and other issues related to climate change. As originally introduced by Malta, the draft Resolution stated that climate is the "common heritage of mankind," a concept used in several other environmental instruments. As adopted, however, the Resolution states that "climate change is a common concern of mankind," a term which is not yet defined.

PROTECTION OF GLOBAL CLIMATE FOR PRESENT AND FUTURE GENERATIONS OF MANKIND

The General Assembly,

Welcoming with appreciation the initiative taken by the Government of Malta in proposing for consideration by the Assembly the item entitled "Conservation of climate as part of the common heritage of mankind",

Concerned that certain human activities could change global climate patterns, threatening present and future generations with potentially severe economic and social consequences,

Noting with concern that the emerging evidence indicates that continued growth in atmospheric concentrations of "greenhouse" gases could produce global warming with an eventual rise in sea levels, the effects of which could be disastrous for mankind if timely steps are not taken at all levels,

Recognizing the need for additional research and scientific studies into all sources and causes of climate change,

Concerned also that emissions of certain substances are depleting the ozone layer and thereby exposing the earth's surface to increased ultra-violet radiation, which may pose a threat to, *inter alia*, human health, agricultural productivity and animal and marine life, and reaffirming in this context the appeal, contained in its resolution 42/182 of 11 December 1987, to all States that have not yet done so to consider becoming parties to the Vienna Convention for the Protection of the Ozone Layer, adopted on 22 March 1985, and the Montreal Protocol on Substances that Deplete the Ozone Layer, adopted on 16 September 1987, as soon as possible,

Recalling its resolutions 42/186 and 42/187 of 11 December 1987 on the Environmental Perspective to the Year 2000 and Beyond and on the report of the World Commission on Environment and Development, respectively,

Convinced that changes in climate have an impact on development,

Aware that a considerable amount of valuable work, particularly at the scientific level and in the legal field, has already been initiated on climate change, in particular by the United Nations Environment Programme, the World Meteorological Organization and the International Council of Scientific Unions and under the auspices of individual States,

Welcoming the convening in 1990 of a second World Climate Conference,

Recalling also the conclusions of the meeting held at Villach, Austria, in 1985,[1] which, *inter alia*, recommended a programme on climate change to be promoted by Governments and the scientific community with the collaboration of the World Meteorological Organization, the United Nations Environment Programme and the International Council of Scientific Unions,

Convinced that climate change affects humanity as a whole and should be confronted within a global framework so as to take into account the vital interests of all mankind.

1. *Recognizes* that climate change is a common concern of mankind, since climate is an essential condition which sustains life on earth;

2. *Determines* that necessary and timely action should be taken to deal with climate change within a global framework;

3. *Reaffirms* its resolution 42/184 of 11 December 1987, in which, *inter alia*, it agreed with the Governing Council of the United Nations Environment Programme that the Programme should attach importance to the problem of global climate change and that the Executive Director of the United Nations Environment Programme should ensure that the Programme co-operates closely with the World Meteorological Organization and the International Council of Scientific Unions and maintains an active, influential role in the World Climate Programme;

4. *Considers* that activities in support of the World Climate Programme, approved by the Congress and Executive Council of the World Meteorological Organization and elaborated in the system-wide medium-term environment programme for

---

[1]See *United Nations Environment Programme, Annual Report of the Executive Director, 1985* (UNEP/GC.14/2), chap. IV, paras. 138-140.

the period 1990-1995, which was approved by the Governing Council of the United Nations Environment Programme,[2] should be accorded high priority by the relevant organs and programmes of the United Nations system;

5. *Endorses* the action of the World Meteorological Organization and the United Nations Environment Programme in jointly establishing an Intergovernmental Panel on Climate Change to provide internationally co-ordinated scientific assessments of the magnitude, timing and potential environmental and socio-economic impact of climate change and realistic response strategies, and expresses appreciation for the work already initiated by the Panel;

6. *Urges* Governments, intergovernmental and non-governmental organizations and scientific institutions to treat climate change as a priority issue, to undertake and promote specific, co-operative action-oriented programmes and research so as to increase understanding on all sources and causes of climate change, including its regional aspects and specific time-frames as well as the cause and effect relationship of human activities and climate, and to contribute, as appropriate, with human and financial resources to efforts to protect the global climate;

7. *Calls upon* all relevant organizations and programmes of the United Nations system to support the work of the Intergovernmental Panel on Climate Change;

8. *Encourages* the convening of conferences on climate change, particularly on global warming, at the national, regional and global levels in order to make the international community better aware of the importance of dealing effectively and in a timely manner with all aspects of climate change resulting from certain human activities;

9. *Calls upon* Governments and intergovernmental organizations to collaborate in making every effort to prevent detrimental effects on climate and activities which affect the ecological balance, and also calls upon non-governmental organizations, industry and other productive sectors to play their due role;

10. *Requests* the Secretary-General of the World Meteorological Organization and the Executive Director of the United Nations Environment Programme, utilizing the Intergovernmental Panel on Climate Change, immediately to initiate action leading, as soon as possible, to a comprehensive review and recommendations with respect to:

(*a*) The state of knowledge of the science of climate and climatic change;

(*b*) Programmes and studies on the social and economic impact of climate change, including global warming;

(*c*) Possible response strategies to delay, limit or mitigate the impact of adverse climate change;

(*d*) The identification and possible strengthening of relevant existing international legal instruments having a bearing on climate;

(*e*) Elements for inclusion in a possible future international convention on climate;

11. *Also requests* the Secretary-General to bring the present resolution to the attention of all Governments, as well as intergovernmental organizations, non-governmental organizations in consultative status with the Economic and Social Council and well-established scientific institutions with expertise in matters concerning climate;

12. *Further requests* the Secretary-General to report to the General Assembly at its forty-fourth session on the implementation of the present resolution;

13. *Decides* to include this question in the provisional agenda of its forty-fourth session, without prejudice to the application of the principle of bienniali-zation.

---

[2] See Official Records of the General Assembly, Forty-third Session, Supplement No. 25 (A/43/25), annex, decision SS.I/3.

70th plenary meeting
6 December 1988

* * *

DECLARATION OF THE HAGUE. *Supra,* **p. 247.**

CHAPTER 4
OCEANS

Editors' Introductory Note Regarding Oceans

Oceans cover approximately three-quarters of the Earth's surface. Oceans contain vast amounts and varieties of flora and fauna; they stretch through all the world's climes; and they are subject to overexploitation by humans and to pollution from ships, from land-based sources, from the atmosphere, and from stationary activities at sea or on the sea-bed.

Perhaps fittingly, one of the first multilateral instruments with the principal objective of protecting the environment concerned the oceans: the 1954 International Convention for the Prevention of Pollution of the Sea by Oil, 327 UNTS 3, 12 UST 2989, TIAS 4900. Even prior to that, several multilateral conventions had been concluded to protect fisheries or whales (although, at least in the latter case, the primary purpose originally was to protect the whaling industry that was dependent on the continued supply of whales; see infra, p. 479).

The 1954 Convention was followed over the next three decades by a multitude of multilateral treaties that dealt with various aspects of marine pollution, including prevention, emergencies, and liability. Particularly interesting are the United Nations Environment Programme's regional seas conventions dealing with specific seas, e.g., the convention and four protocols dealing with environmental protection in the Mediterranean Sea. See infra, p. 370.

No attempt was made to provide a comprehensive regime for protecting the marine environment until the Third United Nations Conference on the Law of the Sea (1974-82). The 1982 Law of the Sea Convention that emerged from that conference does provide such a regime. As described in the Editors' Note to that Convention, infra p. 332, that Convention is not yet in force, and there is disagreement about the extent to which its provisions, other than those dealing with the deep sea-bed, now represent customary international law.

A. GENERAL

BRUSSELS INTERNATIONAL CONVENTION ON CIVIL LIABILITY FOR OIL POLLUTION DAMAGE. *Infra,* p. 671.

BRUSSELS INTERNATIONAL CONVENTION ON THE ESTABLISHMENT OF AN INTERNATIONAL FUND FOR COMPENSATION FOR OIL POLLUTION DAMAGE. *Infra,* p. 678.

INTERNATIONAL MARITIME ORGANIZATION CONVENTION ON THE PREVENTION OF MARINE POLLUTION BY DUMPING OF WASTES AND OTHER MATTER

Popular Names: LDC, London Dumping Convention, London Ocean Dumping Convention

Done at London, Mexico City, Moscow and Washington on 29 December 1972, 1046 UNTS 120, 26 UST 2403, TIAS 8165, *reprinted in* 11 ILM 1294 (1972), UNEP3 #59, p.320, 2 IPE 552, IELMT 972: 96.
Entry into Force: 30 August 1975

Depositaries: Mexico; Union of Soviet Socialist Republics; United Kingdom of Great Britain and Northern Ireland; United States of America

Languages: English, French, Russian, Spanish

Parties as of 16 November 1990: Afghanistan; Argentina; Australia; Belgium; Belize; Brazil; Byelorussian Soviet Socialist Republic; Canada; Cape Verde; Chile; China; Costa Rica; Côte d'Ivoire; Cuba; Cyprus; Denmark;* Dominican Republic; Finland; France;** Gabon; German Democratic Republic; Germany, Federal Republic of;*** Greece;** Guatemala; Haiti; Honduras; Hungary; Iceland; Ireland; Italy; Japan; Jordan; Kenya; Kiribati; Libyan Arab Jamahiriya; Malta; Mexico; Monaco; Morocco; Nauru; Netherlands;* New Zealand; Nigeria; Norway; Oman; Panama; Papua New Guinea; Philippines; Poland; Portugal; Saint Lucia; Seychelles; Solomon Islands; South Africa; Spain; Suriname; Sweden; Switzerland; Tunisia; Tuvalu; Ukrainian Soviet Socialist Republic; Union of Soviet Socialist Republics; United Arab Emirates; United Kingdom of Great Britain and Northern Ireland;* United States of America; Yugoslavia; Zaire
Amendments: Amendments (dated 12 October 1978 and 24 September 1980) are not yet in force, as of 1 January 1990.

Editors' Note

The London Dumping Convention was the first of a series of conventions protecting the marine environment that followed closely after the 1972 Stockholm Conference on the Human Environment. The Convention obligates member States

---

* With a geographic extension
**With reservation
*** Includes former East Germany, according to the U.S. Department of State

to take effective measures, both individually and collectively, to prevent marine pollution caused by dumping and to harmonize their policies in this regard. Specifically, a member State is obligated to prohibit or regulate the dumping of substances listed in two annexes (according to factors listed in a third annex) and to take implementing measures (including with respect to punishment) regarding vessels or aircraft registered in its territory, flying its flag, loading in its territory or territorial sea matter to be dumped, or under its jurisdiction and believed to be dumping. More generally, member States are obligated to "promote" measures to protect the marine environment against pollution by specified substances (*see* the Editors' Note to Annex V to MARPOL 73/78, immediately below, regarding subsequent action in this regard), to "endeavour" to enter into regional agreements to prevent marine pollution (*see infra*, p. 369, for such a regime), and to develop procedures for assessing liability and settling disputes regarding dumping (*see* Chapter 25, *infra*, for related instruments). Parties meet regularly to review issues related to the Convention.

CONVENTION ON THE PREVENTION OF MARINE POLLUTION BY DUMPING OF WASTES AND OTHER MATTER

The Contracting Parties to this Convention,

Recognizing that the marine environment and the living organisms which it supports are of vital importance to humanity, and all people have an interest in assuring that it is so managed that is quality and resources are not impaired;

Recognizing that the capacity of the sea to assimilate wastes and render them harmless, and its ability to regenerate natural resources, is not unlimited;

Recognizing that States have, in accordance with the Charter of the United Nations and the principles of international law, the sovereign right to exploit their own resources pursuant to their own environmental policies, and the responsibility to ensure that activities within their jurisdiction or control do not cause damage to the environment of other States or of areas beyond the limits of national jurisdiction;

Recalling Resolution 2749 (XXV) of the General Assembly of the United Nations on the principles governing the sea-bed and the ocean floor and the subsoil thereof, beyond the limits of national jurisdiction;

Noting that marine pollution originates in many sources, such as dumping and discharges through the atmosphere, rivers, estuaries, outfalls and pipelines, and that it is important that States use the best practicable means to prevent such pollution and develop products and processes which will reduce the amount of harmful wastes to be disposed of;

Being convinced that international action to control the pollution of the sea by dumping can and must be taken without delay but that this action should not preclude discussion of measures to control other sources of marine pollution as soon as possible; and

Wishing to improve protection of the marine environment by encouraging States with a common interest in particular geographical areas to enter into appropriate agreements supplementary to this Convention;

Have agreed as follows:

Article I.

Contracting Parties shall individually and collectively promote the effective control of all sources of pollution of the marine environment, and pledge themselves especially to take all practicable steps to prevent the pollution of the sea by the dumping of waste and other matter that is liable to create hazards to human health, to harm living resources and marine life, to damage amenities or to interfere with other legitimate uses of the sea.

Article II.

Contracting Parties shall, as provided for in the following Articles, take effective measures individually, according to their scientific, technical and economic capabilities, and collectively, to prevent marine pollution caused by dumping and shall harmonize their policies in this regard.

Article III.

For the purposes of this Convention:

1. (*a*) "Dumping" means:

(i) any deliberate disposal at sea of wastes or other matter from vessels, aircraft, platforms or other man-made structures at sea;

(ii) any deliberate disposal at sea of vessels, aircraft, platforms or other man-made structures at sea.

(*b*) "Dumping" does not include:

(i) the disposal at sea of wastes or other matter incidental to, or derived from the normal operations of vessels, aircraft, platforms or other man-made structures at sea and their equipment, other than wastes or other matter transported by or to vessels, aircraft, platforms or other man-made structures at sea, operating for the purpose of disposal of such matter or derived from the treatment of such wastes or other matter on such vessels, aircraft, platforms or structures;

(ii) placement of matter for a purpose other than the mere disposal thereof, provided that such placement is not contrary to the aims of this Convention.

(*c*) The disposal of wastes or other matter directly arising from, or related to the exploration, exploitation and associated off-shore processing of sea-bed mineral resources will not be covered by the provisions of this Convention.

2. "Vessels and aircraft" means waterborne or airborne craft of any type whatsoever. This expression includes air-cushioned craft and floating craft, whether self-propelled or not.

3. "Sea" means all marine waters other than the internal waters of States.

4. "Wastes or other matter" means material and substance of any kind, form or description.

5. "Special permit" means permission granted specifically on application in advance and in accordance with Annex II and Annex III.

6. "General permit" means permission granted in advance and in accordance with Annex III.

7. The "Organisation" means the Organisation designated by the Contracting Parties in accordance with Article XIV (2).

Article IV.

1. In accordance with the provisions of this Convention, Contracting Parties shall prohibit the dumping of any wastes or other matter in whatever form or condition except as otherwise specified below:

(*a*) the dumping of wastes or other matter listed in Annex I is prohibited;

(b) the dumping of wastes or other matter listed in Annex II requires a prior special permit;

(c) the dumping of all other wastes or matter requires a prior general permit.

2. Any permit shall be issued only after careful consideration of all the factors set forth in Annex III, including prior studies of the characteristics of the dumping site, as set forth in Sections B and C of that Annex.

3. No provision of this Convention is to be interpreted as preventing a Contracting Party from prohibiting, insofar as that Party is concerned, the dumping of wastes or other matter not mentioned in Annex I. That Party shall notify such measures to the Organisation.

Article V.

1. The provisions of Article IV shall not apply when it is necessary to secure the safety of human life or of vessels, aircraft, platforms or other man-made structures at sea in cases of *force majeure* caused by stress of weather, or in any case which constitutes a danger to human life or a real threat to vessels, aircraft, platforms or other man-made structures at sea, if dumping appears to be the only way of averting the threat and if there is every probability that the damage consequent upon such dumping will be less than would otherwise occur. Such dumping shall be so conducted as to minimise the likelihood of damage to human or marine life and shall be reported forthwith to the Organisation.

2. A Contracting Party may issue a special permit as an exception to Article IV (1) (a), in emergencies, posing unacceptable risk relating to human health and admitting no other feasible solution. Before doing so the Party shall consult any other country or countries that are likely to be affected and the Organisation which, after consulting other Parties, and international organisations as appropriate, shall, in accordance with Article XIV promptly recommend to the Party the most approximate procedures to adopt. The Party shall follow these recommendations to the maximum extent feasible consistent with the time within which action must be taken and with the general obligation to avoid damage to the marine environment and shall inform the Organisation of the action it takes. The Parties pledge themselves to assist one another in such situations.

3. Any Contracting Party may waive its rights under paragraph (2) at the time of, or subsequent to ratification of, or accession to this Convention.

Article VI.

1. Each Contracting Party shall designate an appropriate authority or authorities to:

(a) issue special permits which shall be required prior to, and for, the dumping of matter listed in Annex II and in the circumstances provided for in Article V (2);

(b) issue general permits which shall be required prior to, and for, the dumping of all other matter;

(c) keep records of the nature and quantities of all matter permitted to be dumped and the location, time and method of dumping;

(d) monitor individually, or in collaboration with other Parties and competent international organisations, the condition of the seas for the purposes of this Convention.

2. The appropriate authority or authorities of a Contracting Party shall issue prior special or general permits in accordance with paragraph (1) in respect of matter intended for dumping:

(a) loaded in its territory;

(b) loaded by a vessel or aircraft registered in its territory or flying its flag, when the loading occurs in the territory of a State not party to this Convention.

3. In issuing permits under sub-paragraphs (1) (*a*) and (*b*) above, the appropriate authority or authorities shall comply with Annex III, together with such additional criteria, measures and requirements as they may consider relevant.

4. Each Contracting Party, directly or through a Secretariat established under a regional agreement, shall report to the Organisation, and where appropriate to other Parties, the information specified in sub-paragraphs (*c*) and (*d*) of paragraph (1) above, and the criteria, measures and requirements it adopts in accordance with paragraph (3) above. The procedure to be followed and the nature of such reports shall be agreed by the Parties in consultation.

Article VII.

1. Each Contracting Party shall apply the measures required to implement the present Convention to all:
(*a*) vessels and aircraft registered in its territory or flying its flag;
(*b*) vessels and aircraft loading in its territory or territorial seas matter which is to be dumped;
(*c*) vessels and aircraft and fixed or floating platforms under its jurisdiction believed to be engaged in dumping.

2. Each Party shall take in its territory appropriate measures to prevent and punish conduct in contravention of the provisions of this Convention.

3. The Parties agree to co-operate in the development of procedures for the effective application of this Convention particularly on the high seas, including procedures for the reporting of vessels and aircraft observed dumping in contravention of the Convention.

4. This Convention shall not apply to those vessels and aircraft entitled to sovereign immunity under international law. However, each Party shall ensure by the adoption of appropriate measures that such vessels and aircraft owned or operated by it act in a manner consistent with the object and purpose of this Convention, and shall inform the Organisation accordingly.

5. Nothing in this Convention shall affect the right of each Party to adopt other measures, in accordance with the principles of international law, to prevent dumping at sea.

Article VIII.

In order to further the objectives of this Convention, the Contracting Parties with common interests to protect in the marine environment in a given geographical area shall endeavour, taking into account characteristic regional features, to enter into regional agreements consistent with this Convention for the prevention of pollution, especially by dumping. The Contracting Parties to the present Convention shall endeavour to act consistently with the objectives and provisions of such regional agreements, which shall be notified to them by the Organisation. Contracting Parties shall seek to co-operate with the Parties to regional agreements in order to develop harmonized procedures to be followed by Contracting Parties to the different conventions concerned. Special attention shall be given to co-operation in the field of monitoring and scientific research.

Article IX.

The Contracting Parties shall promote, through collaboration within the Organisation and other international bodies, support for those Parties which request it for:
(*a*) the training of scientific and technical personnel;
(*b*) the supply of necessary equipment and facilities for research and monitoring;

(*c*) the disposal and treatment of waste and other measures to prevent or mitigate pollution caused by dumping;

preferably within the countries concerned, so furthering the aims and purposes of this Convention.

Article X.

In accordance with the principles of international law regarding State responsibility for damage to the environment of other States or to any other area of the environment, caused by dumping of wastes and other matters of all kinds, the Contracting Parties undertake to develop procedures for the assessment of liability and the settlement of disputes regarding dumping.

Article XI.

The Contracting Parties shall at their first consultative meeting consider procedures for the settlement of disputes concerning the interpretation and application of this Convention.

Article XII.

The Contracting Parties pledge themselves to promote, within the competent specialised agencies and other international bodies, measures to protect the marine environment against pollution caused by:

(*a*) hydrocarbons, including oil, and their wastes;

(*b*) other noxious or hazardous matter transported by vessels for purposes other than dumping;

(*c*) wastes generated in the course of operation of vessels, aircraft, platforms and other man-made structures at sea;

(*d*) radio-active pollutants from all sources, including vessels;

(*e*) agents of chemical and biological warfare;

(*f*) wastes or other matter directly arising from, or related to the exploration, exploitation and associated off-shore processing of sea-bed mineral resources.

The Parties will also promote, within the appropriate international organisation, the codification of signals to be used by vessels engaged in dumping.

Article XIII.

Nothing in this Convention shall prejudice the codification and development of the law of the sea by the United Nations Conference on the Law of the Sea convened pursuant to Resolution 2750 C (XXV) of the General Assembly of the United Nations nor the present or future claims and legal views of any State concerning the law of the sea and the nature and extent of coastal and flag State jurisdiction. The Contracting Parties agree to consult at a meeting to be convened by the Organisation after the Law of the Sea Conference, and in any case not later than 1976, with a view to defining the nature and extent of the right and the responsibility of a coastal State to apply the Convention in a zone adjacent to its coast.

Article XIV.

* * *

4. Consultative or special meetings of the Contracting Parties shall keep under continuing review the implementation of this Convention and may, *inter alia*:

(a)review and adopt amendments to this Convention and its Annexes in accordance with Article XV;
(b)invite the appropriate scientific body or bodies to collaborate with and to advise the Parties or the Organisation on any scientific or technical aspect relevant to this Convention, including particularly the content of the Annexes;
(c)receive and consider reports made pursuant to Article VI (4);
(d)promote co-operation with and between regional organisations concerned with the prevention of marine pollution;
(e)develop or adopt, in consultation with appropriate International Organisations, procedures referred to in Article V (2), including basic criteria for determining exceptional and emergency situations, and procedures for consultative advice and the safe disposal of matter in such circumstances, including the designation of appropriate dumping areas, and recommend accordingly;
(f)consider any additional action that may be required.
5. The Contracting Parties at their first consultative meeting shall establish rules of procedure as necessary.

Article XV.

1. (a) At meetings of the Contracting Parties called in accordance with Article XIV amendments to this Convention may be adopted by a two-thirds majority of those present. An amendment shall enter into force for the Parties which have accepted it on the sixtieth day after two thirds of the Parties shall have deposited an instrument of acceptance of the amendment with the Organisation. Thereafter the amendment shall enter into force for any other Party 30 days after that Party deposits its instrument of acceptance of the amendment.

(b) The Organisation shall inform all Contracting Parties of any request made for a special meeting under Article XIV and of any amendments adopted at meetings of the Parties and of the date on which each such amendment enters into force for each Party.

2. Amendments to the Annexes will be based on scientific or technical considerations. Amendments to the Annexes approved by a two-thirds majority of those present at a meeting called in accordance with Article XIV shall enter into force for each Contracting Party immediately on notification of its acceptance to the Organisation and 100 days after approval by the meeting for all other Parties except for those which before the end of the 100 days make a declaration that they are not able to accept the amendment at that time. Parties should endeavour to signify their acceptance of an amendment to the Organisation as soon as possible after approval at a meeting. A Party may at any time substitute an acceptance for a previous declaration of objection and the amendment previously objected to shall thereupon enter into force for that Party.

* * *

ANNEX I

1. Organohalogen compounds.
2. Mercury and mercury compounds.
3. Cadmium and cadmium compounds.
4. Persistent plastics and other persistent synthetic materials, for example, netting and ropes, which may float or may remain in suspension in the sea in such a manner as to interfere materially with fishing, navigation or other legitimate uses of the sea.
5. Crude oil, fuel, oil, heavy diesel oil, and lubricating oils, hydraulic fluids, and any mixtures containing any of these, taken on board for the purpose of dumping.
6. High-level radio-active wastes or other high-level radio-active matter, defined on public health, biological or other grounds, by the competent international

body in this field, at present the International Atomic Energy Agency, as unsuitable for dumping at sea.

7. Materials in whatever form (e.g. solids, liquids, semi-liquids, gases or in a living state) produced for biological and chemical warfare.

8. The preceding paragraphs of this Annex do not apply to substances which are rapidly rendered harmless by physical, chemical or biological processes in the sea provided they do not:

    (i) make edible marine organisms unpalatable, or

    (ii) endanger human health or that of domestic animals.

The consultative procedure provided for under Article XIV should be followed by a Party if there is doubt about the harmlessness of the substance.

9. This Annex does not apply to wastes or other materials (e.g. sewage sludges and dredged spoils) containing the matters referred to in paragraphs 1-5 above as trace contaminants. Such wastes shall be subject to the provisions of Annexes II and III as appropriate.

ANNEX II

The following substances and materials requiring special care are listed for the purposes of Article VI (1) (*a*).

A.   Wastes containing significant amounts of the matters listed below:

    arsenic

    lead

    copper   and their compounds

    zinc

    organosilicon compounds

    cyanides

    fluorides

    pesticides and their by-products not covered in Annex I.

B.   In the issue of permits for the dumping of large quantities of acids and alkalis, consideration shall be given to the possible presence in such wastes of the substances listed in paragraph A and to the following additional substances:

    beryllium

    chromium

    nickel   and their compounds

    vanadium

C.   Containers, scrap metal and other bulky wastes liable to sink to the sea bottom which may present a serious obstacle to fishing or navigation.

D.   Radio-active wastes or other radio-active matter not included in Annex I. In the issue of permits for the dumping of this matter, the Contracting Parties should take full account of the recommendations of the competent international body in this field, at present the International Atomic Energy Agency.

ANNEX III

Provisions to be considered in establishing criteria governing the issue of permits for the dumping of matter at sea, taking into account Article IV (2), include:

A. Characteristics and composition of the matter

1. Total amount and average composition of matter dumped (e.g. per year).
2. Form, e.g. solid, sludge, liquid, or gaseous.
3. Properties: physical (e.g. solubility and density), chemical and biochemical (e.g. oxygen demand, nutrients) and biological (e.g. presence of viruses, bacteria, yeasts, parasites).

4. Toxicity.
5. Persistence: physical, chemical and biological.
6. Accumulation and biotransformation in biological materials or sediments.
7. Susceptibility to physical, chemical and biochemical changes and interaction in the aquatic environment with other dissolved organic and inorganic materials.
8. Probability of production of taints or other changes reducing marketability of resources (fish, shellfish, etc.).

B. CHARACTERISTICS OF DUMPING SITE AND METHOD OF DEPOSIT

1. Location (e.g. co-ordinates of the dumping area, depth and distance from the coast), location in relation to other areas (e.g. amenity areas, spawning, nursery and fishing areas and exploitable resources).
2. Rate of disposal per specific period (e.g. quantity per day, per week, per month).
3. Methods of packaging and containment, if any.
4. Initial dilution achieved by proposed method of release.
5. Dispersal characteristics (e.g. effects of currents, tides and wind on horizontal transport and vertical mixing).
6. Water characteristics (e.g. temperature, pH, salinity, stratification, oxygen indices of pollution—dissolved oxygen (DO), chemical oxygen demand (COD), biochemical oxygen demand (BOD)—nitrogen present in organic and mineral form including ammonia, suspended matter, other nutrients and productivity).
7. Bottom characteristics (e.g. topography, geochemical and geological characteristics and biological productivity).
8. Existence and effects of other dumpings which have been made in the dumping area (e.g. heavy metal background reading and organic carbon content).
9. In issuing a permit for dumping, Contracting Parties should consider whether an adequate scientific basis exists for assessing the consequences of such dumping, as outlined in this Annex, taking into account seasonal variations.

C. GENERAL CONSIDERATIONS AND CONDITIONS

1. Possible effects on amenities (e.g. presence of floating or stranded material, turbidity, objectionable odour, discolouration and foaming).
2. Possible effects on marine life, fish and shellfish culture, fish stocks and fisheries, seaweed harvesting and culture.
3. Possible effects on other uses of the sea (e.g. impairment of water quality for industrial use, underwater corrosion of structures, interference with ship operations from floating materials, interference with fishing or navigation through deposit of waste or solid objects on the sea floor and protection of areas of special importance for scientific or conservation purposes).
4. The practical availability of alternative land-based methods of treatment, disposal or elimination, or of treatment to render the matter less harmful for dumping at sea.

LONDON INTERNATIONAL CONVENTION FOR THE PREVENTION OF POLLUTION FROM SHIPS, 1973, AS MODIFIED BY THE PROTOCOL OF 1978 RELATING THERETO (MARPOL 73/78), ANNEX V: REGULATIONS FOR THE PREVENTION OF POLLUTION BY GARBAGE FROM SHIPS

Popular Names: Annex V to MARPOL 73/78, Annex V to MARPOL, MARPOL Annex V

Done at London on 2 November 1973, IMCO Doc. MP/CONF/WP.35, TIAS ———, *reprinted in* 12 ILM 1319, 1434 (1973), UNEP3 #59, p.320, 380, 2 IPE 552, IELMT 973: 84, as modified by the 1978 Protocol, done at London on 17 February 1978, TIAS ———, Cmnd 5748, *reprinted in* 17 ILM 546 (1978), 21 IELR 2381, UNEP3 #59, p.382, 19 IPE 9451, IELMT 978: 13.

Entry into Force: Not intended to enter into force on its own, but rather in connection with the Protocol of 1978 Relating to the International Convention for the Prevention of Pollution from Ships, 1973, which came into force on 2 October 1983, at the option of each party to the 1978 Protocol.

Depositary: International Maritime Organization

Languages: English, French, Russian, Spanish

Parties to Optional Annex V as of 18 October 1990 (these States are also parties to the 1978 Protocol): Algeria; Antigua and Barbuda; Australia; Austria; Bahamas; Belgium; China; Colombia; Côte d'Ivoire; Cyprus; Czech and Slovak Federal Republic; Denmark;* Ecuador; Egypt; Finland; France; Gabon; Germany;** Greece; Hungary; Iceland; Italy; Japan; Korea, Democratic People's Republic of; Lebanon; Marshall Islands; Netherlands;* Norway; Oman; Panama; Peru; Poland; Portugal; Saint Vincent and the Grenadines; Suriname; Sweden; Switzerland; Togo; Tunisia; Turkey; Tuvalu; Union of Soviet Socialist Republics; United Kingdom;*** United States of America;*** Uruguay; Yugoslavia

Literature: Guidelines for the Implementation of Annex V of MARPOL 73/78 (IMO 1988).

Editors' Note

The International Convention for the Prevention of Pollution from Ships was finalized in 1973. It was intended to supersede the 1954 International Convention for the Protection of Pollution of the Sea by Oil.

---

*   With geographic extension
** The depositary lists Germany, consisting of the Federal Republic of Germany and the German Democratic Republic, as a party
***With a statement or understanding

The 1973 Convention prohibits the discharge from ships (not including dumping covered by the 1972 London Dumping Convention, *supra* this Chapter, releases associated with exploiting seabed mineral resources, or discharges from non-commercial vessels) of various harmful substances. The term "harmful substances" is defined generally in article 2 and is further detailed in five annexes: Annex I involves oil; Annex II involves noxious liquids in bulk; Annex III involves harmful substances carried in packaged forms, containers, tanks, or wagons; Annex IV involves sewage; and Annex V involves garbage. Annexes III, IV, and V are optional. The 1973 Convention also contains two protocols on reporting and on arbitration.

Before the 1973 Convention was assented to by sufficient States to bring it into force, however, a serious discovery occurred: the provisions of Annex II were so strict that no State—even the most advanced maritime States—had the ability to comply. In order to deal with this situation (so as to allow the regime to become effective), unusual and potentially confusing actions were taken, as follows:

A general diplomatic conference was convened in 1978 to adopt a new treaty in the form of a "protocol" to the 1973 Convention. Because the Convention was not yet in force, the 1978 Protocol is self-described as "relating to" the Convention. The goal was to have a new instrument consisting of the 1973 Convention together with the 1978 amendments thereto. Article 1 of the 1978 Protocol effectively provides that the new intrument consists of (a) the 1978 Protocol and its Annex, and (b) the 1973 Convention as amended by the 1978 Protocol. Article 1 further provides that the provisions of the 1973 Convention and the 1978 Protocol should be "read and interpreted together as one single instrument." In addition to alleviating the obligations in Annex II, the 1978 Protocol modified several other parts of the 1973 Convention. Annex V was not modified by the 1978 Protocol or by the six amendments (three of which are in force) thereto.

In an attempt to achieve one consistent, workable regime, States have been encouraged to become parties to the 1978 Protocol (which incorporates the 1973 Convention as modified and which, contrary to usual practice, can—and has—come into force without the 1973 Convention itself coming into force), but they have been discouraged from becoming Parties to the 1973 Convention. The new conventional regime is thus most clearly denominated "The International Convention for the Prevention of Pollution from Ships, 1973, as modified by the Protocol of 1978 relating thereto," or, more simply, the "1973 Convention as modified by the 1978 Protocol" or even "MARPOL 73/78."

Nomenclature aside, the convoluted process described above has resulted in some legal uncertainty, e.g., regarding whether article 15 of the 1973 Convention can be merged with article V of the 1978 Protocol. No consolidated single text of MARPOL 73/78 has been issued.

Annex V to MARPOL 73/78 contains seven Regulations, the first of which defines terms. Regulation 2 provides that the Annex applies to all ships. Regulation 3 prohibits the disposal into the sea of all plastics, regardless of the distance from shore, and provides that the disposal of other types of garbage shall be as far as practicable from shore and no closer than certain distances (depending on the type of garbage), subject to provisions regarding drilling rigs (Regulation 4) and special areas (Regulation 5) and exceptions (Regulation 6). Regulation 7 obligates parties to provide adequate reception facilities for garbage in ports and terminals.

INTERNATIONAL CONVENTION FOR THE PREVENTION OF POLLUTION FROM SHIPS, 1973, AS AMENDED BY THE 1978 PROTOCOL, ANNEX V:
Regulations for the Prevention of Pollution by Garbage from Ships

Regulation 1
Definitions

For the purposes of this Annex:

(1) "Garbage" means all kinds of victual, domestic and operational waste excluding fresh fish and parts thereof, generated during the normal operation of the ship and liable to be disposed of continuously or periodically except those substances which are defined or listed in other Annexes to the present Convention.

(2) "Nearest land". The term "from the nearest land" means from the baseline from which the territorial sea of the territory in question is established in accordance with international law except that, for the purposes of the present Convention "from the nearest land" off the north eastern coast of Australia shall mean from a line drawn from a point on the coast of Australia in latitude 11° South, longitude 142°08' East to a point in latitude 10°35' South,
longitude 141°55' East-thence to a point latitude 10°00' South,
longitude 142°00' East, thence to a point latitude 9°10' South,
longitude 143°52' East, thence to a point latitude 9°00' South,
longitude 144°30' East, thence to a point latitude 13°00' South,
longitude 144°00' East, thence to a point latitude 15°00' South,
longitude 146°00' East, thence to a point latitude 18°00' South,
longitude 147°00' East, thence to a point latitude 21°00' South,
longitude 153°00' East, thence to a point on the coast of Australia in latitude 24°42' South, longitude 153°15' East.

(3) "Special area" means a sea area where for recognized technical reasons in relation to its oceanographical and ecological condition and to the particular character of its traffic the adoption of special mandatory methods for the prevention of sea pollution by garbage is required. Special areas shall include those listed in Regulation 5 of this Annex.

Regulation 2
Application

The provisions of this Annex shall apply to all ships.

Regulation 3
Disposal of Garbage Outside Special Areas

(1) Subject to the provisions of Regulations 4, 5 and 6 of this Annex:
    (a)   the disposal into the sea of all plastics, including but not limited to synthetic ropes, synthetic fishing nets and plastic garbage bags is prohibited;

(b)   the disposal into the sea of the following garbage shall be made as far as practicable from the nearest land but in any case is prohibited if the distance from the nearest land is less than:
  (i)   25 nautical miles for dunnage, lining and packing materials which will float;
  (ii) 12 nautical miles for food wastes and all other garbage including paper products, rags, glass, metal, bottles, crockery and similar refuse;

(c)   disposal into the sea of garbage specified in sub-paragraph (b)(ii) of this Regulation may be permitted when it is passed through a comminuter or grinder and made as far as practicable from the nearest land but in any case is prohibited if the distance from the nearest land is less than 3 nautical miles. Such comminuted or ground garbage shall be capable of passing through a screen with openings no greater than 25 millimetres.

(2) When the garbage is mixed with other discharges having different disposal or discharge requirements the more severe requirements shall apply.

Regulation 4
Disposals from Drilling Rigs

(1) Fixed or floating platforms engaged in the exploration, exploitation and associated offshore processing of sea-bed mineral resources, and all other ships when alongside such platforms or within 500 metres of such platforms, are forbidden to dispose of any materials regulated by this Annex, except as permitted by paragraph (2) of this Regulation.

(2) The disposal into the sea of food wastes when passed through a comminuter or grinder from such fixed or floating drilling rigs located more than 12 nautical miles from land and all other ships when positioned as above. Such comminuted or ground food wastes shall be capable of passing through a screen with openings no greater than 25 millimetres.

Regulation 5
Disposal of Garbage within Special Areas

(1) For the purpose of this Annex the special areas are the Mediterranean Sea area, the Baltic Sea area, the Black Sea area, the Red Sea area and the "Gulfs area" which are defined as follows:

(a)   The Mediterranean Sea area means the Mediterranean Sea proper including the gulfs and seas therein with the boundary between the Mediterranean and the Black Sea constituted by the 41°N parallel and bounded to the west by the Straits of Gibraltar at the meridian of 5°36'W.

(b)   The Baltic Sea area means the Baltic Sea proper with the Gulf of Bothnia and the Gulf of Finland and the entrance to the Baltic Sea bounded by the parallel of the Skaw in the Skagerrak at 57°44.8'N.

(c)   The Black Sea area means the Black Sea proper with the boundary between the Mediterranean and the Black Sea constituted by the parallel 41°N.

(d)   The Red Sea area means the Red Sea proper including the Gulfs of Suez and Aqaba bounded at the south by the rhumb line between Ras si Ane (12°8.5'N, 43°19.6'E) and Husn Murad (12°40.4'N,43°30.2'W).

(e)   The "Gulfs area" means the sea area located north west of the rhumb line between Ras al Hadd (22°30'N, 59°48'E) and Ras al Fasteh (25°04'N, 61°25'E).

(2) Subject to the provisions of Regulation 6 of this Annex:

(a)   disposal into the sea of the following is prohibited:

     (i)   all plastics, including but not limited to synthetic ropes, synthetic fishing nets and plastic garbage bags;

     (ii)   all other garbage, including paper products, rags, glass, metal, bottles, crockery, dunnage, lining and packing materials;

(b)   disposal into the sea of food wastes shall be made as far as practicable from land, but in any case not less than 12 nautical miles from the nearest land.

(3) When the garbage is mixed with other discharges having different disposal or discharge requirements the more severe requirements shall apply.

(4) Reception facilities within special areas.

(a)   The Government of each party to the Convention, the coast line of which borders a special area undertakes to ensure that as soon as possible in all ports within a special area, adequate reception facilities are provided in accordance with Regulation 7 of this Annex, taking into account the special needs of ships operating in these areas.

(b)   The Government of each party concerned shall notify the Organization of the measures taken pursuant to sub-paragraph (a) of this Regulation. Upon receipt of sufficient notifications the Organization shall establish a date from which the requirements of this Regulation in respect of the area in question shall take effect. The Organization shall notify all parties of the date so established no less than twelve months in advance of that date.

(c)   After date so established, ships calling also at ports in these special areas where such facilities are not yet available, shall fully comply with the requirements of this Regulation.

Regulation 6
Exception

Regulations 3, 4 and 5 of this Annex shall not apply to:

(a)   the disposal of garbage from a ship necessary for the purpose of securing the safety of a ship, the health of its personnel, or saving life at sea;

(b)   the escape of garbage resulting from damage to a ship or its equipment provided all reasonable precautions have been taken before and after the occurrence of the damage, for the purpose of preventing or minimizing the escape;

(c)   the accidental loss of synthetic fishing nets or synthetic material incidental to the repair of such nets, provided that all reasonable precautions have been taken to prevent such loss.

Regulation 7
Reception Facilities

(1) The Government of each party to the Convention undertakes to ensure the provisions of facilities at ports and terminals for the reception of garbage, without causing undue delay to ships, and according to the needs of the ships using them.

(2) The Government of each party shall notify the Organization for transmission to the parties concerned of all cases where the facilities provided under this Regulation are alleged to be inadequate.

UNITED NATIONS CONVENTION ON THE LAW OF THE SEA

Popular Name: Law of the Sea Convention, Montego Bay Convention

Done at Montego Bay on 10 December 1982, The Law of the Sea: Official Text of the United Nations Convention on the Law of the Sea with Annexes and Index, U.N. Doc. A/CONF.62/122, at 14, 22-23, 37-38, 45, 70-85, 111 (1983), Cmnd 8941, Misc 11 (1983), *reprinted in* 21 ILM 1261 (1982), IPE(2) II/A/10-12-82.
Entry into Force: Not yet in force as of 1 September 1990

Depositary: United Nations

Languages: Arabic, Chinese, English, French, Russian, Spanish

Parties as of 1 September 1990: Antigua and Barbuda; Bahamas; Bahrain; Belize; Botswana; Brazil;* Cameroon; Cape Verde;* Côte d'Ivoire; Cuba;* Cyprus; Egypt;* Gambia; Ghana; Guinea; Guinea-Bissau;* Iceland; Indonesia; Iraq;* Jamaica; Kenya; Kuwait;* Mali;* Mexico; Namibia; Nicaragua;* Oman;* Paraguay; Philippines;* Saint Lucia; Sao Tome and Principe;* Senegal; Somalia; Sudan;* Tanzania, United Republic of;* Togo; Trinidad and Tobago; Tunisia;* Yemen, Democratic;* Yugoslavia;* Zaire; Zambia; European Economic Community*

Editors' Note

The United Nations Convention on the Law of the Sea, drafted over eight years (1974-1982) at the Third United Nations Conference on the Law of the Sea, covers virtually all aspects of international law for the oceans. It is a complex instrument of 320 articles and nine annexes. It is the first instrument to provide a comprehensive regime to protect and preserve the marine environment.

The environmental provisions are primarily located in Part XII of the Convention, titled Protection and Preservation of the Marine Environment (arts. 192-237). Other provisions deal specifically with pollution in international straits (art. 43), conservation and utilization of living resources in the exclusive economic zone (arts. 61-68), management and conservation of living resources of the high seas (arts. 116-20), and protection of the marine environment from activities in the sea-bed and ocean floor beyond the limits of national jurisdiction (art. 145).

The principal obligation of Part XII is set forth in article 192: "States have the obligation to protect and preserve the marine environment." Article 194 elaborates on that general obligation in several respects, most notably in paragraph 1:

States shall take, individually or jointly as appropriate, all measures consistent with this Convention that are necessary to prevent, reduce and control pollution of the marine environment from any source, using for this purpose the

---

* With a declaration

best practicable means at their disposal and in accordance with their capabilities, and they shall endeavour to harmonize their policies in this connection.

Other provisions of Part XII deal with pollution from land-based sources (art. 207), pollution from sea-bed activities subject to national jurisdiction (art. 208), pollution from activities on the sea-bed or ocean floor beyond the limits of national jurisdiction (art. 209; *see also* art. 145), pollution by dumping (art. 210), pollution from vessels (art. 211), pollution from the atmosphere (art. 212), global and regional cooperation (arts. 197-201), technical assistance to developing States (arts. 202-203), monitoring and assessment (arts. 204-06), enforcement (arts. 213-34), responsibility and liability (art. 235), sovereign immunity (art. 236), and obligations under other marine-environment conventions (art. 237).

A particularly interesting question involves the Convention's treatment of developing countries. Depending on the precise circumstances, the contextual qualification "using . . . the best practicable means at their disposal and in accordance with their capabilities" in article 194(1) (quoted above) may have the effect of allowing developing countries to take less stringent measures than developed countries. Article 207 provides that States "shall endeavour to establish global and *regional* rules . . . taking into account *characteristic regional features, the economic capacity of developing States and their need for economic development*" (emphasis added). Finally, article 203 provides that States shall provide technical assistance to developing States regarding preserving and protecting the marine environment, and article 204 provides that international organizations shall provide preferential treatment to developing States.

The Convention is not yet in force, primarily because of opposition by the United States regarding the Convention's treatment of deep sea-bed mining; and it is not expected to come into force until the United States agrees to become a party. Nevertheless, preparatory work is proceeding regarding the sea-bed authority. The extent to which the provisions of the Convention other than those concerning the sea-bed represent customary international law and hence are binding on States is unsettled.

UNITED NATIONS CONVENTION ON THE LAW OF THE SEA

PART I. INTRODUCTION

Article 1
Use of terms and scope

1. For the purposes of this Convention:
(1) "Area" means the sea-bed and ocean floor and subsoil thereof, beyond the limits of national jurisdiction;

* * *

(4) "pollution of the marine environment" means the introduction by man, directly or indirectly, of substances or energy into the marine environment, including estuaries, which results or is likely to result in such deleterious effects as harm to living resources and marine life, hazards to human health, hindrance to marine activities, including fishing and other legitimate uses of the sea, impairment of quality for use of sea water and reduction of amenities;
(5) (a) "dumping" means:

(i)   any deliberate disposal of wastes or other matter from vessels, air-craft, platforms or other man-made structures at sea;

(ii) any deliberate disposal of vessels, aircraft, platforms or other man-made structures at sea;

(b)   "dumping" does not include:

(i)   the disposal of wastes or other matter incidental to, or derived from the normal operations of vessels, aircraft, platforms or other man-made structures at sea and their equipment, other than wastes or other matter transported by or to vessels, aircraft, platforms or other man-made structures at sea, operating for the purpose of disposal of such matter or derived from the treatment of such wastes or other matter on such vessels, aircraft, platforms or structures;

(ii) placement of matter for a purpose other than the mere disposal thereof, provided that such placement is not contrary to the aims of this Convention.

* * *

PART II. TERRITORIAL SEA AND CONTIGUOUS ZONE
* * *

Article 19
Meaning of innocent passage

1. Passage is innocent so long as it is not prejudicial to the peace, good order or security of the coastal State. Such passage shall take place in conformity with this Convention and with other rules of international law.

2. Passage of a foreign ship shall be considered to be prejudicial to the peace, good order or security of the coastal State if in the territorial sea it engages in any of the following activities:

*   *   *

(h)   any act of wilful and serious pollution contrary to this Convention;

* * *

Part III. STRAITS USED FOR INTERNATIONAL NAVIGATION

* * *

Article 43
Navigational and safety aids and other improvements and the prevention, reduction and control of pollution

User States and States bordering a strait should by agreement co-operate:
(a) in the establishment and maintenance in a strait of necessary navigational and safety aids or other improvements in aid of international navigation; and
(b) for the prevention, reduction and control of pollution from ships.

* * *

PART V. EXCLUSIVE ECONOMIC ZONE
* * *

Article 61
Conservation of the living resources

1. The coastal State shall determine the allowable catch of the living resources in its exclusive economic zone.

2. The coastal State, taking into account the best scientific evidence available to it, shall ensure through proper conservation and management measures that the maintenance of the living resources in the exclusive economic zone is not endangered by over-exploitation. As appropriate, the coastal State and competent international organizations, whether subregional, regional or global, shall co-operate to this end.

3. Such measures shall also be designed to maintain or restore populations of harvested species at levels which can produce the maximum sustainable yield, as qualified by relevant environmental and economic factors, including the economic needs of coastal fishing communities and the special requirements of developing States, and taking into account fishing patterns, the interdependence of stocks and any generally recommended international minimum standards, whether subregional, regional or global.

4. In taking such measures the coastal State shall take into consideration the effects on species associated with or dependent upon harvested species with a view to maintaining or restoring populations of such associated or dependent species above levels at which their reproduction may become seriously threatened.

5. Available scientific information, catch and fishing effort statistics, and other data relevant to the conservation of fish stocks shall be contributed and exchanged on a regular basis through competent international organizations, whether subregional, regional or global, where appropriate and with participation by all States concerned, including States whose nationals are allowed to fish in the exclusive economic zone.

Article 62
Utilization of the living resources

1. The coastal State shall promote the objective of optimum utilization of the living resources in the exclusive economic zone without prejudice to article 61.

2. The coastal State shall determine its capacity to harvest the living resources of the exclusive economic zone. Where the coastal State does not have the capacity to harvest the entire allowable catch, it shall, through agreements or other arrangements and pursuant to the terms, conditions, laws and regulations referred to in paragraph 4, give other States access to the surplus of the allowable catch, having particular regard to the provisions of articles 69 and 70, especially in relation to the developing States mentioned therein.

3. In giving access to other States to its exclusive economic zone under this article, the coastal State shall take into account all relevant factors, including, *inter alia*, the significance of the living resources of the area to the economy of the coastal State concerned and its other national interests, the provisions of articles 69 and 70, the requirements of developing States in the subregion or region in harvesting part of the surplus and the need to minimize economic dislocation in States whose nationals have habitually fished in the zone or which have made substantial efforts in research and identification of stocks.

4. Nationals of other States fishing in the exclusive economic zone shall comply with the conservation measures and with the other terms and conditions established in the laws and regulations of the coastal State. These laws and regulations shall be consistent with this Convention and may relate, *inter alia*, to the following:

(a) licensing of fishermen, fishing vessels and equipment, including payment of fees and other forms or remuneration, which, in the case of developing coastal States, may consist of adequate compensation in the field of financing, equipment and technology relating to the fishing industry;

(b) determining the species which may be caught, and fixing quotas of catch, whether in relation to particular stocks or groups of stocks or catch per vessel over a period of time or to the catch by nationals of any State during a specified period;

(c) regulating seasons and areas of fishing, the types, sizes and amount of gear, and the types, sizes and number of fishing vessels that may be used;

(d) fixing the age and size of fish and other species that may be caught;

(e) specifying information required of fishing vessels, including catch and effort statistics and vessel position reports;

(f) requiring, under the authorization and control of the coastal State, the conduct of specified fisheries research programmes and regulating the conduct of such research, including the sampling of catches, disposition of samples and reporting of associated scientific data;

(g) the placing of observers or trainees on board such vessels by the coastal State;

(h) the landing of all or any part of the catch by such vessels in the ports of the coastal State;

(i) terms and conditions relating to joint ventures or other co-operative arrangements;

(j) requirements for the training of personnel and the transfer of fisheries technology, including enhancement of the coastal State's capability of undertaking fisheries research;

(k) enforcement procedures.

5. Coastal States shall give due notice of conservation and management laws and regulations.

Article 63
Stocks occurring within the exclusive economic zones of two or more coastal States or both within the exclusive economic zone and in an area beyond and adjacent to it

1. Where the same stock or stocks of associated species occur within the exclusive economic zones of two or more coastal States, these States shall seek, either directly or through appropriate subregional or regional organizations, to agree upon the measures necessary to co-ordinate and ensure the conservation and development of such stocks without prejudice to the other provisions of this Part.

2. Where the same stock or stocks of associated species occur both within the exclusive economic zone and in an area beyond and adjacent to the zone, the coastal State and the States fishing for such stocks in the adjacent area shall seek, either directly or through appropriate subregional or regional organizations, to agree upon the measures necessary for the conservation of these stocks in the adjacent area.

Article 64
Highly migratory species

1. The coastal State and other States whose nationals fish in the region for the highly migratory species listed in Annex I shall co-operate directly or through appropriate international organizations with a view to ensuring conservation and promoting the objective of optimum utilization of such species throughout the region, both within and beyond the exclusive economic zone. In regions for which no appropriate international organization exists, the coastal State and other States

whose nationals harvest these species in the region shall co-operate to establish such an organization and participate in its work.

2. The provisions of paragraph 1 apply in addition to the other provisions of this Part.

Article 65
Marine mammals

Nothing in this Part restricts the right of a coastal State or the competence of an international organization, as appropriate, to prohibit, limit or regulate the exploitation of marine mammals more strictly than provided for in this Part. States shall co-operate with a view to the conservation of marine mammals and in the case of cetaceans shall in particular work through the appropriate international organizations for their conservation, management and study.

Article 66
Anadromous stocks

1. States in whose rivers anadromous stocks originate shall have the primary interest in and responsibility for such stocks.

2. The State of origin of anadromous stocks shall ensure their conservation by the establishment of appropriate regulatory measures for fishing in all waters landward of the outer limits of its exclusive economic zone and for fishing provided for in paragraph 3(b). The State of origin may, after consultations with the other States referred to in paragraphs 3 and 4 fishing these stocks, establish total allowable catches for stocks originating in its rivers.

3.   (a) Fisheries for anadromous stocks shall be conducted only in waters landward of the outer limits of exclusive economic zones, except in cases where this provision would result in economic dislocation for a State other than the State of origin. With respect to such fishing beyond the outer limits of the exclusive economic zone, States concerned shall maintain consultations with a view to achieving agreement on terms and conditions of such fishing giving due regard to the conservation requirements and the needs of the State of origin in respect of these stocks.

(b)   The State of origin shall co-operate in minimizing economic dislocation in such other States fishing these stocks, taking into account the normal catch and the mode of operations of such States, and all the areas in which such fishing has occurred.

(c)   States referred to in subparagraph (b), participating by agreement with the State of origin in measures to renew anadromous stocks, particularly by expenditures for that purpose, shall be given special consideration by the State of origin in the harvesting of stocks originating in its rivers.

(d)   Enforcement of regulations regarding anadromous stocks beyond the exclusive economic zone shall be by agreement between the State of origin and the other States concerned.

4. In cases where anadromous stocks migrate into or through the waters landward of the outer limits of the exclusive economic zone of a State other than the State of origin, such State shall co-operate with the State of origin with regard to the conservation and management of such stocks.

5. The State of origin of anadromous stocks and other States fishing these stocks shall make arrangements for the implementation of the provisions of this article, where appropriate, through regional organizations.

Article 67
Catadromous species

1. A coastal State in whose waters catadromous species spend the greater part of their life cycle shall have responsibility for the management of these species and shall ensure the ingress and egress of migrating fish.

2. Harvesting of catadromous species shall be conducted only in waters landward of the outer limits of exclusive economic zones. When conducted in exclusive economic zones, harvesting shall be subject to this article and the other provisions of this Convention concerning fishing in these zones.

3. In cases where catadromous fish migrate through the exclusive economic zone of another State, whether as juvenile or maturing fish, the management, including harvesting, of such fish shall be regulated by agreement between the State mentioned in paragraph 1 and the other State concerned. Such agreement shall ensure the rational management of the species and take into account the responsibilities of the State mentioned in paragraph 1 for the maintenance of these species.

Article 68
Sedentary species

This Part does not apply to sedentary species as defined in article 77, paragraph 4.

* * *

PART VII. HIGH SEAS
* * *

Article 116
Right to fish on the high seas

All States have the right for their nationals to engage in fishing on the high seas subject to:
(a)   their treaty obligations;
(b)   the rights and duties as well as the interests of coastal States provided for, *inter alia*, in article 63, paragraph 2, and articles 64 to 67; and
(c)   the provisions of this section.

Article 117
Duty of States to adopt with respect to their nationals measures for the conservation of the living resources of the high seas

All States have the duty to take, or to co-operate with other States in taking, such measures for their respective nationals as may be necessary for the conservation of the living resources of the high seas.

Article 118
Co-operation of States in the conservation and management of living resources

States shall co-operate with each other in the conservation and management of living resources in the areas of the high seas. States whose nationals exploit identical living resources, or different living resources in the same area, shall enter into negotiations with a view to taking the measures necessary for the conservation of the living resources concerned. They shall, as appropriate, co-operate to establish subregional or regional fisheries organizations to this end.

Article 119
Conservation of the living resources of the high seas

1. In determining the allowable catch and establishing other conservation measures for the living resources in the high seas, States shall:

(a)   take measures which are designed, on the best scientific evidence available to the States concerned, to maintain or restore populations of harvested species at levels which can produce the maximum sustainable yield, as qualified by relevant environmental and economic factors, including the special requirements of developing States, and taking into account fishing patterns, the interdependence of stocks and any generally recommended international minimum standards, whether subregional, regional or global;

(b)   take into consideration the effects on species associated with or dependent upon harvested species with a view to maintaining or restoring populations of such associated or dependent species above levels at which their reproduction may become seriously threatened.

2. Available scientific information, catch and fishing effort statistics, and other data relevant to the conservation of fish stocks shall be contributed and exchanged on a regular basis through competent international organizations, whether subregional, regional or global, where appropriate and with participation by all States concerned.

3. States concerned shall ensure that conservation measures and their implementation do not discriminate in form or in fact against the fishermen of any State.

Article 120
Marine mammals

Article 65 also applies to the conservation and management of marine mammals in the high seas.

* * *

PART XI. THE AREA
* * *

Article 145
Protection of the marine environment

Necessary measures shall be taken in accordance with this Convention with respect to activities in the Area to ensure effective protection for the marine environment from harmful effects which may arise from such activities. To this end the Authority shall adopt appropriate rules, regulations and procedures for *inter alia*:

(a)   the prevention, reduction and control of pollution and other hazards to the marine environment, including the coastline, and of interference with the ecological balance of the marine environment, particular attention being paid to the need for protection from harmful effects of such activities as drilling, dredging, excavation, disposal of waste, construction and operation or maintenance of installations, pipelines and other devices related to such activities;

(b)   the protection and conservation of the natural resources of the Area and the prevention of damage to the flora and fauna of the marine environment.

* * *

PART XII. PROTECTION AND PRESERVATION OF THE MARINE ENVIRONMENT

Section 1. general provisions

Article 192
General obligation

States have the obligation to protect and preserve the marine environment.

Article 193
Sovereign right of States to exploit their natural resources

States have the sovereign right to exploit their natural resources pursuant to their environmental policies and in accordance with their duty to protect and preserve the marine environment.

Article 194
Measures to prevent, reduce and control pollution of the marine environment

1. States shall take, individually or jointly as appropriate, all measures consistent with this Convention that are necessary to prevent, reduce and control pollution of the marine environment from any source, using for this purpose the best practicable means at their disposal and in accordance with their capabilities, and they shall endeavour to harmonize their policies in this connection.

2. States shall take all measures necessary to ensure that activities under their jurisdiction or control are so conducted as not to cause damage by pollution to other States and their environment, and that pollution arising from incidents or activities under their jurisdiction or control does not spread beyond the areas where they exercise sovereign rights in accordance with this Convention.

3. The measures taken pursuant to this Part shall deal with all sources of pollution of the marine environment. These measures shall include, *inter alia*, those designed to minimize to the fullest possible extent:

   (a) the release of toxic, harmful or noxious substances, especially those which are persistent, from land-based sources, from or through the atmosphere or by dumping;

   (b) pollution from vessels, in particular measures for preventing accidents and dealing with emergencies, ensuring the safety of operations at sea, preventing intentional and unintentional discharges, and regulating the design, construction, equipment, operation and manning of vessels;

   (c) pollution from installations and devices used in exploration or exploitation of the natural resources of the sea-bed and subsoil, in particular measures for preventing accidents and dealing with emergencies, ensuring the safety of operations at sea, and regulating the design, construction, equipment, operation and manning of such installations or devices;

   (d) pollution from other installations and devices operating in the marine environment, in particular measures for preventing accidents and dealing with emergencies, ensuring the safety of operations at sea, and regulating the design, construction, equipment, operation and manning of such installations or devices.

4. In taking measures to prevent, reduce or control pollution of the marine environment, States shall refrain from unjustifiable interference with activities carried out by other States in the exercise of their rights and in pursuance of their duties in conformity with this Convention.

5. The measures taken in accordance with this Part shall include those necessary to protect and preserve rare or fragile ecosystems as well as the habitat of depleted, threatened or endangered species and other forms of marine life.

Article 195
Duty not to transfer damage or hazards or transform one type of pollution into another

In taking measures to prevent, reduce and control pollution of the marine environment, States shall act so as not to transfer, directly or indirectly, damage or hazards from one area to another or transform one type of pollution into another.

Article 196
Use of technologies or introduction of alien or new species

1. States shall take all measures necessary to prevent, reduce and control pollution of the marine environment resulting from the use of technologies under their jurisdiction or control, or the intentional or accidental introduction of species, alien or new, to a particular part of the marine environment, which may cause significant and harmful changes thereto.

2. This article does not affect the application of this Convention regarding the prevention, reduction and control of pollution of the marine environment.

SECTION 2. GLOBAL AND REGIONAL CO-OPERATION

Article 197
Co-operation on a global or regional basis

States shall co-operate on a global basis and, as appropriate, on a regional basis, directly or through competent international organizations, in formulating and elaborating international rules, standards and recommended practices and procedures consistent with this Convention, for the protection and preservation of the marine environment, taking into account characteristic regional features.

Article 198
Notification of imminent or actual damage

When a State becomes aware of cases in which the marine environment is in imminent danger of being damaged or has been damaged by pollution, it shall immediately notify other States it deems likely to be affected by such damage, as well as the competent international organizations.

Article 199
Contingency plans against pollution

In the cases referred to in article 198, States in the area affected, in accordance with their capabilities, and the competent international organizations shall co-operate, to the extent possible, in eliminating the effects of pollution and preventing or minimizing the damage. To this end, States shall jointly develop and promote contingency plans for responding to pollution incidents in the marine environment.

Article 200
Studies, research programmes and exchange of information and data

States shall co-operate, directly or through competent international organizations, for the purpose of promoting studies, undertaking programmes of scientific research and encouraging the exchange of information and data acquired about pollution of the marine environment. They shall endeavour to participate actively in regional and global programmes to acquire knowledge for the assessment of the nature and extent of pollution, exposure to it, and its pathways, risks and remedies.

Article 201
Scientific criteria for regulations

In the light of the information and data acquired pursuant to article 200, States shall co-operate, directly or through competent international organizations, in establishing appropriate scientific criteria for the formulation and elaboration of rules, standards and recommended practices and procedures for the prevention, reduction and control of pollution of the marine environment.

Section 3. Technical Assistance

Article 202
Scientific and technical assistance to developing States

States shall, directly or through competent international organizations:
(a) promote programmes of scientific, educational, technical and other assistance to developing States for the protection and preservation of the marine environment and the prevention, reduction and control of marine pollution. Such assistance shall include, *inter alia*:
    (i) training of their scientific and technical personnel;
    (ii) facilitating their participation in relevant international programmes;
    (iii) supplying them with necessary equipment and facilities;
    (iv) enhancing their capacity to manufacture such equipment;
    (v) advice on and developing facilities for research, monitoring, educational and other programmes;
(b) provide appropriate assistance, especially to developing States, for the minimization of the effects of major incidents which may cause serious pollution of the marine environment;
(c) provide appropriate assistance, especially to developing States, concerning the preparation of environmental assessments.

Article 203
Preferential treatment for developing States

Developing States shall, for the purposes of prevention, reduction and control of pollution of the marine environment or minimization of its effects, be granted preference by international organizations in:
(a) the allocation of appropriate funds and technical assistance; and
(b) the utilization of their specialized services.

Section 4. Monitoring and Environmental Assessment

Article 204
Monitoring of the risks or effects of pollution

1. States shall, consistent with the rights of other States, endeavour, as far as practicable, directly or through the competent international organizations, to observe, measure, evaluate and analyse, by recognized scientific methods, the risks or effects of pollution of the marine environment.

2. In particular, States shall keep under surveillance the effects of any activities which they permit or in which they engage in order to determine whether these activities are likely to pollute the marine environment.

Article 205
Publication of reports

States shall publish reports of the results obtained pursuant to article 204 or provide such reports at appropriate intervals to the competent international organizations, which should make them available to all States.

Article 206
Assessment of potential effects of activities

When States have reasonable grounds for believing that planned activities under their jurisdiction or control may cause substantial pollution of or significant and harmful changes to the marine environment, they shall, as far as practicable, assess the potential effects of such activities on the marine environment and shall communicate reports of the results of such assessments in the manner provided in article 205.

Section 5. International Rules and National Legislation to Prevent, Reduce and Control Pollution of the Marine Environment

Article 207
Pollution from land-based sources

1. States shall adopt laws and regulations to prevent, reduce and control pollution of the marine environment from land-based sources, including rivers, estuaries, pipelines and outfall structures, taking into account internationally agreed rules, standards and recommended practices and procedures.
2. States shall take other measures as may be necessary to prevent, reduce and control such pollution.
3. States shall endeavour to harmonize their policies in this connection at the appropriate regional level.
4. States, acting especially through competent international organizations or diplomatic conference, shall endeavour to establish global and regional rules, standards and recommended practices and procedures to prevent, reduce and control pollution of the marine environment from land-based sources, taking into account characteristic regional features, the economic capacity of developing States and their need for economic development. Such rules, standards and recommended practices and procedures shall be re-examined from time to time as necessary.
5. Laws, regulations, measures, rules, standards and recommended practices and procedures referred to in paragraphs 1, 2 and 4 shall include those designed to minimize, to the fullest extent possible, the release of toxic, harmful or noxious substances, especially those which are persistent, into the marine environment.

Article 208
Pollution from sea-bed activities subject to national jurisdiction

1. Coastal States shall adopt laws and regulations to prevent, reduce and control pollution of the marine environment arising from or in connection with sea-bed activities subject to their jurisdiction and from artificial islands, installations and structures under their jurisdiction, pursuant to articles 60 and 80.

2. States shall take other measures as may be necessary to prevent, reduce and control such pollution.

3. Such laws, regulations and measures shall be no less effective than international rules, standards and recommended practices and procedures.

4. States shall endeavour to harmonize their policies in this connection at the appropriate regional level.

5. States, acting especially through competent international organizations or diplomatic conference, shall establish global and regional rules, standards and recommended practices and procedures to prevent, reduce and control pollution of the marine environment referred to in paragraph 1. Such rules, standards and recommended practices and procedures shall be re-examined from time to time as necessary.

Article 209
Pollution from activities in the Area

1. International rules, regulations and procedures shall be established in accordance with Part XI to prevent, reduce and control pollution of the marine environment from activities in the Area. Such rules, regulations and procedures shall be re-examined from time to time as necessary.

2. Subject to the relevant provisions of this section, States shall adopt laws and regulations to prevent, reduce and control pollution of the marine environment from activities in the Area undertaken by vessels, installations, structures and other devices flying their flag or of their registry or operating under their authority, as the case may be. The requirements of such laws and regulations shall be no less effective than the international rules, regulations and procedures referred to in paragraph 1.

Article 210
Pollution by dumping

1. States shall adopt laws and regulations to prevent, reduce and control pollution of the marine environment by dumping.

2. States shall take other measures as may be necessary to prevent, reduce and control such pollution.

3. Such laws, regulations and measures shall ensure that dumping is not carried out without the permission of the competent authorities of States.

4. States, acting especially through competent international organizations or diplomatic conference, shall endeavour to establish global and regional rules, standards and recommended practices and procedures to prevent, reduce and control such pollution. Such rules, standards and recommended practices and procedures shall be re-examined from time to time as necessary.

5. Dumping within the territorial sea and the exclusive economic zone or onto the continental shelf shall not be carried out without the express prior approval of the coastal State, which has the right to permit, regulate and control such dumping after due consideration of the matter with other States which by reason of their geographical situation may be adversely affected thereby.

6. National laws, regulations and measures shall be no less effective in preventing, reducing and controlling such pollution than the global rules and standards.

Article 211
Pollution from vessels

1. States, acting through the competent international organization or general diplomatic conference, shall establish international rules and standards to prevent,

reduce and control pollution of the marine environment from vessels and promote the adoption, in the same manner, wherever appropriate, of routeing systems designed to minimize the threat of accidents which might cause pollution of the marine environment, including the coastline, and pollution damage to the related interests of coastal States. Such rules and standards shall, in the same manner, be re-examined from time to time as necessary.

2. States shall adopt laws and regulations for the prevention, reduction and control of pollution of the marine environment from vessels flying their flag or of their registry. Such laws and regulations shall at least have the same effect as that of generally accepted international rules and standards established through the competent international organization or general diplomatic conference.

3. States which establish particular requirements for the prevention, reduction and control of pollution of the marine environment as a condition for the entry of foreign vessels into their ports or internal waters or for a call at their off-shore terminals shall give due publicity to such requirements and shall communicate them to the competent international organization. Whenever such requirements are established in identical form by two or more coastal States in an endeavour to harmonize policy, the communication shall indicate which States are participating in such co-operative arrangements. Every State shall require the master of a vessel flying its flag or of its registry, when navigating within the territorial sea of a State participating in such co-operative arrangements, to furnish, upon the request of that State, information as to whether it is proceeding to a State of the same region participating in such co-operative arrangements and, if so, to indicate whether it complies with the port entry requirements of that State. This article is without prejudice to the continued exercise by a vessel of its right of innocent passage or to the application of article 25, paragraph 2.

4. Coastal States may, in the exercise of their sovereignty within their territorial sea, adopt laws and regulations for the prevention, reduction and control of marine pollution from foreign vessels, including vessels exercising the right of innocent passage. Such laws and regulations shall, in accordance with Part II, section 3, not hamper innocent passage of foreign vessels.

5. Coastal States, for the purpose of enforcement as provided for in section 6, may in respect of their exclusive economic zones adopt laws and regulations for the prevention, reduction and control of pollution from vessels conforming to and giving effect to generally accepted international rules and standards established through the competent international organization or general diplomatic conference.

6. (a) Where the international rules and standards referred to in paragraph 1 are inadequate to meet special circumstances and coastal States have reasonable grounds for believing that a particular, clearly defined area of their respective exclusive economic zones is an area where the adoption of special mandatory measures for the prevention of pollution from vessels is required for recognized technical reasons in relation to its oceanographical and ecological conditions, as well as its utilization or the protection of its resources and the particular character of its traffic, the coastal States, after appropriate consultations through the competent international organization with any other States concerned, may, for that area, direct a communication to that organization, submitting scientific and technical evidence in support and information on necessary reception facilities. Within 12 months after receiving such a communication, the organization shall determine whether the conditions in that area correspond to the requirements set out above. If the organization so determines, the coastal States may, for that area, adopt laws and regulations for the prevention, reduction and control of pollution from vessels implementing such international rules and standards or navigational practices as are made applicable, through the organization, for special areas. These laws and regulations shall not become applicable to foreign vessels until 15 months after the submission of the communication to the organization.

(b) The coastal States shall publish the limits of any such particular, clearly defined area.

(c) If the coastal States intend to adopt additional laws and regulations for the same area for the prevention, reduction and control of pollution from vessels, they shall, when submitting the aforesaid communication, at the same time notify the organization thereof. Such additional laws and regulations may relate to discharges or navigational practices but shall not require foreign vessels to observe design, construction, manning or equipment standards other than generally accepted international rules and standards; they shall become applicable to foreign vessels 15 months after the submission of the communication to the organization, provided that the organization agrees within 12 months after the submission of the communication.

7. The international rules and standards referred to in this article should include *inter alia* those relating to prompt notification to coastal States, whose coastline or related interests may be affected by incidents, including maritime casualties, which involve discharges or probability of discharges.

Article 212
Pollution from or through the atmosphere

1. States shall adopt laws and regulations to prevent, reduce and control pollution of the marine environment from or through the atmosphere, applicable to the air space under their sovereignty and to vessels flying their flag or vessels or aircraft of their registry, taking into account internationally agreed rules, standards and recommended practices and procedures and the safety of air navigation.

2. States shall take other measures as may be necessary to prevent, reduce and control such pollution.

3. States, acting especially through competent international organizations or diplomatic conference, shall endeavour to establish global and regional rules, standards and recommended practices and procedures to prevent, reduce and control such pollution.

Section 6. Enforcement

Article 213
Enforcement with respect to pollution from land-based sources

States shall enforce their laws and regulations adopted in accordance with article 207 and shall adopt laws and regulations and take other measures necessary to implement applicable international rules and standards established through competent international organizations or diplomatic conference to prevent, reduce and control pollution of the marine environment from land-based sources.

Article 214
Enforcement with respect to pollution from sea-bed activities

States shall enforce their laws and regulations adopted in accordance with article 208 and shall adopt laws and regulations and take other measures necessary to implement applicable international rules and standards established through competent international organizations or diplomatic conference to prevent, reduce and control pollution of the marine environment arising from or in connection with sea-bed activities subject to their jurisdiction and from artificial islands, installations and structures under their jurisdiction, pursuant to articles 60 and 80.

Article 215
Enforcement with respect to pollution from activities in the Area

Enforcement of international rules, regulations and procedures established in accordance with Part XI to prevent, reduce and control pollution of the marine environment from activities in the Area shall be governed by that Part.

Article 216
Enforcement with respect to pollution by dumping

1. Laws and regulations adopted in accordance with this Convention and applicable international rules and standards established through competent international organizations or diplomatic conference for the prevention, reduction and control of pollution of the marine environment by dumping shall be enforced:
   (a) by the coastal State with regard to dumping within its territorial sea or its exclusive economic zone or onto its continental shelf;
   (b) by the flag State with regard to vessels flying its flag or vessels or aircraft of its registry;
   (c) by any State with regard to acts of loading of wastes or other matter occurring within its territory or at its off-shore terminals.
2. No State shall be obliged by virtue of this article to institute proceedings when another State has already instituted proceedings in accordance with this article.

Article 217
Enforcement by flag States

1. States shall ensure compliance by vessels flying their flag or of their registry with applicable international rules and standards, established through the competent international organization or general diplomatic conference, and with their laws and regulations adopted in accordance with this Convention for the prevention, reduction and control of pollution of the marine environment from vessels and shall accordingly adopt laws and regulations and take other measures necessary for their implementation. Flag States shall provide for the effective enforcement of such rules, standards, laws and regulations, irrespective of where a violation occurs.
2. States shall, in particular, take appropriate measures in order to ensure that vessels flying their flag or of their registry are prohibited from sailing, until they can proceed to sea in compliance with the requirements of the international rules and standards referred to in paragraph 1, including requirements in respect of design, construction, equipment and manning of vessels.
3. States shall ensure that vessels flying their flag or of their registry carry on board certificates required by and issued pursuant to international rules and standards referred to in paragraph 1. States shall ensure that vessels flying their flag are periodically inspected in order to verify that such certificates are in conformity with the actual condition of the vessels. These certificates shall be accepted by other States as evidence of the condition of the vessels and shall be regarded as having the same force as certificates issued by them, unless there are clear grounds for believing that the condition of the vessel does not correspond substantially with the particulars of the certificates.
4. If a vessel commits a violation of rules and standards established through the competent international organization or general diplomatic conference, the flag State, without prejudice to articles 218, 220 and 228, shall provide for immediate investigation and where appropriate institute proceedings in respect of the alleged violation irrespective of where the violation occurred or where the pollution caused by such violation has occurred or has been spotted.
5. Flag States conducting an investigation of the violation may request the assistance of any other State whose co-operation could be useful in clarifying the

circumstances of the case. States shall endeavour to meet appropriate requests of flag States.

6. States shall, at the written request of any State, investigate any violation alleged to have been committed by vessels flying their flag. If satisfied that sufficient evidence is available to enable proceedings to be brought in respect of the alleged violation, flag States shall without delay institute such proceedings in accordance with their laws.

7. Flag States shall promptly inform the requesting State and the competent international organization of the action taken and its outcome. Such information shall be available to all States.

8. Penalties provided for by the laws and regulations of States for vessels flying their flag shall be adequate in severity to discourage violations wherever they occur.

Article 218
Enforcement by port States

1. When a vessel is voluntarily within a port or at an off-shore terminal of a State, that State may undertake investigations and, where the evidence so warrants, institute proceedings in respect of any discharge from that vessel outside the internal waters, territorial sea or exclusive economic zone of that State in violation of applicable international rules and standards established through the competent international organization or general diplomatic conference.

2. No proceedings pursuant to paragraph 1 shall be instituted in respect of a discharge violation in the internal waters, territorial sea or exclusive economic zone of another State unless requested by that State, the flag State, or a State damaged or threatened by the discharge violation, or unless the violation has caused or is likely to cause pollution in the internal waters, territorial sea or exclusive economic zone of the State instituting the proceedings.

3. When a vessel is voluntarily within a port or at an off-shore terminal of a State, that State shall, as far as practicable, comply with requests from any State for investigation of a discharge violation referred to in paragraph 1, believed to have occurred in, caused, or threatened damage to the internal waters, territorial sea or exclusive economic zone of the requesting State. It shall likewise, as far as practicable, comply with requests from the flag State for investigation of such a violation, irrespective of where the violation occurred.

4. The records of the investigation carried out by a port State pursuant to this article shall be transmitted upon request to the flag State or to the coastal State. Any proceedings instituted by the port State on the basis of such an investigation may, subject to section 7, be suspended at the request of the coastal State when the violation has occurred within its internal waters, territorial sea or exclusive economic zone. The evidence and records of the case, together with any bond or other financial security posted with the authorities of the port State, shall in that event be transmitted to the coastal State. Such transmittal shall preclude the continuation of proceedings in the port State.

Article 219
Measures relating to seaworthiness of vessels to avoid pollution

Subject to section 7, States which, upon request or on their own initiative, have ascertained that a vessel within one of their ports or at one of their off-shore terminals is in violation of applicable international rules and standards relating to seaworthiness of vessels and thereby threatens damage to the marine environment shall, as far as practicable, take administrative measures to prevent the vessel from sailing. Such States may permit the vessel to proceed only to the nearest appropriate repair yard and, upon removal of the causes of the violation, shall permit the vessel to continue immediately.

Article 220
Enforcement by coastal States

1. When a vessel is voluntarily within a port or at an off-shore terminal of a State, that State may, subject to section 7, institute proceedings in respect of any violation of its laws and regulations adopted in accordance with this Convention or applicable international rules and standards for the prevention, reduction and control of pollution from vessels when the violation has occurred within the territorial sea or the exclusive economic zone of that State.

2. Where there are clear grounds for believing that a vessel navigating in the territorial sea of a State has, during its passage therein, violated laws and regulations of that State adopted in accordance with this Convention or applicable international rules and standards for the prevention, reduction and control of pollution from vessels, that State, without prejudice to the application of the relevant provisions of Part II, section 3, may undertake physical inspection of the vessel relating to the violation and may, where the evidence so warrants, institute proceedings, including detention of the vessel, in accordance with its laws, subject to the provisions of section 7.

3. Where there are clear grounds for believing that a vessel navigating in the exclusive economic zone or the territorial sea of a State has, in the exclusive economic zone, committed a violation of applicable international rules and standards for the prevention, reduction and control of pollution from vessels or laws and regulations of that State conforming and giving effect to such rules and standards, that State may require the vessel to give information regarding its identity and port of registry, its last and its next port of call and other relevant information required to establish whether a violation has occurred.

4. States shall adopt laws and regulations and take other measures so that vessels flying their flag comply with requests for information pursuant to paragraph 3.

5. Where there are clear grounds for believing that a vessel navigating in the exclusive economic zone or the territorial sea of a State has, in the exclusive economic zone, committed a violation referred to in paragraph 3 resulting in a substantial discharge causing or threatening significant pollution of the marine environment, that State may undertake physical inspection of the vessel for matters relating to the violation if the vessel has refused to give information or if the information supplied by the vessel is manifestly at variance with the evident factual situation and if the circumstances of the case justify such inspection.

6. Where there is clear objective evidence that a vessel navigating in the exclusive economic zone or the territorial sea of a State has, in the exclusive economic zone, committed a violation referred to in paragraph 3 resulting in a discharge causing major damage or threat of major damage to the coastline or related interests of the coastal State, or to any resources of its territorial sea or exclusive economic zone, that State may, subject to section 7, provided that the evidence so warrants, institute proceedings, including detention of the vessel, in accordance with its laws.

7. Notwithstanding the provisions of paragraph 6, whenever appropriate procedures have been established, either through the competent international organization or as otherwise agreed, whereby compliance with requirements for bonding or other appropriate financial security has been assured, the coastal State if bound by such procedures shall allow the vessel to proceed.

8. The provisions of paragraphs 3, 4, 5, 6 and 7 also apply in respect of national laws and regulations adopted pursuant to article 211, paragraph 6.

Article 221
Measures to avoid pollution arising from maritime casualties

1. Nothing in this Part shall prejudice the right of States, pursuant to international law, both customary and conventional, to take and enforce measures beyond the territorial sea proportionate to the actual or threatened damage to protect their coastline or related interests, including fishing, from pollution or threat of pollution following upon a maritime casualty or acts relating to such a casualty, which may reasonably be expected to result in major harmful consequences.

2. For the purposes of this article, "maritime casualty" means a collision of vessels, stranding or other incident of navigation, or other occurrence on board a vessel or external to it resulting in material damage or imminent threat of material damage to a vessel or cargo.

Article 222
Enforcement with respect to pollution from or through the atmosphere

States shall enforce, within the air space under their sovereignty or with regard to vessels flying their flag or vessels or aircraft of their registry, their laws and regulations adopted in accordance with article 212, paragraph 1, and with other provisions of this Convention and shall adopt laws and regulations and take other measures necessary to implement applicable international rules and standards established through competent international organizations or diplomatic conference to prevent, reduce and control pollution of the marine environment from or through the atmosphere, in conformity with all relevant international rules and standards concerning the safety of air navigation.

Section 7. Safeguards

Article 223
Measures to facilitate proceedings

In proceedings instituted pursuant to this Part, States shall take measures to facilitate the hearing of witnesses and the admission of evidence submitted by authorities of another State, or by the competent international organization, and shall facilitate the attendance at such proceedings of official representatives of the competent international organization, the flag State and any State affected by pollution arising out of any violation. The official representatives attending such proceedings shall have such rights and duties as may be provided under national laws and regulations or international law.

Article 224
Exercise of powers of enforcement

The powers of enforcement against foreign vessels under this Part may only be exercised by officials or by warships, military aircraft, or other ships or aircraft clearly marked and identifiable as being on government service and authorized to that effect.

Article 225
Duty to avoid adverse consequences in the exercise of the powers of enforcement

In the exercise under this Convention of their powers of enforcement against foreign vessels, States shall not endanger the safety of navigation or otherwise create any hazard to a vessel, or bring it to an unsafe port or anchorage, or expose the marine environment to an unreasonable risk.

Article 226
Investigation of foreign vessels

1.   (a) States shall not delay a foreign vessel longer than is essential for purposes of the investigations provided for in articles 216, 218 and 220. Any physical inspection of a foreign vessel shall be limited to an examination of such certificates, records or other documents as the vessel is required to carry by generally accepted international rules and standards or of any similar documents which it is carrying; further physical inspection of the vessel may be undertaken only after such an examination and only when:

(i)   there are clear grounds for believing that the condition of the vessel or its equipment does not correspond substantially with the particulars of those documents;

(ii) the contents of such documents are not sufficient to confirm or verify a suspected violation; or

(iii) the vessel is not carrying valid certificates and records.

(b)   If the investigation indicates a violation of applicable laws and regulations or international rules and standards for the protection and preservation of the marine environment, release shall be made promptly subject to reasonable procedures such as bonding or other appropriate financial security.

(c)   Without prejudice to applicable international rules and standards relating to the seaworthiness of vessels, the release of a vessel may, whenever it would present an unreasonable threat of damage to the marine environment, be refused or made conditional upon proceeding to the nearest appropriate repair yard. Where release has been refused or made conditional, the flag State of the vessel must be promptly notified, and may seek release of the vessel in accordance with Part XV.

2.   States shall co-operate to develop procedures for the avoidance of unnecessary physical inspection of vessels at sea.

Article 227
Non-discrimination with respect to foreign vessels

In exercising their rights and performing their duties under this Part, States shall not discriminate in form or in fact against vessels of any other State.

Article 228
Suspension and restrictions on institution of proceedings

1. Proceedings to impose penalties in respect of any violation of applicable laws and regulations or international rules and standards relating to the prevention, reduction and control of pollution from vessels committed by a foreign vessel beyond the territorial sea of the State instituting proceedings shall be suspended upon the taking of proceedings to impose penalties in respect of corresponding charges by the flag State within six months of the date on which proceedings were first instituted, unless those proceedings relate to a case of major damage to the coastal State or the flag State in question has repeatedly disregarded its obligation to enforce effectively the applicable international rules and standards in respect of violations committed by its vessels. The flag State shall in due course make available to the State previously instituting proceedings a full dossier of the case and the

records of the proceedings, whenever the flag State has requested the suspension of proceedings in accordance with this article. When proceedings instituted by the flag State have been brought to a conclusion, the suspended proceedings shall be terminated. Upon payment of costs incurred in respect of such proceedings, any bond posted or other financial security provided in connection with the suspended proceedings shall be released by the coastal State.

2. Proceedings to impose penalties on foreign vessels shall not be instituted after the expiry of three years from the date on which the violation was committed, and shall not be taken by any State in the event of proceedings having been instituted by another State subject to the provisions set out in paragraph 1.

3. The provisions of this article are without prejudice to the right of the flag State to take any measures, including proceedings to impose penalties, according to its laws irrespective of prior proceedings by another State.

Article 229
Institution of civil proceedings

Nothing in this Convention affects the institution of civil proceedings in respect of any claim for loss or damage resulting from pollution of the marine environment.

Article 230
Monetary penalties and the observance of recognized rights of the accused

1. Monetary penalties only may be imposed with respect to violations of national laws and regulations or applicable international rules and standards for the prevention, reduction and control of pollution of the marine environment, committed by foreign vessels beyond the territorial sea.

2. Monetary penalties only may be imposed with respect to violations of national laws and regulations or applicable international rules and standards for the prevention, reduction and control of pollution of the marine environment, committed by foreign vessels in the territorial sea, except in the case of a wilful and serious act of pollution in the territorial sea.

3. In the conduct of proceedings in respect of such violations committed by a foreign vessel which may result in the imposition of penalties, recognized rights of the accused shall be observed.

Article 231
Notification to the flag State and other States concerned

States shall promptly notify the flag State and any other State concerned of any measures taken pursuant to section 6 against foreign vessels, and shall submit to the flag State all official reports concerning such measures. However, with respect to violations committed in the territorial sea, the foregoing obligations of the coastal State apply only to such measures as are taken in proceedings. The diplomatic agents or consular officers and where possible the maritime authority of the flag State, shall be immediately informed of any such measures taken pursuant to section 6 against foreign vessels.

Article 232
Liability of States arising from enforcement measures

States shall be liable for damage or loss attributable to them arising from measures taken pursuant to section 6 when such measures are unlawful or exceed those reasonably required in the light of available information. States shall provide for recourse in their courts for actions in respect of such damage or loss.

Article 233
Safeguards with respect to straits used for international navigation

Nothing in sections 5, 6 and 7 affects the legal régime of straits used for international navigation. However, if a foreign ship other than those referred to in section 10 has committed a violation of the laws and regulations referred to in article 42, paragraph 1(a) and (b), causing or threatening major damage to the marine environment of the straits, the States bordering the straits may take appropriate enforcement measures and if so shall respect *mutatis mutandis* the provisions of this section.

Section 8. Ice-Covered Areas

Article 234
Ice-covered areas

Coastal States have the right to adopt and enforce non-discriminatory laws and regulations for the prevention, reduction and control of marine pollution from vessels in ice-covered areas within the limits of the exclusive economic zone, where particularly severe climatic conditions and the presence of ice covering such areas for most of the year create obstructions or exceptional hazards to navigation, and pollution of the marine environment could cause major harm to or irreversible disturbance of the ecological balance. Such laws and regulations shall have due regard to navigation and the protection and preservation of the marine environment based on the best available scientific evidence.

Section 9. Responsibility and Liability

Article 235
Responsibility and liability

1. States are responsible for the fulfilment of their international obligations concerning the protection and preservation of the marine environment. They shall be liable in accordance with international law.

2. States shall ensure that recourse is available in accordance with their legal systems for prompt and adequate compensation or other relief in respect of damage caused by pollution of the marine environment by natural or juridical persons under their jurisdiction.

3. With the objective of assuring prompt and adequate compensation in respect of all damage caused by pollution of the marine environment, States shall co-operate in the implementation of existing international law and the further development of international law relating to responsibility and liability for the assessment of and compensation for damage and the settlement of related disputes, as well as, where appropriate, development of criteria and procedures for payment of adequate compensation, such as compulsory insurance or compensation funds.

Section 10. Sovereign Immunity

Article 236
Sovereign immunity

The provisions of this Convention regarding the protection and preservation of the marine environment do not apply to any warship, naval auxiliary, other vessels or aircraft owned or operated by a State and used, for the time being, only on government non-commercial service. However, each State shall ensure, by the adoption of appropriate measures not impairing operations or operational capabilities of such vessels or aircraft owned or operated by it, that such vessels or aircraft act in a manner consistent, so far as is reasonable and practicable, with this Convention.

Section 11. Obligations Under Other Conventions on the Protection and Preservation of the Marine Environment

Article 237
Obligations under other conventions on the protection and preservation of the marine environment

1. The provisions of this Part are without prejudice to the specific obligations assumed by States under special conventions and agreements concluded previously which relate to the protection and preservation of the marine environment and to agreements which may be concluded in furtherance of the general principles set forth in this Convention.

2. Specific obligations assumed by States under special conventions, with respect to the protection and preservation of the marine environment, should be carried out in a manner consistent with the general principles and objectives of this Convention.

RESTATEMENT (THIRD) OF FOREIGN RELATIONS LAW OF THE UNITED STATES §§ 603-604 AND COMMENTS

Language: English

Editors' Note

The Restatement (Third) of the Foreign Relations Law of the United States is described *supra*, p. 354. Sections 603 and 604 express the American Law Institute's view of international law regarding marine pollution. The Introduction to Part VI (Environment) of the Restatement (Third), reprinted *supra*, p. 197, also discusses marine pollution.

Copyright 1987 by The American Law Institute. Reprinted with permission The American Law Institute.

§ 603 STATE RESPONSIBNILITY FOR MARIŅE POLLUTION

§ 603. State Responsibility for Marine Pollution
   (1) A state is obligated
   (a)   to adopt laws and regulations to prevent, reduce, and control any significant pollution of the marine environment that are no less effective than generally accepted international rules and standards; and
   (b)   to ensure compliance with the laws and regulations adopted pursuant to clause (a) by ships flying its flag, and, in case of a violation, to impose adequate penalties on the owner or captain of the ship.
   (2) A state is obligated to take, individually and jointly with other states, such measures as may be necessary, to the extent practicable under the circumstances, to prevent, reduce, and control pollution causing or threatening to cause significant injury to the marine environment.

Source Note:

This section is based on Articles 194, 207-12, 217, and 220 of the 1982 Convention on the Law of the Sea.

Comment:

a. State responsibility for marine pollution. This section applies the principles of § 601 to marine pollution. In fulfilling their obligations under this section, states must use "the best practicable means at their disposal and in accordance with their capabilities," and must "endeavour to harmonize their policies in this connection." LOS Convention, Article 194(1). In taking measures to prevent, reduce, or control pollution, states are obligated to implement any pertinent international rules and standards, and to refrain from unjustifiable interference with activities carried out by other states in exercise of their rights and in pursuance of their duties in conformity with international law. Articles 194(4) and 213-22.

The measures to be taken must "minimize to the fullest possible extent" the release of toxic, harmful, or noxious substances from land-based sources (such as rivers, estuaries, pipelines, and sewers), from or through the atmosphere, or by dumping of waste. Articles (194(3), 207, 210, and 212. In order to limit pollution from ships, all states must take measures for preventing accidents and dealing with emergencies, ensuring the safety of operations at sea, and preventing harmful discharges, whether intentional or unintentional. Navigational routing systems should also be designed to minimize the danger of accidents. Articles 194(3)(b) and 211(1). For the obligations of flag states, see Comment *b*; for the obligations of states engaged in sea-bed mining, see Comment *c*.

Under the principles of § 601(2) and (3), a state is responsible for injuries caused by pollution resulting from a violation of its obligations under this section to a coast or coastal waters of another state or to the marine areas beyond the limits of national jurisdiction, *i.e.*, areas of the sea not included in internal waters, the territorial sea, or the exclusive economic zone of a state, or in the archipelagic waters of an archipelagic state. See Article 86. State responsibility extends to injuries such as those caused by pollution, *e.g.*, by: toxic or noxious substances flowing down-river into the sea and moving into the coastal waters of a neighboring state; sewage drifting from the coastal waters of one state to the coast of another state; toxic or noxious substances dumped, or garbage or fuel discharged, by ships flying the flag of one state and landing on the coast of another state; or oil spills, mineral tailings, or other discharges from installations for exploration and exploitation of oil or polymetallic nodules that contaminate the high seas or are moved by currents to the waters or coast of another state.

b. Obligations of flag state. The flag state has the primary obligation to ensure that its ships respect generally accepted international anti-pollution rules and standards established through the competent international organization or general diplomatic conference, and that they comply with the state's laws and regulations implementing such rules and standards. A flag state is obligated to prohibit its ships from sailing unless they have complied with such international rules and standards, and have also met standards set by the state's own laws, especially those relating to design, construction, equipment, and manning of ships; to require its ships to carry on board certificates of compliance with the international rules; and to inspect its ships periodically to verify that their condition conforms to the certificates they carry. Other states must accept the certificates issued by the flag state as evidence of the condition of the ship, unless there are clear grounds for believing that the condition of the ship does not correspond substantially to the certificates. Article 217(1)-(3).

The flag state is obligated to provide for penalties for pollution by its vessels adequate in severity to discourage violations. Article 217(8). For further enforcement obligations of the flag state, see § 604, Comment *c*.

c. Obligations of sea-bed mining states. States are obligated to adopt laws, regulations, and other measures for preventing, reducing, and controlling pollution of the marine environment arising from or in connection with their exploration and exploitation of the sea-bed and subsoil, or from artificial islands, installations, and structures under their jurisdiction that are operating in the marine environment. Such laws, regulations, and measures must be no less effective than international rules, standards, and recommended practices and procedures. Articles 194(3)(c) and (d) and 208.

d. Protection of fragile ecosystems. States are obligated to take measures necessary to protect and preserve rare or fragile ecosystems, and the habitat of depleted, threatened, or endangered species and other forms of marine life. Where the area to be protected forms part of a state's exclusive economic zone, the competent international organization may authorize that state to implement special international rules and standards applicable to such zones. Articles 194(5) and 211(6).

A coastal state also has the right to adopt and enforce non-discriminatory laws and regulations for the prevention, reduction, and control of marine pollution from vessels in ice-covered areas within the limits of its exclusive economic zone, where particularly severe climatic conditions and the presence of ice for most of the year create obstructions or exceptional hazards to navigation, and where pollution of the marine environment could cause major harm to, or irreversible disturbance of, the ecological balance. The coastal state is obligated to base such laws and regulations on the best available scientific evidence and to have due regard to navigation. Article 234.

e. Obligation to notify. When a state becomes aware that the marine environment has been injured or is in imminent danger of being injured, it is obligated immediately to notify other states likely to be affected by such injuries as well as the competent global or regional international organization. Article 198.

f. Joint action in emergencies. States in an area affected by a maritime pollution disaster are obligated to cooperate in eliminating the effects of pollution and in preventing or minimizing injury. To be able to deal better with such emergencies, neighboring states are obligated to develop and be ready to put into operation contingency plans for responding to pollution incidents affecting the marine environment in their vicinity. Article 199.

g. Pollution by aircraft. States are responsible under this section for pollution of the marine environment by aircraft of their registry, *e.g.*, by noxious emissions. States are obligated to adopt laws and regulations to prevent, reduce, and control such pollution, taking into account internationally agreed rules, standards, and recommended practices and procedures adopted by the International Civil Aviation Organization, but must not prejudice thereby the safety of air navigation. Article 212.

§ 604. REMEDIES FOR MARINE POLLUTION

(1) A state responsible to another state for a violation of the principles of § 603 is subject to general interstate remedies (§ 902) to prevent, reduce, or terminate the activity threatening or causing pollution, and to pay reparation for injury caused.

(2) A state is obligated to ensure that a remedy is available, in accordance with its legal system, to provide prompt and adequate compensation or other relief for an injury to private interests caused by pollution of the marine environment resulting from a violation of § 603.

(3) In addition to remedies that may be available to it under Subsection (1):

(a)   a coastal state may detain, and institute proceedings against, a foreign ship:

        (i) navigating in its territorial sea, for a violation therein of antipollution laws that the coastal state adopted in accordance with applicable international rules and standards; or

        (ii) navigating in its territorial sea or its exclusive economic zone, for a violation in that zone of applicable international antipollution rules and standards that resulted in a discharge causing or threatening a major injury to the coastal state;

(b) a port state may institute proceedings against a foreign ship that has voluntarily come into that state's port,

        (i) for a violation of the port state's antipollution laws adopted in accordance with applicable international rules and standards, if the violation had occurred in the port state's territorial sea or exclusive economic zone; or

        (ii) for a discharge in violation of applicable international antipollution rules and standards that had occurred beyond the limits of national jurisdiction of any state; and

(c) a port state is obligated to investigate, as far as practicable, whether a foreign ship that has voluntarily come into that state's port was responsible for a discharge in violation of applicable international antipollution rules and standards,

        (i) at the request of another state, where the discharge was alleged to have occurred in waters subject to that state's jurisdiction, or to have caused or threatened damage to that state; or

        (ii) at the request of the flag state, irrespective of where the violation was alleged to have occurred.

Source Note:

This section is based on Articles 211, 217-18, 220, and 228 of the 1982 Convention on the Law of the Sea.

Comment:

a. Ordinary remedies between states. Subsection (1) states that ordinary international remedies are available for violations of obligations under § 603 as for violation of other obligations under international environmental law (§ 602), or of international obligations generally (§ 902). A state is responsible for a violation of international antipollution rules and standards, resulting from an act or omission by state officials or public vessels, or by ships, aircraft, platforms, or other structures at sea, or by natural or juridical persons, that are under the state's jurisdiction.

Interstate remedies may include claims for reparation for injury to the state or its political subdivisions, or injury to its nationals or inhabitants when they are not afforded reparation by domestic remedy in the offending state. See Subsection (2) and Comment *b*. The obligations of states in respect of the common environment are *erga omnes* and any state may pursue remedies for violations that inflict significant injury on that environment (for instance, to obtain termination of the wrongful conduct). See also Comment *c*.

b. Remedies for private injury. Under Subsection (2), when a natural or juridical person for whose acts a state is responsible under § 601 has caused injury to interests of a private person who is not the state's own national or resident, the state must provide to the injured person access to domestic remedies so that prompt and adequate compensation or preventive or injunctive relief may be obtained. See LOS Convention, Article 235. Where the injury results from a violation by a private ship or installation, the owner is presumably liable under domestic law, and the responsibility of the state is invoked only where adequate reparation is not obtained from the person responsible by domestic remedies. If complex patterns of ownership and agency make it difficult to determine who was legally liable under domestic law for the violation causing the injury, the state is responsible for ensuring that the injured person is compensated.

   c. *Enforcement by flag states.* In addition to the remedies set forth in Comments *a* and *b*, if a ship has committed a violation of applicable international rules and standards, the flag state is obligated to investigate immediately and to institute appropriate proceedings, irrespective of the place of the violation or injury. See LOS Convention, Article 217. The state that is the victim of a violation by a ship (or, in case of pollution of the common environment, any state) may complain to the flag state and request that the guilty persons be punished and be enjoined from further pollution (see Articles 217(6) and 235); if dissatisfied with action taken by the flag state, it may invoke against the flag state the remedies available under international law. Subsection (1) and Comment *a*. In addition, if the flag state has repeatedly disregarded its obligations to enforce effectively the applicable international rules and standards in respect of violations committed by its ships, a port state where proceedings against a ship have been instituted under Subsection (3)(b) or (c) may continue such proceedings and impose penalties, regardless of a request of the flag state that the proceedings be transferred to it. See Comment *e*; LOS Convention, Article 228(1).

   d. *Enforcement by coastal states.* The authority of the coastal state to bring proceedings against an offending foreign vessel (Subsection 3(a)) varies according to where the vessel is located and where the violation occurred. The coastal state has jurisdiction to prescribe, adjudicate, and enforce with respect to acts of pollution committed in its ports. The coastal state can also institute proceedings against a ship voluntarily in port, or against its crew, for a violation of its laws that occurred within its territorial sea or exclusive economic zone, provided that its laws were adopted in accordance with applicable international rules and standards. An offshore terminal is assimilated to a port for these purposes. LOS Convention, Article 220(1).

   Where there are clear grounds for believing that a foreign ship, while passing through the territorial sea of the coastal state, violated laws and regulations of that state adopted in accordance with applicable international rules and standards, the coastal state may, subject to certain procedural safeguards (see Article 226), undertake physical inspection of the vessel in the territorial sea in order to ascertain the facts relating to the violation. Where evidence so warrants, the coastal state may institute proceedings against the ship, in accordance with its laws, and may detain the ship pending such proceedings. Article 220(2); see also Articles 19(2)(h), 21(1)(f), and 27.

   When a violation of applicable international antipollution rules and standards is committed in the exclusive economic zone of the coastal state, and the ship is still in the zone or in the territorial sea of the coastal state, that state can take various steps, depending on the gravity of the violation. Where there are clear grounds for believing that a violation has occurred, the coastal state may require the ship to identify itself and its port of registry, indicate its last and its next port of call, and provide other relevant information needed to establish whether a violation has occurred. When there are clear grounds for believing that the violation resulted in "a substantial discharge causing or threatening significant pollution of the marine environment," and the ship either refuses to give information or the information supplied is manifestly at variance with the facts, the coastal state is entitled to proceed with a physical inspection. Only if there is "clear objective evidence" that the ship committed the violation and that the discharge is causing or threatens to cause "major damage to the coastline or related interests of the coastal state, or to any resources of its territorial sea or exclusive economic zone," is that state entitled to institute proceedings in accordance with its laws, and to detain the ship. Article 220(3)-(6).

To ensure that a ship is not unduly detained, appropriate procedures must be established, either through the competent international organization or by special agreement, for bonding or other appropriate financial security. If the ship makes the necessary arrangements, the coastal state is obligated to allow the vessel to proceed. Only monetary penalties may be imposed, unless the violation was committed in the territorial sea and the act of pollution was willful and serious, in which case the vessel may be confiscated and the person responsible may be tried and punished. Articles 220(7) and 230.

The principle of sovereign immunity protects warships, warplanes, and other government ships and aircraft on noncommercial service against coastal state proceedings, but the flag state is obligated to ensure that such ships or aircraft act in a manner consistent, as far as is reasonable and practicable, with applicable international rules and standards. Article 236.

e. Enforcement by port states. The jurisdiction of the port state with respect to a foreign ship voluntarily in its port or off-shore terminal includes authority for the state to investigate and, where the evidence warrants, to institute proceedings with respect to any discharge from that ship that occurred on the high seas. The port state may also institute proceedings if an unlawful discharge outside its coastal waters caused or is likely to cause pollution within those waters. If the discharge occurred in the coastal waters of another state, the port state is obligated to institute proceedings, as far as practicable, when requested by that state. In addition, under Subsection (3)(c), the port state is obligated to conduct an investigation, as far as practicable, when so requested by the flag state, or by a state damaged or threatened by the discharge. LOS Convention, Article 218(1)-(4).

The records of the investigation carried out by a port state must be transmitted to the state that asked for the investigation if it so requests. The state in whose coastal waters the violation took place, but not the state where the injury occurred, is entitled to have the proceedings transferred to it. Once the records, the evidence, and the bonds (or other financial security) are transmitted to the requesting state, the proceedings in the port state must be suspended. Article 218(4).

The flag state is entitled to have penal proceedings against its ship in a foreign state suspended as soon as the flag state has itself instituted proceedings against the ship. However, the state that has instituted the proceedings need not suspend them (1) if the violation was committed in its territorial sea; (2) if the coastal state suffered major damage; or (3) if the flag state "has repeatedly disregarded its obligations to enforce effectively the applicable international rules and standards in respect of violations committed by its vessels." A proceeding that is suspended is to be terminated upon completion of proceedings in the flag state. Article 228(1). If the coastal state is dissatisfied with the action taken by the flag state after the case has been transferred, it may protest both to the flag state and to the competent international organizations; and if the lack of enforcement recurs, the coastal state may refuse to suspend proceedings on a future occasion.

f. Liability for wrongful enforcement measures. If a state has taken measures against a foreign ship that were unlawful or exceeded those reasonably required in the light of available information, it is oligated to pay the flag state for any injury or loss attributable to such measures. It must provide for recourse in its courts for private actions in respect of such injury or loss. LOS Convention, Article 232.

B. ANTARCTIC OCEAN

Editors' Introductory Note Regarding the Antarctic Treaty Regime.
Infra, p. 514.

ANTARCTIC TREATY. *Infra*, p. 515.

CANBERRA CONVENTION ON THE CONSERVATION OF ANTARCTIC MARINE LIVING RESOURCES. *Infra*, p. 520.

WELLINGTON CONVENTION ON THE REGULATION OF ANTARCTIC MINERAL RESOURCES ACTIVITIES. *Infra*, p. 529.

PROTOCOL ON ENVIRONMENTAL PROTECTION TO THE ANTARCTIC TREATY. *Infra*, p. 536

C. ARCTIC OCEAN

PARIS CONVENTION FOR THE PREVENTION OF MARINE POLLUTION FROM LAND-BASED SOURCES

Popular Name: Paris Convention

Done at Paris on 4 June 1974, UKTS No.64 (1978), *reprinted in* UNEP3 #64, p. 430, 13 ILM 352 (1974), 2 IPE 748, IELMT 974: 43.
Entry into Force: 6 May 1978

Depositary: France

Languages: English, French

Parties as of May 1989: Belgium; Denmark; France; Germany, Federal Republic of; Iceland; Ireland; Netherlands; Norway; Portugal; Spain; Sweden; United Kingdom of Great Britain and Northern Ireland;* European Economic Community

Editors' Note

This Convention is directed at controlling pollution from land-based sources in parts of the North Atlantic and Arctic Oceans and the North Sea, more particularly those parts abutting the west and north coasts of Europe. "Pollution from land-based sources" means pollution through watercourses, from the coast, via pipelines,

---

* With geographic extensions

and from man-made structures under the jurisdiction of a member State. Member States are obligated to implement measures (including regarding punishment) to eliminate pollution from some substances identified and to limit strictly pollution from others (the substances are identified in an annex). Research and monitoring obligations are also provided. The Convention further provides a "pledge" to "take all possible steps to prevent" marine pollution generally, and to harmonize policies about pollution from land-based sources.

CONVENTION FOR THE PREVENTION OF MARINE POLLUTION FROM LAND-BASED SOURCES

The Contracting Parties:

Recognizing that the marine environment and the fauna and flora which it supports are of vital importance to all nations;

Mindful that the ecological equilibrium and the legitimate uses of the sea are increasingly threatened by pollution;

Considering the recommendations of the United Nations Conference on the Human Environment, held in Stockholm in June 1972;

Recognizing that concerted action at national, regional and global levels is essential to prevent and combat marine pollution;

Convinced that international action to control the pollution of the sea from land-based sources can and should be taken without delay, as part of progressive and coherent measures to protect the marine environment from pollution, whatever its origin, including current efforts to combat the pollution of international waterways;

Considering that the common interests of States concerned with the same marine area should induce them to cooperate at regional or sub-regional levels;

Recalling the Convention for the Prevention of Marine Pollution by Dumping from Ships and Aircraft concluded in Oslo on 15 February 1972,

Have agreed as follows:

Article 1

1. The Contracting Parties pledge themselves to take all possible steps to prevent pollution of the sea, by which is meant the introduction by man, directly or indirectly, of substances or energy into the marine environment (including estuaries) resulting in such deleterious effects as hazards to human health, harm to living resources and to marine eco-systems, damage to amenities or interference with other legitimate uses of the sea.

2. The Contracting Parties shall adopt individually and jointly measures to combat marine pollution from land-based sources in accordance with the provisions of the present Convention and shall harmonize their policies in this regard.

Article 2

The present Convention shall apply to the maritime area within the following limits:

(a) those parts of the Atlantic and Arctic Oceans and the dependent seas which lie North of 36° north latitude and between 42° west longitude and 51° east longitude, but excluding:

(i) the Baltic Sea and Belts lying to the south and east of lines drawn from Hasenore Head to Gniben Point, from Korshage to Spodsbjerg and from Gilbjerg Head to Kullen, and

    (ii) the Mediterranean Sea and its dependent seas as far as the point of intersection of the parallel of 36° north latitude and the meridian of 5°36' west longitude;

(b)   that part of the Atlantic Ocean north of 59° north latitude and between 44° west longitude and 42° west longitude.

Article 3

For the purpose of the present Convention:

(a)   "Maritime area" means: the high seas, the territorial seas of Contracting Parties and waters on the landward side of the base lines from which the breadth of the territorial sea is measured and extending in the case of watercourses, unless otherwise decided under article 16(c) of the present Convention, up to the freshwater limit;

(b)   "Freshwater limit" means: the place in the watercourse where, at low tide and in a period of low freshwater flow, there is an appreciable increase in salinity due to the presence of seawater;

(c)   "Pollution from land-based sources" means: the pollution of the maritime area

    (i)   through watercourses,

    (ii) from the coast, including introduction through underwater or other pipelines,

    (iii) from man-made structures placed under the jurisdiction of a Contracting Party within the limits of the area to which the present Convention applies.

Article 4

1. The Contracting Parties undertake:

(a)   to eliminate, if necessary by stages, pollution of the maritime area from land-based sources by substances listed in Part I of Annex A to the present Convention;

(b)   to limit strictly pollution of the maritime area from land-based sources by substances listed in Part II of Annex A to the present Convention.

2. In order to carry out the undertakings in paragraph 1 of this Article, the Contracting Parties, jointly or individually as appropriate, shall implement programmes and measures:

(a)   for the elimination, as a matter of urgency, of pollution of the maritime area from land-based sources by substances listed in Part I of Annex A to the present Convention;

(b)   for the reduction or, as appropriate, elimination of pollution of the maritime area from land-based sources by substances listed in Part II of Annex A to the present Convention. These substances shall be discharged only after approval has been granted by the appropriate authorities within each contracting State. Such approval shall be periodically reviewed.

3. The programmes and measures adopted under paragraph 2 of this article shall include, as appropriate, specific regulations or standards governing the quality of the environment, discharges into the maritime area, such discharges into watercourses as affect the maritime area, and the composition and use of substances and products. These programmes and measures shall take into account the latest technical developments.

The programmes shall contain time-limits for their completion.

4. The Contracting Parties may, furthermore, jointly or individually as appropriate, implement programmes or measures to forestall, reduce or eliminate pollution of the maritime area from land-based sources by a substance not then listed in

Annex A to the present Convention, if scientific evidence has established that a serious hazard may be created in the maritime area by that substance and if urgent action is necessary.

Article 5

1. The Contracting Parties undertake to adopt measures to forestall and, as appropriate, eliminate pollution of the maritime area from land-based sources by radio-active substances referred to in Part III of Annex A of the present Convention.

2. Without prejudice to their obligations under other treaties and conventions, in implementing this undertaking the Contracting Parties shall:

(a)   take full account of the recommendations of the appropriate international organisations and agencies;

(b)   take account of the monitoring procedures recommended by these international organisations and agencies;

(c)   co-ordinate their monitoring and study of radio-active substances in accordance with Articles 10 and 11 of the present Convention.

Article 6

1. With a view to preserving and enhancing the quality of the marine environment, the Contracting Parties, without prejudice to the provisions of Article 4, shall endeavour:

(a)   to reduce existing pollution from land-based sources;

(b)   to forestall any new pollution from land-based sources, including that which derives from new substances.

2. In implementing this undertaking, the Contracting Parties shall take account of:

(a)   the nature and quantities of the pollutants under consideration;

(b)   the level of existing pollution;

(c)   the quality and absorptive capacity of the receiving waters of the maritime area;

(d)   the need for an integrated planning policy consistent with the requirement of environmental protection.

Article 7

The Contracting Parties agree to apply the measures they adopt in such a way as to avoid increasing pollution:

—   in the seas outside the area to which the present Convention applies;

—   in the maritime area covered by the present Convention, originating otherwise than from land-based sources.

Article 8

No provision of the present Convention shall be interpreted as preventing the Contracting Parties from Taking more stringent measures to combat marine pollution from land-based sources.

Article 9

1. When pollution from land-based sources originating from the territory of a Contracting Party by substances not listed in Part 1 of Annex A of the present Convention is likely to prejudice the interests of one or more of the other Parties to the present Convention, the Contracting Parties concerned undertake to enter

into consultation, at the request of any one of them, with a view to negotiating a co-operation agreement.

2. At the request of any Contracting Party concerned, the Commission referred to in Article 15 of the present Convention shall consider the question and may make recommendations with a view to reaching a satisfactory solution.

3. The special agreements specified in paragraph 1 of this Article may, among other things, define the areas to which they shall apply, the quality objectives to be achieved, and the methods for achieving these objectives including methods for the application of appropriate standards and the scientific and technical information to be collected.

4. The Contracting Parties signatory to these special agreements shall, through the medium of the Commission, inform the other Contracting Parties of their purport and of the progress made in putting them into effect.

Article 10

The Contracting Parties agree to establish complementary or joint programmes of scientific and technical research, including research into the best methods of eliminating or replacing noxious substances so as to reduce marine pollution from land-based sources, and to transmit to each other the information so obtained. In doing so they shall have regard to the work carried out, in these fields, by the appropriate international organizations and agencies.

Article 11

The Contracting Parties agree to set up progressively and to operate within the area covered by the present Convention a permanent monitoring system allowing:
—   the earliest possible assessment of the existing level of marine pollution;
—   the assessment of the effectiveness of measures for the reduction of marine pollution from land-based sources taken under the terms of the present Convention.

For this purpose the Contracting Parties shall lay down the ways and means of pursuing individually or jointly systematic and ad hoc monitoring programmes. These programmes shall take into account the deployment of research vessels and other facilities in the monitoring area.

The programmes shall take into account similar programmes pursued in accordance with conventions already in force and by the appropriate international organizations and agencies.

Article 12

1. Each Contracting Party undertakes to ensure compliance with the provisions of this Convention and to take in its territory appropriate measures to prevent and punish conduct in contravention of the provisions of the present Convention.

2. The Contracting Parties shall inform the Commission of the legislative and administrative measures they have taken to implement the provisions of the preceding paragraph.

Article 13

The Contracting Parties undertake to assist one another as appropriate to prevent incidents which may result in pollution from land-based sources, to minimize and eliminate the consequences of such incidents, and to exchange information to that end.

Article 14

1. The provisions of the present Convention may not be invoked against a Contracting Party to the extent that the latter is prevented, as a result of pollution having its origin in the territory of a non-Contracting State, from ensuring their full application.

2. However, the said Contracting Party shall endeavour to cooperate with the non-Contracting State so as to make possible the full application of the present Convention.

Article 15

A Commission composed of representatives of each of the Contracting Parties is hereby established. The Commission shall meet at regular intervals and at any time when due to special circumstances it is so decided in accordance with its rules of procedure.

Article 16

It shall be the duty of the Commission:
- (a) to exercise overall supervision over the implementation of the present Convention;
- (b) to review generally the condition of the seas within the area to which the present Convention applies, the effectiveness of the control measures being adopted and the need for any additional or different measures;
- (c) to fix, if necessary, on the proposal of the Contracting Party or Parties bordering on the same watercourse and following a standard procedure, the limit to which the maritime area shall extend in that watercourse;
- (d) to draw up, in accordance with Article 4 of the present Convention, programmes and measures for the elimination or reduction of pollution from land-based sources;
- (e) to make recommendations in accordance with the provisions of Article 9;
- (f) to receive and review information and distribute it to the Contracting Parties in accordance with the provisions of Articles 11, 12 and 17 of the present Convention;
- (g) to make, in accordance with Article 18, recommendations regarding any amendment to the lists of substances included in Annex A to the present Convention;
- (h) to discharge such other functions, as may be appropriate, under the terms of the present Convention.

Article 17

The Contracting Parties, in accordance with a standard procedure, shall transmit to the Commission:
- (a) the results of monitoring pursuant to Article 11;
- (b) the most detailed information available on the substances listed in the Annexes to the present Convention and liable to find their way into the maritime area.

The Contracting Parties shall endeavour to improve progressively techniques for gathering such information which can contribute to the revision of the pollution reduction programmes drawn up in accordance with Article 4 of the present Convention.

Article 18

1. The Commission shall draw up its own Rules of Procedure which shall be adopted by unanimous vote.

2. The Commission shall draw up its own Financial Regulations which shall be adopted by unanimous vote.

3. The Commission shall adopt, by unanimous vote, programmes and measures for the reduction or elimination of pollution from land-based sources as provided for in Article 4, programmes for scientific research and monitoring as provided for in Articles 10 and 11, and decisions under Article 16(c).

The programmes and measures shall commence for and be applied by all Contracting Parties two hundred days after their adoption, unless the Commission specifies another date.

Should unanimity not be attainable, the Commission may nonetheless adopt a programme or measures by a three quarters majority vote of its members. The programmes or measures shall commence for those Contracting Parties which voted for them two hundred days after their adoption, unless the Commission specifies another date, and for any other Contracting Party after it has explicitly accepted the programme or measures, which it may do at any time.

4. The Commission may adopt recommendations for amendments to Annex A to the present Convention by a three quarters majority vote of its members and shall submit them for the approval of the Governments of the Contracting Parties. Any Government of a Contracting Party that is unable to approve an amendment shall notify the depositary Government in writing within a period of two hundred days after the adoption of the Recommendation of amendment in the Commission. Should no such notification be received, the amendment shall enter into force for all Contracting Parties two hundred and thirty days after the vote in the Commission. The depositary Government shall notify the Contracting Parties as soon as possible of the receipt of any notification.

Article 19

Within the area of its competence, the European Economic Community is entitled to a number of votes equal to the number of its member States which are Contracting Parties to the present Convention.

The European Economic Community shall not exercise its right to vote in cases where its member States exercise theirs and conversely.

Article 20

The depositary Government shall convene the first meeting of the Commission as soon as possible after the coming into force of the present Convention.

Article 21

Any dispute between Contracting Parties relating to the interpretation or application of the present Convention, which cannot be settled otherwise by the Parties concerned, for instance by means of inquiry or conciliation within the Commission, shall, at the request of any of those Parties, be submitted to arbitration under the conditions laid down in Annex B to the present Convention.

* * *

Annex A

The allocation of substances to Parts I, II and III below takes account of the following criteria:

(*a*)   persistence;

(*b*)   toxicity or other noxious properties;

(*c*)   tendency to bio-accumulation.

These criteria are not necessarily of equal importance for a particular substance or group of substances, and other factors, such as the location and quantities of the discharge, may need to be considered.

Part I

The following substances are included in this Part

(i)   because they are not readily degradable or rendered harmless by natural processes; and

(ii)   because they may either

    (*a*) give rise to dangerous accumulation of harmful material in the food chain, or

    (*b*) endanger the welfare of living organisms causing undesirable changes in the marine eco-systems, or

    (*c*) interfere seriously with the harvesting of sea foods or with other legitimate uses of the sea; and

(iii)   because it is considered that pollution by these substances necessitates urgent action.

1. Organohalogen compounds and substances which may form such compounds in the marine environment, excluding those which are biologically harmless, or which are rapidly converted in the sea into substances which are biologically harmless.

2. Mercury and mercury compounds.

3. Cadmium and cadmium compounds.

4. Persistent synthetic materials which may float, remain in suspension or sink, and which may seriously interfere with any legitimate use of the sea.

5. Persistent oils and hydrocarbons of petroleum origin.

Part II

The following substances are included in this Part because, although exhibiting similar characteristics to the substances in Part I and requiring strict control, they seem less noxious or are more readily rendered harmless by natural processes:

1. Organic compounds of phosphorous, silicon, and tin and substances which may form such compounds in the marine environment, excluding those which are biologically harmless, or which are rapidly converted in the sea into substances which are biologically harmless.

2. Elemental phosphorus.

3. Non-persistent oils and hydrocarbons of petroleum origin.

4. The following elements and their compounds:

Arsenic	Lead
Chromium	Nickel
Copper	Zinc

5. Substances which have been agreed by the Commission as having a deleterious effect on the taste and/or smell of products derived from the marine environment for human consumption.

Part III

The following substances are included in this Part because, although they display characteristics similar to those of substances listed in Part I and should be subject to stringent controls with the aim of preventing and, as appropriate, eliminating the pollution which they cause, they are already the subject of research, recommendations and, in some cases, measures under the auspices of several international organisations and institutions; those substances are subject to the provisions of Article 5:

—   Radioactive substances, including wastes.

Annex B

Article 1

Unless the parties to the dispute decide otherwise, the arbitration procedure shall be in accordance with the provisions of this Annex.

Article 2

1. At the request addressed by one Contracting Party to another Contracting Party in accordance with Article 21 of the Convention, an arbitral tribunal shall be constituted. The request for arbitration shall state the subject matter of the application including in particular the Articles of the Convention, the interpretation or application of which is in dispute.

2. The claimant shall inform the Commission that he has requested the setting up of an arbitral tribunal, stating the name of the other party to the dispute and the Articles of the Convention the interpretation or application of which is in his opinion in dispute. The Commission shall forward the information thus received to all Contracting Parties to the Convention.

Article 3

The arbitral tribunal shall consist of three members: each of the parties to the dispute shall appoint an arbitrator; the two arbitrators so appointed shall designate by common agreement the third arbitrator who shall be the chairman of the tribunal. The latter shall not be a national of one of the parties to the dispute, nor have his usual place of residence in the territory of one of these parties, nor be employed by any of them, nor have dealt with the case in any other capacity.

Article 4

1. If the chairman of the arbitral tribunal has not been designated within two months of the appointment of the second arbitrator, the Secretary General of the United Nations shall, at the request of either party, designate him within a further two months' period.

2. If one of the parties to the dispute does not appoint an arbitrator within two months of receipt of the request, the other party may inform the Secretary General of the United Nations who shall designate the chairman of the arbitral tribunal

within a further two months' period. Upon designation, the chairman of the arbitral tribunal shall request the party which has not appointed an arbitrator to do so within two months. After such period, he shall inform the Secretary General of the United Nations who shall make this appointment within a further two months' period.

Article 5

1. The arbitral tribunal shall decide according to the rules of international law and, in particular, those of this Convention.
2. Any arbitral tribunal constituted under the provisions of this Appendix shall draw up its own rules of procedure.

Article 6

1. The decisions of the arbitral tribunal, both on the procedure and on the substance, shall be taken by majority voting of its members.
2. The tribunal may take all appropriate measures in order to establish the facts. It may, at the request of one ot [sic] the Parties, recommend indispensable interim measures of protection.
3. If two or more arbitral tribunals constituted under the provisions of this Appendix are seized of requests with identical or analogous subjects, they may inform themselves of the procedures for establishing the facts and take them into account as far as possible.
4. The parties to the dispute shall provide all facilities necessary for the effective running of the procedure.
5. The absence or default of a party to the dispute shall not constitute an impediment to the procedure.

Article 7

1. The award of the arbitral tribunal shall be accompanied by a statement of reasons. It shall be final and binding upon the parties to the dispute.
2. Any dispute which may arise between the parties concerning the interpretation or execution of the award may be submitted by either party to the arbitral tribunal which made the award or, if the latter cannot be seized thereof, to another arbitral tribunal constituted for this purpose in the same manner as the first.

Article 8

The European Economic Community, like any other Contracting Party to the present Convention, has the right to appear as applicant or respondant before the arbitral tribunal.

D. ATLANTIC OCEAN

PARIS CONVENTION FOR THE PREVENTION OF MARINE POLLUTION FROM LAND-BASED SOURCES. *Supra*, p. 360.

G. NORTH AND BALTIC SEAS

PARIS CONVENTION FOR THE PREVENTION OF MARINE POLLUTION FROM LAND-BASED SOURCES. *Supra*, p. 360.

H. MEDITERRANEAN SEA

Editors' Introductory Note Regarding the Mediterranean Sea

Following recommendations from the 1972 United Nations Conference on the Human Environment (*supra*, p. 171), the United Nations Environment Programme (UNEP) commenced a Mediterranean Action Plan (sometimes referred to as Med Plan) in 1975 for marine and coastal pollution control. That effort led to the conclusion of the Convention for the Protection of the Mediterranean Sea Against Pollution and four protocols thereto (on dumping, emergencies, land-based pollution, and specially protected areas). All eighteen Mediterranean States—even countries that normally are aloof or politically antagonistic—have joined together in the Mediterranean environmental regime, which was the first of UNEP's regional seas projects.

Nine other regional seas are now protected—to varying degrees—by regional seas conventions and protocols. Together, more than 125 States and 50 United Nations agencies and other international organizations are involved. *See generally* P. Sands, *Marine Environmental Law* (1988).

BARCELONA CONVENTION FOR THE PROTECTION OF THE MEDITERRANEAN SEA AGAINST POLLUTION

Popular Name: Barcelona Convention, Mediterranean Pollution Convention, Mediterranean Regional Seas Convention

Done at Barcelona on 16 February 1976, UNTS Reg. No. 16908, UNEP Reg. p. 136, *reprinted in* UNEP3 #66, p. 448, 15 ILM 290 (1976), 19 IPE 9497, IELMT 976: 13.

Entry into Force: 12 February 1978

Depositary: Spain

Languages: Arabic, English, French, Spanish

Parties as of 31 August 1990: Albania; Algeria; Cyprus; Egypt; France;* Greece; Israel;** Italy; Lebanon; Libyan Arab Jamahiriya; Malta; Monaco; Morocco;

---

*   With a reservation
** With a declaration

Spain; Syrian Arab Republic;* Tunisia; Turkey; Yugoslavia; European Economic Community

CONVENTION FOR THE PROTECTION OF THE MEDITERRANEAN SEA AGAINST POLLUTION

THE CONTRACTING PARTIES,

Conscious of the economic, social, health and cultural value of the marine environment of the Mediterranean Sea Area,

Fully aware of their responsibility to preserve this common heritage for the benefit and enjoyment of present and future generations,

Recognizing the threat posed by pollution to the marine environment, its ecological equilibrium, resources and legitimate uses,

Mindful of the special hydrographic and ecological characteristics of the Mediterranean Sea Area and its particular vulnerability to pollution,

Noting that existing international conventions on the subject do not cover, in spite of the progress achieved, all aspects and sources of marine pollution and do not entirely meet the special requirements of the Mediterranean Sea Area,

Realizing fully the need for close co-operation among the States and international organizations concerned in a co-ordinated and comprehensive regional approach for the protection and enhancement of the marine environment in the Mediterranean Sea Area,

HAVE AGREED AS FOLLOWS:

Article 1
Geographical coverage

1. For the purposes of this Convention, the Mediterranean Sea Area shall mean the maritime waters of the Mediterranean Sea proper, including its gulfs and seas, bounded to the West by the meridian passing through Cape Spartel lighthouse, at the entrance of the Straits of Gibraltar, and to the East by the southern limits of the Straits of the Dardanellos between Mehmetcik and Kumkale lighthouses.
2. Except as may be otherwise provided in any protocol to this Convention, the Mediterranean Sea Area shall not include internal waters of the Contracting Parties.

Article 2
Definitions

For the purposes of this Convention:

a) "pollution means the introduction by man, directly or indirectly, of substances or energy into the marine environment resulting in such deleterious effects as harm to living resources, hazards to human health, hindrance to marine activities including fishing, impairment of quality for use of sea water and reduction of amenities.

b) "Organization" means the body designated as responsible for carrying out secretariat functions pursuant to article 13 of this Convention.

Article 3
General provisions

1. The Contracting Parties may enter into bilateral or multilateral agreements, including regional or sub-regional agreements, for the protection of the marine

environment of the Mediterranean Sea against pollution, provided that such agreements are consistent with this Convention and conform to international law. Copies of such agreements between Contracting Parties to this Convention shall be communicated to the Organization.

2. Nothing in this Convention shall prejudice the codification and development of the Law of the Sea by the United Nations Conference on the Law of the Sea convened pursuant to resolution 2750 C (XXV) of the General Assembly of the United Nations, nor the present or future claims and legal views of any State concerning the law of the sea and the nature and extent of coastal and flag State jurisdiction.

Article 4
General undertakings

1. The Contracting Parties shall individually or jointly take all appropriate measures in accordance with the provisions of this Convention and those protocols in force to which they are party, to prevent, abate and combat pollution of the Mediterranean Sea Area and to protect and enhance the marine environment in that Area.

2. The Contracting Parties shall co-operate in the formulation and adoption of protocols, in addition to the protocols opened for signature at the same time as this Convention, prescribing agreed measures, procedures and standards for the implementation of this Convention.

3. The Contracting Parties further pledge themselves to promote, within the international bodies considered to be competent by the Contracting Parties, measures concerning the protection of the marine environment in the Mediterranean Sea Area from all types and sources of pollution.

Article 5
Pollution caused by dumping from ships and aircraft

The Contracting Parties shall take all appropriate measures to prevent and abate pollution of the Mediterranean Sea Area caused by dumping from ships and aircraft.

Article 6
Pollution from ships

The Contracting Parties shall take all measures in conformity with international law to prevent, abate and combat pollution of the Mediterranean Sea Area caused by discharges from ships and to ensure the effective implementation in that Area of the rules which are generally recognized at the international level relating to the control of this type of pollution.

Article 7
Pollution resulting from exploration and exploitation of the continental shelf and the seabed and its subsoil

The Contracting Parties shall take all appropriate measures to prevent, abate and combat pollution of the Mediterranean Sea Area resulting from exploration and exploitation of the continental shelf and the seabed and its subsoil.

Article 8
Pollution from land-based sources

The Contracting Parties shall take all appropriate measures to prevent, abate and combat pollution of the Mediterranean Sea Area caused by discharges from rivers, coastal establishments or outfalls, or emanating from any other land-based sources within their territories.

Article 9
Co-operation in dealing with pollution emergencies

1. The Contracting Parties shall co-operate in taking the necessary measures for dealing with pollution emergencies in the Mediterranean Sea Area, whatever the causes of such emergencies, and reducing or eliminating damage resulting therefrom.
2. Any Contracting Party which becomes aware of any pollution emergency in the Mediterranean Sea Area shall without delay notify the Organization and, either through the Organization or directly, any Contracting Party likely to be affected by such emergency.

Article 10
Monitoring

1. The Contracting Parties shall endeavour to establish, in close co-operation with the international bodies which they consider competent, complementary or joint programmes, including, as appropriate, programmes at the bilateral or multilateral levels, for pollution monitoring in the Mediterranean Sea Area and shall endeavour to establish a pollution monitoring system for that Area.
2. For this purpose, the Contracting Parties shall designate the competent authorities responsible for pollution monitoring within areas under their national jurisdiction and shall participate as far as practicable in international arrangements for pollution monitoring in areas beyond national jurisdiction.
3. The Contracting Parties undertake to co-operate in the formulation, adoption and implementation of such annexes to this Convention as may be required to prescribe common procedures and standards for pollution monitoring.

Article 11
Scientific and technological co-operation

1. The Contracting Parties undertake as far as possible to co-operate directly, or when appropriate through competent regional or other international organizations, in the fields of science and technology and to exchange data as well as other scientific information for the purpose of this Convention.
2. The Contracting Parties undertake as far as possible to develop and co-ordinate their national research programmes relating to all types of marine pollution in the Mediterranean Sea Area and to co-operate in the establishment and implementation of regional and other international research programmes for the purposes of this Convention.
3. The Contracting Parties undertake to co-operate in the provision of technical and other possible assistance in fields relating to marine pollution, with priority to be given to the special needs of developing countries in the Mediterranean region.

Article 12
Liability and compensation

The Contracting Parties undertake to co-operate as soon as possible in the formulation and adoption of appropriate procedures for the determination of liability and compensation for damage resulting from the pollution of the marine environment deriving from violations of the provisions of this Convention and applicable protocols.

Article 13
Institutional arrangements

The Contracting Parties designate the United Nations Environment Programme as responsible for carrying out the following secretariat functions:

(i) To convene and prepare the meetings of Contracting Parties and conferences provided for in articles 14, 15 and 16;

(ii) To transmit to the Contracting Parties notifications, reports and other information received in accordance with article [sic] 3, 9 and 20;

(iii) To consider inquiries by, and information from, the Contracting Parties, and to consult with them on questions relating to this Convention and the protocols and annexes thereto;

(iv) To perform the functions assigned to it by the protocols to this Convention;

(v) To perform such other functions as may be assigned to it by the Contracting Parties;

(vi) To ensure the necessary co-ordination with other international bodies which the Contracting Parties consider competent, and in particular, to enter into such administrative arrangements as may be required for the effective discharge of the secretariat functions.

Article 14
Meetings of the Contracting Parties

1. The Contracting Parties shall hold ordinary meetings once every two years and extraordinary meetings at any other time deemed necessary, upon the request of the Organization or at the request of any Contracting Party, provided that such requests are supported by at least two Contracting Parties.

2. It shall be the function of the meetings of the Contracting Parties to keep under review the implementation of this Convention and the protocols and, in particular:

(i) To review generally the inventories carried out by Contracting Parties and competent international organizations on the state of marine pollution and its effects in the Mediterranean Sea Area;

(ii) To consider reports submitted by the Contracting Parties under article 20;

(iii) To adopt, review and amend as required the annexes to this Convention and to the protocols, in accordance with the procedure established in article 17;

(iv) To make recommendations regarding the adoption of any additional protocols or any amendments to this Convention or the protocols in accordance with the provisions of articles 15 and 16;

(v) To establish working groups as required to consider any matters related to this Convention and the protocols and annexes;

(vi) To consider and undertake any additional action that may be required for the achievement of the purposes of this Convention and the protocols.

Article 15
Adoption of additional protocols

1. The Contracting Parties, at a diplomatic conference, may adopt additional protocols to this Convention pursuant to paragraph 2 of article 4.

2. A diplomatic conference for the purpose of adopting additional protocols shall be convened by the Organization at the request of two thirds of the Contracting Parties.

3. Pending the entry into force of this Convention the Organization may, after consulting with the signatories to this Convention, convene a diplomatic conference for the purpose of adopting additional protocols.

Article 16
Amendment of the Convention or protocols

1. Any Contracting Party to this Convention may propose amendments to the Convention. Amendments shall be adopted by a diplomatic conference which shall be convened by the Organization at the request of two thirds of the Contracting Parties.

2. Any Contracting Party to this Convention may propose amendments to any protocol. Such amendments shall be adopted by a diplomatic conference which shall be convened by the Organization at the request of two thirds of the Contracting Parties to the protocol concerned.

3. Amendments to this Convention shall be adopted by a three-fourths majority vote of the Contracting Parties to the Convention which are represented at the diplomatic conference and shall be submitted by the Depositary for acceptance by all Contracting Parties to the Convention. Amendments to any protocol shall be adopted by a three-fourths majority vote of the Contracting Parties to such protocol which are represented at the diplomatic conference and shall be submitted by the Depositary for acceptance by all Contracting Parties to such protocol.

4. Acceptance of amendments shall be notified to the Depositary in writing. Amendments adopted in accordance with paragraph 3 of this article shall enter into force between Contracting Parties having accepted such amendments on the thirtieth day following the receipt by the Depositary of notification of their acceptance by at least three fourths of the Contracting Parties to this Convention or to the protocol concerned, as the case may be.

5. After the entry into force of an amendment to this Convention or to a protocol, any new Contracting Party to this Convention or such protocol shall become a Contracting Party to the instrument as amended.

Article 17
Annexes and amendments to annexes

1. Annexes to this Convention or to any protocol shall form an integral part of the Convention or such protocol, as the case may be.

2. Except as may be otherwise provided in any protocol, the following procedure shall apply to the adoption and entry into force of any amendments to annexes to this Convention or to any protocol, with the exception of amendments to the Annex on Arbitration:

(i)   Any Contracting Party may propose amendments to the Annexes to this Convention or to any protocol at the meetings referred to in article 14:

(ii) Such amendments shall be adopted by a three-fourths majority vote of the Contracting Parties to the instrument in question;

(iii) The Depositary shall without delay communicate the amendments so adopted to all Contracting Parties;

(iv) Any Contracting Party that is unable to approve an amendment to the annexes to this Convention or to any protocol shall so notify in writing the Depositary within a period determined by the Contracting Parties concerned when adopting the amendment;

(v)   The Depositary shall without delay notify all Contracting Parties of any notification received pursuant to the preceding sub-paragraph;

(vi) On expiry of the period referred to in sub-paragraph (iv) above, the amendment to the annex shall become effective for all Contracting Parties to this Convention or to the protocol concerned which have not submitted a notification in accordance with the provisions of that sub-paragraph.

3. The adoption and entry into force of a new annex to this Convention or to any protocol shall be subject to the same procedure as for the adoption and entry into force of an amendment to an annex in accordance with the provisions of paragraph 2 of this article, provided that, if any amendment to the Convention or the protocol concerned is involved, the new annex shall not enter into force until such time as the amendment to the Convention or the protocol concerned enters into force.

4. Amendments to the Annex on Arbitration shall be considered to be amendments to this Convention and shall be proposed and adopted in accordance with the procedures set out in article 16 above.

Article 18
Rules of procedure and financial rules

1. The Contracting Parties shall adopt rules of procedure for their meetings and conferences envisaged in articles 14, 15 and 16 above.

2. The Contracting Parties shall adopt financial rules, prepared in consultation with the Organization, to determine, in particular, their financial participation.

Article 19
Special exercise of voting right

Within the areas of their competence, the European Economic Community and any regional economic grouping referred to in article 24 of this Convention shall exercise their right to vote with a number of votes equal to the number of their member States which are Contracting Parties to this Convention and to one or more protocols; the European Economic Community and any grouping as referred to above shall not exercise their right to vote in cases where the member States concerned exercise theirs, and conversely.

Article 20
Reports

The Contracting Parties shall transmit to the Organization reports on the measures adopted in the implementation of this Convention and of Protocols to which they are Parties, in such form and at such intervals as the meetings of Contracting Parties may determine.

Article 21
Compliance control

The Contracting Parties undertake to co-operate in the development of procedures enabling them to control the application of this Convention and the protocols.

Article 22
Settlement of disputes

1. In case of a dispute between Contracting Parties as to the interpretation or application of this Convention or the protocols, they shall seek a settlement of the dispute through negotiation or any other peaceful means of their own choice.

2. If the Parties concerned cannot settle their dispute through the means mentioned in the preceding paragraph, the dispute shall upon common agreement be submitted to arbitration under the conditions laid down in Annex A to this Convention.

3. Nevertheless, the Contracting Parties may at anytime declare that they recognize as compulsory *ipso-facto* and without special agreement, in relation to any other

Party accepting the same obligation, the application of the arbitration procedure in conformity with the provisions of Annex A. Such declaration shall be notified in writing to the Depositary, who shall communicate it to the other Parties.

Article 23
Relationship between the Convention and protocols

1. No one may become a Contracting Party to this Convention unless it becomes at the same time a Contracting Party to at least one of the protocols. No one may become a Contracting Party to a protocol unless it is, or becomes at the same time, a Contracting Party to this Convention.
2. Any protocol to this Convention shall be binding only on the Contracting Parties to the protocol in question.
3. Decisions concerning any protocol pursuant to articles 14, 16 and 17 of this Convention shall be taken only by the Parties to the protocol concerned.

Article 24
Signature

This Convention, the Protocol for the Prevention of Pollution of the Mediterranean Sea by Dumping from Ships and Aircraft and the Protocol concerning cooperation in Combating Pollution of the Mediterranean Sea by Oil and Other Harmful Substances in Cases of Emergency shall be open for signature in Barcelona on 16 February 1976 and in Madrid from 17 February 1976 to 16 February 1977 by any State invited as a participant in the Conference of Plenipotentiaries of the Coastal States of the Mediterranean Region on the Protection of the Mediterranean Sea, held in Barcelona from 2 to 16 February 1976, and by any State entitled to sign any protocol in accordance with the provisions of such protocol. They shall also be open until the same date for signature by the European Economic Community and by any similar regional economic grouping at least one member of which is a coastal State of the Mediterranean Sea Area and which exercise competences in fields covered by this Convention, as well as by any protocol affecting them.

* * *

BARCELONA PROTOCOL FOR THE PREVENTION OF POLLUTION OF THE MEDITERRANEAN SEA BY DUMPING FROM SHIPS AND AIRCRAFT

Popular Name: Barcelona Dumping Protocol, Mediterranean Dumping Protocol

Done at Barcelona on 16 February 1976, UNTS Reg. No. 16908, UNEP Reg. p. 138, *reprinted in* 15 ILM 300 (1976), 19 IPE 9515, IELMT 967: 14.
Entry into Force: 12 February 1978

Depositary: Spain

Languages: Arabic, English, French, Spanish

Parties as of 31 August 1990: Albania; Algeria; Cyprus; Egypt; France;* Greece; Israel; Italy; Lebanon; Libyan Arab Jamahiriya; Malta; Monaco; Morocco; Spain;

---

* With a reservation

Syrian Arab Republic; Tunisia; Turkey; Yugoslavia; European Economic Community

PROTOCOL FOR THE PREVENTION OF POLLUTION OF THE MEDITERRANEAN SEA BY DUMPING FROM SHIPS AND AIRCRAFT

The Contracting Parties to the Present Protocol,

Being Parties to the Convention for the Protection of the Mediterranean Sea against Pollution,

Recognizing the danger posed to the marine environment by pollution caused by the dumping of wastes or other matter from ships and aircraft,

Considering that the coastal States of the Mediterranean Sea have a common interest in protecting the marine environment from this danger,

Bearing in mind the Convention on the Prevention of Marine Pollution by Dumping of Wastes and other Matter, adopted in London in 1972.

HAVE AGREED AS FOLLOWS:

Article 1

The Contracting Parties to this Protocol (hereinafter referred to as "the Parties") shall take all appropriate measures to prevent and abate pollution of the Mediterranean Sea Area caused by dumping from ships and aircraft.

Article 2

The area to which this Protocol applies shall be the Mediterranean Sea Area as defined in article 1 of the Convention for the Protection of the Mediterranean Sea against Pollution (hereinafter referred to as "the Convention").

Article 3

For the purposes of this Protocol:

1. "Ships and aircraft" means waterborne or airborne craft of any type whatsoever. This expression includes air-cushioned craft and floating craft, whether self-propelled or not, and platforms and other man-made structures at sea and their equipment.
2. "Wastes or other matter" means material and substances of any kind, form or description.
3. "Dumping" means:
    (a)   Any deliberate disposal at sea of wastes or other matter from ships or aircraft;
    (b)   Any deliberate disposal at sea of ships or aircraft.
4. "Dumping" does not include:
    (a)   The disposal at sea of wastes or other matter incidental to, or derived from, the normal operations of vessels or aircraft and their equipment, other than wastes or other matter transported by or to vessels or aircraft, operating for the purpose of disposal of such matter, or derived from the treatment of such wastes or other matter on such vessels or aircraft;
    (b)   Placement of matter for a purpose other than the mere disposal thereof, provided that such placement is not contrary to the aims of this Protocol.
5. "Organization" means the body referred to in article 13 of the Convention.

Article 4

The dumping into the Mediterranean Sea Area of wastes or other matter listed in Annex I to this Protocol is prohibited.

Article 5

The dumping into the Mediterranean Sea Area of wastes or other matter listed in Annex II to this Protocol requires, in each case, a prior special permit from the competent national authorities.

Article 6

The dumping into the Mediterranean Sea Area of all other wastes or other matter requires a prior general permit from the competent national authorities.

Article 7

The permits referred to in articles 5 and 6 above shall be issued only after careful consideration of all the factors set forth in Annex III to this Protocol. The Organization shall receive records of such permits.

Article 8

The provisions of articles 4, 5 and 6 shall not apply in case of *force majeure* due to stress of weather or any other cause when human life or the safety of a ship or aircraft is threatened. Such dumpings shall immediately be reported to the Organization and, either through the Organization or directly, to any Party or Parties likely to be affected, together with full details of the circumstances and of the nature and quantities of the wastes or other matter dumped.

Article 9

If a Party in a critical situation of an exceptional nature considers that wastes or other matter listed in Annex I to this Protocol cannot be disposed of on land without unacceptable danger or damage, above all for the safety of human life, the Party concerned shall forthwith consult the Organization. The Organization, after consulting the Parties to this Protocol, shall recommend methods of storage or the most satisfactory means of destruction or disposal under the prevailing circumstances. The Party shall inform the Organization of the steps adopted in pursuance of these recommendations. The Parties pledge themselves to assist one another in such situations.

Article 10

1. Each Party shall designate one or more competent authorities to:
   (a)   Issue the special permits provided for in article 5;
   (b)   Issue the general permits provided for in article 6;
   (c)   Keep records of the nature and quantities of the wastes or other matter permitted to be dumped and of the location, date and method of dumping.
2. The competent authorities of each Party shall issue the permits provided for in articles 5 and 6 in respect of the wastes or other matter intended for dumping:
   (a)   Loaded in its territory;
   (b)   Loaded by a ship or aircraft registered in its territory or flying its flag, when the loading occurs in the territory of a State not Party to this Protocol.

Article 11

1. Each Party shall apply the measures required to implement this Protocol to all:
    (a) Ships and aircraft registered in its territory or flying its flag;
    (b) Ships and aircraft loading in its territory wastes or other matter which are to be dumped;
    (c) Ships and aircraft believed to be engaged in dumping in areas under its jurisdiction in this matter.

2. This Protocol shall not apply to any ships or aircraft owned or operated by a State Party to this Protocol and used for the time being only on Government noncommercial service. However, each Party shall ensure by the adoption of appropriate measures not impairing the operations or operational capabilities of such ships or aircraft owned or operated by it, that such ships and aircraft act in a manner consistent, so far as is reasonable and practicable, with this Protocol.

Article 12

Each Party undertakes to issue instructions to its maritime inspection ships and aircraft and to other appropriate services to report to its authorities any incidents or conditions in the Mediterranean Sea Area which give rise to suspicions that dumping in contravention of the provisions of this Protocol has occurred or is about to occur. That Party shall, if it considers it appropriate, report accordingly to any other Party concerned.

Article 13

Nothing in this Protocol shall affect the right of each Party to adopt other measures, in accordance with international law, to prevent pollution due to dumping.

Article 14

1. Ordinary meetings of the Parties to this Protocol shall be held in conjunction with ordinary meetings of the Contracting Parties to the Convention held pursuant to article 14 of the Convention. The Parties to this Protocol may also hold extraordinary meetings in conformity with article 14 of the Convention.

2. It shall be the function of the meetings of the Parties to this Protocol:
    (a) To keep under review the implementation of this Protocol, and to consider the efficacy of the measures adopted and the need for any other measures, in particular in the form of annexes;
    (b) To study and consider the records of the permits issued in accordance with articles 5, 6 and 7 and of the dumping which has taken place;
    (c) To review and amend as required any annex to this Protocol;
    (d) To discharge such other functions as may be appropriate for the implementation of this Protocol.

3. The adoption of amendments to the annexes to this Protocol pursuant to article 17 of the Convention shall require a three-fourths majority vote of the Parties.

Article 15

1. The provisions of the Convention relating to any protocol shall apply with respect to the present Protocol.

2. The rules of procedure and the financial rules adopted pursuant to article 18 of the Convention shall apply with respect to this Protocol, unless the Parties to this Protocol agree otherwise.

BARCELONA PROTOCOL CONCERNING CO-OPERATION IN COMBATING POLLUTION OF THE MEDITERRANEAN SEA BY OIL AND OTHER HARMFUL SUBSTANCES IN CASES OF EMERGENCY

Popular Name: Barcelona Emergency Protocol, Mediterranean Emergency Protocol

Done at Barcelona on 16 February 1976, UNTS Reg. No. 16908, UNEP Reg. p. 140, *reprinted in* 15 ILM 306 (1976), 19 IPE 9506, IELMT 976: 15.
Entry into Force: 12 February 1978

Depositary: Spain

Languages: Arabic, English, French, Spanish

Parties as of 31 August 1990: Albania; Algeria; Cyprus; Egypt; France;* Greece; Israel; Italy; Lebanon; Libyan Arab Jamahiriya; Malta; Monaco; Morocco; Spain; Syrian Arab Republic; Tunisia; Turkey; Yugoslavia; European Economic Community

PROTOCOL CONCERNING CO-OPERATION IN COMBATING POLLUTION OF THE MEDITERRANEAN SEA BY OIL AND OTHER HARMFUL SUBSTANCES IN CASES OF EMERGENCY

The Contracting Parties to the Present Protocol,

Being Parties to the Convention for the Protection of the Mediterranean Sea against Pollution,
Recognizing that grave pollution of the sea by oil and other harmful substances in the Mediterranean Sea Area involves a danger for the coastal States and the marine eco-system,
Considering that the co-operation of all the coastal States of the Mediterranean is called for to combat this pollution,
Bearing in mind the International Convention for the Prevention of Pollution from Ships, 1973, the International Convention relating to Intervention on the High Seas in Cases of Oil Pollution Casualties, 1969, as well as the Protocol relating to Intervention on the High Seas in Cases of Marine Pollution by Substances Other than Oil, 1973,
Further taking into account the International Convention on Civil Liability for Oil Pollution Damage, 1969,
HAVE AGREED AS FOLLOWS:

Article 1

The Contracting Parties to this Protocol (hereinafter referred to as "the Parties") shall co-operate in taking the necessary measures in cases of grave and

---

* With a reservation

imminent danger to the marine environment, the coast or related interests of one or more of the Parties due to the presence of massive quantities of oil or other harmful substances resulting from accidental causes or an accumulation of small discharges which are polluting or threatening to pollute the sea within the area defined in Article 1 of the Convention for the Protection of the Mediterranean Sea against Pollution (hereinafter referred to as "the Convention").

Article 2

For the purpose of this Protocol, the term "related interests" means the interests of a coastal State directly affected or threatened and concerning, among others:
- (a) activities in coastal waters, in ports or estuaries, including fishing activities;
- (b) the historical and tourist appeal of the area in question, including water sports and recreation;
- (c) the health of the coastal population;
- (d) the preservation of living resources.

Article 3

The Parties shall endeavour to maintain and promote, either individually or through bilateral or multilateral co-operation, their contingency plans and means for combating pollution of the sea by oil and other harmful substances. These means shall include, in particular, equipment, ships, aircraft and manpower prepared for operations in cases of emergency.

Article 4

The Parties shall develop and apply, either individually or through bilateral or multilateral co-operation, monitoring activities covering the Mediterranean Sea Area in order to have as precise information as possible on the situation referred to in article 1 of this Protocol.

Article 5

In the case of release or loss overboard of harmful substances in packages, freight containers, portable tanks or road and rail tank wagons, the Parties shall co-operate as far as practicable in the salvage and recovery of such substances so as to reduce the danger of pollution of the marine environment.

Article 6

1. Each Party undertakes to disseminate to the other Parties information concerning:
- (a) The competent national organization or authorities responsible for combating pollution of the sea by oil and other harmful substances;
- (b) The competent national authorities responsible for receiving reports of pollution of the sea by oil and other harmful substances and for dealing with matters concerning measures of assistance between Parties;
- (c) New ways in which pollution of the sea by oil and other harmful substances may be avoided, new measures of combating pollution and the development of research programmes.

2. Parties which have agreed to exchange information directly between themselves shall nevertheless communicate such information to the regional centre. The latter shall communicate this information to the other Parties and, on a basis of reciprocity, to coastal States of the Mediterranean Sea Area which are not Parties to this Protocol.

Article 7

The Parties undertake to co-ordinate the utilization of the means of communication at their disposal in order to ensure, with the necessary speed and reliability, the reception, transmission and dissemination of all reports and urgent information which relate to the occurrences and situations referred to in article 1. The regional centre shall have the necessary means of communication to enable it to participate in this co-ordinated effort and, in particular, to fulfil the functions assigned to it by paragraph 2 of article 10.

Article 8

1. Each Party shall issue instructions to the masters of ships flying its flag and to the pilots of aircraft registered in its territory requiring them to report by the most rapid and adequate channels in the circumstances, and in accordance with Annex I to this Protocol, either to a Party or to the regional centre:
   (a) All accidents causing or likely to cause pollution of the sea by oil or other harmful substances;
   (b) The presence, characteristics and extent of spillages of oil or other harmful substances observed at sea which are likely to present a serious and imminent threat to the marine environment or to the coast or related interests of one or more of the Parties.
2. The information collected in accordance with paragraph 1 shall be communicated to the other Parties likely to be affected by the pollution:
   (a) by the Party which has received the information, either directly or preferably, through the regional centre; or
   (b) by the regional centre.
   In case of direct communication between Parties, the regional centre shall be informed of the measures taken by these Parties.
3. In consequence of the application of the provisions of paragraph 2, the Parties are not bound by the obligation laid down in article 9, paragraph 2, of the Convention.

Article 9

1. Any Party faced with a situation of the kind defined in article 1 of this Protocol shall:
   (a) Make the necessary assessments of the nature and extent of the casualty or emergency or, as the case may be, of the type and approximate quantity of oil or other harmful substances and the direction and speed or drift of the spillage;
   (b) Take every practicable measure to avoid or reduce the effects of pollution;
   (c) Immediately inform all other Parties, either directly or through the regional centre, of these assessments and of any action which it has taken or which it intends to take to combat the pollution;
   (d) Continue to observe the situation for as long as possible and report thereon in accordance with article 8.
2. Where action is taken to combat pollution originating from a ship, all possible measures shall be taken to safeguard the persons present on board and, to the extent possible, the ship itself. Any Party which takes such action shall inform the Inter-Governmental Maritime Consultative Organization.

Article 10

1. Any Party requiring assistance for combating pollution by oil or other harmful substances polluting or threatening to pollute its coasts may call for assistance from other Parties, either directly or through the regional centre referred to in article 6,

starting with the Parties which appear likely to be affected by the pollution. This assistance may comprise, in particular, expert advice and the supply to or placing at the disposal of the Party concerned of products, equipment and nautical facilities. Parties so requested shall use their best endeavours to render this assistance.

2. Where the Parties engaged in an operation to combat pollution cannot agree on the organization of the operation, the regional centre may, with their approval, co-ordinate the activity of the facilities put into operation by these Parties.

Article 11

The application of the relevant provisions of articles 6, 7, 8, 9 and 10 of this Protocol relating to the regional centre shall be extended, as appropriate, to sub-regional centres in the event of their establishment, taking into account their objectives and functions and their relationship with the said regional centre.

Article 12

1. Ordinary meetings of the Parties to this Protocol shall be held in conjunction with ordinary meetings of the Contracting Parties to the Convention, held pursuant to article 14 of the Convention. The Parties to this Protocol may also hold extraordinary meetings as provided in article 14 of the Convention.

2. It shall be the function of the meetings of the Parties to this Protocol, in particular:

    (a)   To keep under review the implementation of this Protocol, and to consider the efficacy of the measures adopted and the need for any other measures, in particular in the form of annexes;

    (b)   To review and amend as required any annex to this Protocol;

    (c)   To discharge such other functions as may be appropriate for implementation of this Protocol.

Article 13

1. The provisions of the Convention relating to any protocol shall apply with respect to the present Protocol.

2. The rules of procedure and the financial rules adopted pursuant to article 18 of the Convention shall apply with respect to this Protocol, unless the Parties to this Protocol agree otherwise.

* * *

ATHENS PROTOCOL FOR THE PROTECTION OF THE MEDITERRANEAN SEA AGAINST POLLUTION FROM LAND-BASED SOURCES

Popular Name: Athens Protocol, Mediterranean Land-Based Sources Protocol

Done at Athens on 17 May 1980, UNTS Reg. No. 22281, UNEP Reg. p.142, *reprinted in* 19 ILM 869 (1980).
Entry into Force: 17 June 1983

Depositary: Spain

Languages: Arabic, English, French, Spanish

Parties as of 31 August 1990: Albania; Algeria; Cyprus; Egypt; France;* Greece; Italy; Libyan Arab Jamahiriya; Malta; Monaco; Morocco; Tunisia; Turkey; Yugoslavia; European Economic Community

PROTOCOL FOR THE PROTECTION OF THE MEDITERRANEAN SEA AGAINST POLLUTION FROM LAND-BASED SOURCES

The Contracting Parties to the present Protocol,
Being Parties to the Convention for the Protection of the Mediterranean Sea against Pollution, adopted at Barcelona on 16 February 1976,
Desirous of implementing article 4, paragraph 2, and articles 8 and 15 of the said Convention,
Noting the rapid increase of human activities in the Mediterranean Sea Area, particularly in the fields of industrialization and urbanization, as well as the seasonal increase in the coastal population due to tourism,
Recognizing the danger posed to the marine environment and to human health by pollution from land-based sources and the serious problems resulting therefrom in many coastal waters and river estuaries of the Mediterranean Sea, primarily due to the release of untreated, insufficiently treated or inadequately disposed domestic or industrial discharges,
Recognizing the differences in levels of development between the coastal States, and taking account of the economic and social imperatives of the developing countries,
Determined to take in close co-operation the necessary measures to protect the Mediterranean Sea against pollution from land-based sources,
Have agreed as follows:

Article 1

The Contracting Parties to this Protocol (hereinafter referred to as "the Parties") shall take all appropriate measures to prevent, abate, combat and control pollution of the Mediterranean Sea Area caused by discharges from rivers, coastal establishments or outfalls, or emanating from any other land-based sources within their territories.

Article 2

For the purposes of this Protocol:
(a) "The Convention" means the Convention for the Protection of the Mediterranean Sea against Pollution, adopted at Barcelona on 16 February 1976;
(b) "Organization" means the body referred to in article 13 of the Convention;
(c) "Freshwater limit" means the place in watercourses where, at low tides and in a period of low freshwater flow, there is an appreciable increase in salinity due to the presence of sea water.

Article 3

The area to which this Protocol applies (hereinafter referred to as the "Protocol Area") shall be:

---

* With a reservation

(a)   the Mediterranean Sea Area as defined in article 1 of the Convention;
(b)   waters on the landward side of the baselines from which the breadth of the territorial sea is measured and extending, in the case of watercourses, up to the freshwater limit;
(c)   saltwater marshes communicating with the sea.

Article 4

1. This Protocol shall apply:
(a)   to polluting discharges reaching the Protocol Area from land-based sources within the territories of the Parties, in particular:
—   directly, from outfalls discharging into the sea or through coastal disposal;
—   indirectly, through rivers, canals or other watercourses, including underground watercourses, or through run-off;
(b)   to pollution from land-based sources transported by the atmosphere, under conditions to be defined in an additional annex to this Protocol and accepted by the Parties in conformity with the provisions of article 17 of the Convention.
2. This Protocol shall also apply to polluting discharges from fixed man-made off-shore structures which are under the jurisdiction of a Party and which serve purposes other than exploration and exploitation of mineral resources of the continental shelf and the sea-bed and its sub-soil.

Article 5

1. The Parties undertake to eliminate pollution of the Protocol Area from land-based sources by substances listed in annex I to this Protocol.
2. To this end they shall elaborate and implement, jointly or individually, as appropriate, the necessary programmes and measures.
3. These programmes and measures shall include, in particular, common emission standards and standards for use.
4. The standards and the time-tables for the implementation of the programmes and measures aimed at eliminating pollution from land-based sources shall be fixed by the Parties and periodically reviewed, if necessary every two years, for each of the substances listed in annex I, in accordance with the provisions of article 15 of this Protocol.

Article 6

1. The Parties shall strictly limit pollution from land-based sources in the Protocol Area by substances or sources listed in annex II to this Protocol.
2. To this end they shall elaborate and implement, jointly or individually, as appropriate, suitable programmes and measures.
3. Discharges shall be strictly subject to the issue, by the competent national authorities, of an authorization taking due account of the provisions of annex III to this Protocol.

Article 7

1. The Parties shall progressively formulate and adopt, in co-operation with the competent international organizations, common guidelines and, as appropriate, standards or criteria dealing in particular with:
(a)   the length, depth and position of pipelines for coastal outfalls, taking into account, in particular, the methods used for pretreatment of effluents;
(b)   special requirements for effluents necessitating separate treatment;

(c)   the quality of sea water used for specific purposes that is necessary for the protection of human health, living resources and ecosystems;

(d)   the control and progressive replacement of products, installations and industrial and other processes causing significant pollution of the marine environment;

(e)   specific requirements concerning the quantities of the substances listed in annexes I and II discharged, their concentration in effluents and methods of discharging them.

2. Without prejudice to the provisions of article 5 of this Protocol, such common guidelines, standards or criteria shall take into account local ecological, geographical and physical characteristics, the economic capacity of the Parties and their need for development, the level of existing pollution and the real absorptive capacity of the marine environment.

3. The programmes and measures referred to in articles 5 and 6 shall be adopted by taking into account, for their progressive implementation, the capacity to adapt and reconvert existing installations, the economic capacity of the Parties and their need for development.

Article 8

Within the framework of the provisions of, and the monitoring programmes provided for in, article 10 of the Convention, and if necessary in co-operation with the competent international organizations, the Parties shall carry out at the earliest possible date monitoring activities in order:

(a)   systematically to assess, as far as possible, the levels of pollution along their coasts, in particular with regard to the substances or sources listed in annexes I and II, and periodically to provide information in this respect;

(b)   to evaluate the effects of measures taken under this Protocol to reduce pollution of the marine environment.

Article 9

In conformity with article 11 of the Convention, the Parties shall co-operate as far as possible in scientific and technological fields related to pollution from land-based sources, particularly research on inputs, pathways and effects of pollutants and on the development of new methods for their treatment, reduction or elimination. To this end the Parties shall, in particular, endeavour to:

(a)   exchange scientific and technical information;

(b)   co-ordinate their research programmes.

Article 10

1. The Parties shall, directly or with the assistance of competent regional or other international organizations or bilaterally, co-operate with a view to formulating and, as far as possible, implementing programmes of assistance to developing countries, particularly in the fields of science, education and technology, with a view to preventing pollution from land-based sources and its harmful effects in the marine environment.

2. Technical assistance would include, in particular, the training of scientific and technical personnel, as well as the acquisition, utilization and production by those countries of appropriate equipment on advantageous terms to be agreed upon among the Parties concerned.

Article 11

1. If discharges from a watercourse which flows through the territories of two or more Parties or forms a boundary between them are likely to cause pollution of

the marine environment of the Protocol Area, the Parties in question, respecting the provisions of this Protocol in so far as each of them is concerned, are called upon to co-operate with a view to ensuring its full application.

2. A Party shall not be responsible for any pollution originating on the territory of a non-contracting State. However, the said Party shall endeavour to co-operate with the said State so as to make possible full application of the Protocol.

Article 12

1. Taking into account article 22, paragraph 1, of the Convention, when land-based pollution originating from the territory of one Party is likely to prejudice directly the interests of one or more of the other Parties, the Parties concerned shall, at the request of one or more of them, undertake to enter into consultation with a view to seeking a satisfactory solution.

2. At the request of any Party concerned, the matter shall be placed on the agenda of the next meeting of the Parties held in accordance with article 14 of this Protocol; the meeting may make recommendations with a view to reaching a satisfactory solution.

Article 13

1. The Parties shall inform one another through the Organization of measures taken, of results achieved and, if the case arises, of difficulties encountered in the application of this Protocol. Procedures for the collection and submission of such information shall be determined at the meetings of the Parties.

2. Such information shall include, *inter alia*:
   (a)   statistical data on the authorizations granted in accordance with article 6 of this Protocol;
   (b)   data resulting from monitoring as provided for in article 8 of this Protocol;
   (c)   quantities of pollutants discharged from their territories;
   (d)   measures taken in accordance with articles 5 and 6 of this Protocol.

Article 14

1. Ordinary meetings of the Parties shall take place in conjunction with ordinary meetings of the Contracting Parties to the Convention held pursuant to article 14 of the Convention. The Parties may also hold extraordinary meetings in accordance with article 14 of the Convention.

2. The functions of the meetings of the Parties to this Protocol shall be, *inter alia*:
   (a)   to keep under review the implementation of this Protocol and to consider the efficacy of the measures adopted and the advisability of any other measures, in particular in the form of annexes;
   (b)   to revise and amend any annex to this Protocol, as appropriate;
   (c)   to formulate and adopt programmes and measures in accordance with articles 5, 6 and 15 of this Protocol;
   (d)   to adopt, in accordance with article 7 of this Protocol, common guidelines, standards or criteria, in any form decided upon by the Parties;
   (e)   to make recommendations in accordance with article 12, paragraph 2, of this Protocol;
   (f)   to consider the information submitted by the Parties under article 13 of this Protocol;
   (g)   to discharge such other functions as may be appropriate for the application of this Protocol.

Article 15

1. The meeting of the Parties shall adopt, by a two-thirds majority, the programmes and measures for the abatement of the elimination of pollution from land-based sources which are provided for in articles 5 and 6 of this Protocol.

2. The Parties which are not able to accept a programme or measures shall inform the meeting of the Parties of the action they intend to take as regards the programme or measures concerned, it being understood that these Parties may, at any time, give their consent to the programme or measures that have been adopted.

Article 16

1. The provisions of the Convention relating to any Protocol shall apply with respect to this Protocol.

2. The rules of procedure and the financial rules adopted pursuant to article 18 of the Convention shall apply with respect to this Protocol, unless the Parties to this Protocol agree otherwise.

3. This Protocol shall be open for signature, at Athens from 17 May 1980 to 16 June 1980, and at Madrid from 17 June 1980 to 16 May 1981, by any State invited to the Conference of Plenipotentiaries of the Coastal States of the Mediterranean Region for the Protection of the Mediterranean Sea against Pollution from Land-Based Sources held at Athens from 12 May to 17 May 1980. It shall also be open until the same dates for signature by the European Economic Community and by any similar regional economic grouping of which at least one member is a coastal State of the Mediterranean Sea Area and which exercises competence in fields covered by this Protocol.

4. This Protocol shall be subject to ratification, acceptance or approval. Instruments of ratification, acceptance or approval shall be deposited with the Government of Spain, which will assume the functions of Depositary.

5. As from 17 May 1981, this Protocol shall be open for accession by the States referred to in paragraph 3 above, by the European Economic Community and by any grouping referred to in that paragraph.

6. This Protocol shall enter into force on the thirtieth day following the deposit of at least six instruments of ratification, acceptance or approval of, or accession to, the Protocol by the Parties referred to in paragraph 3 of this article.

* * *

GENEVA PROTOCOL CONCERNING MEDITERRANEAN SPECIALLY PROTECTED AREAS

Popular Name: Geneval Protocol, Mediterranean Specially Protected Areas Protocol

Done at Geneva on 3 April 1982, UNTS Reg. No. 24079
Entry into Force: 23 March 1986

Depositary: Spain

Languages: Arabic, English, French, Spanish

Parties as of 31 August 1990: Albania; Algeria; Cyprus; Egypt; France;* Greece; Israel;* Italy; Libyan Arab Jamahiriya; Malta; Monaco;* Morocco; Spain; Tunisia;* Turkey;* Yugoslavia; European Economic Community

PROTOCOL CONCERNING MEDITERRANEAN SPECIALLY PROTECTED AREAS

The Contracting Parties to the present Protocol,

* * *

Stressing the importance of protecting and, as appropriate, improving the state of the natural resources and natural sites of the Mediterranean Sea, as well as of their cultural heritage in the region, among other means by the establishment of specially protected areas including marine areas and their environment,

* * *

Have agreed as follows:

Article 1

1. The Contracting Parties to this Protocol (hereinafter referred to as "the Parties") shall take all appropriate measures with a view to protecting those marine areas which are important for the safeguard of the natural resources and natural sites of the Mediterranean Sea Area, as well as for the safeguard of their cultural heritage in the region.

2. Nothing in this Protocol shall prejudice the codification and development of the law of the sea by the United Nations Conference on the Law of the Sea convened pursuant to resolution 2750 C (XXV) of the General Assembly of the United Nations, nor the present or future claims and legal views of any State concerning the law of the sea and the nature and extent of coastal and flag State jurisdiction.

Article 2

For the purposes of the designation of specially protected areas (hereinafter referred to as "protected areas"), the area to which this Protocol applies shall be the Mediterranean Sea Area as defined in article 1 of the Convention for the Protection of the Mediterranean Sea against Pollution (hereinafter referred to as "the Convention"); it being understood that, for the purposes of the present Protocol, it shall be limited to the territorial waters of the Parties and may include waters on the landward side of the baseline from which the breadth of the territorial sea is measured and extending, in the case of watercourses, up to the freshwater limit. It may also include wetlands or coastal areas designated by each of the Parties.

Article 3

1. The Parties shall, to the extent possible, establish protected areas and shall endeavour to undertake the action necessary in order to protect those areas and, as appropriate, restore them, as rapidly as possible.

---

* With a reservation or declaration

2. Such areas shall be established in order to safeguard in particular:

a)   —sites of biological and ecological value;
       —the genetic diversity, as well as satisfactory population levels, of species, and their breeding grounds and habitats;
       —representative types of ecosystems, as well as ecological processes;

b)   sites of particular importance because of their scientific, aesthetic, historical, archeological, cultural or educational interest.

Article 4

The Parties to this Protocol shall, at their first meeting, formulate and adopt, if necessary in co-operation with the competent international organizations, common guidelines and, if needed, standards or criteria dealing in particular with:

a)   the selection of protected areas;
b)   the establishment of protected areas;
c)   the management of protected areas;
d)   the notification of information on protected areas.

Article 5

The Parties may strengthen the protection of a protected area by establishing, within the area to which this Protocol applies, one or more buffer areas in which activities are less severely restricted while remaining compatible with the purposes of the protected area.

Article 6

1. If a Party intends to establish a protected area contiguous to the frontier or to the limits of the zone of national jurisdiction of another Party, the competent authorities of the two Parties shall endeavour to consult each other with a view to reaching agreement on the measures to be taken and shall, among other things, examine the possibility of the establishment by the other Party of a corresponding protected area or the adoption by it of any other appropriate measure.

2. If a Party intends to establish a protected area contiguous to the frontier or to the limits of the zone of national jurisdiction of a State which is not a party to this Protocol, the Party shall endeavour to work together with the competent authorities of that State with a view to holding the consultations referred to in the preceding paragraph.

3. If contiguous protected areas are established by two Parties, or by one Party and by a State which is not a party to this Protocol, special agreements may provide for the means whereby the consultation or the collaboration contemplated in paragraphs 1 and 2 respectively may take place.

4. If a State which is not a party to this Protocol intends to establish a protected area contiguous to the frontier or to the limits of the zone of national jurisdiction of a Party to this Protocol, the latter shall endeavour to work together with that State with a view to holding consultations, and possibly concluding a special agreement as referred to in paragraph 3.

Article 7

The Parties, having regard to the objectives pursued and taking into account the characteristics of each protected area, shall, in conformity with the rules of international law, progressively take the measures required, which may include:

a)   the organization of a planning and management system;
b)   the prohibition of the dumping or discharge of wastes or other matter which may impair the protected area;

c)   the regulation of the passage of ships and any stopping or anchoring;
d)   the regulation of fishing and hunting and of the capture of animals and harvesting of plants;
e)   the prohibition of the destruction of plant life or animals and of the introduction of exotic species;
f)   the regulation of any act likely to harm or disturb the fauna or flora, including the introduction of indigenous zoological or botanical species;
g)   the regulation of any activity involving the exploration or exploitation of the sea-bed or its subsoil or a modification of the sea-bed profile;
h)   the regulation of any activity involving a modification of the profile of the soil or the exploitation of the subsoil of the land part of a marine protected area;
i)   the regulation of any archaeological activity and of the removal of any object which may be considered as an archaeological object;
j)   the regulation of trade in and import and export of animals, parts of animals, plants, parts of plants and archaeological objects which originate in protected areas and are subject to measures of protection;
k)   any other measure aimed at safeguarding ecological and biological processes in protected areas.

Article 8

1. The Parties shall give appropriate publicity to the establishment of protected areas, as well as of the areas provided for in article 5, and to their markings and the regulations applying thereto.
2. The information referred to in the preceding paragraph shall be notified to the Organization designated in article 13 of the Convention (hereinafter referred to as "the Organization") which shall compile and keep up to date a directory of protected areas in the area to which this Protocol applies. The Parties shall supply the Organization with all the information necessary for that purpose.

Article 9

1. The Parties shall, in promulgating protective measures, take into account the traditional activities of their local populations. To the fullest extent possible, no exemption which is allowed for this reason shall be such as:
a)   to endanger either the maintenance of ecosystems protected under the terms of the present Protocol or the biological processes contributing to the maintenance of those ecosystems;
b)   to cause either the extinction of, or any substantial reduction in, the number of individuals making up the species or animal and plant populations within the protected ecosystems, or any ecologically connected species or populations, particularly migratory species and rare, endangered or endemic species.
2. Parties which allow exemptions with regard to protective measures or do not apply such measures strictly shall inform the Organization accordingly.

Article 10

The Parties shall encourage and develop scientific and technical research on their protected areas and on the ecosystems and archaeological heritage of those areas.

Article 11

The Parties shall endeavour to inform the public as widely as possible of the significance and interest of the protected areas and of the scientific knowledge which may be gained from them from the point of view of both nature conservation and archaeology. Such information should have an appropriate place in education programmes concerning the environment and history. The Parties should also endeavour to promote the participation of their public and their nature conservation organizations in appropriate measures which are necessary for the protection of the areas concerned.

Article 12

The Parties shall, to the extent possible, establish a co-operation programme to co-ordinate the establishment, planning, management and conservation of protected areas, with a view to creating a network of protected areas in the Mediterranean region, taking fully into account existing networks, especially that of biosphere reserves of UNESCO. There shall be regular exchanges of information concerning the characteristics of the protected areas, the experience acquired and the problems encountered.

Article 13

The Parties shall, in accordance with the procedures set forth in article 14, exchange scientific and technical information concerning current or planned research and the results expected. They shall, to the fullest extent possible, co-ordinate their research. They shall, moreover, endeavour to define jointly or to standardize the scientific methods to be applied in the selection, management and monitoring of protected areas.

Article 14

1. In applying the principles of co-operation set forth in articles 12 and 13, the Parties shall forward to the Organization:
   a)   comparable information for monitoring the biological development of the Mediterranean environment;
   b)   reports, publications and information of a scientific, administrative and legal nature, in particular:
      — on the measures taken by the Parties in pursuance of this Protocol for the protection of the protected areas;
      — on the species present in the protected areas;
      — on any threats to those areas, especially those which may come from sources of pollution outside their control.

2. The Parties shall designate persons responsible for protected areas. Those persons shall meet at least once every two years to discuss matters of joint interest and especially to propose recommendations concerning scientific, administrative and legal information as well as the standardization and processing of data.

Article 15

1. The Parties shall, directly or with the assistance of competent regional or other international organizations or bilaterally, co-operate, on the entry into force of this Protocol, in formulating and implementing programmes of mutual assistance and of assistance to those developing countries which express a need for it in the selection, establishment and management of protected areas.

2. The programmes contemplated in the preceding paragraph should relate, in particular, to the training of scientific and technical personnel, scientific research, and the acquisition, utilization and production by those countries of appropriate equipment on advantageous terms to be agreed among the Parties concerned.

Article 16

Changes in the delimitation or legal status of a protected area or the suppression of all or part of such an area may not take place except under a similar procedure to that followed for its establishment.

Article 17

1. The ordinary meetings of the Parties to this Protocol shall be held in conjunction with the ordinary meetings of the Contracting Parties to the Convention held pursuant to article 14 of the Convention. The Parties may also hold extraordinary meetings in conformity with that article.

2. It shall be the function of the meetings of the Parties to this Protocol, in particular:

a)   to keep under review the implementation of this Protocol;

b)   to consider the efficacy of the measures adopted, having regard in particular to the area to which the Protocol applies, and to examine the need for other measures, in particular in the form of annexes, or for envisaging, if necessary, an alteration to that area, in conformity with the provisions of article 16 of the Convention;

c)   to adopt, review and amend as required any annex to this Protocol;

d)   to monitor the establishment and development of the network of protected areas provided by article 12, and to adopt guidelines to facilitate the establishment and development of that system and to increase co-operation among the Parties;

e)   to consider the recommendations made by the meetings of the persons responsible for the protected areas, as provided by article 14, paragraph 2;

f)   to consider reports transmitted by the Parties to the Organization under article 20 of the Convention and any other information which the Parties may transmit to the Organization or to the meeting of the Parties.

Article 18

1. The provisions of the Convention relating to any protocol shall apply with respect to the present Protocol.

2. The rules of procedure and the financial rules adopted pursuant to article 18, paragraph 2, of the Convention shall apply with respect to this Protocol, unless the Parties to this Protocol agree otherwise.

3. This Protocol shall be open for signature, at Geneva on 3 and 4 April 1982, and at Madrid from 5 April 1982 to 2 April 1983 by any Contracting Party to the Convention and any State invited to the Conference of Plenipotentiaries on the Protocol concerning Mediterranean Specially Protected Areas held at Geneva on 2 and 3 April 1982. It shall also be open for signature from 5 April 1982 to 2 April 1983 by any regional economic grouping of which at least one member is a coastal State of the Mediterranean Sea Area and which exercises competence in fields covered by this Protocol.

4. This Protocol shall be subject to ratification, acceptance or approval. Instruments of ratification, acceptance or approval shall be deposited with the Government of Spain, which will assume the functions of Depositary.

5. As from 3 April 1983, this Protocol shall be open for accession by the Contracting Parties to the Convention and by any State or grouping referred to in paragraph 3.

6. This Protocol shall enter into force on the thirtieth day following the deposit of at least six instruments of ratification, acceptance or approval of, or accession to, the Protocol.

* * *

CHAPTER 5
FRESH WATERS

A. GENERAL

Editors' Introductory Note Regarding the International Law Association's Helsinki and Seoul Rules

The International Law Association (ILA), founded in 1873, is a private membership association with approximately 4000 members worldwide that studies and advances international law. Headquartered in London, it has branches in about 40 countries. It has consultative status, as a non-governmental organization, with several U.N. agencies and bodies.

The ILA's Helsinki Rules on International Watercourses, adopted in 1966 together with an extensive commentary, have been very influential in shaping approaches to the sharing, management, and protection of international watercourses. The Helsinki Rules are not in the form of an international agreement, but they are often referred to as stating customary international law. Among other things, the Helsinki Rules have helped promote treating the entire drainage basin as an integrated whole, including surface and ground waters. The ILA adopted a short set of rules regarding ground waters in 1986 at Seoul, again accompanied by in-depth comments.

INTERNATIONAL LAW ASSOCIATION HELSINKI RULES ON THE USES OF THE WATERS OF INTERNATIONAL RIVERS

Popular Name: Helsinki Rules

Done at Helsinki on 20 August 1966, *in* I.L.A., Report of the Fifty-Second Conference 484 (1967), *reprinted in* 11 IPE 5741.

Language: English

THE HELSINKI RULES

CHAPTER 1
GENERAL

Article I

The general rules of international law as set forth in these chapters are applicable to the use of the waters of an international drainage basin except as may be provided otherwise by convention, agreement or binding custom among the basin States.

Article II

An international drainage basin is a geographical area extending over two or more States determined by the watershed limits of the system of waters, including surface and underground waters, flowing into a common terminus.

Article III

A "basin State" is a state the territory of which includes a portion of an international drainage basin.

CHAPTER 2
EQUITABLE UTILIZATION OF THE WATERS OF AN INTERNATIONAL DRAINAGE BASIN

Article IV

Each basin State is entitled, within its territory, to a reasonable and equitable share in the beneficial uses of the waters of an international drainage basin.

Article V

(1) What is a reasonable and equitable share within the meaning of Article IV is to be determined in the light of all the relevant factors in each particular case.

(2) Relevant factors which are to be considered include, but are not limited to:

(a) the geography of the basin, including in particular the extent of the drainage area in the territory of each basin State;

(b) the hydrology of the basin, including in particular the contribution of water by each basin State;

(c) the climate affecting the basin;

(d) the past utilization of the waters of the basin, including in particular existing utilization;

(e) the economic and social needs of each basin State;

(f) the population dependent on the waters of the basin in each basin State;

(g) the comparative costs of alternative means of satisfying the economic and social needs of each basin State;

(h) the availability of other resources;

(i) the avoidance of unnecessary waste in the utilization of waters of the basin;

(j)   the practicability of compensation to one or more of the co-basin States as a means of adjusting conflicts among uses; and

(k)   the degree to which the needs of a basin State may be satisfied, without causing substantial injury to a co-basin State;

(3) The weight to be given to each factor is to be determined by its importance in comparison with that of other relevant factors. In determining what is a reasonable and equitable share, all relevant factors are to be considered together and a conclusion reached on the basis of the whole.

Article VI

A use or category of uses is not entitled to any inherent preference over any other use or category of uses.

Article VII

A basin State may not be denied the present reasonable use of the waters of an international drainage basin to reserve for a co-basin State a future use of such waters.

Article VIII

1. An existing reasoanble use may continue in operation unless the factors justifying its continuance are outweighed by other factors leading to the conclusion that it be modified or terminated so as to accommodate a competing incompatible use.

2. (a) A use that is in fact operational is deemed to have been an existing use from the time of the initiation of construction directly related to the use or, where such construction is not required, the undertaking of comparable acts of actual implementation.

(b) Such a use continues to be an existing use until such time as it is discontinued with the intention that it be abandoned.

3. A use will not be deemed an existing use if at the time of becoming operational it is incompatible with an already existing reasonable use.

CHAPTER 3
POLLUTION

Article IX

As used in this Chapter, the term "water pollution" refers to any detrimental change resulting from human conduct in the natural composition, content, or quality of the waters of an international drainage basin.

Article X

1. Consistent with the principle of equitable utilization of the waters of an international drainage basin, a State

(a)   must prevent any new form of water pollution or any increase in the degree of existing water pollution in an international drainage basin which would cause substantial injury in the territory of a co-basin State, and

(b)   should take all reasonable measures to abate existing water pollution in an international drainage basin to such an extent that no substantial damage is caused in the territory of a co-basin State.

2. The rule stated in paragraph 1 of this Article applies to water pollution originating:

(a)   within a territory of the State, or
(b)   outside the territory of the State, if it is caused by the State's conduct.

Article XI

1. In the case of a violation of the rule stated in paragraph 1(a) of Article X of this Chapter, the State responsible shall be required to cease the wrongful conduct and compensate the injured co-basin State for the injury that has been caused to it.

2. In a case falling under the rule stated in paragraph 1(b) of Article X, if a State fails to take reasonable measures, it shall be required promptly to enter into negotiations with the injured State with a view toward reaching a settlement equitable under the circumstances.

CHAPTER 4
NAVIGATION

Article XII

1. This Chapter refers to those rivers and lakes portions of which are both navigable and separate or traverse the territories of two or more States.

2. Rivers or lakes are "navigable" if in their natural or canalized state they are currently used for commercial navigation or are capable by reason of their natural condition of being so used.

3. In this Chapter the term "riparian State" refers to a State through or along which the navigable portion of a river flows or a lake lies.

Article XIII

Subject to any limitations or qualifications referred to in these Chapters, each riparian State is entitled to enjoy rights of free navigation on the entire course of a river or lake.

Article XIV

"Free navigation", as the term is used in this Chapter, includes the following freedom for vessels of a riparian State on a basis of equality:
(a)   freedom of movement on the entire navigable course of the river or lake;
(b)   freedom to enter ports and to make use of plants and docks; and
(c)   freedom to transport goods and passengers, either directly or through trans-shipment, between the territory of one riparian State and the territory of another riparian State and between the territory of a riparian State and the open sea.

Article XV

A riparian State may exercise rights of police, including but not limited to the protection of public safety and health, over that portion of the river or lake subject to its jurisdiction, provided the exercise of such rights does not unreasonably interfere with the enjoyment of the rights of free navigation defined in Articles XIII and XIV.

Article XVI

Each riparian State may restrict or prohibit the loading by vessels of a foreign State of goods and passengers in its territory for discharge in such territory.

Article XVII

A riparian State may grant rights of navigation to non-riparian States on rivers or lakes within its territory.

Article XVIII

Each riparian State is, to the extent of the means available or made available to it, required to maintain in good order that portion of the navigable course of a river or lake within its jurisdiction.

Article XIX

The rules stated in this Chapter are not applicable to the navigation of vessels of war or of vessels performing police or administrative functions, or, in general, exercising any other form of public authority.

Article XX

In time of war, other armed conflict, or public emergency constituting a threat to the life of the State, a riparian State may take measures derogating from its obligations under this Chapter to the extent strictly required by the exigencies of the situation, provided that such measures are not inconsistent with its other obligations under international law. The riparian State shall in any case facilitate navigation for humanitarian purposes.

CHAPTER 5
TIMBER FLOATING

Article XXI

The floating of timber on a watercourse which flows through or between the territories of two or more States is governed by the following Articles except in cases in which floating is governed by rules of navigation according to applicable law or custom binding upon the riparians.

Article XXII

The States riparian to an international watercourse utilized for navigation may determine by common consent whether and under what conditions timber floating may be permitted upon the watercourse.

Article XXIII

1. It is recommended that each State riparian to an international watercourse not used for navigation should, with due regard to other uses of the watercourse, authorise the co-riparian States to use the watercourse and its banks within the territory of each riparian State for the floating of timber.

2. This authorization should extend to all necessary work along the banks by the floating crew and to the installation of such facilities as may be required for the timber floating.

Article XXIV

If a riparian State requires permanent installation for floating inside a territory of a co-riparian State or if it is necessary to regulate the flow of the watercourse, all questions connected with these installations and measures should be determined by agreement between the States concerned.

Article XXV

Co-riparian States of a watercourse which is, or is to be used for floating timber should negotiate in order to come to an agreement governing the administrative regime of floating, and if necessary to establish a joint agency or commission in order to facilitate the regulation of floating in all aspects.

CHAPTER 6
PROCEDURES FOR THE PREVENTION AND SETTLEMENT OF DISPUTES

Article XXVI

This Chapter relates to procedures for the prevention and settlement of international disputes as to the legal rights or other interests of basin States and of other States in the waters of an international drainage basin.

Article XXVII

1. Consistently with the Charter of the United Nations, States are under an obligation to settle international disputes as to their legal rights or other interests by peaceful means in such a manner that international peace and security, and justice are not endangered.

2. It is recommended that States resort progressively to the means of prevention and settlement of disputes stipulated in Articles XXIX to XXXIV of this Chapter.

Article XXVIII

1. States are under a primary obligation to resort to means of prevention and settlement of disputes stipulated in the applicable treaties binding upon them.

2. States are limited to the means of prevention and settlement of disputes stipulated in treaties binding upon them only to the extent provided by the applicable treaties.

Article XXIX

1. With a view to preventing disputes from arising between basin States as to their legal rights or other interests, it is recommended that each basin State furnish relevant and reasonably available information to the other basin States concerning the waters of a drainage basin within its territory and its use of, and activities with respect to such waters.

2. A State, regardless of its location in a drainage basin, should in particular furnish to any other basin State, the interests of which may be substantially affected, notice of any proposed construction or installation which would alter the regime of the basin in a way which might give rise to a dispute as defined in Article XXVI. The notice should include such essential facts as will permit the recipient to make an assessment of the probable effect of the proposed alteration.

3. A State providing the notice referred to in paragraph 2 of this Article should afford to the recipient a reasonable period of time to make an assessment of the probable effect of the proposed construction or installation and to submit its views thereon to the State furnishing the notice.

4. If a State has failed to give the notice referred to in paragraph 2 of this Article, the alteration by the State in the regime of the drainage basin shall not be given the weight normally accorded to temporal priority in use in the event of a determination of what is a reasonable and equitable share of the waters of the basin.

Article XXX

In case of a dispute between States as to their legal rights or other interests, as defined in Article XXVI, they should seek a solution by negotiation.

Article XXXI

1. If a question or dispute arises which relates to the present or future utilization of the waters of an international drainage basin, it is recommended that the basin States refer the question or dispute to a joint agency and that they request the agency to survey the international drainage basin and to formulate plans or recommendations for the fullest and most efficient use thereof in the interests of all such States.

2. It is recommended that the joint agency be instructed to submit reports on all matters within its competence to the appropriate authorities of the member States concerned.

3. It is recommended that the member States of the joint agency in appropriate cases invite non-basin States which by treaty enjoy a right in the use of the waters an [sic] an international drainage basin to associate themselves with the work of the joint agency or that they be permitted to appear before the agency.

Article XXXII

If a question or a dispute is one which is considered by the States concerned to be incapable of resolution in the manner set forth in Article XXXI, it is recommended that they seek the good offices, or jointly request the mediation of a third State, of a qualified international organisation or of a qualified person.

Article XXXIII

1. If the States concerned have not been able to resolve their dispute through negotiation or have been unable to agree on the measures described in Article XXXI and XXXII, it is recommended that they form a commission of inquiry or an ad hoc conciliation commission, which shall endeavour to find a solution, likely to be accepted by the States concerned, of any dispute as to their legal rights.

2. It is recommended that the conciliation commission be constituted in the manner set forth in the Annex.

Article XXXIV

It is recommended that the States concerned agree to submit their legal disputes to an *ad hoc* arbitral tribunal, to a permanent arbitral tribunal or to the International Court of Justice if:

(a) A commission has not been formed as provided in Article XXXIII, or

(b) The commission has not been able to find a solution to be recommended, or

(c) A solution recommended has not been accepted by the States concerned, and

(d) An agreement has not been otherwise arrived at.

Article XXXV

It is recommended that in the event of arbitration the States concerned have recourse to the Model Rules on Arbitral Procedure prepared by the International Law Commission of the United Nations at its tenth session in 1958.

Article XXXVI

Recourse to arbitration implies the undertaking by the States concerned to consider the award to be given as final and to submit in good faith to its execution.

Article XXXVII

The means of settlement referred to in the preceding Articles of this Chapter are without prejudice to the utilization of means of settlement recommended to, or required of, members of regional arrangements or agencies and of other international organizations.

ANNEX
MODEL RULES FOR THE CONSTITUTION OF THE CONCILIATION COMMISSION FOR THE SETTLEMENT OF A DISPUTE
(In implementation of Article XXXIII of Chapter 6)

Article I

The members of the Commission, including the President, shall be appointed by the States concerned.

Article II

If the States concerned cannot agree on these appointments, each State shall appoint two members. The members thus appointed shall choose one more member who shall be the President of the Commission. If the appointed members do not agree, the member-president shall be appointed, at the request of any State concerned, by the President of the International Court of Justice, or, if he does not make the appointment, by the Secretary-General of the United Nations.

Article III

The membership of the Commission should include persons who, by reason or their special competence, are qualified to deal with disputes concerning international drainage basins.

Article IV

If a member of the Commission abstains from performing his office or is unable to discharge his responsibilities, he shall be replaced by the procedure set out in Article I or Article II of this Annex, according to the manner in which he was originally appointed. If, in the case of—
  (1)   a member originally appointed under Article I, the States fail to agree as to a replacement; or
  (2)   a member originally appointed under Article II, the State involved fails to replace the member;
a replacement shall be chosen, at the request of any State concerned, by the President of the International Court of Justice or, if he does not choose the replacement, by the Secretary-General of the United Nations.

Article V

In the absence of agreement to the contrary between the parties, the Conciliation Commission shall determine the place of its meetings and shall lay down its own procedure.

INTERNATIONAL LAW ASSOCIATION SEOUL RULES ON INTERNATIONAL GROUNDWATERS

Popular Name: Seoul Groundwater Rules, Seoul Rules

Done at Seoul on 30 August 1986, I.L.A., Report of the Sixty-Second Conference 251 (1987).

Language: English

Copyright 1987 by the International Law Association. Reprinted with permission from the International Law Association

Rules on International Groundwaters

Article 1
THE WATERS OF INTERNATIONAL AQUIFERS*

The waters of an aquifer that is intersected by the boundary between two or more States are international groundwaters and such an aquifer with its waters forms an international basin or part thereof. Those States are basin States within the meaning of the Helsinki Rules whether or not the aquifer and its waters form with surface waters part of a hydraulic system flowing into a common terminus.

*The term 'aquifer' as here employed comprehends all underground water bearing strata capable of yielding water on a practicable basis, whether these are in other instruments or contexts called by another name such as "groundwater reservoir", "groundwater catchment area," etc. including the waters in fissured or fractured rock formations and the structures containing deep, so-called "fossil waters".

Article 2
HYDRAULIC INTERDEPENDENCE

1. An aquifer that contributes water to, or receives water from, surface waters of an international basin constitutes part of that international basin for the purposes of the Helsinki Rules.
2. An aquifer intersected by the boundary between two or more States that does not contribute water to, or receive water from, surface waters of an international drainage basin constitutes an international drainage basin for the purpose of the Helsinki Rules.
3. Basin States, in exercising their rights and performing their duties under international law, shall take into account any interdependence of the groundwater and other waters, including any interconnections between aquifers, and any leaching into aquifers caused by activities in areas under their jurisdiction.

Article 3
PROTECTION OF GROUNDWATER

1. Basin States shall prevent or abate the pollution of international groundwaters in accordance with international law applicable to existing, new, increased and highly dangerous pollution. Special consideration shall be given to the long-term effects of the pollution of groundwater.
2. Basin States shall consult and exchange relevant available information and data at the request of any one of them
   (a)   for the purpose of preserving the groundwaters of the basin from degradation and protecting from impairment the geologic structure of the aquifers, including recharge areas;
   (b)   for the purpose of considering joint or parallel quality standards and environmental protection measures applicable to international groundwaters and their aquifers.
3. Basin States shall co-operate, at the request of any one of them, for the purpose of collecting and analyzing additional needed information and data pertinent to the international groundwaters or their aquifers.

Article 4
GROUNDWATER MANAGEMENT AND SURFACE WATERS

Basin States should consider the integrated management, including conjunctive use with surface waters, of their international groundwaters at the request of any one of them.

INTERNATIONAL LAW COMMISSION DRAFT ARTICLES ON THE LAW OF NON-NAVIGATIONAL USES OF INTERNATIONAL WATERCOURSES

Popular Name: ILC Draft Rules on Watercourses

July 1991, Report of the International Law Commission on the Work of its Forth-Third Session, 46 U.N. GAOR Supp. (No. 10) at 161, U.N. Doc. A/46/10 (1991).

Languages: Arabic, Chinese, English, French, Russian, Spanish

Editors' Note

The U.N. International Law Commission (ILC) is a U.N. organ composed of 35 individuals nominated by their governments in a process designed to achieve geographic representation. Members are elected for five-year terms. The Commission, which meets annually, is charged with the codification and progressive development of international law. It selects topics for study in consultation with the U.N. General Assembly, and then appoints a member as the topic's special rapporteur to direct the study. The ILC's reports are reviewed annually by the Sixth (Law) Committee of the General Assembly.

The ILC included the topic "The law of the non-navigational uses of international watercourses" on its work program in 1971. Since 1974, when the ILC appointed the topic's first special rapporteur, there have been four special rapporteurs: Richard Kearney, 1974-76 (U.S.); Stephen Schwebel, 1977-81 (U.S.); Jens

Evensen, 1982-84 (Norway); and Stephen McCaffrey, 1985-present (U.S.). Because the interests of upstream and downstream states are typically diametrically opposed, this topic has been one of the most politically contentious undertaken by the ILC in its approximately 45 years of existence. That three of the topic's four special rapporteurs have been from the United States reflects the fact that the United States is almost equally an upstream and a downstream State.

In 1991, the ILC approved a complete set of draft articles (reproduced below). The closing date for comments on the draft articles is 1 January 1993. Of particular interest regarding the environment is the interaction of draft Articles 5 (equitable and reasonable utilization) and 7 (obligation not to cause appreciable harm): can a use that causes appreciable harm to another State nevertheless be equitable and reasonable? The ILC recently concluded that a harmful use cannot be equitable and reasonable, although some accommodation may be required.

THE LAW OF THE NON-NAVIGATIONAL USES OF INTERNATIONAL WATERCOURSES

PART I
INTRODUCTION

Article 1
Scope of the present articles

1. The present articles apply to uses of international watercourses and of their waters for purposes other than navigation and to measures of conservation related to the uses of those watercourses and their waters.

2. The use of international watercourses for navigation is not within the scope of the present articles except in so far as other uses affect navigation or are affected by navigation.

Article 2
Use of terms

For the purposes of the present articles:
(a)   "international watercourse" means a watercourse, parts of which are situated in different States;
(b)   "watercourse" means a system of surface and underground waters constituting by virtue of their physical relationship a unitary whole and flowing into a common terminus;
(c)   "watercourse State" means a State in whose territory part of an international watercourse is situated.

Article 3
Watercourse agreements

1. Watercourse States may enter into one or more agreements, hereinafter referred to as "watercourse agreements", which apply and adjust the provisions of the present articles to the characteristics and uses of a particular international watercourse or part thereof.

2. Where a watercourse agreement is concluded between two or more watercourse States, it shall define the waters to which it applies. Such an agreement may be entered into with respect to an entire international watercourse or with respect

to any part thereof or a particular project, programme or use, provided that the agreement does not adversely affect, to an appreciable extent, the use by one or more other watercourse States of the waters of the watercourse.

3. Where a watercourse State considers that adjustment or application of the provisions of the present articles is required because of the characteristics and uses of a particular international watercourse, watercourse States shall consult with a view to negotiating in good faith for the purpose of concluding a watercourse agreement or agreements.

Article 4
Parties to watercourse agreements

1. Every watercourse State is entitled to participate in the negotiation of and to become a party to any watercourse agreement that applies to the entire international watercourse, as well as to participate in any relevant consultations.

2. A watercourse State whose use of an international watercourse may be affected to an appreciable extent by the implementation of a proposed watercourse agreement that applies only to a part of the watercourse or to a particular project, programme or use is entitled to participate in consultations on, and in the negotiation of, such an agreement, to the extent that its use is thereby affected, and to become a party thereto.

PART II
GENERAL PRINCIPLES

Article 5
Equitable and reasonable utilization and participation

1. Watercourse States shall in their respective territories utilize an international watercourse in an equitable and reasonable manner. In particular, an international watercourse shall be used and developed by watercourse States with a view to attaining optimal utilization thereof and benefits therefrom consistent with adequate protection of the watercourse.

2. Watercourse States shall participate in the use, development and protection of an international watercourse in an equitable and reasonable manner. Such participation includes both the right to utilize the watercourse and the duty to cooperate in the protection and development thereof, as provided in the present articles.

Article 6
Factors relevant to equitable and reasonable utilization

1. Utilization of an international watercourse in an equitable and reasonable manner within the meaning of article 5 requires taking into account all relevant factors and circumstances, including:
   (a) geographic, hydrographic, hydrological, climatic, ecological and other factors of a natural character;
   (b) the social and economic needs of the watercourse States concerned;
   (c) the effects of the use or uses of the watercourse in one watercourse State on other watercourse States;
   (d) existing and potential uses of the watercourse;
   (e) conservation, protection, development and economy of use of the water resources of the watercourse and the costs of measures taken to that effect;

(f)   the availability of alternatives, of corresponding value, to a particular planned or existing use.

2. In the application of article 5 or paragraph 1 of this article, watercourse States concerned shall, when the need arises, enter into consultations in a spirit of cooperation.

Article 7
Obligation not to cause appreciable harm

Watercourse States shall utilize an international watercourse in such a way as not to cause appreciable harm to other watercourse States.

Article 8
General obligation to cooperate

Watercourse States shall cooperate on the basis of sovereign equality, territorial integrity and mutual benefit in order to attain optimal utilization and adequate protection of an international watercourse.

Article 9
Regular exchange of data and information

1. Pursuant to article 8, watercourse States shall on a regular basis exchange reasonably available data and information on the condition of the watercourse, in particular that of a hydrological, meteorological, hydrogeological and ecological nature, as well as related forecasts.

2. If a watercourse State is requested by another watercourse State to provide data or information that is not reasonably available, it shall employ its best efforts to comply with the request but may condition its compliance upon payment by the requesting State of the reasonable costs of collecting and, where appropriate, processing such data or information.

3. Watercourse States shall employ their best efforts to collect and, where appropriate, to process data and information in a manner which facilitates its utilization by the other watercourse States to which it is communicated.

Article 10
Relationship between uses

1. In the absence of agreement or custom to the contrary, no use of an international watercourse enjoys inherent priority over other uses.

2. In the event of a conflict between uses of an international watercourse, it shall be resolved with reference to the principles and factors set out in articles 5 to 7, with special regard being given to the requirements of vital human needs.

PART III
PLANNED MEASURES

Article 11
Information concerning planned measures

Watercourse States shall exchange information and consult each other on the possible effects of planned measures on the condition of an international watercourse.

Article 12
Notification concerning planned measures with possible adverse effects

Before a watercourse State implements or permits the implementation of planned measures which may have an appreciable adverse effect upon other watercourse States, it shall provide those States with timely notification thereof. Such notification shall be accompanied by available technical data and information in order to enable the notified States to evaluate the possible effects of the planned measures.

Article 13
Period for reply to notification

Unless otherwise agreed, a watercourse State providing a notification under article 12 shall allow the notified States a period of six months within which to study and evaluate the possible effects of the planned measures and to communicate their findings to it.

Article 14
Obligations of the notifying State during the period for reply

During the period referred to in article 13, the notifying State shall cooperate with the notified States by providing them, on request, with any additional data and information that is available and necessary for an accurate evaluation, and shall not implement or permit the implementation of the planned measures without the consent of the notified States.

Article 15
Reply to notification

1. The notified States shall communicate their findings to the notifying State as early as possible.
2. If a notified State finds that implementation of the planned measures would be inconsistent with the provisions of articles 5 or 7, it shall communicate this finding to the notifying State within the period referred to in article 13, together with a documented explanation setting forth the reasons for the finding.

Article 16
Absence of reply to notification

If, within the period referred to in article 13, the notifying State receives no communication under paragraph 2 of article 15, it may, subject to its obligations under articles 5 and 7, proceed with the implementation of the planned measures, in accordance with the notification and any other data and information provided to the notified States.

Article 17
Consultations and negotiations concerning planned measures

1. If a communication is made under paragraph 2 of article 15, the notifying State and the State making the communication shall enter into consultations and negotiations with a view to arriving at an equitable resolution of the situation.
2. The consultations and negotiations shall be conducted on the basis that each State must in good faith pay reasonable regard to the rights and legitimate interests of the other State.

3. During the course of the consultations and negotiations, the notifying State shall, if so requested by the notified State at the time it makes the communication, refrain from implementing or permitting the implementation of the planned measures for a period not exceeding six months.

Article 18
Procedures in the absence of notification

1. If a watercourse State has serious reason to believe that another watercourse State is planning measures that may have an appreciable adverse effect upon it, the former State may request the latter to apply the provisions of article 12. The request shall be accompanied by a documented explanation setting forth the reasons for such belief.

2. In the event that the State planning the measures nevertheless finds that it is not under an obligation to provide a notification under article 12, it shall so inform the other State, providing a documented explanation setting forth the reasons for such finding. If this finding does not satisfy the other State, the two States shall, at the request of that other State, promptly enter into consultations and negotiations in the manner indicated in paragraphs 1 and 2 of article 17.

3. During the course of the consultations and negotiations, the State planning the measures shall, if so requested by the other State at the time it requests the initiation of consultations and negotiations, refrain from implementing or permitting the implementation of those measures for a period not exceeding six months.

Article 19
Urgent implementation of planned measures

1. In the event that the implementation of planned measures is of the utmost urgency in order to protect public health, public safety or other equally important interests, the State planning the measures may, subject to articles 5 and 7, immediately proceed to implementation, notwithstanding the provisions of article 14 and paragraph 3 of article 17.

2. In such cases, a formal declaration of the urgency of the measures shall be communicated to the other watercourse States referred to in article 12 together with the relevant data and information.

3. The State planning the measures shall, at the request of the States referred to in paragraph 2, promptly enter into consultations and negotiations with it in the manner indicated in paragraphs 1 and 2 of article 17.

PART IV
PROTECTION AND PRESERVATION

Article 20
Protection and preservation of ecosystems

Watercourse States shall, individually or jointly, protect and preserve the ecosystems of international watercourses.

Article 21
Prevention, reduction and control of pollution

1. For the purposes of this article, "pollution of an international watercourse" means any detrimental alteration in the composition or quality of the waters of an international watercourse which results directly or indirectly from human conduct.

2. Watercourse States shall, individually or jointly, prevent, reduce and control pollution of an international watercourse that may cause appreciable harm to other watercourse States or to their environment, including harm to human health or safety, to the use of the waters for any beneficial purpose or to the living resources of the watercourse. Watercourse States shall take steps to harmonize their policies in this connection.

3. Watercourse States shall, at the request of any of them, consult with a view to establishing lists of substances, the introduction of which into the waters of an international watercourse is to be prohibited, limited, investigated or monitored.

Article 22
Introduction of alien or new species

Watercourse States shall take all measures necessary to prevent the introduction of species, alien or new, into an international watercourse which may have effects detrimental to the ecosystem of the watercourse resulting in appreciable harm to other watercourse States.

Article 23
Protection and preservation of the marine environment

Watercourse States shall, individually or jointly, take all measures with respect to an international watercourse that are necessary to protect and preserve the marine environment, including estuaries, taking into account generally accepted international rules and standards.

PART V
HARMFUL CONDITIONS AND EMERGENCY SITUATIONS

Article 24
Prevention and mitigation of harmful conditions

Watercourse States shall, individually or jointly, take all appropriate measures to prevent or mitigate conditions that may be harmful to other watercourse States, whether resulting from natural causes or human conduct, such as flood or ice conditions, water-borne diseases, siltation, erosion, salt-water intrusion, drought or desertification.

Article 25
Emergency situations

1. For the purposes of this article, "emergency" means a situation that causes, or poses an imminent threat of causing, serious harm to watercourse States or other States and that results suddenly from natural causes, such as floods, the breaking up of ice, landslides or earthquakes, or from human conduct as for example in the case of industrial accidents.

2. A watercourse State shall, without delay and by the most expeditious means available, notify other potentially affected States and competent international organizations of any emergency originating within its territory.

3. A watercourse State within whose territory an emergency originates shall, in cooperation with potentially affected States and, where appropriate, competent international organizations, immediately take all practicable measures necessitated by the circumstances to prevent, mitigate and eliminate harmful effects of the emergency.

4. When necessary, watercourse States shall jointly develop contingency plans for responding to emergencies, in cooperation, where appropriate, with other potentially affected States and competent international organizations.

PART VI
MISCELLANEOUS PROVISIONS

Article 26
Management

1. Watercourse States shall, at the request of any of them, enter into consultations concerning the management of an international watercourse, which may include the establishment of a joint management mechanism.
2. For the purposes of this article, "management" refers, in particular, to:
(a)　planning the sustainable development of an international watercourse and providing for the implementation of any plans adopted; and
(b)　otherwise promoting rational and optimal utilization, protection and control of the watercourse.

Article 27
Regulation

1. Watercourse States shall cooperate where appropriate to respond to needs or oppoertunities for regulation of the flow of the waters of an international watercourse.
2. Unless they have otherwise agreed, watercourse States shall participate on an equitable basis in the construction and maintenance or defrayal of the costs of such regulation works as they may have agreed to undertake.
3. For the purposes of this article, "regulation" means the use of hydraulic works or any other continuing measure to alter, vary or otherwise control the flow of the waters of an international watercourse.

Article 28
Installations

1. Watercourse States shall, within their respective territories, employ their best efforts to maintain and protect installations, facilities and other works related to an international watercourse.
2. Watercourse States shall, at the request of any of them which has serious reason to believe that it may suffer appreciable adverse effects, enter into consultations with regard to:
(a)　the safe operation or maintenance of installations, facilities or other works related to an international watercourse; or
(b)　the protection of installations, facilities or other works from wilful or negligent acts or the forces of nature.

Article 29
International watercourses and installations in time of armed conflict

International watercourses and related installations, facilities and other works shall enjoy the protection accorded by the principles and rules of international law applicable in international and internal armed conflict and shall not be used in violation of those principles and rules.

Article 30
Indirect procedures

In cases where there are serious obstacles to direct contacts between watercourse States, the States concerned shall fulfil their obligations of cooperation provided for in the present articles, including exchange of data and information, notification, communication, consultations and negotiations, through any indirect procedure accepted by them.

Article 31
Data and information vital to national defence or security

Nothing in the present articles obliges a watercourse State to provide data or information vital to its national defence or security. Nevertheless, that State shall cooperate in good faith with the other watercourse States with a view to providing as much information as possible under the circumstances.

Article 32
Non-discrimination

Watercourse States shall not discriminate on the basis of nationality or residence in granting access to judicial and other procedures, in accordance with their legal systems, to any natural or juridical person who has suffered appreciable harm as a result of an activity related to an international watercourse or is exposed to a threat thereof.

C. AMERICAS

CANADA-UNITED STATES: WASHINGTON TREATY RELATING TO THE BOUNDARY WATERS AND QUESTIONS ARISING ALONG THE BOUNDARY BETWEEN THE UNITED STATES AND CANADA

Popular Name: Boundary Waters Treaty, 1909 Boundary Waters Treaty

Done at Washington on 11 January 1909, United States-Great Britain, 36 Stat. 2448, T.S. No. 548, 12 Bevans 319, 102 BFSP 137, LEG/SER.B/12, p. 261, *reprinted in* 10 IPE 5158.

Entry into Force: 5 May 1910

Language: English

Editors' Note

The 1909 Boundary Waters Treaty provides, *inter alia*, that "the waters herein defined as boundary waters and the waters flowing across the boundary shall not be polluted on either side to the injury of health or property on the other." It also establishes a binational mechanism, the International Joint Commission (IJC), for helping resolve boundary-water disputes.

The IJC, which is composed of three members from each nation, is a quasi-judicial body with mandatory jurisdiction and binding authority to approve or disapprove the quantitative—but not the qualitative—aspects of projects such as boundary-water diversions or obstructions. The United States and Canada may also jointly refer environmental matters to the IJC for its binding or nonbinding recommendation. No disputes have been referred for the former, but more than 100 disputes have been referred to the IJC for nonbinding consideration. The IJC normally proceeds by first appointing a joint board of experts to report on the factual aspects of the dispute, which frequently has resulted in eliminating much of the controversy by resolving factual disagreements or misunderstandings. The IJC's recommendations normally have been followed, at least in spirit.

TREATY BETWEEN THE UNITED STATES AND GREAT BRITAIN RELATING TO BOUNDARY WATERS BETWEEN THE UNITED STATES AND CANADA.

* * *

Preliminary Article

For the purposes of this treaty boundary waters are defined as the waters from main shore to main shore of the lakes and rivers and connecting waterways, or the portions thereof, along which the international boundary between the United States and the Dominion of Canada passes. [sic] including all bays, arms, and inlets thereof, but not including tributary waters which in their natural channels would flow into such lakes, rivers, and waterways, or waters flowing from such lakes, rivers, and waterways, or the waters of rivers flowing across the boundary.

Article I

The High Contracting Parties agree that the navigation of all navigable boundary waters shall forever continue free and open for the purposes of commerce to the inhabitants and to the ships, vessels, and boats of both countries equally, subject, however, to any laws and regulations of either country, within its own territory, not inconsistent with such privilege of free navigation and applying equally and without discrimination to the inhabitants, ships, vessels, and boats of both countries.

It is further agreed that so long as this treaty shall remain in force, this same right of navigation shall extend to the waters of Lake Michigan and to all canals connecting boundary waters, and now existing or which may hereafter be constructed on either side of the line. Either of the High Contracting Parties may adopt rules and regulations governing the use of such canals within its own territory and may charge tolls for the use thereof, but all such rules and regulations and all tolls charged shall apply alike to the subjects or citizens of the High Contracting Parties and the ships, vessels, and boats of both of the High Contracting Parties, and they shall be placed on terms of equality in the use thereof.

Article II

Each of the High Contracting Parties reserves to itself or to the several State Governments on the one side and the Dominion or Provincial Governments on the other as the case may be, subject to any treaty provisions now existing with respect thereto, the exclusive jurisdiction and control over the use and diversion, whether temporary or permanent, of all waters on its own side of the line which in their natural channels would flow across the boundary or into boundary waters; but it is agreed that any interference with or diversion from their natural channel of such waters on either side of the boundary, resulting in any injury on the other side of the boundary, shall give rise to the same rights and entitle the injured parties to the same legal remedies as if such injury took place in the country where such diversion or interference occurs; but this provision shall not apply to cases already existing or to cases expressly covered by special agreement between the parties hereto.

It is understood, however, that neither of the High Contracting Parties intends by the foregoing provision to surrender any right, which it may have, to object to any interference with or diversions of waters on the other side of the boundary the effect of which would be productive of material injury to the navigation interests on its own side of the boundary.

Article III

It is agreed that, in addition to the uses, obstructions, and diversions heretofore permitted or hereafter provided for by special agreement between the Parties hereto, no further or other uses or obstructions or diversions, whether temporary or permanent, of boundary waters on either side of the line, affecting the natural level or flow of boundary waters on the other side of the line, shall be made except by authority of the United States or the Dominion of Canada within their respective jurisdictions and with the approval, as hereinafter provided, of a joint commission, to be known as the International Joint Commission.

The foregoing provisions are not intended to limit or interfere with the existing rights of the Government of the United States on the one side and the Government of the Dominion of Canada on the other, to undertake and carry on governmental works in boundary waters for the deepening of channels, the construction of breakwaters, the improvement of harbors, and other governmental works for the benefit of commerce and navigation, provided that such works are wholly on its own side of the line and do not materially affect the level or flow of the boundary waters on the other, nor are such provisions intended to interfere with the ordinary use of such waters for domestic and sanitary purposes.

Article IV

The High Contracting Parties agree that, except in cases provided for by special agreement between them, they will not permit the construction or maintenance on their respective sides of the boundary of any remedial or protective works or any dams or other obstructions in waters flowing from boundary waters or in waters at a lower level than the boundary in rivers flowing across the boundary, the effect of which is to raise the natural level of waters on the other side of the boundary unless the construction or maintenance thereof is approved by the aforesaid International Joint Commission.

It is further agreed that the waters herein defined as boundary waters and waters flowing across the boundary shall not be polluted on either side to the injury of health or property on the other.

Article V

The High Contracting Parties agree that it is expedient to limit the diversion of waters from the Niagara River so that the level of Lake Erie and the flow of the stream shall not be appreciably affected. It is the desire of both Parties to accomplish this object with the least possible injury to investments which have already been made in the construction of power plants on the United States side of the river under grants of authority from the State of New York, and on the Canadian side of the river under licenses authorized by the Dominion of Canada and the Province of Ontario.

So long as this treaty shall remain in force, no diversion of the waters of the Niagara River above the Falls from the natural course and stream thereof shall be permitted except for the purposes and to the extent hereinafter provided.

The United States may authorize and permit the diversion within the State of New York of the waters of said river above the Falls of Niagara, for power purposes, not exceeding in the aggregate a daily diversion at the rate of twenty thousand cubic feet of water per second.

The United Kingdom, by the Dominion of Canada, or the Province of Ontario, may authorize and permit the diversion within the Province of Ontario of the waters of said river above the Falls of Niagara, for power purposes, not exceeding in the aggregate a daily diversion at the rate of thirty-six thousand cubic feet of water per second.

The prohibitions of this article shall not apply to the diversion of water for sanitary or domestic purposes, or for the service of canals for the purposes of navigation.

Article VI

The High Contracting Parties agree that the St. Mary and Milk Rivers and their tributaries (in the State of Montana and the Provinces of Alberta and Saskatchewan) are to be treated as one stream for the purposes of irrigation and power, and the waters thereof shall be apportioned equally between the two countries, but in making such equal apportionment more than half may be taken from one river and less than half from the other by either country so as to afford a more beneficial use to each. It is further agreed that in the division of such waters during the irrigation season, between the 1st of April and 31st of October, inclusive, annually, the United States is entitled to a prior appropriation of 500 cubic feet per second of the waters of the Milk River, or so much of such amount as constitutes three-fourths of its natural flow, and that Canada is entitled to a prior appropriation of 500 cubic feet per second of the flow of St. Mary River, or so much of such amount as constitutes three-fourths of its natural flow.

The channel of the Milk River in Canada may be used at the convenience of the United States for the conveyance, while passing through Canadian territory, of waters diverted from the St. Mary River. The provisions of Article II of this treaty shall apply to any injury resulting to property in Canada from the conveyance of such waters through the Milk River.

The measurement and apportionment of the water to be used by each country shall from time to time be made jointly by the properly constituted reclamation officers of the United States and the properly constituted irrigation officers of His Majesty under the direction of the International Joint Commission.

Article VII

The High Contracting Parties agree to establish and maintain an International Joint Commission of the United States and Canada composed of six commissioners, three on the part of the United States appointed by the President thereof, and three on the part of the United Kingdom appointed by His Majesty on the recommendation of the Governor in Council of the Dominion of Canada.

Article VIII

This International Joint Commission shall have jurisdiction over and shall pass upon all cases involving the use or obstruction or diversion of the waters with respect to which under Articles III and IV of this treaty the approval of this Commission is required, and in passing upon such cases the Commission shall be governed by the following rules or principles which are adopted by the High Contracting Parties for this purpose:

The High Contracting Parties shall have, each on its own side of the boundary, equal and similar rights in the use of the waters hereinbefore defined as boundary waters.

The following order of precedence shall be observed among the various uses enumerated hereinafter for these waters, and no use shall be permitted which tends materially to conflict with or restrain any other use which is given preference over it in this order of precedence:

(1) Uses for domestic and sanitary purposes;

(2) Uses for navigation, including the service of canals for the purposes of navigation;

(3) Uses for power and for irrigation purposes.

The foregoing provisions shall not apply to or disturb any existing uses of boundary waters on either side of the boundary.

The requirement for an equal division may in the discretion of the Commission be suspended in cases of temporary diversions along boundary waters at points where such equal division can not be made advantageously on account of local conditions, and where such diversion does not diminish elsewhere the amount available for use on the other side.

The Commission in its discretion may make its approval in any case conditional upon the construction of remedial or protective works to compensate so far as possible for the particular use or diversion proposed, and in such cases may require that suitable and adequate provision, approved by the Commission, be made for the protection and indemnity against injury of any interests on either side of the boundary.

In cases involving the elevation of the natural level of waters on either side of the line as a result of the construction or maintenance on the other side of remedial or protective works or dams or other obstructions in boundary waters or in waters flowing therefrom or in waters below the boundary in rivers flowing across the boundary, the Commission shall require, as a condition of its approval thereof, that suitable and adequate provision, approved by it, be made for the protection and indemnity of all interests on the other side of the line which may be injured thereby.

The majority of the Commissioners shall have power to render a decision. In case the Commission is evenly divided upon any question or matter presented to it for decision, separate reports shall be made by the Commissioners on each side to their own Government. The High Contracting Parties shall thereupon endeavor to agree upon an adjustment of the question or matter of difference, and if an agreement is reached between them, it shall be reduced to writing in the form of a protocol, and shall be communicated to the Commissioners, who shall take such further proceedings as may be necessary to carry out such agreement.

Article IX

The High Contracting Parties further agree that any other questions or matters of difference arising between them involving the rights, obligations, or interests of either in relation to the other or to the inhabitants of the other, along the common frontier between the United States and the Dominion of Canada, shall be referred from time to time to the International Joint Commission for examination and report, whenever either the Government of the United States or the Government of the Dominion of Canada shall request that such questions or matters of difference be so referred.

The International Joint Commission is authorized in each case so referred to examine into and report upon the facts and circumstances of the particular questions and matters referred, together with such conclusions and recommendations as may be appropriate, subject, however, to any restrictions or exceptions which may be imposed with respect thereto by the terms of the reference.

Such reports of the Commission shall not be regarded as decisions of the questions or matters so submitted either on the facts or the law, and shall in no way have the character of an arbitral award.

The Commission shall make a joint report to both Governments in all cases in which all or a majority of the Commissioners agree, and in case of disagreement the minority may make a joint report to both Governments, or separate reports to their respective Governments.

In case the Commission is evenly divided upon any question or matter referred to it for report, separate reports shall be made by the Commissioners on each side to their own Government.

Article X

Any questions or matters of difference arising between the High Contracting Parties involving the rights, obligations, or interests of the United States or of the Dominion of Canada either in relation to each other or to their respective inhabitants, may be referred for decision to the International Joint Commission by the consent of the two Parties, it being understood that on the part of the United States any such action will be by and with the advice and consent of the Senate, and on the part of His Majesty's Government with the consent of the Governor General in Council. In each case so referred, the said Commission is authorized to examine into and report upon the facts and circumstances of the particular questions and matters referred, together with such conclusions and recommendations as may be appropriate, subject, however, to any restrictions or exceptions which may be imposed with respect thereto by the terms of the reference.

A majority of the said Commission shall have power to render a decision or finding upon any of the questions or matters so referred.

If the said Commission is equally divided or otherwise unable to render a decision or finding as to any questions or matters so referred, it shall be the duty of the Commissioners to make a joint report to both Governments, or separate reports to their respective Governments, showing the different conclusions arrived at with regard to the matters or questions so referred, which questions or matters shall thereupon be referred for decision by the High Contracting Parties to an umpire chosen in accordance with the procedure prescribed in the fourth, fifth, and sixth paragraphs of Article XLV of The Hague Convention for the pacific settlement of international disputes, dated October 18, 1907. Such umpire shall have power to render a final decision with respect to those matters and questions so referred on which the Commission failed to agree.

Article XI

A duplicate original of all decisions rendered and joint reports made by the Commission shall be transmitted to and filed with the Secretary of State of the United States and the Governor General of the Dominion of Canada, and to them shall be addressed all communications of the Commission.

Article XII

The International Joint Commission shall meet and organize at Washington promptly after the members thereof are appointed, and when organized the Commission may fix such times and places for its meetings as may be necessary, subject at all times to special call or direction by the two Governments. Each Commissioner, upon the first joint meeting of the Commission after his appointment, shall, before proceeding with the work of the Commission, make and subscribe a solemn declaration in writing that he will faithfully and impartially perform the duties imposed upon him under this treaty, and such declaration shall be entered on the records of the proceedings of the Commission.

The United States and Canadian sections of the Commission may each appoint a secretary, and these shall act as joint secretaries of the Commission at its joint sessions, and the Commission may employ engineers and clerical assistants from time to time as it may deem advisable. The salaries and personal expenses of the Commission and of the secretaries shall be paid by their respective Governments, and all reasonable and necessary joint expenses of the Commission, incurred by it, shall be paid in equal moieties by the High Contracting Parties.

The Commission shall have power to administer oaths to witnesses, and to take evidence on oath whenever deemed necessary in any proceeding, or inquiry, or matter within its jurisdiction under this treaty, and all parties interested therein shall be given convenient opportunity to be heard, and the High Contracting Parties agree to adopt such legislation as may be appropriate and necessary to give the Commission the powers above mentioned on each side of the boundary, and to provide for the issue of subpœnas and for compelling the attendance of witnesses in proceedings before the Commission. The Commission may adopt such rules of procedure as shall be in accordance with justice and equity, and may make such examination in person and through agents or employees as may be deemed advisable.

Article XIII

In all cases where special agreements between the High Contracting Parties hereto are referred to in the foregoing articles, such agreements are understood and intended to include not only direct agreements between the High Contracting Parties, but also any mutual arrangement between the United States and the Dominion of Canada expressed by concurrent or reciprocal legislation on the part of Congress and the Parliament of the Dominion.

Article XIV

The present treaty shall be ratified by the President of the United States of America, by and with the advice and consent of the Senate thereof, and by His Britannic Majesty. The ratifications shall be exchanged at Washington as soon as possible and the treaty shall take effect on the date of the exchange of its ratifications. It shall remain in force for five years, dating from the day of exchange of ratifications, and thereafter until terminated by twelve months' written notice given by either High Contracting Party to the other.

In faith whereof the respective plenipotentiaries have signed this treaty in duplicate and have hereunto affixed their seals.

Done at Washington the 11th day of January, in the year of our Lord one thousand nine hundred and nine.

ELIHU ROOT [SEAL]
JAMES BRYCE [SEAL]

PROTOCOL OF EXCHANGE

On proceeding to the exchange of the ratifications of the treaty signed at Washington on January 11, 1909, between the United States and Great Britain, relating to boundary waters and questions arising along the boundary between the United States and the Dominion of Canada, the undersigned plenipotentiaries, duly authorized thereto by their respective Governments, hereby declare that nothing in this treaty shall be construed as affecting, or changing, any existing territorial, or riparian rights in the water, or rights of the owners of lands under water, on either side of the international boundary at the rapids of the St. Mary's River at Sault Ste. Marie, in the use of the waters flowing over such lands, subject to the requirements of navigation in boundary waters and of navigation canals, and without prejudice to the existing right of the United States and Canada, each to use the waters of the St. Mary's River, within its own territory; and further, that nothing in this treaty shall be construed to interfere with the drainage of wet, swamp, and overflowed lands into streams flowing into boundary waters, and also that this declaration shall be deemed to have equal force and effect as the treaty itself and to form an integral part thereto.

The exchange of ratifications then took place in the usual form.

IN WITNESS WHEREOF, they have signed the present Protocol of Exchange and have affixed their seals thereto.

DONE at Washington this 5th day of May, one thousand nine hundred and ten.

PHILANDER C KNOX [SEAL]
JAMES BRYCE [SEAL]

CANADA-UNITED STATES: GREAT LAKES WATER QUALITY AGREEMENT, 1978, AS AMENDED BY THE 1983 AND 1987 PROTOCOLS

Popular Name: Great Lakes Water Quality Agreement

Done at Ottawa on 22 November 1978, United States-Canada, 30 UST 1383, TIAS 9257, *as amended* 16 October 1983, TIAS 10798, and 18 November 1987, *consolidated in* International Joint Commission, Revised Great Lakes Water Quality Agreement of 1978 (1988), *reprinted in* 26 IPE 19.
Entry into Force: 22 November 1978

Languages: English, French

Editors' Note

In 1964 Canada and the United States, concerned about the growing pollution of Lake Erie and Lake Ontario, submitted a Reference of the issues to the International Joint Commission. In so doing, they invoked the Reference procedure provided in Article 9 of the 1909 Boundary Waters Treaty, *supra* this Chapter. After six years of studies, the Commission issued a report which focussed on problems of phosphate pollution and eutrophication of the lakes and recommended phosphate control programs, new water quality objectives, and a new international board to coordinate the programs. The 1972 Great Lakes Water Quality Agreement, *reprinted in* 11 ILM 694 (1972), was a direct response to this Reference report.

In 1978 Canada and the United States negotiated a new agreement which covered all the Great Lakes. It maintained the basic institutional structure of the 1972 agreement: the International Joint Commission to advise the parties, with a water quality board of representatives from state and provincial governments to monitor water quality, and a scientific advisory board to address research issues. The 1978 Agreement made two very important changes from its 1972 predecessor. It severely restricted the discharge of toxic chemicals in the Lakes and introduced the concept of ''the Great Lakes basin ecosystem,'' which recognized that pollution management in the Lakes required more than controlling direct discharges into them.

The 1987 Protocol to the agreement carries forward the basin ecosystem approach by calling for controls on groundwater contamination that can reach the Lakes and on airborne transport of contaminants to the Lakes.

The 1978 Great Lakes Water Quality Agreement is an executive agreement.

PROTOCOL AMENDING THE 1978 AGREEMENT BETWEEN THE UNITED STATES OF AMERICA AND CANADA ON GREAT LAKES WATER QUALITY, AS AMENDED ON OCTOBER 16, 1983

The Government of the United States of America and the Government of Canada,

REAFFIRMING their commitment to achieving the purpose and objectives of the 1978 Agreement between the United States of America and Canada on Great Lakes Water Quality, as amended on October 16, 1983;

HAVING developed and implemented cooperative programs and measures to achieve such purpose and objectives;

RECOGNIZING the need for strengthened efforts to address the continuing contamination of the Great Lakes Basin Ecosystem, particularly by persistent toxic substances;

ACKNOWLEDGING that many of these toxic substances enter the Great Lakes System from the air, from ground water infiltration, from sediments in the Lakes and from the runoff of non-point sources;

AWARE that further research and program development is now required to enable effective actions to be taken to address the continuing contamination of the Great Lakes;

DETERMINED to improve management processes for achieving Agreement objectives and to demonstrate firm leadership in the implementation of control measures;

Have agreed as follows:

AGREEMENT BETWEEN CANADA AND THE UNITED STATES OF AMERICA ON GREAT LAKES WATER QUALITY, 1978

The Government of Canada and the Government of the United States of America,

Having in 1972 and 1978 entered into Agreements on Great Lakes Water Quality;

Reaffirming their determination to restore and enhance water quality in the Great Lakes System;

Continuing to be concerned about the impairment of water quality on each side of the boundary to an extent that is causing injury to health and property on the other side, as described by the International Joint Commission;

Reaffirming their intent to prevent further pollution of the Great Lakes Basin Ecosystem owing to continuing population growth, resource development and increasing use of water;

Reaffirming in a spirit of friendship and cooperation the rights and obligations of both countries under the Boundary Waters Treaty, signed on January 11, 1909, and in particular their obligation not to pollute boundary waters;

Continuing to recognize the rights of each country in the use of its Great Lakes waters;

Having decided that the Great Lakes Water Quality Agreements of 1972 and 1978 and subsequent reports of the International Joint Commission provide a sound basis for new and more effective cooperative actions to restore and enhance water quality in the Great Lakes Basin Ecosystem;

Recognizing that restoration and enhancement of the boundary waters can not be achieved independently of other parts of the Great Lakes Basin Ecosystem with which these waters interact;

Concluding that the best means to preserve the aquatic ecosystem and achieve improved water quality throughout the Great Lakes System is by adopting common objectives, developing and implementing cooperative programs and other measures, and assigning special responsibilities and functions to the International Joint Commission;

Have agreed as follows:

ARTICLE I
DEFINITIONS

As used in this Agreement:
(a) "Agreement" means the present Agreement as distinguished from the Great Lakes Water Quality Agreement of April 15, 1972;
(b) "Annex" means any of the Annexes to this Agreement, each of which is attached to and forms an integral part of this Agreement;
(c) "Boundary waters of the Great Lakes System" or "boundary waters" means boundary waters, as defined in the Boundary Waters Treaty, that are within the Great Lakes System;
(d) "Boundary Waters Treaty" means the Treaty between the United States and Great Britain Relating to Boundary Waters, and Questions Arising Between the United States and Canada, signed at Washington on January 11, 1909;
(e) "Compatible regulations" means regulations no less restrictive than the agreed principles set out in this Agreement;
(f) "General Objectives" are broad descriptions of water quality conditions consistent with the protection of the beneficial uses and the level of environmental quality which the Parties desire to secure and which will provide overall water management guidance;
(g) "Great Lakes Basin Ecosystem" means the interacting components of air, land, water and living organisms, including *humans*, within the drainage basin of the St. Lawrence River at or upstream from the point at which this river becomes the international boundary between Canada and the United States;
(h) "Great Lakes System" means all of the streams, rivers, lakes and other bodies of water that are within the drainage basin on the St. Lawrence River at or upstream from the point at which this river becomes the international boundary between Canada and the United States;
(i) "Harmful quantity" means any quantity of a substance that if discharged into receiving water would be inconsistent with the achievement of the General and Specific Objectives;

(j) "Hazardous Polluting substance" means any element or compound identified by the Parties which, if discharged in any quantity into or upon receiving waters or adjoining shorelines, would present an imminent and substantial danger to public health or welfare; for this purpose, "public health or welfare" encompasses all factors affecting the health and welfare of *humans* including but not limited to human health, and the conservation and protection of flora and fauna, public and private property, shorelines and beaches;

(k) "International Joint Commission" or "Commission" means the International Joint Commission established by the Boundary Waters Treaty;

(l) "Monitoring" means a scientifically designed system of continuing standardized measurements and observations and the evaluation thereof;

(m) "Objectives" means the General Objectives adopted pursuant to Article III and the Specific Objectives adopted pursuant to Article IV of this Agreement;

(n) "Parties" means the Government of Canada and the Government of the United States of America;

(o) "Phosphorus" means the element phosphorus present as a constituent of various organic and inorganic complexes and compounds;

(p) "Research" means development, *interpretation and* demonstration *of advanced scientific knowledge for the resolution of issues* but does not include monitoring and surveillance of water or air quality;

(q) "Science Advisory Board" means the Great Lakes Science Advisory Board of the International Joint Commission established pursuant to Article VIII of this Agreement;

(r) "Specific Objectives" means the concentration or quantity of a substance or level of effect that the Parties agree, after investigation, to recognize as a maximum or minimum desired limit for a defined body of water or portion thereof, taking into account the beneficial uses or level of environmental quality which the Parties desire to secure and protect;

(s) "State and Provincial Governments" means the Governments of the States of Illinois, Indiana, Michigan, Minnesota, New York, Ohio, Wisconsin, and the Commonwealth of Pennsylvania, and the Government of the Province of Ontario;

(t) "Surveillance" means specific observations and measurements relative to control and management;

(u) "Terms of Reference" means the Terms of Reference for the Joint Institutions and the Great Lakes Regional Office established pursuant to this Agreement, which are attached to and form an integral part of this Agreement;

(v) "Toxic substance" means a substance which can cause death, disease, behavioural abnormalities, cancer, genetic mutations, physiological or reproductive malfunctions or physical deformities in any organism or its offspring, or which can become poisonous after concentration in the food chain or in combination with other substances;

(w) "Tributary waters of the Great Lakes System" or "tributary waters" means all that waters within the Great Lakes System that are not boundary waters;

(x) "Water Quality Board" means the Great Lakes Water Quality Board of the International Joint Commission established pursuant to Article VIII of this Agreement.

ARTICLE II
PURPOSE

The purpose of the Parties is to restore and maintain the chemical, physical, and biological integrity of the waters of the Great Lakes Basin Ecosystem. In order to achieve this purpose, the Parties agree to make a maximum effort to develop programs, practices and technology necessary for a better understanding of the Great Lakes Basin Ecosystem and to eliminate or reduce to the maximum extent practicable the discharge of pollutants into the Great Lakes System.

Consistent with the provisions of this Agreement, it is the policy of the Parties that:

(a) The discharge of toxic substances in toxic amounts be prohibited and the discharge of any or all persistent toxic substances be virtually eliminated;

(b) Financial assistance to construct publicly owned waste treatment works be provided by a combination of local, state, provincial, and federal participation; and

(c) Coordinated planning processes and best management practices be developed and implemented by the respective jurisdictions to ensure adequate control of all sources of pollutants.

ARTICLE III
GENERAL OBJECTIVES

The Parties adopt the following General Objectives for the Great Lakes System. These waters should be:

(a) Free from substances that directly or indirectly enter the waters as a result of human activity and that will settle to form putrescent or otherwise objectionable sludge deposits, or that will adversely affect aquatic life or waterfowl;

(b) Free from floating materials such as debris, oil, scum, and other immiscible substances resulting from human activities in amounts that are unsightly or deleterious;

(c) Free from materials and heat directly or indirectly entering the water as a result of human activity that alone, or in combination with other materials, will produce colour, odour, taste, or other conditions in such a degree as to interfere with beneficial uses;

(d) Free from materials and heat directly or indirectly entering the water as a result of human activity that alone, or in combination with other materials, will produce conditions that are toxic or harmful to human, animal, or aquatic life; and

(e) Free from nutrients directly or indirectly entering the waters as a result of human activity in amounts that create growths of aquatic life that interfere with beneficial uses.

ARTICLE IV
SPECIFIC OBJECTIVES

1. The Parties adopt the Specific Objectives for the boundary waters of the Great Lakes System as set forth in Annex 1, subject to the following:

(a) The Specific Objectives adopted pursuant to this Article represent the minimum levels of water quality desired in the boundary waters of the Great Lakes System and are not intended to preclude the establishment of more stringent requirements.

(b) The determination of the achievement of Specific Objectives shall be based on statistically valid sampling data.

(c) Notwithstanding the adoption of Specific Objectives, all reasonable and practicable measures shall be taken to maintain or improve the existing water quality in those areas of the boundary waters of the Great Lakes System where such water quality is better than that prescribed by the Specific Objectives, and in those areas having outstanding natural resource value.

(d)   The responsible regulatory agencies shall not consider flow augmentation as a substitute for adequate treatment to meet the Specific Objectives.

(e)   The Parties recognize that in certain areas of inshore waters natural phenomena exist which, despite the best efforts of the Parties, will prevent the achievement of some of the Specific Objectives. As early as possible, these areas should be identified explicitly by the appropriate jurisdictions and reported to the International Joint Commission.

(f)   *The Parties recognize that there are areas in the boundary waters of the Great Lakes System where, due to human activity, one or more of the General or Specific Objectives of the Agreement are not being met. Pending virtual elimination of persistent toxic substances in the Great Lakes System, the Parties, in cooperation with State and Provincial Governments and the Commission, shall identify and work toward the elimination of:*
(i)   Areas of Concern pursuant to Annex 2;
(ii) Critical Pollutants pursuant to Annex 2; and
(iii) Point Source Impact Zones pursuant to Annex 2.

2. The Specific Objectives for the boundary waters of the Great Lakes System or for particular portions thereof shall be kept under review by the Parties and the International Joint Commission, which shall make appropriate recommendations.

3. The Parties shall consult on:

(a)   The establishment of Specific Objectives to protect beneficial uses from the combined effects of pollutants; and

(b)   The control of pollutant loading rates for each lake basin to protect the integrity of the ecosystem over the long term.

ARTICLE V
STANDARDS, OTHER REGULATORY REQUIREMENTS, AND RESEARCH

1. Water quality standards and other regulatory requirements of the Parties shall be consistent with the achievement of the General and Specific Objectives. The Parties shall use their best efforts to ensure that water quality standards and other regulatory requirements of the State and Provincial Governments shall similarly be consistent with the achievement of these Objectives. Flow augmentation shall not be considered as a substitute for adequate treatment to meet water quality standards or other regulatory requirements.

2. The Parties shall use their best efforts to ensure that:

(a)   The principal research funding agencies in both countries orient the research programs of their organizations in response to research priorities identified by the Science Advisory Board and recommended by the Commission;

(b)   Mechanisms be developed for appropriate cost-effective international cooperation; *and*

(c)   *Research priorities are undertaken in accordance with Annex 17.*

ARTICLE VI
PROGRAMS AND OTHER MEASURES

1. The Parties, *in cooperation with State and Provincial Governments,* shall continue to develop and implement programs and other measures to fulfil the purpose of this Agreement and to meet the General and Specific Objectives. Where present treatment is inadequate to meet the General and Specific Objectives, additional treatment shall be required. The programs and measures shall include the following:

(a)   *Pollution from Municipal Sources.* Programs for the abatement, control and prevention of municipal discharges and urban drainage into the Great

Lakes System. These programs shall be completed and in operation as soon as practicable, and in the case of municipal sewage treatment facilities no later than December 31, 1982. These programs shall include:

(i) Construction and operation of waste treatment facilities in all municipalities having sewer systems to provide levels of treatment consistent with the achievement of phosphorus requirements and the General and Specific Objectives, taking into account the effects of waste from other sources;

(ii) Provisions of financial resources to ensure prompt construction of needed facilities;

(iii) Establishment of requirements for construction and operating standards for facilities;

(iv) Establishment of pre-treatment requirements for all industrial plants discharging waste into publicly owned treatment works where such industrial wastes are not amenable to adequate treatment or removal using conventional municipal treatment processes;

(v) Development and implementation of practical programs for reducing pollution from storm, sanitary, and combined sewer discharges; and

(vi) Establishment of effective enforcement programs to ensure that the above pollution abatement requirements are fully met.

(b) *Pollution from Industrial Sources.* Programs for the abatement, control and prevention of pollution from industrial sources entering the Great Lakes System. These programs shall be completed and in operation as soon as practicable and in any case no later than December 31, 1983, and shall include:

(i) Establishment of waste treatment or control requirements expressed as effluent limitations (concentrations and/or loading limits for specific pollutants where possible) for all industrial plants, including power generating facilities, to provide levels of treatment or reduction or elimination of inputs of substances and effects consistent with the achievement of the General and Specific Objectives and other control requirements, taking into account the effects of waste from other sources;

(ii) Requirements for the substantial elimination of discharges into the Great Lakes System of persistent toxic substances;

(iii) Requirements for the control of thermal discharges;

(iv) Measures to control the discharge of radioactive materials into the Great Lakes System;

(v) Requirements to minimize adverse environmental impacts of water intakes;

(vi) Development and implementation of programs to meet industrial pre-treatment requirements as specified under sub-paragraph (a)(iv) above; and

(vii) Establishment of effective enforcement programs to ensure the above pollution abatement requirements are fully met.

(c) *Inventory of Pollution Abatement Requirements.* Preparation of an inventory of pollution abatement requirements for all municipal and industrial facilities discharging into the Great Lakes System in order to gauge progress toward the earliest practicable completion and operation of the programs listed in sub-paragraphs (a) and (b) above. This inventory, prepared and revised annually, shall include compliance schedules and status of compliance with monitoring and effluent restrictions, and shall be made available to the International Joint Commission and to the public. In the initial preparation of this inventory, priority shall be given to the problem areas previously identified by the Water Quality Board.

(d)   *Eutrophication.* Programs and measures for the reduction and control of inputs of phosphorus and other nutrients, in accordance with the provisions of Annex 3.

(e)   *Pollution from Agricultural, Forestry and Other Land Use Activities.* Measures for the abatement and control of pollution from agricultural, forestry and other land use activities including:

(i)   Measures for the control of pest control products used in the Great Lakes Basin to ensure that pest control products likely to have long-term deleterious effects on the quality of water or its biota be used only as authorized by the responsible regulatory agencies; that inventories of pest control products used in the Great Lakes Basin be established and maintained by appropriate agencies; and that research and educational programs be strengthened to facilitate integration of cultural, biological and chemical pest control techniques;

(ii) Measures for the abatement and control of pollution from animal husbandry operations, including encouragement to appropriate agencies to adopt policies and regulations regarding utilization of animal wastes, and site selection and disposal of liquid and solid wastes, and to strengthen educational and technical assistance programs to enable farmers to establish waste utilization, handling and disposal systems;

(iii) Measures governing the hauling and disposal of liquid and solid wastes, including encouragement to appropriate regulatory agencies to ensure proper location, design, and regulation governing land disposal, and to ensure sufficient, adequately trained technical and administrative capability to review plans and to supervise and monitor systems for application of wastes on land;

(iv) Measures to review and supervise road salting practices and salt storage to ensure optimum use of salt and all-weather protection of salt stores in consideration of long-term environmental impact;

(v)   Measures to control soil losses from urban and suburban as well as rural areas:

(vi) Measures to encourage and facilitate improvements in land use planning and management programs to take account of impacts on Great Lakes water quality;

(vii) Other advisory programs and measures to abate and control inputs of nutrients, toxic substances and sediments from agricultural, forestry and other land use activities;

(viii)Consideration of future recommendations from the International Joint Commission based on the Pollution from Land Use Activities Reference; *and*

(ix) *Conduct further non-point source programs in accordance with Annex 13.*

(f)   *Pollution from Shipping Activities.* Measures for the abatement and control of pollution from shipping sources, including;

(i)   Programs and compatible regulations to prevent discharges of harmful quantities of oil and hazardous polluting substances, in accordance with Annex 4;

(ii) Compatible regulations for the control of discharges of vessel wastes, in accordance with Annex 5;

(iii) Such compatible regulations to abate and control pollution from shipping sources as may be deemed desirable in the light of continuing reviews and studies to be undertaken in accordance with Annex 6;

(iv) Programs and any necessary compatible regulations in accordance with Annexes 4 and 5, for the safe and efficient handling of shipboard generated wastes, including oil, hazardous polluting substances, garbage, waste water and sewage, and for their subsequent disposal, including the type and quantity of reception facilities and, if applicable, treatment standards; and

(v) Establishment by the Canadian Coast Guard and the United States Coast Guard of a coordinated system for aerial and surface surveillance for the purpose of enforcement of regulations and the early identification, abatement and clean-up of spills of oil, hazardous polluting substances or other pollution.

(g) *Pollution from Dredging Activities.* Measures for the abatement and control of pollution from all dredging activities, including the development of criteria for the identification of polluted sediments and compatible programs for disposal of polluted dredged material, in accordance with Annex 7. Pending the development of compatible criteria and programs, dredging operations shall be conducted in a manner that will minimize adverse effects on the environment.

(h) *Pollution from Onshore and Offshore Facilities.* Measures for the abatement and control of pollution from onshore and offshore facilities, including programs and compatible regulations for the prevention of discharges of harmful quantities of oil and hazardous polluting substances, in accordance with Annex 8.

(i) *Contingency Plan.* Maintenance of a joint contingency plan for use in the event of a discharge or the imminent threat of a discharge of oil or hazardous polluting substances, in accordance with Annex 9.

(j) *Hazardous Polluting Substances.* Implementation of Annex 10 concerning hazardous polluting substances. The Parties shall further consult from time to time for the purpose of revising the list of hazardous polluting substances and of identifying harmful quantities of these substances.

(k) *Persistent Toxic Substances.* Measures for the control of inputs of persistent toxic substances including control programs for their production, use, distribution and disposal, in accordance with Annex 12.

(l) *Airborne Toxic Substances.* Programs to identify pollutant sources and relative source contributions, including the more accurate definition of wet and dry deposition rates, for those substances which may have significant adverse effects of environmental quality including the indirect effects of impairment of tributary water quality through atmospheric deposition in drainage basins. In cases where significant contributions to Great Lakes pollution from atmospheric sources are identified, the Parties agree to consult on appropriate remedial programs. *The Parties shall conduct such programs in accordance with Annex 15.*

(m) *Surveillance and Monitoring.* Implementation of a coordinated surveillance and monitoring program in the Great Lakes System, in accordance with Annex 11, to assess compliance with pollution control requirements and achievement of the Objectives, to provide information for measuring local and whole lake response to control measures, and to identify emerging problems;

(n) *Remedial Action Plans. Measures to ensure the development and implementation of Remedial Action Plans for Areas of Concern pursuant to Annex 2;*

(o) *Lakewide Management Plans. Measures to ensure the development and implementation of Lakewide Management Plans to address Critical Pollutants pursuant to Annex 2;*

(p) *Pollution from Contaminated Sediments. Measures for the abatement and control of pollution from all contaminated sediments, including the development of chemical and biological criteria for assessing the signifi-cance of the relative contamination arising from the sediments and com-patible programs for remedial action for polluted sediments in accor-dance with Annex 14; and*

(q)   *Pollution from Contaminated Groundwater and Subsurface Sources. Pro-grams for the assessment and control of contaminated groundwater and subsurface sources entering the boundary waters of the Great Lakes System pursuant to Annex 16.*

2. The Parties shall develop and implement such additional programs as they jointly decide are necessary and desirable to fulfil the purpose of this Agreement and to meet the General and Specific Objectives.

ARTICLE VII
POWERS, RESPONSIBILITIES AND FUNCTIONS OF THE INTERNATIONAL JOINT COMMISSION

1. The International Joint Commission shall assist in the implementation of this Agreement. Accordingly, the Commission is hereby given, by a Reference pursuant to Article IX of the Boundary Waters Treaty, the following responsibilities:

(a)   Collation, analysis and dissemination of data and information supplied by the Parties and State and Provincial Governments relating to the quality of the boundary waters of the Great Lakes System and to pollution that enters the boundary waters from tributary waters and other sources;

(b)   Collection, analysis and dissemination of data and information concern-ing the General and Specific Objectives and the operation and effective-ness of the programs and other measures established pursuant to this Agreement;

(c)   Tendering of advice and recommendations to the Parties and to the State and Provincial Governments on problems of and matters related to the quality of the boundary waters of the Great Lakes System including specific recommendations concerning the General and Specific Objec-tives, legislation, standards and other regulatory requirements, programs and other measures, and intergovernmental agreements relating to the quality of these waters;

(d)   Tendering of advice and recommendations to the Parties in connection with matters covered under the Annexes to this Agreement;

(e)   Provision of assistance in the coordination of the joint activities envisaged by this Agreement;

(f)   Provision of assistance in and advice on matters related to research in the Great Lakes Basin Ecosystem, including identification of objectives for research activities, tendering of advice and recommendations concern-ing research to the Parties and to the State and Provincial Governments, and dissemination of information concerning research to interested per-sons and agencies;

(g)   Investigations of such subjects related to the Great Lakes Basin Ecosys-tem as the Parties may from time to time refer to it.

2. In the discharge of its responsibilities under this Reference, the Commission may exercise all of the powers conferred upon it by the Boundary Waters Treaty and by any legislation passed pursuant thereto including the power to conduct public hearings and to compel the testimony of witnesses and the production of documents.

3. The Commission shall make a full report to the Parties and to the State and Provincial Governments no less frequently than biennially concerning progress toward the achievement of the General and Specific Objectives including, as appro-priate, matters related to Annexes to this Agreement. This report shall include an assessment of the effectiveness of the programs and other measures undertaken

pursuant to this Agreement, and advice and recommendations. In alternate years, the Commission may submit a summary report. The Commission may at any time make special reports to the Parties, to the State and Provincial Governments and to the public concerning any problem of water quality in the Great Lakes System.

4. The Commission may in its discretion publish any report, statement or other document prepared by it in the discharge of its functions under this Reference.

5. The Commission shall have authority to verify independently the data and other information submitted by the Parties and by the State and Provincial Governments through such tests or other means as appear appropriate to it, consistent with the Boundary Waters Treaty and with applicable legislation.

6. The Commission shall carry out its responsibilities under this Reference utilizing principally the services of the Water Quality Board and the Science Advisory Board established under Article VIII of this Agreement. The Commission shall also ensure liaison and coordination between the institutions established under this Agreement and other institutions which may address concerns relevant to the Great Lakes Basin Ecosystem, including both those within its purview, such as those Boards related to Great Lakes levels and air pollution matters, and other international bodies as appropriate.

ARTICLE VIII
JOINT INSTITUTIONS AND REGIONAL OFFICE

1. To assist the International Joint Commission in the exercise of the powers and responsibilities assigned to it under this Agreement, there shall be two Boards:

   (a)   A Great Lakes Water Quality Board which shall be the principal advisor to the Commission. The Board shall be composed of an equal number of members from Canada and the United States, including representatives from the Parties and each of the State and Provincial Governments; and

   (b)   A Great Lakes Science Advisory Board which shall provide advice on research to the Commission and to the Water Quality Board. The Board shall further provide advice on scientific matters referred to it by the Commission, or by the Water Quality Board in consultation with the Commission. The Science Advisory Board shall consist of managers of Great Lakes research programs and recognized experts on Great Lakes water quality problems and related fields.

2. The members of the Water Quality Board and the Science Advisory Board shall be appointed by the Commission after consultation with the appropriate government or governments concerned. The functions of the Boards shall be as specified in the Terms of Reference appended to this Agreement.

3. To provide administrative support and technical assistance to the two Boards, and to provide a public information service for the programs, including public hearings, undertaken by the International Joint Commission and by the Boards, there shall be a Great Lakes Regional Office of the International Joint Commission. Specific duties and organization of the Office shall be as specified in the Terms of Reference appended to this Agreement.

4. The Commission shall submit an annual budget of anticipated expenses to be incurred in carrying out its responsibilities under this Agreement to the Parties for approval. Each Party shall seek funds to pay one-half of the annual budget so approved, but neither Party shall be under an obligation to pay a larger amount than the other toward this budget.

ARTICLE IX
SUBMISSION AND EXCHANGE OF INFORMATION

1. The International Joint Commission shall be given at its request any data or other information relating to water quality in the Great Lakes System in accordance with procedures established by the Commission.

2. The Commission shall make available to the Parties and to the State and Provincial Governments upon request all data or other information furnished to it in accordance with this Article.

3. Each Party shall make available to the other at its request any data or other information in its control relating to water quality in the Great Lakes System.

4. Notwithstanding any other provision of this Agreement, the Commission shall not release without the consent of the owner any information identified as proprietary information under the law of the place where such information has been acquired.

ARTICLE X
CONSULTATION AND REVIEW

1. Following the receipt of each report submitted to the Parties by the International Joint Commission in accordance with paragraph 3 of Article VII of this Agreement, the Parties shall consult on the recommendations contained in such report and shall consider such action as may be appropriate, including:

- (a)   The modification of existing Objectives and the adoption of new Objectives;
- (b)   The modification or improvement of programs and joint measures; and
- (c)   The amendment of this Agreement or any Annex thereto.

   Additional consultations may be held at the request of either Party on any matter arising out of the implementation of this Agreement.

2. When a Party becomes aware of a special pollution problem that is of joint concern and requires an immediate response, it shall notify and consult the other Party forthwith about appropriate remedial action.

3. *The Parties, in cooperation with State and Provincial Governments, shall meet twice a year to coordinate their respective work plans with regard to the implementation of this Agreement and to evaluate progress made.*

4. The Parties shall conduct a comprehensive review of the operation and effectiveness of this Agreement following *every* third biennial report of the Commission required under Article VII of this Agreement.

ARTICLE XI
IMPLEMENTATION

1. The obligations undertaken in this Agreement shall be subject to the appropriation of funds in accordance with the constitutional procedures of the Parties.

2. The Parties commit themselves to seek:

- (a)   The appropriation of the funds required to implement this Agreement, including the funds needed to develop and implement the programs and other measures provided for in Article VI of this Agreement, and the funds required by the International Joint Commission to carry out its responsibilities effectively;
- (b)   The enactment of any additional legislation that may be necessary in order to implement the programs and other measures provided for in Article VI of this Agreement; and
- (c)   The cooperation of the State and Provincial Governments in all matters relating to this Agreement.

ARTICLE XII
EXISTING RIGHTS AND OBLIGATIONS

   Nothing in this Agreement shall be deemed to diminish the rights and obligations of the Parties as set forth in the Boundary Waters Treaty.

ARTICLE XIII
AMENDMENT

1. This Agreement, the Annexes, and the Terms of Reference may be amended by agreement of the Parties. The Annexes may also be amended as provided therein, subject to the requirement that such amendments shall be within the scope of this Agreement. All such amendments to the Annexes shall be confirmed by an exchange of notes or letters between the Parties through diplomatic channels which shall specify the effective date or dates of such amendments.
2. All amendments to this Agreement, the Annexes, and the Terms of Reference shall be communicated promptly to the International Joint Commission.

ARTICLE XIV
ENTRY INTO FORCE AND TERMINATION

This Agreement shall enter into force upon signature by the duly authorized representatives of the Parties, and shall remain in force for a period of five years and thereafter until terminated upon twelve months' notice given in writing by one of the Parties to the other.

ARTICLE XV
SUPERSESSION

This Agreement supersedes the Great Lakes Water Quality Agreement of April 15, 1972, and shall be referred to as the "Great Lakes Water Quality Agreement of 1978."

IN WITNESS WHEREOF the undersigned representatives, duly authorized by their respective Governments, have signed this Agreement.

DONE in duplicate at Ottawa in the English and French languages, both versions being equally authentic, this 22nd day of November 1978.

IN FOI DE QUOI, les représentants soussignées, dûment authorisés par leur Gouvernement respectif, ont signé le présent Accord.

FAIT en double exemplaire à Ottawa en français et en anglais, chaque version faisant également foi, ce 22ème jour de novembre 1978.

TERMS OF REFERENCE
FOR THE JOINT INSTITUTIONS AND THE GREAT LAKES REGIONAL OFFICE

1. *Great Lakes Water Quality Board*
    (a)   This Board shall be the principal advisor to the International Joint Commission with regard to the exercise of all the functions, powers, and responsibilities (other than those functions and responsibilities of the Science Advisory Board pursuant to paragraph 2 of these Terms of Reference) assigned to the Commission under this Agreement. In addition, the Board shall carry out such other functions, related to the water quality of the boundary waters of the Great Lakes System, as the Commission may request from time to time.
    (b)   The Water Quality Board, at the direction of the Commission, shall:
        (i)   Make recommendations on the development and implementation of programs to achieve the purpose of this Agreement;
        (ii)   Assemble and evaluate information evolving from such programs;
        (iii) Identify deficiencies in the scope and funding of such programs and evaluate the adequacy and compatibility of results;

        (iv) Examine the appropriateness of such programs in the light of present and future socio-economic imperatives; and

        (v) Advise the Commission on the progress and effectiveness of such programs and submit appropriate recommendations.

(c)   The Water Quality Board, on behalf of the Commission, shall undertake liaison and coordination between the institutions established under this Agreement and other institutions and jurisdictions which may address concerns relevant to the Great Lakes Basin Ecosystem so as to ensure a comprehensive and coordinated approach to planning and to the resolution of problems, both current and anticipated.

(d)   The Water Quality Board shall report to the Commission periodically as appropriate, or as required by the Commission, on all aspects relating to the operation and effectiveness of this Agreement.

2. *Great Lakes Science Advisory Board*

(a)   This Board shall be the scientific advisor to the Commission and the Water Quality Board.

(b)   The Science Advisory Board shall be responsible for developing recommendations on all matters related to research and the development of scientific knowledge pertinent to the identification, evaluation and resolution of current and anticipated problems related to Great Lakes water quality.

(c)   To effect these responsibilities the Science Advisory Board shall:

        (i) Review scientific information in order to:

            a.   examine the impact and adequacy of research and the reliability of research results, and ensure the dissemination of such results;

            b.   identify additional research requirements;

            c.   identify specific research programs for which international cooperation is desirable; and

        (ii) Advise jurisdictions of relevant research needs, solicit their involvement and promote coordination.

(d)   The Science Advisory Board shall seek analyses, assessments and recommendations from other scientific, professional, academic, governmental or intergovernmental groups relevant to Great Lakes Basin Ecosystem research.

(e)   The Science Advisory Board shall report to the Commission and the Water Quality Board periodically as appropriate, or as required by the Commission, on all matters of a scientific or research nature relating to the operation and effectiveness of this Agreement.

3. *The Great Lakes Regional Office*

(a)   This Office, located at Windsor, Ontario, shall assist the Commission and the two Boards in the discharge of the functions specified in subparagraph (b) below.

(b)   The Office shall perform the following functions:

        (i) Provide administrative support and technical assistance for the Water Quality Board and the Science Advisory Board and their sub-organizations, to assist the Boards in discharging effectively the responsibilities, duties and functions assigned to them.

        (ii) Provide a public information service for the programs, including public hearings, undertaken by the Commission and its Boards.

(c)   The Office shall be headed by a Director who shall be appointed by the Commission in consultation with the Parties and with the Co-Chairmen of the Boards. The position of Director shall alternate between a Canadian citizen and a United States citizen. The term of office for the Director shall be determined in the review referred to in subparagraph (d) below.

(d)   The Parties, mindful of the need to staff the Great Lakes Regional Office to carry out the functions assigned the Commission by this Agreement, shall, within six months from the date of entry into force of this Agreement, complete a review of the staffing of the Office. This review shall be conducted by the Parties based upon recommendations of the Commission after consultation with the Co-Chairmen of the Boards. Subsequent reviews may be requested by either Party, or recommended by the Commission, in order to ensure that the staffing of the Regional Office is maintained at a level and character commensurate with its assigned functions.

(e)   Consistent with the responsibilities assigned to the Commission, and under the general supervision of the Water Quality Board, the Director shall be responsible for the management of the Regional Office and its staff in carrying out the functions described herein.

(f)   The Co-Chairmen of the Boards, in consultation with the Director, will determine the activities which they wish the Office to carry out on behalf of, or in support of the Boards, within the current capability of the Office and its staff. The Director is responsible to the Co-Chairmen of each Board for activities carried out on behalf of, or in support of such Board, by the Office or individual staff members.

(g)   The Commission, in consultation with the Director, will determine the public information activities to be carried out on behalf of the Commission by the Regional Office.

(h)   The Director shall be responsible for preparing an annual budget to carry out the functions of the Boards and the Regional Office for submission jointly by the two Boards to the Commission for approval and procurement of resources.

Editors' Introductory Note Regarding the Amazon Basin. *Infra,* p. 545.

BRASILIA TREATY FOR AMAZONIAN CO-OPERATION.
Infra, p. 545.

AMAZON DECLARATION. *Infra*, p. 551.

E. EUROPE

ECONOMIC COMMISSION FOR EUROPE DECLARATION OF POLICY ON PREVENTION AND CONTROL OF WATER POLLUTION, INCLUDING TRANSBOUNDARY POLLUTION

Popular Name: ECE Declaration on Water Pollution

Adopted 23 April 1980, ECE Doc. ECE/DEC/B(XXXV), E/1980/28, *reprinted in* 6 EPL 148 (1980), 26 IPE 280.

Language: English

Editors' Note

In 1966, the ECE (described *supra*, p. 249) issued a Declaration of Policy on Water Pollution Control. The ECE developed and expanded upon those principles in its 1980 Declaration, which takes a comprehensive, integrated, long-term approach to water pollution. The 1980 Declaration, for example, considers both surface water and groundwater, both sea water and fresh water, all aspects of each drainage basin, and interactions among air, land, and water pollutants; and it calls for coordinated policy and participation at the local, national, and international levels, and for effective information and education programs. The Declaration also incorporates a broad polluter-pays principle: "as far as possible, the direct or indirect costs attributable to pollution should be borne by the polluter."

ECE DECLARATION OF POLICY ON PREVENTION AND CONTROL OF WATER POLLUTION, INCLUDING TRANSBOUNDARY POLLUTION

The Economic Commission for Europe,

* * *

1. *Decides* to adopt the Principles on prevention and control of water pollution, including transboundary pollution set forth in the appendix to this Decision, which complete and develop the Principles contained in the 1966 Declaration;
2. *Recommends* to ECE Governments that they consider the possibility of applying these Principles in formulating and carrying out their water policies and in their international co-operation;
3. *Invites* the member Governments to report in depth to the Commission at three year intervals, through the Committee on Water Problems, on the action taken by them in this regard;

* * *

PRINCIPLES

1. The conservation of water resources and the prevention and control of water pollution are integral parts of a comprehensive national policy in environmental protection and call for active participation of national and local public authorities and water users as well as close international co-operation. The rational utilization of water resources, both surface and underground, as a basic element in the framework of long-term water management, should be viewed as an effective support to the policy of prevention and control of water pollution, taking into account the special features of each drainage basin.
2. Water pollution control should be handled taking account of possible interactions of pollutants on air, land and water.
3. The aim of water pollution control is to preserve, as far as possible, the natural quality of surface and ground water, to protect the environment which depends on such water, and to decrease existing levels of water pollution in order to protect

public health and to allow the satisfaction of the needs of such water, under the best economic conditions and in sufficient quantity, in particular for: [1]
— providing drinking water of sufficiently good quality for human health;
— preserving the aquatic flora and fauna;
— providing water for industry;
— providing water for agriculture, in particular irrigation and animal consumption;
— recreation (sports and leisure) with due regard to sanitary and aesthetic requirements.

4. Governments should adopt a long-term policy directed towards the reduction of existing water pollution and its prevention in the future. To this end a series of interrelated measures should be developed including, so far as necessary, the improvement of water legislation and its implementation, the use of all legal and administrative measures, integrated land-use planning, and the application of suitable economic incentives to encourage, *inter alia*, the conservation of water, the optimization of water resources management, the elimination of pollutants, in particular, at source the development of low- and non-waste technology, including recycling of water, and research and development.

5. Important tools in water pollution control are standardization and monitoring of water quality in rivers and lakes or standardization and monitoring of effluents, or an appropriate combination of both; the quantitative and qualitative assessment of waste water and its treatment with due regard to the interests of water users and environmental protection. In setting criteria and standards, all types of water resources (surface, ground and sea water) and/or effluents should be covered. The criteria and standards themselves should, as far as possible, reflect public health, drinking water supply and environmental protection requirements and should also satisfy the demand for water in the industrial, agricultural, fisheries and other sectors of the economy.

6. Pollution of the aquatic environment by dangerous substances that are toxic, persistent and bioaccumulative should be prevented by using the best available technology and eliminated within a reasonable period of time.

7. Governments should organize the implementation of water pollution control measures as part of their national policy of environmental protection, within the framework of their institutions and taking into account the nature of the problems to be solved. In this connexion, it may be desirable that States, within the limits of their constitutional and legislative competence, have at their disposal appropriate organs at the central or regional levels or at the level of the various hydrographic basins. It may be desirable that the central responsibility for water pollution control be vested in one authority or co-ordinating body on a sufficiently high level. This authority or body should carry out its work in collaboration with other authorities and within the framework of water resources, water utilization and public health policies in general. Furthermore, bodies such as committees, commissions, etc., composed of representatives of the public authorities, of representatives of users and independent experts may be entrusted with the task of helping and advising the above-mentioned organs.

8. To promote water pollution control and to protect both surface and underground water, it is essential to establish laws which prohibit all discharges of liquid and solid wastes from domestic, industrial and agricultural activities to surface waters and aquifers unless they have been authorized by the competent authority in charge of water pollution control. However, regulations for discharges of limited importance and special derogations, if appropriate, could be implemented in particular cases. In deciding whether to permit these discharges, the appropriate competent authority should ensure that the effluents are treated at least by the best practicable

---

[1]Apart from drinking water, these uses are not necessarily listed in order of importance.

technology possible and that they will not endanger public health or life in general and should take particular account of the following factors:

(a) the capacity of the receiving water to assimilate materials being discharged, taking into account the physical, chemical, biological, microbiological and radio-active characteristics of these materials;

(b) the evaluation of the environmental, social and economic advantages and disadvantages of possible methods of treatment and disposal.

9. Each country should take all appropriate steps to prevent pollution of the sea, namely by the direct or indirect introduction by man into the marine environment—including estuaries—of substances or energy which may endanger human health, harm living resources and the marine ecosystem, affect amenities or interfere with other legitimate uses of the sea. Governments should therefore seek: to reduce progressively land-based pollution provoked by toxic, non-degradable and bioaccumulative substances enumerated in the appropriate supplements to different international conventions; to prohibit or to set up controls by specific permits, according to the different international conventions, of the discharge of these substances from their territories into the sea; and to carry out the principles set out in the convention pertaining to the reduction and prohibition of pollution caused in coastal areas and estuaries by exploration and exploitation of the resources of the sea.

10. It is essential that legislation on water use and pollution control should be drawn up and applied in such a way that if violations occur effective sanctions can be imposed. The competent authorities should be authorized to take immediate action in case of need.

11. The general principle should be adopted that, as far as possible, the direct or indirect costs attributable to pollution should be borne by the polluter. Each State should use the most suitable economic incentives in order to discourage pollution and encourage the reduction of polluting discharges and the development of new technologies which are less polluting. Strategies for water pollution control should include, in addition to the installation of effluent treatment plants, the adoption of preventive measures at the earliest possible stage in the production processes, especially through the incorporation of low- and non-waste technology, water recycling and the rational use of chemicals and fertilizers in agriculture and forestry, as well as the implementation of land-use policies.

12. States should establish information and educational programmes in order to influence individual behaviour in relation to water utilization and pollution and to promote the acceptance of responsibility for dealing with water problems.

13. States sharing water resources[2] should undertake, on the basis of their national policies, concerted action to improve the quality of surface and groundwater, to control pollution and to guard against accidental pollution. These States should, by means of bilateral or multilateral agreements define their mutual relations on water pollution control, especially through the widest possible exchange of information and through consultations at an early stage in regard to activities likely to have significant adverse effects on water quality in the territory of the other States. In these agreements, water quality standards and/or emission standards for a particular water body should be established, where necessary. These agreements would also stipulate the obligations of the States in solving water pollution problems, including their scientific and technological aspects. Provision should be made in particular for the use of existing structures of co-operation and for seeking new ones, as appropriate, to meet fully the interests of expanding and intensifying international relations.

---

[2]The term "shared water resources" is used only for the uniformity of the text and its use does not prejudice the position of the countries supporting the terms "transboundary waters" or "international waters" in any of the problems involved.

14. International co-operation on water problems, within the United Nations Economic Commission for Europe and other competent international organizations operating within the ECE region should facilitate the exchange of experience between countries and help them to find the most appropriate solutions through the exchange of available information, especially on ways of predicting and effectively avoiding adverse environmental consequences of economic activities and new technology. This co-operation should include: exchange of scientific and technical information including experience of structure, design and technology of waste water treatment plants, and on the development and introduction of low- and non-waste technology; exchange of researchers, specialists, trainees; carrying out joint studies; comparison of long-term national policies for rational water use and water protection; organization of scientific and technical meetings; and comparison of water quality criteria and standards as well as their methods of application.

Editors' Introductory Note Regarding Protection of the Rhine River Against Pollution

The Rhine basin is one of the most densely populated and highly industrialized parts of Europe, and it is subject to pollution from human habitation as well as industrial and agricultural activities. International efforts to deal with such pollution date at least to the nineteenth century, but there was no concerted anti-pollution program until after World War II.

The International Commission for the Protection of the Rhine Against Pollution was established in 1965, pursuant to the Berne Convention. The Rhine Commission was directed to investigate the nature, extent, and origin of pollution of the Rhine, propose measures to protect the Rhine against pollution, and prepare bases for possible future conventional regimes. The Berne Convention did not impose any substantive obligations on the member States. Various types of pollution—e.g., chemical and thermal—continued to plague the Rhine.

In 1976, two additional conventions were concluded. The 1976 Rhine Chemical Convention seeks to eliminate certain toxic substances and to reduce pollution from other, less dangerous substances. As the European Economic Community has authority to regulate in this area, it is a party to this Convention. The Rhine Commission has a major role in implementing this Convention.

The 1976 Rhine Chlorides Convention was intended to combat the high salinity of the Rhine by reducing the discharge of waste salts into the Rhine from potassium mines and other sources in France. The costs of doing that are shared among four countries: Federal Republic of Germany, 30%; France, 30%; Netherlands; 34%; and Switzerland, 6%. Downstream States such as the Netherlands apparently reached the conclusion that it is less expensive to pay for part of the costs of preventing the pollution than to experience the damage from the pollution. The increasing incidence of arrangements such as this has led some to question the prevalence or appropriateness of the polluter-pays principle at the inter-State level (described *infra*, p. 706).

BERNE CONVENTION ON THE INTERNATIONAL COMMISSION FOR THE PROTECTION OF THE RHINE AGAINST POLLUTION

Popular Name: Berne Convention

Done at Berne on 29 April 1963, 994 UNTS 3, *reprinted in* UNEP3 #29, p.176, 10 IPE 4820, IELMT 963: 31.
Entry into Force: 1 May 1965

Depositary: Switzerland

Languages: Dutch, French, German

Parties as of September 1990: France; Germany, Federal Republic of;* Luxembourg; Netherlands;* Switzerland

[Translation]

AGREEMENT ON THE INTERNATIONAL COMMISSION FOR THE PROTECTION OF THE RHINE AGAINST POLLUTION

The Governments of the Federal Republic of Germany, the French Republic, the Grand Duchy of Luxembourg, the Kingdom of the Netherlands and the Swiss Confederation,
Concerned to protect the quality of the waters of the Rhine,
Endeavouring to prevent future pollution and to improve the present state of the river,
Convinced of the urgency of that mission,
Desiring to strengthen the co-operation which has existed in that field between the signatory Governments since 1950,
Have agreed as follows:

Article 1

The signatory Governments shall continue to co-operate in the protection of the waters of the Rhine downstream from the Untersee in the framework of the International Commission for the Protection of the Rhine against Pollution.

Article 2

1. The Commission shall:
(*a*)   prepare, commission and avail itself of the results of all investigations necessary to determine the nature, extent and origin of the pollution of the Rhine;

---

* With geographic extension or limitation

(b)   propose to the signatory Governments appropriate measures to protect the Rhine against pollution;

(c)   prepare the bases for possible future arrangements between the signatory Governments concerning the protection of the waters of the Rhine.

2. The Commission's competence shall also extend to all other matters which the signatory Governments refer to it by common consent.

Article 3

1. The Commission shall consist of delegations from the signatory Governments. Each Government shall appoint not more than four delegates, one of whom shall be the head of the delegation.

2. Each delegation may call upon experts for assistance in the consideration of specific questions. The Commission shall determine the conditions governing their participation in its work.

Article 4

1. The chairmanship of the Commission shall rotate every three years among the delegations, in the order in which the signatory Governments are listed in the preamble; the delegation which holds the chairmanship shall appoint one of its members as chairman.

2. As a general rule, the chairman shall not speak on behalf of his delegation at meetings of the Commission.

Article 5

1. The Commission shall hold one regular session each year, which shall be convened by the chairman.

2. Special sessions shall be convened by the chairman at the request of two delegations.

3. The chairman shall draw up the agenda. Each delegation shall have the right to include any item it wants discussed in that agenda. The order of priority shall be decided by the Commission by majority vote.

Article 6

1. Each delegation shall have one vote.

2. Decisions of the Commission, unless otherwise provided by this Agreement, shall be taken in the presence of all delegations and shall be unanimous; they may be taken by a written procedure under conditions to be determined by the rules of procedure.

3. The abstention of only one delegation shall not constitute an obstacle to unanimity.

Article 7

1. The Commission shall establish a working group for current investigations and may, when necessary, establish others for specific purposes.

2. The working groups shall be composed of delegates or experts appointed by each delegation.

3. The Commission shall determine the mandate of each working group, fix the maximum number of its members and appoint its chairman.

Article 8

In its investigations and in availing itself of their results, the Commission may use the services of a scientific institution which offers all the requisite guarantees of independence.

Article 9

The Commission may, for the purpose of considering special problems, use the services of competent individuals or agencies.

Article 10

The Commission shall co-operate with the international commissions for the Rhine and its tributaries and may decide to co-operate with other organizations for water protection.

Article 11

The Commission shall submit an annual report of its activities to the signatory Governments, which shall include, *inter alia*, the results of investigations undertaken and an analysis of such results.

Article 12

1. Each signatory Government shall bear the cost of its representation in the Commission and the working groups and the cost of current investigations undertaken in its territory.

2. The costs relating to the work of the Commission shall be apportioned among the signatory Governments in the following manner:

Federal Republic of Germany 28%
French Republic 28%
Grand Duchy of Luxembourg 2%
Kingdom of the Netherlands 28%
Swiss Confederation 14%

TOTAL 100%

The Commission may, in certain cases, decide on a different apportionment.

Article 13

The Commission shall establish its own rules of procedure.

Article 14

The working languages of the Commission shall be German and French.

Article 15

1. Each of the signatory Governments shall notify the Government of the Swiss Confederation of the completion, on its part, of the constitutional procedures required for the entry into force of this Agreement; the Government of the Swiss Confederation shall immediately confirm the date of receipt of such notification and shall inform the other signatory Governments. The Agreement shall enter into force on the first day of the month following receipt of the last notification.

2. Upon the expiry of a period of three years after its entry into force, this Agreement may be denounced at any time by any of the signatory Governments,

subject to six months' notice, by means of a declaration sent to the Government of the Swiss Confederation.

Article 16

This Agreement, prepared in one copy in the German, French and Dutch languages, all three texts being equally authentic, shall be deposited in the archives of the Government of the Swiss Confederation, which shall transmit an authenticated copy thereof to each of the signatory Governments.

PROTOCOL OF SIGNATURE

Upon signing the Agreement on the International Commission for the Protection of the Rhine against Pollution, the signatory Governments have agreed on the following points:

Ad article 2, paragraph 1 (a)

For all investigations carried out in accordance with article 2, paragraph 1 (*a*), the Commission shall, in accordance with the provisions of article 6, take a decision on the subject and scope of the investigation. Such investigations shall in principle be carried out by the competent national bodies.

Ad article 4, paragraph 1

The term of service of the first chairman shall expire at the end of the third calendar year beginning after the entry into force of this Agreement.

Ad article 8

The Government of the Federal Republic of Germany proposes to the Commission that the scientific institution referred to in article 8 should be an independent technical secretariat to be established at the Federal Institute of Hydrology at Koblenz. The said secretariat shall be subject, in connexion with its work, only to the authority of the Commission, which, acting through its chairman, shall convey all relevant instructions to the secretariat.

The secretariat shall, giving due regard to article 2 and the addendum to it, assist the working groups provided for in article 7 and the competent national bodies in carrying out their investigations and availing themselves of the results obtained. It shall, in particular, make arrangements for the publication of the Commission's reports. Each signatory Government may at any time send representatives to the secrtariat to obtain information concerning its activity and possibly to take part in its work.

The signatory Governments agree that their representatives in the Commission shall, within two months after the entry into force of the Agreement, accept the proposal of the Government of the Federal Republic of Germany for a period of five years.

They agree that the Commission may, by means of a resolution, extend the mandate of the Institute at Koblenz, choose any other institution or adopt any other provisions.

Ad article 10

The co-operation provided for in article 10 shall be carried on, in particular, with the international commissions for the protection of the Moselle, the Saar and

Lake Constance and also with the central commission for Rhine navigation. In that connexion, an effort shall be made principally to maintain regular and complete exchanges of information.

Ad article 12, paragraph 2

The apportionment provided for in article 12, paragraph 2, shall not apply to the measures proposed in accordance with article 2, paragraph 1 (*b*), for the protection of the Rhine.

BONN CONVENTION ON THE PROTECTION OF THE RHINE RIVER AGAINST CHEMICAL POLLUTION

Popular Name: Rhine Chemical Convention

Done at Bonn on 3 December 1976, 1124 UNTS 375, *reprinted in* 16 UNEP3 #70, p.468, ILM 242 (1977), 25 IPE 440, IELMT 976: 89.
Entry into Force: 1 February 1979

Depositary: Switzerland

Languages: Dutch, French, German

Parties as of 1 September 1990: France; Germany, Federal Republic of; Luxembourg; Netherlands; Switzerland; European Economic Community

[Translation]

AGREEMENT FOR THE PROTECTION OF THE RHINE AGAINST CHEMICAL POLLUTION

The Government of the Federal Republic of Germany, the Government of the French Republic, the Government of the Grand Duchy of Luxembourg, the Government of the Kingdom of the Netherlands, the Government of the Swiss Confederation and the European Economic Community,

Referring to the Agreement of 29 April 1963 and the Additional Agreement of 3 December 1976 on the International Commission for the Protection of the Rhine against Pollution,

Considering that chemical pollution of the waters of the Rhine is a threat to its flora and fauna and also has undesirable effects on sea water,

Conscious of the dangers for certain uses of the waters of the Rhine that may result from such pollution,

Desiring to improve the quality of the waters of the Rhine with these uses in mind,

Considering that the Rhine is also used for other purposes, in particular for shipping and for receiving effluents,

Convinced that international action to protect the waters of the Rhine against chemical pollution must be evaluated in conjunction with other efforts to protect these waters, in particular efforts aimed at the conclusion of agreements to counter pollution by chlorides and thermal pollution, and that such action forms part of the continuing and interrelated measures to protect both fresh water and sea water against pollution,

Considering the action taken by the European Economic Community to protect the waters, in particular under the Council's directive of 4 May 1976 concerning pollution resulting from specific dangerous substances discharged into the water environment of the Community,

Referring to the results of the ministerial conferences held on 25 and 26 October 1972 in The Hague, 4 and 5 December 1973 in Bonn and 1 April 1976 in Paris, on protection of the Rhine against pollution,

Have agreed as follows:

Article 1

(1) In order to improve the quality of the waters of the Rhine, the Contracting Parties, in accordance with the following provisions, shall take appropriate action:

(a)   To eliminate pollution of the surface waters of the Rhine basin by the dangerous substances included in the families and groupings of substances specified in annex I (hereinafter referred to as "substances listed in annex I"); they shall aim gradually to eliminate discharges of these substances, taking into account the findings of research carried out by specialists on each of these substances, as well as the technical means available;

(b)   To reduce pollution of the waters of the Rhine by those dangerous substances included in the families and groups of substances listed in annex II (hereinafter referred to as "substances listed in annex II").

(2) When taking the action referred to in paragraph 1, reasonable consideration shall be given to the fact that the waters of the Rhine are used for the following purposes:

(a)   Supplying drinking water for human consumption,

(b)   Consumption by domestic and wild animals,

(c)   Conserving and developing the natural flora and fauna, and maintaining the self-purifying capacity of the waters,

(d)   Fishing,

(e)   Recreation, taking hygienic and aesthetic requirements into consideration,

(f)   Direct or indirect supply of fresh water to agricultural land,

(g)   Production of water for industrial uses,

and the need to preserve an acceptable quality of sea water.

(3) The provisions of this Agreement are only the first step towards achieving the aim referred to in paragraph 1 of this article.

(4) Annex A of this Agreement provides a description of what the Contracting Parties understand by the term "Rhine" for purposes of implementing the Agreement.

Article 2

(1) The Governments Parties to this Agreement shall, in accordance with the provisions of annex III, paragraph 1, draw up a national list of those discharges into the surface waters of the Rhine basin that may contain substances covered in annex I to which emission standards may be applicable.

(2) The Governments shall, in accordance with the provisions of annex III, paragraph 2, inform the International Commission for the Protection of the Rhine against Pollution (hereinafter referred to as "the International Commission"), of

the items on this list, which shall be updated regularly and at least once every three years.

(3) The proposals made by the International Commission, referred to in article 6, paragraph 3, may, if necessary, contain a list of various substances listed in annex II.

Article 3

(1) Every discharge into the surface waters of the Rhine basin that may contain one of the substances listed in annex I shall require prior approval by the competent authority of the Government concerned.

(2) In the case of discharges of those substances into the surface waters of the Rhine basin and when required for the implementation of this Agreement, in the case of discharges of those substances into drains, the approval shall specify emission standards which shall not exceed the limits set in article 5.

(3) So far as current discharges of those substances are concerned, the approval shall set a deadline for compliance with its terms. This deadline shall not exceed the limits set in article 5, paragraph 3.

(4) Approval shall be given only for a limited period. It may be renewed in the light of any changes made in the limits referred to in article 5.

Article 4

(1) The emission standards specified in the approval granted under article 3 shall determine:

(a)　The permissible maximum concentration of a substance in discharges; in cases of dilution, the limits referred to in article 5, paragraph 2, subparagraph (a), shall be divided by the dilution factor;

(b)　The permissible maximum quantity of a substance in discharges over one or more fixed periods of time; if necessary, this maximum may also be expressed as a unit of weight of the pollutant per unit of the characteristic component of the polluting action (for instance, per unit of weight of raw material or per unit of product).

(2) If the discharger declares that he cannot comply with the prescribed emission standards, or if the competent authority of the Government concerned confirms this, permission shall be refused.

(3) If the emission standards are not being adhered to, the competent authority of the Government concerned shall take all appropriate steps to ensure that the terms of the approval are complied with and, where necessary, that the discharge is forbidden.

Article 5

(1) The International Commission shall propose the limits referred to in article 3, paragraph 2, and, where necessary, their applicability to discharges into drains. These limits shall be set in accordance with the procedure laid down in article 14. Once adopted, they shall be included in annex IV.

(2) These limits shall be determined:

(a)　By the permissible maximum concentration of a substance in the discharges; and

(b)　Where appropriate, by the permissible maximum quantity of such a substance, expressed as a unit of weight of the pollutant per unit of the component characteristic of the polluting action (for instance, per unit of weight of raw material or per unit of product).

Where appropriate, the limits applicable to industrial effluents shall be determined by sector and by product type.

The limits applicable to the substances listed in annex I shall be determined primarily on the basis of:
—Toxicity,
—Persistence,
—Bio-accumulation,
taking into consideration the best technical facilities available.

(3) The International Commission shall propose to the Parties to the Agreement the deadlines referred to in article 3, paragraph 3, taking into account the distinctive characteristics of the industrial sectors concerned and, where appropriate, of product types. These deadlines shall be established in accordance with the procedure laid down in article 14.

(4) The International Commission shall use the findings obtained at the international measurement points in order to establish to what extent the content of substances listed in annex I in the waters of the Rhine has changed after implementation of the foregoing provisions.

(5) The International Commission, if this is required from the point of view of the quality of the waters of the Rhine, may propose other measures aimed at reducing the pollution of the waters of the Rhine, particularly with regard to toxicity, persistence and bio-accumulation of the substance concerned. These proposals shall be adopted in accordance with the procedure laid down in article 14.

Article 6

(1) Every discharge of one of the substances listed in annex II which could detrimentally affect the quality of the waters of the Rhine shall be regulated by the national authorities with a view to introducing rigorous restrictions.

(2) The Governments Parties to this Agreement shall endeavour, within a period of two years from the entry into force of this Agreement, to establish national programmes reducing pollution of the waters of the Rhine by the substances listed in annex II; for their implementation they shall apply in particular the measures indicated in paragraphs 1, 4, 6 and 7 of this article.

(3) Before establishing these national programmes, the Contracting Parties shall confer in the International Commission in order to co-ordinate them. To this end, the International Commission shall regularly compare the draft national programmes in order to ensure their compatibility in terms of aims and means, and shall make proposals, in particular for the achievement of common aims relating to reducing the pollution of the waters of the Rhine. These proposals shall be adopted in accordance with the procedure laid down in article 14 of this Agreement. Comparison of national draft programmes shall not be allowed to cause delays in the implementation, at the national or regional level, of measures intended to reduce the pollution of the waters of the Rhine.

(4) For each discharge that may contain one of the substances listed in annex II, prior authorization shall be required from the competent authority of the Government concerned which establishes the emission standards. The standards shall be determined in terms of the quality goals indicated in paragraph 5.

(5) The programmes referred to in paragraph 2 of this article shall prescribe quality goals for the waters of the Rhine.

(6) The programmes may also include specific provisions concerning the composition and use of substances or groups of substances and of products, and shall take account of the latest economically viable technical developments.

(7) The programmes shall set deadlines for their implementation.

(8) The International Commission shall be provided with a summary of the programmes and the results of their implementation.

Article 7

(1) The Contracting Parties shall take all necessary statutory and administrative action in order to guarantee that storage of the substances listed in annexes I and II is organized so as to a avoid any danger of polluting the waters of the Rhine.

(2) The International Commission shall, as necessary, propose to the Contracting Parties appropriate measures for protecting groundwater in order to prevent pollution of the waters of the Rhine by the substances covered in annexes I and II.

Article 8

(1) The Contracting Parties shall ensure that discharges are regulated in accordance with this Agreement.

(2) They shall inform the International Commission annually of their experiences.

Article 9

Implementation of the measures adopted under this Agreement shall in no case lead to a direct or indirect increase in the pollution of the waters of the Rhine.

Article 10

(1) In order to monitor the proportion of substances covered in annexes I and II in the waters of the Rhine, each Government concerned shall be responsible for the installation and operation of measuring instruments and systems, at the agreed measurement stations on the Rhine, which shall serve to determine the concentration of these substances.

(2) Each Government concerned shall inform the International Commission regularly, and at least once annually, of the results of this monitoring process.

(3) The International Commission shall prepare an annual report which summarizes the results of the monitoring process and makes it possible to keep track of the changes in the quality of the waters of the Rhine.

Article 11

When a Government Party to this Agreement discovers in the waters of the Rhine a sudden and large increase of substances listed in annexes I and II, or becomes aware of an accident which may result in a serious threat to the quality of those waters, it shall immediately inform the International Commission and those Contracting Parties which may be affected, using a procedure to be established by the International Commission.

Article 12

(1) The Contracting Parties shall regularly inform the International Commission of the experience they have acquired through implementation of this Agreement.

(2) The International Commission shall draw up, as necessary, recommendations for progressive improvement in the implementation of this Agreement.

Article 13

The International Commission shall draw up recommendations for achieving comparability of results through the use of appropriate methods of measurement and analysis.

Article 14

(1) Annexes I to IV, which form an integral part of this Agreement, may be amended and supplemented in order to bring them into line with scientific and technical developments or to make the efforts to counter chemical pollution of the waters of the Rhine more effective.

(2) To this end, the International Commission shall recommend such amendments or additions as it deems useful.

(3) The amended or supplemented texts shall enter into force after their unanimous adoption by the Contacting Parties.

Article 15

Any dispute between the Contracting Parties, relating to the interpretation or implementation of this Agreement, which cannot be settled by negotiation shall, unless the Parties to the dispute decide otherwise, be submitted, at the request of either of them, to arbitration in accordance with the provisions of annex B which forms an integral part of this Agreement.

Article 16

In implementing this Agreement the European Economic Community and its member States shall take action with regard to those areas which fall within their respective jurisdictions.

* * *

Annex A

For the purposes of this Agreement, the Rhine begins where it leaves Lake Constance and includes those river arms through which it freely reaches the North Sea up to the coastline, including the IJssel up to Kampen.

When drawing up the national programmes referred to in article 6 of this Agreement—so far as quality goals are concerned—and when co-ordinating these programmes within the International Commission, the distinction between fresh river water and brackish river water shall be taken into consideration as necessary.

Annex B

Arbitration

(1) Except where the parties to the dispute decide otherwise, the arbitration procedure shall be carried out in accordance with the provisions of this annex.

(2) The Arbitration Tribunal shall consist of three members: each party to the dispute shall appoint one arbitrator and the two arbitrators thus appointed shall designate, by mutual agreement, the third arbitrator who shall be Chairman of the Tribunal. If, within two months after the appointment of the second arbitrator, the Chairman of the Arbitration Tribunal has not been designated, the President of the European Court of Human Rights shall appoint him within a further period of two months at the request of the party which first took action.

(3) If, within two months after receipt of the request referred to in article 15 of this Agreement, one of the parties to the dispute has not appointed a member of the Tribunal as required, the other party may bring the matter before the President

of the European Court of Human Rights, who shall designate the Chairman of the Arbitration Tribunal within a further period of two months. As soon as the Chairman of the Arbitration Tribunal has been designated, he shall request the party that has not appointed an arbitrator to do so within a period of two months. At the end of this period, he shall bring the matter before the President of the European Court of Human Rights, who shall make the designation within a further period of two months.

(4) If, in the cases referred to in the foregoing paragraphs, the President of the European Court of Human Rights is unable to act or if he is a national of one of the parties to the dispute, the designation of the Chairman of the Arbitration Tribunal or the appointment of the arbitrator shall be made by the Vice-President of the Court or by the most senior member of the Court who is not prevented from acting and who is not a national of one of the parties to the dispute.

(5) The foregoing provisions shall apply, *mutatis mutandis*, to the filling of vacancies as they occur.

(6) The Arbitration Tribunal shall take its decisions on the basis of the rules of international law and, in particular, the provisions of this Agreement.

(7) The Arbitration Tribunal shall take its decisions, on both procedural and substantive matters, by a majority vote; the absence or abstention of one of the members of the Court appointed by the parties shall not prevent the Tribunal from reaching a decision. In the event of a tie the Chairman shall have the casting vote. The decisions of the Tribunal shall be binding on the parties. The parties shall defray the expenses of the member whom they have appointed and shall share the other costs equally. In all other respects the Arbitration Tribunal shall establish its own rules of procedure.

(8) In the case of a dispute between two Contracting Parties of which one is a State member of the European Economic Community, itself a Contracting Party, the other Party shall address its request both to the member State and to the Community which, within a period of two months after receipt of the request, shall together inform the Party whether the member State, the Community, or the member State and the Community jointly will be a party to the dispute. If such notification is not made within the designated period, the member State and the Community shall be deemed, for purposes of the provisions of this annex, to be one and the same party to the dispute. The same shall apply when the member State and the Community jointly constitute a party to the dispute.

Annex I

Families and Groups of Substances

Annex I specifies some individual substances forming part of the following families and groups of substances which are to be selected principally on the basis of their toxicity, persistence and bio-accumulation, except for substances which are biologically harmless or which rapidly become biologically harmless:

(1) Organic halogen compounds and substances which may produce such compounds in water;
(2) Organic phosphorus compounds;
(3) Organic tin compounds;
(4) Substances which have been shown to have a carcinogenic effect in or through the action of water,*

---

* To the extent that some substances in annex II have carcinogenic properties, they are included under category 4 of this annex.

(5) Mercury and mercury compounds;
(6) Cadmium and cadmium compounds;
(7) Stable mineral oils and stable petroleum-base hydrocarbons.

Annex II

Families and Groups of Substances

Annex II specifies:

—Substances forming part of the families and groups of substances listed in annex I for which the limits referred to in article 5 of this Agreement have not been established;

—Certain individual substances and certain categories of substances forming part of the families and groups of substances mentioned below, that have a detrimental effect on water; this effect may, however, be limited to a particular area and will depend on the characteristics of the waters which receive them and on their situation.

Families and groups of substances as referred to under the second dash above:

(1) The following metalloids and metals and their compounds:

(1) Zinc;	(6) Selenium;	(11) Tin;	(16) Vanadium;
(2) Copper;	(7) Arsenic;	(12) Barium;	(17) Cobalt;
(3) Nickel;	(8) Antimony;	(13) Beryllium;	(18) Thallium;
(4) Chromium;	(9) Molybdenum;	(14) Borium;	(19) Tellurium;
(5) Lead;	(10) Titanium;	(15) Uranium;	(20) Silver;

(2) Biocides and their derivatives not specified in annex I;

(3) Substances detrimental to the taste and/or smell of water-derived products intended for human consumption, and also compounds which may produce such substances in the waters;

(4) Toxic or stable organic silicon compounds and substances which could produce such compounds in water, except for those which are biologically harmless or which in water are rapidly converted into harmless substances;

(5) Inorganic phosphorus compounds and elementary phosphorus;

(6) Non-stable mineral oils and non-stable petroleum-based carbohydrates;

(7) Cyanides, fluorides;

(8) Substances which upset the oxygen balance, such as ammonia, nitrites.

Annex III

(1) The national list referred to in article 2, paragraph 1, of this Agreement concerns the dischargers, the discharge points, the substances discharged, classified by type, and the amount of these substances.

(2) The listed items, mentioned in article 2, paragraph 2, refer to respective total quantities of the various substances listed in annex I which are discharged into the waters of the Rhine basin between the measurement points proposed by the International Commission and adopted by all Contracting Parties.

Annex IV

Limits (Article 5)

Substance or group of substances	Origin	Limit expressed as the maximum concentration of a substance	Limit expressed as the maximum quantity of a substance	Deadline for current discharges	Remarks

BONN CONVENTION ON THE PROTECTION OF THE RHINE RIVER AGAINST POLLUTION BY CHLORIDES

Popular Name: Rhine Chloride Convention

Done at Bonn on 3 December 1976, *reprinted in* 16 ILM 265 (1977), 26 IPE 1, IELMT 976: 90.
Entry into Force: 5 July 1985

Depositary: Switzerland

Languages: Dutch, French, German

Parties as of September 1990: France; Germany, Federal Republic of; Luxembourg; Netherlands; Switzerland

[Translation]

CONVENTION ON THE PROTECTION OF THE RHINE AGAINST POLLUTION BY CHLORIDES

The Government of the Federal Republic of Germany, The Government of the French Republic, The Government of the Grand Duchy of Luxembourg, The Government of the Kingdom of the Netherlands, and the Government of the Swiss Confederation,
Referring to the Agreement of April 29, 1963 concerning the International Commission for the Protection of the Rhine against Pollution,
Considering the present amount of chloride ions in the Rhine,
Aware of the damage that could result therefrom,
Referring to the findings and results of the Conference of Ministers on the Pollution of the Rhine, which took place at The Hague on October 25-26, 1972, during the course of which the desire was expressed to improve progressively the quality of the waters of the Rhine so that at the German-Netherlands border the chloride ion content will not be greater than 200 mg/l,
Have agreed on the following:

Article 1

1. The Contracting Parties will strengthen their cooperation for the purpose of fighting against the pollution of the Rhine by chloride ions on the basis, during an initial stage, of the provisions of this Convention.

2. Annex A to the Convention specifies what the Contracting Parties understand by the term "Rhine" for the purposes of the application of the aforementioned Convention.

Article 2

1. The discharge of chloride ions into the Rhine will be reduced by at least 60 kg/s of chloride ions (annual average). This objective will be achieved gradually and in French territory.

2. In order to achieve the objective indicated in the preceding paragraph, the French Government will, under the conditions set forth in Annex I of this Convention, install an injection system in the sub-soil of Alsace in order to reduce over a period of ten years the discharges from the Alsace Potassium Mines by an initial quantity of 20 kg/s of chloride ions. The installation shall be constructed as soon as possible, no later than 18 months after the entry into force of the Convention. The French Government will report regularly to the International Commission for the Protection of the Rhine against Pollution (hereinafter designated "the International Commission").

3. The Contracting Parties are agreed that the French Government will, after consideration of the results obtained during the initial stage described in paragraph 2, take all steps necessary to achieve before January 1, 1980 the objective set forth in paragraph 1, by injection into the Alsatian sub-soil or by other means, subject to an agreement on the technical terms and conditions of the project and on the financing of the costs relating thereto.

4. The French Government will present an over-all plan on the technical terms and conditions and the costs of the measures to be taken pursuant to paragraph 3.

Article 3

1. The Contracting Parties will take in their own territory, the necessary measures to prevent an increase in the amounts of chloride ions discharged into the Rhine basin. The national concentration figures are shown in Annex II.

2. An increase in the amounts of chloride ions from isolated discharges shall be admissible only to the extent that the Contracting Parties concerned will offset such concentration in their respective territories or if a general method of offsetting it is found within the framework of the International Commission. This provision shall not hinder the application of Article 6.

3. A Contracting Party may, in exceptional cases and for imperative reasons, after having requested the opinion of the International Commission, authorize an increase in concentration without immediately offsetting it.

4. The Contracting Parties will control all discharges of chloride ions greater than 1 kg/s in the basin of the Rhine in their territory.

5. Each Contracting Party will send an annual report to the International Commission which shall indicate as precisely as possible the increase in the chloride-ion concentration in the waters of the Rhine. This report shall be based on all significant data from pertinent national programs and shall distinguish discharges greater than 1 Kg/s from other discharges. Should such a distinction be impossible to make, it must be reported to the International Commission.

6. The Annex mentioned previously in paragraph 1 as well as the maximum concentration of 1 kg/s of chloride ions shall be reviewed each year by the International Commission as the situation develops. If necessary, the International Commission shall propose changes in the Annex to the Governments.

Article 4

1. The French Government, on its own initiative or at the request of another Contracting Party, may have the process of injection or resorption of chloride ions halted when there is evidence of serious danger to the environment and particularly to the water table.

2. The French Government, or any other requesting Party, will immediately inform the International Commission of the situation and will provide data on the extent and nature of the danger.

3. The French Government will immediately take the steps rendered necessary by the situation and will report them to the International Commission. When the situation is no longer considered dangerous, the chloride-ion injection or resorption process is to be resumed without delay.

4. The Contracting Parties will, at the request of one of them, consult among themselves within the International Commission if the need for additional measures should arise.

Article 5

If the process of injection or resorption of chloride ions causes damage for which compensation cannot be guaranteed fully or in part by the constructors of the works or by third parties, the Contracting Parties will consult among themselves at the request of one among them regarding a possible contribution that may be paid to the French Government.

Article 6

The International Commission shall present to the Contracting Parties within four years of the entry into force of the Convention proposals concerning the means to achieve progressively a new chloride-ion concentration limitation over the entire course of the Rhine.

Article 7

1. The expenses resulting from injection as provided in Article 2 paragraph 2 and from the preparatory works will be assumed by the French Party.

2. The Contracting Parties mentioned below will contribute to the total cost of 132 million French francs by means of a lump sum payment, prorated as follows:

Federal Republic of Germany	30%
Kingdom of the Netherlands	34%
Swiss Confederation	6%

The payments shall be made no later than three months after the entry into force of this Convention.

3. The Contracting Parties will deliberate, following the presentation of the over-all plan provided for in Article 2 (4) and at the request of the French Government, on the financing of the measures to be carried out in application of Article 2 (3) on the basis of the prorating given in paragraph 2 above. The costs of preliminary research, particularly relating to studies and exploration, and, in addition, the unforeseen expenses not covered by the financing of the first stage shall likewise be included in the financing plan.

Article 8

The payments specified in Article 7 (2) shall be made in French francs to account No. 440-09/line 1 in the Central Accounting Agency of the French Treasury.

Article 9

When, following the entry into force of this Convention, the International Commission ascertains that at one of the measuring points the load and concentration of chloride ions shows a continuing tendency to increase, it shall request each Contracting Party in whose territory the cause of this increase is located to take the necessary steps to halt it.

Article 10

1. If any difficulties should result from the application of Article 9, and a period of six months has gone by since such difficulties were noted by the International Commission, the latter, in order to present a report to the Governments, may call upon the services of an independent expert at the request of a Contracting Party.

2. The expenses relating to the inquiry, including the expert's fee shall be divided among the Contracting Parties mentioned below, as follows:

Federal Republic of Germany	two sevenths ($^2/_7$)
French Republic	two sevenths ($^2/_7$)
Kingdom of the Netherlands	two sevenths ($^2/_7$)
Swiss Confederation	one seventh ($^1/_7$)

The International Commission may, in certain cases, establish a different method for dividing the expenses.

Article 11

When a Contracting Party notes a sudden and sizeable increase in chloride ions in the waters of the Rhine or has knowledge of an accident that may seriously endanger the quality of those waters, it will report it without delay to the International Commission and to the Contracting Parties likely to be affected, according to a procedure to be established by the International Commission.

Article 12

1. Each Contracting Party concerned will be responsible at the appropriate measuring stations, for the installation and operation of the measuring equipment and systems serving to check the concentration of chloride ions in the waters of the Rhine.

2. The chloride-ion concentrations shall be determined on the basis of the measurements carried out according to the recommendations of the International Commission. ·

3. The Contracting Parties will report to the International Commission regularly and at least every six months the results of the checks carried out pursuant to paragraph 1 above.

Any dispute between the Contracting Parties regarding the interpretation or application of the present Convention that cannot be settled by negotiation shall, except when the Parties to the dispute decide otherwise, be subject, at the request of one of them, to arbitration in accordance with the provisions of Annex B. The latter, as well as Annexes A, I, and II shall form an integral part of this Convention.

* * *

ANNEX A

For the purposes of this Convention, the Rhine begins at the outlet from the lower lake and includes the branches of the river up to the fresh-water limit from which its waters flow freely into the North Sea, including the IJssel up to Kampen.

The fresh-water limit is the area where at low tide and at a time when the discharge of fresh water is low, a sizeable increase in the chloride content is noted owing to the presence of sea water. This area is, for the Nieuwe Maas, 1000 kilometers downstream from the Constance Bridge over the Rhine. The other fresh-water limit points shall be established by the International Commission, bearing in mind the methods for determining the limit as defined above.

ANNEX B
ARBITRATION

1. Unless the parties to the dispute decide otherwise, the procedure for arbitration shall be conducted in accordance with the provisions contained in this annex.

2. The Arbitral Tribunal shall be composed of three members. Each of the parties to the dispute shall name an arbitrator and the two arbitrators thus appointed shall designate by common accord a third arbitrator, who will become the Chief Arbitrator of the Tribunal.

If at the end of two months following the designation of the second arbitrator the Chief Arbitrator of the Tribunal has not been designated, the President of the European Court of Human Rights shall, at the request of the most diligent party, appoint one within a new two-month period.

3. If, within two months following the receipt of the request referred to in Article 13 of the Convention, one of the parties to the dispute does not appoint a member of the Tribunal, the other party may request the President of the European Court of Human Rights to appoint the Chief Arbitrator of the Arbitral Tribunal within a new two-month period. Upon his designation, the Chief Arbitrator of the Arbitral Tribunal shall request the party that has not named an arbitrator to do so within two months. If no action has been taken during that time, he shall then request the President of the European Court of Human Rights to make the appointment within a new two-month time limit.

4. If, in the cases referred to in the preceding paragraphs, the President of the European Court of Human Rights is unable to do so or if he is a national of one of the parties to the dispute, the designation of the Chief Arbitrator of the Arbitral Tribunal or the naming of an arbitrator shall fall to the Vice President of the Court, or to the oldest member of the Court who is able to do so and who is not a national of one of the parties to the dispute.

5. The foregoing provisions shall apply according to the case, in order to fill seats that have become vacant.

6. The Arbitral Tribunal shall hand down a decision according to the rules of international law and, in particular, according to the provisions of this Convention.

7. The decisions of the Arbitral Tribunal, on procedure as well as on the merits of the case, shall be adopted by a majority vote of its members, the absence or abstention of one of the members of the tribunal designated by the parties not precluding a decision on the part of the Tribunal. In the event of a tie vote, the Chief Arbitrator's vote shall prevail. The decisions of the Tribunal shall be binding on the parties. The latter shall bear the expenses of the arbitrator they have designated and shall divide the other expenses equally among themselves. On other points, the Arbitral Tribunal itself shall decide the procedure it will follow.

Annex II
NATIONAL CONCENTRATIONS RESULTING FROM CHLORIDE-ION DISCHARGES GREATER THAN 1 KG/S IN DIFFERENT SECTIONS OF THE RIVER

Sections of the River	in Switzerland		in France		in Germany		in the Netherlands	
	Average (1)	Maximum (2)	Average (1)	Maximum (2)	Average (1)	Maximum (2)	Average (1)	Maximum (2)
Stein am Rhein—Kembs	10							
Kembs—Seltz/Maxau			130 (3)		4.2	4.2		
Seltz/Maxau—Mainz					15.8	17.5		
Mainz—Braubach/Coblenz					9.9	10.0		
Braubach/Coblenz—Bimmen/Lobith			38 (4)		105	123.6		
Bimmen/Lobith—mouth of the river	10		168 (3)		134.9			

(1) Long-term average annual concentration after steps taken regarding discharges.
(2) Maximum admissible concentration (reached from time to time, for example at a time of increased flow).
(3) This value diminishes as the measures referred to in Article 2 are carried out.
(4) The chloride-ion discharges are modulated so that the concentration resulting from discharges greater than 1 kg/s of chloride ions does not exceed 400 mg/l of chloride ions at the Hauconcourt measuring station on the Moselle river. The indicated annual average load must not be exceeded.

CHAPTER 6
LAND AND SOIL

A. GENERAL

UNITED NATIONS FOOD & AGRICULTURE ORGANIZATION WORLD SOIL CHARTER

Adopted on 25 November 1981, 21 FAO Conf Resolution 8/81, *reprinted in* 50 FAO SB 79.
Languages: Arabic, Chinese, English, French, Russian, Spanish

Editors' Note

The formulation of a World Soil Charter was first recommended to FAO by the 1974 World Food Conference in Rome (Resolution VI). A text for the proposed Code was considered at the Sixth Session of FAO's Committee on Agriculture and by the 79th session of the FAO Council in 1981; that same year, the FAO Conference at its 21st session adopted the World Soil Charter.

WORLD SOIL CHARTER

PRINCIPLES

1. Among the major resources available to man is land, comprising soil, water and associated plants and animals: the use of these resources should not cause their degradation or destruction because man's existence depends on their continued productivity.
2. Recognizing the paramount importance of land resources for the survival and welfare of people and economic independence of countries, and also the rapidly increasing need for more food production, it is imperative to give high priority to promoting optimum land use, to maintaining and improving soil productivity and to conserving soil resources.
3. Soil degradation means partial or total loss of productivity from the soil, either quantitatively, qualitatively, or both, as a result of such processes as soil erosion by water or wind, salinization, waterlogging, depletion of plant nutrients, deterioration of soil structure, desertification and pollution. In addition, significant areas of soil are lost daily to non-agricultural uses. These developments are alarming in the light of the urgent need for increasing production of food, fibres and wood.
4. Soil degradation directly affects agriculture and forestry by diminishing yields and upsetting water regimes, but other sectors of the economy and the environment as a whole, including industry and commerce, are often seriously affected as well through, for example, floods or the silting up of rivers, dams and ports.
5. It is a major responsibility of governments that land-use programmes include measures toward the best possible use of the land, ensuring long-term maintenance and improvement of its productivity, and avoiding losses of productive soil. The land users themselves should be involved, thereby ensuring that all resources available are utilized in the most rational way.

6. The provision of proper incentives at farm level and a sound technical, institutional and legal framework are basic conditions to achieve good land use.

7. Assistence given to farmers and other land users should be of a practical service-oriented nature and should encourage the adoption of measures of good land husbandry.

8. Certain land-tenure structures may constitute an obstacle to the adoption of sound soil management and conservation measures on farms. Ways and means should be pursued to overcome such obstacles with respect to the rights, duties and responsibilities of land owners, tenants and land users alike, in accordance with the recommendations of the World Conference on Agrarian Reform and Rural Development (Rome, 1979).

9. Land users and the broad public should be well informed of the need and the means of improving soil productivity and conservation. Particular emphasis should be placed on education and extension programmes and training of agricultural staff at all levels.

10. In order to ensure optimum land use, it is important that a country's land resources be assessed in terms of their suitability at different levels of inputs for different types of land use, including agriculture, grazing and forestry.

11. Land having the potential for a wide range of uses should be kept in flexible forms of use so that future options for other potential uses are not denied for a long period of time or forever. The use of land for non-agricultural purposes should be organized in such a way as to avoid, as much as possible, the occupation or permanent degradation of good-quality soils.

12. Decisions about the use and management of land and its resources should favour the long-term advantage rather than the short-term expedience that may lead to exploitation, degradation and possible destruction of soil resources.

13. Land conservation measures should be included in land development at the planning stage and the costs included in development planning budgets.

GUIDELINES FOR ACTION

Acceptance of these Principles would require the following action:

By governments

i. Develop a policy for wise land use according to land suitability for different types of utilization and the needs of the country.

ii. Incorporate principles of rational land use and management and conservation of soil resources into appropriate resource legislation.

iii. Develop an institutional framework for monitoring and supervising soil management and soil conservation, and for coordination between organizations involved in the use of the countries' land resources in order to ensure the most rational choice among possible alternatives.

iv. Assess both new lands and the lands already being used for their suitability for different uses and the likely hazards of degradation. Provide decision makers with alternative land uses which both satisfy communities' aspirations and use the land according to its capabilities.

v. Implement education, training and extension programmes at all levels in soil management and conservation.

vi. Disseminate as widely as possible information and knowledge about soil erosion and methods of controlling it both at the farm level and at the scale of entire watersheds, stressing the importance of soil resources for the benefit of people and development.

vii. Establish links between local government administrations and land users for the implementation of the soils policy and emphasize the need to put proven soil conservation techniques into practice, and to integrate appropriate measures in forestry and agriculture for the protection of the environment.

viii. Strive to create socio-economic and institutional conditions favourable to rational land resource management and conservation. These conditions will include providing security of land tenure and adequate financial incentives (e.g., subsidies, taxation relief, credit) to the land user. Give encouragement particularly to groups willing to work in cooperation with each other and with their government to achieve appropriate land use, soil conservation and improvement.

ix. Conduct research programmes which will provide sound scientific backing to practical soil improvements and soil conservation work in the field, and which give due consideration to prevailing socio-economic conditions.

By international organizations

i. Continue and intensify efforts to create awareness and encourage cooperation among all sectors of the international community, by assisting where required to mount publicity campaigns, conduct seminars and conferences and to provide suitable technical publications.

ii. Assist governments, especially of developing countries, on request, to establish appropriate legislation, institutions and procedures to enable them to mount, implement and monitor appropriate land-use and soil-conservation programmes.

iii. Promote cooperation between governments in adopting sound land-use practices, particularly in the large international watersheds.

iv. Pay particular attention to the needs of agricultural development projects which include the conservation and improvement of soil resources, the provision of inputs and incentives at the level of the farm and of the watershed, and the establishment of the necessary institutional structures as the major components.

v. Support research programmes relevant to soil conservation, not only of a technical nature but also research into social and economic issues which are linked to the whole question of soil conservation and land resource management.

vi. Ensure the storage, compilation and dissemination of experience and information related to soil conservation programmes and of the results obtained in different agro-ecological regions of the world.

CHAPTER 7
OUTER SPACE

Editors' Introductory Note Regarding Outer Space

Almost immediately upon the birth of the "Space Age" with the launching of the first Sputnik in 1957, the UN General Assembly took leadership in developing the international law that would evidently be necessary to control this new technology for the benefit of the world community. It did so by first establishing the Committee on the Peaceful Uses of Outer Space (COPUOS) (A/RES/1472(XIV)), with a Scientific and Technical and a Legal Sub-Committee, all of which meet annually and report to the Assembly. On the basis of the work of these bodies, the Assembly on 13 December 1963 adopted the Declaration of Legal Principles Governing the Activities of States in the Exploration and Use of Outer Space (A/RES/1962(XVII)), and thereupon instructed COPUOS to embody the concepts set out in the Declaration in a set of treaty instruments.

After some preliminary work, the Legal Sub-Committee of COPUOS, then the Committee itself, and finally the General Assembly at their respective sessions in 1966 considered and adopted (A/RES/2222(XXI) of 19 December 1966) the Treaty on Principles Governing the Activities of States in the Exploration and Use of Outer Space, including the Moon and Other Celestial Bodies, which furnishes a general basis for the peaceful uses of outer space and provides a framework for developing international law for that frontier. Like the 1963 Declaration, the so-called Outer Space Treaty is general in nature, setting out various prohibitions, allocation of responsibilities and other rules regarding space activities. From the environmental point of view Article IX is of special importance, in providing that space activities must be carried out so as not to affect adversely either space itself or the earth.

Following the adoption of the Outer Space Treaty, COPUOS, through its standing Sub-Committees, formulated and the General Assembly adopted four further treaties that elaborate certain concepts set out in the 1963 Declaration and the 1966 Treaty. One of these is the Convention on International Liability for Damage Caused by Space Objects (A/RES/2777(XXVI) of 29 November 1971), first considered by the Legal Sub-Committee at its second session in 1963, which allocates liability and the procedure for the presentation and settlement of any claims.

Another of these treaties is the Agreement Governing the Activities of States on the Moon and other Celestial Bodies (A/RES/34/68 of 5 December 1979), which was under consideration by the Legal Sub-Committee and its parent bodies from 1972 through 1979. Article 7(1) of that treaty (which is not reproduced herein) requires States Parties to take measures to "prevent the disruption of the existing balance of [the moon's] environment, whether by introducing adverse changes in that environment, by its harmful contamination through the introduction of extra-environmental matter or otherwise" and also to "avoid harmfully affecting the

459

environment of the earth through the introduction of extraterrestrial matter or otherwise.'' The next paragraph requires States to inform the UN Secretary-General of the measures they adopt in compliance with those provisions and in any event in advance of any placement of radioactive materials on the moon; finally a third paragraph foresees the possibility of designating on the moon certain areas ''as international scientific preserves.''

TREATY ON PRINCIPLES GOVERNING THE ACTIVITIES OF STATES IN THE EXPLORATION AND USE OF OUTER SPACE, INCLUDING THE MOON AND OTHER CELESTIAL BODIES

Popular Name: Outer Space Treaty

Done at London, Moscow, and Washington on 27 January 1967, A/RES/ 2222(XXI), 610 UNTS 205, 18 UST 2410, TIAS 6347, *reprinted in* 6 ILM 386 (1967), 1 IPE 30, IELMT 967: 07.
Entry into Force: 10 October 1967

Depositaries: Union of Soviet Socialist Republics; United Kingdom of Great Britain and Northern Ireland; United States of America

Languages: Chinese, English, French, Russian, Spanish

Parties as of 1 January 1990: Afghanistan; Antigua and Barbuda; Argentina; Australia; Austria; Bahamas; Bangladesh; Barbados; Belgium; Benin; Brazil; Brunei Darussalam; Bulgaria; Burkina Faso; Burma; Byelorussian Soviet Socialist Republic; Canada; Chile; China; Cuba; Cyprus; Czech and Slovak Federal Republic; Denmark; Dominica; Dominican Republic; Ecuador; Egypt; El Salvador; Fiji; Finland; France; German Democratic Republic; Germany, Federal Republic of; Greece; Grenada; Guinea-Bissau; Hungary; Iceland; India; Iraq; Ireland; Israel; Italy; Jamaica; Japan; Kenya; Korea, Republic of; Kuwait; Lao People's Democratic Republic; Lebanon; Libyan Arab Jamahiriya; Madagascar; Mali; Mauritius; Mexico; Mongolia; Morocco; Nepal; Netherlands;* New Zealand; Niger; Norway; Pakistan; Papua New Guinea; Peru; Poland; Romania; Saint Kitts and Nevis; Saint Lucia; San Marino; Saudi Arabia; Seychelles; Sierra Leone; Singapore; South Africa; Spain; Sri Lanka; Swaziland; Sweden; Switzerland; Syrian Arab Republic; Thailand; Togo; Tonga; Tunisia; Turkey; Uganda; Ukrainian Soviet Socialist Republic; Union of Soviet Socialist Republics; United Kingdom of Great Britain and Northern Ireland;* United States of America; Uruguay; Venezuela; Viet Nam; Yemen, Democratic; Zambia

---

*With a geographic extension

Treaty on Principles Governing the Activities of States in the Exploration and Use of Outer Space, Including the Moon and Other Celestial Bodies

* * *

Article I

The exploration and use of outer space, including the moon and other celestial bodies, shall be carried out for the benefit and in the interests of all countries, irrespective of their degree of economic or scientific development, and shall be the province of all mankind.

Outer space, including the moon and other celestial bodies, shall be free for exploration and use by all States without discrimination of any kind, on a basis of equality and in accordance with international law, and there shall be free access to all areas of celestial bodies.

There shall be freedom of scientific investigation in outer space, including the moon and other celestial bodies, and States shall facilitate and encourage international co-operation in such investigation.

* * *

Article IX

In the exploration and use of outer space, including the moon and other celestial bodies, States Parties to the Treaty shall be guided by the principle of co-operation and mutual assistance and shall conduct all their activities in outer space, including the moon and other celestial bodies, with due regard to the corresponding interests of all other States Parties to the Treaty. States Parties to the Treaty shall pursue studies of outer space, including the moon and other celestial bodies, and conduct exploration of them so as to avoid their harmful contamination and also adverse changes in the environment of the Earth resulting from the introduction of extraterrestrial matter and, where necessary, shall adopt appropriate measures for this purpose. If a State Party to the Treaty has reason to believe that an activity or experiment planned by it or its nationals in outer space, including the moon and other celestial bodies, would cause potentially harmful interference with activities of other States Parties in the peaceful exploration and use of outer space, including the moon and other celestial bodies, it shall undertake appropriate international consultations before proceeding with any such activity or experiment. A State Party to the Treaty which has reason to believe that an activity or experiment planned by another State Party in outer space, including the moon and other celestial bodies, would cause potentially harmful interference with activities in the peaceful exploration and use of outer space, including the moon and other celestial bodies, may request consultation concerning the activity or experiment.

* * *

CONVENTION ON THE INTERNATIONAL LIABILITY FOR DAMAGE CAUSED BY SPACE OBJECTS

Popular Name: Space Liability Convention

Done at London, Moscow, and Washington on 29 March 1972, A/RES/
2777(XXXVI), 961 UNTS 187, 24 UST 2389, TIAS 7762, *reprinted in* 17 IPE
8629, IELMT 972: 24.

Entry into Force: 1 September 1972

Depositaries: Union of Soviet Socialist Republics; United Kingdom
                       of Great Britain and Northern Ireland; United States of
                       America

Languages: Chinese, English, French, Russian, Spanish

Parties as of 1 January 1990: Antigua and Barbuda; Argentina; Australia; Austria;*
   Belgium; Benin; Botswana; Brazil; Bulgaria; Byelorussian Soviet Socialist Re-
   public; Canada;* Chile; China, Republic of (Taiwan); Cuba; Cyprus; Czech and
   Slovak Federal Republic; Denmark;* Dominica; Dominican Republic; Ecuador;
   Fiji; Finland; France; Gabon; German Democratic Republic; Germany, Federal
   Republic of;*** Greece; Grenada; Hungary; India; Iran, Islamic Republic of;
   Iraq; Ireland;* Israel; Italy; Japan; Kenya; Korea, Republic of; Kuwait; Laos;
   Liechtenstein; Luxembourg; Mali; Malta; Mexico; Mongolia; Morocco; Nether-
   lands; New Zealand;* Niger; Pakistan; Panama; Papua New Guinea; Poland;
   Qatar; Romania; Saint Kitts and Nevis; Saint Lucia; Saint Vincent and the
   Grenadines; Saudi Arabia; Senegal; Seychelles; Singapore; Solomon Islands;
   Spain; Sri Lanka; Sweden;* Switzerland; Syrian Arab Republic; Togo; Trinidad
   and Tobago; Tunisia; Ukrainian Soviet Socialist Republic; Union of Soviet So-
   cialist Republics; United Kingdom of Great Britain and Northern Ireland;***
   United States of America; Uruguay; Venezuela; Yugoslavia; Zambia; European
   Space Agency;** European Telecommunications Satellite Organization**

CONVENTION ON INTERNATIONAL LIABILITY FOR DAMAGE CAUSED BY SPACE OBJECTS

The States Parties to this Convention,
Recognizing the common interest of all mankind in furthering the exploration
and use of outer space for peaceful purposes,

* * *

*   With a declaration
** Declaration of acceptance in accordance with art. XXII
***With a geographic extension

Recognizing the need to elaborate effective international rules and procedures concerning liability for damage caused by space objects and to ensure, in particular, the prompt payment under the terms of this Convention of a full and equitable measure of compensation to victims of such damage,

* * *

Have agreed on the following:

ARTICLE I

For the purposes of this Convention:
(a)   The term "damage" means loss of life, personal injury or other impairment of health; or loss of or damage to property of States or of persons, natural or juridical, or property of international intergovernmental organizations;
(b)   The term "launching" includes attempted launching;
(c)   The term "launching State" means:
    (i)   A State which launches or procures the launching of a space object;
    (ii) A State from whose territory or facility a space object is launched;
(d)   The term "space object" includes component parts of a space object as well as its launch vehicle and parts thereof.

ARTICLE II

A launching State shall be absolutely liable to pay compensation for damage caused by its space object on the surface of the earth or to aircraft in flight.

ARTICLE III

In the event of damage being caused elsewhere than on the surface of the earth to a space object of one launching State or to persons or property on board such a space object by a space object of another launching State, the latter shall be liable only if the damage is due to its fault or the fault of persons for whom it is responsible.

ARTICLE IV

1. In the event of damage being caused elsewhere than on the surface of the earth to a space object of one launching State or to persons or property on board such a space object by a space object of another launching State, and of damage thereby being caused to a third State or to its natural or juridical persons, the first two States shall be jointly and severally liable to the third State, to the extent indicated by the following:
(a)   If the damage has been caused to the third State on the surface of the earth or to aircraft in flight, their liability to the third State shall be absolute;
(b)   If the damage has been caused to a space object of the third State or to persons or property on board that space object elsewhere than on the surface of the earth, their liability to the third State shall be based on the fault of either of the first two States or on the fault of persons for whom either is responsible.

2. In all cases of joint and several liability referred to in paragraph 1 of this article, the burden of compensation for the damage shall be apportioned between the first two States in accordance with the extent to which they were at fault; if the extent of the fault of each of these States cannot be established, the burden of

compensation shall be apportioned equally between them. Such apportionment shall be without prejudice to the right of the third State to seek the entire compensation due under this Convention from any or all of the launching States which are jointly and severally liable.

* * *

ARTICLE VI

1. Subject to the provisions of paragraph 2 of this article, exoneration from absolute liability shall be granted to the extent that a launching State establishes that the damage has resulted either wholly or partially from gross negligence or from an act or omission done with intent to cause damage on the part of a claimant State or of natural or juridical persons it represents.

2. No exoneration whatever shall be granted in cases where the damage has resulted from activities conducted by a launching State which are not in conformity with international law including, in particular, the Charter of the United Nations and the Treaty on Principles Governing the Activities of States in the Exploration and Use of Outer Space, including the Moon and Other Celestial Bodies.

ARTICLE VII

The provisions of this Convention shall not apply to damage caused by a space object of a launching State to:
(a)   Nationals of that launching State;
(b)   Foreign nationals during such time as they are participating in the opera-
       tion of that space object from the time of its launching or at any stage
       thereafter until its descent, or during such time as they are in the immedi-
       ate vicinity of a planned launching or recovery area as the result of an
       invitation by that launching State.

ARTICLE VIII

1. A State which suffers damage, or whose natural or juridical persons suffer damage, may present to a launching State a claim for compensation for such damage.

2. If the State of nationality has not presented a claim, another State may, in respect of damage sustained in its territory by any natural or juridical person, present a claim to a launching State.

3. If neither the State of nationality nor the State in whose territory the damage was sustained has presented a claim or notified its intention of presenting a claim, another State may, in respect of damage sustained by its permanent residents, present a claim to a launching State.

* * *

ARTICLE X

1. A claim for compensation for damage may be presented to a launching State not later than one year following the date of the occurrence of the damage or the identification of the launching State which is liable.

2. If, however, a State does not know of the occurrence of the damage or has not been able to identify the launching State which is liable, it may present a claim within one year following the date on which it learned of the aforementioned facts; however, this period shall in no event exceed one year following the date on which the State could reasonably be expected to have learned of the facts through the exercise of due diligence.

3. The time-limits specified in paragraphs 1 and 2 of this article shall apply even if the full extent of the damage may not be known. In this event, however, the claimant State shall be entitled to revise the claim and submit additional documentation after the expiration of such time-limits until one year after the full extent of the damage is known.

* * *

ARTICLE XII

The compensation which the launching State shall be liable to pay for damage under this Convention shall be determined in accordance with international law and the principles of justice and equity, in order to provide such reparation in respect of the damage as will restore the person, natural or juridical, State or international organization on whose behalf the claim is presented to the condition which would have existed if the damage had not occurred.

* * *

ARTICLE XIV

If no settlement of a claim is arrived at through diplomatic negotiations as provided for in article IX, within one year from the date on which the claimant State notifies the launching State that it has submitted the documentation of its claim, the parties concerned shall establish a Claims Commission at the request of either party.

ARTICLE XIX
* * *

2. The decision of the Commission shall be final and binding if the parties have so agreed; otherwise the Commission shall render a final and recomendatory award, which the parties shall consider in good faith. The Commission shall state the reasons for its decision or award.

* * *

ARTICLE XXI

If the damage caused by a space object presents a large-scale danger to human life or seriously interferes with the living conditions of the population or the functioning of vital centers, the States Parties, and in particular the launching State, shall examine the possibility of rendering appropriate and rapid assistance to the State which has suffered the damage, when it so requests. However, nothing in this article shall affect the rights or obligations of the States Parties under this Convention.

ARTICLE XXII

1. In this Convention, with the exception of articles XXIV to XXVII, references to States shall be deemed to apply to any international intergovernmental organization which conducts space activities if the organization declares its acceptance of the rights and obligations provided for in this Convention and if a majority of the States members of the organization are States Parties to this Convention and to the Treaty on Principles Governing the Activities of States in the Exploration and Use of Outer Space, including the Moon and Other Celestial Bodies.

* * *

CHAPTER 8
BIOLOGICAL RESOURCES

A. GENERAL

WASHINGTON CONVENTION ON NATURE PROTECTION AND WILDLIFE PRESERVATION IN THE WESTERN HEMISPHERE. *Supra*, p.212

WASHINGTON CONVENTION ON INTERNATIONAL TRADE IN ENDANGERED SPECIES OF WILD FAUNA AND FLORA

Popular Name: CITES

Done at Washington on 3 March 1973, 993 UNTS 243, 27 UST 1087, TIAS 8249, UKTS No.101 (1976), Cmnd 6647, *reprinted in* 12 ILM 1088 (1973), UNEP3 #57, p.289, 5 IPE 2228, IELMT 973: 08; as amended in Bonn on 22 June 1979, US Sen. Exec. Print C, 96:2 Cong.
Entry into Force: 1 July 1975; 13 April 1987 (amendment)

Depositary: Switzerland

Languages: Chinese, English, French, Russian, Spanish

Parties as of 16 November 1990: Afghanistan;* Algeria;* Argentina;* Australia; Austria; Bahamas;* Bangladesh;* Belgium; Belize; Benin;* Bolivia;* Botswana; Brazil; Brunei;* Burkina Faso;* Burundi;* Cameroon;* Canada; Central African Republic;* Chad;* Chile; China;* Colombia; Congo;* Costa Rica;* Cuba;* Cyprus; Denmark;*** Dominican Republic;* Ecuador; Egypt; Ethiopia;* Finland; France; Gabon;* Gambia;* German Democratic Republic;* Germany, Federal Republic of;*** Ghana;* Guatemala;* Guinea;* Guinea-Bissau;* Guyana;* Honduras;* Hungary;* India; Indonesia; Iran, Islamic Republic of; Israel;* Italy; Japan; Jordan; Kenya; Kiribati;* Liberia;* Liechtenstein; Luxembourg; Madagascar; Malawi;* Malaysia;* Malta;* Mauritius; Monaco;* Morocco; Mozambique;* Nepal; Netherlands; New Zealand;* Nicaragua;* Niger; Nigeria; Norway; Pakistan; Panama; Papua New Guinea; Paraguay; Peru; Philippines;* Poland;* Portugal;*** Rwanda; Saint Lucia;* Saint Vincent and the Grenadines;* Senegal; Seychelles; Singapore; Somalia;* South Africa; Spain;* Sri

---

*   Not a party to the 1979 amendment.
** Withdrew but re-acceded on 8 February 1990
***With a geographic extension

466

Lanka;* Sudan;* Suriname; Sweden; Switzerland; Tanzania, United Republic of;* Thailand;* Togo; Trinidad and Tobago; Tunisia; Tuvalu;*/*** Union of Soviet Socialist Republics; United Arab Emirates;*/** United Kingdom of Great Britain and Northern Ireland;*** United States of America;* Uruguay; Vanuatu;* Venezuela;* Zaire;* Zambia;* Zimbabwe

Amendments:	A 1979 amendment (adding finance authority to article XI(3)(a)) became effective on 13 April 1987, as indicated above. An amendment adopted at Gaborone on 30 April 1983, to provide accession by regional economic integration organizations, is not in force as of 30 November 1990. The October 1989 modification to the appendix, prohibiting trade in ivory, became effective on 18 January 1990, except with respect to Botswana, Malawi, South Africa, Zambia, and Zimbabwe.
Literature:	D. Favre, *International Trade in Endangered Species: A Guide to CITES* (1989); S. Lyster, *International Wildlife Law* 239 (1985)

Editors' Note

International trade in endangered species has been highly profitable. While the trade dates back centuries, the volume of the trade expanded greatly about thirty years ago. In response, the International Union for the Conservation of Nature and Natural Resources called in 1963 for an international agreement to control trade in endangered species. Countries successfully concluded an international agreement ten years later.

The Convention operates through a permit system. It prohibits commercial trade in species threatened with extinction and controls trade in those whose survival could be threatened if trade in them were not controlled. Exporters of listed species need a CITES permit for shipment. The Convention only controls trade in those species that countries have agreed to list in the appendices. Individual countries can also list in a separate appendix those species for which they control export and thus enlist the help of other countries in enforcing their export prohibitions.

Every two years a Conference of the Parties meets to review the implementation of the CITES Convention and, as appropriate, to revise the species on the lists. Parties can enter reservations to the listing of any particular specie, which has arguably limited the effectiveness of efforts to control trade. Five countries objected to the ban on trade in ivory, which otherwise became effective 18 January 1990.

In the United States, the Endangered Species Act of 1973, 16 U.S.C. § 1538, and regulations issued pursuant thereto, 50 C.F.R. § 17.23 (1990), implement the CITES Convention.

CONVENTION ON INTERNATIONAL TRADE IN ENDANGERED SPECIES OF WILD FAUNA AND FLORA, AS AMENDED IN 1979

The Contracting States,

Recognizing that wild fauna and flora in their many beautiful and varied forms are an irreplaceable part of the natural systems of the earth which must be protected for this and the generations to come;

Conscious of the ever-growing value of wild fauna and flora from aesthetic, scientific, cultural, recreational and economic points of view;

Recognizing that peoples and States are and should be the best protectors of their own wild fauna and flora;

Recognizing, in addition, that international cooperation is essential for the protection of certain species of wild fauna and flora against over-exploitation through international trade;

Convinced of the urgency of taking appropriate measures to this end;

Have agreed as follows:

Article I. Definitions

For the purpose of the present Convention, unless the context otherwise requires:

(a) "Species" means any species, subspecies, or geographically separate populations thereof;

(b) "Specimen" means:

(i) any animal or plant, whether alive or dead;

(ii) in the case of an animal: for species included in Appendices I and II, any readily recognizable part or derivative thereof; and for species included in Appendix III, any readily recognizable part or derivative thereof specified in Appendix III in relation to the species; and

(iii) in the case of a plant: for species included in Appendix I, any readily recognizable part or derivative thereof; and for species included in Appendices II and III, any readily recognizable part or derivative thereof specified in Appendices II and III in relation to the species;

(c) "Trade" means export, re-export, import and introduction from the sea;

(d) "Re-export" means export of any specimen that has previously been imported;

(e) "Introduction from the sea" means transportation into a State of specimens of any species which were taken in the marine environment not under the jurisdiction of any State;

(f) "Scientific Authority" means a national scientific authority designated in accordance with Article IX;

(g) "Management Authority" means a national management authority designated in accordance with Article IX;

(h) "Party" means a State for which the present Convention has entered into force.

Article II. Fundamental Principles

1. Appendix I shall include all species threatened with extinction which are or may be affected by trade. Trade in specimens of these species must be subject

to particularly strict regulation in order not to endanger further their survival and must only be authorized in exceptional circumstances.

2. Appendix II shall include:

(a)   all species which although not necessarily now threatened with extinction may become so unless trade in specimens of such species is subject to strict regulation in order to avoid utilization incompatible with their survival; and

(b)   other species which must be subject to regulation in order that trade in specimens of certain species referred to in sub-paragraph (a) of this paragraph may be brought under effective control.

3. Appendix III shall include all species which any Party identifies as being subject to regulation within its jurisdiction for the purpose of preventing or restricting exploitation, and as needing the cooperation of other parties in the control of trade.

4. The Parties shall not allow trade in specimens of species included in Appendices I, II and III except in accordance with the provisions of the present Convention.

Article III. Regulation of Trade in Specimens of Species Included in Appendix I

1. All trade in specimens of species included in Appendix I shall be in accordance with the provisions of this Article.

2. The export of any specimen of a species included in Appendix I shall require the prior grant and presentation of an export permit. An export permit shall only be granted when the following conditions have been met:

(a)   a Scientific Authority of the State of export has advised that such export will not be detrimental to the surival of that species;

(b)   a Management Authority of the State of export is satisfied that the specimen was not obtained in contravention of the laws of that State for the protection of fauna and flora;

(c)   a Management Authority of the State of export is satisfied that any living specimen will be so prepared and shipped as to minimize the risk of injury, damage to health or cruel treatment; and

(d)   a Management Authority of the State of export is satisfied that an import permit has been granted for the specimen.

3. The import of any specimen of a species included in Appendix I shall require the prior grant and presentation of an import permit and either an export permit or a re-export certificate. An import permit shall only be granted when the following conditions have been met:

(a)   a Scientific Authority of the State of import has advised that the import will be for purposes which are not detrimental to the survival of the species involved;

(b)   a Scientific Authority of the State of import is satisfied that the proposed recipient of a living specimen is suitably equipped to house and care for it; and

(c)   a Management Authority of the State of import is satisfied that the specimen is not to be used for primarily commercial purposes.

4. The re-export of any specimen of a species included in Appendix I shall require the prior grant and presentation of a re-export certificate. A re-export certificate shall only be granted when the following conditions have been met:

(a)   a Management Authority of the State of re-export is satisfied that the specimen was imported into that State in accordance with the provisions of the present Convention;

    (*b*)   a Management Authority of the State of re-export is satisfied that any living specimen will be so prepared and shipped as to minimize the risk of injury, damage to health or cruel treatment; and

    (*c*)   a Management Authority of the State of re-export is satisfied that an import permit has been granted for any living specimen.

    5. The introduction from the sea of any specimen of a species included in Appendix I shall require the prior grant of a certificate from a Management Authority of the State of introduction. A certificate shall only be granted when the following conditions have been met:

    (*a*)   a Scientific Authority of the State of introduction advises that the introduction will not be detrimental to the survival of the species involved;

    (*b*)   a Management Authority of the State of introduction is satisfied that the proposed recipient of a living specimen is suitably equipped to house and care for it; and

    (*c*)   a Management Authority of the State of introduction is satisfied that the specimen is not to be used for primarily commercial purposes.

Article IV. Regulation of Trade in Specimens of Species Included in Appendix II

    1. All trade in specimens of species included in Appendix II shall be in accordance with the provisions of this Article.

    2. The export of any specimen of a species included in Appendix II shall require the prior grant and presentation of an export permit. An export permit shall only be granted when the following conditions have been met:

    (*a*)   a Scientific Authority of the State of export has advised that such export will not be detrimental to the survival of that species;

    (*b*)   a Management Authority of the State of export is satisfied that the specimen was not obtained in contravention of the laws of that State for the protection of fauna and flora; and

    (*c*)   a Management Authority of the State of export is satisfied that any living specimen will be so prepared and shipped as to minimize the risk of injury, damage to health or cruel treatment.

    3. A Scientific Authority in each Party shall monitor both the export permits granted by that State for specimens of species included in Appendix II and the actual exports of such specimens. Whenever a Scientific Authority determines that the export of specimens of any such species should be limited in order to maintain that species throughout its range at a level consistent with its role in the ecosystems in which it occurs and well above the level at which that species might become eligible for inclusion in Appendix I, the Scientific Authority shall advise the appropriate Management Authority of suitable measures to be taken to limit the grant of export permits for specimens of that species.

    4. The import of any specimen of a species included in Appendix II shall require the prior presentation of either an export permit or a re-export certificate.

    5. The re-export of any specimen of a species included in Appendix II shall require the prior grant and presentation of a re-export certificate. A re-export certificate shall only be granted when the following conditions have been met:

    (*a*)   a Management Authority of the State of re-export is satisfied that the specimen was imported into that State in accordance with the provisions of the present Convention; and

    (*b*)   a Management Authority of the State of re-export is satisfied that any living specimen will be so prepared and shipped as to minimize the risk of injury, damage to health or cruel treatment.

6. The introduction from the sea of any specimen of a species included in Appendix II shall require the prior grant of a certificate from a Management Authority of the State of introduction. A certificate shall only be granted when the following conditions have been met:

(a) a Scientific Authority of the State of introduction advises that the introduction will not be detrimental to the survival of the species involved; and

(b) a Management Authority of the State of introduction is satisfied that any living specimen will be so handled as to minimize the risk of injury, damage to health or cruel treatment.

7. Certificates referred to in paragraph 6 of this Article may be granted on the advice of a Scientific Authority, in consultation with other national scientific authorities or, when appropriate, international scientific authorities, in respect of periods not exceeding one year for total numbers of specimens to be introduced in such periods.

Article V. Regulation of Trade in Specimens of Species Included in Appendix III

1. All trade in specimens of species included in Appendix III shall be in accordance with the provisions of this Article.

2. The export of any specimen of a species included in Appendix III from any State which has included that species in Appendix III shall require the prior grant and presentation of an export permit. An export permit shall only be granted when the following conditions have been met:

(a) a Management Authority of the State of export is satisfied that the specimen was not obtained in contravention of the laws of that State for the protection of fauna and flora; and

(b) a Management Authority of the State of export is satisfied that any living specimen will be so prepared and shipped as to minimize the risk of injury, damage to health or cruel treatment.

3. The import of any specimen of a species included in Appendix III shall require, except in circumstances to which paragraph 4 of this Article applies, the prior presentation of a certificate of origin and, where the import is from a State which has included that species in Appendix III, an export permit.

4. In the case of re-export, a certificate granted by the Management Authority of the State of re-export that the specimen was processed in that State or is being re-exported shall be accepted by the State of import as evidence that the provisions of the present Convention have been complied with in respect of the specimen concerned.

Article VI. Permits and Certificates

1 Permits and certificates granted under the provisions of Articles III, IV, and V shall be in accordance with the provisions of this Article.

2. An export permit shall contain the information specified in the model set forth in Appendix IV, and may only be used for export within a period of six months from the date on which it was granted.

3. Each permit or certificate shall contain the title of the present Convention, the name and any identifying stamp of the Management Authority granting it and a control number assigned by the Management Authority.

4. Any copies of a permit or certificate issued by a Management Authority shall be clearly marked as copies only and no such copy may be used in place of the original, except to the extent endorsed thereon.

5. A separate permit or certificate shall be required for each consignment of specimens.

6. A Management Authority of the State of import of any specimen shall cancel and retain the export permit or re-export certificate and any corresponding import permit presented in respect of the import of that specimen.

7. Where appropriate and feasible a Management Authority may affix a mark upon any specimen to assist in identifying the specimen. For these purposes ''mark'' means any indelible imprint, lead seal or other suitable means of identifying a specimen, designed in such a way as to render its imitation by unauthorized persons as difficult as possible.

Article VII. Exemptions and Other Special Provisions Relating to Trade

1. The provisions of Articles III, IV and V shall not apply to the transit or trans-shipment of specimens through or in the territory of a Party while the specimens remain in Customs control.

2. Where a Management Authority of the State of export or re-export is satisfied that a specimen was acquired before the provisions of the present Convention applied to that specimen, the provisions of Articles III, IV and V shall not apply to that specimen where the Management Authority issues a certificate to that effect.

3. The provisions of Articles III, IV and V shall not apply to specimens that are personal or household effects. This exemption shall not apply where:

    (a)   in the case of specimens of a species included in Appendix I, they were acquired by the owner outside his State of usual residence, and are being imported into that State; or

    (b)   in the case of specimens of species included in Appendix II:

        (i)   they were acquired by the owner outside his State of usual residence and in a State where removal from the wild occurred;

        (ii) they are being imported into the owner's State of usual residence; and

        (iii) the State where removal from the wild occurred requires the prior grant of export permits before any export of such specimens;

unless a Management Authority is satisfied that the specimens were acquired before the provisions of the present Convention applied to such specimens.

4. Specimens of an animal species included in Appendix I bred in captivity for commercial purposes, or of a plant species included in Appendix I artificially propagated for commercial purposes, shall be deemed to be specimens of species included in Appendix II.

5. Where a Management Authority of the State of export is satisfied that any specimen of an animal species was bred in captivity or any specimen of a plant species was artificially propagated, or is a part of such an animal or plant or was derived therefrom, a certificate by that Management Authority to that effect shall be accepted in lieu of any of the permits or certificates required under the provisions of Articles III, IV or V.

6. The provisions of Articles III, IV and V shall not apply to the non-commercial loan, donation or exchange between scientists or scientific institutions registered by a Management Authority of their State, of herbarium specimens, other preserved, dried or embedded museum specimens, and live plant material which carry a label issued or approved by a Management Authority.

7. A Management Authority of any State may waive the requirements of Articles III, IV and V and allow the movement without permits or certificates of

specimens which form part of a travelling zoo, circus, menagerie, plant exhibition of other travelling exhibition provided that:

(a)   the exporter or importer registers full details of such specimens with that Management Authority;

(b)   the specimens are in either of the categories specified in paragraphs 2 or 5 of this Article; and

(c)   the Management Authority is satisfied that any living specimen will be so transported and cared for as to minimize the risk of injury, damage to health or cruel treatment.

Article VIII. Measures to be Taken by the Parties

1. The Parties shall take appropriate measures to enforce the provisions of the present Convention and to prohibit trade in specimens in violation thereof. These shall include measures:

(a)   to penalize trade in, or possession of, such specimens, or both; and

(b)   to provide for the confiscation or return to the State of export of such specimens.

2. In addition to the measures taken under paragraph 1 of this Article, a Party may, when it deems it necessary, provide for any method of internal reimbursement for expenses incurred as a result of the confiscation of a specimen traded in violation of the measures taken in the application of the provisions of the present Convention.

3. As far as possible, the Parties shall ensure that specimens shall pass through any formalities required for trade with a minimum of delay. To facilitate such passage, a Party may designate ports of exit and ports of entry at which specimens must be presented for clearance. The Parties shall ensure further that all living specimens, during any period of transit, holding or shipment, are properly cared for so as to minimize the risk of injury, damage to health or cruel treatment.

4. Where a living specimen is confiscated as a result of measures referred to in paragraph 1 of this Article:

(a)   the specimen shall be entrusted to a Management Authority of the State of confiscation;

(b)   the Management Authority shall, after consultation with the State of export, return the specimen to that State at the expense of that State, or to a rescue centre or such other place as the Management Authority deems appropriate and consistent with the purposes of the present Convention; and

(c)   the Management Authority may obtain the advice of a Scientific Authority, or may, whenever it considers it desirable, consult the Secretariat in order to facilitate the decision under sub-paragraph (b) of this paragraph, including the choice of a rescue centre or other place.

5. A rescue centre as referred to in paragraph 4 of this Article means an institution designated by a Management Authority to look after the welfare of living specimens, particularly those that have been confiscated.

6. Each Party shall maintain records of trade in specimens of species included in Appendices I, II and III which shall cover:

(a)   the names and addresses of exporters and importers; and

(b)   the number and type of permits and certificates granted; the States with which such trade occurred; the numbers or quantities and types of specimens, names of species as included in Appendices I, II and III and, where applicable, the size and sex of the specimens in question.

7. Each Party shall prepare periodic reports on its implementation of the present Convention and shall transmit to the Secretariat:

(a) an annual report containing a summary of the information specified in sub-paragraph (b) of paragraph 6 of this Article; and

(b) a biennial report on legislative, regulatory and administrative measures taken to enforce the provisions of the present Convention.

8. The information referred to in paragraph 7 of this Article shall be available to the public where this is not inconsistent with the law of the Party concerned.

Article IX. Management and Scientific Authorities

1. Each Party shall designate for the purposes of the present Convention:

(a) one or more Management Authorities competent to grant permits or certificates on behalf of that Party; and

(b) one or more Scientific Authorities.

2. A State depositing an instrument of ratification, acceptance, approval or accession shall at that time inform the Depositary Government of the name and address of the Management Authority authorized to communicate with other Parties and with the Secretariat.

3. Any changes in the designations or authorizations under the provisions of this Article shall be communicated by the Party concerned to the Secretariat for transmission to all other Parties.

4. Any Management Authority referred to in paragraph 2 of this Article shall if so requested by the Secrtariat or the Management Authority of another Party, communicate to it impression of stamps, seals or other devices used to authenticate permits or certificates.

Article X. Trade with States not Party to the Convention

Where export or re-export is to, or import is from, a State not a party to the present Convention, comparable documentation issued by the competent authorities in that State which substantially conforms with the requirements of the present Convention for permits and certificates may be accepted in lieu thereof by any Party.

Article XI. Conference of the Parties

1. The Secretariat shall call a meeting of the Conference of the Parties not later than two years after the entry into force of the present Convention.

2. Thereafter the Secretariat shall convene regular meetings at least once every two years, unless the Conference decides otherwise, and extraordinary meetings at any time on the written request of at least one-third of the Parties.

3. At meetings, whether regular or extraordinary, the Parties shall review the implementation of the present Convention and may:

(a)   make such provision as may be necessary to enable the Secretariat to carry out its duties, and adopt financial provisions;

(b)   consider and adopt amendments to Appendices I and II in accordance with Article XV;

(c)   review the progress made towards the restoration and conservation of the species included in Appendices I, II and III;

(d)   receive and consider any reports presented by the Secretariat or by any Party; and

(e)   where appropriate, make recommendations for improving the effectiveness of the present Convention.

4. At each regular meeting, the Parties may determine the time and venue of the next regular meeting to be held in accordance with the provisions of paragraph 2 of this Article.

5. At any meeting, the Parties may determine and adopt rules of procedure for the meeting.

6. The United Nations, its Specialized Agencies and the International Atomic Energy Agency, as well as any State not a Party to the present Convention, may be represented at meetings of the Conference by observers, who shall have the right to participate but not to vote.

7. Any body or agency technically qualified in protection, conservation or management of wild fauna and flora, in the following categories, which has informed the Secretariat of its desire to be represented at meetings of the Conference by observers, shall be admitted unless at least one-third of the Parties present object:

(a)   international agencies or bodies, either governmental or non-governmental, and national governmental agencies and bodies; and

(b)   national non-governmental agencies or bodies which have been approved for this purpose by the State in which they are located. Once admitted, these observers shall have the right to participate but not to vote.

* * *

Article XIII. International Measures

1. When the Secretariat in the light of information received is satisfied that any species included in Appendices I or II is being affected adversely by trade in specimens of that species or that the provisions of the present Convention are not being effectively implemented, it shall communicate such information to the authorized Management Authority of the Party or Parties concerned.

2. When any Party receives a communication as indicated in paragraph 1 of this Article, it shall, as soon as possible, inform the Secretariat of any relevant facts insofar as its laws permit and, where appropriate, propose remedial action. Where the Party considers that an inquiry is desirable, such inquiry may be carried out by one or more persons expressly authorized by the Party.

3. The information provided by the Party or resulting from any inquiry as specified in paragraph 2 of this Article shall be reviewed by the next Conference of the Parties which may make whatever recommendations it deems appropriate.

Article XIV. Effect on Domestic Legislation and International Conventions

1. The provisions of the present Convention shall in no way affect the right of Parties to adopt:

(*a*)   stricter domestic measures regarding the conditions for trade, taking possession or transport of specimens of species included in Appendices I, II and III, or the complete prohibition thereof; or

(*b*)   domestic measures restricting or prohibiting trade, taking possession, or transport of species not included in Appendices I, II or III.

2. The provisions of the present Convention shall in no way affect the provisions of any domestic measures or the obligations of Parties deriving from any treaty, convention, or international agreement relating to other aspects of trade, taking possession, or transport of specimens which is in force or subsequently may enter into force for any Party including any measure pertaining to the Customs, public health, veterinary or plant quarantine fields.

3. The provisions of the present Convention shall in no way affect the provisions of, or the obligations deriving from, any treaty, convention or international agreement concluded or which may be concluded between States creating a union or regional trade agreement establishing or maintaining a common external customs control and removing customs control between the parties thereto insofar as they relate to trade among the States members of that union or agreement.

4. A State party to the present Convention, which is also a party to any other treaty, convention or international agreement which is in force at the time of the coming into force of the present Convention and under the provisions of which protection is afforded to marine species included in Appendix II, shall be relieved of the obligations imposed on it under the provisions of the present Convention with respect to trade in specimens of species included in Appendix II that are taken by ships registered in that State and in accordance with the provisions of such other treaty, convention or international agreement.

5. Notwithstanding the provisions of Articles III, IV and V, any export of a specimen taken in accordance with paragraph 4 of this Article shall only require a certificate from a Management Authority of the State of introduction to the effect that the specimen was taken in accordance with the provisions of the other treaty, convention or international agreement in question.

6. Nothing in the present Convention shall prejudice the codification and development of the law of the sea by the United Nations Conference on the Law of the Sea convened pursuant to Resolution 2750 C (XXV)[1] of the General Assembly of the United Nations nor the present or future claims and legal views of any State concerning the law of the sea and the nature and extent of coastal and flag State jurisdiction.

---

[1]United Nations, *Official Records of the General Assembly, Twenty-Fifth Session, Supplement No. 28* (A/8028), p. 25.

Article XV. Amendments to Appendices I and II

1. The following provisions shall apply in relation to amendments to Appendices I and II at meetings of the Conference of the Parties:

(a) Any Party may propose an amendment to Appendix I or II for consideration at the next meeting. The text of the proposed amendment shall be communicated to the Secretariat at least 150 days before the meeting. The Secretariat shall consult the other Parties and interested bodies on the amendment in accordance with the provisions of sub-paragraphs (b) and (c) of paragraph 2 of this Article and shall communicate the response to all Parties not later than 30 days before the meeting.

(b) Amendments shall be adopted by a two-thirds majority of Parties present and voting. For these purposes "Parties present and voting" means Parties present and casting an affirmative or negative vote. Parties abstaining from voting shall not be counted among the two-thirds required for adopting an amendment.

(c) Amendments adopted at a meeting shall enter into force 90 days after that meeting for all Parties except those which make a reservation in accordance with paragraph 3 of this Article.

2. The following provisions shall apply in relation to amendments to Appendices I and II between meetings of the Conference of the Parties:

(a) Any Party may propose an amendment to Appendix I or II for consideration between meetings by the postal procedures set forth in this paragraph.

(b) For marine species, the Secretariat shall, upon receiving the text of the proposed amendment, immediately communicate it to the Parties. It shall also consult inter-governmental bodies having a function in relation to those species especially with a view to obtaining scientific data these bodies may be able to provide and to ensuring coordination with any conservation measures enforced by such bodies. The Secretariat shall communicate the views expressed and data provided by these bodies and its own findings and recommendations to the Parties as soon as possible.

(c) For species other than marine species, the Secretariat shall, upon receiving the text of the proposed amendment, immediately communicate it to the Parties, and, as soon as possible thereafter, its own recommendations.

(d) Any Party may, within 60 days of the date on which the Secretariat communicated its recommendations to the Parties under sub-paragraphs (b) or (c) of this paragraph, transmit to the Secretariat any comments on the proposed amendment together with any relevant scientific data and information.

(e) The Secretariat shall communicate the replies received together with its own recommendations to the Parties as soon as possible.

(f) If no objection to the proposed amendment is received by the Secretariat within 30 days of the date the replies and recommendations were communicated under the provisions of sub-paragraph (e) of this paragraph, the amendment shall enter into force 90 days later for all Parties except those which make a reservation in accordance with paragraph 3 of this Article.

(g) If an objection by any Party is received by the Secretariat, the proposed amendment shall be submitted to a postal vote in accordance with the provisions of sub-paragraphs (h), (i) and (j) of this paragraph.

(h) The Secretariat shall notify the Parties that notification of objection has been received.

(*i*)   Unless the Secretariat receives the votes for, against or in abstention from at least one-half of the Parties within 60 days of the date of notification under sub-paragraph (*h*) of this paragraph, the proposed amendment shall be referred to the next meeting of the Conference for further consideration.

(*j*)   Provided that votes are received from one-half of the Parties, the amendment shall be adopted by a two-thirds majority of Parties casting an affirmative or negative vote.

(*k*)   The Secretariat shall notify all Parties of the result of the vote.

(*l*)   If the proposed amendment is adopted it shall enter into force 90 days after the date of the notification by the Secretariat of its acceptance for all Parties except those which make a reservation in accordance with paragraph 3 of this Article.

3. During the period of 90 days provided for by sub-paragraph (*c*) of paragraph 1 or sub-paragraph (*l*) of paragraph 2 of this Article any Party may by notification in writing to the Depositary Government make a reservation with respect to the amendment. Until such reservation is withdrawn the Party shall be treated as a State not a party to the present Convention with respect to trade in the species concerned.

Article XVI. Appendix III and Amendments Thereto

1. Any party may at any time submit to the Secretariat a list of species which it identifies as being subject to regulation within its jurisdiction for the purpose mentioned in paragraph 3 of Article II. Appendix III shall include the names of the Parties submitting the species for inclusion therein, the scientific names of the species so submitted, and any parts or derivatives of the animals or plants concerned that are specified in relation to the species for the purposes of sub-paragraph (*b*) of Article I.

2. Each list submitted under the provisions of paragraph 1 of this Article shall be communicated to the Parties by the Secretariat as soon as possible after receiving it. The list shall take effect as part of Appendix III 90 days after the date of such communication. At any time after the communication of such list, any Party may by notification in writing to the Depositary Government enter a reservation with respect to any species or any parts or derivatives, and until such reservation is withdrawn, the State shall be treated as a State not a Party to the present Convention with respect to trade in the species or part or derivative concerned.

3. A Party which has submitted a species for inclusion in Appendix III may withdraw it at any time by notification to the Secretariat which shall communicate the withdrawal to all Parties. The withdrawal shall take effect 30 days after the date of such communication.

4. Any Party submitting a list under the provisions of paragraph 1 of this Article shall submit to the Secretariat a copy of all domestic laws and regulations applicable to the protection of such species, together with any interpretations which the Party may deem appropriate or the Secretariat may request. The Party shall, for as long as the species in question is included in Appendix III, submit any amendments of such laws and regulations or any new interpretations as they are adopted.

* * *

CANBERRA CONVENTION ON THE CONSERVATION OF
ANTARCTIC MARINE LIVING RESOURCES. *Infra*, p. 520.

C. Fauna

WASHINGTON INTERNATIONAL CONVENTION FOR THE REGULATION OF WHALING AND 1956 PROTOCOL, WITH ATTACHED SCHEDULE AS AMENDED BY THE INTERNATIONAL WHALING COMMISSION AT THE 42ND ANNUAL MEETING, JULY 1990

Popular Name: Whaling Convention

Done at Washington on 2 December 1946, 161 UNTS 72, 62 Stat. 1716, TIAS 1849, 4 Bevans 248, UKTS No.5 (1949), *reprinted in* 7 IPE 3498, IELMT 946: 89, *amended by* Protocol done at Washington on 19 November 1956, 338 UNTS 366, 10 UST 952, TIAS 4228, UKTS No.68 (1959), *reprinted in* 7 IPE 3539, IELMT 956: 87, *and by* Schedule done July 1990.

Entry into Force: Convention, 10 November 1948; Protocol, 4 May 1959; Schedule, 16 October 1990 (continuing and amending earlier schedules)

Depositary: United States of America, International Whaling Commission

Language: English

Parties (to both the Convention and the Protocol) as of 1 January 1990: Antigua and Barbuda; Argentina;* Australia; Brazil; Chile;* China; Denmark; Finland; France; Germany, Federal Republic of; Iceland; India; Ireland; Japan; Kenya; Korea, Republic of; Mexico; Monaco; Netherlands;** New Zealand; Norway; Oman; Peru; Saint Lucia; Saint Vincent and the Grenadines; Senegal; Seychelles; Solomon Islands; South Africa; Spain; Sweden; Switzerland; Union of Soviet Socialist Republics; United Kingdom of Great Britain and Northern Ireland; United States of America; Uruguay

Withdrawals: Canada; Dominca; Panama

Amendments: The schedule is amended annually.

Literature: S. Lyster, *International Wildlife Law* 17 (1985)

---

* Indicates a reservation
**With a geographic extension

Editors' Note

By the early 1900s, the world's whale population was severely depleted as a result of overexploitation. Unilateral attempts by countries to regulate whaling off their coasts failed because most whaling occurred on the high seas, and whalers interpreted the traditional doctrine of freedom of the seas to include the harvest of whales without restriction. In 1902, the International Council for the Exploration of the Sea was established and began to press for an international solution to whale depletion that would be based upon scientific information and principles. The 1931 Convention for the Regulation of Whales, 155 LNTS 349, 49 Stat. 3079, TS 880, 3 Bevans 26, which resulted from those and other efforts, banned the harvest of two species and imposed other restrictions; but several major whaling States did not become party to it. Moreover, it did not provide for enforcement measures, specific penalties, a permanent commission, or easy modification to take account of new scientific evidence.

The International Whaling Convention of 1946, which superseded the 1931 convention, utilized several novel features in an attempt to correct these deficiencies. The 1946 Convention instituted a schedule, which is updated annually in light of new scientific evidence, to regulate whale harvesting practices and set harvest limits for various whale species. The schedule identifies protected species, establishes seasons and harvest areas, and sets size limits, whaling methods, and catch quotas. The Convention also created a permanent International Whaling Commission, composed of one representative from each member State, which meets annually to oversee whale research and amend the schedule accordingly. The Commission reaches decisions by a simple majority vote except when amending the schedule, which requires a ¾ majority vote. States that object to an amendment within 90 days are not bound by the amendment, unless they withdraw their objection. Each member State is obligated to enforce the Convention and schedule against its own nationals.

In 1946, the Convention set a single maximum quota for annual whale harvesting. Individual quotas for various species later replaced the single quota. A limited international observer scheme was established to aid in enforcing catch quotas, pursuant to a 1956 amending protocol that also added harvesting via helicopters and other aircraft. In 1982, the Commission amended the schedule (para. 10(e)) to institute a moratorium on all commercial whaling, thus allowing only aboriginal whaling and whaling for scientific research. Several States objected to the amendment, however, and thus are not bound by it. The Commission reviewed the moratorium in 1990 and extended it to 1991.

Critics argue that inherent problems render the Convention ineffective. For example, the Convention's objective remains to conserve and expand whale populations for the whaling industry, even though the majority of member States are now nonwhaling countries (the initial members were whaling countries). Moreover, the ability to avoid the effect of an amendment to the schedule by filing a timely objection allows objecting States to undermine the Convention. Furthermore, States such as Iceland and Japan have been accused of utilizing the scientific-research exception to eviscerate the 1982 moratorium.

The whales covered by the 1946 Whaling Convention are also listed in Appendix I to the Convention on International Trade in Endangered Species, *supra* p. 479.

INTERNATIONAL CONVENTION FOR THE REGULATION OF WHALING

Washington, 2nd December, 1946

The Governments whose duly authorised representatives have subscribed hereto,

Recognizing the interest of the nations of the world in safeguarding for future generations the great natural resources represented by the whale stocks;

Considering that the history of whaling has seen over-fishing of one area after another and of one species of whale after another to such a degree that it is essential to protect all species of whales from further over-fishing;

Recognizing that the whale stocks are susceptible of natural increases if whaling is properly regulated, and that increases in the size of whale stocks will permit increases in the number of whales which may be captured without endangering these natural resources;

Recognizing that it is in the common interest to achieve the optimum level of whale stocks as rapidly as possible without causing widespread economic and nutritional distress;

Recognizing that in the course of achieving these objectives, whaling operations should be confined to those species best able to sustain exploitation in order to give an interval for recovery to certain species of whales now depleted in numbers;

Desiring to establish a system of international regulation for the whale fisheries to ensure proper and effective conservation and development of whale stocks on the basis of the principles embodied in the provisions of the International Agreement for the Regulation of Whaling, signed in London on 8th June, 1937, and the protocols to that Agreement signed in London on 24th June, 1938, and 26th November, 1945; and

Having decided to conclude a convention to provide for the proper conservation of whale stocks and thus make possible the orderly development of the whaling industry;

Have agreed as follows: —

Article I

1. This Convention includes the Schedule attached thereto which forms an integral part thereof. All references to "Convention" shall be understood as including the said Schedule either in its present terms or as amended in accordance with the provisions of Article V.

2. This Convention applies to factory ships, land stations, and whale catchers under the jurisdiction of the Contracting Governments and to all waters in which whaling is prosecuted by such factory ships, land stations, and whale catchers.

Article II

As used in this Convention: —

1. "Factory ship" means a ship in which or on which whales are treated whether wholly or in part;

2. "Land station" means a factory on the land at which whales are treated whether wholly or in part;

3. "Whale catcher" means a ship used for the purpose of hunting, taking, towing, holding on to, or scouting for whales;

4. "Contracting Government" means any Government which has deposited an instrument of ratification or has given notice of adherence to this Convention.

Article III

1. The Contracting Governments agree to establish an International Whaling Commission, hereinafter referred to as the Commission, to be composed of one member from each Contracting Government. Each member shall have one vote and may be accompanied by one or more experts and advisers.

2. The Commission shall elect from its own members a Chairman and Vice-Chairman and shall determine its own Rules of Procedure. Decisions of the Commission shall be taken by a simple majority of those members voting except that a three-fourths majority of those members voting shall be required for action in pursuance of Article V. The Rules of Procedure may provide for decisions otherwise than at meetings of the Commission.

3. The Commission may appoint its own Secretary and staff.

4. The Commission may set up, from among its own members and experts or advisers, such committees as it considers desirable to perform such functions as it may authorize.

5. The expenses of each member of the Commission and of his experts and advisers shall be determined by his own Government.

6. Recognizing that specialized agencies related to the United Nations will be concerned with the conservation and development of whale fisheries and the products arising therefrom and desiring to avoid duplication of functions, the Contracting Governments will consult among themselves within two years after the coming into force of this Convention to decide whether the Commission shall be brought within the framework of a specialized agency related to the United Nations.

7. In the meantime the Government of the United Kingdom of Great Britain and Northern Ireland shall arrange, in consultation with the other Contracting Governments, to convene the first meeting of the Commission, and shall initiate the consultation referred to in paragraph 6 above.

8. Subsequent meetings of the Commission shall be convened as the Commission may determine.

Article IV

1. The Commission may either in collaboration with or through independent agencies of the Contracting Governments or other public or private agencies, establishments, or organizations, or independently

(a)   encourage, recommend, or if necessary, organize studies and investigations relating to whales and whaling;

(b)   collect and analyze statistical information concerning the current condition and trend of the whale stocks and the effects of whaling activities thereon;

(c)   study, appraise, and disseminate information concerning methods of maintaining and increasing the populations of whale stocks.

2. The Commission shall arrange for the publication of reports of its activities, and it may publish independently or in collaboration with the International Bureau for Whaling Statistics at Sandefjord in Norway and other organizations and agencies such reports as it deems appropriate, as well as statistical, scientific, and other pertinent information relating to whales and whaling.

Article V

1. The Commission may amend from time to time the provisions of the Schedule by adopting regulations with respect to the conservation and utilization of whale resources, fixing (*a*) protected and unprotected species; (*b*) open and closed seasons; (*c*) open and closed waters, including the designation of sanctuary areas; (*d*) size limits for each species; (*e*) time, methods, and intensity of whaling (including the maximum catch of whales to be taken in any one season); (*f*) types and specifications of gear and apparatus and appliances which may be used; (*g*) methods of measurement; and (*h*) catch returns and other statistical and biological records.

2. These amendments of the Schedule (*a*) shall be such as are necessary to carry out the objectives and purposes of this Convention and to provide for the conservation, development, and optimum utilization of the whale resources; (*b*) shall be based on scientific findings; (*c*) shall not involve restrictions on the number or nationality of factory ships or land stations, nor allocate specific quotas to any factory or ship or land station or to any group of factory ships or land stations; and (*d*) shall take into consideration the interests of the consumers of whale products and the whaling industry.

3. Each of such amendments shall become effective with respect to the Contracting Governments ninety days following notification of the amendment by the Commission to each of the Contracting Governments, except that (*a*) if any Government presents to the Commission objection to any amendment prior to the expiration of this ninety-day period, the amendment shall not become effective with respect to any of the Governments for an additional ninety days; (*b*) thereupon, any other Contracting Government may present objection to the amendment at any time prior to the expiration of the additional ninety-day period, or before the expiration of thirty days from the date of receipt of the last objection received during such additional ninety-day period, whichever date shall be the later; and (*c*) thereafter, the amendment shall become effective with respect to all Contracting Governments which have not presented objection but shall not become effective with respect to any Government which has so objected until such date as the objection is withdrawn. The Commission shall notify each Contracting Government immediately upon receipt of each objection and withdrawal and each Contracting Government shall acknowledge receipt of all notifications of amendments, objections, and withdrawals.

4. No amendments shall become effective before 1st July, 1949.

Article VI

The Commission may from time to time make recommendations to any or all Contracting Governments on any matters which relate to whales or whaling and to the objectives and purposes of this Convention.

Article VII

The Contracting Governments shall ensure prompt transmission to the International Bureau for Whaling Statistics at Sandefjord in Norway, or to such other body as the Commission may designate, of notifications and statistical and other information required by this Convention in such form and manner as may be prescribed by the Commission.

Article VIII

1. Notwithstanding anything contained in this Convention any Contracting Government may grant to any of its nationals a special permit authorizing that national to kill, take and treat whales for purposes of scientific research subject to

such restrictions as to number and subject to such other conditions as the Contracting Government thinks fit, and the killing, taking, and treating of whales in accordance with the provisions of this Article shall be exempt from the operation of this Convention. Each Contracting Government shall report at once to the Commission all such authorizations which it has granted. Each Contracting Government may at any time revoke any such special permit which it has granted.

2. Any whales taken under these special permits shall so far as practicable be processed and the proceeds shall be dealt with in accordance with directions issued by the Government by which the permit was granted.

3. Each Contracting Government shall transmit to such body as may be designated by the Commission, in so far as practicable, and at intervals of not more than one year, scientific information available to that Government with respect to whales and whaling, including the results of research conducted pursuant to paragraph I of this Article and to Article IV.

4. Recognizing that continuous collection and analysis of biological data in connection with the operations of factory ships and land stations are indispensable to sound and constructive management of the whale fisheries, the Contracting Governments will take all practicable measures to obtain such data.

Article IX

1. Each Contracting Government shall take appropriate measures to ensure the application of the provisions of this Convention and the punishment of infractions against the said provisions in operations carried out by persons or by vessels under its jurisdiction.

2. No bonus or other remuneration calculated with relation to the results of their work shall be paid to the gunners and crews of whale catchers in respect of any whales the taking of which is forbidden by this Convention.

3. Prosecution for infractions against or contraventions of this Convention shall be instituted by the Government having jurisdiction over the offence.

4. Each Contracting Government shall transmit to the Commission full details of each infraction of the provisions of this Convention by persons or vessels under the jurisdiction of that Government as reported by its inspectors. This information shall include a statement of measures taken for dealing with the infraction and of penalties imposed.

Article X

1. This Convention shall be ratified and the instruments of ratification shall be deposited with the Government of the United States of America.

2. Any Government which has not signed this Convention may adhere thereto after it enters into force by a notification in writing to the Government of the United States of America.

3. The Government of the United States of America shall inform all other signatory Governments and all adhering Governments of all ratifications deposited and adherences received.

4. This Convention shall, when instruments of ratification have been deposited by at least six signatory Governments, which shall include the Governments of the Netherlands, Norway, the Union of Soviet Socialist Republics, the United Kingdom of Great Britain and Northern Ireland, and the United States of America, enter into force with respect to those Governments and shall enter into force with respect to each Government which subsequently ratifies or adheres on the date of the deposit of its instrument of ratification or the receipt of its notification of adherence.

5. The provisions of the Schedule shall not apply prior to 1st July, 1948. Amendments to the Schedule adopted pursuant to Article V shall not apply prior to 1st July, 1949.

Article XI

Any Contracting Government may withdraw from this Convention on 30th June, of any year by giving notice on or before 1st January, of the same year to the depository Government, which upon receipt of such a notice shall at once communicate it to the other Contracting Governments. Any other Contracting Government may, in like manner, within one month of the receipt of a copy of such a notice from the depository Government give notice of withdrawal, so that the Convention shall cease to be in force on 30th June, of the same year with respect to the Government giving such notice of withdrawal.

This Convention shall bear the date on which it is opened for signature and shall remain open for signature for a period of fourteen days thereafter.

In witness whereof the undersigned, being duly authorized, have signed this Convention.

Done in Washington this second day of December, 1946, in the English language, the original of which shall be deposited in the archives of the Government of the United States of America. The Government of the United States of America shall transmit certified copies thereof to all the other signatory and adhering Governments.

PROTOCOL TO THE INTERNATIONAL CONVENTION FOR THE REGULATION OF WHALING

The Contracting Governments to * * * the 1946 Whaling Convention, desiring to extend the application of that Convention to helicopters and other aircraft and to include provisions on methods of inspection among those Schedule provisions which may be amended by the Commission, agree as follows:

Article I

Subparagraph 3 of Article II of the 1946 Whaling Convention shall be amended to read as follows:

"3. 'whale catcher' means a helicopter, or other aircraft, or a ship, used for the purpose of hunting, taking, killing, towing, holding on to, or scouting for whales."

Article II

Paragraph 1 of Article V of the 1946 Whaling Convention shall be amended by deleting the word "and" preceding clause (h), substituting a semicolon for the period at the end of the paragraph, and adding the following language: "and (i) methods of inspection".

Article III

1. This Protocol shall be open for signature and ratification or for adherence on behalf of any Contracting Government to the 1946 Whaling Convention.

2. This Protocol shall enter into force on the date upon which instruments of ratification have been deposited with, or written notifications of adherence have been received by, the Government of the United States of America on behalf of all the Contracting Governments to the 1946 Whaling Convention.

* * *

INTERNATIONAL WHALING COMMISSION

SCHEDULE

As amended by the Commission at the 42nd Annual Meeting, July 1990, and replacing that dated October 1989

* * *

Classification of Stocks
    10. All stocks of whales shall be classified in one of three categories according to the advice of the Scientific Committee as follows:
* * *

    (*e*) Notwithstanding the other provisions of paragraph 10, catch limits for the killing for commercial purposes of whales from all stocks for the 1986 coastal and the 1985/86 pelagic seasons and thereafter shall be zero. This provision will be kept under review, based upon the best scientific advice, and by 1990 at the latest the Commission will undertake a comprehensive assessment of the effects of this decision on whale stocks and consider modification of this provision and the establishment of other catch limits.*

* * *

OSLO AGREEMENT ON THE CONSERVATION OF POLAR BEARS

Popular Name: Polar Bear Convention

Done at Oslo on 15 November 1973, 27 UST 3918, TIAS 8409, *reprinted in* 13 ILM 13 (1973), UNEP3 #61, p.401, 5 IPE 2276, IELMT 973: 85.

Entry into Force: 26 May 1976

Depositary: Norway

Language: English

Parties as of 1 January 1990: Canada;** Denmark; Norway; Union of Soviet Socialist Republics; United States of America

---

*The Governments of Japan, Norway, Peru and the Union of Soviet Socialist Republics lodged objection to paragraph 10(*e*) within the prescribed period. For all other Contracting Governments this paragraph came into force on 3 February 1983. Peru withdrew its objection on 22 July 1983.
The Government of Japan withdrew its objections with effect from 1 May 1987 with respect to commercial pelagic whaling: from 1 October 1987 with respect to commercial coastal whaling for minke and Bryde's whales; and from 1 April 1988 with respect to commercial coastal sperm whaling.
The objections of Norway and the Union of Soviet Socialist Republics not having been withdrawn, the paragraph is not binding upon these Governments.
**With a statement

Editors' Note

The Polar Bear Agreement is intended to protect polar bears by increasing and coordinating research, restricting the "taking" (e.g., hunting, killing, and capturing) of polar bears, and preserving the ecosystems (including consideration of migration patterns) of which the polar bear is a part. Killing is permitted for certain purposes, but even that is subject to limits of sound conservation practices. Two of the parties (Norway and the Soviet Union) have gone beyond the Agreement's requirements to ban totally the killing of polar bears.

Commercial trade in skins of bears killed for some permitted purposes is banned. Polar bears are also listed in Appendix II of CITES, *supra* p. 470, with the result that parties to CITES (which includes all five parties to the Polar Bear Agreement) must limit international trade in polar bears and their parts and products to a level that is not detrimental to their survival as a species.

No secretariat or other administrative machinery is specified in the Agreement.

AGREEMENT ON CONSERVATION OF POLAR BEARS

THE GOVERNMENTS of Canada, Denmark, Norway, the Union of Soviet Socialist Republics, and the United States of America,

RECOGNIZING the special responsibilities and special interests of the States of the Arctic Region in relation to the protection of the fauna and flora of the Arctic Region;

RECOGNIZING that the polar bear is a significant resource of the Arctic Region which requires additional protection;

HAVING DECIDED that such protection should be achieved through co-ordinated national measures taken by the States of the Arctic Region;

DESIRING to take immediate action to bring further conservation and management measures into effect;

HAVE AGREED AS FOLLOWS:

ARTICLE I

1. The taking of polar bears shall be prohibited except as provided in Article III.

2. For the purpose of this Agreement, the term "taking" includes hunting, killing and capturing.

ARTICLE II

Each Contracting Party shall take appropriate action to protect the ecosystems of which polar bears are a part, with special attention to habitat components such as denning and feeding sites and migration patterns, and shall manage polar bear populations in accordance with sound conservation practices based on the best available scientific data.

ARTICLE III

1. Subject to the provisions of Articles II and IV, any Contracting Party may allow the taking of polar bears when such taking is carried out:
   (a)   for *bona fide* scientific purposes; or

(b)   by that Party for conservation purposes; or

(c)   to prevent serious disturbance of the management of other living resources, subject to forfeiture to that Party of the skins and other items of value resulting from such taking; or

(d)   by local people using traditional methods in the exercise of their traditional rights and in accordance with the laws of that Party; or

(e)   wherever polar bears have or might have been subject to taking by traditional means by its nationals.

2. The skins and other items of value resulting from taking under sub-paragraphs (b) and (c) of paragraph 1 of this Article shall not be available for commercial purposes.

ARTICLE IV

The use of aircraft and large motorized vessels for the purpose of taking polar bears shall be prohibited, except where the application of such prohibition would be inconsistent with domestic laws.

ARTICLE V

A Contracting Party shall prohibit the exportation from, the importation and delivery into, and traffic within, its territory of polar bears or any part or product thereof taken in violation of this Agreement.

ARTICLE VI

1. Each Contracting Party shall enact and enforce such legislation and other measures as may be necessary for the purpose of giving effect to this Agreement.

2. Nothing in this Agreement shall prevent a Contracting Party from maintaining or amending existing legislation or other measures or establishing new measures on the taking of polar bears so as to provide more stringent controls than those required under the provisions of this Agreement.

ARTICLE VII

The Contracting Parties shall conduct national research programmes on polar bears, particularly research relating to the conservation and management of the species. They shall as appropriate coordinate such research with research carried out by other Parties, consult with other Parties on the management of migrating polar bear populations, and exchange information on research and management programmes, research results and data on bears taken.

ARTICLE VIII

Each Contracting Party shall take action as appropriate to promote compliance with the provisions of this Agreement by nationals of States not party to this Agreement.

ARTICLE IX

The Contracting Parties shall continue to consult with one another with the object of giving further protection to polar bears.

* * *

BONN CONVENTION ON THE CONSERVATION OF MIGRATORY SPECIES OF WILD ANIMALS, PLUS RESOLUTION ON ASSISTANCE TO DEVELOPING COUNTRIES

Popular Names: Bonn Convention, Migratory Animals Convention

Done at Bonn on 23 June 1979, Misc 11 (1980), Cmnd 7888, *reprinted in* UNEP3 #76, p.500, 19 ILM 15 (1980), 23 IPE 1.

Entry into Force: 1 November 1983

Depositary: Federal Republic of Germany

Languages: English, French, German, Russian, Spanish; official (but not "authentic") versions also in Arabic and Chinese, as per article XX of the Convention

Parties as of 15 November 1990: Belgium; Benin; Burkina Faso; Cameroon; Chile; Denmark; Egypt; Finland; Germany, Federal Republic of; France; Ghana; Hungary; India; Ireland; Israel; Italy; Luxembourg; Mali; Netherlands;* Niger; Nigeria; Norway; Pakistan; Panama; Portugal; Senegal; Somalia; Spain; Sri Lanka; Sweden; Tunisia; United Kingdom of Great Britain and Northern Ireland; Uruguay; Zaire; European Economic Community

Literature: S. Lyster, *International Wildlife Law* 275 (1985)

Editors' Note

Migratory species can be threatened with extinction if even only one country in the migratory range does not adequately protect the species. The Migratory Species Convention, which was negotiated pursuant to Recommendation 32 of the Action Plan of the 1972 UN Conference on the Human Environment, attempts to resolve that problem through a two-level approach. Member States are prohibited (with limited exceptions) from "taking" (e.g., hunting, killing, and capturing) endangered species listed in Appendix I and are obligated to "endeavour to" conserve their habitats. Member States also "shall endeavour to conclude AGREEMENTS" benefiting species listed in Appendix II which have an unfavorable conservation status. Guidelines are provided regarding the object and contents of those AGREEMENTS. Appendices I and II, which may be modified by a vote of two-thirds of the members voting for or against the modification at a Conference of the Parties, were amended in 1985 and 1988.

---

*With a geographic extension

The Convention, which the Federal Republic of Germany took the lead in drafting, is similar to CITES (*supra*, p. 000) in many respects (especially in the final clauses). Unlike the World Heritage Convention, the Migratory Species Convention does not make special provision for developing States, whose participation is essential to protect many species. The Conference, however, passed a nonbinding Resolution on Assistance to Developing Countries, which is reproduced immediately following the Convention.

CONVENTION ON THE CONSERVATION OF MIGRATORY SPECIES OF WILD ANIMALS

THE CONTRACTING PARTIES

RECOGNIZING that wild animals in their innumerable forms are an irreplaceable part of the earth's natural system which must be conserved for the good of mankind;

AWARE that each generation of man holds the resources of the earth for future generations and has an obligation to ensure that this legacy is conserved and, where utilized, is used wisely;

CONSCIOUS of the ever-growing value of wild animals from environmental, ecological, genetic, scientific, aesthetic, recreational, cultural, educational, social and economic points of view;

CONCERNED particularly with those species of wild animals that migrate across or outside national jurisdictional boundaries;

RECOGNIZING that the States are and must be the protectors of the migratory species of wild animals that live within or pass through their national jurisdictional boundaries;

CONVINCED that conservation and effective management of migratory species of wild animals require the concerted action of all States within the national jurisdictional boundaries of which such species spend any part of their life cycle;

RECALLING Recommendation 32 of the Action Plan adopted by the United Nations Conference on the Human Environment (Stockholm, 1972) and noted with satisfaction at the Twenty-seventh Session of the General Assembly of the United Nations.

HAVE AGREED as follows:

Article I
Interpretation

1. For the purpose of this Convention:
   a) "Migratory species" means the entire population or any geographically separate part of the population of any species or lower taxon of wild animals, a significant proportion of whose members cyclically and predictably cross one or more national jurisdictional boundaries;
   b) "Conservation status of a migratory species" means the sum of the influences acting on the migratory species that may affect its long-term distribution and abundance;
   c) "Conservation status" will be taken as "favourable" when:
      (1) population dynamics data indicate that the migratory species is maintaining itself on a long-term basis as a viable component of its ecosystems;
      (2) the range of the migratory species is neither currently being reduced, nor is likely to be reduced, on a long-term basis;

(3) there is, and will be in the foreseeable future, sufficient habitat to maintain the population of the migratory species on a long-term basis; and

(4) the distribution and abundance of the migratory species approach historic coverage and levels to the extent that potentially suitable ecosystems exist and to the extent consistent with wise wildlife management;

d) "Conservation status" will be taken as "unfavourable" if any of the conditions set out in sub-paragraph (c) of this paragraph is not met;

e) "Endangered" in relation to a particular migratory species means that the migratory species is in danger of extinction throughout all or a significant portion of its range;

f) "Range" means all the areas of land or water that a migratory species inhabits, stays in temporarily, crosses or overflies at any time on its normal migration route;

g) "Habitat" means any area in the range of a migratory species which contains suitable living conditions for that species;

h) "Range State" in relation to a particular migratory species means any State (and where appropriate any other Party referred to under sub-paragraph k) of this paragraph) that exercises jurisdiction over any part of the range of that migratory species, or a State, flag vessels of which are engaged outside national jurisdictional limits in taking that migratory species;

i) "Taking" means taking, hunting, fishing, capturing, harassing, deliberate killing, or attempting to engage in any such conduct;

j) "AGREEMENT" means an international agreement relating to the conservation of one or more migratory species as provided for in Articles IV and V of this Convention; and

k) "Party" means a State or any regional economic integration organization constituted by sovereign States which has competence in respect of the negotiation, conclusion and application of international agreements in matters covered by this Convention for which this Convention is in force.

2. In matters within their competence, the regional economic integration organizations which are Parties to this Convention shall in their own name exercise the rights and fulfil the responsibilities which this Convention attributes to their member States. In such cases the member States of these organizations shall not be entitled to exercise such rights individually.

3. Where this Convention provides for a decision to be taken by either a two-thirds majority or a unanimous decision of "the Parties present and voting" this shall mean "the Parties present and casting an affirmative or negative vote". Those abstaining from voting shall not be counted amongst "the Parties present and voting" in determining the majority.

Article II
Fundamental Principles

1. The Parties acknowledge the importance of migratory species being conserved and of Range States agreeing to take action to this end whenever possible and appropriate, paying special attention to migratory species the conservation status of which is unfavourable, and taking individually or in co-operation appropriate and necessary steps to conserve such species and their habitat.

2. The Parties acknowledge the need to take action to avoid any migratory species becoming endangered.

3. In particular, the Parties:

a) should promote, co-operate in and support research relating to migratory species;

b)   shall endeavour to provide immediate protection for migratory species included in Appendix I; and

c)   shall endeavour to conclude AGREEMENTS covering the conservation and management of migratory species included in Appendix II.

Article III
Endangered Migratory Species: Appendix I

1. Appendix I shall list migratory species which are endangered.
2. A migratory species may be listed in Appendix I provided that reliable evidence, including the best scientific evidence available, indicates that the species is endangered.
3. A migratory species may be removed from Appendix I when the Conference of the Parties determines that:
    a)   reliable evidence, including the best scientific evidence available, indicates that the species is no longer endangered, and
    b)   the species is not likely to become endangered again because of loss of protection due to its removal from Appendix I.
4. Parties that are Range States of a migratory species listed in Appendix I shall endeavour:
    a)   to conserve and, where feasible and appropriate, restore those habitats of the species which are of importance in removing the species from danger of extinction;
    b)   to prevent, remove, compensate for or minimize, as appropriate, the adverse effects of activities or obstacles that seriously impede or prevent the migration of the species; and
    c)   to the extent feasible and appropriate, to prevent, reduce or control factors that are endangering or are likely to further endanger the species, including strictly controlling the introduction of, or controlling or eliminating, already introduced exotic species.
5. Parties that are Range States of a migratory species listed in Appendix I shall prohibit the taking of animals belonging to such species. Exceptions may be made to this prohibition only if:
    a)   the taking is for scientific purposes;
    b)   the taking is for the purpose of enhancing the propagation or survival of the affected species;
    c)   the taking is to accommodate the needs of traditional subsistence users of such species; or
    d)   extraordinary circumstances so require;
    provided that such exceptions are precise as to content and limited in space and time. Such taking should not operate to the disadvantage of the species.
6. The Conference of the Parties may recommend to the Parties that are Range States of a migratory species listed in Appendix I that they take further measures considered appropriate to benefit the species.
7. The Parties shall as soon as possible inform the Secretariat of any exceptions made pursuant to paragraph 5 of this Article.

Article IV
Migratory Species to Be the Subject of AGREEMENTS: Appendix II

1. Appendix II shall list migratory species which have an unfavourable conservation status and which require international agreements for their conservation and management, as well as those which have a conservation status which would significantly benefit from the international co-operation that could be achieved by an international agreement.

2. If the circumstances so warrant, a migratory species may be listed both in Appendix I and Appendix II.
3. Parties that are Range States of migratory species listed in Appendix II shall endeavour to conclude AGREEMENTS where these would benefit the species and should give priority to those species in an unfavourable conservation status.
4. Parties are encouraged to take action with a view to concluding agreements for any population or any geographically separate part of the population of any species or lower taxon of wild animals, members of which periodically cross one or more national jurisdictional boundaries.
5. The Secretariat shall be provided with a copy of each AGREEMENT concluded pursuant to the provisions of this Article.

Article V
Guidelines for AGREEMENTS

1. The object of each AGREEMENT shall be to restore the migratory species concerned to a favourable conservation status or to maintain it in such a status. Each AGREEMENT should deal with those aspects of the conservation and management of the migratory species concerned which serve to achieve that object.
2. Each AGREEMENT should cover the whole of the range of the migratory species concerned and should be open to accession by all Range States of that species, whether or not they are Parties to this Convention.
3. An AGREEMENT should, wherever possible, deal with more than one migratory species.
4. Each AGREEMENT should:
   a) identify the migratory species covered;
   b) describe the range and migration route of the migratory species;
   c) provide for each Party to designate its national authority concerned with the implementation of the AGREEMENT;
   d) establish, if necessary, appropriate machinery to assist in carrying out the aims of the AGREEMENT, to monitor its effectiveness, and to prepare reports for the Conference of the Parties;
   e) provide for procedures for the settlement of disputes between Parties to the AGREEMENT; and
   f) at a minimum, prohibit, in relation to a migratory species of the Order Cetacea, any taking that is not permitted for that migratory species under any other multilateral agreement and provide for accession to the AGREEMENT by States that are not Range States of that migratory species.
5. Where appropriate and feasible, each AGREEMENT should provide for, but not be limited to:
   a) periodic review of the conservation status of the migratory species concerned and the identification of the factors which may be harmful to that status;
   b) co-ordinated conservation and management plans;
   c) research into the ecology and population dynamics of the migratory species concerned, with special regard to migration;
   d) the exchange of information on the migratory species concerned, special regard being paid to the exchange of the results of research and of relevant statistics;
   e) conservation and, where required and feasible, restoration of the habitats of importance in maintaining a favourable conservation status, and protection of such habitats from disturbances, including strict control of the introduction of, or control of already introduced, exotic species detrimental to the migratory species;

f) maintenance of a network of suitable habitats approprirately [sic] disposed in relation to the migration routes;

g) where it appears desirable, the provision of new habitats favourable to the migratory species or reintroduction of the migratory species into favourable habitats;

h) elimination of, to the maximum extent possible, or compensation for activities and obstacles which hinder or impede migration;

i) prevention, reduction or control of the release into the habitat of the migratory species of substances harmful to that migratory species;

j) measures based on sound ecological principles to control and manage the taking of the migratory species;

k) procedures for co-ordinating action to suppress illegal taking;

l) exchange of information on substantial threats to the migratory species;

m) emergency procedures whereby conservation action would be considerably and rapidly strengthened when the conservation status of the migratory species is seriously affected; and

n) making the general public aware of the contents and aims of the AGREEMENT.

Article VI
Range States

1. A list of the Range States of migratory species listed in Appendices I and II shall be kept up to date by the Secretariat using information it has received from the Parties.

2. The Parties shall keep the Secretariat informed in regard to which of the migratory species listed in Appendices I and II they consider themselves to be Range States, including provision of information on their flag vessels engaged outside national jurisdictional limits in taking the migratory species concerned and, where possible, future plans in respect of such taking.

3. The Parties which are Range States for migratory species listed in Appendix I or Appendix II should inform the Conference of the Parties through the Secretariat, at least six months prior to each ordinary meeting of the Conference, on measures that they are taking to implement the provisions of this Convention for these species.

Article VII
The Conference of the Parties

1. The Conference of the Parties shall be the decision-making organ of this Convention.

2. The Secretariat shall call a meeting of the Conference of the Parties not later than two years after the entry into force of this Convention.

3. Thereafter the Secretariat shall convene ordinary meetings of the Conference of the Parties at intervals of not more than three years, unless the Conference decides otherwise, and extraordinary meetings at any time on the written request of at least one-third of the Parties.

4. The Conference of the Parties shall establish and keep under review the financial regulations of this Convention. The Conference of the Parties shall, at each of its ordinary meetings, adopt the budget for the next financial period. Each Party shall contribute to this budget according to a scale to be agreed upon by the Conference. Financial regulations, including the provisions on the budget and the scale of contributions as well as their modifications, shall be adopted by unanimous vote of the Parties present and voting.

5. At each of its meetings the Conference of the Parties shall review the implementation of this Convention and may in particular:

* * *

7. Any meeting of the Conference of the Parties shall determine and adopt rules of procedure for that meeting. Decisions at a meeting of the Conference of the Parties shall require a two-thirds majority of the Parties present and voting, except where otherwise provided for by this Convention.
8. The United Nations, its Specialized Agencies, the International Atomic Energy Agency, as well as any State not a party to this Convention and, for each AGREEMENT, the body designated by the parties to that AGREEMENT, may be represented by observers at meetings of the Conference of the Parties.
9. Any agency or body technically qualified in protection, conservation and management of migratory species, in the following categories, which has informed the Secretariat of its desire to be represented at meetings of the Conference of the Parties by observers, shall be admitted unless at least one-third of the Parties present object:
    a)   international agencies or bodies, either governmental or non-governmental, and national governmental agencies and bodies; and
    b)   national non-governmental agencies or bodies which have been approved for this purpose by the State in which they are located.
Once admitted, these observers shall have the right to participate but not to vote.

Article VIII
The Scientific Council

1. At its first meeting, the Conference of the Parties shall establish a Scientific Council to provide advice on scientific matters.
2. Any Party may appoint a qualified expert as a member of the Scientific Council. In addition, the Scientific Council shall include as members qualified experts selected and appointed by the Conference of the Parties; the number of these experts, the criteria for their selection and the terms of their appointments shall be as determined by the Conference of the Parties.

* * *

Article IX
The Secretariat

1. For the purposes of this Convention a Secretariat shall be established.
2. Upon entry into force of this Convention, the Secretariat is provided by the Executive Director of the United Nations Environment Programme. To the extent and in the manner he considers appropriate, he may be assisted by suitable intergovernmental or non-governmental, international or national agencies and bodies technically qualified in protection, conservation and management of wild animals.
3. If the United Nations Environment Programme is no longer able to provide the Secretariat, the Conference of the Parties shall make alternative arrangements for the Secretariat.

* * *

Article XI
Amendment of the Appendices

1. Appendices I and II may be amended at any ordinary or extraordinary meeting of the Conference of the Parties.
2. Proposals for amendment may be made by any Party.
3. The text of any proposed amendment and the reasons for it, based on the best scientific evidence available, shall be communicated to the Secretariat at least

one hundred and fifty days before the meeting and shall promptly be communicated by the Secretariat to all Parties. Any comments on the text by the Parties shall be communicated to the Secretariat not less than sixty days before the meeting begins. The Secretariat shall, immediately after the last day for submission of comments, communicate to the Parties all comments submitted by that day.

4. Amendments shall be adopted by a two-thirds majority of Parties present and voting.

5. An amendment to the Appendices shall enter into force for all Parties ninety days after the meeting of the Conference of the Parties at which it was adopted, except for those Parties which make a reservation in accordance with paragraph 6 of this Article.

6. During the period of ninety days provided for in paragraph 5 of this Article, any Party may by notification in writing to the Depositary make a reservation with respect to the amendment. A reservation to an amendment may be withdrawn by written notification to the Depositary and thereupon the amendment shall enter into force for that Party ninety days after the reservation is withdrawn.

* * *

Resolution on Assistance to Developing Countries

THE CONFERENCE,

RECOGNIZING the sacrifices made by developing countries for the maintenance, restoration and improvement of the habitats of migratory species of wild animals;

RECOGNIZING also that implementation of the Convention on Conservation of Migratory Species of Wild Animals and any Agreement made pursuant to the Convention regarding the conservation and management of species covered therein, depends on the collection and analysis of scientific data relating to the distribution, ecology, population dynamics and conservation status of migratory species;

CONSCIOUS that an important element of development lies in the conservation and management of living natural resources and that migratory species constitute a significant part of these resources;

AWARE that implementation of the Convention in some developing countries will necessitate assistance in research on conservation and management of migratory species and their habitats and in the establishment or expansion of appropriate scientific and administrative institutions;

REQUESTS the Parties to the Convention to promote financial, technical and training assistance in support of the conservation efforts made by developing countries;

URGES international and national organizations to give a priority in their aid programmes relating to the management and conservation of migratory species of wild animals and their habitats in developing countries, enabling these countries better to pursue efforts for the conservation of these species for the purpose of implementing the Convention.

RAMSAR CONVENTION ON WETLANDS OF INTERNATIONAL IMPORTANCE ESPECIALLY AS WATERFOWL HABITAT, AS AMENDED 3 DECEMBER 1982

Popular Names: Ramsar Convention, Wetlands Convention

Done at Ramsar on 2 February 1971, 996 UNTS 245, UKTS No.34 (1976), Cmnd 6465, *reprinted in* 11 ILM 969 (1972), UNEP3 #47, p.246, 5 IPE 2161, IELMT 971: 09; amended 3 December 1982.

Entry into Force: 21 December 1975

Depositary: United Nations Educational, Scientific and Cultural Organization (UNESCO)

Languages: English, French, German, Russian

Parties as of 1 January 1990: Algeria; Australia; Austria; Belgium; Bulgaria; Canada; Chile; Denmark; Egypt; Finland; France; Gabon; German Democratic Republic; Germany, Federal Republic of;* Greece; Hungary, Iceland; India; Iran, Islamic Republic of; Ireland; Italy; Japan; Jordan; Mali; Malta; Mauritania; Mexico; Morocco; Netherlands;* New Zealand; Niger; Norway; Pakistan; Poland; Portugal; Senegal; South Africa; Spain; Suriname; Sweden; Switzerland; Tunisia; Union of Soviet Socialist Republics; United Kingdom of Great Britain and Northern Ireland;* United States of America; Uruguay; Venezuela; Viet Nam; Yugoslavia.

Amendments: 28 May 1987 (not yet in force, as of 14 December 1990)

Editors' Note

Wetlands, including marshes, fens, peatlands, and marine water less than six meters deep, constitute one of Earth's most important wildlife habitats and flood-control systems. The Ramsar Convention is intended to protect wetlands from human destruction via, for example, drainage and pollution. Member States are obligated: to designate suitable wetlands in their territory for inclusion in the "List of Wetlands of International Importance," with particular attention paid to migratory waterfowl; to "promote conservation of wetlands" on the List; and to promote the conservation of wetlands (whether or not on the List) and waterfowl by establishing and maintaining nature reserves. In contrast to the World Heritage Convention's listing procedure (*see infra*, p. 554), listing under the Ramsar Convention is unilateral, and each State is required to list a wetland at the time it consents to be a party.

*With a geographic extension

As of 27 June 1990, 480 wetlands were listed, covering more than 30 million hectares. Also in contrast to the World Heritage Convention, the Ramsar Convention does not provide for assisting developing States.

CONVENTION ON WETLANDS OF INTERNATIONAL IMPORTANCE ESPECIALLY AS WATERFOWL HABITAT

Ramsar, 2.2.1971
as amended by the Paris Protocol of 3.12.1982

The Contracting Parties,

Recognizing the interdependence of Man and his environment;

Considering the fundamental ecological functions of wetlands as regulators of water regimes and as habitats supporting a characteristic flora and fauna, especially waterfowl;

Being convinced that wetlands constitute a resource of great economic, cultural, scientific, and recreational value, the loss of which would be irreparable;

Desiring to stem the progressive encroachment on and loss of wetlands now and in the future;

Recognizing that waterfowl in their seasonal migrations may transcend frontiers and so should be regarded as an international resource;

Being confident that the conservation of wetlands and their flora and fauna can be ensured by combining far-sighted national policies with co-ordinated international action;

Have agreed as follows:

Article 1

1. For the purpose of this Convention wetlands are areas of marsh, fen, peatland or water, whether natural or artificial, permanent or temporary, with water that is static or flowing, fresh, brackish or salt, including areas of marine water the depth of which at low tide does not exceed six metres.
2. For the purpose of this Convention waterfowl are birds ecologically dependent on wetlands.

Article 2

1. Each Contracting Party shall designate suitable wetlands within its territory for inclusion in a List of Wetlands of International Importance, hereinafter referred to as "the List" which is maintained by the bureau established under Article 8. The boundaries of each wetland shall be precisely described and also delimited on a map and they may incorporate riparian and coastal zones adjacent to the wetlands, and islands or bodies of marine water deeper than six metres at low tide lying within the wetlands, especially where these have importance as waterfowl habitat.
2. Wetlands should be selected for the List on account of their international significance in terms of ecology, botany, zoology, limnology or hydrology. In the first instance wetlands of international importance to waterfowl at any season should be included.
3. The inclusion of a wetland in the List does not prejudice the exclusive sovereign rights of the Contracting Party in whose territory the wetland is situated.

4. Each Contracting Party shall designate at least one wetland to be included in the List when signing this Convention or when depositing its instrument of ratification or accession, as provided in Article 9.
5. Any Contracting Party shall have the right to add to the List further wetlands situated within its territory, to extend the boundaries of those wetlands already included by it in the List, or, because of its urgent national interests, to delete or restrict the boundaries of wetlands already included by it in the List and shall, at the earliest possible time, inform the organization or government responsible for the continuing bureau duties specified in Article 8 of any such changes.
6. Each Contracting Party shall consider its international responsibilities for the conservation, management and wise use of migratory stocks of waterfowl, both when designating entries for the List and when exercising its right to change entries in the List relating to wetlands within its territory.

Article 3

1. The Contracting Parties shall formulate and implement their planning so as to promote the conservation of the wetlands included in the List, and as far as possible the wise use of wetlands in their territory.
2. Each Contracting Party shall arrange to be informed at the earliest possible time if the ecological character of any wetland in its territory and included in the List has changed, is changing or is likely to change as the result of technological developments, pollution or other human interference. Information on such changes shall be passed without delay to the organization or government responsible for the continuing bureau duties specified in Article 8.

Article 4

1. Each Contracting Party shall promote the conservation of wetlands and waterfowl by establishing nature reserves on wetlands, whether they are included in the List or not, and provide adequately for their wardening.
2. Where a Contracting Party in its urgent national interest, deletes or restricts the boundaries of a wetland included in the List, it should as far as possible compensate for any loss of wetland resources, and in particular it should create additional nature reserves for waterfowl and for the protection, either in the same area or elsewhere, of an adequate portion of the original habitat.
3. The Contracting Parties shall encourage research and the exchange of data and publications regarding wetlands and their flora and fauna.
4. The Contracting Parties shall endeavour through management to increase waterfowl populations on appropriate wetlands.
5. The Contracting Parties shall promote the training of personnel competent in the fields of wetland research, management and wardening.

Article 5

The Contracting Parties shall consult with each other about implementing obligations arising from the Convention especially in the case of a wetland extending over the territories of more than one Contracting Party or where a water system is shared by Contracting Parties. They shall at the same time endeavour to coordinate and support present and future policies and regulations concerning the conservation of wetlands and their flora and fauna.

Article 6[1]

1. The Contracting Parties shall, as the necessity arises, convene Conferences on the Conservation of Wetlands and Waterfowl.

2. The Conferences shall have an advisory character and shall be competent, inter alia:
   (a)   to discuss the implementation of this Convention;
   (b)   to discuss additions to and changes in the List;
   (c)   to consider information regarding changes in the ecological character of wetlands included in the List provided in accordance with paragraph 2 of Article 3;
   (d)   to make general or specific recommendations to the Contracting Parties regarding the conservation, management and wise use of wetlands and their flora and fauna;
   (e)   to request relevant international bodies to prepare reports and statistics on matters which are essentially international in character affecting wetlands;
3. The Contracting Parties shall ensure that those responsible at all levels for wetlands management shall be informed of, and take into consideration, recommendations of such Conferences concerning the conservation, management and wise use of wetlands and their flora and fauna.

Article 7[1]

1. The representatives of the Contracting Parties at such Conferences should include persons who are experts on wetlands or waterfowl by reason of knowledge and experience gained in scientific, administrative or other appropriate capacities.
2. Each of the Contracting Parties represented at a Conference shall have one vote, recommendations being adopted by a simple majority of the votes cast, provided that not less than half the Contracting Parties cast votes.

Article 8

1. The International Union for Conservation of Nature and Natural Resources shall perform the continuing bureau duties under this Convention until such time as another organization or government is appointed by a majority of two-thirds of all Contracting Parties.
2. The continuing bureau duties shall be, inter alia:
   (a)   to assist in the convening and organizing of Conferences specified in Article 6;
   (b)   to maintain the List of Wetlands of International Importance and to be informed by the Contracting Parties of any additions, extensions, deletions or restrictions concerning wetlands included in the List provided in accordance with paragraph 5 of Article 2;
   (c)   to be informed by the Contracting Parties of any changes in the ecological character of wetlands included in the List provided in accordance with paragraph 2 of Article 3;
   (d)   to forward notification of any alterations to the List, or changes in character of wetlands included therein, to all Contracting Parties and to arrange for these matters to be discussed at the next Conference;
   (e)   to make known to the Contracting Party concerned, the recommendations of the Conferences in respect of such alterations to the List or of changes in the character of wetlands included therein.

---

1 These articles have been amended by the Conference of the Parties on 28.5.1987; these amendments are not yet in force (see separate document).

Article 9

1. This Convention shall remain open for signature indefinitely.
2. Any member of the United Nations or of one of the Specialized Agencies or of the International Atomic Energy Agency or Party to the Statute of the International Court of Justice may become a Party to this Convention by:
   (a) signature without reservation as to ratification;
   (b) signature subject to ratification followed by ratification;
   (c) accession.
3. Ratification or accession shall be effected by the deposit of an instrument of ratification or accession with the Director-General of the United Nations Educational, Scientific and Cultural Organization (hereinafter referred to as "the Depositary").

Article 10

1. This Convention shall enter into force four months after seven States have become Parties to this Convention in accordance with paragraph 2 of Article 9.
2. Thereafter this Convention shall enter into force for each Contracting Party four months after the day of its signature without reservation as to ratification, or its deposit of an instrument of ratification or accession.

Article 10 bis

1. This Convention may be amended at a meeting of the Contracting Parties convened for that purpose in accordance with this article.
2. Proposals for amendment may be made by any Contracting Party.
3. The text of any proposed amendment and the reasons for it shall be communicated to the organization or government performing the continuing bureau duties under the Convention (hereinafter referred to as "the Bureau") and shall promptly be communicated by the Bureau to all Contracting Parties. Any comments on the text by the Contracting Parties shall be communicated to the Bureau within three months of the date on which the amendments were communicated to the Contracting Parties by the Bureau. The Bureau shall, immediately after the last day for submission of comments, communicate to the Contracting Parties all comments submitted by that day.
4. A meeting of Contracting Parties to consider an amendment communicated in accordance with paragraph 3 shall be convened by the Bureau upon the written request of one third of the Contracting Parties. The Bureau shall consult the Parties concerning the time and venue of the meeting.
5. Amendments shall be adopted by a two-thirds majority of the Contracting Parties present and voting.
6. An amendment adopted shall enter into force for the Contracting Parties which have accepted it on the first day of the fourth month following the date on which two thirds of the Contracting Parties have deposited an instrument of acceptance with the Depositary. For each Contracting Party which deposits an instrument of acceptance after the date on which two thirds of the Contracting Parties have deposited an instrument of acceptance, the amendment shall enter into force on the first day of the fourth month following the date of the deposit of its instrument of acceptance.

Article 11

1. This Convention shall continue in force for an indefinite period.
2. Any Contracting Party may denounce this Convention after a period of five years from the date on which it entered into force for that Party by giving written

notice thereof to the Depositary. Denunciation shall take effect four months after the day on which notice thereof is received by the Depositary.

Article 12

1. The Depositary shall inform all States that have signed and acceded to this Convention as soon as possible of:
   (a)   signatures to the Convention;
   (b)   deposits of instruments of ratification of this Convention;
   (c)   deposits of instruments of accession to this Convention;
   (d)   the date of entry into force of this Convention;
   (e)   notifications of denunciation of this Convention.
2. When this Convention has entered into force, the Depositary shall have it registered with the Secretariat of the United Nations in accordance with Article 102 of the Charter.

IN WITNESS WHEREOF, the undersigned, being duly authorized to that effect, have signed this Convention.

DONE at Ramsar this 2nd day of February 1971, in a single original in the English, French, German and Russian languages, all texts being equally authentic[2] which shall be deposited with the Depositary which shall send true copies thereof to all Contracting Parties.

D. FLORA

UNITED NATIONS FOOD AND AGRICULTURE ORGANIZATION: INTERNATIONAL UNDERTAKING ON PLANT GENETIC RESOURCES, AND AGREED INTERPRETATION

Popular Name: FAO Plant Genetics Undertaking

Adopted at Rome on 23 November 1983, 22 FAO Conf Resolution 8/83; Agreed Interpretation adopted 29 November 1989, 25 FAO Conf Resolution 5/89.

Entry into Force: 23 November 1983 (Undertaking)

Depositary: Food and Agriculture Organization

Languages: Arabic, Chinese, English, French, Russian, Spanish

Editors' Note

The global rate of extinction of species has been increasing. There is particular concern about declining genetic diversity in plants. In response, under the auspices

---

2 Pursuant to the Final Act of the Conference to conclude the Protocol, the Depositary provided the second Conference of the Contracting Parties with official versions of the Convention in the Arabic, Chinese and Spanish languages, prepared in consultation with interested Governments and with the assistance of the Bureau.

of the United Nations Food and Agricultural Organization (FAO), States adopted an International Undertaking on Plant Genetic Resources, which is not legally binding. The Undertaking declares that plant genetic resources are "the heritage of mankind" and sets forth principles for protecting and exploiting the germplasm. While a substantial number of developing countries have committed themselves to the Undertaking, important developed countries have declined to do so, primarily on the grounds that it does not adequately protect proprietary rights in materials developed from plant genetic resources.

In 1989, the FAO Conference adopted an Agreed Interpretation that recognizes Plant Breeders' Rights and Farmers' Rights (reproduced below). That FAO Conference also adopted a statement on Farmers' Rights, which are described as follows:

Farmers' Rights means rights arising from the past, present and future contributions of farmers in conserving, improving, and making available plant genetic resources, particularly those in the centres of origin/diversity. These rights are vested in the International Community, as trustee for present and future generations of farmers, for the purpose of ensuring full benefits to farmers, and supporting the continuation of their contributions, as well as the attainment of the overall purposes of the International Undertaking. . . .

25 FAO Conf Resolution 5/89 (29 November 1989).

The International Board for Plant Genetic Resources (IBPGR), established in 1974 by the Consultative Group on International Agricultural Research (CGIAR) of the World Bank, FAO and United Nations Development Programme, has as its charge "to promote the collection, conservation, evaluation, utilization and exchange of plant genetic resources." It has sponsored many germplasm collection missions and works with over three dozen centers worldwide to store germplasm. It predates the Undertaking and continues to function independently of the Undertaking.

INTERNATIONAL UNDERTAKING ON PLANT GENETIC RESOURCES

I. GENERAL
Article 1—Objective

1. The objective of this Undertaking is to ensure that plant genetic resources of economic and/or social interest, particularly for agriculture, will be explored, preserved, evaluated and made available for plant breeding and scientific purposes. This Undertaking is based on the universally accepted principle that plant genetic resources are a heritage of mankind and consequently should be avilable [sic] without restriction.

Article 2—Definitions and Scope

2.1 In this Undertaking:
   (a)   "plant genetic resources" means the reproductive or vegetative propagating material of the following categories of plants:

    (i) cultivated varieties (cultivars) in current use and newly developed varieties;

    (ii) obsolete cultivars;

    (iii) primitive cultivars (land races);

    (iv) wild and weed species, near relatives of cultivated varieties;

    (v) special genetic stocks (including elite and current breeders' lines and mutants);

(b) "base collection of plant genetic resources" means a collection of seed stock or vegetative propagating material (ranging from tissue cultures to whole plants) held for long-term security in order to preserve the genetic variation for scientific purposes and as a basis for plant breeding;

(c) "active collection" means a collection which complements a base collection, and is a collection from which seed samples are drawn for distribution, exchange and other purposes such as multiplication and evaluation;

(d) "institution" means an entity established at the international or national level, with or without legal personality, for purposes related to the exploration, collection, conservation, maintenance, evaluation or exchange of plant genetic resources;

(e) "centre" means an institution holding a base or active collection of plant genetic resources, as described in Article 7.

2.2 This Undertaking relates to the plant genetic resources described in para. 2.1(a), of all species of economic and/or social interest, particularly for agriculture at present or in the future, and has particular reference to food crops.

Article 3—Exploration of Plant Genetic Resources

3.1 Governments adhering to this Undertaking will organize or arrange for missions of exploration, conducted in accordance with recognized scientific standards, to identify potentially valuable plant genetic resources that are in danger of becoming extinct in the country concerned, as well as other plant genetic resources in the country which may be useful for development but whose existence or essential characteristics are at present unknown, in particular:

(a) known land races or cultivars in danger of becoming extinct due to their abandonment in favour of the cultivation of new cultivars;

(b) the wild relatives of cultivated plants in areas identified as centres of genetic diversity or natural distribution;

(c) species which are not actually cultivated but may be used for the benefit of mankind as a source of food or raw materials (such as fibres, chemical compounds, medicine or timber).

3.2 Special efforts will be made, in the context of Article 3.1, where the danger of extinction of plant species is certain, or is likely, having regard to circumstances such as the clearance of vegetation from tropical rain forests and semi-arid lands with a view to the expansion of cultivated areas.

Article 4—Preservation, Evaluation and Documentation of Plant Genetic Resources

4.1 Appropriate legislative and other measures will be maintained and, where necessary, developed and adopted to protect and preserve the plant genetic resources of plants growing in areas of their natural habitat in the major centres of genetic diversity.

4.2 Measures will be taken, if necessary through international cooperation, to ensure the scientific collection and safeguarding of material in areas where important plant genetic resources are in danger of becoming extinct on account of agricultural or other development.

4.3 Appropriate measures will also be taken with respect to plant genetic resources held, outside their natural habitats, in gene banks or living collections of plants. Governments and institutions adhering to this Undertaking will, in particular, ensure that the said resources are conserved and maintained in such a way as to preserve their valuable characteristics for use in scientific research and plant breeding, and are also evaluated and fully documented.

Article 5—Availability of Plant Genetic Resources

5. It will be the policy of adhering Governments and institutions having plant genetic resources under their control to allow access to samples of such resources, and to permit their export, where the resources have been requested for the purposes of scientific research, plant breeding or genetic resource conservation. The samples will be made available free of charge, on the basis of mutual exchange or on mutually agreed terms.

II. INTERNATIONAL COOPERATION
Article 6—General

6. International cooperation will, in particular, be directed to:
   (a) establishing or strengthening the capabilities of developing countries, where appropriate on a national or sub-regional basis, with respect to plant genetic resources activities, including plant survey and identification, plant breeding and seed multiplication and distribution, with the aim of enabling all countries to make full use of plant genetic resources for the benefit of their agricultural development;
   (b) intensifying international activities in preservation, evaluation, documentation, exchange of plant genetic resources, plant breeding, germ plasm maintenance, and seed multiplication. This would include activities carried out by FAO and other concerned agencies in the UN System; it would also include activities of other institutions, including those supported by the CGIAR. The aim would be to progressively cover all plant species that are important for agriculture and other sectors of the economy, in the present and for the future;
   (c) supporting the arrangements outlined in Article 7, including the participation in such arrangements of governments and institutions, where appropriate and feasible;
   (d) considering measures, such as the strengthening or establishment of funding mechanisms, to finance activities relating to plant genetic resources.

Article 7—International Arrangements

7.1 The present international arrangements, being carried out under the auspices of FAO and other organizations in the United Nations Systems, by national and regional institutions and institutions supported by the CGIAR, in particular the IBPGR, for the exploration, collection, conservation, maintenance, evaluation, documentation, exchange and use of plant genetic resources will be further developed and, where necessary, complemented in order to develop a global system so as to ensure that:
   (a) there develops an internationally coordinated network of national, regional and international centres, including an international network of base collections in gene banks, under the auspices or the jurisdiction of FAO, that have assumed the responsibility to hold, for the benefit of the international community and on the principle of unrestricted exchange, base or active collections of the plant genetic resources of particular plant species;

(b)   the number of such centres will be progressively increased so as to achieve as complete a coverage as necessary, in terms of species and geographical distribution, account also being taken of the need for duplication, of the resources to be safeguarded and preserved;

(c)   the activities of the centres that are related to the exploration, collection, conservation, maintenance, rejuvenation, evaluation and exchange of plant genetic resources will be carried out with due account being taken of scientific standards;

(d)   sufficient support in funds and facilities will be provided, at the national and international levels, to enable the centres to carry out their tasks;

(e)   a global information system, under the coordination of FAO, relating to plant genetic resources maintained in the aforementioned collections, and linked to systems established at the national, sub-regional and regional levels, will be developed on the basis of relevant arrangements that already exist;

(f)   early warning will be given to FAO, or to any institution designated by FAO, of any hazards that threaten the efficient maintenance and operation of a centre, with a view to prompt international action to safeguard the material maintained by the centre;

(g)   the IBPGR pursues and develops its present activities, within its terms of reference, in liaison with FAO;

(h)   (i) the general expansion and improvement of related professional and institutional capability within developing countries, including training within appropriate institutions in both developd and developing countries, is adequately funded; and
(ii) the overall activity within the Undertaking ultimately ensures a significant improvement in the capacity of developing countries for the production and distribution of improved crop varieties, as required to support major increases in agricultural production, especially in developing countries.

7.2 Within the context of the global system any Governments or institutions that agree to participate in the Undertaking, may, furthermore, notify the Director-General of FAO that they wish the base collection or collections for which they are responsible to be recognized as part of the international network of base collections in gene banks, under the auspices or the jurisdiction of FAO. The centre concerned will, whenever requested by FAO, make material in the base collection available to participants in the Undertaking, for purposes of scientific research, plant breeding or genetic resource conservation, free of charge, on the basis of mutual exchange or on mutually agreed terms.

Article 8—Financial Security

8.1 Adhering Governments, and financing agencies, will, individually and collectively, consider adopting measures that would place activities relevant to the objective of this Undertaking on a firmer financial basis, with special consideration for the need of developing countries to strengthen their capabilities in genetic resource activities, plant breeding and seed multiplication.

8.2 Adhering Governments, and financing agencies, will, in particular, explore the possibility of establishing mechanisms which would guarantee the availability of funds that could be immediately mobilized to meet situations of the kind referred to in Article 7.1(f).

8.3 Adhering Governments and institutions, and financing agencies, will give special consideration to requests from FAO for extra-budgetary funds, equipment or services needed to meet situations of the kind referred to in Article 7.1(f).

8.4 The funding of the establishment and operation of the international network, insofar as it imposes additional costs on FAO, in the main will be funded from extra-budgetary resources.

Article 9—Monitoring of Activities and Related Action by FAO

9.1 FAO will keep under continuous review the international situation concerning the exploration, collection, conservation, documentation, exchange and use of plant genetic resources.
9.2 FAO will, in particular, establish an intergovernmental body to monitor the operation of the arrrangements [sic] referred to in Article 7, and to take or recommend measures that are necessary or desirable in order to ensure the comprehensiveness of the global system and the efficiency of its operations in line with the Undertaking.
9.3 In the performance of its responsibilities outlined in Part II of this Undertaking, FAO will act in consultation with those Governments that have indicated to FAO their intention to support the arrangements referred to in Article 7.

III. OTHER PROVISIONS
Article 10—Phytosanitary Measures

10. This Undertaking is without prejudice to any measures taken by Governments—in line with the provisions of the International Plant Protection Convention, adopted in Rome on 6 December 1951—to regulate the entry of plant genetic resources with the aim of preventing the introduction or spread of plant pests.

Article 11—Information on the Implementation of this Undertaking

11. At the time of adhering, Governments and institutions will advise the Director-General of FAO of the extent to which they are in a position to give effect to the principles contained in the Undertaking. At yearly intervals, they will provide the Director-General of FAO with information on the measures that they have taken or propose to take to achieve the objective of this Undertaking.

Resolution 4/89
Agreed Interpretation of
the International Undertaking

THE CONFERENCE,
Recognizing that:
    plant genetic resources are a common heritage of mankind to be preserved, and to be freely available for use, for the benefit of present and future generations,
Further recognizing that:
    (a)   the International Undertaking on Plant Genetic Resources constitutes a formal framework aimed at ensuring conservation, use and availability of plant genetic resources,
    (b)   some countries have not adhered to the Undertaking and others have adhered with reservation because of possible conflict of certain provisions of the Undertaking with their international obligations and existing national regulations,
    (c)   these reservations and constraints may be overcome through an agreed interpretation of the Undertaking which recognizes Plant Breeders' Rights and Farmers' Rights,

Endorses the agreed interpretation set forth hereinafter which is intended to lay the basis for an equitable and therefore solid and lasting, global system and thereby to facilitate the withdrawal of reservations which countries have made with regard to the International Undertaking, and to secure the adherence of others:

Agreed Interpretation

1. Plant Breeders' Rights as provided for under UPOV (International Union for the Protection of New Varieties of Plant) are not incompatible with the International Undertaking;
2. a state may impose only such minimum restrictions on the free exchange of materials covered by Article 2.1 (a) of the International Undertaking as are necessary for it to conform to its national and international obligations;
3. states adhering to the Undertaking recognize the enormous contribution that farmers of all regions have made to the conservation and development of plant genetic resources, which constitute the basis of plant production throughout the world, and which form the basis for the concept of Farmers' Rights;
4. the adhering states consider that the best way to implement the concept of Farmers' Rights is to ensure the conservation, management and use of plant genetic resources, for the benefit of present and future generations of farmers. This could be achieved through appropriate means, monitored by the Commission on Plant Genetic Resources, including in particular the International Fund for Plant Genetic Resources, already established by FAO. To reflect the responsibility of those countries which have benefitted most from the use of germplasm, the Fund would benefit from being supplemented by further contributions from adhering governments, on a basis to be agreed upon, in order to ensure for the Fund a sound and recurring basis. The International Fund should be used to support plant genetic conservation, management and utilization programmes, particularly within developing countries, and those which are important sources of plant genetic material. Special priority should be placed on intensified educational programmes for biotechnology specialists, and strengthening the capabilities of developing countries in genetic resource conservation and management, as well as the improvement of plant breeding and seed production.
5. It is understood that:
   (a) the term "free access" does not mean free of charge, and
   (b) the benefits to be derived under the International Undertaking are part of a reciprocal system, and should be limited to countries adhering to the INTERNATIONAL UNDERTAKING.

INTERNATIONAL TROPICAL TIMBER AGREEMENT

Popular Name: ITTA

Done at Geneva on 18 November 1983, U.N. Doc. TD/TIMBER/11/Rev.1 (1984).

Entry into Force: 1 April 1985

Depositary: United Nations

Languages: Arabic, English, French, Russian, Spanish

Parties as of 1 September 1990: Australia; Austria; Belgium; Cameroon; Canada; China; Colombia; Congo; Denmark; Ecuador; Egypt; Finland; France; Gabon;*

Germany, Federal Republic of; Ghana; Greece; Honduras;* India; Indonesia; Ireland; Italy; Japan; Liberia; Luxembourg; Malaysia; Nepal; Netherlands; Norway; Panama; Papua New Guinea; Portugal; Korea, Republic of; Spain; Sweden; Switzerland; Thailand; Togo; Trinidad and Tobago; Union of Soviet Socialist Republics; United Kingdom of Great Britain and Northern Ireland; United States of America*

Editors' Note

The 1983 International Tropical Timber Agreement was negotiated under the auspices of the United Nations Conference on Trade and Development (UNCTAD) to promote trade in tropical timber. The major producing and consuming countries are parties to the agreement. The convention provides for the creation of the International Tropical Timber Organization (ITTO), which is headquartered in Japan. The ITTO is charged with monitoring market conditions, conducting studies, and providing technical assistance.

The Agreement contains only a few environmental provisions, but these have received increasing attention. One of the objectives of the agreement is to develop national policies "aimed at sustainable utilization and conservation of tropical forests and their genetic resources, and at maintaining the ecological balance in the regions concerned." This is to be accomplished by expanding and diversifying the tropical timber trade, improving forest management and use of woods, and reforestation.

On 21 May 1990, the International Tropical Timber Organization issued "ITTO Guidelines for the Sustainable Management of Natural Tropical Forests," which are voluntary guidelines for the parties. As of the end of 1990, it had conducted one field investigation of forest management in Sarawak, Malaysia; others are planned.

INTERNATIONAL TROPICAL TIMBER AGREEMENT

PREAMBLE

The Parties to this Agreement,
Recalling the Declaration and the Programme of Action on the Establishment of a New International Economic Order adopted by the General Assembly,[1]
Recalling resolutions 93 (IV) and 124 (V) on the Integrated Programme for Commodities adopted by the United nations [sic] Conference on Trade and Development at its fourth and fifth sessions,
Recognizing the importance of, and the need for, proper and effective conservation and development of tropical timber forests with a view to ensuring their optimum utilization while maintaining the ecological balance of the regions concerned and of the biosphere,
Recognizing the importance of tropical timber to the economies of members, particularly to the exports of producing members and the supply requirements of consuming members,

---

*Provisional application
[1]General Assembly resolutions 3201 (S-VI) and 3202 (S-VI) of 1 May 1974.

Desiring to establish a framework of international cooperation between producing and consuming members in finding solutions to the problems facing the tropical timber economy,

Have agreed as follows:

CHAPTER I. OBJECTIVES
Article 1
Objectives

With a view to achieving the relevant objectives adopted by the United Nations Conference on Trade and Development in its resolutions 93 (IV) and 124 (V) on the Integrated Programme for Commodities, for the benefit of both producing and consuming members and bearing in mind the sovereignty of producing members over their natural resources, the objectives of the International Tropical Timber Agreement, 1983 (hereinafter referred to as "this Agreement") are:

* * *

(*f*) To encourage members to support and develop industrial tropical timber reforestation and forest management activities;

* * *

(*h*) To encourage the development of national policies aimed at sustainable utilization and conservation of tropical forests and their genetic resources, and at maintaining the ecological balance in the regions concerned.

CHAPTER II. DEFINITIONS
Article 2
Definitions

For the purposes of this Agreement:

(1) "Tropical timber" means non-coniferous tropical wood for industrial uses, which grows or is produced in the countries situated between the Tropic of Cancer and the Tropic of Capricorn. The term covers logs, sawnwood, veneer sheets and plywood. Plywood which includes in some measure conifers of tropical origin shall also be covered by this definition;

(2) "Further processing" means the transformation of logs into primary wood products, semi-finished and finished products made wholly or almost wholly of tropical timber;

(3) "Member" means a Government or an intergovernmental organization referred to in article 5 which has consented to be bound by this Agreement whether it is in force provisionally or definitively;

(4) "Producing member" means any country with tropical forest resources and/or a net exporter of tropical timber in volume terms which is listed in annex A and which becomes a party to this Agreement, or any country with tropical forest resources and/or a net exporter of tropical timber in volume terms which is not so listed and which becomes a party to this Agreement and which the Council, with the consent of that country, declares to be a producing member;

(5) "Consuming member" means any country listed in annex B which becomes a party to this Agreement, or any country not so listed which becomes a party to this Agreement and which the Council, with the consent of that country, declars to be a consuming member;

* * *

CHAPTER III. ORGANIZATION
AND ADMINISTRATION
Article 3
Establishment, Headquarters and Structure of The
International Tropical Timber Organization

1. The International Tropical Timber Organization is hereby established to administer the provisions and supervise the operation of this Agreement.

2. The Organization shall function through the International Tropical Timber Council established under article 6, the committees and other subsidiary bodies referred to in article 24, and the Executive Director and staff.

3. The Council shall, at its first session, decide on the location of the headquarters of the Organization.

4. The headquarters of the Organization shall at all times be located in the territory of a member.

Article 4
Membership in the Organization

There shall be two categories of membership in the Organization, namely:
(a)   Producing; and
(b)   Consuming.

* * *

CHAPTER IV. INTERNATIONAL
TROPICAL TIMBER COUNCIL
Article 6
Composition of the International
Tropical Timber Council

1. The highest authority of the Organization shall be the International Tropical Timber Council, which shall consist of all the members of the Organization.

2. Each member shall be represented in the Council by one representative and may designate alternates and advisers to attend sessions of the Council.

3. An alternate representative shall be empowered to act and vote on behalf of the representative during the latter's absence or in special circumstances.

Article 7
Powers and Functions of the Council

1. The Council shall exercise all such powers and perform or arrange for the performance of all such functions as are necessary to carry out the provisions of this Agreement.

* * *

Article 10
Distribution of Votes

1. The producing members shall together hold 1,000 votes and the consuming members shall together hold 1,000 votes.

2. The votes of the producing members shall be distributed as follows:
(a)   Four hundred votes shall be distributed equally among the three producing regions of Africa, Asia-Pacific and Latin America. The votes thus allocated to each of these regions shall then be distributed equally among the producing members of that region;

(b)   Three hundred votes shall be distributed among the producing members in accordance with their respective shares of the total tropical forest resources of all producing members; and

(c)   Three hundred votes shall be distributed among the producing members in proportion to the average of the values of their respective net exports of tropical timber during the most recent three-year period for which definitive figures are available.

3. Notwithstanding the provisions of paragraph 2 of this article, the total votes allocated to the producing members from the African region, calculated in accordance with paragraph 2 of this article, shall be distributed equally among all producing members from the African region. If there are any remaining votes, each of these votes shall be allocated to a producing member from the African region: the first to the producing member which is allocated the highest number of votes calculated in accordance with paragraph 2 of this article, the second to the producing member which is allocated the second highest number of votes, and so on until all the remaining votes have been distributed.

4. For purposes of the calculation of the distribution of votes under paragraph 2(b) of this article, "tropical forest resources" means productive closed broadleaved forests as defined by the Food and Agriculture Organization of the United Nations (FAO).

5. The votes of the consuming members shall be distributed as follows: each consuming member shall have 10 initial votes; the remaining votes shall be distributed among the consuming members in proportion to the average volume of their respective net imports of tropical timber during the three-year period commencing four calendar years prior to the distribution of votes.

6. The Council shall distribute the votes for each financial year at the beginning of its first session of that year in accordance with the provisions of this article. Such distribution shall remain in effect for the rest of that year, except as provided for in paragraph 7 of this article.

7. Whenever the membership of the Organization changes or when any member has its voting rights suspended or restored under any provision of this Agreement, the Council shall redistribute the votes within the affected category or categories of members in accordance with the provisions of this article. The Council shall, in that event, decide when such redistribution shall become effective.

8. There shall be no fractional votes.

* * *

Article 12
Decisions and Recommendations of the Council

1. The Council shall endeavour to take all decisions and to make all recommendations by consensus. If consensus cannot be reached, the Council shall take all decisions and make all recommendations by a simple distributed majority vote, unless this Agreement provides for a special vote.

* * *

Article 14
Co-operation and Co-ordination
with Other Organizations

1. The Council shall make whatever arrangements are appropriate for consultation or co-operation with the United Nations and its organs, such as the United Nations Conference on Trade and Development (UNCTAD), the United Nations Industrial Development Organization (UNIDO), the United Nations Environment Programme (UNEP), the United Nations Development Programme (UNDP) and

the International Trade Centre UNCTAD/GATT (ITC), and with the Food and Agriculture Organization of the United Nations (FAO) and such other specialized agencies of the United Nations and intergovernmental, governmental and non-governmental organizations as may be appropriate.

2. The Organization shall, to the maximum extent possible, utilize the facilities, services and expertise of existing intergovernmental, governmental or non-governmental organizations, in order to avoid duplication of efforts in achieving the objectives of this Agreement and to enhance the complementarity and the efficiency of their activities.

* * *

Article 23
Projects

* * *

5. Research and development projects should relate to at least one of the following five areas:
- (a) Wood utilization, including the utilization of lesser-known and lesser-used species;
- (b) Natural forest development;
- (c) Reforestation development;
- (d) Harvesting, logging infrastructure, training of technical personnel;
- (e) Institutional framework, national planning.

* * *

Article 25
Functions of the Committees

* * *

2. The Committee on Reforestation and Forest Management shall:
- (a) Keep under regular review the support and assistance being provided at a national and international level for reforestation and forest management for the production of industrial tropical timber;
- (b) Encourage the increase of technical assistance to national programmes for reforestation and forest management;
- (c) Assess the requirements and identify all possible sources of financing for reforestation and forest management;
- (d) Review regularly future needs of international trade in industrial tropical timber and, on this basis, identify and consider appropriate possible schemes and measures in the field of reforestation and forest management;
- (e) Facilitate transfer of knowledge in the field of reforestation and forest management with the assistance of competent organizations;
- (f) Co-ordinate and harmonize these activities for co-operation in the field of reforestation and forest management with the relevant activities pursued elsewhere, such as those under FAO, UNEP, the World Bank, regional banks and other competent organizations.

CHAPTER 9
SPECIFIC ECOSYSTEMS

A. ANTARCTICA

Editors' Introductory Note Regarding the Antarctic Treaty Regime

Antarctica is the fifth largest continent, covering 14 million square kilometers. Since James Cook's voyage in 1772, explorers have been attracted to Antarctica. In the 1950s, Antarctica became a subject of scientific interest. Countries designated 1957-58 as the International Geophysical Year to promote international scientific cooperation in Antarctica. In 1959 they agreed to a treaty which would facilitate scientific research in the region.

The Antarctic Treaty puts "on ice" all national claims of sovereignty to any part of the continent, declares that the area can only be used for peaceful purposes, promotes and protects freedom of scientific investigation in Antarctica, bans nuclear explosions and disposal of radioactive wastes, and provides for consultative meetings of the parties to exchange information and agree upon measures to further the objectives of the Treaty. It establishes two tiers of membership: consultative parties, who have the right to vote, and non-consultative parties, who do not. Parties achieve consultative status by having claims to Antarctica at the time the Treaty was negotiated or by conducting a "substantial scientific research activity" in Antarctica.

As countries have recognized the resource potential of Antarctica, they have negotiated additional arrangements for the region. The emerging Antarctic treaty regime includes the Antarctic Treaty of 1959, the recommendations of Consultative Meetings of the parties, the Agreed Measures for the Conservation of Antarctic Flora and Fauna of 1965, the 1972 Convention for the Conservation of Antarctic Seals, the 1980 Convention for the Conservation of Antarctic Marine Living Resources, the 1988 Convention on the Regulation of Antarctic Mineral Resource Activities and the 1991 Protocol on Environmental Protection to the Antarctic Treaty.

The minerals or "Wellington" convention has yet to enter into force, because it requires all claimant States to ratify the agreement. Article 7 of the 1991 Protocol, which had not been signed when this book went to final printing, prohibits all mineral resources activities except for scientific research. The 1991 Protocol thus would effectively replace the Wellington convention (which contains several innovative provisions) as the relevant instrument regarding mineral exploitation. The 1991 Protocol also contains a Schedule on Arbitration and four annexes—Environmental Impact Assessment, Conservation of Antarctic Fauna and Flora, Waste Disposal and Waste Management, and Prevention of Marine Pollution.

ANTARCTIC TREATY

Popular Name: Antarctic Treaty

Done at Washington on 1 December 1959, 402 UNTS 71, 12 UST 794, TIAS 4780, UKTS No.97 (1982), Cmnd 1535, *reprinted in* UNEP3 #21, p.150, 1 IPE 18, IELMT 959: 91.

Entry into Force: 23 June 1961

Depositary: United States of America

Languages: English, French, Russian, Spanish

Parties as of 1 January 1990: Argentina;* Australia;* Austria; Belgium;* Brazil;* Bulgaria; Canada; Chile;* China;* Cuba; Czech and Slovak Federal Republic; Denmark; Ecuador; Finland;* France;* German Democratic Republic;* Germany, Federal Republic of;* Greece; Hungary; India;* Italy;* Japan;* Korea, Democratic People's Republic of; Korea, Republic of;* Netherlands;** New Zealand;* Norway;* Papua New Guinea; Peru;* Poland;* Romania; South Africa;* Spain;* Sweden; Union of Soviet Socialist Republics;* United Kingdom of Great Britain and Northern Ireland;* United States of America;* Uruguay.*

THE ANTARCTIC TREATY

The Governments of Argentina, Australia, Belgium, Chile, the French Republic, Japan, New Zealand, Norway, the Union of South Africa, the Union of Soviet Socialist Republics, the United Kingdom of Great Britain and Northern Ireland, and the United States of America,

Recognizing that it is in the interest of all mankind that Antarctica shall continue forever to be used exclusively for peaceful purposes and shall not become the scene or object of international discord;

Acknowledging the substantial contributions to scientific knowledge resulting from international cooperation in scientific investigation in Antarctica;

Convinced that the establishment of a firm foundation for the continuation and development of such cooperation on the basis of freedom of scientific investigation in Antarctica as applied during the International Geophysical Year accords with the interests of science and the progress of all mankind;

Convinced also that a treaty ensuring the use of Antarctica for peaceful purposes only and the continuance of international harmony in Antarctica will further the purposes and principles embodied in the Charter of the United Nations;

---

* Consultative Members under article IX of the Treaty
**With a geographic extension

Have agreed as follows:

Article I

1. Antarctica shall be used for peaceful purposes only. There shall be prohibited, *inter alia*, any measures of a military nature, such as the establishment of military bases and fortifications, the carrying out of military maneuvers, as well as the testing of any type of weapons.

2. The present Treaty shall not prevent the use of military personnel or equipment for scientific research or for any other peaceful purpose.

Article II

Freedom of scientific investigation in Antarctica and cooperation toward that end, as applied during the International Geophysical Year, shall continue, subject to the provisions of the present Treaty.

Article III

1. In order to promote international cooperation in scientific investigation in Antarctica, as provided for in Article II of the present Treaty, the Contracting Parties agree that, to the greatest extent feasible and practicable:
   (a)   information regarding plans for scientific programs in Antarctica shall be exchanged to permit maximum economy and efficiency of operations;
   (b)   scientific personnel shall be exchanged in Antarctica between expeditions and stations;
   (c)   scientific observations and results from Antarctica shall be exchanged and made freely available.

2. In implementing this Article, every encouragement shall be given to the establishment of cooperative working relations with those Specialized Agencies of the United Nations and other international organizations having a scientific or technical interest in Antarctica.

Article IV

1. Nothing contained in the present Treaty shall be interpreted as:
   (a)   a renunciation by any Contracting Party of previously asserted rights of or claims to territorial sovereignty in Antarctica;
   (b)   a renunciation or diminution by any Contracting Party of any basis of claim to territorial sovereignty in Antarctica which it may have whether as a result of its activities or those of its nationals in Antarctica, or otherwise;
   (c)   prejudicing the position of any Contracting Party as regards its recognition or non-recognition of any other State's right of or claim or basis of claim to territorial sovereignty in Antarctica.

2. No acts or activities taking place while the present Treaty is in force shall constitute a basis for asserting, supporting or denying a claim to territorial sovereignty in Antarctica or create any rights of sovereignty in Antarctica. No new claim, or enlargement of an existing claim, to territorial sovereignty in Antarctica shall be asserted while the present Treaty is in force.

Article V

1. Any nuclear explosions in Antarctica and the disposal there of radioactive waste material shall be prohibited.

2. In the event of the conclusion of international agreements concerning the use of nuclear energy, including nuclear explosions and the disposal of radioactive waste material, to which all of the Contracting Parties whose representatives are entitled to participate in the meetings provided for under Article IX are parties, the rules established under such agreements shall apply in Antarctica.

Article VI

The provisions of the present Treaty shall apply to the area south of 60° South Latitude, including all ice shelves, but nothing in the present Treaty shall prejudice or in any way affect the rights, or the exercise of the rights, of any State under international law with regard to the high seas within that area.

Article VII

1. In order to promote the objectives and ensure the observance of the provisions of the present Treaty, each Contracting Party whose representatives are entitled to participate in the meetings referred to in Article IX of the Treaty shall have the right to designate observers to carry out any inspection provided for by the present Article. Observers shall be nationals of the Contracting Parties which designate them. The names of observers shall be communicated to every other Contracting Party having the right to designate observers, and like notice shall be given of the termination of their appointment.

2. Each observer designated in accordance with the provisions of paragraph 1 of this Article shall have complete freedom of access at any time to any or all areas of Antarctica.

3. All areas of Antarctica, including all stations, installations and equipment within those areas, and all ships and aircraft at points of discharging or embarking cargoes or personnel in Antarctica, shall be open at all times to inspection by any observers designated in accordance with paragraph 1 of this Article.

4. Aerial observation may be carried out at any time over any or all areas of Antarctica by any of the Contracting Parties having the right to designate observers.

5. Each Contracting Party shall, at the time when the present Treaty enters into force for it, inform the other Contracting Parties, and thereafter shall give them notice in advance, of

(a) all expeditions to and within Antarctica, on the part of its ships or nationals, and all expeditions to Antarctica organized in or proceeding from its territory;

(b) all stations in Antarctica occupied by its nationals; and

(c) any military personnel or equipment intended to be introduced by it into Antarctica subject to the conditions prescribed in paragraph 2 of Article I of the present Treaty.

Article VIII

1. In order to facilitate the exercise of their functions under the present Treaty, and without prejudice to the respective positions of the Contracting Parties relating to jurisdiction over all other persons in Antarctica, observers designated under paragraph 1 of Article VII and scientific personnel exchanged under subparagraph 1(b) of Article III of the Treaty, and members of the staffs accompanying any such persons, shall be subject only to the jurisdiction of the Contracting Party of which they are nationals in respect of all acts or omissions occurring while they are in Antarctica for the purpose of exercising their functions.

2. Without prejudice to the provisions of paragraph 1 of this Article, and pending the adoption of measures in pursuance of subparagraph 1(e) of Article IX,

the Contracting Parties concerned in any case of dispute with regard to the exercise of jurisdiction in Antarctica shall immediately consult together with a view to reaching a mutually acceptable solution.

Article IX

1. Representatives of the Contracting Parties named in the preamble to the present Treaty shall meet at the City of Canberra within two months after the date of entry into force of the Treaty, and thereafter at suitable intervals and places, for the purpose of exchanging information, consulting together on matters of common interest pertaining to Antarctica, and formulating and considering, and recommending to their Governments, measures in furtherance of the principles and objectives of the Treaty, including measures regarding:

(a)   use of Antarctica for peaceful purposes only;
(b)   facilitation of scientific research in Antarctica;
(c)   facilitation of international scientific cooperation in Antarctica;
(d)   facilitation of the exercise of the rights of inspection provided for in Article VII of the Treaty;
(e)   questions relating to the exercise of jurisdiction in Antarctica;
(f)   preservation and conservation of living resources in Antarctica.

2. Each Contracting Party which has become a party to the present Treaty by accession under Article XIII shall be entitled to appoint representatives to participate in the meetings referred to in paragraph 1 of the present Article, during such time as that Contracting Party demonstrates its interest in Antarctica by conducting substantial scientific research activity there, such as the establishment of a scientific station or the despatch of a scientific expedition.

3. Reports from the observers referred to in Article VII of the present Treaty shall be transmitted to the representatives of the Contracting Parties participating in the meetings referred to in paragraph 1 of the present Article.

4. The measures referred to in paragraph 1 of this Article shall become effective when approved by all the Contracting Parties whose representatives were entitled to participate in the meetings held to consider those measures.

5. Any or all of the rights established in the present Treaty may be exercised as from the date of entry into force of the Treaty whether or not any measures facilitating the exercise of such rights have been proposed, considered or approved as provided in this Article.

Article X

Each of the Contracting Parties undertakes to exert appropriate efforts, consistent with the Charter of the United Nations, to the end that no one engages in any activity in Antarctica contrary to the principles or purposes of the present Treaty.

Article XI

1. If any dispute arises between two or more of the Contracting Parties concerning the interpretation or application of the present Treaty, those Contracting Parties shall consult among themselves with a view to having the dispute resolved by negotiation, inquiry, mediation, conciliation, arbitration, judicial settlement or other peaceful means of their own choice.

2. Any dispute of this character not so resolved shall, with the consent, in each case, of all parties to the dispute, be referred to the International Court of Justice for settlement; but failure to reach agreement on reference to the International Court shall not absolve parties to the dispute from the responsibility of continuing to seek to resolve it by any of the various peaceful means referred to in paragraph 1 of this Article.

Article XII

1. (a) The present Treaty may be modified or amended at any time by unanimous agreement of the Contracting Parties whose representatives are entitled to participate in the meetings provided for under Article IX. Any such modification or amendment shall enter into force when the depositary Government has received notice from all such Contracting Parties that they have ratified it.

(b) Such modification or amendment shall thereafter enter into force as to any other Contracting Party when notice of ratification by it has been received by the depositary Government. Any such Contracting Party from which no notice of ratification is received within a period of two years from the date of entry into force of the modification or amendment in accordance with the provisions of subparagraph 1(a) of this Article shall be deemed to have withdrawn from the pres nt [sic] Treaty on the date of the expiration of such period.

2. (a) If after the expiration of thirty years from the date of entry into force of the present Treaty, any of the Contracting Parties whose representatives are entitled to participate in the meetings provided for under Article IX so requests by a communication addressed to the depositary Government, a Conference of all the Contracting Parties shall be held as soon as practicable to review the operation of the Treaty.

(b) Any modification or amendment to the present Treaty which is approved at such a Conference by a majority of the Contracting Parties there represented, including a majority of those whose representatives are entitled to participate in the meetings provided for under Article IX, shall be communicated by the depositary Government to all the Contracting Parties immediately after the termination of the Conference and shall enter into force in accordance with the provisions of paragraph 1 of the present Article.

(c) If any such modification or amendment has not entered into force in accordance with the provisions of subparagraph 1(a) of this Article within a period of two years after the date of its communication to all the Contracting Parties, any Contracting Party may at any time after the expiration of that period give notice to the depositary Government of its withdrawal from the present Treaty; and such withdrawal shall take effect two years after the receipt of the notice by the depositary Government.

Article XIII

1. The present Treaty shall be subject to ratification by the signatory States. It shall be open for accession by any State which is a Member of the United Nations, or by any other State which may be invited to accede to the Treaty with the consent of all the Contracting Parties whose representatives are entitled to participate in the meetings provided for under Article IX of the Treaty.

2. Ratification of or accession to the present Treaty shall be effected by each State in accordance with its constitutional processes.

3. Instruments of ratification and instruments of accession shall be deposited with the Government of the United States of America, hereby designated as the depositary Government.

4. The depositary Government shall inform all signatory and acceding States of the date of each deposit of an instrument of ratification or accession, and the date of entry into force of the Treaty and of any modification or amendment thereto.

5. Upon the deposit of instruments of ratification by all the signatory States, the present Treaty shall enter into force for those States and for States which have deposited instruments of accession. Thereafter the Treaty shall enter into force for any acceding State upon the deposit of its instrument of accession.

6. The present Treaty shall be registered by the depositary Government pursuant to Article 102 of the Charter of the United Nations.

Article XIV

The present Treaty, done in the English, French, Russian and Spanish languages, each version being equally authentic, shall be deposited in the archives of the Government of the United States of America, which shall transmit duly certified copies thereof to the Governments of the signatory and acceding States.

CANBERRA CONVENTION ON THE CONSERVATION OF ANTARCTIC MARINE LIVING RESOURCES

Popular Names: Antarctic Marine Living Resources Convention, Canberra Convention, CCAMLR

Done at Canberra on 20 May 1980, 33 UST 3476, TIAS 10240, UKTS No.48 (1982), Cmnd 8714, *reprinted in* 19 ILM 841 (1980).

Entry into Force: 7 April 1982

Depositary: Australia

Languages: English, French, Russian, Spanish

Parties as of 1 January 1990: Argentina;* Australia; Belgium; Brazil; Canada; Chile; Finland; France;* German Democratic Republic; Germany, Federal Republic of; Greece; India; Italy; Japan; Korea, Republic of; New Zealand; Norway; Poland; South Africa; Spain; Sweden; Union of Soviet Socialist Republics; United Kingdom of Great Britain and Northern Ireland; United States of America; Uruguay; European Economic Community

Literature: S. Lyster, *International Wildlife Law* 156 (1985)

CONVENTION ON THE CONSERVATION OF ANTARCTIC MARINE LIVING RESOURCES

The Contracting Parties,
   RECOGNISING the importance of safeguarding the environment and protecting the integrity of the ecosystem of the seas surrounding Antarctica;
   NOTING the concentration of marine living resources found in Antarctic waters and the increased interest in the possibilities offered by the utilization of these resources as a source of protein;
   CONSCIOUS of the urgency of ensuring the conservation of Antarctic marine living resources;
   CONSIDERING that it is essential to increase knowledge of the Antarctic marine ecosystem and its components so as to be able to base decisions on harvesting on sound scientific information;

---
*With declaration

BELIEVING that the conservation of Antractic marine living resources calls for international co-operation with due regard for the provisions of the Antractic Treaty and with the active involvement of all States engaged in research or harvesting activities in Antarctic waters;

RECOGNISING the prime responsibilities of the Antarctic Treaty Consultative Parties for the protection and preservation of the Antarctic environment and, in particular, their responsibilities under Article IX, paragraph 1 (f) of the Antarctic Treaty in respect of the preservation and conservation of living resources in Antarctica;

RECALLING the action already taken by the Antarctic Treaty Consultative Parties including in particular the Agreed Measures for the Conservation of Antarctic Fauna and Flora, as well as the provisions of the Convention for the Conservation of Antarctic Seals;

BEARING in mind the concern regarding the conservation of Antarctic marine living resources expressed by the Consultative Parties at the Ninth Consultative Meeting of the Antarctic Treaty and the importance of the provisions of Recommendation IX-2 which led to the establishment of the present Convention;

BELIEVING that it is in the interest of all mankind to preserve the waters surrounding the Antarctic continent for peaceful purposes only and to prevent their becoming the scene or object of international discord;

RECOGNISING, in the light of the foregoing, that it is desirable to establish suitable machinery for recommending, promoting, deciding upon and co-ordinating the measures and scientific studies needed to ensure the conservation of Antarctic marine living organisms;

HAVE AGREED as follows:

ARTICLE I

1. This Convention applies to the Antarctic marine living resources of the area south of 60° South latitutde and to the Antarctic marine living resources of the area between that latitude and the Antarctic Convergence which form part of the Antarctic marine ecosystem.
2. Antarctic marine living resources means the populations of fin fish, molluscs, crustaceans and all other species of living organisms, including birds, found south of the Antarctic Convergence.
3. The Antarctic marine ecosystem means the complex of relationships of Antarctic marine living resources with each other and with their physical environment.
4. The Antarctic Convergence shall be deemed to be a line joining the following points along parallels of latitude and meridians of longtitude: 50°S, 0°; 50°S, 30°E; 45°S, 30°E; 45°S, 80°E; 55°S, 80°E; 55°S, 150°E; 60°S, 150°E; 60°S, 50°W; 50°S, 50°W; 50°S, 0°.

ARTICLE II

1. The objective of this Convention is the conservation of Antarctic marine living resources.
2. For the purposes of this Convention, the term "conservation" includes rational use.
3. Any harvesting and associated activities in the area to which this Convention applies shall be conducted in accordance with the provisions of this Convention and with the following principles of conservation:
   (a) prevention of decrease in the size of any harvested population to levels below those which ensure its stable recruitment. For this purpose its size should not be allowed to fall below a level close to that which ensures the greatest net annual increment;

(b)   maintenance of the ecological relationships between harvested, dependent and related populations of Antarctic marine living resources and the restoration of depleted populations to the levels defined in sub-paragraph (a) above; and

(c)   prevention of changes or minimization of the risk of changes in the marine ecosystem which are not potentially reversible over two or three decades, taking into account the state of available knowledge of the direct and indirect impact of harvesting, the effect of the introduction of alien species, the effects of associated activities on the marine ecosystem and of the effects of environmental changes, with the aim of making possible the sustained conservation of Antarctic marine living resources.

ARTICLE III

The Contracting Parties, whether or not they are Parties to the Antarctic Treaty, agree that they will not engage in any activities in the Antarctic Treaty area contrary to the principles and purposes of that Treaty and that, in their relations with each other, they are bound by the obligations contained in Articles I and V of the Antarctic Treaty.

ARTICLE IV

1. With respect to the Antarctic Treaty area, all Contracting Parties, whether or not they are Parties to the Antarctic Treaty, are bound by Articles IV and VI of the Antarctic Treaty in their relations with each other.
2. Nothing in this Convention and no acts or activities taking place while the present Convention is in force shall:
    (a)   constitute a basis for asserting, supporting or denying a claim to territorial sovereignty in the Antarctic Treaty area or create any rights of sovereignty in the Antarctic Treaty area;
    (b)   be interpreted as a renunciation or diminution by any Contracting Party of, or as prejudicing, any right or claim or basis of claim to exercise coastal state jurisdiction under international law within the area to which this Convention applies;
    (c)   be interpreted as prejudicing the position of any Contracting Party as regards its recognition or non-recognition of any such right, claim or basis of claim;
    (d)   affect the provision of Article IV, paragraph 2, of the Antarctic Treaty that no new claim, or enlargement of an existing claim, to territorial sovereignty in Antarctica shall be asserted while the Antarctic Treaty is in force.

ARTICLE V

1. The Contracting Parties which are not Parties to the Antarctic Treaty acknowledge the special obligations and responsibilities of the Antarctic Treaty Consultative Parties for the protection and preservation of the environment of the Antarctic Treaty area.
2. The Contracting Parties which are not Parties to the Antarctic Treaty agree that, in their activities in the Antarctic Treaty area, they will observe as and when appropriate the Agreed Measures for the Conservation of Antarctic Fauna and Flora and such other measures as have been recommended by the Antarctic Treaty Consultative Parties in fulfilment of their responsibility for the protection of the Antarctic environment from all forms of harmful human interference.

3. For the purposes of this Convention, "Antarctic Treaty Consultative Parties" means the Contracting Parties to the Antarctic Treaty whose Representatives participate in meetings under Article IX of the Antarctic Treaty.

ARTICLE VI

Nothing in this Convention shall derogate from the rights and obligations of Contracting Parties under the International Convention for the Regulation of Whaling and the Convention for the Conservation of Antarctic Seals.

ARTICLE VII

1. The Contracting Parties hereby establish and agree to maintain the Commission for the Conservation of Antarctic Marine Living Resources (hereinafter referred to as "the Commission").
2. Membership in the Commission shall be as follows:
   - (a) each Contracting Party which participated in the meeting at which this Convention was adopted shall be a Member of the Commission;
   - (b) each State Party which has acceded to this Convention pursuant to Article XXIX shall be entitled to be a Member of the Commission during such time as that acceding Party is engaged in research or harvesting activities in relation to the marine living resources to which this Convention applies;
   - (c) each regional economic integration organization which has acceded to this Convention pursuant to Article XXIX shall be entitled to be a Member of the Commission during such time as its States members are so entitled;
   - (d) a Contracting Party seeking to participate in the work of the Commission pursuant to sub-paragraphs (b) and (c) above shall notify the Depositary of the basis upon which it seeks to become a Member of the Commission and of its willingness to accept conservation measures in force. The Depositary shall communicate to each Member of the Commission such notification and accompanying information. Within two months of receipt of such communication from the Depositary, any Member of the Commission may request that a special meeting of the Commission be held to consider the matter. Upon receipt of such request, the Depositary shall call such a meeting. If there is no request for a meeting, the Contracting Party submitting the notification shall be deemed to have satisfied the requirements for Commission Membership.
3. Each Member of the Commission shall be represented by one representative who may be accompanied by alternate representatives and advisers.

ARTICLE VIII

The Commission shall have legal personality and shall enjoy in the territory of each of the States Parties such legal capacity as may be necessary to perform its function and achieve the purposes of this Convention. The privileges and immunities to be enjoyed by the Commission and its staff in the territory of a State Party shall be determined by agreement between the Commission and the State Party concerned.

ARTICLE IX

1. The function of the Commission shall be to give effect to the objective and principles set out in Article II of this Convention. To this end, it shall:
   - (a) facilitate research into and comprehensive studies of Antarctic marine living resources and of the Antarctic marine ecosystem;

(b)   compile data on the status of and changes in population of Antarctic marine living resources and on factors affecting the distribution, abundance and productivity of harvested species and dependent or related species or populations;

(c)   ensure the acquisition of catch and effort statistics on harvested populations;

(d)   analyse, disseminate and publish the information referred to in sub-paragraphs (b) and (c) above and the reports of the Scientific Committee;

(e)   identify conservation needs and analyse the effectiveness of conservation measures;

(f)   formulate, adopt and revise conservation measures on the basis of the best scientific evidence available, subject to the provisions of paragraph 5 of this Article;

(g)   implement the system of observation and inspection established under Article XXIV of this Convention;

(h)   carry out such other activities as are necessary to fulfil the objective of this Convention.

2. The conservation measures referred to in paragraph 1 (f) above include the following:

(a)   the designation of the quantity of any species which may be harvested in the area to which this Convention applies;

(b)   the designation of regions and sub-regions based on the distribution of populations of Antarctic marine living resources;

(c)   the designation of the quantity which may be harvested from the populations of regions and sub-regions;

(d)   the designation of protected species;

(e)   the designation of the size, age and, as appropriate, sex of species which may be harvested;

(f)   the designation of open and closed seasons for harvesting;

(g)   the designation of the opening and closing of areas, regions or sub-regions for purposes of scientific study or conservation, including special areas for protection and scientific study;

(h)   regulation of the effort employed and methods of harvesting, including fishing gear, with a view, inter alia, to avoiding undue concentration of harvesting in any region or sub-region;

(i)   the taking of such other conservation measures as the Commission considers necessary for the fulfilment of the objective of this Convention, including measures concerning the effects of harvesting and associated activities on components of the marine ecosystem other than the harvested populations.

3. The Commission shall publish and maintain a record of all conservation measures in force.

4. In exercising its functions under paragraph 1 above, the Commission shall take full account of the recommendations and advice of the Scientific Committee.

5. The Commission shall take full account of any relevant measures or regulations established or recommended by the Consultative Meetings pursuant to Article IX of the Antarctic Treaty or by existing fisheries commissions responsible for species which may enter the area to which this Convention applies, in order that there shall be no inconsistency between the rights and obligations of a Contracting Party under such regulations or measures and conservation measures which may be adopted by the Commission.

6. Conservation measures adopted by the Commission in accordance with this Convention shall be implemented by Members of the Commission in the following manner:

(a)   the Commission shall notify conservation measures to all Members of the Commission;

(b)   conservation measures shall become binding upon all Members of the Commission 180 days after such notification, except as provided in sub-paragraphs (c) and (d) below;

(c)   if a Member of the Commission, within ninety days following the notification specified in sub-paragraph (a), notifies the Commission that it is unable to accept the conservation measure, in whole or in part, the measure shall not, to the extent stated, be binding upon that Member of the Commission;

(d)   in the event that any Member of the Commission invokes the procedure set forth in sub-paragraph (c) above, the Commission shall meet at the request of any Member of the Commission to review the conservation measure. At the time of such meeting and within thirty days following the meeting, any Member of the Commission shall have the right to declare that it is no longer able to accept the conservation measure, in which case the Member shall no longer be bound by such measure.

ARTICLE X

1. The Commission shall draw the attention of any State which is not a Party to this Convention to any activity undertaken by its nationals or vessels which, in the opinion of the Commission, affects the implementation of the objective of this Convention.
2. The Commission shall draw the attention of all Contracting Parties to any activity which, in the opinion of the Commission, affects the implementation by a Contracting Party of the objective of this Convention or the compliance by that Contracting Party with its obligations under this Convention.

ARTICLE XI

The Commission shall seek to co-operate with Contracting Parties which may exercise jurisdiction in marine areas adjacent to the area to which this Convention applies in respect of the conservation of any stock or stocks of associated species which occur both within those areas and the area to which this Convention applies, with a view to harmonizing the conservation measures adopted in respect of such stocks.

ARTICLE XII

1. Decisions of the Commission on matters of substance shall be taken by consensus. The question of whether a matter is one of substance shall be treated as a matter of substance.
2. Decisions on matters other than those referred to in paragraph 1 above shall be taken by a simple majority of the Members of the Commission present and voting.
3. In Commission consideration of any item requiring a decision, it shall be made clear whether a regional economic integration organization will participate in the taking of the decision and, if so, whether any of its member States will also participate. The number of Contracting Parties so participating shall not exceed the number of member States of the regional economic integration organization which are Members of the Commission.
4. In the taking of decisions pursuant to this Article, a regional economic integration organization shall have only one vote.

ARTICLE XIII

1. The headquarters of the Commission shall be estalished at Hobart, Tasmania, Australia.

2. The Commission shall hold a regular annual meeting. Other meetings shall also be held at the request of one-third of its members and as otherwise provided in this Convention. The first meeting of the Commission shall be held within three months of the entry into force of this Convention, provided that among the Contracting Parties there are at least two States conducting harvesting activities within the area to which this Convention applies. The first meeting shall, in any event, be held within one year of the entry into force of this Convention. The Depositary shall consult with the signatory States regarding the first Commission meeting, taking into account that a broad representation of such States is necessary for the effective operation of the Commission.
3. The Depositary shall convene the first meeting of the Commission at the headquarters of the Commission. Thereafter, meetings of the Commission shall be held at its headquarters, unless it decides otherwise.
4. The Commission shall elect from among its members a Chairman and Vice-Chairman, each of whom shall serve for a term of two years and shall be eligible for re-election for one additional term. The first Chairman shall, however, be elected for an initial term of three years. The Chairman and Vice-Chairman shall not be representatives of the same Contracting Party.
5. The Commission shall adopt and amend as necessary the rules of procedure for the conduct of its meetings, except with respect to the matters dealt with in Article XII of this Convention.
6. The Commission may establish such subsidiary bodies as are necessary for the performance of its functions.

ARTICLE XIV

1. The Contracting Parties hereby establish the Scientific Committee for the Conservation of Antarctic Marine Living Resources (hereinafter referred to as ''the Scientific Committee'') which shall be a consultative body to the Commission. The Scientific Committee shall normally meet at the headquarters of the Commission unless the Scientific Committee decides otherwise.
2. Each Member of the Commission shall be a member of the Scientific Committee and shall appoint a representative with suitable scientific qualifications who may be accompanied by other experts and advisers.
3. The Scientific Committee may seek the advice of other scientists and experts as may be required on an ad hoc basis.

ARTICLE XV

1. The Scientific Committee shall provide a forum for consultation and co-operation concerning the collection, study and exchange of information with respect to the marine living resources to which this Convention applies. It shall encourage and promote co-operation in the field of scientific research in order to extend knowledge of the marine living resources of the Antarctic marine ecosystem.
2. The Scientific Committee shall conduct such activities as the Commission may direct in pursuance of the objective of this Convention and shall:
   (a) establish criteria and methods to be used for determinations concerning the conservation measures referred to in Article IX of this Convention;
   (b) regularly assess the status and trends of the populations of Antarctic marine living resources;
   (c) analyse data concerning the direct and indirect effects of harvesting on the populations of Antarctic marine living resources;
   (d) assess the effects of proposed changes in the methods or levels of harvesting and proposed conservation measures;

(e)   transmit assessments, analyses, reports and recommendations to the Commission as requested or on its own initiative regarding measures and research to implement the objective of this Convention;

(f)   formulate proposals for the conduct of international and national programs of research into Antarctic marine living resources.

3. In carrying out its functions, the Scientific Committee shall have regard to the work of other relevant technical and scientific organizations and to the scientific activities conducted within the framework of the Antarctic Treaty.

ARTICLE XVI

1. The first meeting of the Scientific Committee shall be held within three months of the first meeting of the Commission. The Scientific Committee shall meet thereafter as often as may be necessary to fulfil its functions.

2. The Scientific Committee shall adopt and amend as necessary its rules of procedure. The rules and any amendments thereto shall be approved by the Commission. The rules shall include procedures for the presentation of minority reports.

3. The Scientific Committee may establish, with the approval of the Commission, such subsidiary bodies as are necessary for the performance of its functions.

* * *

ARTICLE XIX

* * *

3. Each Member of the Commission shall contribute to the budget. Until the expiration of five years after the entry into force of this Convention, the contribution of each Member of the Commission shall be equal. Thereafter the contribution shall be determined in accordnce with two criteria: the amount harvested and an equal sharing among all Members of the Commission. The Commission shall determine by consensus the proportion in which these two criteria shall apply.

* * *

ARTICLE XX

1. The Members of the Commission shall, to the greatest extent possible, provide annually to the Commission and to the Scientific Committee such statistical, biological and other data and information as the Commission and Scientific Committee may require in the exercise of their functions.

2. The Members of the Commission shall provide, in the manner and at such intervals as may be prescribed, information about their harvesting activities, including fishing areas and vessels, so as to enable reliable catch and effort statistics to be compiled.

3. The Members of the Commission shall provide to the Commission at such intervals as may be prescribed information on steps taken to implement the conservation measures adopted by the Commission.

4. The Members of the Commission agree that in any of their harvesting activities, advantage shall be taken of opportunities to collect data needed to assess the impact of harvesting.

ARTICLE XXI

1. Each Contracting Party shall take appropriate measures within its competence to ensure compliance with the provisions of this Convention and with conservation measures adopted by the Commission to which the Party is bound in accordance with Article IX of this Convention.

2. Each Contracting Party shall transmit to the Commission information on measures taken pursuant to paragraph 1 above, including the imposition of sanctions for any violation.

ARTICLE XXII

1. Each Contracting Party undertakes to exert appropriate efforts, consistent with the Charter of the United Nations, to the end that no one engages in any activity contrary to the objective of this Convention.
2. Each Contracting Party shall notify the Commission of any such activity which comes to its attention.

ARTICLE XXIII

1. The Commission and the Scientific Committee shall co-operate with the Antarctic Treaty Consultative Parties on matters falling within the competence of the latter.
2. The Commission and the Scientific Committee shall co-operate, as appropriate, with the Food and Agriculture Organisation of the United Nations and with other Specialised Agencies.
3. The Commission and the Scientific Committee shall seek to develop co-operative working relationships, as appropriate, with inter-governmental and non-governmental organizations which could contribute to their work, including the Scientific Committee on Antarctic Research, the Scientific Committee on Oceanic Research and the International Whaling Commission.
4. The Commission may enter into agreements with the organizations referred to in this Article and with other organizations as may be appropriate. The Commission and the Scientific Committee may invite such organizations to send observers to their meetings and to meetings of their subsidiary bodies.

ARTICLE XXIV

1. In order to promote the objective and ensure observance of the provisions of this Convention, the Contracting Parties agree that a system of observation and inspection shall be established.
2. The system of observation and inspection shall be elaborated by the Commission on the basis of the following principles:
   (a) Contracting Parties shall co-operate with each other to ensure the effective implementation of the system of observation and inspection, taking account of the existing international practice. This system shall include, inter alia, procedures for boarding and inspection by observers and inspectors designated by the Members of the Commission and procedures for flag state prosecution and sanctions on the basis of evidence resulting from such boarding and inspections. A report of such prosecutions and sanctions imposed shall be included in the information referred to in Article XXI of this Convention;
   (b) in order to verify compliance with measures adopted under this Convention, observation and inspection shall be carried out on board vessels engaged in scientific research or harvesting of marine living resources in the area to which this Convention applies, through observers and inspectors designated by the Members of the Commission and operating under terms and conditions to be established by the Commission;
   (c) designated observers and inspectors shall remain subject to the jurisdiction of the Contracting Party of which they are nationals. They shall report to the Member of the Commission by which they have been designated which in turn shall report to the Commission.

3. Pending the establishment of the system of observation and inspection, the Members of the Commission shall seek to establish interim arrangements to designate observers and inspectors and such designated observers and inspectors shall be entitled to carry out inspections in accordance with the principles set out in paragraph 2 above.

* * *

WELLINGTON CONVENTION ON THE REGULATION OF ANTARCTIC MINERAL RESOURCE ACTIVITIES

Popular Names: Antarctic Mineral Resource Convention, CRAMRA, Wellington Convention

Done at Wellington on 2 June 1988, U.N. Doc. AMR/SCM/88/78 (1988), *reprinted in* 27 ILM 868 (1988).

Entry into Force: Not yet in force as of December 1990

Depositary: New Zealand

Languages: Chinese, English, French, Russian, Spanish

CONVENTION ON THE REGULATION OF ANTARCTIC MINERAL RESOURCE ACTIVITIES

* * *

Article 2
Objectives and General Principles

1. This Convention is an integral part of the Antarctic Treaty system, comprising the Antarctic Treaty, the measures in effect under that Treaty, and its associated separate legal instruments, the prime purpose of which is to ensure that Antarctica shall continue forever to be used exclusively for peaceful purposes and shall not become the scene or object of international discord. The Parties provide through this Convention, the principles it establishes, the rules it prescribes, the institutions it creates and the decisions adopted pursuant to it, a means for:
  (a)   assessing the possible impact on the environment of Antarctic mineral resource activities;
  (b)   determining whether Antarctic mineral resource activities are acceptable;
  (c)   governing the conduct of such Antarctic mineral resource activities as may be found acceptable; and
  (d)   ensuring that any Antarctic mineral resource activities are undertaken in strict conformity with this Convention.
2. In implementing this Convention, the Parties shall ensure that Antarctic mineral resource activities, should they occur, take place in a manner consistent with all the components of the Antarctic Treaty system and the obligations flowing therefrom.

3. In relation to Antarctic mineral resource activities, should they occur, the Parties acknowledge the special responsibility of the Antarctic Treaty Consultative Parties for the protection of the environment and the need to:

(a)   protect the Antarctic environment and dependent and associated eco-systems;
(b)   respect Antarctica's significance for, and influence on, the global environment;
(c)   respect other legitimate uses of Antarctica;
(d)   respect Antarctica's scientific value and aesthetic and wilderness qualities;
(e)   ensure the safety of operations in Antarctica;
(f)   promote opportunities for fair and effective participation of all Parties; and
(g)   take into account the interests of the international community as a whole.

Article 3
Prohibition of Antarctic Mineral Resource Activities Outside this Convention

No Antarctic mineral resource activities shall be conducted except in accordance with this Convention and measures in effect pursuant to it and, in the case of exploration or development, with a Management Scheme approved pursuant to Article 48 or 54.

Article 4
Principles Concerning Judgments on Antarctic Mineral Resource Activities

1. Decisions about Antarctic mineral resource activities shall be based upon information adequate to enable informed judgments to be made about their possible impacts and no such activities shall take place unless this information is available for decisions relevant to those activities.

2. No Antarctic mineral resource activity shall take place until it is judged, based upon assessment of its possible impacts on the Antarctic environment and on dependent and on associated ecosystems, that the activity in question would not cause:

(a)   significant adverse effects on air and water quality;
(b)   significant changes in atmospheric, terrestrial or marine environments;
(c)   significant changes in the distribution, abundance or productivity of populations of species of fauna or flora;
(d)   further jeopardy to endangered or threatened species or populations of such species; or
(e)   degradation of, or substantial risk to, areas of special biological, scientific, historic, aesthetic or wilderness significance.

3. No Antarctic mineral resource activity shall take place until it is judged, based upon assessment of its possible impacts, that the activity in question would not cause signfiicant adverse effects on global or regional climate or weather patterns.

4. No Antarctic mineral resource activity shall take place until it is judged that:

(a)   technology and procedures are available to provide for safe operations and compliance with paragraphs 2 and 3 above;
(b)   there exists the capacity to monitor key environmental parameters and ecosystem components so as to identify any adverse effects of such activity and to provide for the modification of operating procedures as may be necessary in the light of the results of monitoring or increased knowledge of the Antarctic environment or dependent or associated ecosystems; and
(c)   there exists the capacity to respond effectively to accidents, particularly those with potential environmental effects.

5. The judgments referred to in paragraphs 2, 3 and 4 above shall take into account the cumulative impacts of possible Antarctic mineral resource activities both by themselves and in combination with other such activities and other uses of Antarctica.

* * *

Article 6
Cooperation and International Participation

In the implementation of this Convention cooperation within its framework shall be promoted and encouragement given to international participation in Antarctic mineral resource activities by interested Parties which are Antarctic Treaty Consultative Parties and by other interested Parties, in particular, developing countries in either category. Such participation may be realised through the Parties themselves and their Operators.

* * *

Article 7
Compliance with this Convention

1. Each Party shall take appropriate measures within its competence to ensure compliance with this Convention and any measures in effect pursuant to it.
2. If a Party is prevented by the exercise of jurisdiction by another Party from ensuring compliance in accordance with paragraph 1 above, it shall not, to the extent that it is so prevented, bear responsibility for that failure to ensure compliance.

* * *

Article 8
Response Action and Liability

1. An Operator undertaking any Antarctic mineral resource activity shall take necessary and timely response action, including prevention, containment, clean up and removal measures, if the activity results in or threatens to result in damage to the Antarctic environment or dependent or associated ecosystems. The Operator, through its Sponsoring State, shall notify the Executive Secretary, for circulation to the relevant institutions of this Convention and to all Parties, of action taken pursuant to this paragraph.
2. An Operator shall be strictly liable for:
   (a) damage to the Antarctic environment or dependent or associated ecosystems arising from its Antarctic mineral resource activities, including payment in the event that there has been no restoration to the *status quo ante*;
   (b) loss of or impairment to an established use, as referred to in Article 15, or loss of or impairment to an established use of dependent or associated ecosystems, arising directly out of damage described in subparagraph (a) above;
   (c) loss of or damage to property of a third party or loss of life or personal injury of a third party arising directly out of damage described in subparagraph (a) above; and
   (d) reimbursement of reasonable costs by whomsoever incurred relating to necessary response action, including prevention, containment, clean up and removal measures, and action taken to restore the *status quo ante* where Antarctic mineral resource activities undertaken by that Operator result in or threaten to result in damage to the Antarctic environment or dependent or associated ecosystems.

3. (a) Damage of the kind referred to in paragraph 2 above which would not have occurred or continued if the Sponsoring State had carried out its obligations under this Convention with respect to its Operator shall, in accordance with international law, entail liability of that Sponsoring State. Such liability shall be limited to that portion of liability not satisfied by the Operator or otherwise.

   (b)   Nothing in subparagraph (a) above shall affect the application of the rules of international law applicable in the event that damage not referred to in that subparagraph would not have occurred or continued if the Sponsoring State had carried out its obligations under this Convention with respect to its Operator.

4. An Operator shall not be liable pursuant to paragraph 2 above if it proves that the damage has been caused directly by, and to the extent that it has been caused directly by:

   (a)   an event constituting in the circumstances of Antarctica a natural disaster of an exceptional character which could not reasonably have been foreseen; or

   (b)   armed conflict, should it occur notwithstanding the Antarctic Treaty, or an act of terrorism directed against the activities of the Operator, against which no reasonable precautionary measures could have been effective.

5. Liability of an Operator for any loss of life, personal injury or loss of or damage to property other than that governed by this Article shall be regulated by applicable law and procedures.

6. If an Operator proves that damage has been caused totally or in part by an intentional or grossly negligent act or omission of the party seeking redress, that Operator may be relieved totally or in part from its obligation to pay compensation in respect of the damage suffered by such party.

7. (a)   Further rules and procedures in respect of the provisions on liability set out in this Article shall be elaborated through a separate Protocol which shall be adopted by consensus by the members of the Commission and shall enter into force according to the procedure provided for in Article 62 for the entry into force of this Convention.

   (b)   Such rules and procedures shall be designed to enhance the protection of the Antarctic environment and dependent and associated ecosystems.

   (c)   Such rules and procedures:

      (i)   may contain provisions for appropriate limits on liability, where such limits can be justified;

      (ii) without prejudice to Article 57, shall prescribe means and mechanisms such as a claims tribunal or other fora by which claims against Operators pursuant to this Article may be assessed and adjudicated;

      (iii) shall ensure that a means is provided to assist with immediate response action, and to satisfy liability under paragraph 2 above in the event, *inter alia*, that an Operator liable is financially incapable of meeting its obligation in full, that it exceeds any relevant limits of liability, that there is a defence to liability or that the loss or damage is of undetermined origin. Unless it is determined during the elaboration of the Protocol that there are other effective means of meeting these objectives, the Protocol shall establish a Fund or Funds and make provision in respect of such Fund or Funds, *inter alia*, for the following:

      — financing by Operators or on industry wide bases;

      — ensuring the permanent liquidity and mandatory supplementation thereof in the event of insufficiency;

      — reimbursement of costs of response action, by whomsoever incurred.

8. Nothing in paragraphs 4, 6 and 7 above or in the Protocol adopted pursuant to paragraph 7 shall affect in any way the provisions of paragraph 1 above.

9. No application for an exploration or development permit shall be made until the Protocol provided for in paragraph 7 above is in force for the Party lodging such application.

10. Each Party, pending the entry into force for it of the Protocol provided for in paragraph 7 above, shall ensure, consistently with Article 7 and in accordance with its legal system, that recourse is available in its national courts for adjudicating liability claims pursuant to paragraphs 2, 4 and 6 above against Operators which are engaged in prospecting. Such recourse shall include the adjudication of claims against any Operator it has sponsored. Each Party shall also ensure, in accordance with its legal system, that the Commission has the right to appear as a party in its national courts to pursue relevant liability claims under paragraph 2(a) above.

11. Nothing in this Article or in the Protocol provided for in paragraph 7 above shall be construed so as to:

    (a)   preclude the application of existing rules on liability, and the development in accordance with international law of further such rules, which may have application to either States or Operators; or

    (b)   affect the right of an Operator incurring liability pursuant to this Article to seek redress from another party which caused or contributed to the damage in question.

12. When compensation has been paid other than under this Convention liability under this Convention shall be offset by the amount of such payment.

* * *

Article 12
Inspection Under This Convention

1. In order to promote the objectives and principles and to ensure the observance of this Convention and measures in effect pursuant to it, all stations, installations and equipment relating to Antarctic mineral resource activities in the area in which these activities are regulated by this Convention, as well as ships and aircraft supporting such activities at points of discharging or embarking cargoes or personnel anywhere in that area shall be open at all times to inspection by:

    (a)   observers designated by any member of the Commission who shall be nationals of that member; and

    (b)   observers designated by the Commission or relevant Regulatory Committees.

2. Aerial inspection may be carried out at any time over the area in which Antarctic mineral resource activities are regulated by this Convention.

* * *

Article 13
Protected Areas

1. Antarctic mineral resource activities shall be prohibited in any area designated as a Specially Protected Area or a Site of Special Scientific Interest under Article IX(1) of the Antarctic Treaty. Such activities shall also be prohibited in any other area designated as a protected area in accordance with Article IX(1) of the Antarctic Treaty, except to the extent that the relevant measure provides otherwise. Pending any designation becoming effective in accordance with Article IX(4) of the Antarctic Treaty, no Antarctic mineral resource activities shall take place in any such area which would prejudice the purpose for which it was designated.

2. The Commission shall also prohibit or restrict Antarctic mineral resource activities in any area which, for historic, ecological, environmental, scientific or other reasons, it has designated as a protected area.

* * *

CHAPTER III: PROSPECTING
Article 37
Prospecting

1. Prospecting shall not confer upon any Operator any right to Antarctic mineral resources.

2. Prospecting shall at all times be conducted in compliance with this Convention and with measures in effect pursuant to this Convention, but shall not require authorisation by the institutions of this Convention.

* * *

7. The Sponsoring State shall notify the Commission at least nine months in advance of the commencement of planned prospecting. The notification shall be accompanied by such fees as may be established by the Commission in accordance with Article 21(1)(p) and shall:

* * *

    (d)   provide an assessment of the possible environmental and other impacts of the prospecting, taking into account possible cumulative impacts as referred to in Article 4(5);

    (e)   describe the measures, including monitoring programmes, to be adopted to avoid harmful environmental consequences or undue interference with other established uses of Antarctica, and outline the measures to be put into effect in the event of any accident and contingency plans for evacuation in an emergency;

CHAPTER IV: EXPLORATION
Article 39
Requests for Identification of an Area for Possible Exploration and Development

1. Any Party may submit to the Executive Secretary a notification requesting that the Commission identify an area for possible exploration and development of a particular mineral resource or resources.

2. Any such notification shall be accompanied by such fees as may be established by the Commission in accordance with Article 21(1)(p) and shall contain:

* * *

    (c)   a detailed description of the physical and environmental characteristics of the proposed area;

* * *

    (e)   a detailed assessment of the environmental and other impacts of possible exploration and development for the resource or resources involved, taking into account Articles 15 and 26(4);

* * *

Article 41
Action by the Commission

1. The Commission shall, as soon as possible after receipt of the report of the Special Meeting of Parties, consider whether or not it will identify an area as

requested. Taking full account of the views and giving special weight to the conclusions of the Special Meeting of Parties, and taking full account of the views and the conclusions of the Advisory Committee, the Commission shall determine whether such identification would be consistent with this Convention. For this purpose:

(a) the Commission shall ensure that an area to be identified shall be such that, taking into account all factors relevant to such identification, including the physical, geological, environmental and other characteristics of such area, it forms a coherent unit for the purposes of resource management. The Commission shall thus consider whether an area to be identified should include all or part of that which was requested in the notification and, subject to the necessary assessments having been made, adjacent areas not covered by that notification;

* * *

2. After it has completed its consideration in accordance with paragraph 1 above, the Commission shall identify an area for possible exploration and development if there is a consensus of Commission members that such identification is consistent with this Convention.

* * *

Article 51
Suspension, Modification or Cancellation of the Management Scheme and Monetary Penalties

1. If a Regulatory Committee determines that exploration or development authorised pursuant to a Management Scheme has resulted or is about to result in impacts on the Antarctic environment or dependent or associated ecosystems beyond those judged acceptable pursuant to this Convention, it shall suspend the relevant activities and as soon as possible modify the Management Scheme so as to avoid such impacts. If such impacts cannot be avoided by the modification of the Management Scheme, the Regulatory Committee shall suspend it, or cancel it and the exploration or development permit.

* * *

Article 52
Monitoring in Relation to Management Schemes

1. Each Regulatory Committee shall monitor the compliance of Operators with Management Schemes within its area of competence.
2. Each Regulatory Committee, taking into account the advice of the Advisory Committee, shall monitor and assess the effects on the Antarctic environment and on dependent and on associated ecosystems of Antarctic mineral resource activities within its area of competence, particularly by reference to key environmental parameters and ecosystem components.
3. Each Regulatory Committee shall, as appropriate, inform the Commission and the Advisory Committee in a timely fashion of monitoring under this Article.

CHAPTER V: DEVELOPMENT
Article 53
Application for a Development Permit

1. At any time during the period in which an approved Management Scheme and exploration permit are in force for an Operator, the Sponsoring State may, on behalf of that Operator, lodge with the Regulatory Committee an application for a development permit.

2. An application shall be accompanied by the fees established by the Regulatory Committee in accordance with Article 43(2)(b) and shall contain:

(a) an updated description of the planned development identifying any modifications proposed to the approved Management Scheme and any additional measures to be taken, consequent upon such modifications, to ensure consistency with this Convention, including any measures in effect pursuant thereto and the general requirements referred to in Article 43(3);

* * *

Article 54
Examination of Applications and Issue of Development Permits

* * *

3. The Regulatory Committee shall consider whether:

* * *

(b) the planned development would cause previously unforeseen impacts on the Antarctic environment or dependent or associated ecosystems, either as a result of any modifications referred to in subparagraph (a) above or in the light of increased knowledge.

* * *

PROTOCOL ON ENVIRONMENTAL PROTECTION TO THE ANTARCTIC TREATY

Expected to be signed in October 1991, XI ATSCM/2 (21 June 1991).

Entry into Force: Not yet in force (as of 15 August 1991)

Depositary: United States of America

Languages: English, French, Russian, Spanish
                        Protocol on Environmental Protection to the Antarctic Treaty

PROTOCOL ON ENVIRONMENTAL PROTECTION TO THE ANTARTIC TREATY

* * *

Article 2
Objective and Designation

The Parties commit themselves to the comprehensive protection of the Antarctic environment and dependent and associated ecosystems and hereby designate Antarctica as a natural reserve, devoted to peace and science.

Article 3
Environmental Principles

1. The protection of the Antarctic environment and dependent and associated ecosystems and the intrinsic value of Antarctica, including its wilderness and aesthetic values and its value as an area for the conduct of scientific research, in particular research essential to understanding the global environment, shall be fundamental considerations in the planning and conduct of all activities in the Antarctic Treaty area.

2. To this end:

(a)   activities in the Antarctic Treaty area shall be planned and conducted so as to limit adverse impacts on the Antarctic environment and dependent and associated ecosystems;

(b)   activities in the Antarctic Treaty area shall be planned and conducted so as to avoid:

    (i)   adverse effects on climate or weather patterns;

    (ii)   significant adverse effects on air or water quality;

    (iii)   significant changes in the atmospheric, terrestrial (including aquatic), glacial or marine environments;

    (iv)   detrimental changes in the distribution, abundance or productivity of species or populations of species of fauna and flora;

    (v)   further jeopardy to endangered or threatened species or populations of such species; or

    (vi)   degradation of, or substantial risk to, areas of biological, scientific, historic, aesthetic or wilderness significance;

(c)   activities in the Antarctic Treaty area shall be planned and conducted on the basis of information sufficient to allow prior assessments of, and informed judgments about, their possible impacts on the Antarctic environment and dependent and associated ecosystems and on the value of Antarctica for the conduct of scientific research; such judgments shall take full account of:

    (i)   the scope of the activity, including its area, duration and intensity;

    (ii)   the cumulative impacts of the activity, both by itself and in combination with other activities in the Antarctic Treaty area;

    (iii)   whether the activity will detrimentally affect any other activity in the Antarctic Treaty area;

    (iv)   whether technology and procedures are available to provide for environmentally safe operations;

    (v)   whether there exists the capacity to monitor key environmental parameters and ecosystem components so as to identify and provide early warning of any adverse effects of the activity and to provide for such modification of operating procedures as may be necessary in the light of the results of monitoring or increased knowledge of the Antarctic environment and dependent and associated ecosystems; and

    (vi)   whether there exists the capacity to respond promptly and effectively to accidents, particularly those with potential environmental effects;

(d)   regular and effective monitoring shall take place to allow assessment of the impacts of ongoing activities, including the verification of predicted impacts;

(e)   regular and effective monitoring shall take place to facilitate early detection of the possible unforeseen effects of activities carried on both within and outside the Antarctic Treaty area on the Antarctic environment and dependent and associated ecosystems.

3. Activities shall be planned and conducted in the Antarctic Treaty area so as to accord priority to scientific research and to preserve the value of Antarctica

as an area for the conduct of such research, including research essential to understanding the global environment.

4. Activities undertaken in the Antarctic Treaty area pursuant to scientific research programmes, tourisme [sic] and all other governmental and non-governmental activities in the Antarctic Treaty area for which advance notice is required in accordance with Article VII (5) of the Antarctic Treaty, including associated logistic support activities, shall:

(a)   take place in a manner consistent with the principles in this Article; and
(b)   be modified, suspended or cancelled if they result in or threaten to result in impacts upon the Antarctic environment or dependent or associated ecosystems inconsistent with those principles

Article 4
Relationship with the Other Components of the Antarctic Treaty System

1. This Protocol shall supplement the Antarctic Treaty and shall neither modify nor amend that Treaty.

2. Nothing in this Protocol shall derogate from the rights and obligations of the Parties to this Protocol under the other international instruments in force within the Antarctic Treaty system.

Article 5
Consistency with the Other Components of the Antarctic Treaty System

The Parties shall consult and co-operate with the Contracting Parties to the other international instruments in force within the Antarctic Treaty system and their respective institutions with a view to ensuring the achievement of the objectives and principles of this Protocol and avoiding any interference with the achievement of the objectives and principles of those instruments or any inconsistency between the implementation of those instruments and of this Protocol.

Article 6
Co-operation

1. The Parties shall co-operate in the planning and conduct of activities in the Antarctic Treaty area. To this end, each Party shall endeavour to:

(a)   promote co-operative programmes of scientific, technical and educational value, concerning the protection of the Antarctic environment and dependent and associated ecosystems;
(b)   provide appropriate assistance to other Parties in the preparation of environmental impact assessments;
(c)   provide to other Parties upon request information relevant to any potential environmental risk and assistance to minimize the effects of accidents which may damage the Antarctic environment or dependent and associated ecosystems;
(d)   consult with other Parties, with regard to the choice of sites for prospective stations and other facilities so as to avoid the cumulative impacts caused by their excessive concentration in any location;
(e)   where appropriate, undertake joint expeditions and share the use of stations and other facilities; and
(f)   carry out such steps as may be agreed upon at Antarctic Treaty Consultative Meetings.

2. Each Party undertakes, to the extent possible, to share information that may be helpful to other Parties in planning and conducting their activities in the Antarctic Treaty area, with a view to the protection of the Antarctic environment and dependent and associated ecosystems.

3. The Parties shall co-operate with those Parties which may exercise jurisdiction in areas adjacent to the Antarctic Treaty area with a view to ensuring that activities in the Antarctic Treaty area do not have adverse environmental impacts on those areas.

Article 7
Prohibition of Mineral Resource Activities

Any activity relating to mineral resources, other than scientific research, shall be prohibited.

Article 8
Environmental Impact Assessment

1. Proposed activities referred to in paragraph 2 below shall be subject to the procedures set out in Annex I for prior assessment of the impacts of those activities on the Antarctic environment or on dependent or associated ecosystems according to whether those activities are identified as having:
   (a)   less than a minor or transitory impact;
   (b)   a minor or transitory impact; or
   (c)   more than a minor or transitory impact.

2. Each Party shall ensure that the assessment procedures set out in Annex I are applied in the planning processes leading to decisions about any activities undertaken in the Antarctic Treaty area pursuant to scientific research programmes, tourism and all other governmental and non-governmental activities in the Antarctic Treaty area for which advance notice is required under Article VII (5) of the Antarctic Treaty, including associated logistic support activities.

3. The assessment procedures set out in Annex I shall apply to any change in an activity whether the change arises from an increase or decrease in the intensity of an existing activity, from the addition of an activity, the decommissioning of a facility, or otherwise.

4. Where activities are planned jointly by more than one Party, the Parties involved shall nominate one of their number to coordinate the implementation of the environmental impact assessment procedures set out in Annex I.

Article 9
Annexes

1. The Annexes to this Protocol shall form an integral part thereof.

2. Annexes, additional to Annexes I-IV, may be adopted and become effective in accordance with Article IX of the Antarctic Treaty.

3. Amendments and modifications to Annexes may be adopted and become effective in accordance with Article IX of the Antarctic Treaty, provided that any Annex may itself make provision for amendments and modifications to become effective on an accelerated basis.

4. Annexes and any amendments and modifications thereto which have become effective in accordance with paragraphs 2 and 3 above shall, unless an Annex itself provides otherwise in respect of the entry into effect of any amendment or modification thereto, become effective for a Contracting Party to the Antarctic Treaty which is not an Antarctic Treaty Consultative Party, or which was not an Antarctic Treaty Consultative Party at the time of the adoption, when notice of approval of that Contracting Party has been received by the Depositary.

5. Annexes shall, except to the extent that an Annex provides otherwise, be subject to the procedures for dispute settlement set out in Articles 18 to 20.

Article 10
Antarctic Treaty Consultative Meetings

1. Antarctic Treaty Consultative Meetings shall, drawing upon the best scientific and technical advice available:
  (a)   define, in accordance with the provisions of this Protocol, the general policy for the comprehensive protection of the Antarctic environment and dependent and associated ecosystems; and
  (b)   adopt measures under Article IX of the Antarctic Treaty for the implementation of this Protocol.

2. Antarctic Treaty Consultative Meetings shall review the work of the Committee and shall draw fully upon its advice and recommendations in carrying out the tasks referred to in paragraph 1 above, as well as upon the advice of the Scientific Committee on Antarctic Research.

Article 11
Committee for Environmental Protection

1. There is hereby established the Committee for Environmental Protection.

2. Each Party shall be entitled to be a member of the Committee and to appoint a representative who may be accompanied by experts and advisers.

3. Observer status in the Committee shall be open to any Contracting Party to the Antarctic Treaty which is not a Party to this Protocol.

4. The Committee shall invite the President of the Scientific Committee on Antarctic Research and the Chairman of the Scientific Committee for the Conservation of Antarctic Marine Living Resources to participate as observers at its sessions. The Committee may also, with the approval of the Antarctic Treaty Consultative Meeting, invite such other relevant scientific, environmental and technical organisations which can contribute to its work to participate as observers at its sessions.

5. The Committee shall present a report on each of its sessions to the Antarctic Treaty Consultative Meeting. The report shall cover all matters considered at the session and shall reflect the views expressed. The report shall be circulated to the Parties and to observers attending the session, and shall thereupon be made publicly available.

6. The Committee shall adopt its rules of procedure which shall be subject to approval by the Antarctic Treaty Consultative Meeting.

Article 12
Functions of the Committee

1. The functions of the Committee shall be to provide advice and formulate recommendations to the Parties in connection with the implementation of this Protocol, including the operation of its Annexes, for consideration at Antarctic Treaty Consultative Meetings, and to perform such other functions as may be referred to it by the Antarctic Treaty Consultative Meetings. In particular, it shall provide advice on:
  (a)   the effectiveness of measures taken pursuant to this Protocol;
  (b)   the need to update, strengthen or otherwise improve such measures;
  (c)   the need for additional measures, including the need for additional Annexes, where appropriate;
  (d)   the application and implementation of the environmental impact assessment procedures set out in Article 8 and Annex I;

(e) means of minimizing or mitigating environmental impacts of activities in the Antarctic Treaty area;

(f) procedures for situations requiring urgent action, including response action in environmental emergencies;

(g) the operation and further elaboration of the Antarctic Protected Area system;

(h) inspection procedures, including formats for inspection reports and checklists for the conduct of inspections;

(i) the collection, archiving, exchange and evaluation of information related to environmental protection;

(j) the state of the Antarctic environment; and

(k) the need for scientific research, including environmental monitoring, related to the implementation of this Protocol.

2. In carrying out its functions, the Committee shall, as appropriate, consult with the Scientific Committee on Antarctic Research, the Scientific Committee for the Conservation of Antarctic Marine Living Resources and other relevant scientific, environmental and technical organizations.

Article 13
Compliance with this Protocol

1. Each Party shall take appropriate measures within its competence, including the adoption of laws and regulations, administrative actions and enforcement measures, to ensure compliance with this Protocol.

2. Each Party shall exert appropriate efforts, consistent with the Charter of the United Nations, to the end that no one engages in any activity contrary to this Protocol.

3. Each Party shall notify all other Parties of the measures it takes pursuant to paragraphs 1 and 2 above.

4. Each Party shall draw the attention of all other Parties to any activity which in its opinion affects the implementation of the objectives and principles of this Protocol.

5. The Antarctic Treaty Consultative Meetings shall draw the attention of any State which is not a Party to this Protocol to any activity undertaken by that State, its agencies, instrumentalities, natural or juridical persons, ships, aircraft or other means of transport which affects the implementation of the objectives and principles of this Protocol.

Article 14
Inspection

1. In order to promote the protection of the Antarctic environment and dependent and associated ecosystems, and to ensure compliance with this Protocol, the Antarctic Treaty Consultative Parties shall arrange, individually or collectively, for inspections by observers to be made in accordance with Article VII of the Antarctic Treaty.

2. Observers are:

(a) observers designated by any Antarctic Treaty Consultative Party who shall be nationals of that Party; and

(b) any observers designated at Antarctic Treaty Consultative Meetings to carry out inspections under procedures to be established by an Antarctic Treaty Consultative Meeting.

3. Parties shall co-operate fully with observers undertaking inspections, and shall ensure that during inspections, observers are given access to all parts of stations, installations, equipment, ships and aircraft open to inspection under Article

VII (3) of the Antarctic Treaty, as well as to all records maintained thereon which are called for pursuant to this Protocol.

4. Reports of inspections shall be sent to the Parties whose stations, installations, equipment, ships or aircraft are covered by the reports. After those Parties have been given the opportunity to comment, the reports and any comments thereon shall be circulated to all the Parties and to the Committee, considered at the next Antarctic Treaty Consultative Meeting, and thereafter made publicly available.

Article 15
Emergency Response Action

1. In order to respond to environmental emergencies in the Antarctic Treaty area, each Party agrees to:
(a)   provide for prompt and effective response action to such emergencies which might arise in the performance of scientific research programmes, tourism and all other governmental and non-governmental activities in the Antarctic Treaty area for which advance notice is required under Article VII (5) of the Antarctic Treaty, including associated logistic support activities.
(b)   establish contingency plans for response to incidents with potential adverse effects on the Antarctic environment or dependent and associated ecosystems.
2. To this end, the Parties shall:
(a)   co-operate in the formulation and implementation of such contingency plans; and
(b)   establish procedures for inmediate [sic] notification of, and co-operative response to, environmental emergencies.
3. In the implementation of this Article, the Parties shall draw upon the advice of the appropriate international organisations.

Article 16
Liability

Consistent with the objectives of this Protocol for the comprehensive protection of the Antarctic environment and dependent and associated ecosystems, the Parties undertake to elaborate rules and procedures relating to liability for damage arising from activities taking place in the Antarctic Treaty area and covered by this Protocol. Those rules and procedures shall be included in one or more Annexes to be adopted in accordance with Article 9 (2).

Article 17
Annual Report by Parties

1. Each Party shall report annually on the steps taken to implement this Protocol. Such reports shall include notifications made in accordance with Article 13 (3), contingency plans established in accordance with Article 15 and any other notifications and information called for pursuant to this Protocol for which there is no other provision concerning the circulation and exchange of information.
2. Reports made in accordance with paragraph 1 above shall be circulated to all Parties and to the Committee, considered at the next Antarctic Treaty Consultative Meeting, and made publicly available.

Article 18
Dispute Settlement

If a dispute arises concerning the interpretation or application of this Protocol, the parties to the dispute shall, at the request of any one of them, consult among themselves as soon as possible with a view to having the dispute resolved by negotiation, inquiry, mediation, conciliation, arbitration, judicial settlement or other peaceful means to which the parties to the dispute agree.

Article 19
Choice of Dispute Settlement Procedure

1. Each Party, when signing, ratifying, accepting, approving or acceding to this Protocol, or at any time thereafter, may choose, by written declaration, one or both of the following means for the settlement of disputes concerning the interpretation or application of Articles 7, 8 and 15 and, except to the extent that an Annex provides otherwise, the provisions of any Annex and, insofar as it relates to these Articles and provisions, Article 13:
    (a)   the International Court of Justice;
    (b)   the Arbitral Tribunal.

2. A declaration made under paragraph 1 above shall not affect the operation of Article 18 and Article 20 (2).

3. A Party which has not made a declaration under paragraph 1 above or in respect of which a declaration is no longer in force shall be deemed to have accepted the competence of the Arbitral Tribunal.

4. If the parties to a dispute have accepted the same means for the settlement of a dispute, the dispute may be submitted only to that procedure, unless the parties otherwise agree.

5. If the parties to a dispute have not accepted the same means for the settlement of a dispute, or if they have both accepted both means, the dispute may be submitted only to the Arbitral Tribunal, unless the parties otherwise agree.

6. A declaration made under paragraph 1 above shall remain in force until it expires in accordance with its terms or until three months after written notice of revocation has been deposited with the Depositary.

7. A new declaration, a notice of revocation or the expiry of a declaration shall not in any way affect proceedings pending before the International Court of Justice or the Arbitral Tribunal, unless the parties to the dispute otherwise agree.

8. Declarations and notices referred to in this Article shall be deposited with the Depositary who shall transmit copies thereof to all Parties.

Article 20
Dispute Settlement Procedure

1. If the parties to a dispute concerning the interpretation or application of Articles 7, 8 or 15 or, except to the extent that an Annex provides otherwise, the provisions of any Annex or, insofar as it relates to this [sic] Articles and provisions, Article 13, have not agreed on a means for resolving it within 12 months of the request for consultation pursuant to Article 18, the dispute shall be referred, at the request of any party to the dispute, for settlement in accordance with the procedure determined by Article 19 (4) and (5).

2. The Arbitral Tribunal shall not be competent to decide or rule upon any matter within the scope of Article IV of the Antarctic Treaty. In addition, nothing in this Protocol shall be interpreted as conferring competence or jurisdiction on the International Court of Justice or any other tribunal established for the purpose of settling disputes between Parties to decide or otherwise rule upon any matter within the scope of Article IV of the Antarctic Treaty.

* * *

Article 24
Reservations

Reservations to this Protocol shall not be permitted.

Article 25
Modification or Amendment

[1. Except for the adoption and modification of Annexes in accordance with Article 9, this Protocol may be modified or amended at any time in accordance with the procedures set forth in Article XII (1) (a) and (b) of the Antarctic Treaty.

2. If, after the expiration of 50 years from the date of entry into force of this Protocol, any of the Antarctic Treaty Consultative Parties so requests by a communication addressed to the Depositary, a conference shall be held as soon as practicable to review the operation of this Protocol.

3. A modification or amendment proposed at any Review Conference called pursuant to paragraph 2 above shall be adopted by a majority of the Parties, including ¾ of the States that where [sic] Antarctic Treaty Consultative Parties at the time of adoption of this Protocol.

4. Any modification or amendment adopted pursuant to paragraph 3 of this Article shall enter into force upon ratification by ¾ of the Consultative Parties, including the ratifications of all States that were Consultative Parties at the time of adoption of this Protocol.

5. With respect to Article 7, the Parties agree that the prohibition on Antarctic mineral resource activities contained therein shall continue unless there is in force a binding legal regime on Antarctic mineral resource activities that includes an agreed means for determining whether, and, if so, under which conditions, any such activities would be acceptable. This regime shall fully safeguard the interests of all States referred to in Article IV of the Antarctic Treaty and apply the principles thereof. Therefore, if a modification or amendment to Article 7 is proposed at a Review Conference referred to in paragraph 2 above, it shall include such a binding legal regime.

6. If any such modification or amendment has not entered into force within 3 years of the date of its communication to all Parties, any Party may at any time thereafter give notice to the Depositary of its withdrawal from this Protocol, and such withdrawal shall take effect 2 years after receipt of the notice by the Depositary.]

* * *

B. MEDITERRANEAN SEA

Editors' Introductory Note on the Mediterranean Sea. *Supra*, p. 370.

BARCELONA CONVENTION FOR THE PROTECTION OF THE MEDITERRANEAN SEA AGAINST POLLUTION. *Supra*, p. 370.

BARCELONA PROTOCOL FOR THE PREVENTION OF POLLUTION OF THE MEDITERRANEAN SEA BY DUMPING FROM SHIPS AND AIRCRAFT. *Supra*, p. 377.

BARCELONA PROTOCOL CONCERNING CO-OPERATION IN COMBATING POLLUTION OF THE MEDITERRANEAN SEA BY OIL AND OTHER HARMFUL SUBSTANCES IN CASES OF EMERGENCY. *Supra,* p. 381.

ATHENS PROTOCOL FOR THE PROTECTION OF THE MEDITERRANEAN SEA AGAINST POLLUTION FROM LAND-BASED SOURCES. *Supra,* p. 384.

GENEVA PROTOCOL CONCERNING MEDITERRANEAN SPECIALLY PROTECTED AREAS. *Supra,* p. 389.

C. PARTICULAR RIVER BASINS

Editors' Introductory Note Regarding the Amazon Basin

In 1978 the countries in the Amazon Basin, at the urging of Brazil, agreed to a treaty to foster co-ordination and cooperation in the use of the Amazon Basin. Under the auspices of the Treaty, parties have held technical meetings on navigational, health, and related issues.

In 1989, the Presidents of the States party to the Amazon Treaty issued the Amazon Declaration, which focused on the problems of ensuring environmentally sustainable development of the region. The Declaration, while non-binding, is important because it is the first time that parties have used the institutional framework of the Amazon Treaty explicitly to address environmental concerns.

Also in 1989, parties to the Treaty agreed to set up four new commissions, which include an Amazonia Special Environmental Commission and an Amazonia Special Commission on Indigenous Affairs.

These developments illustrate a theme common to several international environmental agreements: the evolution of an international agreement created primarily to co-ordinate and facilitate resource development into one which is also used to address issues of conservation and environmentally sustainable resource development.

BRASILIA TREATY FOR AMAZONIAN COOPERATION

Popular Name: Amazon Basin Treaty, Amazon Treaty, Brasilia Treaty

Done at Brasilia on 3 July 1978, *reprinted in* UNEP Reg. p.164, UNEP3 #75, p. 496, 17 ILM 1045 (1978), 18 IPE 9017.

Entry into Force: 2 August 1980

Depositary: Brazil

Languages: English, Dutch, Portuguese, Spanish

Parties as of 1 October 1991: Bolivia; Brazil; Colombia; Ecuador; Guyana; Peru; Suriname; Venezuela

BRASILIA TREATY FOR AMAZONIAN COOPERATION

The Republics of Bolivia, Brazil, Colombia, Ecuador, Guyana, Peru, Suriname and Venezuela,

CONSCIOUS of the importance to each one of the Parties of their respective Amazonian regions as an integral part of their respective territories,

INSPIRED by the common aim of pooling the efforts being made, both within their respective territories as well as among themselves, to promote the harmonious development of the Amazon region, to permit an equitable distribution of the benefits of said development among the Contracting Parties so as to raise the standard of living of their peoples and so as to achieve total incorporation of their Amazonian territories into their respective national economies,

CONSCIOUS of the usefulness of sharing national experiences in matters pertaining to the promotion of regional development,

CONSIDERING that, so as to achieve overall development of their respective Amazonian territories, it is necessary to maintain a balance between economic growth and conservation of the environment,

CONSCIOUS that both socio-economic development as well as conservation of the environment are responsibilities inherent in the sovereignty of each State, and that cooperation among the Contracting Parties shall facilitate fulfillment of these responsibilities, by continuing and expanding the joint efforts being made for the ecological conservation of the Amazon region,

CONFIDENT that cooperation among the Latin American nations on specific matters which they have in common shall contribute to progress on the road towards the integration and solidarity of all Latin America,

CONVINCED that this Treaty represents the beginning of a process of cooperation which shall benefit their respective countries and the Amazon region as a whole,

RESOLVE to sign the following Treaty:

ARTICLE I

The Contracting Parties agree to undertake joint actions and efforts to promote the harmonious development of their respective Amazonian territories in such a way that these joint actions produce equitable and mutually beneficial results and achieve also the preservation of the environment, and the conservation and rational utilization of the natural resources of those territories.

Paragraph: to this end, they would exchange information and prepare operational agreements and understandings as well as the pertinent legal instruments which will permit the aims of the present Treaty to be attained.

ARTICLE II

This Treaty shall be in force in the territories of the Contracting Parties in the Amazonian Basin as well as in any territory of a Contracting Party which, by virtue of its geographical, ecological or economic characteristics is considered closely connected with that Basin.

ARTICLE III

In accordance with and without prejudice to the rights granted by unilateral acts, to the provisions of bilateral treaties among the Parties and to the principles and rules of International Law, the Contracting Parties mutually guarantee on a reciprocal basis that there shall be complete freedom of commercial navigation on the Amazon and other international Amazonian rivers, observing the fiscal and police regulations in force now or in the future within the territory of each. Such regulations should, insofar as possible, be uniform and favour said nagigation[sic] and trade.

Paragraph: This article shall not apply to cabotage.

ARTICLE IV

The Contracting Parties declare that the exclusive use and utilization of natural resources within their respective territories is a right inherent in the sovereignty of each state and that the exercise of this right shall not be subject to any restrictions other than those arising from International Law.

ARTICLE V

Taking account of the importance and multiplicity of the functions which the Amazonian rivers have in the process of economic and social development of the region, the Contracting Parties shall make efforts aimed at achieving rational utilization of the hydro resources.

ARTICLE VI

In order to enable the Amazonian rivers to become an effective communication link among the Contracting Parties and with the Atlantic Ocean, the riparian states interested in any specific problem affecting free and unimpeded navigation shall, as circumstances may warrant, undertake national, bilateral or multilateral measures aimed at improving and making the said rivers navigable.

Paragraph: For this purpose, they shall carry out studies into the means for eliminating physical obstacles to the said navigation as well as the economic and financial implications so as to put into effect the most appropriate operational measures.

ARTICLE VII

Taking into account the need for the exploitation of the flora and fauna of the Amazon region to be rationally planned so as to maintain the ecological balance within the region and preserve the species, the Contracting Parties decide to:

a. Promote scientific research and exchange information and technical personnel among the competent agencies within the respective countries so as to increase their knowledge of the flora and fauna of their Amazon territories and prevent and control diseases in said territories.
b. Establish a regular system for the proper exchange of information on the conservationist measures adopted or to be adopted by each State in its Amazonian territories; these shall be the subject of an annual report to be presented by each country.

ARTICLE VIII

The Contracting Parties decide to promote coordination of the present health services in their respective Amazonian territories and to take other appropriate measures to improve the sanitary conditions in the region and perfect methods for preventing and combating epidemics.

ARTICLE IX

The Contracting Parties agree to establish close cooperation in the fields of scientific and technological research, for the purpose of creating more suitable conditions for the acceleration of the economic and social development of the region.

Paragraph One: For purposes of this Treaty, the technical and scientific cooperation among the Contracting Parties may be as follows:

a.   Joint or coordinated implementation of research and development programmes;

b.   Creation and operation of research institutions or centres for improvement and experimental production;

c.   Organization of seminars and conferences, exchange of information and documentation, and organization of means for their dissemination.

Paragraph Two: The Contracting Parties may, whensoever they deem it necessary and convenient, request the participation of international agencies in the execution of studies, programmes and projects resulting from the forms of technical and scientific cooperation defined in Paragraph One of this Article.

ARTICLE X

The Contracting Parties agree on the advisability of creating a suitable physical infrastructure among their respective countries, especially in relation to transportation and communications. They therefore undertake to study the most harmonious ways of establishing or improving road, river, air and telecommunication links bearing in mind the plans and programmes of each country aimed at attaining the priority goal of fully incorporating those respective Amazonian territories into their respective national economies.

ARTICLE XI

In order to increase the rational utilisation of the human and natural resources of their respective Amazonian territories, the Contracting Parties agree to encourage joint studies and measures aimed at promoting the economic and social development of said territories and generating complementary methods for reinforcing the actions envisaged in the national plans of their respective territories.

ARTICLE XII

The Contracting Parties recognise the benefit to be derived by developing, under equitable and mutually beneficial conditions, retail trade of products for local consumption among the respective Amazonian border populations, by means of suitable bilateral or multilateral agreements.

ARTICLE XIII

The Contracting Parties shall cooperate to increase the flow of tourists, both national and from third countries, in their respective Amazonian territories, without prejudice to national regulations for the protection of indigenous cultures and natural resources.

ARTICLE XIV

The Contracting Parties shall cooperate in ensuring that measures adopted for the conservation of ethnological, and archeological wealth of the Amazon region are effective.

ARTICLE XV

The Contracting Parties shall seek to maintain a permanent exchange of information and cooperation among themselves and with the agencies for Latin American cooperation in the areas pertaining to matters covered by this Treaty.

ARTICLE XVI

The decisions and commitments adopted by the Contracting Parties under this Treaty shall not be to the detriment of projects and undertakings executed within their respective territories, according to International Law and fair practice between neighboring and friendly countries.

ARTICLE XVII

The Contracting Parties shall present initiatives for undertaking studies for the elaboration of programmes of common interest for developing their Amazonian territories and in general terms provide for the fulfillment of the actions contemplated in the present Treaty.

Paragraph: The Contracting Parties agree to give special attention to the consideration of initiatives presented by the least developed countries which require joint action and efforts by the Contracting Parties.

ARTICLE XVIII

Nothing contained in this Treaty shall in any way limit the rights of the Contracting Parties to conclude bilateral or multilateral agreements on specific or generic matters, provided that these are not contrary to the achievement of the common aims for cooperation in the Amazonian region stated in this instrument.

ARTICLE XIX

Neither the signing of this Treaty nor its execution shall have any effect on any other international treaties in force between the Parties nor on any differences with regard to limits or territorial rights which may exist between the Parties nor shall the signing or implementation of this Treaty be interpreted or invoked to imply acceptance or renunciation, affirmation or modification, direct or indirect, express or tacit, of the position or interpretation that each Contracting Party may hold on these matters.

ARTICLE XX

Notwithstanding the fact that more adequate frequency for meetings can be established at a later date, the Ministers of Foreign Affairs of the Contracting Parties shall convene meetings when deemed opportune or advisable, in order to establish the basic guidelines for common policies, for assessing and evaluating the general development or the process of Amazonian cooperation and for taking decisions designed to carry out the aims set out in this document.

Paragraph One: Meetings of Foreign Affairs Ministers shall be convened at the request of any of the Contracting Parties, provided that the request has the support of no fewer than four Member States.

Paragraph Two: The first meeting of Foreign Affairs Ministers shall be held within a period of two years following the date of entry into force of this Treaty. The venue and date of the first meeting shall be established by agreement among the Ministries of Foreign Affairs of the Contracting Parties.

Paragraph Three: Designation of the host country for the meetings shall be by rotation and in alphabetical order.

ARTICLE XXI

The Amazonian Cooperation Council comprising of top level diplomatic representatives shall meet once a year. Its duties shall be as follows:

1. To ensure that the aims and objectives of the Treaty are complied with.
2. To be responsible for carrying out the decisions taken at meetings of Foreign Affairs Ministers.
3. To recommend to the Parties the advisability and the appropriateness of convening meetings of Foreign Affairs Ministers and of drawing-up the corresponding Agenda.
4. To take under consideration initiatives and plans present [sic] by the Parties as well as to adopt decisions for undertaking bilateral or multilateral studies and plans, the execution of which as the case may be, shall be the duty of the Permanent National Commissions.
5. To evaluate the implementation of plans of bilateral or multilateral interest.
6. To draw-up the Rules and Regulations for its proper functioning.

Paragraph One: The Council shall hold special meetings through the initiative of any of the Contracting Parties with the support of the majority of the rest.

Paragraph Two: The venue of regular meetings shall be rotated in alphabetical order among the Contracting Parties.

ARTICLE XXII

The functions of the Secretariat shall be performed *pro-tempore* by the Contracting Party in whose territory the next regular meeting of the Amazonian Cooperation Council is scheduled to be held.

Paragraph: The *pro-tempore* Secretariat shall send the pertinent documentation to the Parties.

ARTICLE XXIII

The Contracting Parties shall create Permanent National Commissions charged with enforcing in their respective territories the provisions set out in this Treaty, as well as carrying out the decisions taken at meetings of Foreign Affairs Ministers and by the Amazonian Cooperation Council, without jeopardizing other tasks assigned them by the State.

ARTICLE XXIV

Whenever necessary, the Contracting Parties may set up special Commissions to study specific problems or matters related to the aims of this Treaty.

ARTICLE XXV

Decisions at meetings held in accordance with Articles XX and XXI shall always require the unanimous vote of the Member Countries of this Treaty. Decisions made at meetings held in accordance with Article XXIV shall always require the unanimous vote of the participating countries.

ARTICLE XXVI

The Contracting Parties agree that the present Treaty shall not be susceptible to interpretative reservation or statements.

ARTICLE XXVII

This Treaty shall remain in force for an unlimited period of time, and shall not be open to adherence.

ARTICLE XXVIII

This Treaty shall be ratified by all the Contracting Parties and the instruments of ratification shall be deposited with the Government of the Federative Republic of Brazil.

Paragraph One: This Treaty shall become effective thirty days after the last instrument of ratification has been deposited by the Contracting Parties.

Paragraph Two: The intention to denounce this Treaty shall be communicated by a Contracting Party to the remaining Contracting Parties at least ninety days prior to formal delivery of the instrument of denunciation to the Government of the Federative Republic of Brazil. This Treaty shall cease to have effect for the Contracting Party denouncing it one year after the denunciation has been formalized.

Paragraph Three: This Treaty shall be drawn up in English, Dutch, Portuguese and Spanish, all having equal validity.

IN WITNESS WHEREOF the undersigned Ministers of Foreign Affairs have signed the present Treaty.

EXECUTED in the city of Brasilia, on 3 July 1978 to be deposited in the archives of the Ministry of Foreign Affairs of Brazil which shall provide the other signatory countries with true copies.

AMAZON DECLARATION

Popular Name: Amazon Declaration

Done in Manaus, Brazil on 6 May 1989, A/44/75, Annex, E/1989/79, Annex, *reprinted in* 28 ILM 1303 (1989).

Languages: English, Dutch, Portuguese, Spanish

Signatories: Bolivia; Brazil; Colombia; Ecuador; Guyana; Peru; Suriname; Venezuela

THE AMAZON DECLARATION, ADOPTED AT MANAUS, BRAZIL, ON 6 MAY 1989 BY THE PRESIDENTS OF THE STATES PARTIES TO THE TREATY FOR AMAZONIAN CO-OPERATION

The Presidents of the States Parties to the Treaty for Amazonian Co-operation, meeting at Manaus, Brazil, on 6 May 1989 for the purpose of undertaking a joint reflection on their common interests in the Amazon region and, in particular, on the future of co-operation for the development and protection of the rich heritage of their respective Amazon territories, adopted the following:

THE AMAZON DECLARATION

1. In the spirit of friendship and understanding that inspires our fraternal dialogue, we affirm our willingness to give full political impetus to the concerted efforts being undertaken by our Governments within the framework of the Treaty for Amazonian Co-operation, signed on 3 July 1978, and also within the framework of their bilateral relations, with a view to promoting co-operation between our countries in all areas of common interest for the sustainable development of the Amazon region. Therefore, we commit ourselves to give the necessary impetus to the decisions contained in the Declaration of San Francisco de Quito, adopted by our Ministers for Foreign Affairs on 7 March 1989.

2. Conscious of the importance of protecting the cultural, economic and ecological heritage of our Amazon regions and of the necessity of using this potential to promote the economic and social development of our peoples, we reiterate that our Amazon heritage must be preserved through the rational use of the resources of the region, so that present and future generations may benefit from this legacy of nature.

3. We express our support for the recently created Amazonia Special Environmental Commission and the Amazonia Special Commission on Indigenous Affairs, aimed at fostering development, conserving the natural resources, the environment and the respective Amazonian populations, and we reiterate our full respect for the right of indigenous populations of the Amazonian region to have adopted all measures aimed at maintaining and preserving the integrity of these human groups, their cultures and their ecological habitats, subject to the exercise of that right which is inherent in the sovereignty of each State. Furthermore, we reiterate our support for actions aimed at strengthening the institutional structure of the Treaty for Amazonian Co-operation, in accordance with the Declaration of San Francisco de Quito.

4. We reaffirm the sovereign right of each country to manage freely its natural resources, bearing in mind the need for promoting the economic and social development of its people and the adequate conservation of the environment. In the exercise of our sovereign responsibility to define the best ways of using and conserving this wealth and in addition to our national efforts and to the co-operation among our countries, we express our willingness to accept co-operation from countries in other regions of the world, as well as from international organizations, which might contribute to the implementation of national and regional projects and programmes that we decide freely to adopt without external impositions, in accordance with the priorities of our Governments.

5. We recognize that the defence of our environment requires the study of measures, both bilateral and regional, to prevent contamination-causing accidents and to deal with their consequences once they have occurred.

6. We stress that the protection and conservation of the environment in the region, one of the essential objectives of the Treaty for Amazonian Co-operation to which each of our nations is firmly committed, cannot be achieved without improvement of the distressing social and economic conditions that oppress our peoples and that are aggravated by an increasingly adverse international context.

7. We denounce the grave conditions of the foreign debt and of its service, which transform us into net exporters of capital to the creditor countries, at the cost of intolerable sacrifices for our peoples. We reiterate that the debt cannot be paid on the present conditions and in the present circumstances and that the problem of debt should be dealt with on the principle of co-responsibility, in terms that permit the reactivation of the process of economic growth and development in each of our countries, an essential condition for the protection, conservation, exploitation and rational utilization of our natural heritage.

8. We emphasize the need for the concerns expressed in the highly developed countries in relation to the conservation of the Amazon environment to be translated into measures of co-operation in the financial and technological fields. We call for the establishment of new resource flows in additional and concessional terms to projects oriented to environmental protection in our countries, including pure and applied scientific research, and we object to attempts to impose conditionalities in the allocation of international resources for development. We expect the establishment of conditions to allow free access to scientific knowledge, to clean technologies and to technologies to be used in environmental protection and we reject any attempts made to use legitimate ecological concerns to realize commercial profits. This approach is based above all on the fact that the principal causes for the deterioration of the environment on a world-wide scale are the patterns of industrialization and consumption as well as waste in the developed countries.

9. Conscious of the global risks for human life and environmental quality represented by the existence of nuclear weapons and other weapons of mass destruction, and concern with preserving our region from these dangers, we reaffirm the commitments our countries have made to use nuclear energy exclusively for peaceful purposes and we urge the countries that possess nuclear weapons immediately to cease the testing of such weapons and to promote the progressive elimination of their arsenals. Likewise, we repudiate the deposit of radioactive and other toxic wastes that may harm the ecosystems in the Amazonian region. We stress the need for appropriate measures to be taken to reduce the risks of environmental contamination in the peaceful use of nuclear energy. Furthermore, we express our support for the aims and objectives of the Treaty for the Prohibition of Nuclear Weapons in Latin America.

10. Convinced of the need to intensify the process of consultation and dialogue among our countries on all issues regarding the development of the region, including those set forth in the Treaty for Amazonian Co-operation, and certain that our co-operation strengthens integration and solidarity in Latin America, we affirm our decision to unite efforts in a vigorous and pioneering joint action, aimed at ensuring a future of peace, co-operation and prosperity for the nations of the Amazon region. Therefore, we are deciding to meet yearly.

D. GREAT LAKES

CANADA-UNITED STATES: GREAT LAKES WATER QUALITY AGREEMENT. *Supra,* p. 419.

CHAPTER 10
CULTURAL HERITAGE

UNITED NATIONS EDUCATIONAL, SCIENTIFIC & CULTURAL ORGANIZATION CONVENTION FOR THE PROTECTION OF THE WORLD CULTURAL AND NATURAL HERITAGE, AND THE WORLD HERITAGE LIST

Popular Name: World Heritage Convention

Done at Paris on 16 November 1972, 1972 UNJYB 89, U.N. Doc. ST/LEG/ SER.C/10, 27 UST 37, TIAS 8226, *reprinted in* 11 ILM 1358 (1972), UNEP3 #55, p.276, 14 IPE 7238, IELMT 972: 86.

Entry into Force: 17 December 1975

Depositary: United Nations Educational, Scientific, and Cultural Organization (UNESCO)

Languages: Arabic, English, French, Russian, Spanish

Parties as of 1 January 1990: Afghanistan; Algeria; Antigua and Barbuda; Argentina; Australia; Bangladesh; Benin; Bolivia; Brazil;** Bulgaria;** Burkina Faso; Burundi; Byelorussian Soviet Socialist Republic; Cameroon; Canada; Cape Verde; Central African Republic; Chile; China; Colombia; Costa Rica; Côte d'Ivoire; Cuba; Cyprus; Denmark;** Dominican Republic; Ecuador; Egypt; Ethiopia; Finland; France;** Gabon; German Democratic Republic; Germany, Federal Republic of; Ghana; Greece; Guatemala; Guinea; Guyana; Haiti; Honduras; Hungary; India; Iran, Islamic Republic of; Iraq; Italy; Jamaica; Jordan; Korea, Republic of; Laos; Lebanon; Libyan Arab Jamahiriya; Luxembourg; Madagascar; Malawi; Malaysia; Maldives; Mali; Malta; Mauritania; Mexico; Monaco; Morocco; Mozambique; Nepal; New Zealand;* Nicaragua; Niger; Nigeria; Norway;** Oman;** Pakistan; Panama; Paraguay; Peru; Philippines; Poland; Portugal; Qatar; Saint Christopher and Nevis; Saudi Arabia; Senegal; Seychelles; Spain; Sri Lanka; Sudan; Sweden; Switzerland; Syrian Arab Republic;*** Tanzania, United Republic of; Thailand; Tunisia; Turkey; Uganda; Ukrainian Soviet Socialist Republic; Union of Soviet Socialist Republics; United Kingdom of Great Britain and Northern Ireland; United States of America; Viet Nam; Yemen; Yemen, Democratic; Yugoslavia; Zaire; Zambia; Zimbabwe

Literature: S. Lyster, *International Wildlife Law* 208 (1985)

---

*   With a geographic extension
**   With reservation
***With a statement

Editors' Note

The World Heritage Convention makes certain natural and cultural sites part of the world heritage, which is to be conserved for present and future generations. Under the Convention, States nominate their own natural and cultural sites for inclusion on an international list of world heritage sites. Parties to the agreement decide at an international meeting which sites to list. States are obligated to protect listed sites. A modest international fund is available to assist States in protecting the sites. The Convention is administered by the United Nations Educational, Scientific and Cultural Organization (UNESCO), which has a secretariat for cultural heritages and one for natural heritages.

The origins of the Convention lie in two separate efforts to conserve world heritages: one to conserve cultural properties; the other, to conserve natural sites.

The initiative to conserve cultural properties was centered in UNESCO. Since World War II, countries have been particularly concerned with preserving monuments and other important cultural properties. In 1954 a Convention on the Protection of Cultural Property in the Event of Armed Conflict was concluded at the Hague. This was followed by individual international campaigns under UNESCO auspices to save specific cultural sites and by the eventual establishment of the International Council on Monuments and Sites in 1975. Thereafter UNESCO adopted a series of resolutions authorizing the creation of a new convention which would provide security for cultural heritage of universal worth. A convention for cultural heritage was drafted by Spring 1971.

At the same time, the International Union for Conservation of Nature and Natural Resources (IUCN) prepared a draft convention to provide international protection for national parks, some historic structures, sites, and important wildlife areas. The sites were to become part of a World Heritage Trust. The United States was instrumental in urging the creation of such a trust and the negotiation of an appropriate convention.

In 1972, after considerable diplomatic deliberations, the two drafts were combined into a single convention, which became effective in 1975. The United States was the first to ratify the World Heritage Convention, following a unanimous Senate vote. The operational rules for implementing the Convention were finalized in 1977. As of 10 July 1990, 112 countries were parties to the Convention. Also as of 10 July 1990, the World Heritage List established pursuant to the Convention contained 322 sites (234 cultural, 75 natural, and 13 mixed sites), one of which was the subject of important litigation in Australia that interpreted and applied the Convention. *See* Australia v. Tasmania, 57 Australian Law Reports 450 (1983).

CONVENTION FOR THE PROTECTION OF THE WORLD CULTURAL AND NATURAL HERITAGE

The General Conference of the United Nations Educational, Scientific and Cultural Organization meeting in Paris from 17 October to 21 November 1972, at its seventeenth session,

Noting that the cultural heritage and the natural heritage are increasingly threatened with destruction not only by the traditional causes of decay, but also by changing social and economic conditions which aggravate the situation with even more formidable phenomena of damage or destruction,

Considering that deterioration or disappearance of any item of the cultural or natural heritage constitutes a harmful impoverishment of the heritage of all the nations of the world,

Considering that protection of this heritage at the national level often remains incomplete because of the scale of the resources which it requires and of the insufficient economic, scientific and technical resources of the country where the property to be protected is situated,

Recalling that the Constitution of the Organization provides that it will maintain, increase and diffuse knowledge, by assuring the conservation and protection of the world's heritage, and recommending to the nations concerned the necessary international conventions,

Considering that the existing international conventions, recommendations and resolutions concerning cultural and natural property demonstrate the importance, for all the peoples of the world, of safeguarding this unique and irreplaceable property, to whatever people it may belong,

Considering that parts of the cultural or natural heritage are of outstanding interest and therefore need to be preserved as part of the world heritage of mankind as a whole,

Considering that, in view of the magnitude and gravity of the new dangers threatening them, it is incumbent on the international community as a whole to participate in the protection of the cultural and natural heritage of outstanding universal value, by the granting of collective assistance which, although not taking the place of action by the State concerned, will serve as an effective complement thereto,

Considering that it is essential for this purpose to adopt new provisions in the form of a convention establishing an effective system of collective protection of the cultural and natural heritage of outstanding universal value, organized on a permanent basis and in accordance with modern scientific methods,

Having decided, at its sixteenth session, that this question should be made the subject of an international convention,

Adopts this sixteenth day of November 1972 this Convention.

I. DEFINITIONS OF THE CULTURAL AND THE NATURAL HERITAGE

Article 1

For the purposes of this Convention, the following shall be considered as "cultural heritage":

monuments: architectural works, works of monumental sculpture and painting, elements or structures of an archaeological nature, inscriptions, cave dwellings and combinations of features, which are of outstanding universal value from the point of view of history, art or science;

groups of buildings: groups of separate or connected buildings which, because of their architecture, their homogeneity or their place in the landscape, are of outstanding universal value from the point of view of history, art or science;

sites: works of man or the combined works of nature and of man, and areas including archaeological sites which are of outstanding universal value from the historical, aesthetic, ethnological or anthropological points of view.

Article 2

For the purposes of this Convention, the following shall be considered as "natural heritage";

natural features consisting of physical and biological formations or groups of such formations, which are of outstanding universal value from the aesthetic or scientific point of view;

geological and physiographical formations and precisely delineated areas which constitute the habitat of threatened species of animals and plants of outstanding universal value from the point of view of science or conservation;
natural sites or precisely delineated natural areas of outstanding universal value from the point of view of science, conservation or natural beauty.

Article 3

It is for each State Party to this Convention to identify and delineate the different properties situated on its territory mentioned in Articles 1 and 2 above.

II. NATIONAL PROTECTION AND INTERNATIONAL PROTECTION OF THE CULTURAL AND NATURAL HERITAGE

Article 4

Each State Party to this Convention recognizes that the duty of ensuring the identification, protection, conservation, presentation and transmission to future generations of the cultural and natural heritage referred to in Articles 1 and 2 and situated on its territory, belongs primarily to that State. It will do all it can to this end, to the utmost of its own resources and, where appropriate, with any international assistance and co-operation, in particular, financial, artistic, scientific and technical, which it may be able to obtain.

Article 5

To ensure that effective and active measures are taken for the protection, conservation and presentation of the cultural and natural heritage situated on its territory, each State Party to this Convention shall endeavour, in so far as possible, and as appropriate for each country:
- (a) to adopt a general policy which aims to give the cultural and natural heritage a function in the life of the community and to integrate the protection of that heritage into comprehensive planning programmes;
- (b) to set up within its territories, where such services do not exist, one or more services for the protection, conservation and presentation of the cultural and natural heritage with an appropriate staff and possessing the means to discharge their functions;
- (c) to develop scientific and technical studies and research and to work out such operating methods as will make the State capable of counteracting the dangers that threaten its cultural or natural heritage;
- (d) to take the appropriate legal, scientific, technical, administrative and financial measures necessary for the identification, protection, conservation, presentation and rehabilitation of this heritage; and
- (e) to foster the establishment or development of national or regional centres for training in the protection, conservation and presentation of the cultural and natural heritage and to encourage scientific research in this field.

Article 6

1. Whilst fully respecting the sovereignty of the States on whose territory the cultural and natural heritage mentioned in Articles 1 and 2 is situated, and without prejudice to property rights provided by national legislation, the States Parties to this Convention recognize that such heritage constitutes a world heritage for whose protection it is the duty of the international community as a whole to co-operate.
2. The States Parties undertake, in accordance with the provisions of this Convention, to give their help in the identification, protection, conservation and preservation of the cultural and natural heritage referred to in paragraphs 2 and 4 of Article 11 if the States on whose territory it is situated so request.
3. Each State Party to this Convention undertakes not to take any deliberate measures which might damage directly or indirectly the cultural and natural heritage referred to in Articles 1 and 2 situated on the territory of other States Parties to this Convention.

Article 7

For the purpose of this Convention, international protection of the world cultural and natural heritage shall be understood to mean the establishment of a system of international co-operation and assistance designed to support States Parties to the Convention in their efforts to conserve and identify that heritage.

III. INTERGOVERNMENTAL COMMITTEE FOR THE PROTECTION OF THE WORLD CULTURAL AND NATURAL HERITAGE

Article 8

1. An Intergovernmental Committee for the Protection of the Cultural and Natural Heritage of Outstanding Universal Value, called "the World Heritage Committee", is hereby established within the United Nations Educational, Scientific and Cultural Organization. It shall be composed of 15 States Parties to the Convention, elected by States Parties to the Convention meeting in general assembly during the ordinary session of the General Conference of the United Nations Educational, Scientific and Cultural Organization. The number of States members of the Committee shall be increased to 21 as from the date of the ordinary session of the General Conference following the entry into force of this Convention for at least 40 States.
2. Election of members of the Committee shall ensure an equitable representation of the different regions and cultures of the world.
3. A representative of the International Centre for the Study of the Preservation and Restoration of Cultural Property (Rome Centre), a representative of the International Council of Monuments and Sites (ICOMOS) and a representative of the International Union for Conservation of Nature and Natural Resources (IUCN), to whom may be added, at the request of States Parties to the Convention meeting in general assembly during the ordinary sessions of the General Conference of the United Nations Educational, Scientific and Cultural Organization, representatives of other intergovernmental or non-governmental organizations, with similar objectives, may attend the meetings of the Committee in an advisory capacity.

Article 9

1. The term of office of States members of the World Heritage Committee shall extend from the end of the ordinary session of the General Conference during which they are elected until the end of its third subsequent ordinary session.

2. The term of office of one-third of the members designated at the time of the first election shall, however, cease at the end of the first ordinary session of the General Conference following that at which they were elected; and the term of office of a further third of the members designated at the same time shall cease at the end of the second ordinary session of the General Conference following that at which they were elected. The names of these members shall be chosen by lot by the President of the General Conference of the United Nations Educational, Scientific and Cultural Organization after the first election.
3. States members of the Committee shall choose as their representatives persons qualified in the field of the cultural or natural heritage.

Article 10

1. The World Heritage Committee shall adopt its Rules of Procedure.
2. The Committee may at any time invite public or private organizations or individuals to participate in its meetings for consultation on particular problems.
3. The Committee may create such consultative bodies as it deems necessary for the performance of its functions.

Article 11

1. Every State Party to this Convention shall, in so far as possible, submit to the World Heritage Committee an inventory of property forming part of the cultural and natural heritage, situated in its territory and suitable for inclusion in the list provided for in paragraph 2 of this Article. This inventory, which shall not be considered exhaustive, shall include documentation about the location of the property in question and its significance.
2. On the basis of the inventories submitted by States in accordance with paragraph 1, the Committee shall establish, keep up to date and publish, under the title of "World Heritage List, [sic] a list of properties forming part of the cultural heritage and natural heritage, as defined in Articles 1 and 2 of this Convention, which it considers as having outstanding universal value in terms of such criteria as it shall have established. An updated list shall be distributed at least every two years.
3. The inclusion of a property in the World Heritage List requires the consent of the State concerned. The inclusion of a property situated in a territory, sovereignty or jurisdiction over which is claimed by more than one State shall in no way prejudice the rights of the parties to the dispute.
4. The Committee shall establish, keep up to date and publish, whenever circumstances shall so require, under the title of "List of World Heritage in Danger", a list of the property appearing in the World Heritage List for the conservation of which major operations are necessary and for which assistance has been requested under this Convention. This list shall contain an estimate of the cost of such operations. The list may include only such property forming part of the cultural and natural heritage as is threatened by serious and specific dangers, such as the threat of disappearance caused by accelerated deterioration, large-scale public or private projects or rapid urban or tourist development projects; destruction caused by changes in the use or ownership of the land; major alterations due to unknown causes; abandonment for any reason whatsoever; the outbreak or the threat of an armed conflict; calamities and cataclysms; serious fires, earthquakes, landslides; volcanic eruptions; changes in water level, floods, and tidal waves. The Committee may at any time, in case of urgent need, make a new entry in the List of World Heritage in Danger and publicize such entry immediately.

5. The Committee shall define the criteria on the basis of which a property belonging to the cultural or natural heritage may be included in either of the lists mentioned in paragraphs 2 and 4 of this article.
6. Before refusing a request for inclusion in one of the two lists mentioned in paragraphs 2 and 4 of this article, the Committee shall consult the State Party in whose territory the cultural or natural property in question is situated.
7. The Committee shall, with the agreement of the States concerned, co-ordinate and encourage the studies and research needed for the drawing up of the lists referred to in paragraphs 2 and 4 of this article.

Article 12

The fact that a property belonging to the cultural or natural heritage has not been included in either of the two lists mentioned in paragraphs 2 and 4 of Article 11 shall in no way be construed to mean that it does not have an outstanding universal value for purposes other than those resulting from inclusion in these lists.

Article 13

1. The World Heritage Committee shall receive and study requests for international assistance formulated by States Parties to this Convention with respect to property forming part of the cultural or natural heritage, situated in their territories, and included or potentially suitable for inclusion in the lists referred to in paragraphs 2 and 4 of Article 11. The purpose of such requests may be to secure the protection, conservation, presentation or rehabilitation of such property.
2. Requests for international assistance under paragraph 1 of this article may also be concerned with identification of cultural or natural property defined in Articles 1 and 2, when preliminary investigations have shown that further inquiries would be justified.
3. The Committee shall decide on the action to be taken with regard to these requests, determine where appropriate, the nature and extent of its assistance, and authorize the conclusion, on its behalf, of the necessary arrangements with the government concerned.
4. The Committee shall determine an order of priorities for its operations. It shall in so doing bear in mind the respective importance for the world cultural and natural heritage of the property requiring protection, the need to give international assistance to the property most representative of a natural environment or of the genius and the history of the peoples of the world, the urgency of the work to be done, the resources available to the States on whose territory the threatened property is situated and in particular the extent to which they are able to safeguard such property by their own means.
5. The Committee shall draw up, keep up to date and publicize a list of property for which international assistance has been granted.
6. The Committee shall decide on the use of the resources of the Fund established under Article 15 of this Convention. It shall seek ways of increasing these resources and shall take all useful steps to this end.
7. The Committee shall co-operate with international and national governmental and non-governmental organizations having objectives similar to those of this Convention. For the implementation of its programmes and projects, the Committee may call on such organizations, particularly the International Centre for the Study of the Preservation and Restoration of Cultural Property (the Rome Centre), the International Council of Monuments and Sites (ICOMOS)and the International Union for Conservation of Nature and Natural Resources (IUCN), as well as on public and private bodies and individuals.

8. Decisions of the Committee shall be taken by a majority of two-thirds of its members present and voting. A majority of the members of the Committee shall constitute a quorum.

Article 14

1. The World Heritage Committee shall be assisted by a Secretariat appointed by the Director-General of the United Nations Educational, Scientific and Cultural Organization.
2. The Director-General of the United Nations Educational, Scientific and Cultural Organization, utilizing to the fullest extent possible the services of the International Centre for the Study of the Preservation and the Restoration of Cultural Property (the Rome Centre), the International Council of Monuments and Sites (ICOMOS) and the International Union for Conservation of Nature and Natural Resources (IUCN) in their respective areas of competence and capability, shall prepare the Committee's documentation and the agenda of its meetings and shall have the responsibility for the implementation of its decisions.

IV. FUND FOR THE PROTECTION OF THE WORLD CULTURAL AND NATURAL HERITAGE

Article 15

1. A Fund for the Protection of the World Cultural and Natural Heritage of Outstanding Universal Value, called "the World Heritage Fund", is hereby established.
2. The Fund shall constitute a trust fund, in conformity with the provisions of the Financial Regulations of the United Nations Educational, Scientific and Cultural Organization.
3. The resources of the Fund shall consist of:
   (a) compulsory and voluntary contributions made by the States Parties to this Convention,
   (b) contributions, gifts or bequests which may be made by:
      (i) other States;
      (ii) the United Nations Educational, Scientific and Cultural Organization, other organizations of the United Nations system, particularly the United Nations Development Programme or other intergovernmental organizations;
      (iii) public or private bodies or individuals;
   (c) any interest due on the resources of the Fund;
   (d) funds raised by collections and receipts from events organized for the benefit of the Fund; and
   (e) all other resources authorized by the Fund's regulations, as drawn up by the World Heritage Committee.
4. Contributions to the Fund and other forms of assistance made available to the Committee may be used only for such purposes as the Committee shall define. The Committee may accept contributions to be used only for a certain programme or project, provided that the Committee shall have decided on the implementation of such programme or project. No political conditions may be attached to contributions made to the Fund.

Article 16

1. Without prejudice to any supplementary voluntary contribution, the States Parties to this Convention undertake to pay regularly, every two years, to the World

Heritage Fund, contributions, the amount of which, in the form of a uniform percentage applicable to all States, shall be determined by the General Assembly of States Parties to the Convention, meeting during the sessions of the General Conference of the United Nations Educational, Scientific and Cultural Organization. This decision of the General Assembly requires the majority of the States Parties present and voting, which have not made the declaration referred to in paragraph 2 of this Article. In no case shall the compulsory contribution of States Parties to the Convention exceed 1% of the contribution to the Regular Budget of the United Nations Educational, Scientific and Cultural Organization.

2. However, each State referred to in Article 31 or in Article 32 of this Convention may declare, at the time of the deposit of its instruments of ratification, acceptance or accession, that it shall not be bound by the provisions of paragraph 1 of this Article.

3. A State Party to the Convention which has made the declaration referred to in paragraph 2 of this Article may at any time withdraw the said declaration by notifying the Director-General of the United Nations Educational, Scientific and Cultural Organization. However, the withdrawal of the declaration shall not take effect in regard to the compulsory contribution due by the State until the date of the subsequent General Assembly of States Parties to the Convention.

4. In order that the Committee may be able to plan its operations effectively, the contributions of States Parties to this Convention which have made the declaration referred to in paragraph 2 of this Article, shall be paid on a regular basis, at least every two years, and should not be less than the contributions which they should have paid if they had been bound by the provisions of paragraph 1 of this Article.

5. Any State Party to the Convention which is in arrears with the payment of its compulsory or voluntary contribution for the current year and the calendar year immediately preceding it shall not be eligible as a Member of the World Heritage Committee, although this provision shall not apply to the first election.

The terms of office of any such State which is already a member of the Committee shall terminate at the time of the elections provided for in Article 8, paragraph 1 of this Convention.

Article 17

The States Parties to this Convention shall consider or encourage the establishment of national, public and private foundations or associations whose purpose is to invite donations for the protection of the cultural and natural heritage as defined in Articles 1 and 2 of this Convention.

Article 18

The States Parties to this Convention shall give their assistance to international fund-raising campaigns organized for the World Heritage Fund under the auspices of the United Nations Educational, Scientific and Cultural Organization. They shall facilitate collections made by the bodies mentioned in paragraph 3 of Article 15 for this purpose.

V. CONDITIONS AND ARRANGEMENTS FOR INTERNATIONAL ASSISTANCE

Article 19

Any State Party to this Convention may request international assistance for property forming part of the cultural or natural heritage of outstanding universal value situated within its territory. It shall submit with its request such information and documentation provided for in Article 21 as it has in its possession and as will enable the Committee to come to a decision.

Article 20

Subject to the provisions of paragraph 2 of Article 13, sub-paragraph (c) of Article 22 and Article 23, international assistance provided for by this Convention may be granted only to property forming part of the cultural and natural heritage which the World Heritage Committee has decided, or may decide, to enter in one of the lists mentioned in paragraphs 2 and 4 of Article 11.

Article 21

1. The World Heritage Committee shall define the procedure by which requests to it for international assistance shall be considered and shall specify the content of the request, which should define the operation contemplated, the work that is necessary, the expected cost thereof, the degree of urgency and the reasons why the resources of the State requesting assistance do not allow it to meet all the expenses. Such requests must be supported by experts' reports whenever possible.
2. Requests based upon disasters or natural calamities should, by reasons of the urgent work which they may involve, be given immediate, priority consideration by the Committee, which should have a reserve fund at its disposal against such contingencies.
3. Before coming to a decision, the Committee shall carry out such studies and consultations as it deems necessary.

Article 22

Assistance granted by the World Heritage Committee may take the following forms:
- (a)   studies concerning the artistic, scientific and technical problems raised by the protection, conservation, presentation and rehabilitation of the cultural and natural heritage, as defined in paragraphs 2 and 4 of Article 11 of this Convention;
- (b)   provision of experts, technicians and skilled labour to ensure that the approved work is correctly carried out;
- (c) ·   training of staff and specialists at all levels in the field of identification, protection, conservation, presentation and rehabilitation of the cultural and natural heritage;
- (d)   supply of equipment which the State concerned does not possess or is not in a position to acquire;
- (e)   low-interest or interest-free loans which might be repayable on a long-term basis;
- (f)   the granting, in exceptional cases and for special reasons, of non-repayable subsidies.

Article 23

The World Heritage Committee may also provide international assistance to national or regional centres for the training of staff and specialists at all levels in the field of identification, protection, conservation, presentation and rehabilitation of the cultural and natural heritage.

Article 24

International assistance on a large scale shall be preceded by detailed scientific, economic and technical studies. These studies shall draw upon the most advanced techniques for the protection, conservation, presentation and rehabilitation of the natural and cultural heritage and shall be consistent with the objectives of this Convention. The studies shall also seek means of making rational use of the resources available in the State concerned.

Article 25

As a general rule, only part of the cost of work necessary shall be borne by the international community. The contribution of the State benefiting from international assistance shall constitute a substantial share of the resources devoted to each programme or project, unless its resources do not permit this.

Article 26

The World Heritage Committee and the recipient State shall define in the agreement they conclude the conditions in which a programme or project for which international assistance under the terms of this Convention is provided, shall be carried out. It shall be the responsibility of the State receiving such international assistance to continue to protect, conserve and present the property so safeguarded, in observance of the conditions laid down by the agreement.

VI. EDUCATIONAL PROGRAMMES

Article 27

1. The States Parties to this Convention shall endeavour by all appropriate means, and in particular by educational and information programmes, to strengthen appreciation and respect by their peoples of the cultural and natural heritage defined in Articles 1 and 2 of the Convention.
2. They shall undertake to keep the public broadly informed of the dangers threatening this heritage and of activities carried on in pursuance of this Convention.

Article 28

States Parties to this Convention which receive international assistance under the Convention shall take appropriate measures to make known the importance of the property for which assistance has been received and the rôle played by such assistance.

VII. REPORTS

Article 29

1. The States Parties to this Convention shall, in the reports which they submit to the General Conference of the United Nations Educational, Scientific and Cultural Organization on dates and in a manner to be determined by it, give information on the legislative and administrative provisions which they have adopted and other action which they have taken for the application of this Convention, together with details of the experience acquired in this field.
2. These reports shall be brought to the attention of the World Heritage Committee.
3. The Committee shall submit a report on its activities at each of the ordinary sessions of the General Conference of the United Nations Educational, Scientific and Cultural Organization.

VIII. FINAL CLAUSES

Article 30

This Convention is drawn up in Arabic, English, French, Russian and Spanish, the five texts being equally authoritative.

Article 31

1. This Convention shall be subject to ratification or acceptance by States members of the United Nations Educational, Scientific and Cultural Organization in accordance with their respective constitutional procedures.
2. The instruments of ratification or acceptance shall be deposited with the Director-General of the United Nations Educational, Scientific and Cultural Organization.

Article 32

1. This Convention shall be open to accession by all States not members of the United Nations Educational, Scientific and Cultural Organization which are invited by the General Conference of the Organization to accede to it.
2. Accession shall be effected by the deposit of an instrument of accession with the Director-General of the United Nations Educational, Scientific and Cultural Organization.

Article 33

This Convention shall enter into force three months after the date of the deposit of the twentieth instrument of ratification, acceptance or accession, but only with respect to those States which have deposited their respective intruments of ratification, acceptance or accession on or before that date. It shall enter into force with respect to any other State three months after the deposit of its instrument of ratification, acceptance or accession.

Article 34

The following provisions shall apply to those States Parties to this Convention which have a federal or non-unitary constitutional system:
(a) with regard to the provisions of this Convention, the implementation of which comes under the legal jurisdiction of the federal or central legislative power, the obligations of the federal or central government shall be the same as for those States Parties which are not federal States;
(b) with regard to the provisions of this Convention, the implementation of which comes under the legal jurisdiction of individual constituent States, countries, provinces or cantons that are not obliged by the constitutional system of the federation to take legislative measures, the federal government shall inform the competent authorities of such States, countries, provinces or cantons of the said provisions, with its recommendation for their adoption.

Article 35

1. Each State Party to this Convention may denounce the Convention.
2. The denunciation shall be notified by an instrument in writing, deposited with the Director-General of the United Nations Educational, Scientific and Cultural Organization.

3. The denunciation shall take effect twelve months after the receipt of the instrument of denunciation. It shall not affect the financial obligations of the denouncing State until the date on which the withdrawal takes effect.

Article 36

The Director-General of the United Nations Educational, Scientific and Cultural Organization shall inform the States members of the Organization, the States not members of the Organization which are referred to in Article 32, as well as the United Nations, of the deposit of all the instruments of ratification, acceptance, or accession provided for in Articles 31 and 32, and of the denunciations provided for in Article 35.

Article 37

1. This Convention may be revised by the General Conference of the United Nations Educational, Scientific and Cultural Organization. Any such revision shall, however, bind only the States which shall become Parties to the revising convention.
2. If the General Conference should adopt a new convention revising this Convention in whole or in part, then, unless the new convention otherwise provides, this Convention shall cease to be open to ratification, acceptance or accession, as from the date on which the new revising convention enters into force.

Article 38

In conformity with Article 102 of the Charter of the United Nations, this Convention shall be registered with the Secretariat of the United Nations at the request of the Director-General of the United Nations Educational, Scientific and Cultural Organization.

Done in Paris, this twenty-third day of November 1972, in two authentic copies bearing the signature of the President of the seventeenth session of the General Conference and of the Director-General of the United Nations Educational, Scientific and Cultural Organization, which shall be deposited in the archives of the United Nations Educational, Scientific and Cultural Organization, and certified true copies of which shall be delivered to all the States referred to in Articles 31 and 32 as well as to the United Nations.

UNESCO WORLD HERITAGE LIST

The World Heritage Committee has approved the following properties and natural properties to be included on the World Heritage List. The properties are arranged alphabetically by nominating country. Following is the 1989 updated version.

ALGERIA: 1980 Al Qal'a of Beni Hammad; 1982 Tassili n'Ajjer; 1982 M'zab Valley; 1982 Djemila; 1982 Tipasa; 1982 Timgad.

ARGENTINA: 1981 Los Glaciares; 1984 Iguazu National Park; 1984 Jesuit Missions of the Guarnis; 1984 San Ignacio Mini, Santa Ana, Nuestro Senora de Loreto and Santa Maria Mayor.

AUSTRALIA: 1981 Great Barrier Reef; 1981 Kakadu National Park; 1981 Willandra Lakes Region; 1982 Western Tasmania Wilderness National Parks; 1982 Lord Howe Island Group; 1987 Uluru National Park; 1987 Australian East Coast Temperate and Sub-Tropical Rainforest Parks; 1988 Wet Tropics of Queensland.

BANGLADESH: 1985 Historic Mosque City of Bagerhat; 1985 Ruins of the Buddhist Vihara at Paharpur.

BENIN: 1985 Royal Palaces of Abomey.

BOLIVIA: 1987 The City of Potosi.

BRAZIL: 1980 Historic Town of Ouro Preto; 1982 Historic Center of the Town of Olinda; 1983 Ruins of San Miguel das Missoes; 1984 Iguazu National Park; 1985 Historic Center of Salvador de Bahia; 1985 Sanctuary of Bom Jesus do Congonhas; 1987 The City of Brasilia.

BULGARIA: 1979 Boyana Church; 1979 Madara Rider; 1979 Rock-hewn Churches of Ivanovo; 1979 Thracian Tomb of Kazanlak; 1983 Ancient City of Nessebar; 1983 Srebarna Nature Reserve; 1983 Pirin National Park; 1983 Rila Monastery; 1985 Thracian Tomb of Sveshtari.

CAMEROON: 1987 Dja Faunal Reserve.

CANADA: 1978 L'Anse aux Meadows National Historic Park; 1978 Nahanni National Park; 1979 Dinosaur Provincial Park; 1981 Anthony Island; 1981 Head-Smashed-In Bison Jump Complex; 1983 Wood Buffalo National Park; 1984 Canadian Rocky Mountain Parks (The Burgess Shale Site, previously inscribed on the WHL, is part of the Canadian Rocky Mountain Parks); 1985 Historic Area of Quebec; 1987 Gros Morne National Park.

CANADA AND THE UNITED STATES OF AMERICA: 1979 Kluane National Park and Reserve, Yukon, Canada, Wrangell-St. Elias National Monument, Alaska, U.S.A.

CENTRAL AFRICAN REPUBLIC: 1988 Parc National du Manovo-Gounda St. Floris.

CHINA (PEOPLES REPUBLIC OF): 1987 The Great Wall; 1987 Mount Taishan; 1987 Imperial Palace of the Ming and Qing Dynasties; 1987 Mogao Caves; 1987 The Mausoleum of the First Qin Emporer; 1987 Peking Man Site at Zhoukoudian.

COLOMBIA: 1987 Port, Fortresses and Group of Monuments, Carthagena.

COSTA RICA: 1983 Talamanca Range-La Amistad Reserve.

CUBA: 1982 Old Havana and its Fortifications; 1988 Trinidad and the Valley de los Ingenios.

CYPRUS: 1980 Paphos; 1985 The Painted Churches in the Troodos Region.

ECUADOR: 1978 Galapagos National Park, including the Galapagos Islands; 1978 Old City of Quito; 1983 Sangay National Park.

EGYPT: 1979 Abu Mena; 1979 Ancient Thebes, including its Necropolis; 1979 Islamic Cairo; 1979 Memphis and its Necropolis-the Pyramid Fields from Giza to Dahshur; 1979 Nubian Monuments from Abu Simbel to Philae.

ETHIOPIA: 1978 Rock-hewn Churches of Lalibela; 1978 Simen National Park; 1979 Fasil Ghebbi, Gondar Region; 1980 Aksum; 1980 Lower Valley of the Awash; 1980 Lower Valley of the Omo; 1980 Tiya.

FRANCE: 1979 Chartres Cathedral; 1979 Decorated Grottoes of the Vezere Valley, including the Grotto of Lascaux; 1979 Mont-St. Michel and its Bay; 1979 Palace and Park of Versailles; 1979 Vezelay, Church and Hill; 1981 Amiens Cathedral; 1981 Chateau and Estate of Chambord; 1981 Cistercian Abbey of Fontenay; 1981 Palace and Park of Fontainebleau; 1981 Roman and Romanesque Monuments of Arles; 1981 The Roman Theatre and its Surroundings and the Triumphal Arch of Orange; 1982 The Royal Saltworks of Arc-et-Senans; 1983 Place Stanislas, Place de la Carriere, and Place d' Alliance, Nancy; 1983 Church of Saint-Savin-sur Gartempe; 1983 Classified Site of Cape Girolata, Cape Porto and Scandola Natural Reserve, Corsica; 1985 Pont du Gard (Roman Aqueduct); 1988 Strasbourg, Grande Isle.

GERMANY (FEDERAL REPUBLIC OF): 1978 Aachen Cathedral; 1981 Speyer Cathedral; 1981 Wurzburg Residence, invcluding [sic] the Court Gardens and Residence Square; 1983 Pilgrimage of Church of Wies; 1984 The Castles of Augustusburg and Falkenlust at Bruhl; 1985 St. Mary's Cathedral and St. Michael's Church, Hildesheim; 1986 Monuments of Trier; 1987 Hanseatic City of Lubeck.

GHANA: 1979 Forts and Castles, Volta Greater Accra, Central and Western Regions; 1980 Ashante Traditional Buildings.

GREECE: 1986 Temple of Apollo Epicurius at Bassae; 1987 Archaeological Site of Delphi; 1987 The Acropolis, Athens; 1988 Mount Athos; 1988 Meteora; 1988 Paleochristian and Byzantine Monuments of Thessalonika; 1988 Archaeological Site of Epidaurus; 1988 Medieval City of Rhodes.

GUATEMALA: 1979 Antigua Guatemala; 1979 Tikal National Park; 1981 Archaeological Park and Ruins of Quirigua.

GUINEA AND IVORY COAST: 1981 Mount Nimba Strict Nature Reserve.

HAITI: 1982 The National Historic Park, including, La Ferriere Citadel, the Sans-Souci Palace and Site of Les Ramiers.

HOLY SEE: 1984 Vatican City.

HONDURAS: 1980 Maya Site of Copan; 1982 Rio Platano Biosphere Reserve.

HUNGARY: 1987 Budapest, including the Banks of the Danube with the district of Buda Castle; 1987 Holloko.

INDIA: 1983 Ellora Caves and Ajanta Caves; 1983 Agra Fort; 1983 Taj Mahal; 1984 Sun Temple, Konarak; 1985 Group of Monuments at Mahabalipuram; 1985 Kaziranga National Park; 1985 Manas Wildlife Sanctuary; 1985 Keoladeo National Park; 1986 Churches and Convents of Goa; 1986 Group of Monuments at Khajuraho; 1986 Group of Monuments at Hampi; 1986 Fatehpur Sikri; 1987 Group of Monuments at Pattadakal; 1987 Elephanta Caves; 1987 Brihadisvara Temple, Thanjavur; 1987 Sundarbans National Park; 1988 Nanda Devi National Park.

IRAN: 1979 Meidan-e-Shah, Esfahan; 1979 Persepolis; 1979 Tchoga Zanbil Ziggurat and Complex; 1988 Meidan Emam, Esfahan.

IRAQ: 1985 Hatra.

ITALY: 1979 Rock Drawings in Valcamonica near Bresica; 1980 Church and Dominican Convent of Santa Maria delle Grazie with "The Last Supper" by Leonardo da Vinci; 1980 Historic Center of Rome; 1982 Historic Center of Florence; 1987 Venice and its Lagoon; 1987 Piazza del Duomo, Pisa.

IVORY COAST: 1982 Tai National Park; 1983 Comoe National Park.

IVORY COAST AND GUINEA: See GUINEA AND IVORY COAST

JORDAN (HASHEMITE KINGDOM OF): 1981 The Old City of Jerusalem and its Walls; 1985 Petra; 1985 Quseir Amra.

LEBANON: 1984 Anjar; 1984 Baalbek; 1984 Byblos; 1984 Tyr.

LIBYAN ARAB JAMAHIRIYA (SOCIALIST PEOPLE'S): 1982 Archaeological Site of Leptis Magna; 1982 Archaeological Site of Sabratha; 1982 Archaeological Site of Cyrene (Shahhat); 1985 Rock-art Sites of Tadrart Acacus; 1988 Old Town of Ghadames.

MALAWI: 1984 Lake Malawi National Park.

MALI: 1988 Old Towns of Djenne; 1988 Timbuktu.

MALTA: 1980 City of Valetta; 1980 Ggantija Temples on the Island of Gozo; 1980 Hal Saflieni Hypogeum.

MEXICO: 1987 Historic Center of Mexico City and Xochimilco; 1987 Pre-Hispanic City and National Park of Palenque; 1987 Pre-Hispanic City of Teotihuacan; 1987 Historic Center of Oaxaca and the Archaeological Site of Monte Alban; 1987 Historic Center of Puebla; 1987 Sian Ka'an; 1988 Historic Town of Guanajuato and adjacent mines; 1988 Pre-Hispanic City of Chichen-Itza.

MOROCCO: 1981 Medina of Fez; 1985 Medina of Marrakesh; 1987 Ksar of Ait-Ben-Haddou.

NEPAL: 1979 Kathmandu Valley; 1979 Sagarmatha National Park, including Mt. Everest; 1984 Royal Chitwan National Park.

NEW ZEALAND: 1988 Westland and Mount Cook National Park; 1988 Fiordland National Park.

NORWAY: 1979 Bryggen, the Old Hansiatic Quarter of Bergen; 1979 Urnes Stave Church; 1980 Roros Mining Town; 1985 Rock Drawings of Alta.

OMAN: 1987 Bahla Fort; 1988 Archaeological Sites of Bat, Al-Khutm and Al-Ayn.

PAKISTAN: 1980 Archaeological Ruins at Moenjodaro; 1980 Buddhist Ruins at Takht-i-Bahi and Neighboring City Remains at Sahr-i-Bahol; 1980 Taxila; 1981 Fort and Shalamar Gardens at Lahore; 1981 Historic Monuments of Thatta.

PANAMA: 1980 Fortifications on the Caribbean Side of Panama—Portobelo, San Lorenzo; 1981 Darien National Park.

PERU: 1983 City of Cuzco; 1983 Historic Sanctuary of Machu Picchu; 1985 Archaeological Site of Chavin; 1985 Huascaran National Park; 1987 Manu National Park; 1988 Convent Ensemble of San Francisco de Lima; 1988 Chan Chan Archaeological Zone.

POLAND: 1978 Historic Center of Cracow; 1978 Wieliczka Salt Mines; 1979 Auschwitz Concentration Camp; 1979 Bialowieza National Park; 1980 Historic Center of Warsaw.

PORTUGAL: 1983 Central Zone of the Town of Angra do Heroisma in the Azores; 1983 Monastery of the Hieronymites and Tower of Belem, Lisbon; 1983 Monastery of Batalha; 1983 Convent of Christ in Tomar; 1988 Historic Center of Evora.

SENEGAL: 1978 Island of Goree; 1981 Djoudj National Bird Sanctuary; 1981 Niokolo Koba National Park.

SEYCHELLES: 1982 Aldabra Atoll; 1983 Vallee de Mai Nature Reserve.

SPAIN: 1984 Mosque of Cordoba; 1984 Alhambra and Generalife, Granada; 1984 Burgos Cathedral; 1984 Monastery and Site of the Escurial, Madrid; 1984 Parque Quell, Palacio Quell and Casa Mila, Barcelona; 1985 Altamira Cave; 1985 Old Town of Segovia, including its aqueduct; 1985 Churches of the Kingdom of the Asturias; 1985 Old Town of Santiago de Compostela; 1985 Old Town of Avila, including its extra-muros churches; 1986 Mudejar Architecture of Teruel; 1986 Historic City of Toledo; 1986 Garajonay National Park; 1986 Old Town of Cacheros; 1987 Cathedral, Alcazar and Archivo de Indias, Seville; 1988 Old City of Salamanca.

SRI LANKA: 1982 Sacred City of Anuradhapura; 1982 Ancient City of Polonnaruva; 1982 Ancient City of Sigiriya; 1988 Sinharaja Forest Reserve; 1988 Sacred City of Kandy; 1988 Old Town of Galle and its fortifications.

SWITZERLAND: 1983 Convent of St. Gall; 1983 Benedictine Convent of St. Jean des Soeurs, Munster; 1983 Old City of Berne.

SYRIAN ARAB REPUBLIC: 1979 Ancient City of Damascus; 1980 Site of Palmyra; 1980 Ancient City of Bosra; 1988 Ancient City of Aleppo.

TANZANIA (UNITED REPUBLIC OF): 1979 Ngorongoro Conservation Area, including the Ngorongoro and Empakaai Craters and Olduvai Gorge; 1981 Ruins of Kilwa Kisiwani and Ruins of Songo Mnara; 1981 Serengeti National Park; 1982 Selous Game Reserve; 1987 Kilimanjaro National Park.

TUNISIA: 1979 Roman Amphitheater of El Jem; 1979 Archaeological Site of Carthage; 1979 Medina of Tunis; 1980 Ichkeul National Park; 1985 Punic Town of Kerkuane, including its Necropolis; 1988 Medina of Sousse; 1988 Kairouan.

TURKEY: 1985 Historic Areas of Istanbul; 1985 Goreme National Park and the Rock Sites of Cappadocia; 1985 Great Mosque and Hospital of Divrigi; 1986 Hattusha; 1987 Nemrut Dag; 1988 Xanthos-Letoon; 1988 Hierapolis-Pamukkale.

UNITED KINGDOM: 1986 The Giant's Causeway and Causeway Coast; 1986 Durham Castle and Cathedral; 1986 Ironbridge Gorge; 1986 Studley Royal Park, including the Ruins of Fountains Abbey; 1986 Stonehenge, Avebury and associated sites; 1986 The Castles and Town Walls of King Edward in Gwynedd; 1986 St. Kilda; 1987 Blenheim Palace; 1987 The City of Bath; 1987 Hadrian's Wall; 1987 Palace of Westminster Abbey and St. Margaret's Church; 1988 Henderson Island; 1988 The Tower of London; 1988 Canterbury Cathedral, St. Augustine's Abbey and St. Martin's Church.

UNITED STATES OF AMERICA: 1978 Mesa Verde National Park, Colorado; 1978 Yellowstone National Park, Wyoming/Idaho/Montana; 1979 Everglades National Park, Florida; 1979 Grand Canyon National Park, Arizona; 1979 Independence Hall, Pennsylvania; 1980 Redwood National Park, California; 1981 Mammoth Cave National Park, Kentucky; 1981 Olympic National Park, Washington State; 1982 Cahokia Mounds State Historic Site, Illinois; 1983 Great Smoky Mountains National Park, North Carolina/Tennessee; 1983 San Juan National Historic Site and La Fortaleza, Puerto Rico; 1984 The Statue of Liberty, New York; 1984 Yosemite National Park, California; 1987 Thomas Jefferson's Home—Monticello, and the University of Virginia Campus at Charlottesville, Virginia; 1987 Chaco Culture National Historic Park, New Mexico; 1987 Hawaii Volcanoes National Park, including Mauna Loa, Hawaii.

UNITED STATES OF AMERICA AND CANADA: See CANADA AND THE UNITED STATES OF AMERICA

YEMEN (DEMOCRATIC REPUBLIC OF): 1982 Old Walled City of Shibam; 1988 Old City of Sana'a.

YUGOSLAVIA: 1979 Historic Complex of Split with the Palace Diocletian; 1979 Natural and Culturo-Historic Region of Kotor; 1979 Ohrid Region, including its cultural and historic aspects, and its natural environment; 1979 Old City of Dubrovnik; 1979 Plitvice Lakes National Park; 1979 Stari Ras and Sopocani Monastery; 1980 Durmitor National Park; 1988 Studenica Monastery; 1988 Skocjan Caves.

ZAIRE: 1979 Virunga National Park; 1981 Kahuzi-Biega National Park; 1980 Garamba National Park; 1984 Salonga National Park.

ZIMBABWE: 1984 Mana Pools National Park, Sapi and Chewore Safari Areas; 1988 Great Zimbabwe National Monument; 1988 Khami Ruins National Monument.

PART III
PROTECTION AGAINST PARTICULAR THREATS

CHAPTER 11
POLLUTION GENERALLY

A. GENERAL PRINCIPLES

NORDIC CONVENTION ON THE PROTECTION OF THE ENVIRONMENT. *Supra*, p.235

PARIS CONVENTION FOR THE PREVENTION OF MARINE POLLUTION FROM LAND-BASED SOURCES. *Supra*, p. 360.

ORGANISATION FOR ECONOMIC CO-OPERATION AND DEVELOPMENT COUNCIL RECOMMENDATION ON PRINCIPLES CONCERNING TRANSFRONTIER POLLUTION

Done at Paris on 14 November 1974, OECD Doc. C(74)224 (21 November 1974), *reprinted in* OECD & E 142, 14 ILM 242 (1975), 1 IPE 316.

Languages: English, French

Editors' Note

The Organisation for Economic Co-operation and Development (OECD) is an economic policymaking organization composed of market-oriented countries. Its 24 members are: Australia; Austria; Belgium; Canada; Denmark; Finland; France; Germany; Greece; Iceland; Ireland; Italy; Japan; Luxembourg; Netherlands; New Zealand; Norway; Portugal; Spain; Sweden; Switzerland; Turkey; United Kingdom of Great Britain and Northern Ireland; and United States of America. This OECD Council recommendation contains a set of principles applicable to transfrontier pollution, including nondiscrimination, equal right of hearing, information and consultation, warning, and exchange of information. *See also* the OECD instruments reproduced *infra* at pp. 706 and 708.

OECD PRINCIPLES CONCERNING TRANSFRONTIER POLLUTION

The Council

Considering that the protection and improvement of the environment are common objectives of Member countries;

Considering that the common interests of countries concerned by transfrontier pollution should induce them to co-operate more closely in a spirit of international solidarity and to initiate concerted action for preventing and controlling transfrontier pollution;

Having regard to the Recommendations of the United Nations Conference on the Human Environment held in Stockholm in June 1972 and in particular those Principles of the Declaration on the Human Environment which are relevant to transfrontier pollution;

On the proposal of the Environment Committee:

I. Recommends that, without prejudice to future developments in international law and international co-operation in relation to transfrontier pollution, Member countries should be guided in their environmental policy by the principles concerning transfrontier pollution contained in this Recommendation and its Annex, which is an integral part of this Recommendation.

II. Instructs the Environment Committee to prepare without delay taking account of the work undertaken by other international organisations, a programme of work designed to elaborate further these principles and to facilitate their practical implementation.

III. Recommends Member countries to co-operate in developing international law applicable to transfrontier pollution.

IV. Instructs the Environment Committee, within the framework of its mandate, to examine or investigate further, as the case may be, the issues related to the Principles of the Stockholm Declaration regarding responsibility and liability, taking into account the work undertaken by other international organisations, to submit a first report to the Council on its work by 1 March, 1976 and to seek to formulate as soon as possible Draft Recommendations.

V. Instructs the Environment Committee to investigate further the issues concerning equal right of hearing, to formulate as soon as possible Draft Recommendations and to report to the Council on its work by 1 July, 1975.

ANNEX
Some Principles Concerning Transfrontier Pollution
Title A. Introduction

This Annex sets forth some principles designed to facilitate the development of harmonized environmental policies with a view to solving transfrontier pollution problems. Their implementation should be based on a fair balance of rights and obligations among countries concerned by transfrontier pollution.

These principles should subsequently be supplemented and developed in the light of work undertaken by the OECD or other appropriate international organisations.

For the purpose of these principles, pollution means the introduction by man, directly or indirectly, of substances or energy into the environment resulting in deleterious effects of such a nature as to endanger human health, harm living resources and ecosystems, and impair or interface with amenities and other legitimate uses of the environment.

Unless otherwise specified, these principles deal with pollution originating in one country and having effect within other countries.

Title B.[1] International solidarity

1. Countries should define a concerted long-term policy for the protection and improvement of the environment in zones liable to be affected by transfrontier pollution.

---

[1]The delegate for Spain reserved his position on Title B.

Without prejudice to their rights and obligations under international law and in accordance with their responsibility under Principle 21 of the Stockholm Declaration, countries should seek, as far as possible, an equitable balance of their rights and obligations as regards the zones concerned by transfrontier pollution.

In implementing this concerted policy, countries should among other things:

(a) take account of:

—levels of existing pollution and the present quality of the environment concerned;

—the nature and quantities of pollutants;

—the assimilative capacity of the environment, as established by mutual agreement by the countries concerned, taking into account the particular characteristics and use of the affected zone;

—activities at the source of pollution and activities and uses sensitive to such pollution;

—the situation, prospective use and development of the zones concerned from a socio-economic standpoint:

(b) define:

—environmental quality objectives and corresponding protective measures;

(c) promote:

—guidelines for a land-use planning policy consistent with the requirements both of environmental protection and socio-economic development;

(d) draw up and maintain up to date:

(i) list of particular dangerous substances regarding which efforts should be made to eliminate polluting discharges, if necessary by stages, and

(ii) lists of substances regarding which polluting discharges should be subject to very strict control.

2. Pending the definition of such concerted long-term policies countries should, individually and jointly, take all appropriate measures to prevent and control transfrontier pollution, and harmonize as far as possible their relevant policies.

3. Countries should endeavour to prevent any increase in transfrontier pollution, including that stemming from new or additional substances and activities, and to reduce, and as far as possible eliminate any transfrontier pollution existing between them within time limits to be specified.

Title C. Principle of non-discrimination

4. Countries should initially base their action on the principle of non-discrimination, whereby:

(a) polluters causing transfrontier pollution should be subject to legal or statutory provisions no less severe than those which would apply for any equivalent pollution occurring within their country, under comparable conditions and in comparable zones, taking into account, when appropriate, the special nature and environmental needs of the zone affected;

(b) in particular, without prejudice to quality objectives or standards applying to transfrontier pollution mutually agreed upon by the countries concerned, the levels of transfrontier pollution entering into the zones liable to be affected by such pollution should not exceed those considered acceptable under comparable conditions and in comparable zones inside the country in which it originates, taking into account, when appropriate, the special state of the environment in the affected country;

(c) any country whenever it applies the Polluter-Pays Principle should apply it to all polluters within this country without making any difference according to whether pollution affects this country or another country;

(d) persons affected by transfrontier pollution should be granted no less favourable treatment than persons affected by a similar pollution in the country from which such transfrontier pollution originates.

Title D.[2] Principle of equal right of hearing

5. Countries should make every effort to introduce, where not already in existence, a system affording equal right of hearing, according to which:

(a) whenever a project, a new activity or a course of conduct may create a significant risk of transfrontier pollution and is investigated by public authorities, those who may be affected by such pollution should have the same rights of standing in judicial or administrative proceedings in the country where it originates as those of that country;

(b) whenever transfrontier pollution gives rise to damage in a country, those who are affected by such pollution should have the same rights of standing in judicial or administrative proceedings in the country where such pollution originates as those of that country, and they should be extended procedural rights equivalent to the rights extended to those of that country.

Title E.[3] Principle of information and consultation

6. Prior to the initiation in a country of works or undertakings which might create a significant risk of transfrontier pollution, this country should provide early information to other countries which are or may be affected. It should provide these countries with relevant information and data, the transmission of which is not prohibited by legislative provisions or prescriptions or applicable international conventions, and should invite their comments.

7. Countries should enter into consultation on an existing or foreseeable transfrontier pollution problem at the request of a country which is or may be directly affected and should diligently pursue such consultations on this particular problem over a reasonable period of time.

8. Countries should refrain from carrying out projects or activities which might create a significant risk of transfrontier pollution without first informing the countries which are or may be affected and, except in cases of extreme urgency, providing a reasonable amount of time in the light of circumstances for diligent consultation. Such consultations held in the best spirit of co-operation and good neighbourliness should not enable a country to unreasonably delay or to impede the activities or projects on which consultations are taking place.

Title F. Warning systems and incidents

9. Countries should promptly warn other potentially affected countries of any situation which may cause any sudden increase in the level of pollution in areas outside the country of origin of pollution, and take all appropriate steps to reduce the effects of any such sudden increase.

10. Countries should assist each other, wherever necessary, in order to prevent incidents which may result in transfrontier pollution, and to minimize, and if possible eliminate, the effects of such incidents, and should develop contingency plans to this end.

Title G. Exchange of scientific information, monitoring measures and research

11. Countries concerned should exchange all relevant scientific information and data on transfrontier pollution, when not prohibited by legislative provisions or prescriptions or by applicable international conventions. They should develop and adopt pollution measurement methods providing results which are compatible.

---

[2]The delegate for Spain reserved his position on Title D.
[3]The delegate for Spain reserved his position on Title E.

12. They should, when appropriate, co-operate in scientific and technical research programmes inter alia for identifying the origin and pathways of transfrontier pollution, any damage caused and the best methods of pollution prevention and control, and should share all information and data thus obtained.

They should, where necessary, consider setting up jointly, in zones affected by transfrontier pollution, a permanent monitoring system or network for assessing the levels of pollution and the effectiveness of measures taken by them to reduce pollution.

Title H. Institutions

13. Countries concerned by a particular problem of transfrontier pollution should consider the advantages of co-operation, by setting up international commissions or other bodies, or by strengthening existing institutions, in order to deal more effectively with particular aspects of such problems.

Such institutions could be authorized to collect any data needed for a proper evaluation of the problem and its causes, and make to the countries concerned practical proposals for concerted efforts to combat transfrontier pollution. With the consent of the States concerned, they could also carry out any necessary additional investigations into the origin and degree of pollution, review the effectiveness of any pollution prevention and control measures which have been taken, and publish reports of their findings.

Title I. Disputes

14. Should negotiations and other means of diplomatically settling disputes concerning transfrontier pollution fail, countries should have the opportunity to submit such a dispute to a procedure of legal settlement which is prompt, effective and binding.

Title J. International agreements

15. Countries should endeavour to conclude, where necessary, bilateral or multilateral agreements for the abatement of transfrontier pollution in accordance with the above principles, to bring promptly into force any agreements which may already have been signed.

16. When negotiating new bilateral or multilateral agreements countries should, while taking into account the principles set out above, strive for the application of efficient pollution prevention and control measures in accordance with the Polluter-Pays Principle.

Such agreements could, inter alia, include provisions for practical procedures promoting the prompt and equitable compensation of persons affected by transfrontier pollution, and could also contain procedures facilitating the provision of information and consultation.

INTERNATIONAL LAW ASSOCIATION MONTREAL RULES OF INTERNATIONAL LAW APPLICABLE TO TRANSFRONTIER POLLUTION

Done at Montreal on 4 September 1982, *in* I.L.A., Report of the Sixtieth Conference 1 (1983).

Language: English

Editors' Note

These rules adopted by the International Law Association (described *supra* in the Editors' Introductory Note at p. 395) have influenced international efforts to control transfrontier pollution. By their terms, the rules do not cover pollution that harms a global commons. Inter alia, the rules (which are not in the form of an international agreement) provide that shared natural resources should be utilized in an "equitable and reasonable" manner and set forth factors relevant to determining what is a reasonable and equitable share.

Copyright 1983 by the International Law Association. Reprinted with permission from the International Law Association.

RULES OF INTERNATIONAL LAW APPLICABLE TO TRANSFRONTIER POLLUTION

Article 1 (Applicability)

The following rules of international law concerning transfrontier pollution are applicable except as may be otherwise provided by convention, agreement or binding custom among the States concerned.

Article 2 (Definition)

(1) "Pollution" means any introduction by man, directly or indirectly, of substance or energy into the environment resulting in deleterious effects of such a nature as to endanger human health, harm living resources, ecosystems and material property and impair amenities or interfere with other legitimate uses of the environment.
(2) "Transfrontier pollution" means pollution of which the physical origin is wholly or in part situated within the territory of one State and which has deleterious effects in the territory of another State.

Article 3 (Prevention and Abatement)

(1) Withoug prejudice to the operation of the rules relating to the reasonable and equitable utilisation of shared natural resources States are in their legitimate activities under an obligation to prevent, abate and control transfrontier pollution to such an extent that no substantial injury is caused in the territory of another State.
(2) Furthermore States shall limit new and increased transfrontier pollution to the lowest level that may be reached by measures practicable and reasonable under the circumstances.
(3) States should endeavour to reduce existing transfrontier pollution, below the requirements of paragraph 1 of this Article, to the lowest level that may be reached by measures practicable and reasonable under the circumstances.

Article 4 (Highly dangerous substances)

Notwithstanding the provisions in Article 3 States shall refrain from causing transfrontier pollution by discharging into the environment substances generally considered as being highly dangerous to human health. If such substances are already being discharged, States shall eliminate the polluting discharge within a reasonable time.

Article 5 (Prior Notice)

(1) States planning to carry out activities which might entail a significant risk of transfrontier pollution shall give early notice to States likely to be affected. In particular they shall on their own initiative or upon request of the potentially affected States, communicate such pertinent information as will permit the recipient to make an assessment of the probable effects of the planned activities.

(2) In order to appraise whether a planned activity implies a significant risk of transfrontier pollution, States should make environmental assessment before carrying out such activities.

Article 6 (Consultations)

(1) Upon request of a potentially affected State, the State furnishing the information should enter into consultations on transfrontier pollution problems connected with the planned activities and pursue such consultations in good faith and over a reasonable period of time.

(2) States are under an obligation to enter into consultations whenever transfrontier pollution problems arise in connection with the equitable utilization of a shared natural resource as envisaged in Art. 5.

Article 7 (Emergency situations)

When as a result of an emergency situation or of other circumstances activities already carried out in the territory of a State cause or might cause a sudden increase in the existing level of transfrontier pollution the State of origin is under a duty:

(a) to promptly warn the affected or potentially affected States;
(b) to provide them with such pertinent information as will enable them to minimize the transfrontier pollution damage;
(c) to inform them of the steps taken to abate the cause of the increased transfrontier pollution level.

AFRICAN CONVENTION ON THE CONSERVATION OF NATURE AND NATURAL RESOURCES. *Supra*, p. 202.

UNITED NATIONS CONVENTION ON THE LAW OF THE SEA. *Supra*, p. 332

B. PARTICULAR AREAS OR WATERS

BARCELONA CONVENTION FOR THE PROTECTION OF THE MEDITERRANEAN SEA AGAINST POLLUTION. *Supra*, p. 370.

BERNE CONVENTION ON THE INTERNATIONAL COMMISSION FOR THE PROTECTION OF THE RHINE AGAINST POLLUTION. *Supra*, p. 438.

C. PARTICULAR SUBSTANCES

BONN CONVENTION FOR THE PROTECTION OF THE RHINE RIVER AGAINST CHEMICAL POLLUTION. *Supra*, p. 442.

BONN CONVENTION FOR THE PROTECTION OF THE RHINE RIVER AGAINST POLLUTION BY CHLORIDES. *Supra*, p. 450.

D. EMERGENCIES

Editors' Introductory Note Regarding the IAEA Assistance and Notification Conventions. *Infra*, p. 582.

INTERNATIONAL ATOMIC ENERGY AGENCY CONVENTION ON EARLY NOTIFICATION OF A NUCLEAR ACCIDENT. *Infra*, p. 583.

INTERNATIONAL ATOMIC ENERGY AGENCY CONVENTION ON ASSISTANCE IN THE CASE OF A NUCLEAR ACCIDENT OR RADIOLOGICAL EMERGENCY. *Infra*, p. 587.

BARCELONA PROTOCOL CONCERNING CO-OPERATION IN COMBATING POLLUTION OF THE MEDITERRANEAN SEA BY OIL AND OTHER HARMFUL SUBSTANCES IN CASES OF EMERGENCY. *Supra*, p. 381.

CHAPTER 12
OIL AND OTHER HYDROCARBONS

A. GENERAL

B. EMERGENCIES

581

CHAPTER 13
PEACEFUL NUCLEAR ACTIVITIES

B. EMERGENCIES

Editors' Introductory Note Regarding the IAEA Assistance and Notification Conventions

On 26 April 1986, a faulty experiment caused a nuclear power reactor in Chernobyl, U.S.S.R., to overheat. Subsequent chemical explosions and fires spewed radioactive particles into the atmosphere. The radioactive plume initially drifted northwestward toward Scandinavia, where the existence of the radioactivity was first detected by Swedish monitors, thence southward over Germany, France, and Italy and finally eastward back over the Soviet Union. The plume eventually circled the globe.

The disaster was not disclosed or acknowledged by the Soviet government until days after the accident. By that time, large portions of other countries' populations had been exposed to radiation, including radioactive iodine and cesium.

More than 30 people died from injuries and exposure received in the immediate aftermath of the accident, vast portions of Byelorussia and the Ukraine were evacuated, and increases in cancers, birth deformities, and other medical problems are expected for decades. Assistance, particularly in the form of medical supplies and personnel, was provided to the Soviet Union by the United States and other countries.

The Chernobyl disaster raised many important international legal issues. Two of those—notification and assistance—were the subject of conventions that were negotiated and finalized unusually quickly, within five months after the accident. These conventions were drafted under the auspices of the International Atomic Energy Agency (IAEA), an independent agency of the United Nations. The IAEA's primary responsibility is to ensure that fissionable material is not diverted from peaceful to military uses, but the IAEA also is involved in other safety aspects of non-military nuclear activities.

The first of the two IAEA conventions reproduced here concerns the duty to notify potentially affected States of dangers from nuclear accidents or emergencies, as well as procedures for effectuating that duty. The Notification Convention requires a State to "forthwith notify, directly or [by means of notifying the IAEA], those States which are or may be physically affected" by a "transboundary release that could be of radiological safety significance," when that release occurs or is likely to occur from an accident in facilities or activities of a State or within its jurisdiction or control. The Convention also specifies the types of information to be provided and obligates the IAEA to "forthwith" pass on notifications it receives to affected or potentially affected States.

The second convention—the Assistance Convention—concerns the process and mechanisms for one State's providing assistance to a State in which a nuclear accident or emergency occurs. The Assistance Convention specifies means and responsibility for requesting assistance, for communicating information, for controlling assistance efforts, and for reimbursing costs; and it covers the IAEA's obligations, confidentiality, and privileges and immunities.

INTERNATIONAL ATOMIC ENERGY AGENCY CONVENTION ON EARLY NOTIFICATION OF A NUCLEAR ACCIDENT

Popular Name: IAEA Notification Convention, Notification Convention

Done at Vienna on 26 September 1986, IAEA INFCIRC/335, IAEA Leg Ser. #14, *reprinted in* 25 ILM 1370 (1986).
Entry into Force: 27 October 1986

Depositary: International Atomic Energy Agency (IAEA)

Languages: Arabic, Chinese, English, French, Russian, Spanish

Parties as of 1 January 1990: Australia; Austria; Bangladesh; Bulgaria;* Byelorussian Soviet Socialist Republic;* China;* Cyprus; Czech and Slovak Federal Republic;* Denmark; Egypt;* Finland; France;* German Democratic Republic;* Guatemala; Hungary;* India;* Iraq;* Japan; Jordan; Malaysia;* Mexico; Monaco; Mongolia;* New Zealand; Norway; Poland;* Saudi Arabia;* South Africa;* Sweden; Switzerland; Thailand;* Tunisia; Ukrainian Soviet Socialist Republic;* Union of Soviet Socialist Republics;* United Arab Emirates; United States of America;* Viet Nam;* Yugoslavia; World Health Organization

Literature: A. O. Adede, *The IAEA Notification and Assistance Conventions in Case of a Nuclear Accident* (1987)

CONVENTION ON EARLY NOTIFICATION OF A NUCLEAR ACCIDENT

THE STATES PARTIES TO THIS CONVENTION,
AWARE that nuclear activities are being carried out in a number of States,
NOTING that comprehensive measures have been and are being taken to ensure a high level of safety in nuclear activities, aimed at preventing nuclear accidents and minimizing the consequences of any such accident, should it occur,
DESIRING to strengthen further international co-operation in the safe development and use of nuclear energy,
CONVINCED of the need for States to provide relevant information about nuclear accidents as early as possible in order that transboundary radiological consequences can be minimized,
NOTING the usefulness of bilateral and multilateral arrangements on information exchange in this area,
HAVE AGREED as follows:

---

*Indicates a reservation and/or declaration

Article 1
Scope of application

1. This Convention shall apply in the event of any accident involving facilities or activities of a State Party or of persons or legal entities under its jurisdiction or control, referred to in paragraph 2 below, from which a release of radioactive material occurs or is likely to occur and which has resulted or may result in an international transboundary release that could be of radiological safety significance for another State.

2. The facilities and activities referred to in paragraph 1 are the following:
   - (a)   any nuclear reactor wherever located;
   - (b)   any nuclear fuel cycle facility;
   - (c)   any radioactive waste management facility;
   - (d)   the transport and storage of nuclear fuels or radioactive wastes;
   - (e)   the manufacture, use, storage, disposal and transport of radioisotopes for agricultural, industrial, medical and related scientific and research purposes; and
   - (f)   the use of radioisotopes for power generation in space objects.

Article 2
Notification and information

In the event of an accident specified in article 1 (hereinafter referred to as a "nuclear accident"), the State Party referred to in that article shall:
- (a)   forthwith notify, directly or through the International Atomic Energy Agency (hereinafter referred to as the "Agency"), those States which are or may be physically affected as specified in article 1 and the Agency of the nuclear accident, its nature, the time of its occurrence and its exact location where appropriate; and
- (b)   promptly provide the States referred to in sub-paragraph (a), directly or through the Agency, and the Agency with such available information relevant to minimizing the radiological consequences in those States, as specified in article 5.

Article 3
Other nuclear accidents

With a view to minimizing the radiological consequences, States Parties may notify in the event of nuclear accidents other than those specified in article 1.

Article 4
Functions of the Agency

The Agency shall:
- (a)   forthwith inform States Parties, Member States, other States which are or may be physically affected as specified in article 1 and relevant international intergovernmental organizations (hereinafter referred to as "international organizations") of a notification received pursuant to sub-paragraph (a) of article 2; and
- (b)   promptly provide any State Party, Member State or relevant international organization, upon request, with the information received pursuant to sub-paragraph (b) of article 2.

Article 5
Information to be provided

1. The information to be provided pursuant to sub-paragraph (b) of article 2 shall comprise the following data as then available to the notifying State Party:

(a)   the time, exact location where appropriate, and the nature of the nuclear accident;

(b)   the facility or activity involved;

(c)   the assumed or established cause and the foreseeable development of the nuclear accident relevant to the transboundary release of the radioactive materials;

(d)   the general characteristics of the radioactive release, including, as far as is practicable and appropriate, the nature, probable physical and chemical form and the quantity, composition and effective height of the radioactive release;

(e)   information on current and forecast meteorological and hydrological conditions, necessary for forecasting the transboundary release of the radioactive materials;

(f)   the results of environmental monitoring relevant to the transboundary release of the radioactive materials;

(g)   the off-site protective measures taken or planned;

(h)   the predicted behaviour over time of the radioactive release.

2. Such information shall be supplemented at appropriate intervals by further relevant information on the development of the emergency situation, including its foreseeable or actual termination.

3. Information received pursuant to sub-paragraph (b) of article 2 may be used without restriction, except when such information is provided in confidence by the notifying State Party.

Article 6
Consultations

A State Party providing information pursuant to sub-paragraph (b) of article 2 shall, as far as is reasonably practicable, respond promptly to a request for further information or consultations sought by an affected State Party with a view to minimizing the radiological consequences in that State.

Article 7
Competent authorities and points of contact

1. Each State Party shall make known to the Agency and to other States Parties, directly or through the Agency, its competent authorities and point of contact responsible for issuing and receiving the notification and information referred to in article 2. Such points of contact and a focal point within the Agency shall be available continuously.

2. Each State Party promptly inform the Agency of any changes that may occur in the information referred to in paragraph 1.

3. The Agency shall maintain an up-to-date list of such national authorities and points of contact as well as points of contact of relevant international organizations and shall provide it to States Parties and Member States and to relevant international organizations.

Article 8
Assistance to States Parties

The Agency shall, in accordance with its Statute and upon a request of a State Party which does not have nuclear activities itself and borders on a State having an active nuclear programme but not Party, conduct investigations into the feasibility and establishment of an appropriate radiation monitoring system in order to facilitate the achievement of the objectives of this Convention.

Article 9
Bilateral and multilateral arrangements

In furtherance of their mutual interests, States Parties may consider, where deemed appropriate, the conclusion of bilateral or multilateral arrangements relating to the subject matter of this Convention.

Article 10
Relationship to other international agreements

This Convention shall not affect the reciprocal rights and obligations of States Parties under existing international agreements which relate to the matters covered by this Convention, or under future international agreements concluded in accordance with the object and purpose of this Convention.

Article 11
Settlement of disputes

1. In the event of a dispute between States Parties, or between a State Party and the Agency, concerning the interpretation or application of this Convention, the parties to the dispute shall consult with a view to the settlement of the dispute by negotiation or by any other peaceful means of settling disputes acceptable to them.
2. If a dispute of this character between States Parties cannot be settled within one year from the request for consultation pursuant to paragraph 1, it shall, at the request of any party to such dispute, be submitted to arbitration or referred to the International Court of Justice for decision. Where a dispute is submitted to arbitration, if, within six months from the date of the request, the parties to the dispute are unable to agree on the organization of the arbitration, a party may request the President of the International Court of Justice or the Secretary-General of the United Nations to appoint one or more arbitrators. In cases of conflicting requests by the parties to the dispute, the request to the Secretary-General of the United Nations shall have priority.
3. When signing, ratifying, accepting, approving or acceding to this Convention, a State may declare that it does not consider itself bound by either or both of the dispute settlement procedures provided for in paragraph 2. The other States Parties shall not be bound by a dispute settlement procedure provided for in paragraph 2 with respect to a State Party for which such a declaration is in force.
4. A State Party which has made a declaration in accordance with paragraph 3 may at any time withdraw it by notification to the depositary.

* * *

Article 13
Provisional application

A State may, upon signature or at any later date before this Convention enters into force for it, declare that it will apply this Convention provisionally.

* * *

INTERNATIONAL ATOMIC ENERGY AGENCY CONVENTION ON ASSISTANCE IN THE CASE OF A NUCLEAR ACCIDENT OR RADIOLOGICAL EMERGENCY

Popular Name: Assistance Convention, IAEA Assistance Convention

Done at Vienna on 26 September 1986, UNTS Reg. No. 24643, IAEA INFCIRC/ 336, IAEA Leg Ser. #14, *reprinted in* 25 ILM 1377 (1986).

Entry into Force: 26 February 1987

Depositary: International Atomic Energy Agency (IAEA)

Languages: Arabic, Chinese, English, French, Russian, Spanish

Parties as of 1 January 1990: Australia;* Austria;* Bangladesh; Bulgaria;* Byelor-
ussian Soviet Socialist Republic;* China;* Cyprus; Czech and Slovak Federal
Republic;* Egypt;* France;* German Democratic Republic;* Guatemala; Hun-
gary;* India;* Iraq;* Israel;* Japan;* Jordan; Malaysia;* Mexico; Mongolia;*
New Zealand; Norway;* Poland;* Saudi Arabia;* South Africa;* Switzerland;
Thailand;* Tunisia; Ukrainian Soviet Socialist Republic;* Union of Soviet So-
cialist Republics;* United Arab Emirates;* United States of America;* Viet
Nam;* World Health Organization
Literature: A. O. Adede, *The IAEA Assistance and Notification Conventions in
Case of a Nuclear Accident* (1987)

CONVENTION ON ASSISTANCE IN THE CASE OF A NUCLEAR ACCIDENT OR RADIOLOGICAL EMERGENCY

THE STATES PARTIES TO THIS CONVENTION,
   AWARE that nuclear activities are being carried out in a number of States,
   NOTING that comprehensive measures have been and are being taken to
ensure a high level of safety in nuclear activities, aimed at preventing nuclear
accidents and minimizing the consequences of any such accident, should it occur,
   DESIRING to strengthen further international co-operation in the safe development and use of nuclear energy,
   CONVINCED of the need for an international framework which will facilitate
the prompt provision of assistance in the event of a nuclear accident or radiological
emergency to mitigate its consequences,
   NOTING the usefulness of bilateral and multilateral arrangements on mutual
assistance in this area,
   NOTING the activities of the International Atomic Energy Agency in developing guidelines for mutual emergency assistance arrangements in connection with
a nuclear accident or radiological emergency,
   HAVE AGREED as follows:

---

*Indicates a reservation and/or declaration

Article 1
General provisions

1. The States Parties shall co-operate between themselves and with the International Atomic Energy Agency (hereinafter referred to as the "Agency") in accordance with the provisions of this Convention to facilitate prompt assistance in the event of a nuclear accident or radiological emergency to minimize its consequences and to protect life, property and the environment from the effects of radioactive releases.
2. To facilitate such co-operation States Parties may agree on bilateral or multilateral arrangements or, where appropriate, a combination of these, for preventing or minimizing injury and damage which may result in the event of a nuclear accident or radiological emergency.
3. The States Parties request the Agency, acting within the framework of its Statute, to use its best endeavours in accordance with the provisions of this Convention to promote, facilitate and support the co-operation between States Parties provided for in this Convention.

Article 2
Provision of assistance

1. If a State Party needs assistance in the event of a nuclear accident or radiological emergency, whether or not such accident or emergency originates within its territory, jurisdiction or control, it may call for such assistance from any other State Party, directly or through the Agency, and from the Agency, or, where appropriate, from other international intergovernmental organizations (hereinafter referred to as "international organizations").
2. A State Party requesting assistance shall specify the scope and type of assistance required and, where practicable, provide the assisting party with such information as may be necessary for that party to determine the extent to which it is able to meet the request. In the event that it is not practicable for the requesting State Party to specify the scope and type of assistance required, the requesting State Party and the assisting party shall, in consultation, decide upon the scope and type of assistance required.
3. Each State Party to which a request for such assistance is directed shall promptly decide and notify the requesting State Party, directly or through the Agency, whether it is in a position to render the assistance requested, and the scope and terms of the assistance that might be rendered.
4. States Parties shall, within the limits of their capabilities, identify and notify the Agency of experts, equipment and materials which could be made available for the provision of assistance to other States Parties in the event of a nuclear accident or radiological emergency as well as the terms, especially financial, under which such assistance could be provided.
5. Any State Party may request assistance relating to medical treatment or temporary relocation into the territory of another State Party of people involved in a nuclear accident or radiological emergency.
6. The Agency shall respond, in accordance with its Statute and as provided for in this Convention, to a requesting State Party's or a Member State's request for assistance in the event of a nuclear accident or radiological emergency by:
   (a)   making available appropriate resources allocated for this purpose;
   (b)   transmitting promptly the request to other States and international organizations which, according to the Agency's information, may possess the necessary resources; and
   (c)   if so requested by the requesting State, co-ordinating the assistance at the international level which may thus become available.

Article 3
Direction and control of assistance

Unless otherwise agreed:

(a) the overall direction, control, co-ordination and supervision of the assistance shall be the responsibility within its territory of the requesting State. The assisting party should, where the assistance involves personnel, designate in consultation with the requesting State, the person who should be in charge of and retain immediate operational supervision over the personnel and the equipment provided by it. The designated person should exercise such supervision in co-operation with the appropriate authorities of the requesting State;

(b) the requesting State shall provide, to the extent of its capabilities, local facilities and services for the proper and effective administration of the assistance. It shall also ensure the protection of personnel, equipment and materials brought into its territory by or on behalf of the assisting party for such purpose;

(c) ownership of equipment and materials provided by either party during the periods of assistance shall be unaffected, and their return shall be ensured;

(d) a State Party providing assistance in response to a request under paragraph 5 of article 2 shall co-ordinate that assistance within its territory.

Article 4
Competent authorities and points of contact

1. Each State Party shall make known to the Agency and to other States Parties, directly or through the Agency, its competent authorities and point of contact authorized to make and receive requests for and to accept offers of assistance. Such points of contact and a focal point within the Agency shall be available continuously.

2. Each State Party shall promptly inform the Agency of any changes that may occur in the information referred to in paragraph 1.

3. The Agency shall regularly and expeditiously provide to States Parties, Member States and relevant international organizations the information referred to in paragraphs 1 and 2.

Article 5
Functions of the Agency

The States Parties request the Agency, in accordance with paragraph 3 of article 1 and without prejudice to other provisions of this Convention, to:

(a) collect and disseminate to States Parties and Member States information concerning:
   (i) experts, equipment and materials which could be made available in the event of nuclear accidents or radiological emergencies;
   (ii) methodologies, techniques and available results of research relating to response to nuclear accidents or radiological emergencies;

(b) assist a State Party or a Member State when requested in any of the following or other appropriate matters:
   (i) preparing both emergency plans in the case of nuclear accidents and radiological emergencies and the appropriate legislation;
   (ii) developing appropriate training programmes for personnel to deal with nuclear accidents and radiological emergencies;
   (iii) transmitting requests for assistance and relevant information in the event of a nuclear accident or radiological emergency;

      (iv) developing appropriate radiation monitoring programmes, proce-
dures and standards;

      (v) conducting investigations into the feasibility of establishing appro-
priate radiation monitoring systems;

(c)   make available to a State Party or a Member State requesting assistance
in the event of a nuclear accident or radiological emergency appropriate
resources allocated for the purpose of conducting an initial assessment
of the accident or emergency;

(d)   offer its good offices to the States Parties and Member States in the event
of a nuclear accident or radiological emergency;

(e)   establish and maintain liaison with relevant international organizations
for the purposes of obtaining and exchanging relevant information and
data, and make a list of such organizations available to States Parties,
Member States and the aforementioned organizations.

Article 6
Confidentiality and public statements

1. The requesting State and the assisting party shall protect the confidentiality of
any confidential information that becomes available to either of them in connection with the assistance in the event of a nuclear accident or radiological emergency. Such information shall be used exclusively for the purpose of the assistance agreed upon.
2. The assisting party shall make every effort to co-ordinate with the requesting
State before releasing information to the public on the assistance provided in
connection with a nuclear accident or radiological emergency.

Article 7
Reimbursement of costs

1. An assisting party may offer assistance without costs to the requesting State.
When considering whether to offer assistance on such a basis, the assisting party
shall take into account:
   (a)   the nature of the nuclear accident or radiological emergency;
   (b)   the place of origin of the nuclear accident or radiological emergency;
   (c)   the needs of developing countries;
   (d)   the particular needs of countries without nuclear facilities; and
   (e)   any other relevant factors.
2. When assistance is provided wholly or partly on a reimbursement basis, the
requesting State shall reimburse the assisting party for the costs incurred for the
services rendered by persons or organizations acting on its behalf, and for all
expenses in connection with the assistance to the extent that such expenses
are not directly defrayed by the requesting State. Unless otherwise agreed,
reimbursement shall be provided promptly after the assisting party has presented
its request for reimbursement to the requesting State, and in respect of costs
other than local costs, shall be freely transferrable.
3. Notwithstanding paragraph 2, the assisting party may at any time waive, or
agree to the postponement of, the reimbursement in whole or in part. In considering such waiver or postponement, assisting parties shall give due consideration
to the needs of developing countries.

Article 8
Privileges, immunities and facilities

1. The requesting State shall afford to personnel of the assisting party and personnel acting on its behalf the necessary privileges, immunities and facilities for
the performance of their assistance functions.

2. The requesting State shall afford the following privileges and immunities to personnel of the assisting party or personnel acting on its behalf who have been duly notified to and accepted by the requesting State:
   (a)   immunity from arrest, detention and legal process, including criminal, civil and administrative jurisdiction, of the requesting State, in respect of acts or omissions in the performance of their duties; and
   (b)   exemption from taxation, duties or other charges, except those which are normally incorporated in the price of goods or paid for services rendered, in respect of the performance of their assistance functions.
3. The requesting State shall:
   (a)   afford the assisting party exemption from taxation, duties or other charges on the equipment and property brought into the territory of the requesting State by the assisting party for the purpose of the assistance; and
   (b)   provide immunity from seizure, attachment or requisition of such equipment and property.
4. The requesting State shall ensure the return of such equipment and property. If requested by the assisting party, the requesting State shall arrange, to the extent it is able to do so, for the necessary decontamination of recoverable equipment involved in the assistance before its return.
5. The requesting State shall facilitate the entry into, stay in and departure from its national territory of personnel notified pursuant to paragraph 2 and of equipment and property involved in the assistance.
6. Nothing in this article shall require the requesting State to provide its nationals or permanent residents with the privileges and immunities provided for in the foregoing paragraphs.
7. Without prejudice to the privileges and immunities, all beneficiaries enjoying such privileges and immunities under this article have a duty to respect the laws and regulations of the requesting State. They shall also have the duty not to interfere in the domestic affairs of the requesting State.
8. Nothing in this article shall prejudice rights and obligations with respect to privileges and immunities afforded pursuant to other international agreements or the rules of customary international law.
9. When signing, ratifying, accepting, approving or acceding to this Convention, a State may declare that it does not consider itself bound in whole or in part by paragraphs 2 and 3.
10. A State Party which has made a declaration in accordance with paragraph 9 may at any time withdraw it by notification to the depositary.

Article 9
Transit of personnel, equipment and property

Each State Party shall, at the request of the requesting State or the assisting party, seek to facilitate the transit through its territory of duly notified personnel, equipment and property involved in the assistance to and from the requesting State.

Article 10
Claims and compensation

1. The States Parties shall closely co-operate in order to facilitate the settlement of legal proceedings and claims under this article.
2. Unless otherwise agreed, a requesting State shall in respect of death or of injury to persons, damage to or loss of property, or damage to the environment caused within its territory or other area under its jurisdiction or control in the course of providing the assistance requested:
   (a)   not bring any legal proceedings against the assisting party or persons or other legal entities acting on its behalf;

(b)   assume responsibility for dealing with legal proceedings and claims brought by third parties against the assisting party or against persons or other legal entities acting on its behalf;

(c)   hold the assisting party or persons or other legal entities acting on its behalf harmless in respect of legal proceedings and claims referred to in sub-paragraph (b); and

(d)   compensate the assisting party or persons or other legal entities acting on its behalf for:

    (i)   death of or injury to personnel of the assisting party or persons acting on its behalf;

    (ii) loss of or damage to non-consumable equipment or materials related to the assistance;

except in cases of wilful misconduct by the individuals who caused the death, injury, loss or damage.

3. This article shall not prevent compensation or indemnity available under any applicable international agreement or national law of any State.

4. Nothing in this article shall require the requesting State to apply paragraph 2 in whole or in part to its nationals or permanent residents.

5. When signing, ratifying, accepting, approving or acceding to this Convention, a State may declare:

(a)   that it does not consider itself bound in whole or in part by paragraph 2;

(b)   that it will not apply paragraph 2 in whole or in part in cases of gross negligence by the individuals who caused the death, injury, loss or damage.

6. A State Party which has made a declaration in accordance with paragraph 5 may at any time withdraw it by notification to the depositary.

Article 11
Termination of assistance

The requesting State or the assisting party may at any time, after appropriate consultations and by notification in writing, request the termination of assistance received or provided under this Convention. Once such a request has been made, the parties involved shall consult with each other to make arrangements for the proper conclusion of the assistance.

Article 12
Relationship to other international agreements

This Convention shall not affect the reciprocal rights and obligations of States Parties under existing international agreements which relate to the matters covered by this Convention, or under future international agreements concluded in accordance with the object and purpose of this Convention.

Article 13
Settlement of disputes

1. In the event of a dispute between States Parties, or between a State Party and the Agency, concerning the interpretation or application of this Convention, the parties to the dispute shall consult with a view to the settlement of the dispute by negotiation or by any other peaceful means of settling disputes acceptable to them.

2. If a dispute of this character between States Parties cannot be settled within one year from the request for consultation pursuant to paragraph 1, it shall, at the request of any party to such dispute, be submitted to arbitration or referred to

the International Court of Justice for decision. Where a dispute is submitted to arbitration, if, within six months from the date of the request, the parties to the dispute are unable to agree on the organization of the arbitration, a party may request the President of the International Court of Justice or the Secretary-General of the United Nations to appoint one or more arbitrators. In cases of conflicting requests by the parties to the dispute, the request to the Secretary-General of the United Nations shall have priority.

3. When signing, ratifying, accepting, approving or acceding to this Convention a State may declare that it does not consider itself bound by either or both of the dispute settlement procedures provided for in paragraph 2. The other States Parties shall not be bound by a dispute settlement procedure provided for in paragraph 2 with respect to a State Party for which such a declaration is in force.

4. A State Party which has made a declaration in accordance with paragraph 3 may at any time withdraw it by notification to the depositary.

* * *

Article 15
Provisional application

A State may, upon signature or at any later date before this Convention enters into force for it, declare that it will apply this Convention provisionally.

* * *

CHAPTER 14
ENERGY PRODUCTION (non-nuclear)

(No instruments reproduced)

CHAPTER 15
INDUSTRIAL ACTIVITIES

B. CHEMICAL

**UNITED NATIONS ENVIRONMENT PROGRAMME
GOVERNING COUNCIL DECISION: LONDON GUIDELINES
FOR THE EXCHANGES OF INFORMATION ON
CHEMICALS IN INTERNATIONAL TRADE.** *Infra,* p. 644.

C. MINING

**WELLINGTON CONVENTION ON THE REGULATION OF
ANTARCTIC MINERAL RESOURCE ACTIVITIES.** *Supra,* p.
529.

CHAPTER 16
AGRICULTURAL ACTIVIES

(No instruments reproduced)

CHAPTER 17
WASTE DISPOSAL

C. WASTE WATER

INTERNATIONAL MARITIME ORGANIZATION CONVENTION ON THE PREVENTION OF MARINE POLLUTION BY DUMPING OF WASTES AND OTHER MATTER. *Supra*, p. 318.

D. RADIOACTIVE

INTERNATIONAL ATOMIC ENERGY AGENCY CODE OF PRACTICE ON THE INTERNATIONAL TRANSBOUNDARY MOVEMENT OF RADIOACTIVE WASTE

Popular Name: IAEA Code on Radioactive Waste Movement

Done 21 September 1990, IAEGC(34)/RES/530, IAEA Doc. GC(34)/920.

Languages: Arabic, Chinese, English, French, Russian, Spanish

Editors' Note

In 1988, the IAEA General Conference requested the Director General of the Agency to establish a technical working group of experts to elaborate an "internationally agreed code of practice for international transactions involving nuclear wastes." The Technical Working Group of Experts was composed of experts from 20 member States of the Agency and of observers from five further members and from four international organizations. It met 22-25 May 1989 and 5-9 February 1990, and at its second session agreed on a Code of Practice on the International Transboundary Movement of Radioactive Waste. After reviewing the Code at its June 1990 session, the Agency's Board requested that it be transmitted to the General Conference, which adopted it at its 34th session. This nonbinding instrument in effect supplements the Basel Convention (*infra*, p. 601), to which it refers in its preamble.

CODE OF PRACTICE ON THE INTERNATIONAL TRANSBOUNDARY MOVEMENT OF RADIOACTIVE WASTE

The Group of Experts,*
* * *

DECIDES that the following Code of Practice should serve as guidelines to States for, inter alia, the development and harmonization of policies and laws on the international transboundary movement of radioactive waste.*

I. SCOPE

This Code applies to the international transboundary movement of radioactive waste.

It relies on international standards for the safe transport of radioactive material and the physical protection of nuclear material, as well as the standards for basic nuclear safety and radiation protection and radioactive waste management; it does not establish separate guidance in these areas. Furthermore, this Code, which is advisory, does not affect in any way existing and future arrangements among States which relate to matters covered by it and are compatible with its objectives.[2]

II. DEFINITIONS

For the purpose of this Code:

"*radioactive waste*" is any material that contains or is contaminated with radionuclides at concentrations or radioactivity levels greater than the "exempt quantities"[3] established by the competent authorities and for which no use is foreseen.[4]

"*disposal*" means the emplacement of waste in a repository, or at a given location, without the intention of retrieval.

"*management*" means all activities, administrative and operational, that are involved in the handling, treatment, conditioning, transportation and storage of waste.

"*competent authority*" means an authority designated or otherwise recognized by a government for specific purposes in connection with radiation protection and/or nuclear safety.

III. BASIC PRINCIPLES

---

*Group of Experts established pursuant to General Conference resolution GC(XXXII)/RES/490. "Dumping of Nuclear Wastes".

*The Group of Experts held two meetings: 22-25 May 1989 and 5-9 February 1990. This Code of Practice was adopted by the Group on 9 February 1990.

[2]Nothing in this Code prejudices or affects in any way the exercise by ships and aircraft of all States of maritime and air navigation rights and freedoms under customary international law, as reflected in the 1982 United Nations Convention on the Law of the Sea, and under other relevant international legal instruments.

[3]"*Exempt quantities*", in relation to radioactive waste, are levels of radionuclide concentration, surface contamination, radiation and/or total activity below which the competent authority decides to exempt from regulatory requirements because the individual and collective effective dose equivalents received from them are so low that such levels are not significant for purposes of radiation protection. Such exempt quantities should be agreed by the competent authorities in the countries concerned with the international transboundary radioactive waste movement.

[4]Spent fuel which is not intended for disposal is not considered to be radioactive waste.

GENERAL

1. Every State should take the appropriate steps necessary to ensure that radioactive waste within its territory, or under its jurisdiction or control is safely managed and disposed of, to ensure the protection of human health and the environment.

2. Every State should take the appropriate steps necessary to minimize the amount of radioactive waste, taking into account social, environmental, technological and economic considerations.

INTERNATIONAL TRANSBOUNDARY MOVEMENT

3. It is the sovereign right of every State to prohibit the movement of radioactive waste into, from or through its territory.

4. Every State involved in the international transboundary movement of radioactive waste should take the appropriate steps necessary to ensure that such movement is undertaken in a manner consistent with international safety standards.

5. Every State should take the appropriate steps necessary to ensure that, subject to the relevant norms of international law, the international transboundary movement of radioactive waste takes place only with the prior notification and consent of the sending, receiving and transit States in accordance with their respective laws and regulations.

6. Every State involved in the international transboundary movement of radioactive waste should have a relevant regulatory authority and adopt appropriate procedures as necessary for the regulation of such movement.

7. No receiving State should permit the receipt of radioactive waste for management or disposal unless it has the administrative and technical capacity and regulatory structure to manage and dispose of such waste in a manner consistent with international safety standards. The sending State should satisfy itself in accordance with the receiving State's consent that the above requirement is met prior to the international transboundary movement of radioactive waste.

8. Every State should take the appropriate steps to introduce into its national laws and regulations relevant provisions as necessary for liability, compensation or other remedies for damage that could arise from the international transboundary movement of radioactive waste.

9. Every State should take the appropriate steps necessary, including the adoption of laws and regulations, to ensure that the international transboundary movement of radioactive waste is carried out in accordance with this Code.

INTERNATIONAL CO-OPERATION

10. The sending State should take the appropriate steps necessary to permit readmission into its territory of any radioactive waste previously transferred from its territory if such transfer is not or cannot be completed in conformity with this Code, unless an alternative safe arrangement can be made.[5]

11. States should co-operate at the bilateral, regional and international levels for the purpose of preventing any international transboundary movement of radioactive waste that is not in conformity with this Code.

IV. ROLE OF THE IAEA

The IAEA should continue to collect and disseminate information on the laws, regulations and technical standards pertaining to radioactive waste management and

---

[5]The above would not apply to waste which is associated with, or results from, a service provided by the sending State to the receiving State and which is subject to a contractual arrangement between them that such waste be returned to the receiving State.

disposal, develop relevent technical standards and provide advice and assistance on all aspects of radioactive waste management and disposal, having particular regard to the needs of developing countries.

The IAEA should review this Code as appropriate, taking into account experience gained and technological developments.

BASEL CONVENTION ON THE CONTROL OF TRANSBOUNDARY MOVEMENTS OF HAZARDOUS WASTES AND THEIR DISPOSAL. *Infra,* p. 601.

CANADA-UNITED STATES: AGREEMENT BETWEEN THE UNITED STATES AND CANADA CONCERNING THE TRANSBOUNDARY MOVEMENT OF HAZARDOUS WASTE. *Infra,* p. 616.

MEXICO-UNITED STATES: AGREEMENT FOR COOPERATION ON ENVIRONMENTAL PROGRAMS AND TRANSBOUNDARY PROBLEMS, ANNEX III, TRANSBOUNDARY SHIPMENT OF HAZARDOUS WASTES AND HAZARDOUS SUBSTANCES. *Infra,* p. 621.

CHAPTER 18
HAZARDOUS SUBSTANCES

B. TRANSPORT

BASEL CONVENTION ON THE CONTROL OF TRANSBOUNDARY MOVEMENTS OF HAZARDOUS WASTES AND THEIR DISPOSAL

Popular Name: Basel Convention

Done at Basel on 22 March 1989, U.N. Doc. UNEP/WG.190/4, UNEP/IG.80/3 (1989), *reprinted in* 28 ILM 657 (1989).

Entry into Force: Not yet in force

Depositary: United Nations

Languages: Arabic, Chinese, English, French, Russian, Spanish

Contracting States as of 15 November 1990: Hungary; Jordan; Norway;* Saudi Arabia; Switzerland

Editors' Note

The Basel Convention is designed to control the export of hazardous wastes. The African countries, in particular, have been very concerned about developed countries using Africa as a "dumping ground" for hazardous waste. In May 1988, the Organization of African Unity (OAU) passed a resolution banning the import of hazardous wastes. 28 ILM 568 (1989). The Convention prohibits the export of hazardous wastes to countries that have not consented in writing to the particular shipment or that have prohibited the import of hazardous wastes altogether, and it prohibits the export if the exporting State "has reason to believe that the wastes in question will not be managed in an environmentally sound manner." Consent is also required from transit States.

Work is underway on a liability protocol to the Convention. A nonbinding Code of Practice on the International Transboundary Movement of Radioactive Waste, which in effect supplements the Basel Convention, was adopted by the General Conference of the International Atomic Energy Agency in June 1990 (*supra*, p. 597).

---

*With statement

BASEL CONVENTION ON THE CONTROL OF TRANSBOUNDARY MOVEMENTS OF HAZARDOUS WASTES AND THEIR DISPOSAL

PREAMBLE

The Parties to this Convention,

Aware of the risk of damage to human health and the environment caused by hazardous wastes and other wastes and the transboundary movement thereof,

Mindful of the growing threat to human health and the environment posed by the increased generation and complexity, and transboundary movement of hazardous wastes and other wastes,

Mindful also that the most effective way of protecting human health and the environment from the dangers posed by such wastes is the reduction of their generation to a minimum in terms of quantity and/or hazard potential,

Convinced that States should take necessary measures to ensure that the management of hazardous wastes and other wastes including their transboundary movement and disposal is consistent with the protection of human health and the environment whatever the place of their disposal,

Noting that States should ensure that the generator should carry out duties with regard to the transport and disposal of hazardous wastes and other wastes in a manner that is consistent with the protection of the environment, whatever the place of disposal,

Fully recognizing that any State has the sovereign right to ban the entry or disposal of foreign hazardous wastes and other wastes in its territory,

Recognizing also the increasing desire for the prohibition of transboundary movements of hazardous wastes and their disposal in other States, especially developing countries,

Convinced that hazardous wastes and other wastes should, as far as is compatible with environmentally sound and efficient management, be disposed of in State where they were generated,

Aware also that transboundary movements of such wastes from the State of their generation to any other State should be permitted only when conducted under conditions which do not endanger human health and the environment, and under conditions in conformity with the provisions of this Convention,

Considering that enhanced control of transboundary movement of hazardous wastes and other wastes will act as an incentive for their environmentally sound management and for the reduction of the volume of such transboundary movement,

Convinced that States should take measures for the proper exchange of information on and control of the transboundary movement of hazardous wastes and other wastes from and to those States,

Noting that a number of international and regional agreements have addressed the issue of protection and preservation of the environment with regard to the transit of dangerous goods.

Taking into account the Declaration of the United Nations Conference on the Human Environment (Stockholm, 1972), the Cairo Guidelines and Principles for the Environmentally Sound Management of Hazardous Wastes adopted by the Governing Council of the United Nations Environment Programme (UNEP) by decision 14/30 of 17 June 1987, the Recommendations of the United Nations Committee of Experts on the Transport of Dangerous Goods (formulated in 1957 and updated biennially), relevant recommendations, declarations, instruments and regulations adopted within the United Nations system and the work and studies done within other international and regional organizations,

Mindful of the spirit, principles, aims and functions of the World Charter for Nature adopted by the General Assembly of the United Nations at its thirty-seventh session (1982) as the rule of ethics in respect of the protection of the human environment and the conservation of natural resources,

Affirming that States are responsible for the fulfilment of their international obligations concerning the protection of human health and protection and preservation of the environment, and are liable in accordance with international law,

Recognizing that in the case of a material breach of the provisions of this Convention or any protocol thereto the relevant international law of treaties shall apply,

Aware of the need to continue the development and implementation of environmentally sound low-waste technologies, recycling options, good house-keeping and management systems with a view to reducing to a minimum the generation of hazardous wastes and other wastes,

Aware also of the growing international concern about the need for stringent control of transboundary movement of hazardous wastes and other wastes, and of the need as far as possible to reduce such movement to a minimum,

Concerned about the problem of illegal transboundary traffic in hazardous wastes and other wastes,

Taking into account also the limited capabilities of the developing countries to manage hazardous wastes and other wastes,

Recognizing the need to promote the transfer of technology for the sound management of hazardous wastes and other wastes produced locally, particularly to the developing countries in accordance with the spirit of the Cairo Guidelines and decision 14/16 of the Governing Council of UNEP on Promotion of the transfer of environmental protection technology,

Recognizing also that hazardous wastes and other wastes should be transported in accordance with relevant international conventions and recommendations,

Convinced also that the transboundary movement of hazardous wastes and other wastes should be permitted only when the transport and the ultimate disposal of such wastes is environmentally sound, and

Determined to protect, by strict control, human health and the environment against the adverse effects which may result from the generation and management of hazardous wastes and other wastes,

HAVE AGREED AS FOLLOWS:

Article 1
Scope of the Convention

1. The following wastes that are subject to transboundary movement shall be "hazardous wastes" for the purposes of this Convention:
   (a) Wastes that belong to any category contained in Annex I, unless they do not possess any of the characteristics contained in Annex III; and
   (b) Wastes that are not covered under paragraph (a) but are defined as, or are considered to be, hazardous wastes by the domestic legislation of the Party of export, import or transit.

2. Wastes that belong to any category contained in Annex II that are subject to transboundary movement shall be "other wastes" for the purposes of this Convention.

3. Wastes which, as a result of being radioactive, are subject to other international control systems, including international instruments, applying specifically to radioactive materials, are excluded from the scope of this Convention.

4. Wastes which derive from the normal operations of a ship, the discharge of which is covered by another international instrument, are excluded from the scope of this Convention.

Article 2
Definitions

For the purposes of this Convention:

1. "Wastes" are substances or objects which are disposed of or are intended to be disposed of or are required to be disposed of by the provisions of national law;

2. "Management" means the collection, transport and disposal of hazardous wastes or other wastes, including after-care of disposal sites;

3. "Transboundary movement" means any movement of hazardous wastes or other wastes from an area under the national jurisdiction of one State to or through an area under the national jurisdiction of another State or to or through an area not under the national jurisdiction of any State, provided at least two States are involved in the movement;

4. "Disposal" means any operation specified in Annex IV to this Convention;

5. "Approved site or facility" means a site or facility for the disposal of hazardous wastes or other wastes which is authorized or permitted to operate for this purpose by a relevant authority of the State where the site or facility is located;

6. "Competent authority" means one governmental authority designated by a Party to be responsible, within such geographical areas as the Party may think fit, for receiving the notification of a transboundary movement of hazardous wastes or other wastes, and any information related to it, and for responding to such a notification, as provided in Article 6;

7. "Focal point" means the entity of a Party referred to in Article 5 responsible for receiving and submitting information as provided for in Articles 13 and 15;

8. "Environmentally sound management of hazardous wastes or other wastes" means taking all practicable steps to ensure that hazardous wastes or other wastes are managed in a manner which will protect human health and the environment against the adverse effects which may result from such wastes;

9. "Area under the national jurisdiction of a State" means any land, marine area or airspace within which a State exercises administrative and regulatory responsibility in accordance with international law in regard to the protection of human health or the environment;

10. "State of export" means a Party from which a transboundary movement of hazardous wastes or other wastes is planned to be initiated or is initiated;

11. "State of import" means a Party to which a transboundary movement of hazardous wastes or other wastes is planned or takes place for the purpose of disposal therein or for the purpose of loading prior to disposal in an area not under the national jurisdiction of any State;

12. "State of transit" means any State, other than the State of export or import, through which a movement of hazardous wastes or other wastes is planned or takes place;

13. "States concerned" means Parties which are States of export or import, or transit States, whether or not Parties;

14. "Person" means any natural or legal person;

15. "Exporter" means any person under the jurisdiction of the State of export who arranges for hazardous wastes or other wastes to be exported;

16. "Importer" means any person under the jurisdiction of the State of import who arranges for hazardous wastes or other wastes to be imported;

17. "Carrier" means any person who carries out the transport of hazardous wastes or other wastes;

18. "Generator" means any person whose activity produces hazardous wastes or other wastes or, if that person is not known, the person who is in possession and/or control of those wastes;

19. "Disposer" means any person to whom hazardous wastes or other wastes are shipped and who carries out the disposal of such wastes;

20. "Political and/or economic integration organization" means an organization constituted by sovereign States to which its member States have transferred competence in respect of matters governed by this Convention and which has been duly authorized, in accordance with its internal procedures, to sign, ratify, accept, approve, formally confirm or accede to it;
21. "Illegal traffic" means any transboundary movement of hazardous wastes or other wastes as specified in Article 9.

Article 3
National Definitions of Hazardous Wastes

1. Each Party shall, within six months of becoming a Party to this Convention, inform the Secretariat of the Convention of the wastes, other than those listed in Annexes I and II, considered or defined as hazardous under its national legislation and of any requirements concerning transboundary movement procedures applicable to such wastes.
2. Each Party shall subsequently inform the Secretariat of any significant changes to the information it has provided pursuant to paragraph 1.
3. The Secretariat shall forthwith inform all Parties of the information it has received pursuant to paragraphs 1 and 2.
4. Parties shall be responsible for making the information transmitted to them by the Secretariat under paragraph 3 available to their exporters.

Article 4
General Obligations

1. (a) Parties exercising their right to prohibit the import of hazardous wastes or other wastes for disposal shall inform the other Parties of their decision pursuant to Article 13.
   (b) Parties shall prohibit or shall not permit the export of hazardous wastes and other wastes to the Parties which have prohibited the import of such wastes, when notified pursuant to subparagraph (a) above.
   (c) Parties shall prohibit or shall not permit the export of hazardous wastes and other wastes if the State of import does not consent in writing to the specific import, in the case where that State of import has not prohibited the import of such wastes.
2. Each Party shall take the appropriate measures to:
   (a) Ensure that the generation of hazardous wastes and other wastes within it is reduced to a minimum, taking into account social, technological and economic aspects;
   (b) Ensure the availability of adequate disposal facilities, for the environmentally sound management of hazardous wastes and other wastes, that shall be located, to the extent possible, within it, whatever the place of their disposal;
   (c) Ensure that persons involved in the management of hazardous wastes or other wastes within it take such steps as are necessary to prevent pollution due to hazardous wastes and other wastes arising from such management and, if such pollution occurs, to minimize the consequences thereof for human health and the environment;
   (d) Ensure that the transboundary movement of hazardous wastes and other wastes is reduced to the minimum consistent with the environmentally sound and efficient management of such wastes, and is conducted in a manner which will protect human health and the environment against the adverse effects which may result from such movement;
   (e) Not allow the export of hazardous wastes or other wastes to a State or group of States belonging to an economic and/or political integration

organization that are Parties, particularly developing countries, which have prohibited by their legislation all imports, or if it has reason to believe that the wastes in question will not be managed in an environmentally sound manner, according to criteria to be decided on by the Parties at their first meeting.

(f) Require that information about a proposed transboundary movement of hazardous wastes and other wastes be provided to the States concerned, according to Annex V A, to state clearly the effects of the proposed movement on human health and the environment;

(g) Prevent the import of hazardous wastes and other wastes if it has reason to believe that the wastes in question will not be managed in an environmentally sound manner;

(h) Co-operate in activities with other Parties and interested organizations, directly and through the Secretariat, including the dissemination of information on the transboundary movement of hazardous wastes and other wastes, in order to improve the environmentally sound management of such wastes and to achieve the prevention of illegal traffic;

3. The Parties consider that illegal traffic in hazardous wastes or other wastes is criminal.

4. Each Party shall take appropriate legal, administrative and other measures to implement and enforce the provisions of this Convention, including measures to prevent and punish conduct in contravention of the Convention.

5. A Party shall not permit hazardous wastes or other wastes to be exported to a non-Party or to be imported from a non-Party.

6. The Parties agree not to allow the export of hazardous wastes or other wastes for disposal within the area south of 60° South latitude, whether or not such wastes are subject to transboundary movement.

7. Furthermore, each Party shall:

(a) Prohibit all persons under its national jurisdiction from transporting or disposing of hazardous wastes or other wastes unless such persons are authorized or allowed to perform such types of operations;

(b) Require that hazardous wastes and other wastes that are to be the subject of a transboundary movement be packaged, labelled, and transported in conformity with generally accepted and recognized international rules and standards in the field of packaging, labelling, and transport, and that due account is taken of relevant internationally recognized practices;

(c) Require that hazardous wastes and other wastes be accompanied by a movement document from the point at which a transboundary movement commences to the point of disposal.

8. Each Party shall require that hazardous wastes or other wastes, to be exported, are managed in an environmentally sound manner in the State of import or elsewhere. Technical guidelines for the environmentally sound management of wastes subject to this Convention shall be decided by the Parties at their first meeting.

9. Parties shall take the appropriate measures to ensure that the transboundary movement of hazardous wastes and other wastes only be allowed if:

(a) The State of export does not have the technical capacity and the necessary facilities, capacity or suitable disposal sites in order to dispose of the wastes in question in an environmentally sound and efficient manner; or

(b) The wastes in question are required as a raw material for recycling or recovery industries in the State of import; or

(c) The transboundary movement in question is in accordance with other criteria to be decided by the Parties, provided those criteria do not differ from the objectives of this Convention.

10. The obligation under this Convention of States in which hazardous wastes and other wastes are generated to require that those wastes are managed in an

environmentally sound manner may not under any circumstances be transferred to the States of import or transit.

11. Nothing in this Convention shall prevent a Party from imposing additional requirements that are consistent with the provisions of this Convention, and are in accordance with the rules of international law, in order better to protect human health and the environment.

12. Nothing in this Convention shall affect in any way the sovereignty of States over their territorial sea established in accordance with international law, and the sovereign rights and the jurisdiction which States have in their exclusive economic zones and their continental shelves in accordance with international law, and the exercise by ships and aircraft of all States of navigational rights and freedoms as provided for in international law and as reflected in relevant international instruments.

13. Parties shall undertake to review periodically the possibilities for the reduction of the amount and/or the pollution potential of hazardous wastes and other wastes which are exported to other States, in particular to developing countries.

Article 5
Designation of Competent Authorities and Focal Point

To facilitate the implementation of this Convention, the Parties shall:

1. Designate or establish one or more competent authorities and one focal point. One competent authority shall be designated to receive the notification in case of a State of transit.

2. Inform the Secretariat, within three months of the date of the entry into force of this Convention for them, which agencies they have designated as their focal point and their competent authorities.

3. Inform the Secretariat, within one month of the date of decision, of any changes regarding the designation made by them under paragraph 2 above.

Article 6
Transboundary Movement between Parties

1. The State of export shall notify, or shall require the generator or exporter to notify, in writing, through the channel of the competent authority of the State of export, the competent authority of the States concerned of any proposed transboundary movement of hazardous wastes or other wastes. Such notification shall contain the declarations and information specified in Annex V A, written in a language acceptable to the State of import. Only one notification needs to be sent to each State concerned.

2. The State of import shall respond to the notifier in writing, consenting to the movement with or without conditions, denying permission for the movement, or requesting additional information. A copy of the final response of the State of import shall be sent to the competent authorities of the States concerned which are Parties.

3. The State of export shall not allow the generator or exporter to commence the transboundary movement until it has received written confirmation that:

(a)   The notifier has received the written consent of the State of import; and

(b)   The notifier has received from the State of import confirmation of the existence of a contract between the exporter and the disposer specifying environmentally sound management of the wastes in question.

4. Each State of transit which is a Party shall promptly acknowledge to the notifier receipt of the notification. It may subsequently respond to the notifier in writing, within 60 days, consenting to the movement with or without conditions, denying permission for the movement, or requesting additional information. The State of

export shall not allow the transboundary movement to commence until it has received the written consent of the State of transit. However, if at any time a Party decides not to require prior written consent, either generally or under specific conditions, for transit transboundary movements of hazardous wastes or other wastes, or modifies its requirements in this respect, it shall forthwith inform the other Parties of its decision pursuant to Article 13. In this latter case, if no response is received by the State of export within 60 days of the receipt of a given notification by the State of transit, the State of export may allow the export to proceed through the State of transit.

5. In the case of a transboundary movement of wastes where the wastes are legally defined as or considered to be hazardous wastes only:

    (a)   By the State of export, the requirements of paragraph 9 of this Article that apply to the importer or disposer and the State of import shall apply *mutatis mutandis* to the exporter and State of export, respectively;

    (b)   By the State of import, or by the States of import and transit which are Parties, the requirements of paragraphs 1, 3, 4 and 6 of this Article that apply to the exporter and State of export shall apply *mutatis mutandis* to the importer or disposer and State of import, respectively; or

    (c)   By any State of transit which is a Party, the provisions of paragraph 4 shall apply to such State.

6. The State of export may, subject to the written consent of the States concerned, allow the generator or the exporter to use a general notification where hazardous wastes or other wastes having the same physical and chemical characteristics are shipped regularly to the same disposer via the same customs office of exit of the State of export via the same customs office of entry of the State of import, and, in the case of transit, via the same customs office of entry and exit of the State or States of transit.

7. The States concerned may make their written consent to the use of the general notification referred to in paragraph 6 subject to the supply of certain information, such as the exact quantities or periodical lists of hazardous wastes or other wastes to be shipped.

8. The general notification and written consent referred to in paragraphs 6 and 7 may cover multiple shipments of hazardous wastes or other wastes during a maximum period of 12 months.

9. The Parties shall require that each person who takes charge of a transboundary movement of hazardous wastes or other wastes sign the movement document either upon delivery or receipt of the wastes in question. They shall also require that the disposer inform both the exporter and the competent authority of the State of export of receipt by the disposer of the wastes in question and, in due course, of the completion of disposal as specified in the notification. If no such information is received within the State of export, the competent authority of the State of export or the exporter shall so notify the State of import.

10. The notification and response required by this Article shall be transmitted to the competent authority of the Parties concerned or to such governmental authority as may be appropriate in the case of non-Parties.

11. Any transboundary movement of hazardous wastes or other wastes shall be covered by insurance, bond or other guarantee as may be required by the State of import or any State of transit which is a Party.

Article 7
Transboundary Movement from a Party through States which are not Parties

Paragraph 2 of Article 6 of the Convention shall apply *mutatis mutandis* to transboundary movement of hazardous wastes or other wastes from a Party through a State or States which are not Parties.

Article 8
Duty to Re-import

When a transboundary movement of hazardous wastes or other wastes to which the consent of the States concerned has been given, subject to the provisions of this Convention, cannot be completed in accordance with the terms of the contract, the State of export shall ensure that the wastes in question are taken back into the State of export, by the exporter, if alternative arrangements cannot be made for their disposal in an environmentally sound manner, within 90 days from the time that the importing State informed the State of export and the Secretariat, or such other period of time as the States concerned agree. To this end, the State of export and any Party of transit shall not oppose, hinder or prevent the return of those wastes to the State of export.

Article 9
Illegal Traffic

1. For the purpose of this Convention, any transboundary movement of hazardous wastes or other wastes:
   (a)   without notification pursuant to the provisions of this Convention to all States concerned; or
   (b)   without the consent pursuant to the provisions of this Convention of a State concerned; or
   (c)   with consent obtained from States concerned through falsification, mis-representation or fraud; or
   (d)   that does not conform in a material way with the documents; or
   (e)   that results in deliberate disposal (e.g. dumping) of hazardous wastes or other wastes in contravention of this Convention and of general principles of international law,
shall be deemed to be illegal traffic.
2. In case of a transboundary movement of hazardous wastes or other wastes deemed to be illegal traffic as the result of conduct on the part of the exporter or generator, the State of export shall ensure that the wastes in question are:
   (a)   taken back by the exporter or the generator or, if necessary, by itself into the State of export, or, if impracticable,
   (b)   are otherwise disposed of in accordance with the provisions of this Convention,
within 30 days from the time the State of export has been informed about the illegal traffic or such other period of time as States concerned may agree. To this end the Parties concerned shall not oppose, hinder or prevent the return of those wastes to the State of export.
3. In the case of a transboundary movement of hazardous wastes or other wastes deemed to be illegal traffic as the result of conduct on the part of the importer or disposer, the State of import shall ensure that the wastes in question are disposed of in an environmentally sound manner by the importer or disposer or, if necessary, by itself within 30 days from the time the illegal traffic has come to the attention of the State of import or such other period of time as the States concerned may agree. To this end, the Parties concerned shall co-operate, as necessary, in the disposal of the wastes in an environmentally sound manner.
4. In cases where the responsibility for the illegal traffic cannot be assigned either to the exporter or generator or to the importer or disposer, the Parties concerned or other Parties, as appropriate, shall ensure, through co-operation, that the wastes in question are disposed of as soon as possible in an environmentally sound manner either in the State of export or the State of import or elsewhere as appropriate.

5. Each Party shall introduce appropriate national/domestic legislation to prevent and punish illegal traffic. The Parties shall co-operate with a view to achieving the objects of this Article.

Article 10
International Co-operation

1. The Parties shall co-operate with each other in order to improve and achieve environmentally sound management of hazardous wastes and other wastes.
2. To this end, the Parties shall:
    (a)   Upon request, make available information, whether on a bilateral or multilateral basis, with a view to promoting the environmentally sound management of hazardous wastes and other wastes, including harmonization of technical standards and practices for the adequate management of hazardous wastes and other wastes;
    (b)   Co-operate in monitoring the effects of the management of hazardous wastes on human health and the environment;
    (c)   Co-operate, subject to their national laws, regulations and policies, in the development and implementation of new environmentally sound low-waste technologies and the improvement of existing technologies with a view to eliminating, as far as practicable, the generation of hazardous wastes and other wastes and achieving more effective and efficient methods of ensuring their management in an environmentally sound manner, including the study of the economic, social and environmental effects of the adoption of such new or improved technologies;
    (d)   Co-operate actively, subject to their national laws, regulations and policies, in the transfer of technology and management systems related to the environmentally sound management of hazardous wastes and other wastes. They shall also co-operate in developing the technical capacity among Parties, especially those which may need and request technical assistance in this field;
    (e)   Co-operate in developing appropriate technical guidelines and/or codes of practice.
3. The Parties shall employ appropriate means to co-operate in order to assist developing countries in the implementation of subparagraphs a, b and c of paragraph 2 of Article 4.
4. Taking into account the needs of developing countries, co-operation between Parties and the competent international organizations is encouraged to promote, *inter alia*, public awareness, the development of sound management of hazardous wastes and other wastes and the adoption of new low-waste technologies.

Article 11
Bilateral, Multilateral and Regional Agreements

1. Notwithstanding the provisions of Article 4 paragraph 5, Parties may enter into bilateral, mutilateral, or regional agreements or arrangements regarding transboundary movement of hazardous wastes or other wastes with Parties or non-Parties provided that such agreements or arrangements do not derogate from the environmentally sound management of hazardous wastes and other wastes as required by this Convention. These agreements or arrangements shall stipulate provisions which are not less environmentally sound than those provided for by this Convention in particular taking into account the interests of developing countries.
2. Parties shall notify the Secretariat of any bilateral, multilateral or regional agreements or arrangements referred to in paragraph 2 and those which they have entered into prior to the entry into force of this Convention for them, for the purpose

of controlling transboundary movements of hazardous wastes and other wastes which take place entirely among the Parties to such agreements. The provisions of this Convention shall not affect transboundary movements which take place pursuant to such agreements provided that such agreements are compatible with the environmentally sound management of hazardous wastes and other wastes as required by this Convention.

Article 12
Consultations on Liability

The Parties shall co-operate with a view to adopting, as soon as practicable, a protocol setting out appropriate rules and procedures in the field of liability and compensation for damage resulting from the transboundary movement and disposal of hazardous wastes and other wastes.

Article 13
Transmission of Information

1. The Parties shall, whenever it comes to their knowledge, ensure that, in the case of an accident occurring during the transboundary movement of hazardous wastes or other wastes or their disposal, which are likely to present risks to human health and the environment in other States, those states are immediately informed.
2. The Parties shall inform each other, through the Secretariat, of:
   (a)   Changes regarding the designation of competent authorities and/or focal points, pursuant to Article 5;
   (b)   Changes in their national definition of hazardous wastes, pursuant to Article 3;
   and, as soon as possible,
   (c)   Decisions made by them not to consent totally or partially to the import of hazardous wastes or other wastes for disposal within the area under their national jurisdiction;
   (d)   Decisions taken by them to limit or ban the export of hazardous wastes or other wastes;
   (e)   Any other information required pursuant to paragraph 4 of this Article.
3. The Parties, consistent with national laws and regulations, shall transmit, through the Secretariat, to the Conference of the Parties established under Article 15, before the end of each calendar year, a report on the previous calendar year, containing the following information:
   (a)   Competent authorities and focal points that have been designated by them pursuant to Article 5;
   (b)   Information regarding transboundary movements of hazardous wastes or other wastes in which they have been involved, including:
      (i)   The amount of hazardous wastes and other wastes exported, their category, characteristics, destination, any transit country and disposal method as stated on the response to notification;
      (ii) The amount of hazardous wastes and other wastes imported, their category, characteristics, origin, and disposal methods;
      (iii) Disposals which did not proceed as intended;
      (iv) Efforts to achieve a reduction of the amount of hazardous wastes or other wastes subject to transboundary movement;
   (c)   Information on the measures adopted by them in implementation of this Convention;
   (d)   Information on available qualified statistics which have been compiled by them on the effects on human health and the environment of the generation, transportation and disposal of hazardous wastes or other wastes;

(e)   Information concerning bilateral, multilateral and regional agreements and arrangements entered into pursuant to Article 11 of this Convention;

(f)   Information on accidents occurring during the transboundary movement and disposal of hazardous wastes and other wastes and on the measures undertaken to deal with them;

(g)   Information on disposal options operated within the area of their national jurisdiction;

(h)   Information on measures undertaken for development of technologies for the reduction and/or elimination of production of hazardous wastes and other wastes; and

(i)   Such other matters as the Conference of the Parties shall deem relevant.

4. The Parties, consistent with national laws and regulations, shall ensure that copies of each notification concerning any given transboundary movement of hazardous wastes or other wastes, and the response to it, are sent to the Secretariat when a Party considers that its environment may be affected by that transboundary movement has requested that this should be done.

Article 14
Financial Aspects

1. The Parties agree that, according to the specific needs of different regions and subregions, regional or sub-regional centres for training and technology transfers regarding the management of hazardous wastes and other wastes and the minimization of their generation should be established. The Parties shall decide on the establishment of appropriate funding mechanisms of a voluntary nature.

2. The Parties shall consider the establishment of a revolving fund to assist on an interim basis in case of emergency situations to minimize damage from accidents arising from transboundary movements of hazardous wastes and other wastes or during the disposal of those wastes.

Article 15
Conference of the Parties

1. A Conference of the Parties is hereby established. The first meeting of the Conference of the Parties shall be convened by the Executive Director of UNEP not later than one year after the entry into force of this Convention. Thereafter, ordinary meetings of the Conference of the Parties shall be held at regular intervals to be determined by the Conference at its first meeting.

2. Extraordinary meetings of the Conference of the Parties shall be held at such other times as may be deemed necessary by the Conference, or at the written request of any Party, provided that, within six months of the request being communicated to them by the Secretariat, it is supported by at least one third of the Parties.

3. The Conference of the Parties shall by consensus agree upon and adopt rules of procedure for itself and for any subsidiary body it may establish, as well as financial rules to determine in particular the financial participation of the Parties under this Convention.

4. The Parties at their first meeting shall consider any additional measures needed to assist them in fulfilling their responsibilities with respect to the protection and the preservation of the marine environment in the context of this Convention.

5. The Conference of the Parties shall keep under continuous review and evaluation the effective implementation of this Convention, and, in addition, shall:

(a)   Promote the harmonization of appropriate policies, strategies and measures for minimizing harm to human health and the environment by hazardous wastes and other wastes;

(b)   Consider and adopt, as required, amendments to this Convention and its annexes, taking into consideration, *inter alia*, available scientific, technical, economic and environmental information;

(c)   Consider and undertake any additional action that may be required for the achievement of the purposes of this Convention in the light of experience gained in its operation and in the operation of the agreements and arrangements envisaged in Article 11;

(d)   Consider and adopt protocols as required; and

(e)   Establish such subsidiary bodies as are deemed necessary for the implementation of this Convention.

6. The United Nations, its specialized agencies, as well as any State not party to this Convention, may be represented as observers at meetings of the Conference of the Parties. Any other body or agency, whether national or international, governmental or non-governmental, qualified in fields relating to hazardous wastes or other wastes which has informed the Secretariat of its wish to be represented as an observer at a meeting of the Conference of the Parties, may be admitted unless at least one third of the Parties present object. The admission and participation of observers shall be subject to the rules of procedure adopted by the Conference of the Parties.

7. The Conference of the Parties shall undertake three years after the entry into force of this Convention, and at least every six years thereafter, an evaluation of its effectiveness and, if deemed necessary, to consider the adoption of a complete or partial ban of transboundary movements of hazardous wastes and other wastes in light of the latest scientific, environmental, technical and economic information.

Article 16
Secretariat

1. The functions of the Secretariat shall be:

(a)   To arrange for and service meetings provided for in Article 15 and 17;

(b)   To prepare and transmit reports based upon information received in accordance with Articles 3, 4, 6, 11 and 13 as well as upon information derived from meetings of subsidiary bodies established under Article 15 as well as upon, as appropriate, information provided by relevant intergovernmental and non-governmental entities;

(c)   To prepare reports on its activities carried out in implementation of its functions under this Convention and present them to the Conference of the Parties;

(d)   To ensure the necessary coordination with relevant international bodies, and in particular to enter into such administrative and contractual arrangements as may be required for the effective discharge of its functions;

(e)   To communicate with focal points and competent authorities established by the Parties in accordance with Article 5 of this Convention;

(f)   To compile information concerning authorized national sites and facilities to Parties available for the disposal of their hazardous wastes and other wastes and to circulate this information among Parties;

(g)   To receive and convey information from and to Parties on;

—sources of technical assistance and training;

—available technical and scientific know-how;

—sources of advice and expertise; and

—availability of resources

with a view to assisting them, upon request, in such areas as:

—the handling of the notification system of this Convention;

—the management of hazardous wastes and other wastes;

—environmentally sound technologies relating to hazardous wastes and other wastes, such as low- and non-waste technology;

—the assessment of disposal capabilities and sites;
—the monitoring of hazardous wastes and other wastes; and
—emergency responses;

(h)   To provide Parties, upon request, with information on consultants or consulting firms having the necessary technical competence in the field, which can assist them to examine a notification for a transboundary movement, the concurrence of a shipment of hazardous wastes or other wastes with the relevant notification, and/or the fact that the proposed disposal facilities for hazardous wastes or other wastes are environmentally sound, when they have reason to believe that the wastes in question will not be managed in an environmentally sound manner. Any such examination would not be at the expense of the Secretariat;

(i)   To assist Parties upon request in their identification of cases of illegal traffic and to circulate immediately to the Parties concerned any information it has received regarding illegal traffic;

(j)   To co-operate with Parties and with relevant and competent international organizations and agencies in the provision of experts and equipment for the purpose of rapid assistance to States in the event of an emergency situation; and

(k)   To perform such other functions relevant to the purposes of this Convention as may be determined by the Conference of the Parties.

2. The secretariat functions will be carried out on an interim basis by UNEP until the completion of the first meeting of the Conference of the Parties held pursuant to Article 15.

3. At its first meeting, the Conference of the Parties shall designate the Secretariat from among those existing competent intergovernmental organizations which have signified their willingness to carry out the secretariat functions under this Convention. At this meeting, the Conference of the Parties shall also evaluate the implementation by the interim Secretariat of the functions assigned to it, in particular under paragraph 1 above, and decide upon the structures appropriate for those functions.

Article 17
Amendment of the Convention

1. Any Party may propose amendments to this Convention and any Party to a protocol may propose amendments to that protocol. Such amendments shall take due account, *inter alia*, of relevant scientific and technical considerations.

2. Amendments to this Convention shall be adopted at a meeting of the Conference of the Parties. Amendments to any protocol shall be adopted at a meeting of the Parties to the protocol in question. The text of any proposed amendment to this Convention or to any protocol, except as may otherwise be provided in such protocol, shall be communicated to the Parties by the Secretariat at least six months before the meeting at which it is proposed for adoption. The Secretariat shall also communicate proposed amendments to the signatories to this Convention for information.

3. The Parties shall make every effort to reach agreement on any proposed amendment to this Convention by consensus. If all efforts at consensus have been exhausted, and no agreement reached, the amendment shall as a last resort be adopted by a three-fourths majority vote of the Parties present and voting at the meeting, and shall be submitted by the Depositary to all Parties for ratification, approval, formal confirmation or acceptance.

4. The procedure mentioned in paragraph 3 above shall apply to amendments to any protocol, except that a two-thirds majority of the Parties to that protocol present and voting at the meeting shall suffice for their adoption.

5. Instruments of ratification, approval, formal confirmation or acceptance of amendments shall be deposited with the Depositary. Amendments adopted in accordance with paragraphs 3 or 4 above shall enter into force between Parties having accepted them on the ninetieth day after the receipt by the Depositary of their instrument of ratification, approval, formal confirmation or acceptance by at least three-fourths of the Parties who accepted the amendments to the protocol concerned, except as may otherwise be provided in such protocol. The amendments shall enter into force for any other Party on the ninetieth day after that Party deposits its instrument of ratification, approval, formal confirmation or acceptance of the amendments.

6. For the purpose of this Article, "Parties present and voting" means Parties present and casting an affirmative or negative vote.

Article 18
Adoption and Amendment of Annexes

1. The annexes to this Convention or to any protocol shall form an integral part of this Convention or of such protocol, as the case may be and, unless expressly provided otherwise, a reference to this Convention or its protocols constitutes at the same time a reference to any annexes thereto. Such annexes shall be restricted to scientific, technical and administrative matters.

2. Except as may be otherwise provided in any protocol with respect to its annexes, the following procedure shall apply to the proposal, adoption and entry into force of additional annexes to this Convention or of annexes to a protocol:

  (a)   Annexes to this Convention and its protocols shall be proposed and adopted according to the procedure laid down in Article 17, paragraphs 2, 3 and 4;

  (b)   Any Party that is unable to accept an additional annex to this Convention or an annex to any protocol to which it is party shall so notify the Depositary, in writing, within six months from the date of the communication of the adoption by the Depositary. The Depositary shall without delay notify all Parties of any such notification received. A Party may at any time substitute an acceptance for a previous declaration of objection and the annexes shall thereupon enter into force for that Party;

  (c)   On the expiry of six months from the date of the circulation of the communication by the Depositary, the annex shall become effective for all Parties to this Convention or to any protocol concerned, which have not submitted a notification in accordance with the provision of subparagraph (b) above.

3. The proposal, adoption and entry into force of amendments to annexes to this Convention or to any protocol shall be subject to the same procedure as for the proposal, adoption and entry into force of annexes to the Convention or annexes to a protocol. Annexes and amendments thereto shall take due account, *inter alia*, of relevant scientific and technical considerations.

4. If an additional annex or an amendment to an annex involves an amendment to this Convention or to any protocol, the additional annex or amended annex shall not enter into force until such time as the amendment to this Convention or to the protocol enters into force.

Article 19
Verification

Any Party which has reason to believe that another Party is acting or has acted in breach of its obligations under this Convention may inform the Secretariat thereof, and in such an event, shall simultaneously and immediately inform, directly or through the Secretariat, the Party against whom the allegations are made. All relevant information should be submitted by the Secretariat to the Parties.

Article 20
Settlement of Disputes

1. In case of a dispute between Parties as to the interpretation or application of, or compliance with, this Convention or any protocol thereto, they shall seek a settlement of the dispute through negotiation or any other peaceful means of their own choice.
2. If the Parties concerned cannot settle their dispute through the means mentioned in the preceding paragraph, the dispute, if the parties to the dispute agree, shall be submitted to the International Court of Justice or to arbitration under the conditions set out in Annex VI on Arbitration. However, failure to reach common agreement on submission of the dispute to the International Court of Justice or to arbitration shall not absolve the Parties from the responsibility of continuing to seek to resolve it by the means referred to in paragraph 1.
3. When ratifying, accepting, approving, formally confirming or acceding to this Convention, or at any time thereafter, a State or political and/or economic integration organization may declare that it recognizes as compulsory *ipso facto* and without special agreement, in relation to any Party accepting the same obligation:
    (a)   submission of the dispute to the International Court of Justice; and/or
    (b)   arbitration in accordance with the procedures set out in Annex VI.
Such declaration shall be notified in writing to the Secretariat which shall communicate it to the Parties.

* * *

Article 26
Reservations and Declarations

1. No reservation or exception may be made to this Convention.
2. Paragraph 1 of this Article does not preclude a State or political and/or economic integration organizations, when signing, ratifying, accepting, approving, formally confirming or acceding to this Convention, from making declarations or statements, however phrased or named, with a view, *inter alia*, to the harmonization of its laws and regulations with the provisions of this Convention, provided that such declarations or statements do not purport to exclude or to modify the legal effects of the provisions of the Convention in their application to that State.

* * *

CANADA-UNITED STATES: AGREEMENT BETWEEN THE UNITED STATES AND CANADA CONCERNING THE TRANSBOUNDARY MOVEMENT OF HAZARDOUS WASTE

Popular Name: Canada-U.S. Hazardous Waste Agreement

Done at Ottawa 28 October 1986, United States-Canada, TIAS ————.

Entry into Force: 8 November 1986

Languages: English, French

Editors' Note

This agreement provides that the exporting country must notify the importing country of proposed transboundary shipments of hazardous wastes, defined according to each country's municipal law. If no response is received within 30 days after receipt of the notification, the importing State is presumed not to object to the shipment. The exporting country must readmit hazardous waste returned by the importing or transiting country.

AGREEMENT BETWEEN THE GOVERNMENT OF THE UNITED STATES OF AMERICA AND THE GOVERNMENT OF CANADA CONCERNING THE TRANSBOUNDARY MOVEMENT OF HAZARDOUS WASTE

The Government of the United States of America (the United States), and the Government of Canada (Canada), hereinafter called "The Parties":

RECOGNIZING that severe health and environmental damage may result from the improper treatment, storage, and disposal of hazardous waste;

SEEKING to ensure that the treatment, storage, and disposal of hazardous waste are conducted so as to reduce the risks to public health, property, and environmental quality;

RECOGNIZING that the close trading relationship and the long common border between the United States and Canada engender opportunities for a generator of hazardous waste to benefit from using the nearest appropriate disposal facility, which may involve the transboundary shipment of hazardous waste;

RECOGNIZING further that the most effective and efficient means of achieving environmentally sound management procedures for hazardous waste crossing the United States-Canada border is through cooperative efforts and coordinated regulatory schemes;

BELIEVING that a bilateral agreement is needed to facilitate the control of transboundary shipments of hazardous waste between the United States and Canada;

REAFFIRMING Principle 21 of the 1972 Declaration of the United Nations Conference on the Human Environment, adopted at Stockholm, which asserts that states have, in accordance with the Charter of the United Nations and the principles of international law, the sovereign right to exploit their own resources pursuant to their own environmental policies and the responsibility to ensure that activities within their jurisdiction or control do not cause damage to the environment of other states or of areas beyond the limits of national jurisdiction;

TAKING into account OECD Council Decisions and Recommendations on transfrontier movements of hazardous wastes, the UNEP Cairo Guidelines and Principles for the Environmentally Sound Management of Hazardous Waste, and resolutions of the London Dumping Convention,

Have agreed as follows:

ARTICLE 1
Definitions

For the purposes of this Agreement:
   (a)   "Designated Authority" means, in the case of the United States of America, the Environmental Protection Agency and, in the case of Canada, the Department of the Environment.
   (b)   "Hazardous Waste" means with respect to Canada, waste dangerous goods, and with respect to the United States, hazardous waste subject to

a manifest requirement in the United States, as defined by their respective national legislations and implementing regulations.

(c)   "Country of Export" means the country from which the shipment of hazardous waste originated.

(d)   "Country of Import" means the country to which hazardous waste is sent for the purpose of treatment, storage (with the exception of short-term storage incidental to transportation) or disposal.

(e)   "Country of Transit" means the country which is neither the country of export nor the country of import, through whose land territory or internal waters hazardous waste is transported, or in whose ports such waste is unloaded for further transportation.

(f)   "Consignee" means the treatment, storage (with the exception of short-term storage incidental to transportation) or disposal facility in the country of import and the name of the person operating the facility.

(g)   "Exporter" means, in the case of the United States, the person defined as exporter, and in the case of Canada, the person defined as consignor, under their respective national laws and regulations governing hazardous waste.

ARTICLE 2
General Obligation

The Parties shall permit the export, import, and transit of hazardous waste across their common border for treatment, storage, or disposal pursuant to the terms of their domestic laws, regulations and administrative practices, and the provisions of this Agreement.

ARTICLE 3
Notification to the Importing Country

(a)   The designated authority of the country of export shall notify the designated authority of the country of import of proposed transboundary shipments of hazardous waste.

(b)   The notice referred to in paragraph (a) of this article may cover an individual shipment or a series of shipments extending over a twelve month or lesser period and shall contain the following information:

(i)   The exporter's name, address and telephone number, and if required in the country of export, the identification number.

(ii) for each hazardous waste type and for each consignee:

(1) A description of the hazardous waste to be exported, as identified by the waste identification number, the classification and the shipping name as required on the manifest in the country of export;

(2) The estimated frequency or rate at which such waste is to be exported and the period of time over which such waste is to be exported;

(3) The estimated total quantity of the hazardous waste in units as specified by the manifest required in the country of export;

(4) The point of entry into the country of import;

(5) The name and address of the transporter(s) and the means of transportation, such as the mode of transportation (air, highway, rail, water, etc.) and type(s) of container (drums, boxes, tanks, etc.);

(6) A description of the manner in which the waste will be treated, stored or disposed of in the importing country;

(7) The name and site address of the consignee;

(8) An approximate date of the first shipment to each consignee, if available.

(c) The designated authority of the country of import shall have 30 days from the date of receipt of the notice provided pursuant to paragraphs (a) and (b) of this article to respond to such notice, indicating its consent (conditional or not) or its objection to the export. Such response will be transmitted to the designated authority of the country of export. The date of receipt of the notice will be identified in an acknowledgement of receipt made immediately by the designated authority of the country of import to the country of export.

(d) If no response is received by the designated authority of the country of export within the 30 day period referred to in paragraph (c) of this article, the country of import shall be considered as having no objection to the export of hazardous waste described in the notice and the export may take place conditional upon the persons importing the hazardous waste complying with all the applicable laws of the country of import.

(e) The country of import shall have the right to amend the terms of the proposed shipment(s) as described in the notice.

(f) The consent of the country of import, whether express, tacit, or conditional, provided pursuant to paragraphs (c) and (d) of this article, may be withdrawn or modified for good cause. The Parties will withdraw or modify such consent insofar as possible at the most appropriate time for the persons concerned.

ARTICLE 4
Notification to the Transit Country

(a) The designated authority of the country of export shall notify the designated authority of the country of transit of the proposed shipment of hazardous waste at least 7 days prior to the date of the shipment. The notice shall include the information specified in paragraph (b) of Article 3, with the following exceptions:

(i) The points of entry into and departure from the country of transit shall be provided in lieu of the entry point(s) into the country of import; and

(ii) A description of the approximate length of time the hazardous waste will remain in the country of transit and the nature of its handling while there shall be submitted instead of a description of the treatment, storage, or disposal of the waste in the country of import.

ARTICLE 5
Cooperative Efforts

1. The Parties will cooperate to ensure, to the extent possible, that all transboundary shipments of hazardous waste comply with the manifest requirements of both countries.

2. The Parties will cooperate in monitoring and spot-checking transboundary shipments of hazardous waste to ensure, to the extent possible, that such shipments conform to the requirements of the applicable legislation and of this Agreement.

3. To the extent any implementing regulations are necessary to comply with this Agreement, the Parties will act expeditiously to issue such regulations consistent with domestic law. Pending such issuance, the Parties will make best efforts to provide notification in accordance with this Agreement where current regulatory authority is insufficient. The Parties will provide each other with a diplomatic note upon the issuance and the coming into effect of any such regulations.

ARTICLE 6
Readmission of Exports

The country of export shall readmit any shipment of hazardous waste that may be returned by the country of import or transit.

ARTICLE 7
Enforcement

The Parties shall ensure, to the extent possible, that within their respective jurisdictions, their domestic laws and regulations are enforced with respect to the transportation, storage, treatment and disposal of transboundary shipments of hazardous waste.

ARTICLE 8
Protection of Confidential Information

If the provision of technical information pursuant to articles 3 and 4 would require the disclosure of information covered by agreement(s) of confidentiality between a Party and an exporter, the country of export shall make every effort to obtain the consent of the concerned person for the purpose of conveying any such information to the country of import or transit. The country of import or transit shall make every effort to protect the confidentiality of such information conveyed.

ARTICLE 9
Insurance

The Parties may require, as a condition of entry, that any transboundary movement of hazardous waste be covered by insurance or other financial guarantee in respect to damage to third parties caused during the entire movement of hazardous waste, including loading and unloading.

ARTICLE 10
Effects on International Agreements

Nothing in this Agreement shall be deemed to diminish the obligations of the Parties with respect to disposal of hazardous waste at sea contained in the 1972 London Dumping Convention.

ARTICLE 11
Domestic Law

The provisions of this Agreement shall be subject to the applicable laws and regulations of the Parties.

ARTICLE 12
Amendment

This Agreement may be amended by mutual written consent of the Parties or their authorized representatives.

ARTICLE 13
Entry into Force

This Agreement shall enter into force on November 8, 1986 and continue in force for five years. It will automatically be renewed for additional five year periods unless either Party gives written notice of termination to the other at least three months prior to the expiration of any five year period. In any five year period, this Agreement may be terminated upon one year written notice given by one Party to the other.

* * *

MEXICO-UNITED STATES: AGREEMENT FOR COOPERATION ON ENVIRONMENTAL PROGRAMS AND TRANSBOUNDARY PROBLEMS, ANNEX III, TRANSBOUNDARY SHIPMENT OF HAZARDOUS WASTES AND HAZARDOUS SUBSTANCES

Popular Name: Mexico-U.S. Hazardous Wastes Agreement

Done at Washington on 12 November 1986, *reprinted in* 26 ILM 25 (1987).

Entry into Force: 29 January 1987

Languages: English, Spanish

Editors' Note

This Annex, which is one of five addressing environmental issues between these two countries, sets forth procedures for transboundary shipments of hazardous waste between Mexico and the United States, which require 45-day notice to the importing country and give that country the right to consent or object to the shipment; and it requires readmission of hazardous wastes returned by the importing country. The Annex also requires notice of transboundary shipments of other hazardous substances if the exporting country becomes aware of such shipments, notice of regulatory action banning or severely restricting a pesticide or chemical, and readmission of all such substances that were illegally imported. Annex III also covers hazardous waste generated from raw materials admitted in bond, such as those used in maquiladoras.

ANNEX III TO THE AGREEMENT BETWEEN THE UNITED STATES OF AMERICA AND THE UNITED MEXICAN STATES ON COOPERATION FOR THE PROTECTION AND IMPROVEMENT OF THE ENVIRONMENT IN THE BORDER AREA:

AGREEMENT OF COOPERATION BETWEEN THE UNITED STATES OF AMERICA AND THE UNITED MEXICAN STATES REGARDING THE TRANSBOUNDARY SHIPMENTS OF HAZARDOUS WASTES AND HAZARDOUS SUBSTANCES

PREAMBLE

The Government of the United States of America ("the United States"), and the Government of the United Mexican States ("Mexico"), ("the Parties"),

Recognizing that health and environmental damage may result from improper activities associated with hazardous waste;

Realizing the potential risks to public health, property and the environment associated with hazardous substances;

Seeking to ensure that activities associated with the transboundary shipment of hazardous waste are conducted so as to reduce or prevent the risks to public health, property and environmental quality, by effectively cooperating in regard to their export and import;

Seeking also to safeguard the quality of public health, property and environment from unreasonable risks by effectively regulating the export and import of hazardous substances;

Considering that transboundary shipments of hazardous waste and hazardous substances between the Parties, if carried out illegally and thus without the supervision and control of the competent authorities, or if improperly managed could endanger the public health, property and environment, particularly in the United States/Mexico border area;

Recognizing that the close trading relationship and the long common border between the Parties make it necessary to cooperate regarding transboundary shipments of hazardous waste and hazardous substances without unreasonably affecting the trade of goods and services;

Reaffirming Principle 21 of the 1972 Declaration of the United Nations Conference on the Human Environment, adopted at Stockholm, which provides that States have, in accordance with the Charter of the United Nations and the principles of international law, the sovereign right to exploit their own resources pursuant to their own environmental policies and the responsibility to ensure that activities within their jurisdiction or control do not cause damage to the environment of other States or of areas beyond the limits of national jurisdiction;

Recognizing that Article 3 of the Agreement between the Parties on Cooperation for the Protection and Improvement of the Environment in the Border Area of 1983 provides that the Parties may conclude specific arrangements for the solution of common problems in the border area as annexes to that Agreement;

Have agreed as follows:

ARTICLE I
Definitions

1. "Designated Authority" means, in the case of the United States, the Environmental Protection Agency and, in the case of Mexico, the Secretariat of Urban Development and Ecology through the Subsecretariat of Ecology.

2. "Hazardous waste" means any waste, as designated or defined by the applicable designated authority pursuant to national policies, laws or regulations,

which if improperly dealt with in activities associated with them, may result in health or environmental damage.

3. "Hazardous substance" means any substance, as designated or defined by the applicable national policies, laws or regulations, including pesticides or chemicals, which when improperly dealt with in activities associated with them, may produce harmful effects to public health, property or the environment, and is banned or severely restricted by the applicable designated authority.

4. "Activities" associated with hazardous waste or hazardous substances means, as applicable, their handling, transportation, treatment, recycling, storage, application, distribution, reuse or other utilization.

5. "Country of export" means the Party from which the transboundary movement of hazardous waste or hazardous substances is to be initiated.

6. "Country of import" means the Party to which the hazardous waste or hazardous substances are to be sent. This does not include "transit", as meaning transport of hazardous waste or hazardous substances through the territory of a Party without being imported through its Customs under applicable laws and regulations.

7. "Consignee" means the facility in the country of import which will ultimately receive the hazardous waste or hazardous substances.

8. "Exporter" means the physical or juridical person, whether public or private, acting on his behalf or as a contractor or subcontractor expressly or implicitly defined as exporter under the national laws and regulations of the country of export which specifically govern hazardous waste or hazardous substances.

9. "Banned or severely restricted" means final regulatory action, as designated or defined by the applicable designated authority, pursuant to national policies, laws or regulations:

a)   Prohibiting, cancelling or suspending all or virtually all registered uses of a pesticide for human health or environmental reasons.

b)   Prohibiting or severely limiting the manufacture, processing, distribution or use of a chemical for human health or environmental reasons.

ARTICLE II
General Obligations

1. Transboundary shipments of hazardous waste and hazardous substances across the common border of the Parties shall be governed by the terms of this Annex and their domestic laws and regulations.

2. Each Party shall ensure, to the extent practicable, that its domestic laws and regulations are enforced with respect to transboundary shipments of hazardous waste and hazardous substances, and other substances as the Parties may mutually agree through appendices to this Annex, that pose dangers to public health, property and the environment.

3. Each Party shall cooperate in monitoring and spot-checking transboundary shipments across the common border of hazardous waste and hazardous substances to ensure, to the extent practicable, that such shipments conform to the requirements of this Annex and its national laws and regulations. To this effect, a program of cooperation in this area should be concluded through an Appendix to this Annex, including the exchange of information resulting from the monitoring and spot-checking of transboundary shipments which may be useful to the other Party.

HAZARDOUS WASTE
ARTICLE III
Notification to the Importing Country

1. The designated authority of the country of export shall notify the designated authority of the country of import of transboundary shipments of hazardous waste

for which the consent of the country of import is required under the laws or regulations of the country of export, with a copy of the notification simultaneously sent through diplomatic channels.

2. The notification referred to in paragraph 1 of this Article shall be given at least 45 days in advance of the planned date of export and may cover an individual shipment or a series of shipments extending over a twelve-month or lesser period and shall contain the following information for each shipment:

    a)   The exporter's name, address, telephone number, identification number and other relevant data required in the country of export.

    b)   By consignee, for each hazardous waste type:

        i)   A description of the hazardous waste to be exported, as identified by the waste identification number(s) and the shipping description(s) required in the country of export.

        ii)   The estimated frequency or rate at which such waste is to be exported and the period time over which such waste is to be exported.

        iii)   The estimated total quantity of the hazardous waste in units as specified by the manifest or documents required in the country of export.

        iv)   The point of entry into the country of import.

        v)   The means of transportation, including the mode of transportation and the type of container involved.

        vi)   A description of the treatment or storage to which the waste will be subjected in the country of import.

        vii) The name and site address of the consignee.

3. In order to facilitate compliance with the requirements of the importing country for the exporter to provide information and documents additional to those described in paragraph 2 of this Article, the designated authority of the exporting country will cooperate by making such requirements for information and documents known to the exporter. To that end, the country of import may list such additional required information and documents in appendices to this Annex.

4. The designated authority of the country of import shall have 45 days from the date of acknowledgement of receipt of the notification provided in paragraph 1 of this Article within which to respond to such notification, indicating its consent, with or without conditions, or its objection to the export.

5. The country of import shall have the right to amend the terms of the proposed shipment contained in the notification in order to give its consent.

6. The consent of the country of import provided pursuant to paragraphs 4 and 5 of this Article, may be withdrawn or modified at any time, pursuant to the national policies, laws or regulations of the country of import.

7. Whenever the designated authority of a country of export requires notification of or is otherwise aware of a transboundary shipment that will be transported through the territory of the other Party, it shall, in accordance with its national laws and regulations, notify that Party.

ARTICLE IV
Readmission of Exports

The country of export shall readmit any shipment of hazardous waste that may be returned for any reason by the country of import.

HAZARDOUS SUBSTANCES
ARTICLE V
Notification of Regulatory Actions

1. When a Party has banned or severely restricted a pesticide or chemical, its designated authority shall notify the designated authority of the other Party that such

action has been taken either directly or through an appropriate intergovernmental organization.

2. The notice referred to in paragraph 1 of this Article shall contain the following information, if available:

(a)   the name of the pesticide or chemical that is the object of the regulatory action;

(b)   a concise summary of the regulatory action taken, including the timetable for any further actions that are planned. If the regulatory action bans or restricts certain uses but allows other uses, such information should be included;

(c)   a concise summary of the reason for the regulatory action, including an indication of the potential risks to human health or the environment that are the grounds for the action;

(d)   information concerning registered pesticides or substitute chemicals that could be used in lieu of the banned or severely restricted pesticide or chemical;

(e)   the name and address of the contact point to which a request for further information should be addressed.

ARTICLE VI
Notification of Exports

1. If the country of export becomes aware that an export of a hazardous substance to the country of import is occurring, the designated authority of the country of export shall notify the designated authority of the country of import.

2. The purpose of such notice shall be to remind the country of import of the notification regarding regulatory action provided pursuant to Article 5 and to alert it to the fact that the export is occurring.

3. The notice referred to in paragraph 1 of this Article shall contain the following information, if available:

(a)   the name of the exported hazardous substance;

(b)   for banned or severely restricted chemicals, approximate date(s) of the export;

(c)   a copy of, or reference to, the information provided at the time of the notification of the regulatory action;

(d)   name and address of the contact point for further information.

ARTICLE VII
Timing of the Notifications

1. Notification of regulatory actions, required pursuant to Article 5, shall be transmitted as soon as practicable after the regulatory action has been taken, and in any event not later than 90 days following the taking of such action.

2. When a Party has banned or severely restricted chemicals or pesticides prior to the entry into force of this Annex, its designated authority shall provide an inventory of such prior regulatory actions to the designated authority of the other Party.

3. Notification of exports required pursuant to Article 6, shall be provided at the time the first export of a hazardous substance is occurring to the Country of import following the regulatory action and should recur at the time of the first export of the hazardous substance each subsequent year to that country.

4. When the hazardous substance being exported has been banned or severely restricted prior to the entry into force of this Annex, the first export following the regulatory action shall be considered to be the first export following the provision of the inventory referred to in paragraph 2 of this Article.

ARTICLE VIII
Compliance with Requirements in the Importing Country

In order to facilitate compliance with the requirements in the importing country for the import of hazardous substances, the designated authority of the country of export will cooperate by making such requirements, including expected information and documents, known to the exporter. To that end, the country of import may list such requirements, information and documents in appendices to this Annex.

ARTICLE IX
Readmission of Exports

The country of export shall readmit any shipment of hazardous substances that was not lawfully imported into the country of import.

GENERAL PROVISIONS
ARTICLE X
Additional Arrangements

1. The Parties shall consider and, as appropriate, establish additional arrangements to mitigate or avoid adverse effects on health, property and the environment from improper activities associated with hazardous waste and hazardous substances. Such arrangements may include the sharing of research data as well as the definition of criteria regarding imminent and substantial endangerment and emergency responses, and may be included in appendices to this Annex.

2. The Parties shall consult regarding experience with transboundary shipments of hazardous wastes and hazardous substances and, as problems are identified in the special circumstances of the United States-Mexico border relationship may include through appendices to this Annex, additional cooperation and mutual obligations aimed at achieving when necessary a more stringent control of transboundary shipments, such as provisions to bring uniformity in those relating to both hazardous wastes and hazardous substances regarding compulsory notification to and consent by the importing country for each transboundary shipment, as may become permitted by new national laws and regulations adopted by the Parties.

ARTICLE XI
Hazardous Waste Generated From Raw Materials Admitted In-Bond

Hazardous waste generated in the processes of economic production, manufacturing, processing or repair, for which raw materials were utilized and temporarily admitted, shall continue to be readmitted by the country of origin of the raw materials in accordance with applicable national policies, laws and regulations.

ARTICLE XII
Information Exchange and Assistance

1. The Parties shall, to the extent practicable, provide to each other mutual assistance designed to increase the capability of each Party to enforce its laws applicable to transboundary shipments of hazardous waste or hazardous substances and to take appropriate action with respect to violations of its laws.
  (a)   Such assistance may generally include:
    (i)   the exchange of information;
    (ii) the provision of documents, records and reports;
    (iii) the facilitating of on-site visits to treatment, storage, or disposal facilities;

(iv) assistance provided or required pursuant to any international agreements or treaties in force with respect to the Parties, or pursuant to any arrangement or practice that might otherwise be applicable;

(v) emergency notification of hazardous situations; and

(vi) other forms of assistance mutually agreed upon by the Parties.

(b)   Save in exceptional circumstances, requests for assistance made pursuant to this Article shall be submitted in writing and translated into the language of the requested State.

(c)   The requested State shall provide the requesting State with copies of publicly available records of government departments and agencies in the requested State.

(d)   The requested State may provide any record or information in the possession of a government office or agency, but not publicly available, to the same extent and under the same conditions as it would be available to its own administrative, law enforcement, or judicial authorities.

2. The Parties may establish in an appendix to this Annex a cooperative program relating to the exchange of scientific, technical, and other information for purposes of the development of their own respective regulatory mechanisms controlling hazardous waste and hazardous substances.

ARTICLE XIII
Protection of Confidential Information

The Parties shall adopt procedures to protect the confidentiality of proprietary or sensitive information conveyed pursuant to this Annex, when such procedures do not already exist.

ARTICLE XIV
Damages

1. The country of import may require, as a condition of entry, that any transboundary shipment of hazardous waste or hazardous sustances be covered by insurance, bond or other appropriate and effective guarantee.

2. Whenever a transboundary shipment of hazardous waste or hazardous substances is carried out in violation of this Annex, of the national laws and regulations of the Parties, or of the conditions to which the authorization for import was subject, or whenever the hazardous waste or hazardous substances produce damages to public health, property or the environment in the country of import, the competent authorities of the country of export shall take all practicable measures and initiate and carry out all pertinent legal actions that they are legally competent to undertake, so that when applicable in accordance with its national laws and regulations the physical or juridical persons involved:

a)   return the hazardous waste or hazardous substances to the country of export;

b)   return in as much as practicable the *status quo ante* of the affected ecosystem;

c)   repair, through compensation, the damages caused to persons, property or the environment.

The country of import shall also take, for the same purposes, all practicable measures and initiate and carry out all pertinent legal actions that its authorities are legally competent to undertake.

The country of export shall report to the country of import all measures and legal actions undertaken in the framework of this paragraph, and shall cooperate with the country of import, on the basis of this Annex or of other bilateral treaties and agreements in force between the Parties, and to the extent permitted by its national laws and regulations, to seek in its courts the satisfaction of those matters covered in subparagraphs a) to c) of this paragraph.

3. The provisions of this Annex shall not be deemed to abridge or prejudice the Parties' national laws concerning transboundary shipments, or liability or compensation for damages resulting from activities associated with hazardous waste and hazardous substances.

ARTICLE XV
Effect On Other Instruments

1. Nothing in this Annex shall be construed to prejudice other existing or future agreements concluded between the Parties, or affect the rights or obligations of the Parties under international agreements to which they are Party.

2. The provisions of this Annex shall, in particular, not be deemed to prejudice or otherwise affect the functions entrusted to the International Boundary and Water Commission, in accordance with the 1944 Treaty on the Utilization of Waters of the Colorado and Tijuana Rivers and of the Rio Grande.

* * *

INTERNATIONAL ATOMIC ENERGY AGENCY CODE OF PRACTICE ON THE INTERNATIONAL MOVEMENT OF RADIOACTIVE WASTE. *Supra*, p. 597.

UNITED NATIONS ENVIRONMENT PROGRAMME GOVERNING COUNCIL DECISION: LONDON GUIDELINES FOR THE EXCHANGE OF INFORMATION ON CHEMICALS IN INTERNATIONAL TRADE. *Infra*, p. 644.

CHAPTER 19
NOISE

(No instruments reproduced)

CHAPTER 20
BIOTECHNICAL ACTIVITIES

(No instruments reproduced)

CHAPTER 21
TOURISM

(No instruments reproduced)

CHAPTER 22
MILITARY ACTIVITIES

TREATY BANNING NUCLEAR WEAPONS TESTS IN THE ATMOSPHERE, IN OUTER SPACE AND UNDER WATER

Popular Names: Limited Test Ban Treaty, Partial Test Ban Treaty, PTBT, Test Ban Treaty

Done in Moscow on 5 August 1963, 480 UNTS 43, 14 UST 1313, TIAS 5433, *reprinted in* UNEP3 #31, p.185, 1 IPE 422, IELMT 963: 59.

Entry into Force: 10 October 1963

Depositaries: Union of Soviet Socialist Republics; United Kingdom of Great Britain and Northern Ireland; United States of America

Languages: English, Russian

Parties as of 1 January 1990: Afghanistan; Antigua and Barbuda; Argentina; Australia; Austria; Bahamas; Bangladesh; Belgium; Benin; Bhutan; Bolivia; Botswana; Brazil; Bulgaria; Burma; Byelorussian Soviet Socialist Republic; Canada; Cape Verde; Central African Republic; Chad; Chile; China, Republic of (Taiwan); Colombia; Costa Rica; Côte d'Ivoire; Cyprus; Czech and Slovak Federal Republic; Denmark; Dominican Republic; Ecuador; Egypt; El Salvador; Fiji; Finland; Gabon; Gambia; German Democratic Republic; Germany, Federal Republic of;* Ghana; Greece; Guatemala; Honduras; Hungary; Iceland; India; Indonesia; Iran, Islamic Republic of; Iraq; Ireland; Israel; Italy; Japan; Jordan; Kenya; Korea, Republic of; Kuwait; Laos; Lebanon; Liberia; Libyan Arab Jamahiriya; Luxembourg; Madagascar; Malawi; Malaysia; Malta; Mauritania; Mauritius; Mexico; Mongolia; Morocco; Nepal; Netherlands;* New Zealand; Nicaragua; Niger; Nigeria; Norway; Pakistan; Panama; Papua New Guinea; Peru; Philippines; Poland; Romania; Rwanda; San Marino; Senegal; Seychelles; Sierra Leone; Singapore; South Africa; Spain; Sri Lanka; Sudan; Swaziland; Sweden; Switzerland; Syrian Arab Republic; Tanzania, United Republic of; Thailand; Togo; Tonga; Trinidad and Tobago; Tunisia; Turkey; Uganda; Ukrainian Soviet Socialist Republic; Union of Soviet Socialist Republics; United Kingdom of Great Britain and Northern Ireland; United States of America; Uruguay; Venezuela; Western Samoa; Yemen, Democratic; Yugoslavia; Zaire; Zambia

---

*With a geographic extension

Editors' Note

The Partial Test Ban Treaty had as a goal ending "the contamination of man's environment by radioactive substances." The Treaty obligates member States "to prohibit, to prevent, and not to carry out" any nuclear explosion, at any place under its jurisdiction or control, in the atmosphere, outer space, underwater, or "in any other environment" (primarily underground) if the result is the presence of radioactive debris outside the State under whose jurisdiction or control the explosion is conducted. Withdrawal is permitted on three-months notice only if a party decides that "extraordinary events . . . have jeopardized [its] supreme interests." Efforts are underway in the U.N. General Assembly to develop a comprehensive ban on nuclear tests by amending the Treaty.

TREATY BANNING NUCLEAR WEAPONS TESTS IN THE ATMOSPHERE, IN OUTER SPACE AND UNDER WATER

The Governments of the United States of America, the United Kingdom of Great Britain and Northern Ireland, and the Union of Soviet Socialist Republics, hereinafter referred to as the "Original Parties",

Proclaiming as their principal aim the speediest possible achievement of an agreement on general and complete disarmament under strict international control in accordance with the objectives of the United Nations which would put an end to the armaments race and eliminate the incentive to the production and testing of all kinds of weapons, including nuclear weapons,

Seeking to achieve the discontinuance of all test explosions of nuclear weapons for all time, determined to continue negotiations to this end, and desiring to put an end to the contamination of man's environment by radioactive substances,

Have agreed as follows:

Article I

1. Each of the Parties to this Treaty undertakes to prohibit, to prevent, and not to carry out any nuclear weapon test explosion, or any other nuclear explosion, at any place under its jurisdiction or control:

   (a)   in the atmosphere; beyond its limits, including outer space; or underwater, including territorial waters or high seas; or

   (b)   in any other environment if such explosion causes radioactive debris to be present outside the territorial limits of the State under whose jurisdiction or control such explosion is conducted. It is understood in this connection that the provisions of this subparagraph are without prejudice to the conclusion of a treaty resulting in the permanent banning of all nuclear test explosions, including all such explosions underground, the conclusion of which, as the Parties have stated in the Preamble to this Treaty, they seek to achieve.

2. Each of the Parties to this Treaty undertakes furthermore to refrain from causing, encouraging, or in any way participating in, the carrying out of any nuclear weapon test explosion, or any other nuclear explosion, anywhere which would take place in any of the environments described, or have the effect referred to, in paragraph 1 of this Article.

Article II

1. Any Party may propose amendments to this Treaty. The text of any proposed amendment shall be submitted to the Depositary Governments which shall

circulate it to all Parties to this Treaty. Thereafter, if requested to do so by one-third or more of the Parties, the Depositary Governments shall convene a conference, to which they shall invite all the Parties, to consider such amendment.

2. Any amendment to this Treaty must be approved by a majority of the votes of all the Parties to this Treaty, including the votes of all of the Original Parties. The amendment shall enter into force for all Parties upon the deposit of instruments of ratification by a majority of all the Parties, including the instruments of ratification of all of the Original Parties.

* * *

Article IV

This Treaty shall be of unlimited duration.

Each Party shall in exercising its national sovereignty have the right to withdraw from the Treaty if it decides that extraordinary events, related to the subject matter of this Treaty, have jeopardized the supreme interests of its country. It shall give notice of such withdrawal to all other Parties to the Treaty three months in advance.

* * *

CONVENTION ON THE PROHIBITION OF MILITARY OR ANY OTHER HOSTILE USE OF ENVIRONMENTAL MODIFICATION TECHNIQUES

Popular Name: ENMOD Convention

Done at Geneva on 18 May 1977, A/RES/31/72, 1108 UNTS 151, 31 UST 333, TIAS 9614, *reprinted in* UNEP 3 #72, p.479, 1976 UNJYB 125, 16 ILM 88 (1977), 16 IPE 8058, IELMT 977: 37.

Entry into Force: 5 October 1978

Depositary: United Nations

Languages: Arabic, Chinese, English, French, Russian, Spanish

Parties as of 31 December 1989: Afghanistan; Antigua and Barbuda; Argentina;* Australia; Bangladesh; Belgium; Benin; Brazil; Bulgaria; Byelorussian Soviet Socialist Republic; Canada; Cape Verde; Cuba; Cyprus; Czech and Slovak Federal Republic; Denmark; Egypt; Finland; German Democratic Republic; Germany, Federal Republic of;** Ghana; Greece; Guatemala;* Hungary; India; Ireland; Italy; Japan; Korea, People's Democratic Republic of; Korea, Republic of;* Kuwait;* Laos; Malawi; Mongolia; Netherlands;** New Zealand;** Norway; Pakistan; Papua New Guinea; Poland; Romania; Sao Tome and Principe; Solomon Islands; Spain; Sri Lanka; Sweden; Switzerland;* Tunisia; Ukrainian

---

* With a reservation
**With a geographic extension

Soviet Socialist Republic; Union of Soviet Socialist Republics; United Kingdom of Great Britain and Northern Ireland;** United States of America; Viet Nam; Yemen

Editors' Note

This Convention (ENMOD) was drafted during the Viet Nam War when there was concern about the potential use of environmental modification techniques, such as large-scale cloud seeding and lightning modification, as weapons of war. Laos was the twentieth State to ratify the Convention, which put it into effect.

ENMOD obligates member States not to engage—or to assist others to engage—in military or other hostile use of environmental modification techniques having widespread, long-lasting, or severe effects as the means of injuring another member State. "Environmental modification techniques" are defined as techniques for changing the "dynamics, composition or structure of the Earth, including its biota, lithosphere, hydrosphere and atmosphere, or of outer space." Peaceful environmental modification is not affected. ENMOD provides for setting up an impartial fact-finding body, at the request of any member State, to ascertain whether a treaty violation is occurring.

CONVENTION ON THE PROHIBITION OF MILITARY OR ANY OTHER HOSTILE USE OF ENVIRONMENTAL MODIFICATION TECHNIQUES

The States Parties to this Convention,

Guided by the interest of consolidating peace, and wishing to contribute to the cause of halting the arms race, and of bringing about general and complete disarmament under strict and effective international control, and of saving mankind from the danger of using new means of warfare,

Determined to continue negotiations with a view to achieving effective progress towards further measures in the field of disarmament,

Recognizing that scientific and technical advances may open new possibilities with respect to modification of the environment,

Recalling the Declaration of the United Nations Conference on the Human Environment, adopted at Stockholm on 16 June 1972,

Realizing that the use of environmental modification techniques for peaceful purposes could improve the interrelationship of man and nature and contribute to the preservation and improvement of the environment for the benefit of present and future generations,

Recognizing, however, that military or any other hostile use of such techniques could have effects extremely harmful to human welfare,

Desiring to prohibit effectively military or any other hostile use of environmental modification techniques in order to eliminate the dangers to mankind from such use, and affirming their willingness to work towards the achievement of this objective,

Desiring also to contribute to the strengthening of trust among nations and to the further improvement of the international situation in accordance with the purposes and principles of the Charter of the United Nations,

Have agreed as follows:

Article I

1. Each State Party to this Convention undertak s [sic] not to engage in military or any other hostile use of environmental modification techniques having widespread, long-lasting or severe effects as the means of destruction, damage or injury to any other State Party.

2. Each State Party to this Convention undertakes not to assist, encourage or induce any State, group of States or international organization to engage in activities contrary to the provisions of paragraph 1 of this article.

Article II

As used in article I, the term "environmental modification techniques" refers to any technique for changing—through the deliberate manipulation of natural processes—the dynamics, composition or structure of the Earth, including its biota, lithosphere, hydrosphere and atmosphere, or of outer space.

Article III

1. The provisions of this Convention shall not hinder the use of environmental modification techniques for peaceful purposes and shall be without prejudice to the generally recognized principles and applicable rules of international law concerning such use.

2. The States Parties to this Convention undertake to facilitate, and have the right to participate in, the fullest possible exchange of scientific and technological information on the use of environmental modification techniques for peaceful purposes. States Parties in a position to do so shall contribute, alone or together with other States or international organizations, to international economic and scientific co-operation in the preservation, improvement and peaceful utilization of the environment, with due consideration for the needs of the developing areas of the world.

Article IV

Each State Party to this Convention undertakes to take any measures it considers necessary in accordance with its constitutional processes to prohibit and prevent any activity in violation of the provisions of the Convention anywhere under its jurisdiction or control.

Article V

1. The States Parties to this Convention undertake to consult one another and to co-operate in solving any problems which may arise in relation to the objectives of, or in the application of the provisions of, the Convention. Consultation and co-operation pursuant to this article may also be undertaken through appropriate international procedures within the framework of the United Nations and in accordance with its Charter. These international procedures may include the services of appropriate international organizations, as well as of a Consultative Committee of Experts as provided for in paragraph 2 of this article.

2. For the purposes set forth in paragraph 1 of this article, the Depositary shall, within one month of the receipt of a request from any State Party to this Convention, convene a Consultative Committee of Experts. Any State Party may appoint an expert to the Committee whose functions and rules of procedure are set out in the annex, which constitutes an integral part of this Convention. The Committee shall transmit to the Depositary a summary of its findings of fact, incorporating all views and information presented to the Committee during its proceedings. The Depositary shall distribute the summary to all States Parties.

3. Any State Party to this Convention which has reason to believe that any other State Party is acting in breach of obligations deriving from the provisions of the Convention may lodge a complaint with the Security Council of the United Nations. Such a complaint should include all relevant information as well as all possible evidence supporting its validity.

4. Each State Party to this Convention undertakes to co-operate in carrying out any investigation which the Security Council may initiate, in accordance with the provisions of the Charter of the United Nations, on the basis of the complaint received by the Council. The Security Council shall inform the States Parties of the results of the investigation.

5. Each State Party to this Convention undertakes to provide or support assistance, in accordance with the provisions of the Charter of the United Nations, to any State Party which so requests, if the Security Council decides that such Party has been harmed or is likely to be harmed as a result of violation of the Convention.

Article VI

1. Any State Party to this Convention may propose amendments to the Convention. The text of any proposed amendment shall be submitted to the Depositary, who shall promptly circulate it to all States Parties.

2. An amendment shall enter into force for all States Parties to this Convention which have accepted it, upon the deposit with the Depositary of instruments of acceptance by a majority of States Parties. Thereafter it shall enter into force for any remaining State Party on the date of deposit of its instrument of acceptance.

Article VII

This Convention shall be of unlimited duration.

Article VIII

1. Five years after the entry into force of this Convention, a conference of the States Parties to the Convention shall be convened by the Depositary at Geneva, Switzerland. The conference shall review the operation of the Convention with a view to ensuring that its purposes and provisions are being realized, and shall in particular examine the effectiveness of the provisions of paragraph 1 of article I in eliminating the dangers of military or any other hostile use of environmenal modification techniques.

2. At intervals of not less than five years thereafter, a majority of the States Parties to this Convention may obtain, by submitting a proposal to this effect to the Depositary, the convening of a conference with the same objectives.

3. If no conference has been convened pursuant to paragraph 2 of this article within ten years following the conclusion of a previous conference, the Depositary shall solicit the views of all States Parties to this Convention concerning the convening of such a conference. If one third or ten of the States Parties, whichever number is less, respond affirmatively, the Depositary shall take immediate steps to convene the conference.

* * *

Annex to the Convention
Consultative Committee of Experts

1. The Consultative Committee of Experts shall undertake to make appropriate findings of fact and provide expert views relevant to any problem raised pursuant to paragraph 1 of article V of this Convention by the State Party requesting the convening of the Committee.

2. The work of the Consultative Committee of Experts shall be organized in such a way as to permit it to perform the functions set forth in paragraph 1 of this annex. The Committee shall decide procedural questions relative to the organization of its work, where possible by consensus, but otherwise by a majority of those present and voting. There shall be no voting on matters of substance.

3. The Depositary or his representative shall serve as the Chairman of the Committee.

4. Each expert may be assisted at meetings by one or more advisers.

5. Each expert shall have the right, through the Chairman, to request from States, and from international organizations, such information and assistance as the expert considers desirable for the accomplishment of the Committee's work.

UNITED NATIONS GENERAL ASSEMBLY RESOLUTION ON THE HISTORICAL RESPONSIBILITY OF STATES FOR THE PROTECTION OF NATURE FOR THE BENEFIT OF PRESENT AND FUTURE GENERATIONS

Adopted on 30 October 1980, U.N. Doc. A/RES/35/8, 1980 UNJYB 726, *reprinted in* IPE(2) I/C/30-10-80.

Languages: Arabic, Chinese, English, French, Russian, Spanish

Editors' Note

At the 35th regular session of the U.N. General Assembly, the Soviet Union proposed the adoption of a draft resolution on the Historical Responsibility of States for the Preservation of Nature for Present and Future Generations (A/35/L.7). After consideration of the draft solely in plenary, the Assembly adopted the proposed text at the same session, on 30 October 1980: 68 in favor, 0 opposed, and 47 abstentions.

HISTORICAL RESPONSIBILITY OF STATES FOR THE PRESERVATION OF NATURE FOR PRESENT AND FUTURE GENERATIONS

The General Assembly,

Having considered the item entitled "Historical responsibility of States for the preservation of nature for present and future generations";

Conscious of the disastrous consequences which a war involving the use of nuclear weapons and other weapons of mass destruction would have on man and his environment,

Noting that the continuation of the arms race, including the testing of various types of weapons, especially nuclear weapons, and the accumulation of toxic chemicals are adversely affecting the human environment and damaging the vegetable and animal world,

Bearing in mind that the arms race is diverting material and intellectual resources from the solution of the urgent problems of preserving nature,

Attaching great importance to the development of planned, constructive international co-operation in solving the problems of preserving nature,

Recognizing that the prospects for solving problems so universal as the preservation of nature are closely linked to the strengthening and development of international détente and the creation of conditions which would banish war from the life of mankind,

Noting with satisfaction the drafting and signature in recent years of a number of international agreements designed to preserve the environment,

Determined to preserve nature as a prerequisite for the normal life of man,

1. *Proclaims* the historical responsibility of States for the preservation of nature for present and future generations;

2. *Draws the attention* of States to the fact that the continuing arms race has pernicious effects on the environment and reduces the prospects for the necessary international co-operation in preserving nature on our planet;

3. *Calls upon* States, in the interests of present and future generations, to demonstrate due concern and take the measures, including legislative measures, necessary for preserving nature, and also to promote international co-operation in this field;

4. *Requests* the Secretary-General, with the co-operation of the United Nations Environment Programme, to prepare a report on the pernicious effects of the arms race on nature and to seek the views of States on possible measures to be taken at the international level for the preservation of nature;

5. *Decides* to include in the provisional agenda of its thirty-sixth session an item entitled "Historical responsibility of States for the preservation of nature for present and future generations: report of the Secretary-General".

49th plenary meeting
30 October 1980

WORLD CHARTER FOR NATURE. *Supra*, p. 184.

INTERNATIONAL LAW COMMISSION DRAFT ARTICLES ON THE NON-NAVIGATIONAL USES OF INTERNATIONAL WATERCOURSES. *Supra*, p. 404.

CHAPTER 23
DISASTERS

A. GENERAL

**INTERNATIONAL ATOMIC ENERGY AGENCY
CONVENTION ON EARLY NOTIFICATION OF A NUCLEAR
ACCIDENT.** *Supra*, p. 583.

**INTERNATIONAL ATOMIC ENERGY AGENCY
CONVENTION ON ASSISTANCE IN THE CASE OF A
NUCLEAR ACCIDENT OR RADIOLOGICAL EMERGENCY.**
Supra, p. 587.

PART IV:
TECHNIQUES OF ENVIRONMENTAL PROTECTION

CHAPTER 24
ENVIRONMENTAL DECISIONMAKING

A. ENVIRONMENTAL IMPACT STATEMENTS

WELLINGTON CONVENTION ON THE REGULATION OF ANTARCTIC MINERAL RESOURCE ACTIVITIES. *Supra*, p. 529.

PROTOCOL ON ENVIRONMENTAL PROTECTION TO THE ANTARCTIC TREATY. *Supra*, p. 536.

VIENNA CONVENTION ON THE PROTECTION OF THE OZONE LAYER, 1985, DECISIONS OF THE SECOND MEETING OF THE PARTIES TO THE MONTREAL PROTOCOL. *Supra*, p. 276.

B. EXCHANGE OF AND ACCESS TO INFORMATION

CANADA-UNITED STATES OF AMERICA: AGREEMENT CONCERNING THE TRANSBOUNDARY MOVEMENT OF HAZARDOUS WASTE. *Supra*, p. 616.

MEXICO-UNITED STATES OF AMERICA: LA PAZ AGREEMENT FOR COOPERATION ON ENVIRONMENTAL PROGRAMS AND TRANSBOUNDARY PROBLEMS. *Supra*, p. 621.

BASEL CONVENTION ON THE CONTROL OF TRANSBOUNDARY MOVEMENTS OF HAZARDOUS WASTES AND THEIR DISPOSAL. *Supra*, p. 601.

UNITED NATIONS ENVIRONMENT PROGRAMME GOVERNING COUNCIL DECISION: LONDON GUIDELINES FOR THE EXCHANGE OF INFORMATION ON CHEMICALS IN INTERNATIONAL TRADE

Popular Names: London Chemical Guidelines, UNEP Chemical Guidelines

Done at London on 25 May 1989, U.N. Doc. UNEP/PIC.WG.2/4 at 9 (1989), UNEP GC/DEC/15/30.

Languages: Arabic, Chinese, English, French, Russian, Spanish

Editors' Note

This set of guidelines is based on the principle of prior informed consent (PIC), i.e., that an international shipment of a banned or severely restricted chemical should not occur without the prior informed consent of the importing country.

LONDON GUIDELINES FOR THE EXCHANGE OF INFORMATION ON CHEMICALS IN INTERNATIONAL TRADE (AMENDED, 1989)

Introduction to the Guidelines

1. This set of Guidelines is addressed to Governments with a view to assisting them in the process of increasing chemical safety in all countries through the exchange of information on chemicals in international trade. They have been developed on the basis of common elements and principles derived from relevant existing bilateral, regional and global instruments and national regulations, drawing upon experience already gained through their preparation and implementation.
2. The Guidelines are general in nature and are aimed at enhancing the sound management of chemicals through the exchange of scientific, technical, economic and legal information. Special provisions have been included regarding the exchange of information on banned or severely restricted chemicals in international trade, which call for co-operation between exporting and importing countries in the light of their joint responsibility for the protection of human health and the environment at the global level. To this end, all references in these Guidelines to a Government or Governments shall be deemed to apply equally to regional economic integration organizations for matters falling within their areas of competence.
3. The Guidelines are without prejudice to the provisions of particular systems or procedures included in existing or future national legislation and bilateral, regional and multilateral instruments for the exchange of information on chemicals; rather, they have been prepared with a view to assisting States in the process of developing such arrangements.
4. These Guidelines do not preclude States from instituting broader and more frequent information exchange or other systems involving consultation with importing countries on banned or severely restricted chemicals designed to gain experience with alternative procedures.

5. These Guidelines provide a mechanism for importing countries to formally record and disseminate their decisions regarding the future importation of chemicals which have been banned or severely restricted and outlines the shared responsibilities of importing and exporting countries and exporting industries in ensuring that these decisions are heeded.

6. The importance of technical and financial assistance to enhance decision-making and training in the safe use of chemicals is recognized by the Guidelines.

7. These Guidelines are complementary to existing instruments developed by the United Nations and the World Health Organization and to the International Code of Conduct on the Distribution and Use of Pesticides of the Food and Agriculture Organization of the United Nations, which is the primary guidance for the management of pesticides internationally. These Guidelines should be implemented in a non-duplicative manner for the different classes of chemicals covered by existing instruments.

8. Although the Guidelines have not been prepared specifically to address the situation of developing countries, they nevertheless provide a framework for the establishment of procedures for the effective use of information on chemicals in these countries. Implementation of the Guidelines should thus help them to avoid serious and costly health and environmental problems due to ignorance about the risks associated with the use of chemicals, particularly those that have been banned or severely restricted in other States.

PART I
GENERAL PROVISIONS

1. *Definitions*

For the purposes of the Guidelines:

(a)   "Chemical" means a chemical substance whether by itself or in a mixture or preparation, whether manufactured or obtained from nature and includes such substances used as industrial chemicals and pesticides;

(b)   "Banned chemical" means a chemical which has, for health or environmental reasons, been prohibited for all uses by final governmental regulatory action;

(c)   "Severely restricted chemical" means a chemical for which, for health or environmental reasons, virtually all uses have been prohibited nationally by final government regulatory action, but for which certain specific uses remain authorized;

(d)   "International trade" means export or import of chemicals;

(e)   "Export" and "import" mean, in their respective connotations, the movement of a chemical from one State to another State, but exclude mere transit operations;

(f)   "Management" means the handling, supply, transport, storage, treatment, application, or other use of a chemical subsequent to its initial manufacture or formulation;

(g)   "Prior informed consent" (PIC) refers to the *principle* that international shipment of a chemical that is banned or severely restricted in order to protect human health or the environment should not proceed without the agreement, where such agreement exists, or contrary to the decision, of the designated national authority in the importing country;

(h)   "Prior informed consent procedure" (PIC procedure) means the *procedure* for formally obtaining and disseminating the decisions of importing countries as to whether they wish to receive future shipments of chemicals which have been banned or severely restricted. A specific procedure was established for selecting chemicals for initial implementation of the PIC procedures. These include chemicals which have been previously banned or severely restricted as well as certain pesticide formulations which are acutely toxic. This is explained in annex II.

2. *General principles*

(a)   Both States of export and States of import should protect human health and the environment against potential harm by exchanging information on chemicals in international trade;

(b)   In their activities with regard to chemicals, States should act, in so far as is applicable, in accordance with principle 21 of the Declaration of the United Nations Conference on the Human Environment;

(c)   States taking measures to regulate chemicals with a view to protecting human, animal or plant life or health, or the environent, should ensure that regulations and standards for this purpose do not create unnecessary obstacles to international trade;

(d)   States should ensure that governmental control measures or actions taken with regard to an imported chemical for which information has been received in implementation of the Guidelines are not more restrictive than those applied to the same chemical produced for domestic use or imported from a State other than the one that supplied the information;

(e)   States with more advanced systems for the safe management of chemicals should share their experience with those countries in need of improved systems;

(f)   Both States of import and States of export should, as appropriate, strengthen their existing infrastructures and institutions in the following way:

    (i)   Establishing and strengthening legislative and regulatory systems and other mechanisms for improving control and management of chemicals. This may include development of model legislation or regulations, in light of these Guidelines and other relevant guidelines prepared by other organizations;

    (ii) Creating national registers of toxic chemicals, including both industrial chemicals and pesticides;

    (iii) Preparing and updating manuals, directories and documentation for better utilization of facilities for information collection and dissemination at the country level and to on-line facilities at the regional level.

3. *Exemptions*

These Guidelines should not apply to:

(a)   Pharmaceuticals, including narcotics, drugs and psychotropic substances;[1]

(b)   Radioactive materials;

(c)   Chemicals imported for the purposes of research or analysis in quantities not likely to affect the environment or human health;

(d)   Chemicals imported as personal or household effects, in quantities reasonable for these uses;

(e)   Food additives.[1]

4. *Effects on other instruments*

(a)   States should take the necessary measures with regard to implementation of these Guidelines.

(b)   The provisions of these Guidelines do not affect the obligations of States deriving from any relevant international agreement to which they are or may become party.

5. *Institutional arrangements*

---

[1]It is open to States to apply these Guidelines to pharmaceuticals and food additives if they wish to do so.

5.1 UNEP and FAO should develop an information exchange system to ensure that designated national authorities of importing and exporting countries have a single contact point for obtaining information and communicating decisions on chemicals subject to the PIC procedure;

5.2 UNEP should share with FAO the operational responsibility for the implementation of the PIC procedure and jointly manage and implement common elements including the selection of chemicals to be included in the PIC procedure, preparation of PIC guidance documents, mechanisms for information sharing, and creation of data bases;

5.3 UNEP should collaborate with FAO in reviewing the implementation of the PIC procedure, including participation, responses, and violations of importing country decisions;

5.4 For purposes of international communications, each State should designate a national governmental authority (or authorities) competent to perform the administrative functions related to the exchange of information and decisions regarding importation of chemicals included in the PIC procedure;[2]

5.5 The designated national authority should be authorized to communicate, directly or as provided by national law or regulation, with designated national authorities of other States and with international organizations concerned, to exchange information, to make and communicate decisions regarding chemicals included in the PIC procedure and to submit reports at the request of such States or organizations or on its own initiative;

5.6 States should ensure that designated national authorities have sufficient national resources to assume responsibility with regard to implementation of these Guidelines;

5.7 States should as soon as possible make available the name and address of their designated national authority to the International Register of Potentially Toxic Chemicals (IRPTC), as well as subsequent changes;

5.8 A register of designated national authorities should be maintained, regularly updated, and disseminated by IRPTC;

5.9 IRPTC should, in addition:
(a) Co-ordinate the network of designated national authorities;
(b) Develop recommendations on practices and procedures, and such joint programmes and measures as may be required to make the Guidelines effective;
(c) Maintain liaison with other concerned intergovernmental and non-governmental organizations;
(d) Keep under review the implementation of these Guidelines, on the basis of periodic reports from designated national authorities and provide biennial reports on the effectiveness of the Guidelines and suggestions for their improvement.

PART II
NOTIFICATION AND INFORMATION REGARDING BANNED AND SEVERELY RESTRICTED CHEMICALS AND OPERATION OF THE PIC PROCEDURE

6. *Notification of control action*
(a) States having taken control action to ban or severely restrict a chemical as defined in these Guidelines should notify IRPTC. IRPTC will disseminate these notifications as provided in these Guidelines;

---

[2]States may designate more than one national authority for different purposes, such as for information exchange and making PIC determinations, or for industrial chemicals and pesticides. Where more than one national authority is designated, the term "designated national authority" in the text of these Guidelines should be interpreted as referring to the authority responsible for the actions being discussed.

(b)   The purpose of the notification regarding control action is to give competent authorities in other States the opportunity to assess the risks associated with the chemical, and to make timely and informed decisions thereon, taking into account local environmental, public health, economic and administrative conditions, and with regard to existing information on toxicology, safety and regulatory aspects;

(c)   The minimum information to be provided for this purpose should be:
   (i)   The chemical identification/specification of the chemical;
   (ii) A summary of the control action taken and of the reasons for it. If the control action bans or restricts certain uses but allows other uses, such information should be included;
   (iii) The fact that additional information is available, and the indication of the contact point in the State of export to which a request for further information should be addressed;

(d)   To the extent practicable, the designated national authority issuing the notification should provide information concerning alternative measures, such as, for example, integrated pest management procedures, non-chemical alternatives and impact mitigation measures;

(e)   Notification of control action should be provided as soon as practicable after the control action is taken.[3] For chemicals banned or severely restricted before the implementation of these Guidelines, an inventory of prior control actions should be provided to IRPTC, unless such information has already been provided and circulated by IRPTC to all designated national authorities.

7. *Operation of the PIC procedure*
   7.1 *Determination of participation in the PIC procedure*
   PIC is a procedure which operates in addition to information exchange and export notification. Those countries which elect to participate in the PIC procedure will have the opportunity to record their decisions regarding future imports of banned or severely restricted chemicals in a formal way.

(a)   Countries may participate in the information exchange procedures under these Guidelines without participating in the PIC procedure;

(b)   All exporting countries are expected to participate in the PIC procedure by respecting the decisions of importing countries;

(c)   IRPTC should invite countries to participate in the PIC procedure with respect to imports. Designated national authorities should reply indicating whether their country will participate. If there is no reply a follow-up letter should be sent 60 days after the first invitation. If there is no response, IRPTC should take additional steps to obtain a decision. If after that, there is still no response then it will be assumed that the country does not wish to participate in the procedure;

(d)   A country may designate one competent body to handle both industrial chemicals and pesticides or may designate separate competent bodies for each;

(e)   A country may elect at any time to participate or not participate in the PIC procedure by communicating its decision to IRPTC;

(f)   IRPTC should make available on request a list of countries who have elected to participate, countries which have elected not to participate and countries which did not respond.

   7.2 *Identification of chemicals for inclusion in the PIC procedure*
(a)   As provided in paragraph 9, IRPTC will notify each participating country of each chemical that is the subject of a notification of a final government control action and that meets the definitions as being banned or severely

---

[3]The form attached as annex I should be used for that purpose.

restricted for environmental or human health reasons for a decision under its conditions of use as to whether that country wishes to permit use and importation of the chemical. An informal consultative process may be used to assist IRPTC in determining whether the control action meets the definitions of the Guidelines;

(b) As provided in paragraph 9, IRPTC should send qualifying control actions, along with PIC decision guidance documents, to the appropriate designated national authority or authorities in each participating country for decision.[4]

7.3 *Response to notification of control action for chemicals identified for inclusion in the PIC procedure*

(a) The designated national authority in each participating importing country shall make an initial response to IRPTC within 90 days. A response may take either of two forms:

    (i) A final decision to permit use and importation, to prohibit use and importation or to permit importation only under specified stated conditions;

    (ii) An interim response which may be:

        a. A statement that importation is under active review but that final decision has not yet been reached;

        b. A request for further information; and/or

        c. A request for assistance in evaluating the chemical.

An interim response may also contain a statement permitting importation with or without stated specified conditions or prohibiting importation during the interim period until a final decision is made;

(b) The designated national authority shall use the form provided to make such response;[5]

(c) IRPTC should send reminders to countries as necessary to encourage a response and should facilitate the provision of technical assistance where requested;

(d) If a participating importing country does not make a response or responds with an interim decision that does not address importation, the *status quo* with respect to importation of the chemical should continue. This means that the chemical should not be exported without the explicit consent of the importing country, unless it is a pesticide which is registered in the importing country or is a chemical the use or importation of which has been allowed by other governmental action of the importing country;

(e) If a country takes a unilateral action which affects the *status quo* with respect to a chemical, it must so notify IRPTC to make IRPTC aware of the decision. Such a unilateral action will be interpreted as superseding any previous decision it has made with respect to the chemical;

(f) When an importing country takes a final or interim decision which affects the *status quo*, it should also communicate this decision to the national competent authority responsible for controlling imports so that it can take appropriate import control actions under its authority.

7.4 *Dissemination of information*

(a) IRPTC will inform designated national authorities of decisions taken by participating importing countries in a timely fashion and should also make these available to industry and other interested parties on request, preferably through a computer data base. This information should also be included in the regular updates of the United Nations Consolidated List of Products whose Consumption and/or Sale have been Banned,

---

[4]The content of a PIC decision guidance document is outlined in annex III.

[5]The content of a form for importing country response is outlined in annex IV.

Withdrawn or Severely Restricted by Governments. Semi-annually, IRPTC will notify all Governments in writing of the status of the decisions by importing countries;

(b)   Governments of exporting countries shall, upon receipt of importing countries' decisions, transmit them to their industry.

8. *Information regarding exports*

(a)   If an export of a chemical banned or severely restricted in the State of export occurs, the State of export should ensure that necessary steps are taken to provide the designated national authority of the State of import with relevant information;[6]

(b)   The purpose of information regarding exports is to remind the State of import of the original notification regarding control action and to alert it to the fact that an export will occur or is occurring;

(c)   The minimum information to be provided for this purpose should be:

    (i) A copy of, or reference to, the information provided at the time of notification of control action;

    (ii) Indication that an export of the chemical concerned will occur or is occurring;

    (iii) An estimate of the quantity to be exported annually as well as any shipment-specific information that might be available;

(d)   States should endeavour to ensure that, to the extent possible, information regarding exports provided or received in implementation of these guidelines is forwarded to the State of final destination and to IRPTC;

(e)   Provision of information regarding exports should take place when the first export following the control action occurs, and should recur periodically or in the case of any significant development of new information or condition surrounding the control action. It is the intention that, in so far as possible, the information should be provided prior to export. Where the chemical has been banned or severely restricted before the adoption of these Guidelines, the "first export following the control action" should be considered to be the first export after adoption of these Guidelines.

9. *Channels of notification and information*

(a)   Notifications of control actions should be addressed to IRPTC for transmission to designated national authorities;

(b)   Participating importing countries should send their response on the prescribed forms to IRPTC for appropriate dissemination;

(c)   PIC decision guidance documents will be transmitted by IRPTC to designated national authorities in participating importing countries for their decision and response and to designated national authorities in other countries for their information;

(d)   Information on exports should be addressed to the national authority designated for this purpose in the State of import.

10. *Feedback*

Designated national authorities of States of import should provide to IRPTC, for the purpose of periodic review pursuant to paragraph 5.9 (d), a summary of action taken as a result of notifications and information received pursuant to paragraphs 6, 7.3 and 8 and information on any difficulties which they have experienced in using these Guidelines.

11. *Confidential data*

(a)   States undertaking information exchange in implementation of these Guidelines should establish internal procedures for the receipt, handling and protection of confidential and proprietary information received from other States;

---

[6]The form attached as annex V should be used for that purpose.

(b)   States receiving notifications and information regarding exports should be responsible for the protection of proprietary rights and the confidentiality of data received under these Guidelines when claimed by the State supplying the information.

12. *Functions of designated national authorities*
    (a)   *Control action*. It should be the function of designated national authorities, with regard to control action taken by States to ban or severely restrict a chemical:
        (i)   To provide notification to IRPTC, in accordance with these Guidelines, that such control action has been taken;
        (ii) To receive from IRPTC notification that such action has been taken in other States, and to ensure its prompt transmittal to all other national authorities concerned;
        (iii) To receive from the United Nations the regular updates of the United Nations Consolidated List of Products Whose Consumption and/or Sale have been Banned, Withdrawn or Severely Restricted by Governments;
        (iv) To reply to the request for participation in the PIC procedures in accordance with paragraph 7.1 of these Guidelines;
        (v)   To respond to notifications of control action in accordance with paragraph 7.3 of these Guidelines, including response to the lists to be circulated in accordance with paragraph 7.2 and annex II;
    (b)   *Imports*. It should be the function of designated national authorities, with regard to imports of banned or severely restricted chemicals:
        (i)   To receive from States of export information on exports, and to ensure the prompt transmittal of such information to all other authorities concerned in the State of import;
        (ii) To transmit to States of export requests for further information as required;
        (iii) To provide feedback information to IRPTC on action taken as a result of notifications and information received and on any difficulties experienced in the exchange of data with States of exports;
        (iv) To advise and assist import control authorities so that they can take appropriate import control actions under their authority;
        (v)   To strengthen national decision-making procedures and import control mechanisms;
        (vi) To ensure that decisions apply uniformly to all sources of import and to domestic production of chemicals for domestic use;
        (vii) To encourage that chemicals subject to PIC be purchased only from sources in exporting countries which are participants in that procedure;
    (c)   *Exports*. It should be the function of designated national authorities, with regard to exports of banned or severely restricted chemicals:
        (i)   To ensure the issuance or transmittal of information on exports;
        (ii) To respond to requests for information from other States, especially as regards sources of precautionary information on safe use and handling of the chemicals concerned;
        (iii) To communicate PIC decisions to their export industry;
        (iv) To implement appropriate procedures, within their authority, designed to ensure that exports do not occur contrary to the PIC decisions of participating importing countries;
    (d)   *Other functions*. Designated national authorities should also consider the need:
        (i)   To provide information regarding applicable national regulations for the management of banned or severely restricted chemicals;

    (ii) To ensure the provision of appropriate precautionary information to persons using or handling the chemicals concerned;

    (iii) To keep records of notifications and information received, issued and transmitted which could be open for public inspection in accordance with national law, except for information classified as confidential or proprietary;

    (iv) To keep records of imports and exports of banned and severely restricted chemicals.

PART III
GENERAL INFORMATION EXCHANGE AND PROVISION OF TECHNICAL ASSISTANCE REGARDING CHEMICALS

13. *Information, advice and assistance*
    (a) For the protection of human health and the environment, States should facilitate:
        (i) The exchange of scientific information (including toxocological and safety data) and technical, economic and legal information concerning the management of chemicals, particularly through designated national governmental authorities and through intergovernmental organizations as appropriate;
        (ii) The provision upon request of technical advice and assistance concerning the management of chemicals to other States, on a bilateral or multilateral basis, taking into account the special needs of developing countries.
    (b) With regard to the export of chemicals, States of export should ensure that, where appropriate, information, advice and assistance is provided to States of import concerned regarding the sound management of such chemicals, including appropriate precautionary information;
    (c) With regard to the use of imported chemicals, States of import should, on the basis of notification and information provided by States of export, take the necessary measures to ensure that users are provided with information, advice and assistance for the sound management of such chemicals, including appropriate precautionary information;
    (d) As far as practicable, precautionary information should be provided in the principal language or languages of the State of import and of the area of intended use, and should be accompanied by suitable pictorial and/or tactile aids and labels.

14. *Classification, packaging and labelling*
    (a) States should recognize that classification, packaging and labelling are important elements in information exchange on chemicals in international trade, and that it is desirable that chemicals exported from their territories are subject to no less stringent requirements of classification, packaging and labelling than comparable products destined for use in the State of export;
    (b) In the development and implementation of existing and future internationally harmonized procedures for the classification, packaging and labelling of chemicals in international trade, States should take into account the special circumstances surrounding the management of chemicals in developing countries;
    (c) In the absence of other standards in the State of import, States should ensure that the classification, packaging and labelling of chemicals exported from their territories conform to recognized and, where appropriate, internationally harmonized procedures and practices for ensuring

the protection of human health and the environment during use of these chemicals.

15. *Technical assistance*
    (a)   IRPTC should encourage funding agencies, such as the development banks and the United Nations Development Programme, and bilateral donors to provide training, technical assistance and funding for institutional strengthening and should further encourage other United Nations organizations to strengthen their activities related to safe management of chemicals;

    (b)   States with more advanced chemical regulatory programmes should provide technical assistance to other countries in developing infrastructure and capacity to manage chemicals within their countries, including implementation of the provisions of these Guidelines. Developing countries with more advanced systems should be particularly encouraged to provide technical assistance to other developing countries with no, or less advanced, systems of chemical management. To the extent possible, donor countries and institutions and recipient countries should inform IRPTC of all such technical assistance activities;

    (c)   Special attention should be devoted by technical assistance and funding authorities to those countries without any regulatory procedures on chemicals in developing a régime for their control;

    (d)   Essential elements of technical assistance needed by developing countries for the management of chemicals include:

    (i) Strengthening existing infrastructure and institutions;

    (ii) Provision for the interchange of experts, including short missions, from developed countries to developing countries and vice versa and in particular from one developing country to another for the purposes of:
        a.   Sharing each other's experience and exchanging ideas;
        b.   Advising on analysis of information on chemical risks and benefits, conducting environmental impact assessment, and disposing of unusable products safely;
        c.   Sharing information on new products and alternatives;
        d.   Ascertaining research and development requirements for local pesticide efficacy studies and development of alternatives;
        e.   Assisting one another in dealing with practical difficulties in implementing these Guidelines;

    (iii) Training to include:
        a.   Technical workshops on a local, regional and international level;
        b.   Awareness campaigns on the safe management of chemicals for industrial and agricultural workers, customs officials and doctors;
        c.   Opportunities for decision makers in developing countries to study systems in countries which have been successfully implementing these Guidelines.

Annex I
Form for Notification of Control Action

Date Received in IRPTC	Country code

UNITED NATIONS ENVIRONMENT PROGRAMME
INTERNATIONAL REGISTER OF POTENTIALLY TOXIC CHEMICALS

LONDON GUIDELINES FOR THE EXCHANGE OF INFORMATION ON CHEMICALS IN INTER-
NATIONAL TRADE

NOTIFICATION SCHEME FOR BANNED AND SEVERELY RESTRICTED CHEMICALS

NOTIFICATION OF CONTROL ACTION

1. Country_____
2. Ministry/department and responsible authority (address, telephone, telefax, telex)_____

3. Name(s) of chemical (chemical name (IUPAC); common name; trade names)_____

4. Specification, if relevant for control action (e.g., for pesticides)_____

5. Code numbers
   —Chemical Abstracts Service Registry No. (CAS)_____
   —Other numbers (specify)_____

6. Control action

Use(s) controlled and summary of control action*	Effective date	Reference to national document

*If the control action bans or restricts certain uses, but allows other uses, such information should be included.

7. Reasons supporting the control action (relevant to protection of human health and the
   environment)

   _____
   _____
   _____
   _____

8. Alternatives_____
   _____
   _____

9. Designated national authority (address,
   telephone, telefax, telex)
   _____
   _____
   _____

10. Contact point where additional informa-
    tion may be obtained (address, telephone,
    telefax, telex)

    _____
    _____
    _____

11. Name and title of official issuing this noti-
    fication (address, telephone, telefax,
    telex)

    _____
    _____
    _____

12. Date_____

Annex IV
Form for Importing Country Response on Prior Informed Consent Chemicals

1. Country_____
2. Ministry/department and responsible authority_____
   _____

3. Name(s) of chemical_____
4. IRPTC reference number_____
5. Is this a registered/approved chemical in your country? Yes   No
6. Country final decision regarding future importation:
   A final decision has been taken to: (check one)
   — Permit importation;
   — Prohibit importation and use;
   — Permit imports only under the following conditions:
   _____
   _____
   _____
   _____

7. Country interim response (answer this section only if no final decision has been taken and reported in 6):
   (a) Nature of interim response:
   — Additional time will be required for a final decision
   — The following additional information is requested:
   _____
   _____
   _____
   _____

   — Technical assistance is requested to assist in reaching a final decision.
   (b) Has or is this chemical being imported into the country? Yes   No
   If yes, may imports be permitted pending a final decision? Yes   No
   Imports permitted only under the following conditions:
   _____
   _____
   _____
   _____

8. Contact point for additional information (include telephone, telex and telefax numbers):
   _____
   _____
   _____

9. Name and title of official issuing this decision: _____
   _____
   _____
   _____

10. Date_____

Annex V
Form for Information Regarding Export

UNITED NATIONS ENVIRONMENT PROGRAMME
INTERNATIONAL REGISTER OF POTENTIALLY TOXIC CHEMICALS

LONDON GUIDELINES FOR THE EXCHANGE OF INFORMATION ON CHEMICALS
IN INTERNATIONAL TRADE

NOTIFICATION SCHEME FOR BANNED AND SEVERELY
RESTRICTED CHEMICALS

INFORMATION REGARDING EXPORT

1. Country of export

2. Ministry/department and responsible authority/ or firm (address, telephone, telefax, telex)

3. Name(s) of chemical (Chemical name (IUPAC); common name; trade names)

4. Specification, if relevant for control action (e.g. for pesticides)

5. Code numbers
   — Chem. Abstr. Service Reg. No. (CAS)

   — Other numbers (specify)

6. Country(ies) of destination

7. Designated national authority(ies) to which this information is addressed (address, telehone, telefax, telex)

8. Notification(s) of control action sent
   — Date(s)

   — Copy attached ☐ Yes ☐ No
   — Reference address of designated national authority

9.

Information regarding export

---

10. Name, title, address, telephone, telefax and telex numbers of person providing this information
11. Date

Annex II
Procedure for Initial Identification of Chemicals for Inclusion in the Prior Informed Consent Procedure

1. Control actions have been taken prior to the adoption of the prior informed consent (PIC) procedure in the London Guidelines for the Exchange of Information on Chemicals in International Trade. Some have been notified to the International Register of Potentially Toxic Chemicals (IRPTC) and some have not been submitted. It is necessary to take these into account in starting up the PIC procedures. The following approach will be used to incorporate previous control actions:

   (a)   Designated national authorities in all States should submit inventories of control actions in accordance with paragraph 6 of these Guidelines, including all information specified in that paragraph, to IRPTC if they have not already done so. Submissions should be made as soon as possible to be available in IRPTC prior to the date of implementation of the PIC procedures;

   (b)   On the basis of these submissions, IRPTC will identify all chemicals banned or severely restricted by five or more countries. These will be introduced into the PIC process according to the following criteria:

      (i)   All chemicals banned or severely restricted as defined in these Guidelines by 10 or more countries should be immediately placed on a list and circulated, with PIC decision guidance documents, to countries participating in these Guidelines for determination regarding future use and importation;

      (ii)   Chemicals banned or severely restricted by 5 or more countries, but by less than 10, should be submitted to an informal consultation to determine whether they meet the definitions of banned and severely restricted for human health or environmental reasons. This determination should be made as expeditiously as possible. Those chemicals that meet the definitions will be circulated as an addition to the list referred to in subparagraph (i) above, with PIC decision guidance documents, for a determination by participating importing countries regarding their future use and importation;

   (c)   Should additional inventories of past control actions be received by IRPTC subsequent to the implementation date of the PIC procedures, they will be added to the original inventory. This updated inventory should be assessed annually in the same manner as the original inventory under step (b) above and incorporated into the PIC procedure as appropriate. These additional chemicals should be circulated to participating importing countries for their consideration and determinations regarding future use and importation under the PIC procedures. This annual reappraisal of the inventory of past control actions should continue until IRPTC has received adequate information from Governments that these reappraisals are no longer essential to the operation of the PIC procedures.

2. Additionally, an Expert Group will consider the problem of acutely hazardous pesticide formulations to determine if there exists a need for a list of such products to supplement the chemicals already subject to the PIC procedure.

3. This Expert Group should be made up of representatives from the World Health Organization (WHO), the Food and Agriculture Organization of the United Nations (FAO), the United Nations Environment Programme (UNEP) and national pesticide registrars. They may call upon the expertise of industry and non-governmental

organizations and other experts as they deem necessary and will review formulations based on the WHO Class 1A compounds.

4. If the Group concludes that there are acutely hazardous pesticide formulations of concern to developing countries which are not already included in the PIC procedure, a supplemental list of such formulations will be recommended for inclusion.

Annex III
Information to be Included in a Prior Informed Consent (PIC) Decision Guidance Document

A prior informed consent (PIC) decision guidance document will be prepared for each chemical placed into the PIC procedures. The document should consist of three parts, containing the following information to the extent it is available. In the case of the initial list, a summary of all control actions to date will be provided. For subsequent control actions, each national action will be provided as received with appropriate references to previous actions for the second and following notifications by additional countries.

(a)   *A summary of the control action*:
   (i)   The common and trade names of the chemical, its specification and numerical identification, using widely recognized chemical numbering systems;
   (ii) Whether a pesticide or industrial chemical, or both;
   (iii) Nature of the control action and date taken;
   (iv) Reasons for the control action;
   (v)   Uses banned;
   (vi) Uses continued in effect, if any;
   (vii) Alternatives considered effective replacements by the country taking the control action, including, e.g., integrated pest management and non-chemical alternatives;
   (viii) A contact for further information in the country taking the control action, including telephone, telefax and telex numbers, in addition to a mailing address;
   (ix) Relevant references supporting the action;
(b)   *Summary information on the chemical, including*:
   (i)   Description of the chemical;
   (ii) Uses and formulations;
   (iii) Chemical and physical properties;
   (iv) Toxicological characteristics;

EUROPEAN ECONOMIC COMMUNITY COUNCIL DIRECTIVE ON THE FREEDOM OF ACCESS TO INFORMATION ON THE ENVIRONMENT

Popular Name: Council Directive on Access to Information, EEC Directive on Access to Information

Done at Luxembourg on 7 June 1990, 33 OJEC No. L 158/56 (1990), *reprinted in* IER 131:7001.

Entry into Force: 7 June 1990

Languages: Danish, Dutch, English, French, German, Greek, Irish, Italian, Portuguese, Spanish

EEC Member States as of 1 September 1990: Belgium; Denmark; France; Germany, Federal Republic of; Greece; Ireland; Italy; Luxembourg; Netherlands; Portugal; Spain; United Kingdom of Great Britain and Northern Ireland

Editors' Note

This Directive of the European Economic Community (described *supra*, p. 233), requires that EEC member States bring into force laws, regulations, and administrative provisions necessary to comply with the Directive by 31 December 1991. This Directive and the Regulation creating the European Environment Agency and the European enironment information and observation network, EEC Council Regulation No. 1210/90 (7 May 1990), 33 OJEC No. 2 120/1 (1990), should result in substantially more information about the environment being available to the public and to policymakers.

COUNCIL DIRECTIVE
OF 7 JUNE 1990
ON THE FREEDOM OF ACCESS TO INFORMATION ON THE ENVIRONMENT

THE COUNCIL OF THE EUROPEAN COMMUNITIES,
Having regard to the Treaty establishing the European Economic Community, and in particular Article 130s thereof,
Having regard to the proposal from the Commission([1]),
Having regard to the opinion of the European Parliament([2]),
Having regard to the opinion of the Economic and Social Committee([3]),

---

([1]) OJ No C 335, 30. 12. 1988, p. 5.
([2]) OJ No C 120, 16. 5. 1989, p. 231.
([3]) OJ No C 139, 5. 6. 1989, p. 47.

Considering the principles and objectives defined by the action programmes of the European Communities on the environment of 1973([4]), 1977([5]) and 1983([6]), and more particularly the action programme of 1987([7]), which calls, in particular, for devising 'ways of improving public access to information held by environmental authorities';

Whereas the Council of the European Communities and the representatives of the Governments of the Member States, meeting within the Council, declared in their resolution of 19 October 1987 on the continuation and implementation of a European Community policy and action programme on the environment (1987 to 1992)([8]) that it was important, in compliance with the respective responsibilities of the Community and the Member States, to concentrate Community action on certain priority areas, including better access to information on the environment;

Whereas the European Parliament stressed, in its opinion on the fourth action programme of the European Communities on the environment([9]), that 'access to information for all must be made possible by a specific Community programme';

Whereas access to information on the environment held by public authorities will improve environmental protection;

Whereas the disparities between the laws in force in the Member States concerning access to information on the environment held by public authorities can create inequality within the Community as regards access to information and/or as regards conditions of competition;

Whereas it is necessary to guarantee to any natural or legal person throughout the Community free access to available information on the environment in written, visual, aural or data-base form held by public authorities, concerning the state of the environment, activities or measures adversely affecting, or likely so to affect the environment, and those designed to protect it;

Whereas, in certain specific and clearly defined cases, it may be justified to refuse a request for information relating to the environment;

Whereas a refusal by a public authority to forward the information requested must be justified;

Whereas it must be possible for the applicant to appeal against the public authority's decision;

Whereas access to information relating to the environment held by bodies with public responsibilities for the environment and under the control of public authorities should also be ensured;

Whereas, as part of an overall strategy to disseminate information on the environment, general information should actively be provided to the public on the state of the environment;

Whereas the operation of this Directive should be subject to a review in the light of the experience gained,

HAS ADOPTED THIS DIRECTIVE:

Article 1

The object of this Directive is to ensure freedom of access to, and dissemination of, information on the environment held by public authorities and to set out the basic terms and conditions on which such information should be made available.

([4]) OJ No C 112, 20. 12. 1973, p. 1.
([5]) OJ No C 139, 13. 6. 1977, p. 1.
([6]) OJ No C 46, 17. 2. 1983, p. 1.
([7]) OJ No C 70, 18. 3. 1987, p. 3.
([8]) OJ No C 289, 29. 10. 1987, p. 3.
([9]) OJ No C 156, 15. 6. 1987, p. 138.

Article 2

For the purposes of this Directive:
- (a) 'information relating to the environment' shall mean any available information in written, visual, aural or data-base form on the state of water, air, soil, fauna, flora, land and natural sites, and on activities (including those which give rise to nuisances such as noise) or measures adversely affecting, or likely so to affect these, and on activities or measures designed to protect these, including administrative measures and environmental management programmes;
- (b) 'public authorities' shall mean any public administration at national, regional or local level with responsibilities, and possessing information, relating to the environment with the exception of bodies acting in a judicial or legislative capacity.

Article 3

1. Save as provided in this Article, Member States shall ensure that public authorities are required to make available information relating to the environment to any natural or legal person at his request and without his having to prove an interest. Member States shall define the practical arrangements under which such information is effectively made available.
2. Member States may provide for a request for such information to be refused where it affects:
—the confidentiality of the proceedings of public authorities, international relations and national defence,
—public security,
—matters which are, or have been, *sub judice*, or under enquiry (including disciplinary enquiries), or which are the subject of preliminary investigation proceedings,
—commercial and industrial confidentiality, including intellectual property,
—the confidentiality of personal data and/or files,
—material supplied by a third party without that party being under a legal obligation to do so,
—material, the disclosure of which would make it more likely that the environment to which such material related would be damaged.
Information held by public authorities shall be supplied in part where it is possible to separate out information on items concerning the interests referred to above.
3. A request for information may be refused where it would involve the supply of unfinished documents or data or internal communications, or where the request is manifestly unreasonable or formulated in too general a manner.
4. A public authority shall respond to a person requesting information as soon as possible and at the latest within two months. The reasons for a refusal to provide the information requested must be given.

Article 4

A person who considers that his request for information has been unreasonably refused or ignored, or has been inadequately answered by a public authority, may seek a judicial or administrative review of the decision in accordance with the relevant national legal system.

Article 5

Member States may make a charge for supplying the information, but such charge may not exceed a reasonable cost.

Article 6

Member States shall take the necessary steps to ensure that information relating to the environment held by bodies with public responsibilities for the environment and under the control of public authorities is made available on the same terms and conditions as those set out in Articles 3, 4 and 5 either via the competent public authority or directly by the body itself.

Article 7

Member States shall take the necessary steps to provide general information to the public on the state of environment by such means as the periodic publication of descriptive reports.

Article 8

Four years after the date referred to in Article 9 (1), the Member States shall report to the Commission on the experience gained in the light of which the Commission shall make a report to the European Parliament and the Council together with any proposal for revision which it may consider appropriate.

Article 9

1.   Member States shall bring into force the laws, regulations and administrative provisions necessary to comply with this Directive by 31 December 1992 at the latest. They shall forthwith inform the Commission thereof.
2. Member States shall communicate to the Commission the main provisions of national law which they adopt in the field governed by this Directive.

Article 10

This Directive is addressed to the Member States.

C. REQUIREMENT TO INTERACT (CONSULT, NEGOTIATE, AGREE)

CANADA-UNITED STATES: AGREEMENT ON AIR QUALITY. *Supra*, p. 263.

AFRICAN CONVENTION ON THE CONSERVATION OF NATURE AND NATURAL RESOURCES. *Supra*, p. 202.

CHAPTER 25
ACCOUNTABILITY (LIABILITY)

Editors' Introductory Note Regarding Accountability (Liability)

International accountability on the part of States or private persons for causing environmental harm raises complex issues. Disagreement exists about the precise circumstances in which States are accountable for international pollution (or other environmental harm) under customary international law (*see infra* the Editors' Introductory Note to part A, this Chapter), and customary norms do not create accountability for private polluters. Moreover, very few conventional regimes exist that specify accountability or provide compensation. Finally, municipal remedies against either State- or private-polluters typically face insuperable barriers in a transnational setting. Efforts to strengthen and clarify customary norms and establish conventional regimes regarding accountability and compensation for environmental harm are thus of great importance.

A. STATES

Editors' Introductory Note
Regarding Accountability of States

Customary international law regarding accountability and compensation for international pollution or other environmental harm is currently subject to vigorous discussion. From a practical perspective, the uncertainty is demonstrated by the events following the Chernobyl disaster (described *supra*, p. 582). Most international law commentators would agree that customary norms prohibit States from causing damage to the environment of another State or of the global commons, yet there have been no diplomatic claims for compensation from the Soviet Union for damage from the Chernobyl disaster.

From a theoretical perspective, the debate has focussed on the United Nations International Law Commission's (described *supra*, p. 404) studies of two topics: "State responsibility" and "international liability for injurious consequences arising out of acts not prohibited by international law." Some commentators take the view that the latter topic is misconceived, because international accountability can be engaged only if a State has acted wrongfully, e.g., by failing to exercise due diligence in regulating private activities within its territory or control, with the result that transfrontier pollution occurs. Other commentators argue that a State can be obligated to pay for damage in another State caused by pollution emanating from the first State (the State of origin) even if the State of origin has exercised due diligence and even if the activity at issue is not ultrahazardous. The Commission, whose study of international liability is still very much in progress, has thus far favored the latter view, although it has not adopted a standard of strict liability.

The so-called Schematic Outline, which has formed the basis of the Commission's work thus far, is reproduced below.

  A separate issue is raised by the Commission's draft articles on State responsibility, which principally deal with rules of attribution and consequences of violating primary rules. The Commission has provisionally—and controversially—approved the concept of "international crime" and has defined it to include certain conduct causing environmental harm.

  The relevant provisions are reproduced below.

UNITED NATIONS INTERNATIONAL LAW COMMISSION RAPPORTEUR'S SCHEMATIC OUTLINE ON INTERNATIONAL LIABILITY FOR INJURIOUS CONSEQUENCES ARISING OUT OF ACTS NOT PROHIBITED BY INTERNATIONAL LAW

Popular Name: ILC Schematic Outline on Liability, ILC Draft Liability Articles

Report of the International Law Commission on the Work of its Thirty-Fourth Session, 37 U.N. GAOR Supp. (No. 10) at 83, U.N. Doc. A/37/10 (1982), A/CN.4/373, Annex, 2 YBILC, pt. 2, at 83 (1983).

Languages: Arabic, Chinese, English, French, Russian, Spanish

SCHEMATIC OUTLINE

Section 1
1. *Scope*

  Activities within the territory or control of a State which give rise or may give rise to loss or injury to persons or things within the territory or control of another State.

  [*Notes*: (1) It is a matter for later review whether this provision needs to be supplemented or adapted, when the operative provisions have been drafted and considered in relation to matters other than losses or injuries arising out of the physical use of the environment.

  (2) Compare this provision, in particular, with the provision contained in section 4, article 1.]

2. *Definitions*

  (*a*) "Acting State" and "affected State" have meanings corresponding to the terms of the provision describing the scope.

  (*b*) "Activity" includes any human activity.

  [*Note*: Should 'activity' also include a lack of activity to remove a natural danger which gives rise or may give rise to loss or injury to another State?]

  (*c*) "Loss or injury" means any loss or injury, whether to the property of a State, or to any person or thing within the territory or control of a State.

(*d*)   "Territory or control" includes, in relation to places not within the territory of the acting State,

    (i)   any activity which takes place within the substantial control of that State; and

    (ii)   any activity conducted on ships or aircraft of the acting State, or by nationals of the acting State, and not within the territory or control of any other State, otherwise than by reason of the presence within that territory of a ship in course of innocent passage, or an aircraft in authorized overflight.

3. *Saving*

Nothing contained in these articles shall affect any right or obligation arising independently of these articles.

Section 2

1. When an activity taking place within its territory or control gives or may give rise to loss or injury to persons or things within the territory or control of another State, the acting State has a duty to provide the affected State with all relevant and available information, including a specific indication of the kinds and degrees of loss or injury that it considers to be foreseeable and the remedial measures it proposes.

2. When a State has reason to believe that persons or things within its territory or control are being or may be subjected to loss or injury by an activity taking place within the territory or control of another State, the affected State may so inform the acting State, giving as far as its means of knowledge will permit, a specific indication of the kinds and degrees of loss or injury that it considers to be foreseeable; and the acting State has thereupon a duty to provide all relevant and available information, including a specific indication of the kinds and degrees of loss or injury that it considers to be foreseeable; and the acting State has thereupon a duty to provide all relevant and available information, including a specific indication of the kinds and degrees of loss or injury that it considers to be foreseeable, and the remedial measures it proposes.

3. If, for reasons or national or industrial security, the acting State considers it necessary to withhold any relevant information that would otherwise be available, it must inform the affected State that information is being withheld. In any case, reasons of national or industrial security cannot justify a failure to give an affected State a clear indication of the kinds and degrees of loss or injury to which persons and things within the territory or control of that affected State are being or may be subjected; and the affected State is not obliged to rely upon assurances which it has no sufficient means of knowledge to verify.

4. If not satisfied that the measures being taken in relation to the loss or injury foreseen are sufficient to safeguard persons and things within its territory or control, the affected State may propose to the acting State that fact-finding be undertaken.

5. The acting State may itself propose that fact-finding be undertaken; and when such a proposal is made by the affected State, the acting State has a duty to co-operate in good faith to reach agreement with the affected State upon the arrangements for and terms of reference of the inquiry, and upon the establishment of the fact-finding machinery. Both States shall furnish the inquiry with all relevant and available information.

6. Unless the States concerned otherwise agree,

(*a*)   there should be joint fact-finding machinery, with reliance upon experts, to gather relevant information, assess its implications and, to the extent possible, recommend solutions;

(*b*) the report should be advisory, not binding the States concerned.

7. The acting State and the affected State shall contribute to the costs of the fact-finding machinery on an equitable basis.

8. Failure to take any step required by the rules contained in this section shall not in itself give rise to any right of action. Nevertheless, unless it is otherwise agreed, the acting State has a continuing duty to keep under review the activity that gives or may give rise to loss or injury; to take whatever remedial measures it considers necessary and feasible to safeguard the interests of the affected State; and, as far as possible, to provide information to the affected State about the action it is taking.

Section 3

1. If (*a*) it does not prove possible within a reasonable time either to agree upon the establishment and terms of reference of fact-finding machinery or for the fact-finding machinery to complete its terms of reference; or (*b*) any State concerned is not satisfied with the findings, or believes that other matters should be taken into consideration; or (*c*) the report of the fact-finding machinery so recommends, the States concerned have a duty to enter into negotiations at the request of any one of them with a view to determining whether a regime is necessary and what form it should take.

2. Unless the States concerned otherwise agree, the negotiations shall apply the principles set out in section 5; shall also take into account, as far as applicable, any relevant factor including those set out in section 6; and may be guided by reference to any of the matters set out in section 7.

3. Any agreement concluded pursuant to the negotiations shall, in accordance with its terms, satisfy the rights and obligations of the States parties under the present articles; it may also stipulate the extent to which these rights and obligations replace any other rights and obligations of the parties.

4. Failure to take any step required by the rules contained in this section shall not in itself give rise to any right of action. Nevertheless, unless it is otherwise agreed, the acting State has a continuing duty to keep under review the activity that gives or may give rise to loss or injury; to take or continue whatever remedial measures it considers necessary and feasible to safeguard the interests of the affected State; and, as far as possible, to provide information to the affected State about the action it is taking.

Section 4

1. If any activity does give rise to loss or injury, and the rights and obligations of the acting and affected States under the present articles in respect of any such loss or injury have not been specified in an agreement between those States, those rights and obligations shall be determined in accordance with the provisions of this section. The States concerned shall negotiate in good faith to achieve this purpose.

2. Reparation shall be made by the acting State to the affected State in respect of any such loss or injury, unless it is established that the making of reparation for a loss or injury of that kind or character is not in accordance with the shared expectations of those States.

3. The reparation due to the affected State under the preceding article shall be ascertained in accordance with the shared expectations of the States concerned and the principles set out in section 5; and account shall be taken of the reasonableness of the conduct of the parties, having regard to the record of any exchanges or negotiations between them and to the remedial measures taken by the acting State to safeguard the interests of the affected State. Account may also be taken of any relevant factors including those set out in section 6, and guidance may be obtained by reference to any of the matters set out in section 7.

4. In the two preceding articles, "shared expectations" include shared expectations which:

(*a*)   have been expressed in correspondence or other exchanges between the States concerned or, in so far as there are no such expressions,

(*b*)   can be implied from common legislative or other standards or patterns of conduct normally observed by the States concerned, or in any regional or other grouping to which they both belong, or in the international community.

Section 5

1. The aim and purpose of the present articles is to ensure to acting States as much freedom of choice, in relation to activities within their territory or control, as is compatibie with adequate protection for the interests of affected States.

2. Adequate protection requires measures of prevention that as far as possible avoid a risk of loss or injury and, in so far as that is not possible, measures of reparation; but the standards of adequate protection should be determined with due regard to the importance of the activity and its economic viability.

3. In so far as may be consistent with the proceeding articles, an innocent victim should not be left to bear his loss or injury; the costs of adequate protection should be distributed with due regard to the distribution of the benefits of the activity, and standards of protection should take into account the means at the disposal of the acting State and the standards applied in the affected State and in regional and international practice.

4. To the extent that an acting State has not made available to an affected State information that is more accessible to the acting State concerning the nature and effects of an activity, and the means of verifying and assessing that information, the affected State shall be allowed a liberal recourse to inferences of fact and circumstantial evidence in order to establish whether the activity does or may give rise to loss or injury.

Section 6

Factors which may be relevant to a balancing of interests include:

1. The degree of probability of loss or injury (i.e. how likely is it to happen?);

2. The seriousness of loss or injury (i.e. an assessment of quantum and degree of severity in terms of the consequences);

3. The probable cumulative effect of losses or injuries of the kind in question—in terms of conditions of life and security of the affected State, and more generally—if reliance is placed upon measures to ensure the provision of reparation rather than prevention (i.e. the acceptable mix between prevention and reparation);

4. The existence of means to prevent loss or injury, having regard to the highest known state of the art of carrying on the activity;

5. The feasibility of carrying on the activity by alternative means or in alternative places;

6. The importance of the activity to the acting State (i.e. how necessary is it to continue or undertake the activity, taking account of economic, social, security or other interests?);

7. The economic viability of the activity considered in relation to the cost of possible means of protection;

8. The availability of alternative activities;

9. The physical and technical capacities of the acting States (considered, for example, in relation to its ability to take measures of prevention or make reparation or to undertake alternative activities);

10. The way in which existing standards of protection compare with:

(*a*)   the standards applied by the affected State; and
(*b*)   the standards applied in regional and international practice;
11. The extent to which the acting State:
(*a*)   has effective control over the activity; and
(*b*)   obtains a real benefit from the activity;
12. The extent to which the affected State shares in the benefits of the activity;
13. The extent to which the adverse effects arise from or affect the use of a shared resource;
14. The extent to which the affected State is prepared to contribute to the cost of preventing or making reparation for loss or injury, or of maximizing its benefits from the activity;
15. The extent to which the interests of:
(*a*)   the affected State, and
(*b*)   the acting State
are compatible with the interests of the general community;
16. The extent to which assistance to the acting State is available from third States or from international organizations;
17. The applicability of relevant principles and rules of international law.

Section 7

Matters which may be relevant in negotiations concerning prevention and reparation include:

I. *Fact-finding and prevention*

1. The identification of adverse effects and of material and non-material loss or injury to which they may give rise;
2. The establishment of procedural means for managing the activity and monitoring its effects;
3. The establishment of requirements concerning the structure and operation of the activity;
4. The taking of measures to assist the affected State in minimizing loss or injury.

II. *Compensation as a means of reparation*

1. A decision as to where primary and residual liability should lie, and whether the liability of some actors should be channelled through others;
2. A decision as to whether liability should be unlimited or limited;
3. The choice of a forum in which to determine the existence of liability and the amounts of compensation payable;
4. The establishment of procedures for the presentation of claims;
5. The identification of compensable loss or injury;
6. The test of the measure of compensation for loss or injury;
7. The establishment of forms and modalities for the payment of compensation awarded;
8. Consideration of the circumstances which might increase or diminish liability or provide an exoneration from it.

III. *Authorities competent to make decisions concerning fact-finding, prevention and compensation*

At different phases of the negotiations the States concerned may find it helpful to place in the hands of their national authorities or courts, international organizations or specially constituted commissions, the responsibility for making recommendations or taking decisions as to the matters referred to in I and II above.

Section 8

Settlement of disputes (taking due account of recently concluded multilateral treaties that provide such measures).

UNITED NATIONS INTERNATIONAL LAW COMMISSION DRAFT ARTICLES ON STATE RESPONSIBILITY

Popular Name: ILC Draft State Responsibility Articles

Report of the International Law Commission on the Work of its Forty-First Session, 44 U.N. GAOR Supp. (No. 10) at 190-93, 218-19, U.N. Doc. A/44/10 (1989), 2 YBILC 1976, pp.96, 108-09.

Languages: Arabic, Chinese, English, French, Russian, Spanish

STATE RESPONSIBILITY

Part One, *Article 19. International crimes and international delicts*

1. An act of a State which constitutes a breach of an international obligation is an internationally wrongful act, regardless of the subject-matter of the obligation breached.

2. An internationally wrongful act which results from the breach of a State of an international obligation so essential for the protection of fundamental interests of the international community that its breach is recognized as a crime by that community as a whole constitutes an international crime.

3. Subject to paragraph 2, and on the basis of the rules of international law in force, an international crime may result, *inter alia*, from:

* * *

(*d*)   a serious breach of an international obligation of essential importance for the safeguarding and preservation of the human environment, such as those prohibiting massive pollution of the atmosphere or of the seas.

4. Any internationally wrongful act which is not an international crime in accordance with paragraph 2 constitutes an international delict.

* * *

Part Two, *Article 5*

1. For the purposes of the present articles, "injured State" means any State a right of which is infringed by the act of another State, if that act constitutes, in accordance with Part One of the present articles, an internationally wrongful act of that State.

* * *

3. In addition, "injured State" means, if the internationally wrongful act constitutes an international crime [and in the context of the rights and obligations of States under articles 14 and 15], all other States.

CONVENTION ON INTERNATIONAL LIABILITY FOR DAMAGE CAUSED BY SPACE OBJECTS. *Supra*, p. 462.

RESTATEMENT (THIRD) OF THE FOREIGN RELATIONS LAW OF THE UNITED STATES. *Supra*, pp. 194, 354.

B. PRIVATE PERSONS

Editors' Introductory Note Regarding Private Liability for Oil Pollution from Spills at Sea

Strict, but limited liability for spills of oil transported at sea is provided by four instruments—two of which are international agreements among States and two of which are agreements among private members of industries related to the carriage of oil at sea (tanker owners and oil companies). These four agreements were in response to incidents such as the Torrey Canyon spill.

The 1969 Convention on Civil Liability for Oil Pollution Damage (CLC), an intergovernmental agreement, establishes strict liability on the part of the shipowner for pollution damage occurring in the territory or the territorial sea of a member State from the escape or discharge of oil, including the cost of preventive measures to mitigate such damage. The CLC also limits the amount of liability if the ship-owner is not at fault or in privity and the shipowner constitutes a fund by obtaining insurance or otherwise as prescribed in the CLC. Two protocols (1976 and 1984) have been negotiated to the CLC; only the 1976 Protocol is in force.

The second intergovernmental convention is the 1971 Convention on the Establishment of an International Fund for Compensation for Oil Pollution Damage. Generally speaking, the Fund Convention increases the amount of compensation available by supplementing compensation from the CLC, and it shifts part of the cost of that compensation from tanker owners to oil companies. The Fund Convention indemnifies shipowners for part of their liability under the CLC; the fund is composed of contributions from persons in member States receiving a specified amount of oil that has been transported by sea. Neither of the two protocols (1976 and 1984) to the Fund Convention are in force.

Ten months before the CLC was concluded, tanker owners entered into the Tanker Owners Voluntary Agreement Concerning Liability for Oil Pollution (TO-VALOP). It is widely thought that the tanker owners acted as they did in order to decrease the likelihood that governments would take more severe steps. In any event, TOVALOP, as amended, parallels—but does not duplicate in many significant details—the coverage of the CLC. TOVALOP provides generally that tanker owners (including bareboat charterers) will compensate persons—including governments—who sustain roughly the same types of damage covered by the CLC, but it also provides that compensation will be paid for measures taken to remove the threat of a discharge of oil even if no discharge occurs. A liability limit similar to that of the CLC applies. Owners of the vast majority of the free world's tanker tonnage are parties to TOVALOP, which has been revised twice (1978 and 1987) and now has a second tier (known as TOVALOP Supplement; the main part of

TOVALOP is referred to as the Standing Agreement) providing increased compensation when the oil spilled is owned by a member of CRISTAL (described below).

The Contract Regarding an Interim Supplement to Tanker Liability for Oil Pollution (CRISTAL) is another agreement among nongovernmental parties—in this case, oil companies. CRISTAL, which antedated the Fund Convention, has the effect of increasing the amount of compensation available from TOVALOP to pay for oil pollution damage and of shifting costs of compensation from tanker owners to persons receiving oil transported by sea.

Compensation under TOVALOP, TOVALOP Supplement, and CRISTAL is not available if the CLC and Fund Convention apply. The United States is a member of neither the CLC nor the Fund Convention, which has jeopardized the continued viability of those conventions and leaves U.S. claimants dependent on TOVALOP, TOVALOP Supplement, CRISTAL, and remedies under domestic legislation.

BRUSSELS INTERNATIONAL CONVENTION ON CIVIL LIABILITY FOR OIL POLLUTION DAMAGE, AS AMENDED BY THE 1976 PROTOCOL

Popular Names: Brussels Convention, Civil Liability Convention, CLC

Done at Brussels on 29 November 1969, U.N. Doc. ST/LEG/SER.C/7, 973 UNTS 3, UKTS No.106 (1975), *reprinted in* UNEP Reg. p.81, 1969 UNJYB 174, 9 ILM 45 (1970), 1 IPE 460, IELMT 969: 88; amended on 19 November 1976 by a Protocol, *reprinted in* 16 ILM 617 (1977), 19 IPE 9443.

Entry into Force: 19 June 1975 (Convention); 8 April 1981 (Protocol)

Depositary: International Maritime Organization

Languages: English, French

Parties as of 18 October 1990: Algeria; Australia;* Bahamas; Belgium;* Belize;**** Benin; Brazil; Cameroon; Canada; Chile; China;* Colombia; Côte d'Ivoire; Cyprus; Denmark; Djibouti; Dominican Republic; Ecuador; Egypt; Fiji; Finland; France; Gabon; Germany;*/** Ghana; Greece; Guatemala;* Iceland; India; Indonesia; Italy; Japan; Kiribati;**** Korea, Republic of; Kuwait; Lebanon; Liberia; Maldives; Monaco; Morocco; Netherlands; New Zealand; Nigeria; Norway; Oman; Panama; Papua New Guinea; Peru;* Poland; Portugal; Qatar; Saint Vincent and the Grenadines; Senegal; Seychelles; Singapore; Solomon Islands;**** South Africa; Spain; Sri Lanka; Sweden; Switzerland; Syrian Arab Republic;* Tunisia; Tuvalu; Union of Soviet Socialist Republics;* United Arab Emirates; United Kingdom of Great Britain and Northern Ireland;*** Vanuatu; Yemen; Yugoslavia

---

*   With a reservation, declaration, or statement
**   The Depositary lists Germany, consisting of the Federal Republic of Germany and the German Democratic Republic, as a party
***   With a geographic extension
****Provisional application

Amendments:1984 Protocol, *reprinted in* 13 EPL 66 (1984), not yet in force as of 18 October 1990

INTERNATIONAL CONVENTION ON CIVIL LIABILITY FOR OIL POLLUTION DAMAGE

The States Parties to the present Convention,

Conscious of the dangers of pollution posed by the worldwide maritime carriage of oil in bulk,

Convinced of the need to ensure that adequate compensation is available to persons who suffer damage caused by pollution resulting from the escape or discharge of oil from ships,

Desiring to adopt uniform international rules and procedures for determining questions of liability and providing adequate compensation in such cases,

Have agreed as follows:

Article I. For the purposes of this Convention:

1. "Ship" means any sea-going vessel and any seaborne craft of any type whatsoever, actually carrying oil in bulk as cargo.

2. "Person" means any individual or partnership or any public or private body, whether corporate or not, including a State or any of its constituent subdivisions.

3. "Owner" means the person or persons registered as the owner of the ship or, in the absence of registration, the person or persons owning the ship. However, in the case of a ship owned by a State and operated by a company which in that State is registered as the ship's operator, "owner" shall mean such company.

4. "State of the ship's registry" means in relation to registered ships the State of registration of the ship, and in relation to unregistered ships the State whose flag the ship is flying.

5. "Oil" means any persistent oil such as crude oil, fuel oil, heavy diesel oil, lubricating oil and whale oil, whether carried on board a ship as cargo or in the bunkers of such a ship.

6. "Pollution damage" means loss or damage caused outside the ship carrying oil by contamination resulting from the escape or discharge of oil from the ship, wherever such escape or discharge may occur, and includes the costs of preventive measures and further loss or damage caused by preventive measures.

7. "Preventive measures" means any reasonable measures taken by any person after an incident has occurred to prevent or minimize pollution damage.

8. "Incident" means any occurrence, or series of occurrences having the same origin, which causes pollution damage.

9. "Organization" means the Inter-Governmental Maritime Consultative Organization.

Article II. This Convention shall apply exclusively to pollution damage caused on the territory including the territorial sea of a Contracting State and to preventive measures taken to prevent or minimize such damage.

Article III. 1. Except as provided in paragraphs 2 and 3 of this Article, the owner of a ship at the time of an incident, or where the incident consists of a series of occurrences at the time of the first such occurrence, shall be liable for any pollution damage caused by oil which has escaped or been discharged from the ship as a result of the incident.

2. No liability for pollution damage shall attach to the owner if he proves that the damage:

(a) resulted from an act of war, hostilities, civil war, insurrection or a natural phenomenon of an exceptional, inevitable and irresistible character, or

(b) was wholly caused by an act or omission done with intent to cause damage by a third party, or

(c) was wholly caused by the negligence or other wrongful act of any Government or other authority responsible for the maintenance of lights or other navigational aids in the exercise of that function.

3. If the owner proves that the pollution damage resulted wholly or partially either from an act or omission done with intent to cause damage by the person who suffered the damage or from the negligence of that person, the owner may be exonerated wholly or partially from his liability to such person.

4. No claim for compensation for pollution damage shall be made against the owner otherwise than in accordance with this Convention. No claim for pollution damage under this Convention or otherwise may be made against the servants or agents of the owner.

5. Nothing in this Convention shall prejudice any right of recourse of the owner against third parties.

Article IV. When oil has escaped or has been discharged from two or more ships, and pollution damage results therefrom, the owners of all the ships concerned, unless exonerated under Article III, shall be jointly and severally liable for all such damage which is not reasonably separable.

Article V. 1. The owner of a ship shall be entitled to limit his liability under this Convention in respect of any one incident to an aggregate amount of 2,000 francs for each ton of the ship's tonnage. However, this aggregate amount shall not in any event exceed 210 million francs.

2. If the incident occurred as a result of the actual fault or privity of the owner, he shall not be entitled to avail himself of the limitation provided in paragraph 1 of this Article.

3. For the purpose of availing himself of the benefit of limitation provided for in paragraph 1 of this Article the owner shall constitute a fund for the total sum representing the limit of his liability with the Court or other competent authority of any one of the Contracting States in which action is brought under Article IX. The fund can be constituted either by depositing the sum or by producing a bank guarantee or other guarantee, acceptable under the legislation of the Contracting State where the fund is constituted, and considered to be adequate by the Court or another competent authority.

4. The fund shall be distributed among the claimants in proportion to the amounts of their established claims.

5. If before the fund is distributed the owner or any of his servants or agents or any person providing him insurance or other financial security has, as a result of the incident in question, paid compensation for pollution damage, such person shall, up to the amount he has paid, acquire by subrogation the rights which the person so compensated would have enjoyed under this Convention.

6. The right of subrogation provided for in paragraph 5 of this Article may also be exercised by a person other than those mentioned therein in respect of any amount of compensation for pollution damage which he may have paid but only to the extent that such subrogation is permitted under the applicable national law.

7. Where the owner or any other person establishes that he may be compelled to pay at a later date in whole or in part any such amount of compensation, with regard to which such person would have enjoyed a right of subrogation under paragraphs 5 or 6 of this Article, had the compensation been paid before the fund was distributed, the Court or other competent authority of the State where the fund

has been constituted may order that a sufficient sum shall be provisionally set aside to enable such person at such later date to enforce his claim against the fund.

8. Claims in respect of expenses reasonably incurred or sacrifices reasonably made by the owner voluntarily to prevent or minimize pollution damage shall rank equally with other claims against the fund.

9. The franc mentioned in this Article shall be a unit consisting of sixty-five-and-a-half milligrams of gold of millesimal fineness nine hundred. The amount mentioned in paragraph 1 of this Article shall be converted into the national currency of the State in which the fund is being constituted on the basis of the official value of that currency by reference to the unit defined above on the date of the constitution of the fund.

10. For the purpose of this Article the ship's tonnage shall be the net tonnage of the ship with the addition of the amount deducted from the gross tonnage on account of engine room space for the purpose of ascertaining the net tonnage. In the case of a ship which cannot be measured in accordance with the normal rules of tonnage measurement, the ship's tonnage shall be deemed to be 40 per cent of the weight in tons (of 2,240 lbs) of oil which the ship is capable of carrying.

11. The insurer or other person providing financial security shall be entitled to constitute a fund in accordance with this Article on the same conditions and having the same effect as if it were constituted by the owner. Such a fund may be constituted even in the event of the actual fault or privity of the owner but its constitution shall in that case not prejudice the rights of any claimant against the owner.

Article VI. 1. Where the owner, after an incident, has constituted a fund in accordance with Article V, and is entitled to limit his liability,

(a) no person having a claim for pollution damage arising out of that incident shall be entitled to exercise any right against any other assets of the owner in respect of such claim;

(b) the Court or other competent authority of any Contracting State shall order the release of any ship or other property belonging to the owner which has been arrested in respect of a claim for pollution damage arising out of that incident, and shall similarly release any bail or other security furnished to avoid such arrest.

2. The foregoing shall, however, only apply if the claimant has access to the Court administering the fund and the fund is actually available in respect of his claim.

Article VII. 1. The owner of a ship registered in a Contracting State and carrying more than 2,000 tons of oil in bulk as cargo shall be required to maintain insurance or other financial security, such as the guarantee of a bank or a certificate delivered by an international compensation fund, in the sums fixed by applying the limits of liability prescribed in Article V, paragraph 1, to cover his liability for pollution damage under this Convention.

2. A certificate attesting that insurance or other financial security is in force in accordance with the provisions of this Convention shall be issued to each ship. It shall be issued or certified by the appropriate authority of the State of the ship's registry after determining that the requirements of paragraph 1 of this Article have been complied with. This certificate shall be in the form of the annexed model and shall contain the following particulars:

(a) name of ship and port of registration;

(b) name and principal place of business of owner;

(c) type of security;

(d) name and principal place of business of insurer or other person giving security and, where appropriate, place of business where the insurance or security is established;

(e) period of validity of certificate which shall not be longer than the period of validity of the insurance or other security.

3. The certificate shall be in the official language or languages of the issuing State. If the language used is neithr English nor French, the text shall include a translation into one of these languages.

4. The certificate shall be carried on board the ship and a copy shall be deposited with the authorities who keep the record of the ship's registry.

5. An insurance or other financial security shall not satisfy the requirements of this Article if it can cease, for reasons other than the expiry of the period of validity of the insurance or security specified in the certificate under paragraph 2 of this Article, before three months have elapsed from the date on which notice of its termination is given to the authorities referred to in paragraph 4 of this Article, unless the certificate has been surrendered to these authorities or a new certificate has been issued within the said period. The foregoing provisions shall similarly apply to any modification which results in the insurance or security no longer satisfying the requirements of this Article.

6. The State of registry shall, subject to the provisions of this Article, determine the conditions of issue and validity of the certificate.

7. Certificates issued or certified under the authority of a Contracting State shall be accepted by other Contracting States for the purposes of this Convention and shall be regarded by other Contracting States as having the same force as certificates issued or certified by them. A Contracting State may at any time request consultation with the State of a ship's registry should it believe that the insurer or guarantor named in the certificate is not financially capable of meeting the obligations imposed by this Convention.

8. Any claim for compensation for pollution damage may be brought directly against the insurer or other person providing financial security for the owner's liability for pollution damage. In such case the defendant may, irrespective of the actual fault or privity of the owner, avail himself of the limits of liability prescribed in Article V, paragraph 1. He may further avail himself of the defences (other than the bankruptcy or winding up of the owner) which the owner himself would have been entitled to invoke. Furthermore, the defendant may avail himself of the defence that the pollution damage resulted from the wilful misconduct of the owner himself, but the defendant shall not avail himself of any other defence which he might have been entitled to invoke in proceedings brought by the owner against him. The defendant shall in any event have the right to require the owner to be joined in the proceedings.

9. Any sums provided by insurance or by other financial security maintained in accordance with paragraph 1 of this Article shall be available exclusively for the satisfaction of claims under this Convention.

10. A Contracting State shall not permit a ship under its flag to which this Article applies to trade unless a certificate has been issued under paragraph 2 or 12 of this Article.

11. Subject to the provisions of this Article, each Contracting State shall ensure, under its national legislation, that insurance or other security to the extent specified in paragraph 1 of this Article is in force in respect of any ship, wherever registered, entering or leaving a port in its territory, or arriving at or leaving an off-shore terminal in its territorial sea, if the ship actually carries more than 2,000 tons of oil in bulk as cargo.

12. If insurance or other financial security is not maintained in respect of a ship owned by a Contracting State, the provisions of this Article relating thereto shall not be applicable to such ship, but the ship shall carry a certificate issued by the appropriate authorities of the State of the ship's registry stating that the ship is owned by that State and that the ship's liability is covered within the limits prescribed by Article V, paragraph 1. Such a certificate shall follow as closely as practicable the model prescribed by paragraph 2 of this Article.

Article VIII. Rights of compensation under this Convention shall be extinguished unless an action is brought thereunder within three years from the date when the damage occurred. However, in no case shall an action be brought after six years from the date of the incident which caused the damage. Where this incident consists of a series of occurrences, the six years' period shall run from the date of the first such occurrence.

Article IX. 1. Where an incident has caused pollution damage in the territory including the territorial sea of one or more Contracting States, or preventive measures have been taken to prevent or minimize pollution damage in such territory including the territorial sea, actions for compensation may only be brought in the Courts of any such Contracting State or States. Reasonable notice of any such action shall be given to the defendant.

2. Each Contracting State shall ensure that its Courts possess the necessary jurisdiction to entertain such actions for compensation.

3. After the fund has been constituted in accordance with Article V the Courts of the State in which the fund is constituted shall be exclusively competent to determine all matters relating to the apportionment and distribution of the fund.

Article X. 1. Any judgment given by a Court with jurisdiction in accordance with Article IX which is enforceable in the State of origin where it is no longer subject to ordinary forms of review shall be recognized in any Contracting State, except:
(*a*)   where the judgment was obtained by fraud; or
(*b*)   where the defendant was not given reasonable notice and a fair opportunity to present his case.

2. A judgment recognized under paragraph 1 of this Article shall be enforceable in each Contract State as soon as the formalities required in that State have been complied with. The formalities shall not permit the merits of the case to be re-opened.

Article XI. 1. The provisions of this Convention shall not apply to warships or other ships owned or operated by a State and used, for the time being, only on Government non-commercial service.

2. With respect to ships owned by a Contracting State and used for commercial purposes, each State shall be subject to suit in the jurisdictions set forth in Article IX and shall waive all defences based on its status as a sovereign State.

Article XII. This Convention shall supersede any International Conventions in force or open for signature, ratification or accession at the date on which the Convention is opened for signature, but only to the extent that such Conventions would be in conflict with it; however, nothing in this Article shall affect the obligations of Contracting States to non-Contracting States arising under such International Conventions.

* * *

Article XV. 1. The present Convention shall enter into force on the ninetieth day following the date on which Governments of eight States including five States each with not less than 1,000,000 gross tons of tanker tonnage have either signed it without reservation as to ratification, acceptance or approval or have deposited instruments of ratification, acceptance, approval or accession with the Secretary-General of the Organization.

* * *

ANNEX

CERTIFICATE OF INSURANCE OR OTHER FINANCIAL SECURITY IN RESPECT FOR CIVIL LIABILITY FOR OIL POLLUTION DAMAGE

Issued in accordance with the provisions of Article VII of the International Convention on Civil Liability for Oil Pollution Damage, 1969

Name of Ship	Distinctive number or letters	Port of registry	Name and address of owner

This is to certify that there is in force in respect of the above-named ship a policy of insurance or other financial security satisfying the requirements of Article VII of the International Convention on Civil Liability for Oil Pollution Damage, 1969.

Type of Security..

Duration of Security ....

Name and Address of the Insurer(s) and/or Guarantor(s)

Name ....

Address ....

This certificate is valid until..

Issued or certified by the Government of ....

....

(Full designation of the State)

At..On..

   (Place)   *(Date)*

....

(Signature and title of issuing or certifying official)

EXPLANATORY NOTES

1. If desired, the designation of the State may include a reference to the competent public authority of the country where the certificate is issued.

2. If the total amount of security has been furnished by more than one source, the amount of each of them should be indicated.

3. If security is furnished in several forms, these should be enumerated.

4. The entry "Duration of the Security" must stipulate the date on which such security takes effect.

BRUSSELS INTERNATIONAL CONVENTION ON THE ESTABLISHMENT OF AN INTERNATIONAL FUND FOR COMPENSATION FOR OIL POLLUTION DAMAGE

Popular Names: Fund Convention, FUND 1971

Done at Brussels on 18 December 1971, 1110 UNTS 57, UKTS No.95(1978), Cmnd 7383, *reprinted in* UNEP Reg. p.98, 1971 UNJYB 103, 11 ILM 284 (1972), UNEP3 #51, p.255, 2 IPE 529, IELMT 971: 94.

Entry into Force: 16 October 1978

Depositary: International Maritime Organization

Languages: English, French

Parties as of 27 November 1990: Algeria; Bahamas; Benin; Canada;* Cameroon; Côte d'Ivoire; Cyprus; Denmark; Djibouti; Fiji; Finland; France; Gabon; Germany, Federal Republic of;* Ghana; Greece; Iceland; India; Indonesia; Italy; Japan; Kuwait; Liberia; Maldives; Monaco; Netherlands; Nigeria; Norway; Oman; Papua New Guinea; Poland; Portugal; Qatar; Seychelles; Spain; Sri Lanka; Sweden; Syrian Arab Republic;* Tunisia; Tuvalu; Union of Soviet Socialist Republics; United Arab Emirates; United Kingdom of Great Britain and Northern Ireland;** Vanuatu; Yugoslavia

Amendments: 1976 Protocol, *reprinted in* 16 ILM 621 (1977), not yet in force as of 16 October 1990; 1984 Protocol, *reprinted in* 13 EPL 61 (1984), not yet in force as of 16 October 1990

INTERNATIONAL CONVENTION ON THE ESTABLISHMENT OF AN INTERNATIONAL FUND FOR COMPENSATION FOR OIL POLLUTION DAMAGE (SUPPLEMENTARY TO THE INTERNATIONAL CONVENTION ON CIVIL LIABILITY FOR OIL POLLUTION DAMAGE, 1969)

The States Parties to the present Convention,

Being Parties to the International Convention on Civil Liability for Oil Pollution Damage, adopted at Brussels on 29 November 1969,

Conscious of the dangers of pollution posed by the world-wide maritime carriage of oil in bulk,

Convinced of the need to ensure that adequate compensation is available to persons who suffer damage caused by pollution resulting from the escape or discharge of oil from ships,

---

* With a reservation, declaration or statement
**With a geographic extension

Considering that the International Convention of 29 November 1969, on Civil Liability for Oil Pollution Damage, by providing a régime for compensation for pollution damage in Contracting States and for the costs of measures, wherever taken, to prevent or minimize such damage, represents a considerable progress towards the achievement of this aim,

Considering however that this régime does not afford full compensation for victims of oil pollution damage in all cases while it imposes an additional financial burden on shipowners,

Considering further that the economic consequences of oil pollution damage resulting from the escape or discharge of oil carried in bulk at sea by ships should not exclusively be borne by the shipping industry but should in part be borne by the oil cargo interests,

Convinced of the need to elaborate a compensation and indemnification system supplementary to the International Convention on Civil Liability for Oil Pollution Damage with a view to ensuring that full compensation will be available to victims of oil pollution incidents and that the shipowners are at the same time given relief in respect of the additional financial burdens imposed on them by the said Convention,

Taking note of the Resolution on the Establishment of an International Compensation Fund for Oil Pollution Damage which was adopted on 29 November 1969 by the International Legal Conference on Marine Pollution Damage,

Have agreed as follows:

General Provisions

Article 1. For the purposes of this Convention:

1. "Liability Convention" means the International Convention on Civil Liability for Oil Pollution Damage, adopted at Brussels on 29 November 1969.

2. "Ship", "Person", "Owner", "Oil", "Pollution Damage", "Preventive Measures", "Incident" and "Organization", have the same meaning as in Article I of the Liability Convention, provided however that, for the purposes of these terms, "oil" shall be confined to persistent hydrocarbon mineral oils.

3. "Contributing Oil" means crude oil and fuel oil as defined in sub-paragraphs (*a*) and (*b*) below:

(*a*)   "Crude Oil" means any liquid hydrocarbon mixture occurring naturally in the earth whether or not treated to render it suitable for transportation. It also includes crude oils from which certain distillate fractions have been removed (sometimes referred to as "topped crudes") or to which certain distillate fractions have been added (sometimes referred to as "spiked" or "reconstituted" crudes).

(*b*)   "Fuel Oil" means heavy distillates or residues from crude oil or blends of such materials intended for use as a fuel for the production of heat or power of a quality equivalent to the "American Society for Testing and Materials' Specification for Number Four Fuel Oil (Designation D 396-69)", or heavier.

4. "Franc" means the unit referred to in Article V, paragraph 9, of the Liability Convention.

5. "Ship's tonnage" has the same meaning as in Article V, paragraph 10, of the Liability Convention.

6. "Ton", in relation to oil, means a metric ton.

7. "Guarantor" means any person providing insurance or other financial security to cover an owner's liability in pursuance of Article VII, paragraph 1, of the Liability Convention.

8. "Terminal installation" means any site for the storage of oil in bulk which is capable of receiving oil from waterborne transportation, including any facility situated off-shore and linked to such site.

9. Where an incident consists of a series of occurrences, it shall be treated as having occurred on the date of the first such occurrence.

Article 2. 1. An International Fund for compensation for pollution damage, to be named "the International Oil Pollution Compensation Fund" and hereinafter referred to as "the Fund", is hereby established with the following aims:

(*a*)   To provide compensation for pollution damage to the extent that the protection afforded by the Liability Convention is inadequate;

(*b*)   To give relief to shipowners in respect of the additional financial burden imposed on them by the Liability Convention, such relief being subject to conditions designed to ensure compliance with safety at sea and other conventions;

(*c*)   To give effect to the related purposes set out in this Convention.

2. The Fund shall in each Contracting State be recognized as a legal person capable under the laws of that State of assuming rights and obligations and of being a party in legal proceedings before the courts of that State. Each Contracting State shall recognize the Director of the Fund (hereinafter referred to as "the Director") as the legal representative of the Fund.

Article 3. This Convention shall apply:

1. With regard to compensation according to Article 4, exclusively to pollution damage caused on the territory including the territorial sea of a Contracting State, and to preventive measures taken to prevent or minimize such damage;

2. With regard to indemnification of shipowners and their guarantors according to Article 5, exclusively in respect of pollution damage caused on the territory, including the territorial sea, of a State party to the Liability Convention by a ship registered in or flying the flag of a Contracting State and in respect of preventive measures taken to prevent or minimize such damage.

Compensation and Indemnification

Article 4. 1. For the purpose of fulfilling its function under Article 2, paragraph 1(*a*), the Fund shall pay compensation to any person suffering pollution damage if such person has been unable to obtain full and adequate compensation for the damage under the terms of the Liability Convention,

(*a*)   Because no liability for the damage arises under the Liability Convention;

(*b*)   Because the owner liable for the damage under the Liability Convention is financially incapable of meeting his obligations in full and any financial security that may be provided under Article VII of that Convention does not cover or is insufficient to satisfy the claims for compensation for the damage; an owner being treated as financially incapable of meeting his obligations and a financial security being treated as insufficient if the person suffering the damage has been unable to obtain full satisfaction of the amount of compensation due under the Liability Convention after having taken all reasonable steps to pursue the legal remedies available to him;

(*c*)   Because the damage exceeds the owner's liability under the Liability Convention as limited pursuant to Article V, paragraph 1, of that Convention or under the terms of any other international Convention in force or open for signature, ratification or accession at the date of this Convention.

Expenses reasonably incurred or sacrifices reasonably made by the owner voluntarily to prevent or minimize pollution damage shall be treated as pollution damage for the purposes of this Article.

2. The Fund shall incur no obligation under the preceding paragraph if:

(a) It proves that the pollution damage resulted from an act of war, hostilities, civil war or insurrection or was caused by oil which has escaped or been discharged from a warship or other ship owned or operated by a State and used, at the time of the incident, only on Government non-commercial service; or

(b) The claimant cannot prove that the damage resulted from an incident involving one or more ships.

3. If the Fund proves that the pollution damage resulted wholly or partially either from an act or omission done with intent to cause damage by the person who suffered the damage or from the negligence of that person, the Fund may be exonerated wholly or partially from its obligation to pay compensation to such person provided, however, that there shall be no such exoneration with regard to such preventive measures which are compensated under paragraph 1. The Fund shall in any event be exonerated to the extent that the shipowner may have been exonerated under Article III, paragraph 3, of the Liability Convention.

4. (a) Except as otherwise provided in subparagraph (b) of this paragraph, the aggregate amount of compensation payable by the Fund under this Article shall in respect of any one incident be limited, so that the total sum of that amount and the amount of compensation actually paid under the Liability Convention for pollution damage caused in the territory of the Contracting States, including any sums in respect of which the Fund is under an obligation to indemnify the owner pursuant to Article 5, paragraph 1, of this Convention, shall not exceed 450 million francs.

(b) The aggregate amount of compensation payable by the Fund under this Article for pollution damage resulting from a natural phenomenon of an exceptional, inevitable and irresistible character shall not exceed 450 million francs.

5. Where the amount of established claims against the Fund exceeds the aggregate amount of compensation payable under paragraph 4, the amount available shall be distributed in such a manner that the proportion between any established claim and the amount of compensation actually recovered by the claimant under the Liability Convention and this Convention shall be the same for all claimants.

6. The Assembly of the Fund (hereinafter referred to as "the Assembly") may, having regard to the experience of incidents which have occurred and in particular the amount of damage resulting therefrom and to changes in the monetary values, decide that the amount of 450 million francs referred to in paragraph 4, sub-paragraphs (a) and (b), shall be changed; provided, however, that this amount shall in no case exceed 900 million francs or be lower than 450 million francs. The changed amount shall apply to incidents which occur after the date of the decision effecting the change.

7. The Fund shall, at the request of a Contracting State, use its good offices as necessary to assist that State to secure promptly such personnel, material and services as are necessary to enable the State to take measures to prevent or mitigate pollution damage arising from an incident in respect of which the Fund may be called upon to pay compensation under this Convention.

8. The Fund may, on conditions to be laid down in the Internal Regulations, provide credit facilities with a view to the taking of preventive measures against pollution damage arising from a particular incident in respect of which the Fund may be called upon to pay compensation under this Convention.

Article 5. 1. For the purpose of fulfilling its function under Article 2, paragraph 1 (b), the Fund shall indemnify the owner and his guarantor for that portion of the aggregate amount of liability under the Liability Convention which:

(a) Is in excess of an amount equivalent to 1,500 francs for each ton of the ship's tonnage or of an amount of 125 million francs, whichever is the less, and (*b*)   Is not in excess of an amount equivalent to 2,000 francs for each ton of the said tonnage or an amount of 210 million francs, whichever is the less,

provided, however, that the Fund shall incur no obligation under this paragraph where the pollution damage resulted from the wilful misconduct of the owner himself.

2. The Assembly may decide that the Fund shall, on conditions to be laid down in the Internal Regulations, assume the obligations of a guarantor in respect of ships referred to in Article 3, paragraph 2, with regard to the portion of liability referred to in paragraph 1 of this Article. However, the Fund shall assume such obligations only if the owner so requests and if he maintains adequate insurance or other financial security covering the owner's liability under the Liability Convention up to an amount equivalent to 1,500 francs for each ton of the ship's tonnage or an amount of 125 million francs, whichever is the less. If the Fund assumes such obligations, the owner shall in each Contracting State be considered to have complied with Article VII of the Liability Convention in respect of the portion of his liability mentioned above.

3. The Fund may be exonerated wholly or partially from its obligations under paragraph 1 towards the owner and his guarantor if the Fund proves that as a result of the actual fault or privity of the owner:

(*a*)   The ship from which the oil causing the pollution damage escaped did not comply with the requirements laid down in:

(i)   The International Convention for the Prevention of Pollution of the Sea by Oil, 1954, as amended in 1962; or

(ii)   The International Convention for the Safety of Life at Sea, 1960; or

(iii) The International Convention on Load Lines, 1966; or

(iv)   The International Regulations for Preventing Collisions at Sea, 1960; or

(v)   Any amendments to the above-mentioned Conventions which have been determined as being of an important nature in accordance with Article XVI(5) of the Convention mentioned under (i), Article IX(*e*) of the Convention mentioned under (ii) or Article 29(3)(*d*) or (4)(*d*) of the Convention mentioned under (iii), provided, however, that such amendments had been in force for at least twelve months at the time of the incident; and

(*b*)   The incident or damage was caused wholly or partially by such non-compliance.

The provisions of this paragraph shall apply irrespective of whether the Contracting State in which the ship was registered or whose flag it was flying is a Party to the relevant Instrument.

4. Upon the entry into force of a new Convention designed to replace, in whole or in part, any of the Instruments specified in paragraph 3, the Assembly may decide at least six months in advance a date on which the new Convention will replace such Instrument or part thereof for the purpose of paragraph 3. However, any State Party to this Convention may declare to the Director before that date that it does not accept such replacement; in which case the decision of the Assembly shall have no effect in respect of a ship registered in, or flying the flag of, that State at the time of the incident. Such a declaration may be withdrawn at any later date and shall in any event cease to have effect when the State in question becomes a party to such new Convention.

5. A ship complying with the requirements in an amendment to an Instrument specified in paragraph 3 or with requirements in a new Convention, where the amendment or Convention is designed to replace in whole or in part such Instrument, shall be considered as complying with the requirements in the said Instrument for the purposes of paragraph 3.

6. Where the Fund, acting as a guarantor by virtue of paragraph 2, has paid compensation for pollution damage in accordance with the Liability Convention, it shall have a right of recovery from the owner if and to the extent that the Fund would have been exonerated pursuant to paragraph 3 from its obligations under paragraph 1 to indemnify the owner.

7. Expenses reasonably incurred and sacrifices reasonably made by the owner voluntarily to prevent or minimize pollution damage shall be treated as included in the owner's liability for the purposes of this Article.

Article 6. 1. Rights to compensation under Article 4 or indemnification under Article 5 shall be extinguished unless an action is brought thereunder or a notification has been made pursuant to Article 7, paragraph 6, within three years from the date when the damage occurred. However, in no case shall an action be brought after six years from the date of the incident which caused the damage.

2. Notwithstanding paragraph 1, the right of the owner or his guarantor to seek indemnification from the Fund pursuant to Article 5, paragraph 1, shall in no case be extinguished before the expiry of a period of six months as from the date on which the owner or his guarantor acquired knowledge of the bringing of an action against him under the Liability Convention.

Article 7. 1. Subject to the subsequent provisions of this Article, any action against the Fund for compensation under Article 4 or indemnification under Article 5 of this Convention shall be brought only before a court competent under Article IX of the Liability Convention in respect of actions against the owner who is or who would, but for the provisions of Article III, paragraph 2, of that Convention, have been liable for pollution damage caused by the relevant incident.

2. Each Contracting State shall ensure that its courts possess the necessary jurisdiction to entertain such actions against the Fund as are referred to in paragraph 1.

3. Where an action for compensation for pollution damage has been brought before a court competent under Article IX of the Liability Convention against the owner of a ship or his guarantor, such court shall have exclusive jurisdictional competence over any action against the Fund for compensation or indemnification under the provisions of Article 4 or 5 of this Convention in respect of the same damage. However, where an action for compensation for pollution damage under the Liability Convention has been brought before a court in a State Party to the Liability Convention but not to this Convention, any action against the Fund under Article 4 or under Article 5, paragraph 1, of this Convention shall at the option of the claimant be brought either before a court of the State where the Fund has its headquarters or before any court of a State Party to this Convention competent under Article IX of the Liability Convention.

4. Each Contracting State shall ensure that the Fund shall have the right to intervene as a party to any legal proceedings instituted in accordance with Article IX of the Liability Convention before a competent court of that State against the owner of a ship or his guarantor.

5. Except as otherwise provided in paragraph 6, the Fund shall not be bound by any judgment or decision in proceedings to which it has not been a party or by any settlement to which it is not a party.

6. Without prejudice to the provisions of paragraph 4, where an action under the Liability Convention for compensation for pollution damage has been brought against an owner or his guarantor before a competent court in a Contracting State, each party to the proceedings shall be entitled under the national law of that State to notify the Fund of the proceedings. Where such notification has been made in accordance with the formalities required by the law of the court seized and in such time and in such a manner that the Fund has in fact been in a position effectively

to intervene as a party to the proceedings, any judgment rendered by the court in such proceedings shall, after it has become final and enforceable in the State where the judgment was given, become binding upon the Fund in the sense that the facts and findings in that judgment may not be disputed by the Fund even if the Fund has not actually intervened in the proceedings.

Article 8. Subject to any decision concerning the distribution referred to in Article 4, paragraph 5, any judgment given against the Fund by a court having jurisdiction in accordance with Article 7, paragraphs 1 and 3, shall, when it has become enforceable in the State of origin and is in that State no longer subject to ordinary forms of review, be recognized and enforceable in each Contracting State on the same conditions as are prescribed in Article X of the Liability Convention.

Article 9. 1. Subject to the provisions of Article 5, the Fund shall, in respect of any amount of compensation for pollution damage paid by the Fund in accordance with Article 4, paragraph 1, of this Convention, acquire by subrogation the rights that the person so compensated may enjoy under the Liability Convention against the owner or his guarantor.

2. Nothing in this Convention shall prejudice any right of recourse or subrogation of the Fund against persons other than those referred to in the preceding paragraph. In any event the right of the Fund to subrogation against such person shall not be less favourable than that of an insurer of the person to whom compensation or indemnification has been paid.

3. Without prejudice to any other rights of subrogation or recourse against the Fund which may exist, a Contracting State or agency thereof which has paid compensation for pollution damage in accordance with provisions of national law shall acquire by subrogation the rights which the person so compensated would have enjoyed under this Convention.

Contributions

Article 10. 1. Contributions to the Fund shall be made in respect of each Contracting State by any person who, in the calendar year referred to in Article 11, paragraph 1, as regards initial contributions and in Article 12, paragraphs 2 (*a*) or (*b*), as regards annual contributions, has received in total quantities exceeding 150,000 tons:

(*a*)   In the ports or terminal installations in the territory of that State contributing oil carried by sea to such ports or terminal installations; and

(*b*)   In any installations situated in the territory of that Contracting State contributing oil which has been carried by sea and discharged in a port or terminal installation of a non-Contracting State, provided that contributing oil shall only be taken into account by virtue of this sub-paragraph on first receipt in a Contracting State after its discharge in that non-Contracting State.

2. (*a*) For the purposes of paragraph 1, where the quantity of contributing oil received in the territory of a Contracting State by any person in a calendar year when aggregated with the quantity of contributing oil received in the same Contracting State in that year by any associated person or persons exceeds 150,000 tons, such person shall pay contributions in respect of the actual quantity received by him notwithstanding that that quantity did not exceed 150,000 tons.

(*b*)   ''Associated person'' means any subsidiary or commonly controlled entity. The question whether a person comes within this definition shall be determined by the national law of the State concerned.

Article 11. 1. In respect of each Contracting State initial contributions shall be made of an amount which shall for each person referred to in Article 10 be calculated on the basis of a fixed sum for each ton of contributing oil received by him during the calendar year preceding that in which this Convention entered into force for that State.

2. The sum referred to in paragraph 1 shall be determined by the Assembly within two months after the entry into force of this Convention. In performing this function the Assembly shall, to the extent possible, fix the sum in such a way that the total amount of initial contributions would, if contributions were to be made in respect of 90 per cent of the quantities of contributing oil carried by sea in the world, equal 75 million francs.

3. The initial contributions shall in respect of each Contracting State be paid within three months following the date at which the Convention entered into force for that State.

* * *

Article 14. 1. Each Contracting State may at the time when it deposits its instrument of ratification or accession or at any time thereafter declare that it assumes itself obligations that are incumbent under this Convention on any person who is liable to contribute to the Fund in accordance with Article 10, paragraph 1, in respect of oil received within the territory of that State. Such declaration shall be made in writing and shall specify which obligations are assumed.

2. Where a declaration under paragraph 1 is made prior to the entry into force of this Convention in accordance with Article 40, it shall be deposited with the Secretary-General of the Organization who shall after the entry into force of the Convention communicate the declaration to the Director.

3. A declaration under paragraph 1 which is made after the entry into force of this Convention shall be deposited with the Director.

4. A declaration made in accordance with this Article may be withdrawn by the relevant State giving notice thereof in writing to the Director. Such notification shall take effect three months after the Director's receipt thereof.

5. Any State which is bound by a declaration made under this Article shall, in any proceedings brought against it before a competent court in respect of any obligation specified in the declaration, waive any immunity that it would otherwise be entitled to invoke.

Article 15. 1. Each Contracting State shall ensure that any person who receives contributing oil within its territory in such quantities that he is liable to contribute to the Fund appears on a list to be established and kept up to date by the Director in accordance with the subsequent provisions of this Article.

2. For the purposes set out in paragraph 1, each Contracting State shall communicate, at a time and in the manner to be prescribed in the Internal Regulations, to the Director the name and address of any person who in respect of that State is liable to contribute to the Fund pursuant to Article 10, as well as data on the relevant quantities of contributing oil received by any such person during the preceding calendar year.

3. For the purposes of ascertaining who are, at any given time, the persons liable to contribute to the Fund in accordance with Article 10, paragraph 1, and of establishing, where applicable, the quantities of oil to be taken into account for any such person when determining the amount of his contribution, the list shall be *prima facie* evidence of the facts stated therein.

Organization and Administration

Article 16. The Fund shall have an Assembly, a Secretariat headed by a Director and, in accordance with the provisions of Article 21, an Executive Committee.

* * *

Voting

Article 32. The following provisions shall apply to voting in the Assembly and the Executive Committee:
(a) Each member shall have one vote;
(b) Except as otherwise provided in Article 33, decisions of the Assembly and the Executive Committee shall be by a majority vote of the members present and voting;
(c) Decisions where a three-fourths or a two-thirds majority is required shall be by a three-fourths or two-thirds majority vote, as the case may be, of those present;
(d) For the purpose of this Article the phrase "members present" means "members present at the meeting at the time of the vote", and the phrase "members present and voting" means "members present and casting an affirmative or negative vote". Members who abstain from voting shall be considered as not voting.

Article 33. 1. The following decisions of the Assembly shall require a three-fourths majority:
(a) An increase in accordance with Article 4, paragraph 6, in the maximum amount of compensation payable by the Fund;
(b) A determination, under Article 5, paragraph 4, relating to the replacement of the Instruments referred to in that paragraph;
(c) The allocation to the Executive Committee of the functions specified in Article 18, paragraph 5.
2. The following decisions of the Assembly shall require a two-thirds majority:
(a) A decision under Article 13, paragraph 3, not to take or continue action against a contributor;
(b) The appointment of the Director under Article 18, paragraph 4;
(c) The establishment of subsidiary bodies, under Article 18, paragraph 9.

* * *

Article 43. 1. This Convention shall cease to be in force on the date when the number of Contracting States falls below three.
2. Contracting States which are bound by this Convention on the date before the day it ceases to be in force shall enable the Fund to exercise its functions as described under Article 44 and shall, for that purpose only, remain bound by this Convention.

Article 44. 1. If this Convention ceases to be in force, the Fund shall nevertheless
(a) Meet its obligations in respect of any incident occurring before the Convention ceased to be in force;
(b) Be entitled to exercise its rights to contributions to the extent that these contributions are necessary to meet the obligations under sub-paragraph (a), including expenses for the administration of the Fund necessary for this purpose.
2. The Assembly shall take all appropriate measures to complete the winding up of the Fund, including the distribution in an equitable manner of any remaining assets among those persons who have contributed to the Fund.
3. For the purposes of this Article the Fund shall remain a legal person.

* * *

TANKER OWNERS VOLUNTARY AGREEMENT CONCERNING LIABILITY FOR OIL POLLUTION, STANDING AGREEMENT AND SUPPLEMENT

Popular Name: TOVALOP

Done on 20 February 1987.

THE TANKER OWNERS VOLUNTARY AGREEMENT CONCERNING LIABILITY FOR OIL POLLUTION ("TOVALOP") STANDING AGREEMENT

Introduction

The Parties to this Agreement are Tanker Owners and Bareboat Charterers.
By means of the Tanker Owners Voluntary Agreement concerning Liability for Oil Pollution dated January 7th, 1969, as amended, (hereinafter called "TOVALOP") the Parties took constructive measures to mitigate and provide compensation for damage by oil pollution from Tankers.
Pending the widespread application of the International Convention on Civil Liability for Oil Pollution Damage, 1969 ("the Liability Convention") and the Protocol thereto adopted in 1984, the Parties have from time to time amended TOVALOP to enhance the benefits and protection available to persons sustaining Pollution Damage.
Accordingly, the Parties, and such other Tanker Owners and Bareboat Charterers as may hereafter become Parties, in consideration of their mutual promises, have agreed with one another and do hereby agree as follows:

I. Definitions

Whenever the following words and phrases appear in the Introduction and other Clauses hereof, they shall have the meaning indicated below:
  (a) "Bareboat Charterer" means the Person(s) who has chartered a Tanker upon terms which provide, among other things, that the Charterer shall have exclusive possession and control of the Tanker during the life of the charter.
  (b) "Cost" or "Costs" means reasonable cost or costs, respectively.
  (c) The "Federation" means The International Tanker Owners Pollution Federation Limited, a Company limited by guarantee and formed pursuant to the laws of England for the purpose of administering this Agreement.
  (d) "Incident" means any occurrence, or series of occurrences having the same origin, which causes Pollution Damage, or which creates the Threat of an escape or discharge of Oil.
  (e) "Liability Convention" means the International Convention on Civil Liability for Oil Pollution Damage, 1969, which entered into force on June 19th, 1975, including legislation and regulations implementing the

provisions hereof which are enacted from time to time by any Contracting State thereunder.

(f) "Oil" means any persistent hydrocarbon mineral oil such as crude oil, fuel oil, heavy diesel oil and lubricating oil whether or not carried as cargo.

(g) "Owner" means the Person or Persons registered as the owner of the Tanker or, in the absence of registration, the Person or Persons owning the Tanker. However, in the case of a Tanker owned by a State and operated by a company which in that State is registered as the Tanker's operator, "Owner" shall mean such company. Notwithstanding the foregoing, in the case of a Tanker under bareboat charter, "Owner" means the Bareboat Charterer.

(h) "Participating Owner" means the Owner of a Tanker who is a Party.

(i) "Party" means a Party to this Agreement.

(j) "Person" means any individual or partnership or any public or private body, whether corporate or not, including a State or any of its constituent sub-divisions.

(k) "Pollution Damage" means loss or damage caused outside the Tanker by contamination resulting from the escape or discharge of Oil from the Tanker, wherever such escape or discharge may occur, provided that the loss or damage is caused on the territory, including the territorial sea, of any State and includes the costs of Preventive Measures, wherever taken, and further loss or damage caused by Preventive Measures but excludes any loss or damage which is remote or speculative, or which does not result directly from such escape or discharge.

(l) "Preventive Measures" means any reasonable measures taken by any Person after an Incident has occurred to prevent or minimise Pollution Damage.

(m) "Tanker" means any sea-going vessel and any sea-borne craft of any type whatsoever, designed and constructed for carrying Oil in bulk as cargo, whether or not it is actually so carrying Oil.

(n) "Threat of an escape or discharge of Oil" means a grave and imminent danger of the escape or discharge of Oil from a Tanker which, if it occurred, would create a serious danger of Pollution Damage, whether or not an escape or discharge in fact subsequently occurs.

(o) "Threat Removal Measures" means reasonable measures taken by any Person after an Incident has occurred for the purposes of removing the Threat of an escape or discharge of Oil.

(p) A Tanker's "Tonnage" shall be the net tonnage of the Tanker with the addition of the amount deducted from the gross tonnage on account of engine room space for the purpose of ascertaining the net tonnage. In the case of a Tanker for which this Tonnage cannot be ascertained, the Tanker's Tonnage shall be deemed to be 40 per cent. of the weight in tons of 2,240 lbs. of Oil which the Tanker is capable of carrying.

(q) "Ton" means a ton of a Tanker's Tonnage.

II. General Conditions

(A) Upon acceptance by the Federation of an application by an Owner in the form annexed hereto as Exhibit "A", that Owner shall become a Party and a member of the Federation.

(B) Each Party shall:

(1) make the terms of this Agreement applicable to all Tankers of which he is or becomes Owner;

(2) at all times be the Owner of a Tanker to which the terms of this Agreement are applied;

(3)   establish and maintain his financial capability to fulfil his obligations under this Agreement to the satisfaction of the Federation;

(4)   dispose of all valid claims against him arising under this Agreement as promptly as is practicable;

(5)   become a member of the Federation and, subject to the Articles of Association of the Federation, remain a member thereof so long as he continues to be a Party hereto;

(6)   abide by the Memorandum and Articles of Association of the Federation and all rules and directives of the Federation; and

(7)   fulfil all his other obligations under this Agreement.

(C) A Party shall forthwith notify the Federation if he shall fail to perform or observe any of the conditions specified in Clause II(B).

(D) A Party shall forthwith cease to be a Party if he shall fail to perform or observe any of the conditions specified in Clause II(B), but without, however, affecting his rights and obligations accrued at the time of such cessation (including his obligation under Clause II(C)) and without limitation to his right at any time thereafter to become a Party.

(E) Without prejudice to the foregoing provisions of this Clause or to the generality of Clause IX the Federation may at any time by notice in writing require a Party to inform it whether or not that Party has failed to perform or observe any of the conditions specified in Clause II(B) and if that Party shall fail to respond to such request within 28 days after the date of that notice, then that Party shall thereupon forthwith cease to be a Party.

III. Duration

(A) This Agreement may be terminated by Special Resolution adopted at a General Meeting of the Members of the Federation convened and conducted in accordance with the Articles of Association of the Federation upon a poll vote in which at least 75 per cent. of the votes cast are in favour of the said Resolution.

(B) A Party may withdraw from this Agreement on any date by giving at least six months prior written notice of withdrawal to the Federation, or in accordance with Clause X.

(C) The withdrawal of a Party from this Agreement under Clause III, or under Clause X, or termination of this Agreement by the Parties shall not affect any rights and obligations of any Party then accrued under this Agreement.

(D) Upon termination of this Agreement the Federation shall continue in existence for such reasonable period as is necessary to wind up its affairs.

IV. Responsibility

(A) Subject to the terms and conditions of this Agreement, the Participating Owner of a Tanker involved in an Incident agrees to assume responsibility hereunder in respect of Pollution Damage caused by Oil which has escaped or which has been discharged from the Tanker, and the Cost of Threat Removal Measures taken as a result of the Incident.

(B) No responsibility for Pollution Damage or for the Cost of Threat Removal Measures shall be assumed if the Incident:

(a)   caused Pollution Damage anywhere in the world for any part of which liability is imposed under the terms of the Liability Convention, or

(b)   resulted from an act of war, hostilities, civil war, insurrection or a natural phenomenon of an exceptional, inevitable and irresistible character, or

(c)   was wholly caused by an act or omission done with intent to cause damage by a third party, or

(d)   was wholly caused by the negligence or other wrongful act of any Government or other authority responsible for the maintenance of lights or other navigational aids in the exercise of that function.

(C) If Pollution Damage or the circumstances which gave rise to Threat Removal Measures resulted wholly or partially from the negligence of the Person who sustained the Pollution Damage or who took the Threat Removal Measures, the Participating Owner shall be exonerated wholly or partially from any responsibility he would otherwise have to such Person under this Agreement.

V. Responsibility for Pollution Damage Where Two or More Tankers are Involved

When Oil has escaped or been discharged from two or more Tankers of Participating Owners and causes Pollution Damage, the Participating Owners concerned, except as exonerated by reason of Clause IV, shall be jointly and severally responsible hereunder in respect of all such Pollution Damage which is not reasonably separable.

VI. Preventive Measures and Threat Removal Measures by the Participating Owner

A Participating Owner of a Tanker involved in an Incident shall exercise his best efforts to take such Preventive Measures and/or Threat Removal Measures as are practicable and appropriate under the circumstances. The taking of such Measures shall not constitute an admission of liability or of responsibility under this Agreement.

Each Participating Owner shall in connection with the establishment and maintenance of financial capability referred to in Clause II(B)(3) make appropriate provision for the reimbursement of the Cost of such Measures.

VII. Limits of Financial Responsibility

(A) The maximum financial responsibility under this Agreement of a Participating Owner in respect of any one Incident shall be One Hundred and Sixty U.S. Dollars (US $160.00) per Ton of each of his Tankers involved in the Incident, or Sixteen Million Eight Hundred Thousand U.S. Dollars (US $16,800,000.00), whichever is less.

(B) When the aggregate of the established claims hereunder exceeds the maximum financial responsibility specified in Clause VII(A), the Participating Owner(s) shall pay that proportion of each of those established claims as the said maximum financial responsibility bears to the total amount of those established claims.

(C) If, before the Participating Owner has satisfied in full his financial responsibility under this Agreement, he or any Person providing him insurance or other financial security has, as a result of the Incident in question, paid compensation for Pollution Damage and/or for the Costs of Threat Removal Measures, then

(a)   the amount of that payment shall be taken into account in assessing the aggregate of established claims under this Agreement in respect of that Incident; and

(b)   the Participating Owner or any Person providing him insurance or other financial security shall, to the extent of that payment, be in the same position as the Person to whom that sum was paid would have been.

(D) Costs incurred by the Participating Owner or any Person providing him insurance or other financial security as a result of the Participating Owner himself taking Preventive Measures and/or Threat Removal Measures shall be treated as if they were claims by Persons other than the Participating Owner and

(a) the amount of those Costs shall be taken into account in assessing the aggregate of established claims under this Agreement in respect of that Incident; and

(b) the Participating Owner or any Person providing him insurance or other financial security shall, to the extent of those Costs, be in the same position as if he were any other Person with a claim under this Agreement.

(E) When a Participating Owner establishes that the aggregate of claims in respect of an Incident may exceed his maximum financial responsibility hereunder, he or any Person providing him insurance or other financial security may in his sole discretion make partial payment to claimants until the full extent of all claims is determined.

VIII. Procedure and Miscellaneous

(A) The Parties hereto authorise the Federation to provide Persons concerned with the escape or discharge of Oil or the Threat thereof with a copy of this Agreement and confirmation that the Owner was, at the time of such escape or discharge or Threat, a Participating Owner.

(B) A Participating Owner may require that any payment hereunder to a Person by him, or on his behalf by anyone providing him insurance or other financial security, shall be conditional upon either that Person assigning to that Participating Owner his right of action, or authorising him to proceed in the name of that Person, in each case up to the amounts paid or to be paid to that Person in relation to the Incident in question.

(C) No responsibility shall arise under this Agreement unless written notice of claim is received by the Participating Owner within two years of the date of the Incident.

(D) Unless otherwise agreed in writing, any payment to a Person by or on behalf of a Participating Owner shall be in full settlement of all said Person's claims against the Participating Owner, the Tanker involved, its master, officers and crew, its charterer(s), manager or operator and their respective officers, agents, employees and affiliates and underwriters, which arise out of the Incident.

(E) Persons making claims hereunder may, in the event of a dispute with a Participating Owner concerning same, commence arbitration proceedings, in accordance with Clause VIII(F) hereof, within three years of the date of the Incident, and these proceedings shall be the exclusive means for enforcing a Participating Owner's responsibility hereunder. Each Participating Owner by becoming a Party to this Agreement, and so long as he remains bound hereby, shall be deemed irrevocably to have offered to any such Person to submit all such disputes to arbitration as provided in said Clause VIII(F).

(F) All claims by any Person or Persons under this Agreement shall, if not otherwise disposed of, be finally settled under the rules of conciliation and arbitration of the International Chamber of Commerce by one or more arbitrators appointed in accordance with said rules. In any such proceeding the Person allegedly having the claim shall have the burden of proving that Oil discharged from the Tanker caused him Pollution Damage or that the Threat thereof necessitated his taking Threat Removal Measures.

(G) Except as provided by Clause V, no Participating Owner shall be responsible under this Agreement in respect of an escape or discharge of Oil or the Threat thereof from the Tanker of another Participating Owner.

(H) This Agreement does not create any rights against the Federation and the Federation shall have no liability hereunder or otherwise to any Person.

(I) No rights or obligations created hereunder or connected herewith may be assigned or transferred except as provided in Clause VIII(B).

(J) No payment made hereunder shall be deemed (i) an admission of, or evidence of liability on the part of the Participating Owner in any proceeding or to any

Person, or (ii) submission to any jurisdiction on the part of the Participating Owner for any purpose whatsoever.

(K) Nothing in this Agreement shall prejudice the right of recourse of a Participating Owner against third parties or vessels.

IX. Interpretation

The Federation shall have the right to make rules and directives from time to time with respect to the interpretation and administration of this Agreement.

X. Amendments

This Agreement may be amended by Special Resolution adopted at a General Meeting of the members of the Federation convened and conducted in accordance with the Articles of Association of the Federation upon a poll vote in which at least 75 per cent. of the votes cast are in favour of said Resolution. A Party who votes against such Resolution shall thereupon have the option, to be exercised by written notice served upon the Federation within sixty days of the date of said Special Resolution, to withdraw from this Agreement, without, however, affecting his rights and obligations accrued at the time of his withdrawal.

XI. Law Governing

This Agreement shall be governed by the laws of England. However, anything herein to the contrary notwithstanding, a Participating Owner shall not be required:

(a) to incur any obligation or take any action, with respect of any Incident in which his Tanker is involved, which would violate the laws or government regulations of the flag State of the Tanker; or

(b) to incur any obligation or take any action which would, if a majority of the stock of the Participating Owner is owned, directly or indirectly by another corporation, partnership or individual, violate any laws or government regulations which may apply to said other corporation, partnership or individual.

Supplement

Introduction

The Parties recognise that (i) while the Standing Agreement (as hereinafter defined) has provided constructive measures to mitigate and provide compensation for Pollution Damage, it does not now provide, in all respects, adequate compensation for all legitimate claims for Pollution Damage, (ii) while the Liability Convention has established, in many jurisdictions, a legal system providing for the compensation of persons who sustain Pollution Damage, it does not provide for compensation of Costs incurred to remove a Threat of an escape or discharge of Oil from a Tanker where no pollution occurs, nor does it provide, in all respects, adequate compensation for all legitimate claims for Pollution Damage and (iii) it will require some time before the Protocol to the Liability Convention will come into force in a substantial number of jurisdictions.

Accordingly, the Parties decided to amend TOVALOP pursuant to Clause X thereof effective from February 20th, 1987 by the adoption of this Supplement (as subsequently amended) so as to provide in respect of an Applicable Incident (as hereinafter defined) enhanced compensation for Pollution Damage and Costs incurred to remove a Threat of an escape or discharge of Oil, but without affecting the provisions of the Standing Agreement which alone shall continue to apply to any Incident which is not an Applicable Incident.

1. Definitions and Interpretation

(1) Whenever the following words and phrases appear in the Introduction to and other Paragraphs of this Supplement, they shall have the meaning set forth below:

(A) "Applicable Incident" means any occurrence or series of occurrences, having the same origin, which causes Pollution Damage by, or which creates the Threat of an escape or discharge of, Oil when the cargo in the Tanker is "owned", as defined in CRISTAL, by an Oil Company Party to CRISTAL.

(B) "CRISTAL" means the Contract Regarding a Supplement to Tanker Liability for Oil Pollution dated January 14, 1971, as the same has been and may from time to time be amended.

(C) "Cristal Limited" means Cristal Limited, a company organised and existing under the Laws of Bermuda.

(D) "Fund" means the International Oil Pollution Compensation Fund established under Article 2 of the Fund Convention.

(E) "Fund Convention" means the International Convention on the Establishment of an International Fund for Compensation for Oil Pollution Damage, 1971, as amended from time to time, but excluding amendments set forth in the protocol thereto adopted at an International Conference held in London in 1984.

(F) "Liability Convention" means the International Convention on Civil Liability for Oil Pollution Damage, 1969, as defined in Clause I(e) of the Standing Agreement but excluding amendments set forth in the Protocol thereto.

(G) "Pollution Damage" means (i) physical loss or damage caused outside the Tanker by contamination resulting from the escape or discharge of Oil from the Tanker, wherever such escape or discharge may occur, including such loss or damage caused by Preventive Measures, and/or (ii) proven economic loss actually sustained, irrespective as to accompanying physical damage, as a direct result of contamination as set out in (i) above, including the Costs of Preventive Measures, and/or (iii) Costs actually incurred in taking reasonable and necessary measures to restore or replace natural resources damaged as a direct result of an Applicable Incident, but excluding any other damage to the environment.

(H) "Preventive Measures" means any reasonable measures taken by any Person after an Applicable Incident has occurred to prevent or minimise Pollution Damage.

(I) "Protocol" means the protocol to the Liability Convention adopted at an Internatioanl Conference held in London in 1984.

(J) "Standing Agreement" means the Tanker Owners Voluntary Agreement concerning Liability for Oil Pollution dated January 7th, 1969, as the same has been and may from time to time be amended, but excluding the provisions of this Supplement thereto.

(K) "Threat Removal Measures" means reasonable measures taken by any Person after an Applicable Incident has occurred for the purposes of removing a Threat of an escape or discharge of Oil.

(L) "Ton" means a ton of a Tanker's gross tonnage as determined in accordance with the provisions of the International Convention on Tonnage Measurement of Ships, 1969, as amended and in force as of the effective date of this Supplement.

(2) (A)   Insofar as they are not varied by this Paragraph 1, words and phrases shall have the same meanings as defined in Clause I of the Standing Agreement whenever they appear in this Supplement.

(B)   References in this Supplement to Clauses I to XI are references to those Clauses in the Standing Agreement, and references to Paragraphs 1 to 5 are references to those Paragraphs in this Supplement.

(C)   References in the Standing Agreement to ''this Agreement'' shall, where the context permits, apply also to the provisions of this Supplement.

(D)   The Standing Agreement alone shall apply to an Incident (as defined in Clause I(d) thereof) which is not an Applicable Incident and shall remain in full force and effect in respect of each such Incident. This Supplement shall not apply to any Incident which is not an Applicable Incident.

(E)   The provisions of this Supplement shall apply to an Applicable Incident in substitution for and to the exclusion of Clauses IV, V and VII of the Standing Agreement. The provisions of all other Clauses of the Standing Agreement shall apply to an Applicable Incident except where those provisions are inconsistent with this Supplement, in which event this Supplement shall prevail.

2. Duration

(A) This Supplement shall cease to apply to an Applicable Incident occurring after 12.00 hours G.M.T. on February 20th, 1992 (or such later date as may be agreed), it being understood that nothing set forth herein shall affect the obligations of a Participating Owner with respect to an Applicable Incident which shall have occurred prior to 12.00 hours G.M.T. on February 20th, 1992.

(B) Upon termination of this Supplement the existence of the Federation shall not be affected, its continued existence being governed by the terms of the Standing Agreement.

3. Financial Responsibility for an Applicable Incident

(A) If an Applicable Incident occurs which does not cause Pollution Damage in a jurisdiction where the provisions of the Fund Convention are in force (but irrespective as to whether or not the provisions of the Liability Convention or any other applicable domestic laws are in force) the Participating Owner of a Tanker involved in that Applicable Incident shall, subject to the provisions of Paragraph 3(C), take such Preventive Measures and/or Threat Removal Measures as are practical and appropriate under the circumstances and, subject as aforesaid and in the following order of priority—

(1)   pay such amount(s) to such Person(s) as may be necessary to fulfil his obligations under the Liability Convention, the Protocol and domestic legislation giving effect thereto or any other law equivalent thereto together with any Costs incurred by the Participating Owner in taking Preventive Measures and/or Threat Removal Measures; and

(2)   compensate any Person who would otherwise remain uncompensated and who (i) sustains Pollution Damage and/or (ii) incurs Costs in taking Preventive Measures and/or Threat Removal Measures.

(B) If an Applicable Incident occurs which causes Pollution Damage in a jurisdiction where the provisions of both the Liability Convention and Fund Convention are in force, the Participating Owner of a Tanker involved in that Applicable Incident shall, subject to the provisions of Paragraph 3(C), take such Preventive Measures and/or Threat Removal Measures as are practical and appropriate under the circumstances and, subject as aforesaid and in the following order of priority—

(1)   pay such amount(s) to such Person(s) as may be necessary to fulfil his obligations under the Liability Convention, the Protocol and domestic

       legislation giving effect thereto or any other law equivalent thereto to-
       gether with any Costs incurred by the Participating Owner in taking
       Preventive Measures and/or Threat Removal Measures;

(2)   compensate Cristal Limited in an amount equal to the amount that the
       Fund has assessed against Oil Company Parties to CRISTAL as a result
       of the Applicable Incident; and

(3)   compensate any Person who would otherwise remain uncompensated and
       who (i) sustains Pollution Damage and/or (ii) incurs Costs in taking
       Preventive Measures and/or Threat Removal Measures.

(C) The responsibilities which a Participating Owner has assumed, pursuant to
Paragraphs 3(A) and (B), shall be subject to the following terms and conditions:

(1)   A Participating Owner shall not be obligated to take Preventive Measures
       or Threat Removal Measures or pay Costs or make any compensation to
       a Person if the Applicable Incident (i) resulted from an act of war,
       hostilities, civil war, insurrection or a natural phenomenon of an excep-
       tional, inevitable and irresistible character, or (ii) was wholly caused by
       an act or omission done with intent to cause damage by a third party or
       (iii) was wholly caused by the negligence or other wrongful act of any
       Government or other authority responsible for the maintenance of lights
       or other navigational aids in the exercise of that function. Notwithstand-
       ing the foregoing provisions of this sub-paragraph (1), a Participating
       Owner shall (irrespective as to whether he bears or would bear any
       liability under the Liability Convention with respect to the Applicable
       Incident) compensate Cristal Limited pursuant to Paragraph 3(B)(2) ex-
       cept when the Applicable Incident (i) resulted from an act of war, hostilit-
       ies, civil war or insurrection or (ii) was wholly caused by an act or
       omission done with intent to cause damage by a third party.

(2)   If Pollution Damage or the circumstances which gave rise to Preventive
       Measures or Threat Removal Measures resulted wholly or partially either
       from an act or omission done with intent to cause damage by, or from
       the negligence of, the Person who sustained the Pollution Damage and/
       or who took the Preventive Measures and/or Threat Removal Measures,
       the Participating Owner shall be proportionately exonerated from any
       responsibility he would otherwise have to such Person.

(3)   The maximum amount of Costs to be incurred in respect of Preventive
       Measures and Threat Removal Measures and compensation to be paid by
       a Participating Owner under Paragraph 3(A) or (B) in respect of any one
       Applicable Incident, shall not exceed an amount equal, in the case of a
       Tanker of Five Thousand (5,000) Tons or less, Three Million Five Hun-
       dred Thousand United States Dollars (US $3,500,000.00) and for a
       Tanker in excess of Five Thousand (5,000) Tons, Three Million Five
       Hundred Thousand United States Dollars (US $3,500,000.00) plus Four
       Hundred and Ninety-Three United States Dollars (US $493.00) for each
       Ton in excess of said Five Thousand (5,000) Tons, subject to a maximum
       of Seventy Million United States Dollars (US $70,000,000.00).

(4)   When Oil has escaped or been discharged from two or more Tankers of
       Participating Owners and/or there is a Threat of an escape or discharge of
       Oil from two or more Tankers of Participating Owners, the Participating
       Owners concerned, subject to the other provisions of Paragraph 3(C),
       shall be jointly and severally responsible for all said Costs and compensa-
       tion under Paragraphs 3(A) and (B) which are not reasonably separable.

(5)   If the maximum sum that can be paid by the Participating Owner(s)
       within the provisions of Paragraph 3(C)(3), after deducting all payments
       made or to be made together with all Costs incurred under Paragraph
       3(A)(1) or, as the case may be, 3(B)(1) and (2), is insufficient to meet all

established claims in respect of an Applicable Incident under Paragraphs 3(A)(2) or (B)(3), then the Participating Owner(s) shall pay that proportion of each of those established claims as the available balance of that maximum sum bears to the total amount of those established claims.

4. Special Provisions

(A) If, before the Participating Owner has satisfied in full his financial responsibility under this Supplement, any Person providing him insurance or other financial security has, as a result of the Applicable Incident in question, made payment pursuant to Paragraphs 3(A) or (B), then

(1) the amount of that payment shall be taken into account in assessing the aggregate of established claims under this Supplement in respect of that Applicable Incident; and

(2) that Person shall, to the extent of that payment, be in the same position as the Person to whom that sum was paid would have been.

(B) When a Participating Owner establishes that the aggregate of claims in respect of an Applicable Incident may exceed the available balance of his maximum financial responsibility hereunder, he or any Person providing him insurance or other financial security may in his sole discretion make partial payment to claimants until the full extent of all claims is determined.

(C) For the purpose of determining the extent to which a Participating Owner has discharged his financial responsibility the amount of any payment made by a Participating Owner under this Supplement in a currency or currencies other than United States Dollars shall be converted to United States Dollars at the buy rate of exchange for said currency(ies) to United States Dollars as quoted by the National Westminster Bank Plc in London on the date of payment.

5. Procedure and Miscellaneous

(A) The provisions of Clauses VIII (B), (D) and (E) of the Standing Agreement shall apply to this Supplement as if references in those Clauses to the Incident were to the Applicable Incident.

(B) No financial responsibility shall arise under Paragraph 3(A) or (B) unless written notice of claim is received by the Participating Owner within two years of the date of the Applicable Incident giving rise thereto, it being understood that this provision shall not apply to the Participating Owner's obligation to compensate Cristal Limited under Paragraph 3(B)(2) which obligation shall not arise unless written notice of claim is received by Cristal Limited from an Oil Company Party and notified in writing to the Participating Owner within one year after the date that payment of the contribution under Article 10 of the Fund Convention is to be made.

(C) In the event that during the period of this Supplement there shall be any change to any oil pollution compensation regime, including CRISTAL, which, in the opinion of the Board of Directors of the Federation, is or may be material to the Parties' obligations hereunder, then the said Board shall further consider the same with a view to making such recommendation to Parties in that regard as it thinks fit.

OIL COMPANIES: CONTRACT REGARDING A SUPPLEMENT TO TANKER LIABILITY FOR OIL POLLUTION

Popular Name: CRISTAL

Done on 14 January 1971, amended thereafter, most recently, effective 23 October 1989.

CONTRACT REGARDING A SUPPLEMENT TO TANKER LIABILITY FOR OIL POLLUTION

Preamble

The Parties to this Contract are various Oil Companies and Cristal Limited (hereinafter referred to as "CRISTAL"), a Company organised and existing under the laws of Bermuda.

The Parties recognize that (i) Tankers carrying bulk Oil cargoes may cause substantial Pollution Damage as a result of the escape or discharge of Oil into the sea, and (ii) Persons who have sustained Pollution Damage are sometimes unable to recover adequate compensation.

Therefore, the Parties have decided by means of this Contract to (i) provide supplemental compensation to such Persons and (ii) reimburse Oil Company Parties their contributions to the Fund, when cargoes are "owned" by Oil Company Parties, all in accordance with the terms and conditions set forth herein.

Clause I.
Definitions

For the purpose of this Contract (including the Preamble):

(A) "Bareboat Charterer" means the Person (or Persons) who has chartered a Tanker upon terms which provide, among other things, that the charterer shall have exclusive possession and control of the Tanker during the life of the charter.

(B) "Cost" or "Costs" means reasonable cost or costs, respectively.

(C) "Fund" means the International Oil Pollution Compensation Fund established under Article 2 of the Fund Convention.

(D) "Fund Convention" means the International Convention on the Establishment of an International Fund for Compensation for Oil Pollution Damage, 1971, as amended from time to time, but excluding amendments set forth in the Protocol thereto adopted at an International Conference held in London in 1984.

(E) "Incident" means any occurrence, or series of occurrences having the same origin, which causes Pollution Damage, or which creates the Threat of an escape or discharge of Oil.

(F) "Liability Convention" means the International Convention on Civil Liability for Oil Pollution Damage, 1969, as amended from time to time, but excluding amendments set forth in the Protocol thereto adopted at an International Conference held in London in 1984.

(G) "Oil" means any persistent hydrocarbon mineral oil including, but not limited to, crude oil, fuel oil, heavy diesel oil and lubricating oil whether carried on board a Tanker as cargo or in the bunkers of such a Tanker.

(H) "Oil Company" means any Person (i) engaged in the production, refining, marketing, storing, trading or terminaling of Oil, or any one or more of whose affiliates are so engaged or (ii) that receives Oil in bulk for its own consumption or use.

(I) "Oil Company Party" means an Oil Company which is a Party to this Contract.

(J) "Owner" means the Person or Persons registered as the owner of the Tanker or, in the absence of registration, the Person or Persons owning the Tanker.

However, in the case of a Tanker owned by a State and operated by a company which in that State is registered as the Tanker's operator, "Owner" shall mean such company. Notwithstanding the foregoing, in the case of a Tanker under bareboat charter, "Owner" means the Bareboat Charterer or any other Person deemed to be an owner under the laws applicable to the Incident.

(K) "Person" means (i) an Owner and (ii) any individual or partnership or any public or private body, whether corporate or not, including a State or any of its constituent subdivisions.

(L) "Preventive Measures" means any reasonable measures taken by any Person after an Incident has occurred to prevent or minimise Pollution Damage.

*(M) "Pollution Damage" means (i) physical loss or damage caused outside the Tanker by contamination resulting from the escape or discharge of Oil from the Tanker, wherever such escape or discharge may occur, including such loss or damage caused by Preventive Measures, and/or (ii) proven economic loss actually sustained, irrespective as to accompanying physical damage, as a direct result of contamination as set out in (i) above, including the Costs of Preventive Measures, and/or (iii) Costs actually incurred in taking reasonable and necessary measures to restore or replace natural resources damaged as a direct result of an Incident, but excluding any other damage to the environment.

(N) "Tanker" means any seagoing vessel and any seaborne craft of any type whatsoever, designed and constructed for carrying Oil in bulk as cargo, and actually so carrying Oil.

(O) "Threat of an escape or discharge of Oil" means a grave and imminent danger of the escape or discharge of Oil from a Tanker, which, if it occurred, would create a serious danger of Pollution Damage, whether or not an escape or discharge in fact subsequently occurs.

(P) "Threat Removal Measures" means reasonable measures taken by any Person after an Incident has occurred for the purposes of removing the Threat of an escape or discharge of Oil.

(Q) "Ton" means a ton of a Tanker's gross tonnage as determined in accordance with the provisions of the International Convention on Tonnage Measurement of Ships, 1969, as amended, and in force at the Effective Date of this Contract.

Clause II.
General Conditions

(A) Any Oil Company may become an Oil Company Party to this Contract and a Member of CRISTAL upon acceptance by CRISTAL of an application in the form attached hereto as "Exhibit A".

(B) The obligations of an Oil Company Party under this Contract shall extend solely to CRISTAL and to the other Oil Company Parties hereto. The obligations of CRISTAL under this Contract shall extend solely to the Oil Company Parties hereto.

Clause III.
Effective Date

(A) This Contract shall be applicable to Incidents which shall have occurred after 12.00 hours G.M.T. on February 20, 1987, (the "Effective Date"), and shall no longer be applicable to Incidents occurring at or after 12.00 hours G.M.T. on February 20, 1992,(or such later date as may be agreed); it being understood that nothing set forth herein shall affect the obligations of CRISTAL with respect to an Incident which occurred prior to the Effective Date.

---

*Amendment effective October 23, 1989.

(B) An Oil Company Party may withdraw from this Contract at any time following the Effective Date, provided that it gives at least six (6) months prior written notice of withdrawal to CRISTAL and such withdrawing Oil Company Party shall have no rights hereunder as of the date of withdrawal; however any such withdrawal shall not affect the obligations of the withdrawing Oil Company Party with respect to Incidents which occurred prior to the said date of withdrawal, which obligations shall be satisfied as set forth in Paragraph (C) of this Clause III.

(C) An Oil Company Party shall satisfy its obligations under Paragraph (B) of this Clause III by, either (i) paying a release assessment calculated by CRISTAL in a manner set forth in the Rules to this Contract or (ii) at CRISTAL's option, contributing to Periodic Calls made after the aforesaid date of withdrawal in accordance with terms and conditions set forth in the Rules to this Contract.

Clause IV.
Compensation and Payments

(A) If an Incident does not cause Pollution Damage in a jurisdiction where the provisions of the Fund Convention are in force, but irrespective as to whether the provisions of the Liability Convention or any applicable domestic law are in force, CRISTAL shall, subject to the conditions and in the amounts set forth in Paragraphs (D) and (E) of this Clause IV, compensate any Person who, (i) sustains Pollution Damage or (ii) incurs Costs in taking Threat Removal Measures.

(B) If an Incident causes Pollution Damage in a jurisdiction where the provisions of both the Liability Convention and the Fund Convention are in force CRISTAL shall, subject to the conditions and in the amounts set forth in Paragraphs (D) and (E) of this Clause IV:

(1) pay an Oil Company Party, an amount equal to the contribution assessed by the Fund or made to the Fund by such Oil Company Party under Article 10 of the Fund Convention, with respect to the amount that the Fund intends to pay or did pay as compensation as a result of an Incident; and,

(2) compensate any Person who (i) sustains Pollution Damage or (ii) incurs Costs in taking Threat Removal Measures and who would otherwise remain uncompensated.

(C) For the purposes of Paragraphs (A) and (B) of this Clause IV, Pollution Damage shall include amounts paid by a Person to compensate another Person for Pollution Damage.

(D) No Payment or Compensation shall be made under either Paragraphs (A) or (B) of this Clause IV except subject to and in accordance with the terms and conditions set forth herein.

(1) It shall be a condition precedent to CRISTAL's obligation to make any payment whatsoever that, at the time of the Incident, the Oil involved in the Incident be "owned" by an Oil Company Party, as provided in Clause V.

(2) No compensation shall be paid to a Person, under either Paragraph (A) or (B) (2) of this Clause IV, if the Incident (i) resulted from an act of war, hostilities, civil war, insurrection or a natural phenomenon of an exceptional, inevitable and irresistible character, or (ii) was wholly caused by an act or omission done with intent to cause damage by a third party, or (iii) was wholly caused by the negligence or other wrongful act of any Government or other authority responsible for the maintenance of lights or other navigational aids in the exercise of that function.

Notwithstanding the foregoing provisions of this Subparagraph (2) CRISTAL shall compensate Oil Company Parties under Paragraph B (1) of this Clause IV except when the Incident resulted from an act of war, hostilities, civil war or insurrection, or was wholly caused by an act or omission done with intent to cause damage by a third party.

(3) If Pollution Damage or the taking of Threat Removal Measures resulted wholly or partially either from an act or omission done with intent to cause damage by, or from the negligence of the Person who sustained the Pollution Damage or who took the Threat Removal Measures, any payment or compensation that would otherwise be payable by CRISTAL to that Person, under either Paragraphs (A) or (B) (2) of this Clause IV, shall be denied or reduced proportionately to the extent of that Person's negligence; however nothing set forth in this Subparagraph shall affect CRISTAL's obligations under Paragraph (B) (1) of this Clause IV, or to the Owner in respect of an Incident which does not result from the wilful misconduct of the Owner or from the unseaworthiness of the Tanker where this occurs with the privity of the Owner.

(4) No payment or compensation shall be made or paid under Paragraphs (A) and (B), of this Clause IV, until evidence, satisfactory to CRISTAL, has been presented demonstrating that claims for Pollution Damage or Costs of Preventive Measures or Threat Removal Measures (including payments made by the Owner to CRISTAL, as agent for Oil Company Party(ies)), and payments or costs incurred by the Owner as a result of the application of the Liability Convention, applicable domestic laws or otherwise have been paid by, or on behalf of, the Owner equal, in the case of a Tanker of Five Thousand (5,000) Tons or less to Three Million Five Hundred Thousand United States Dollars (U.S. $3,500,000.00) and for a Tanker in excess of Five Thousand (5,000) Tons Three Million Five Hundred Thousand United States Dollars (U.S. $3,500,000.00) plus Four Hundred and Ninety Three United States Dollars (U.S. $493.00) for each Ton in excess of said Five Thousand (5,000) Tons, subject to a maximum of Seventy Million United States Dollars (US $70,000,000.00).

(5) (a) The aggregate amount to be paid by CRISTAL, under Paragraph (A), (B) and (D) (8) of this Clause IV, in respect of any one Incident, shall not exceed, after taking into account payments made under Subparagraph (4) of this Clause IV (D) an amount equal to Thirty Six Million United States Dollars (U.S. $36,000,000.00) for a Tanker of Five Thousand (5,000) Tons or less and for a Tanker in excess of Five Thousand (5,000) Tons Thirty Six Million United States Dollars (U.S. $36,000,000.00) plus Seven Hundred and Thirty Three United States Dollars (U.S. $733.00) for each Ton in excess of said Five Thousand (5,000) Tons, subject to a maximum of One Hundred and Thirty Five Million United States Dollars (U.S.$135,000,000.00).

(b) In the event more than one Tanker discharges Oil or poses a Threat of an escape or discharge of Oil in respect of any one Incident, the aggregate amount to be paid by CRISTAL under Subparagraph (5) (a) of this Clause IV (D) shall be established by reference to the tonnage of the largest of said Tankers. For the purpose of establishing under Subparagraph (4) of this Clause IV (D) whether payment or compensation shall be made or paid, payments or Costs incurred by or on behalf of the Owners of all the said Tankers shall be taken into account.

(6) If the maximum amount that can be paid by CRISTAL, pursuant to Paragraph (D) (5) of this Clause IV, is insufficient to reimburse an Oil Company Party(ies), pursuant to Paragraph (B) (1) of this Clause IV, and meet in full all other claims, approved under Paragraphs (A) and (B) (2) of this Clause IV, then CRISTAL shall prorate the amount available among all claims.

(7) No payment or compensation shall be made or paid to a Person entitled, under Paragraphs (A) and (B) (2) of this Clause IV, to make a claim with respect to an Incident, if that Person prosecutes a claim for Pollution Damage or the Cost of Preventive Measures or Threat Removal Measures against any fund established and/or maintained by means of assessments against Oil Companies, irrespective as to whether any said Person is entitled to either indemnification or compensation under the terms of any such fund; provided that nothing set forth herein shall prevent such a Person from asserting, prosecuting or settling a claim, against any said fund for those amounts not satisfied pursuant to this Contract or, under either (i) the Liability Convention or (ii) against the Fund under the Fund Convention, or both, if or to the extent, they are applicable.

(8) No compensation (except any payment to be made pursuant to Paragraph (B) (1) of this Clause IV) shall be made or paid to a Person until such Person has taken all reasonable steps to obtain full compensation for Pollution Damage or for the Cost of Preventive Measures or Threat Removal Measures or any element thereof from any Person, but not including the Owner unless the Pollution Damage or Costs resulted from the wilful misconduct of the Owner or from the unseaworthiness of the Tanker where this occurs with the privity of the Owner, or ship (which shall include but not be limited to a Tanker or any other vessel or ship) liable therefor, and from any other source of compensation available under convention, law or regulation (except for funds established and maintained by means of assessments against Oil Companies as referred to in Subparagraph (7) of this Clause IV (D)); provided, however, that CRISTAL may, in its sole discretion and to the extent permitted under applicable law, advance monies to said Person to partially or fully compensate for the Costs said Person might incur in taking reasonable steps to obtain full compensation as set forth in this Subparagraph (8).

(9) (a) In the event that CRISTAL should determine that it is unreasonable for a Person to take steps or further steps, pursuant to Subparagraph (8) of this Clause IV (D), CRISTAL may require, prior to compensating said Person under Paragraphs (A) or (B) (2) of this Clause IV, that it receive, in a form acceptable to it, documentation or other instrument(s), executed by said Person (but without prejudice to the rights of the Fund under the Fund Convention if it has made a payment to said Person under the Fund Convention), (i) transferring or assigning to CRISTAL any and all rights of any nature or kind, said Person has or might have to seek compensation from any third party (including a government or governmental agency but excluding the Fund) for the compensation to be paid by CRISTAL to said Person for either Pollution Damage and Costs of Preventive Measures or Threat Removal Measures; or (ii) granting irrevocable authority to CRISTAL to institute, in the name of any said Person, legal, equitable or administrative proceedings in any jurisdiction whatsoever to perfect and exercise the aforesaid rights and if any judgment, award, decision or decree is secured to collect the same, in the name of any said Person, and when collected to endorse and negotiate any cheque, money order, bill of exchange, promissory note, transfer or similar instrument so that the proceeds of any such judgment, award, decision or decree shall be the sole property of CRISTAL; and

(b) no payment shall be made under Paragraph (B) (1) of this Clause IV, until CRISTAL has received, in a form acceptable to it, a document or other instrument evidencing settlement in part or in full, as the case may be, the obligations of CRISTAL pursuant to Paragraph (B) (1) of this Clause IV.

(10) For the purposes of Paragraph (D) (3) and (8) of this Clause IV the terms "wilful misconduct", "privity" and "unseaworthiness" shall have the same meaning as they have under the Marine Insurance Act 1906 as interpreted by the English Courts under English Law.

(E) For the purposes of determining the amount of any payments or compensation to be paid by CRISTAL hereunder, CRISTAL shall:

(1) Convert any losses or Costs constituting Pollution Damage, Preventive Measures or Threat Removal Measures either incurred or suffered by a Person or any payment made by or on behalf of an Owner, for the purposes of Paragraph (D) (4) and (5) of this Clause IV, if incurred in a currency(ies) other than United States Dollars to United States Dollars at the buy rate of exchange for said currency(ies) as quoted by the National Westminster Bank Plc in London on the date of the payment by or on behalf of the Owner, or by CRISTAL respectively; except when a limitation fund is established under the provisions of the Liability Convention when the said exchange rate shall be that as quoted on the date that the limitation fund is established.

(2) Convert any payments to be made to an Oil Company Party, pursuant to Paragraph (B) (1) of this Clause IV, if incurred in a currency(ies) other than United States Dollars, to United States Dollars at the buy rate of exchange for said currency(ies) to United States Dollars as quoted by the National Westminster Bank Plc in London on the date that the Fund shall have demanded payment by the Oil Company Party.

(3) The amount of all losses or Costs constituting Pollution Damage, Preventive Measures or Threat Removal Measures shall be determined by CRISTAL in the currency of the jurisdiction where the Incident has occurred or the Costs were incurred by a Person. All payments in compensation therefor made pursuant to Paragraphs (A) or (B) (2) of this Clause VI shall be made by CRISTAL in such currency(ies), if other than United States dollars, by converting the equivalent amount of United States dollars into such currency(ies) at the buy rate of exchange as quoted by the National Westminster Bank Plc in London on the date of payment. If on the date payment of said claim(s) is (are) to be made, an expenditure of United States Dollars (after considering all payments to be made under Paragraph (B) (1) of this Clause IV) is required by CRISTAL in excess of the provisions of Paragraph (D) (5) of this Clause IV, the provisions of Paragraph (D) (6) of this Clause IV shall be applicable.

*Clause V.
Ownership of Shipments

(A) A particular shipment of Oil shall be considered "owned" by an Oil Company Party for the purpose of Clause IV (D) (1) and Clause VII if at the time of the Incident title to the shipment is in either:

(1) said Oil Company Party, or

(2) a Person not an Oil Company Party to whom said Oil Company Party has transferred the shipment, or

(3) a Person not an Oil Company Party but the shipment is being carried by a Tanker owned by or under charter to an Oil Company Party or one of its affiliates, or

(4) a Person not an Oil Company Party who, prior to any Incident involving said shipment, contracted to transfer said shipment to an Oil Company Party, or

---

*Amendment effective May 16, 1988.

(5) a Person not an Oil Company Party who, prior to any Incident involving said shipment, contracted for delivery to, storage, processing or transshipment at or shipment from a terminal or other facility owned, operated, managed, leased, hired or otherwise controlled by an Oil Company Party or in which an Oil Company Party has an interest and an Incident occurs or Polluton Damage is caused in a geographic area within 250 nautical miles in any direction from a point at the geographic centre of said terminal or other facility.

(B) For the purposes of Clause V(A)(2) and (3) such Oil shall be deemed to be so "owned" by an Oil Company Party provided that prior to any Incident involving said shipment of Oil, and in accordance with the Rules of CRISTAL, said Oil Company Party has advised CRISTAL in writing that it elects to be considered the "owner" thereof.

(C) For the purposes of Clause V(A)(5) terminal or other facility shall mean any property, fixed or floating from which Oil can be unloaded from or discharged into a Tanker including, but not limited to oil terminals, tank farms, refineries, single point moorings, floating storage or offshore discharging or loading vessels.

**(D) For the purpose of Clause IV (A) and (B) only, segregated slops of a Tanker carrying any shipment so owned, and bunker oil and lubricating oil intended for use in said Tanker's operation shall be deemed included in such shipment.

Clause VI.
Subrogation

(A) CRISTAL shall, in respect of any amount of compensation paid in accordance with Clause IV (A) and (B) (2), acquire by subrogation the rights that the Person so compensated may enjoy under applicable legislation, law, convention or otherwise against the Owner or its insurers.

(B) Nothing herein shall prejudice any right of recourse or subrogation of CRISTAL against Persons other than those referred to in the preceding Paragraph. In any event, the right of CRISTAL to subrogation against such Person shall not be less favourable than that of an insurer of the Person to whom compensation has been paid.

*Clause VII.
The CRISTAL Fund

(A) (1) CRISTAL, in order to assure its financial capability to make payments in accordance with Clause IV, shall maintain and administer an account, to be known as the "CRISTAL Fund", contributions to which shall be made by each Oil Company Party.

(2) Contributions to the CRISTAL Fund shall be calculated on the basis of the Crude/Fuel Oil Receipts of the Oil Company Parties. For the purpose of this Clause VII, Crude/Fuel Oil Receipts means,

(i) crude oil and fuel oil received at an installation or terminal by an Oil Company Party which has been transported all or part of the way to such installation or terminal by Tanker (excluding any crude oil which is received solely for transhipment for onward transportation by Tanker to an installation or terminal for receipt by an Oil Company Party) and which at the time of receipt is "owned" by an Oil Company Party,

---

**Amendment effective October 23, 1989.
*Amendment effective October 23, 1989.

(ii) crude oil and fuel oil not so received but with respect to which an Oil Company Party has elected, pursuant to Clause V, to be considered the "owner",

(iii) crude oil and fuel oil owned by an Oil Company Party but with respect to which title was transferred at destination to a Person not an Oil Company Party,

(iv) crude oil and fuel oil at the time when it has been retained on board a Tanker for a period of six (6) months and which at that time is owned by an Oil Company Party, together with any such crude oil and fuel oil retained on board such Tanker on the last day of each ensuing calendar year thereafter which, at that time, is owned by an Oil Company Party,

(v) that portion of all crude oil and fuel oil received at a terminal or other facility, defined in Clause V (A) (5) and (C), in which an Oil Company Party has an equity interest, equal to that Oil Company Party's proportional equity interest in said terminal or other facility, as compared to the equity interest(s) of all Oil Company Parties in that terminal or other facility and which is not otherwise either reported or to be reported in the Crude/Fuel Oil Receipts of the Oil Company Party or any other related or affiliated Oil Company Party, and

(vi) crude oil and fuel oil, transported by Tanker, in which an Oil Company Party had title at some point after loading and prior to discharge from the Tanker and which (i) is not included in the Crude/Fuel Oil Receipts of that Oil Company Party or any other related or affiliated Oil Company Party by reason of any other provision of this Paragraph, and/or (ii) had not been sold to another Oil Company Party.

(B) (1) CRISTAL shall from time to time estimate amounts (hereinafter referred to as a "Periodic Call") required to assure the capability of the CRISTAL Fund to make payments in accordance with Clause IV.

(2) Contributions to a Periodic Call shall be calculated by dividing the amount of the Call by the total of the Crude/Fuel Oil Receipts of all the Oil Company Parties as at the date of the Periodic Call during the calendar year preceding the year in which the Periodic Call is made, and multiplying the figure so calculated by the Crude/Fuel Oil Receipts of each Oil Company Party for such preceding year. For the purpose of these calculations the Crude/Fuel Oil Receipts shall be the total of the crude oil and fuel oil as defined in Paragraphs (A) (2) (i), (ii), (iii), (iv), (v) and (vi) of this Clause VII.

(3) However, notwithstanding the foregoing provisions of this Paragraph (B) (1) and (2) of this Clause VII:

(i) each such Oil Company Party (whether or not it had any Crude/Fuel Oil Receipts during such preceding calendar year) shall pay no less than a minimum charge determined by CRISTAL to be reasonable under the circumstances, and

(ii) no Oil Company party shall be liable to contribute to any payment of compensation by CRISTAL in respect to any Incident which occurred before it became a Party to this Contract, and

(iii) any Oil Company Party which becomes a Party hereto shall pay a contribution to any Periodic Call made in the calendar year of joining, subject to the provision of Paragraph (B) (3) (ii) of this Clause VII, and in no event less than the minimum sum referred to in Paragraph (B) (3) (i) of this Clause VII.

(C) Upon the Oil Company Parties deciding on a date beyond which claims will not be accepted under this Contract, any amounts remaining in the CRISTAL

Fund, after the settlement or other disposition of all claims arising from Incidents occurring before the said date and the settlement of all costs and expenses relating to the winding up of CRISTAL, shall be equitably distributed among the Oil Companies that are Parties at the date when CRISTAL is finally dissolved.

Clause VIII.
Notice of Claim

No liability shall arise under Clause IV (A) or (B) (2) unless written notice of claim is received by CRISTAL within two (2) years of the date of the Incident giving rise thereto. In the case of a payment to be made under Clause IV (B) (1) no liability shall arise unless written notice of claim is received by CRISTAL from an Oil Company Party within one year of the date that payment of the Contribution under Article 10 of the Fund Convention is to be made.

Clause IX.
Rules and Directives

In fulfilling its obligations, in accordance with the terms of this Contract, CRISTAL shall be the sole judge in accordance with these terms of the validity of any claim made hereunder, except that CRISTAL, for the purposes of Clause IV (B) (1), will accept the validity of any request for a contribution made by the Fund. CRISTAL shall also have the right to make rules and directives from time to time with respect to interpretation and administration of this Contract.

Clause X.
Amendment

This Contract may be amended by resolution adopted at any Regular or Special Meeting of the Members of CRISTAL upon a vote in which at least seventy five percent (75%) of the votes cast are in favour of said resolution. Amendments to this Contract shall apply only in respect of Incidents which occur after 12.00 hours G.M.T. on the date on which said amendment is adopted by the Members of CRISTAL.

Clause XI.
Law Governing

(A) This Contract shall be construed and shall take effect in accordance with the Laws of England; the Courts of England shall have exclusive jurisdiction over any matter arising therefrom.

(B) This Contract shall not be construed as creating a trust.

(C) A Party hereto shall not be required to incur any obligation or take any action which would violate any laws or government regulations which apply to it or, in the event its stock or shares are owned by another Person, which would violate any laws or government regulations which apply to said Person.

IN WITNESS WHEREOF, the Parties have entered into this Contract upon January 14, 1971, or upon such later date as their applications to become Parties are accepted by CRISTAL.

ORGANISATION FOR ECONOMIC CO-OPERATION AND DEVELOPMENT COUNCIL RECOMMENDATION ON THE IMPLEMENTATION OF THE POLLUTER-PAYS PRINCIPLE

Popular Name: OECD PPP Recommendation, Polluter-Pays Principle

Done at Paris on 14 November 1974, OECD Doc. C(74)223 (21 Nov. 1974), *reprinted in* OECD & E 26 (1986), 14 ILM 234 (1975).

Editors' Note

In 1974, at the same time that it recommended principles regarding transfrontier pollution (*supra*, p. 573), the OECD Council passed this recommendation regarding implementing the polluter-pays principle. The OECD had earlier declared that the polluter-pays principle should be used "for allocating the costs of pollution prevention and control." OECD Council Recommendation of 26 May 1972, C(72)128. This principle essentially requires a person whose activities threaten to create pollution to internalize the costs of preventing that pollution, at least to the extent of meeting pollution-control standards and, by implication, to the extent of paying for damage resulting from a failure to meet those standards. The principle—at least as conceptualized outside the context of the OECD—now probably also requires the internalization of the costs of pollution damage that results even if pollution-control standards have been met. *See also* the immediately following instrument in this Chapter.

THE IMPLEMENTATION OF THE POLLUTER-PAYS PRINCIPLE

THE COUNCIL,

Having regard to Article 5(*b*) of the Convention on the Organisation for Economic Co-operation and Development of 14th December, 1960;

Having regard to the provisions of the General Agreement on Tariffs and Trade;

Having regard to the Recommendation of the Council of 26th May, 1972 on Guiding Principles Concerning International Economic Aspects of Environmental Policies [C(72)128];

Having regard to the Note by the Environment Committee on Implementation of the Polluter-Pays Principle [ENV(73)32(Final)];

Having regard to the possibility, approved by the Council of holding informal consultations on the Guiding Principles within the OECD;

On the proposal of the Environment Committee:

I. REAFFIRMS that:

1. The Polluter-Pays Principle constitutes for Member countries a fundamental principle for allocating costs of pollution prevention and control measures introduced by the public authorities in Member countries;

2. The Polluter-Pays Principle, as defined by the Guiding Principles concerning International Economic Aspects of Environmental Policies, which take account of

particular problems possibly arising for developing countries, means that the polluter should bear the expenses of carrrying [sic] out the measures, as specified in the previous paragraph, to ensure that the environment is in an acceptable state. In other words, the cost of these measures should be reflected in the cost of goods and services which cause pollution in production and/or consumption;

3. Uniform application of this principle, through the adoption of a common basis for Member countries' environmental policies, would encourage the rational use and the better allocation of scarce environmental resources and prevent the appearance of distortions in international trade and investment.

II. NOTES that:

1. There is a close relationship between a country's environmental policy and its overall socio-economic policy;

2. In exceptional circumstances, such as the rapid implementation of a compelling and especially stringent pollution control regime, socio-economic problems may develop of such significance as to justify consideration of the granting of governmental assistance if the environmental policy objectives of a Member country are to be realized within a prescribed and specified time;

3. Aid given for the purpose of stimulating experimentation with new pollution-control technologies and development of new pollution-abatement equipment is not necessarily incompatible with the Polluter-Pays Principle;

4. Where measures taken to promote a country's specific socio-economic objectives, such as the reduction of serious inter-regional imbalances, would have the incidental effect of constituting aid for pollution-control purposes, the granting of such aid would not be inconsistent with the Polluter-Pays Principle.

III. RECOMMENDS that:

1. Member countries continue to collaborate and work closely together in striving for uniform observance of the Polluter-Pays Principle, and therefore that as a general rule they should not assist the polluters in bearing the costs of pollution control whether by means of subsidies, tax advantages or other measures;

2. The granting of any such assistance for pollution control be strictly limited, and in particular comply with every one of the following conditions:

  a)   it should be selective and restricted to those parts of the economy, such as industries, areas or plants, where severe difficulties would otherwise occur;

  b)   it should be limited to well-defined transitional periods, laid down in advance and adapted to the specific socio-economic problems associated with the implementation of a country's environmental programme;

  c)   it should not create significant distortions in international trade and investment.

3. That if a Member country, in cases of exceptional difficulty, gives assistance to new plants, the conditions be even stricter than those applicable to existing plants and that criteria on which to base this differentiation be developed;

4. In accordance with appropriate procedures to be worked out, all systems to provide assistance be notified to Member countries through the OECD Secretariat. Wherever practicable these notifications would occur prior to implementation of such systems;

5. Regardless of whether notification has taken place, consultations, as mentioned in the Guiding Principles on the implementation of such systems, will take place at the request of any Member State.

IV. INVITES the Environment Committee to report to the Council on action take [sic] pursuant to this Recommendation.

ORGANISATION FOR ECONOMIC CO-OPERATION AND DEVELOPMENT COUNCIL RECOMMENDATION ON THE APPLICATION OF THE POLLUTER-PAYS PRINCIPLE TO ACCIDENTAL POLLUTION

Done at Paris on 7 July 1989, OECD Doc. C(89)88(Final) (25 July 1989), *reprinted in* 28 ILM 1321 (1989).

Languages: English, French

Editors' Note

This OECD Council recommendation extends the scope of the polluter-pays principle, *supra*, p. 706, beyond chronic pollution caused by ongoing activity to cover accidental pollution.

COUNCIL
RECOMMENDATION ON THE APPLICATION OF THE POLLUTER-PAYS PRINCIPLE TO ACCIDENTAL POLLUTION

THE COUNCIL,

Having regard to Article 5 b) of the Convention on the Organisation for Economic Co-operation and Development of 14th December 1960;

Having regard to the Recommendation of the Council of 26th May 1972 on Guiding Principles Concerning International Economic Aspects of Environmental Policies [C(72)128];

Having regard to the Recommendation of the Council of 14th November 1974 on the Implementation of the Polluter-Pays Principle [C(74)223];

Having regard to the Recommendation of the Council of 28th April 1981 on Certain Financial Aspects of Action by Public Authorities to Prevent and Control Oil Spills [C(81)32(Final)];

Having regard to the Concluding Statement of the OECD Conference on Accidents Involving Hazardous Substances held in Paris on 9th and 10th February 1988 [C(88)83];

Considering that this Conference concluded that "operators of hazardous installations have the full responsibility for the safe operation of their installations and for taking all appropriate measures to prevent accidents" and that "operators of hazardous installations should take all reasonable measures . . . to take emergency actions in case of an accident";

Considering that such responsibility has repercussions on the allocation of the cost of reasonable measures aimed at preventing accidents in hazardous installations and limiting their consequences and that the Conference concluded that "the Polluter-Pays Principle should be applied, as far as possible, in connection with accidents involving hazardous substances";

Considering that public authorities are often required to take expensive action in case of accidental pollution from hazardous installations and may find it necessary to undertake costly accident preparedness measures in relation to certain hazardous installations;

Considering that closer harmonisation of laws and regulations relating to the allocation of the cost of measures to prevent and control accidental pollution is likely to reduce distortions in international trade and investment;

On the proposal of the Environment Committee,

I. RECOMMENDS that, in applying the Polluter-Pays Principle in connection with accidents involving hazardous substances, Member countries take into account the "Guiding Principles Relating to Accidental Pollution" set out in the Appendix which is an integral part of this Recommendation.

II. INSTRUCTS the Environment Committee to review the actions taken by Member countries pursuant to this Recommendation and to report to the Council within three years of the adoption of this Recommendation.

Appendix

Guiding Principles Relating to Accidental Pollution

Scope and Definition

1. The Guiding Principles described below concern some aspects of the application of the Polluter-Pays Principle to hazardous installations.

2. For the purposes of this Recommendation:

a) "Hazardous installations" means those fixed installations which are defined under applicable law as being capable of giving rise to hazards sufficient to warrant the taking of precautions off-site, excluding nuclear or military installations and hazardous waste repositories (1);

b) "Accidental pollution" means substantial pollution off-site resulting from an accident in a hazardous installation;

c) "Operator of a hazardous installation" means the legal or natural person who under applicable law is in charge of the installation and is responsible for its proper operation (2).

The Polluter-pays Principle

3. According to the Recommendation of the Council of 26th May 1972, on the Guiding Principles Concerning International Economic Aspects of Environmental Policies [C(72)128], the "principle to be used for allocating the costs of pollution prevention and control is the so called Polluter-Pays Principle". The implementation of this principle will "encourage rational use of scarce environmental resources". According to the Recommendation of the Council of 14th November 1974 on the Implementation of the Polluter-Pays Principle [C(74)223], "the Polluter-Pays Principle . . . means that the polluter should bear the expenses of carrying out the pollution prevention and control measures introduced by public authorities in Member countries, to ensure that the environment is in an acceptable state. In other words, the cost of these measures should be reflected in the cost of goods and services which cause pollution in production and/or consumption". In the same Recommendation, the Council recommended that "as a general rule, Member countries should not assist the polluters in bearing the costs of pollution control whether by means of subsidies, tax advantages or other measures".

Application of the Polluter-pays Principle

4. In matters of accidental pollution risks, the Polluter-Pays Principle implies that the operator of a hazardous installation should bear the cost of reasonable measures to prevent and control accidental pollution from that installation which are introduced by public authorities in Member countries in conformity with domestic law

prior to the occurrence of an accident in order to protect human health or the environment.

5. Domestic law which provides that the cost of reasonable measures to control accidental pollution after an accident should be collected as expeditiously as possible from the legal or natural person who is at the origin of the accident, is consistent with the Polluter-Pays Principle.

6. In most instances and notwithstanding issues concerning the origin of the accident, the cost of such reasonable measures taken by the authorities is initially borne by the operator for administrative convenience or for other reasons (3). When a third party is liable for the accident, that party reimburses to the operator the cost of reasonable measures to control accidental pollution taken after an accident.

7. If the accidental pollution is caused solely by an event for which the operator clearly cannot be considered liable under national law, such as a serious natural disaster that the operator cannot reasonably have foreseen, it is consistent with the Polluter-Pays Principle that public authorities do not charge the cost of control measures to the operator.

8. Measures to prevent and control accidental pollution are those taken to prevent accidents in specific installations and to limit their consequences for human health or the environment. They can include, in particular, measures aimed at improving the safety of hazardous installations and accident preparedness, developing emergency plans, acting promptly following an accident in order to protect human health and the environment, carrying out clean-up operations and minimizing without undue delay the ecological effects of accidental pollution. They do not include humanitarian measures or other measures which are strictly in the nature of public services and which cannot be reimbursed to the public authorities under applicable law nor measures to compensate victims for the economic consequences of an accident.

9. Public authorities of Member countries that "have responsibilities in the implementation of policies for prevention of, and response to, accidents involving hazardous substances" (4), may take specific measures to prevent accidents occurring at hazardous installations and to control accidental pollution. Although the cost entailed is as a general rule met by the general budget, public authorities may with a view to achieving a more economically efficient resource allocation, introduce specific fees or taxes payable by certain installations on account of their hazardous nature (e.g., licensing fees), the proceeds of which to be allocated to accidental pollution prevention and control.

10. One specific application of the Polluter-Pays Principle consists in adjusting these fees or taxes, in conformity with domestic law, to cover more fully the cost of certain exceptional measures to prevent and control accidental pollution in specific hazardous installations which are taken by public authorities to protect human health and the environment (e.g., special licensing procedures, execution of detailed inspections, drawing up of installation-specific emergency plans or building up special means of response for the public authorities to be used in connection with a hazardous installation), provided such measures are reasonable and directly connected with accident prevention or with the control of accidental pollution released by the hazardous installation. Lack of laws or regulations on relevant fees or taxes should not, however, prevent public authorities from meeting their responsibilities in connection with accidents involving hazardous substances.

11. A further specific application of the Polluter-Pays Principle consists in charging, in conformity with domestic law, the cost of reasonable pollution control measures decided by the authorities following an accident to the operator of the hazardous installation from which pollution is released. Such measures taken without undue delay by the operator or, in case of need, by the authorities would aim at promptly avoiding the spreading of environmental damage and would concern limiting the release of hazardous substances (e.g., by ceasing emissions at the plant,

by erecting floating barriers on a river), the pollution as such (e.g., by cleaning or decontamination), or its ecological effects (e.g., by rehabilitating the polluted environment).

12. The extent to which prevention and control measures can be considered reasonable will depend on the circumstances under which they are implemented, the nature and extent of the measures, the threats and hazards existing when the decision is taken, the laws and regulations in force, and the interests which must be protected. Prior consultation between operators and public authorities should contribute to the choice of measures which are reasonable, economically efficient, and provide adequate protection of human health and the environment.

13. The pooling among operators of certain financial risks connected with accidents, for instance by means of insurance or within a special compensation or pollution control fund, is consistent with the Polluter-Pays Principle.

Exceptions

14. Exceptions to the Polluter-Pays Principle could be made under special circumstances such as the need for the rapid implementation of stringent measures for accident prevention, provided this does not lead to significant distortions in international trade and investment. In particular, any aid to be granted to operators for prevention or control of accidental pollution should be limited and comply with the conditions set out previously.(5) In the case of existing hazardous installations, compensatory payments or measures for changes in zoning decisions in the framework of the local land use plan might be envisaged with a view to facilitating the relocation of these installations so as to lessen the risks for the exposed population.

15. Likewise, exceptions to the above Guiding Principles could be made in the event of accidental pollution if strict and prompt implementation of the Polluter-Pays Principle would lead to severe socio-economic consequences.

16. The allocation to the person at the origin of the accident or the operator, as the case may be, of the cost of reasonable measures taken by public authorities to control accidental pollution does not affect the possibility under domestic law of requiring the same person to pay other costs connected with the public authorities' response to an accident (e.g., the supply of potable water) or with the occurrence of the accident. In addition, public authorities may, as appropriate, seek compensation from the party liable for the accident for costs incurred by them as a result of the accident when such costs have not yet been paid to the authorities.

Notes

1. Hazardous installations covered by this Recommendation are as defined in the law applicable in the country of the installation (domestic law and in some instances, European Community law). Countries are not prevented from making provisions under their national laws to the effect that the Guiding Principles also apply to installations excluded under subparagraph 2a of this Appendix.
2. The concept of operator is defined in the law applicable in the country of the installation, in which attention may be given to criteria such as ownership of certain hazardous substances or possession of a license or permit.
3. In cases where a party other than the operator has, under the law applicable in the country of the installation, strict liability for an accident, the cost of reasonable control measures taken by the authorities would be charged to that party, not to the operator. Whenever national laws provide a regime of strict liability, this regime would be applied in respect of the reimbursement of costs of control measures taken after the accident.
4. Concluding Statement of the OECD Conference on Accidents Involving Hazardous Substances, C(88)83.

5. Recommendation of the Council of 14th November 1974 on the Implementation of the Polluter-Pays Principle, C(74)223.

WELLINGTON CONVENTION ON THE REGULATION OF ANTARCTIC MINERAL RESOURCE ACTIVITIES. *Supra*, p. 529.

INTERNATIONAL ATOMIC ENERGY AGENCY CODE OF PRACTICE ON THE INTERNATIONAL TRANSBOUNDARY MOVEMENT OF RADIOACTIVE WASTE. *Supra*, p. 597.

CHAPTER 26
SURVEILLANCE & MONITORING

PROTOCOL ON ENVIRONMENTAL PROTECTION TO THE ANTARCTIC TREATY. *Supra*, p. 536.

CHAPTER 27
TRADE (IMPORT AND EXPORT)
RESTRICTIONS

GENERAL AGREEMENT ON TARIFFS AND TRADE (GATT)

Popular Name: GATT

Done at Geneva on 30 October 1947, 55 UNTS 187, *reprinted in* 1 IPE 7.

Entry into Force: Applied provisionally from 1 January 1948

Depositary: United Nations

Languages: English, French

Parties as of 31 December 1989: Antigua and Barbuda; Argentina; Australia; Austria; Bangladesh; Barbados; Belgium; Belize; Benin; Botswana; Brazil; Burkina Faso; Burundi; Canada; Cameroon; Central African Republic; Chad; Chile; Colombia; Congo; Côte d'Ivoire; Cuba; Cyprus; Czech and Slovak Federal Republic; Denmark; Dominican Republic; Egypt; Finland; France; Gabon; Gambia; Germany, Federal Republic of; Ghana; Greece; Guyana; Haiti; Hong Kong; Hungary; Iceland; India; Indonesia; Ireland; Israel; Italy; Jamaica; Japan; Kenya; Korea, Republic of; Kuwait; Luxembourg; Madagascar; Malawi; Malaysia; Maldives; Malta; Mauritania; Mauritius; Mexico; Morocco; Myanmar; Netherlands; New Zealand; Nicaragua; Niger; Nigeria; Norway; Pakistan; Peru; Philippines; Poland; Portugal; Romania; Rwanda; Senegal; Sierra Leone; Singapore; South Africa; Southern Rhodesia; Spain; Sri Lanka; Suriname; Sweden; Switzerland; Tanzania, United Republic of; Thailand; Togo; Trinidad and Tobago; Turkey; Uganda; United Kingdom of Great Britain and Northern Ireland; United States of America; Uruguay; Yugoslavia; Zaire; Zambia

Editors' Note

The General Agreement on Tariffs and Trade (GATT), which is applied "provisionally" by all members, was negotiated after World War II in an effort to establish rules of international trade in order to reduce tariffs and prevent the erection of protective trade barriers. GATT has been amended several times. *See* The Text of the General Agreement on Tariffs and Trade (GATT 1986). GATT member States account for approximately four-fifths of total world trade. In addition to the parties to GATT, approximately 30 other countries apply it in practice. The primary obligation in GATT is to provide, generally speaking, most-favored-nation treatment to all member States regarding concessions and restrictions on the flow of imports and exports, such as customs duties and administrative rules and procedures. That general principle of nondiscrimination is subject to exceptions, but they have not completely swallowed the basic obligation. Multilateral negotiations pursuant to GATT have resulted in lower world tariffs, but nontariff barriers (NTBs) have arisen that restrict international trade. GATT article XX provides that certain types of environmental controls do not constitute impermissible NTBs. It is expected that the role of environmental regulation in affecting world trade will receive increased attention.

Article XX was applied by a GATT panel in *Canada-Measures Affecting Exports of Unprocessed Herring and Salmon*, L/6268 (22 March 1988).

GENERAL AGREEMENT ON TARIFFS AND TRADE

* * *

Article XX
General Exceptions

Subject to the requirement that such measures are not applied in a manner which would constitute a means of arbitrary or unjustifiable discrimination between countries where the same conditions prevail, or a disguised restriction on international trade, nothing in this Agreement shall be construed to prevent the adoption or enforcement by any contracting party of measures:
  I.

* * *

  (*b*)   necessary to protect human, animal or plant life or health;
* * *
  (*f*)   imposed for the protection of national treasures of artistic, historic or archaeological value;
  (*g*)   relating to the conservation of exhaustible natural resources if such measures are made effective in conjunction with restrictions on domestic production or consumption;
* * *

WASHINGTON CONVENTION ON INTERNATIONAL TRADE IN ENDANGERED SPECIES OF WILD FAUNA AND FLORA. *Supra*, p. 466.

CANADA-UNITED STATES FREE TRADE AGREEMENT

Popular Name: Canada-U.S. FTA

Done at Ottawa on 22 December 1987 and 2 January 1988, and at Washington, D.C. and Palm Springs, 23 December 1987 and 2 January 1988, *reprinted in* 27 ILM 281 (1988).

Entry into Force: 2 January 1988

Languages: English, French

Editors' Note

The Canada-United States Free Trade Agreement (FTA) eliminates many barriers to trade between the countries. It prohibits, *inter alia*, federal technical standards for goods, processes, or production methods that would create "unnecessary obstacles" to trade between the two countries. The FTA provides that requirements whose demonstrable purpose is to protect the environment do not constitute such obstacles. The two countries are required to take steps to make their standards compatible. Section 1201 of the FTA also incorporates by reference article XX of the GATT, *supra* p. 714, as does article 7 of the Free Trade Area Agreement between the United States and Israel, 22 April 1985, *reprinted in* 24 ILM 653 (1986). The FTA contains far-reaching provisions for resolving disputes. Section 1201 was applied by an FTA Panel in *Canada's Landing Requirement for Pacific Coast Salmon and Herring* (16 October 1989).

CANADA-UNITED STATES FREE TRADE AGREEMENT

Chapter Six
Technical Standards

Article 601: Scope

1. The provisions of this Chapter shall apply to technical standards related to goods other than agricultural, food, beverage and certain related goods as defined in Chapter Seven (Agriculture).
2. The provisions of this Chapter shall not apply to any measure of a provincial or state government. Accordingly, the Parties need not ensure the observance of these provisions by state or provincial governments.

Article 602: Affirmation of GATT Agreement

The Parties affirm their respective rights and obligations under the GATT *Agreement on Technical Barriers to Trade*.

Article 603: No Disguised Barriers to Trade

Neither Party shall maintain or introduce standards-related measures or procedures for product approval that would create unnecessary obstacles to trade between the territories of the Parties. Unnecessary obstacles to trade shall not be deemed to be created if:
    a)   the demonstrable purpose of such measure or procedure is to achieve a legitimate domestic objective; and
    b)   the measure or procedure does not operate to exclude goods of the other Party that meet that legitimate domestic objective.
* * *

Article 607: Information Exchange

1. Each Party shall promptly provide the other Party with full texts of proposed federal government standards-related measures and product approval procedures

published in official journals in sufficient time to provide persons of the other Party with at least 60 days to develop comments and discuss them with the appropriate regulating authority prior to submitting the comments.

2. Either Party may, in urgent circumstances where delay would frustrate the achievement of a legitimate domestic objective, proceed without prior provision of a text under paragraph 1. In such instances, the texts shall be provided expeditiously after issuance in final form.

3. Where feasible, each Party shall:

    a)   notify the other Party of proposed standards-related measures of state and provincial authorities that may significantly affect bilateral trade; if such notice cannot be provided in advance, it should be provided as expeditiously as possible;

    b)   provide a full text of such proposed state and provincial standards-related measures;

    c)   take such reasonable steps as may be available to it to provide persons of the other Party with information that would facilitate their provision of comments to, and discussions of comments with, appropriate state or provincial authorities; and

    d)   take such reasonable steps as may be available to it to notify the other Party of standards-related measures of major national private organizations.

* * *

Article 609: Definitions

For purposes of this Chapter:

* * *

legitimate domestic objective means an objective whose purpose is to protect health, safety, essential security, the environment, or consumer interests;

* * *

Chapter Twelve
Exceptions for Trade in Goods

Article 1201: GATT Exceptions

Subject to the provisions of Articles 409 and 904, the provisions of Article XX of the *General Agreement on Tariffs and Trade* (GATT) are incorporated into and made a part of this Part of this Agreement.

WASHINGTON CONVENTION ON NATURE PROTECTION AND WILDLIFE PRESERVATION IN THE WESTERN HEMISPHERE. *Supra,* p. 211.

BASEL CONVENTION ON THE CONTROL OF TRANSBOUNDARY MOVEMENTS OF HAZARDOUS WASTES AND THEIR DISPOSAL. *Supra,* p. 601.

CANADA-UNITED STATES: AGREEMENT BETWEEN THE UNITED STATES AND CANADA CONCERNING THE TRANSBOUNDARY MOVEMENT OF HAZARDOUS WASTE. *Supra*, p. 616.

MEXICO-UNITED STATES: AGREEMENT FOR COOPERATION ON ENVIRONMENTAL PROGRAMS AND TRANSBOUNDARY PROBLEMS, ANNEX III, TRANSBOUNDARY SHIPMENT OF HAZARDOUS WASTES AND HAZARDOUS SUBSTANCES. *Supra*, p. 621.

INTERNATIONAL ATOMIC ENERGY AGENCY CODE OF PRACTICE ON THE INTERNATIONAL MOVEMENT OF RADIOACTIVE WASTE. *Supra*, p. 597.

UNITED NATIONS ENVIRONMENT PROGRAMME GOVERNING COUNCIL DECISION: LONDON GUIDELINES FOR THE EXCHANGE OF INFORMATION ON CHEMICALS IN INTERNATIONAL TRADE. *Supra*, p. 644.

CHAPTER 28
ESTABLISHMENT OF AN ORGANIZATION OR ORGAN

A. SPECIFICALLY ENVIRONMENTAL

UNITED NATIONS GENERAL ASSEMBLY RESOLUTION: INSTITUTIONAL AND FINANCIAL ARRANGEMENTS FOR INTERNATIONAL ENVIRONMENTAL CO-OPERATION [DEFINING THE CONSTITUTIVE ELEMENTS OF THE UNITED NATIONS ENVIRONMENT PROGRAMME (UNEP)]

Popular Name: UNEP Statute

Adopted by the United Nations General Assembly on 15 December 1972, G.A. Res. 2997 (XXVII).

Languages: Arabic, Chinese, English, French, Russian, Spanish

Editors' Note

As mentioned in the Editors' Note relating to the Stockholm Declaration (*supra* p. 171), the 1972 Stockholm Conference adopted, *inter alia*, a detailed resolution on institutional and financial arrangements. At its regular session later that year, the General Assembly, in considering the report of the Conference and the report of the U.N. Secretary-General thereon (A/8783 and /Adds. 1-2), adopted a resolution (A/RES/2997(XXVII) of 15 December 1972) enacting, with some slight amendments, the arrangements proposed by the Conference. That resolution has, in effect, become the Statute of the United Nations Environment Programme (UNEP). Four years later the Assembly reviewed and reaffirmed these institutional arrangements (A/RES/31/111 of 16 December 1976).

Although the 1972 resolution does not explicitly establish an organ designated as UNEP, by part I the Assembly established the Governing Council of the Programme and by parts II-IV it called respectively for the establishment of an Environment Secretariat headed by the Executive Director of UNEP, of a voluntary Environment Fund, and of an Environment Co-ordination Board under the auspices of the Administrative Committee on Co-ordination (ACC) of the U.N. System. By a separate resolution (A/RES/3004(XXVII)) adopted at the same meeting, the Assembly decided that the Environment Secretariat be located in Nairobi, which has thus also become the seat of the Environment Fund and the normal meeting place of the UNEP Governing Council. The Co-ordination Board, however, which was established and functioned for some years, was later replaced by ACC by the Inter-Agency Board of Designated Officials for Environmental Matters (DOEM) in which over a dozen U.N. organs and some eight specialized and related agencies participate.

INSTITUTIONAL AND FINANCIAL ARRANGEMENTS FOR INTERNATIONAL ENVIRONMENTAL CO-OPERATION

The General Assembly,

Convinced of the need for prompt and effective implementation by Governments and the international community of measures designed to safeguard and enhance the environment for the benefit of present and future generations of man,

Recognizing that responsibility for action to protect and enhance the environment rests primarily with Governments and, in the first instance, can be exercised more effectively at the national and regional levels,

Recognizing further that environmental problems of broad international significance fall within the competence of the United Nations system,

Bearing in mind that international co-operative programmes in the field of the environment must be undertaken with due respect for the sovereign rights of States and in conformity with the Charter of the United Nations and principles of international law,

Mindful of the sectoral responsibilities of the organizations in the United Nations system,

Conscious of the significance of regional and sub-regional co-operation in the field of the environment and of the important role of the regional economic commissions and other regional intergovernmental organizations,

Emphasizing that problems of the environment constitute a new and important area for international co-operation and that the complexity and interdependence of such problems require new approaches,

Recognizing that the relevant international scientific and other professional communities can make an important contribution to international co-operation in the field of the environment,

Conscious of the need for processes within the United Nations system which would effectively assist developing countries to implement environmental policies and programmes that are compatible with their development plans and to participate meaningfully in international environmental programmes,

Convinced that, in order to be effective, international co-operation in the field of the environment requires additional financial and technical resources,

Aware of the urgent need for a permanent institutional arrangement within the United Nations system for the protection and improvement of the environment,

Taking note of the report of the Secretary-General on the United Nations Conference on the Human Environment.[a]

I
Governing Council of the United Nations Environment Programme

1. *Decides* to establish a Governing Council of the United Nations Environment Programme, composed of fifty-eight members elected by the General Assembly for three-year terms on the following basis:

---

[a]A/8783 and Add.1, Add.1/Corr.1 and Add.2.

(a) Sixteen seats for African States;
(b) Thirteen seats for Asian States;
(c) Six seats for Eastern European States;
(d) Ten seats for Latin American States;
(e) Thirteen seats for Western European and other States.

2. *Decides* that the Governing Council shall have the following main functions and responsibilities:

(a) To promote international co-operation in the field of the environment and to recommend, as appropriate, policies to this end;
(b) To provide general policy guidance for the direction and co-ordination of environmental programmes within the United Nations system;
(c) To receive and review the periodic reports of the Executive Director of the United Nations Environment Programme, referred to in section II, paragraph 2, below, on the implementation of environmental programmes within the United Nations system;
(d) To keep under review the world environmental situation in order to ensure that emerging environmental problems of wide international significance receive appropriate and adequate consideration by Governments;
(e) To promote the contribution of the relevant international scientific and other professional communities to the acquisition, assessment and exchange of environmental knowledge and information and, as appropriate, to the technical aspects of the formulation and implementation of environmental programmes within the United Nations system;
(f) To maintain under continuing review the impact of national and international environmental policies and measures on developing countries, as well as the problem of additional costs that may be incurred by developing countries in the implementation of environmental programmes and projects, and to ensure that such programmes and projects shall be compatible with the development plans and priorities of those countries;
(g) To review and approve annually the programme of utilization of resources of the Environment Fund referred to in section III below;

3. *Decides* that the Governing Council shall report annually to the General Assembly through the Economic and Social Council, which will transmit to the Assembly such comments on the reports as it may deem necessary, particularly with regard to questions of co-ordination and to the relationship of environmental policies and programmes within the United Nations system to overall economic and social policies and priorities;

II
Environment Secretariat

1. *Decides* that a small secretariat shall be established in the United Nations to serve as a focal point for environmental action and co-ordination within the United Nations system in such a way as to ensure a high degree of effective management;

2. *Decides* that the environment secretariat shall be headed by the Executive Director of the United Nations Environment Programme, who shall be elected by the General Assembly on the nomination of the Secretary-General for a term of four years and who shall be entrusted, *inter alia*, with the following responsibilities:

(a) To provide substantive support to the Governing Council of the United Nations Environment Programme;
(b) To co-ordinate, under the guidance of the Governing Council, environmental programmes within the United Nations system, to keep their implementation under review and to assess their effectiveness;

(c)   To advise, as appropriate and under the guidance of the Governing Coun-
        cil, intergovernmental bodies of the United Nations system on the formu-
        lation and implementation of environmental programmes;
(d)   To secure the effective co-operation of, and contribution from, the rele-
        vant scientific and other professional communities in all parts of the
        world;
(e)   To provide, at the request of all parties concerned, advisory services for
        the promotion of international co-operation in the field of the envi-
        ronment;
(f)   To submit to the Governing Council, on his own initiative or upon re-
        quest, proposals embodying medium-range and long-range planning for
        United Nations programmes in the field of the environment;
(g)   To bring to the attention of the Governing Council any matter which he
        deems to require consideration by it;
(h)   To administer, under the authority and policy guidance of the Governing
        Council, the Environment Fund referred to in section III below;
(i)   To report on environmental matters to the Governing Council;
(j)   To perform such other functions as may be entrusted to him by the
        Governing Council;

3. *Decides* that the costs of servicing the Governing Council and providing the
small secretariat referred to in paragraph 1 above shall be borne by the regular
budget of the United Nations and that operational programme costs, programme
support and administrative costs of the Environment Fund established under section
III below shall be borne by the Fund;

III
Environment Fund

1. *Decides* that, in order to provide for additional financing for environmental
programmes, a voluntary fund shall be established, with effect from 1 January
1973, in accordance with existing United Nations financial procedures;
2. *Decides* that, in order to enable the Governing Council of the United Nations
Environment Programme to fulfil its policy-guidance role for the direction and co-
ordination of environmental activities, the Environment Fund shall finance wholly
or partly the costs of the new environmental initiatives undertaken within the United
Nations system—which will include the initiatives envisaged in the Action Plan for
the Human Environment[b] adopted by the United Nations Conference on the Human
Environment, with particular attention to integrated projects, and such other environmental activities as may be decided upon by the Governing Council—and that the
Governing Council shall review these initiatives with a view to taking appropriate
decisions as to their continued financing;
3. *Decides* that the Environment Fund shall be used for financing such programmes
of general interest as regional and global monitoring, assessment and data-collecting
systems, including, as appropriate, costs for national counterparts; the improvement
of environmental quality management; environmental research; information exchange and dissemination; public education and training; assistance for national,
regional and global environmental institutions; the promotion of environmental
research and studies for the development of industrial and other technologies best
suited to a policy of economic growth compatible with adequate environmental
safeguards; and such other programmes as the Governing Council may decide upon,

---

[b]A/CONF.48/14 and Corr. 1, chap. II.

and that in the implementation of such programmes due account should be taken of the special needs of the developing countries;

4. *Decides* that, in order to ensure that the development priorities of developing countries shall not be adversely affected, adequate measures shall be taken to provide additional financial resources on terms compatible with the economic situation of the recipient developing country, and that, to this end, the Executive Director, in co-operation with competent organizations, shall keep this problem under continuing review;

5. *Decides* that the Environment Fund, in pursuance of the objectives stated in paragraphs 2 and 3 above, shall be directed to the need for effective co-ordination in the implementation of international environmental programmes of the organizations in the United Nations system and other international organizations;

6. *Decides* that, in the implementation of programmes to be financed by the Environment Fund, organizations outside the United Nations system, particularly those in the countries and regions concerned, shall also be utilized as appropriate, in accordance with the procedures established by the Governing Council, and that such organizations are invited to support the United Nations environmental programmes by complementary initiatives and contributions;

7. *Decides* that the Governing Council shall formulate such general procedures as are necessary to govern the operations of the Environment Fund;

IV
Environment Co-Ordination Board

1. *Decides* that, in order to provide for the most efficient co-ordination of United Nations environmental programmes, an Environment Co-ordination Board, under the chairmanship of the Executive Director of the United Nations Environment Programme, shall be established under the auspices and within the framework of the Administrative Committee on Co-ordination;

2. *Further decides* that the Environment Co-ordination Board shall meet periodically for the purpose of ensuring co-operation and co-ordination among all bodies concerned in the implementation of environmental programmes and that it shall report annually to the Governing Council of the United Nations Environment Programme;

3. *Invites* the organizations of the United Nations system to adopt the measures that may be required to undertake concerted and co-ordinated programmes with regard to international environmental problems, taking into account existing procedures for prior consultation, particularly on programme and budgetary matters;

4. *Invites* the regional economic commissions and the United Nations Economic and Social Office at Beirut, in co-operation where necessary with other appropriate regional bodies, to intensify further their efforts directed towards contributing to the implementation of environmental programmes in view of the particular need for the rapid development of regional co-operation in this field;

5. *Also invites* other intergovernmental and those non-governmental organizations that have an interest in the field of the environment to lend their full support and collaboration to the United Nations with a view to achieving the largest possible degree of co-operation and co-ordination;

6. *Calls upon* Governments to ensure that appropriate national institutions shall be entrusted with the task of the co-ordination of environmental action, both national and international;

7. *Decides* to review as appropriate, at its thirty-first session, the above institutional arrangements, bearing in mind, *inter alia*, the responsibilities of the Economic and Social Council under the Charter of United Nations.

BERNE CONVENTION ON THE INTERNATIONAL COMMISSION FOR THE PROTECTION OF THE RHINE AGAINST POLLUTION. *Supra*, p. 438.

UNITED NATIONS EDUCATIONAL, SCIENTIFIC AND CULTURAL ORGANIZATION CONVENTION FOR THE PROTECTION OF THE WORLD CULTURAL AND NATURAL HERITAGE. *Supra*, p. 554.

PROTOCOL ON ENVIRONMENTAL PROTECTION TO THE ANTARCTIC TREATY. *Supra*, p. 536.

B. WITH SOME ENVIRONMENTAL FUNCTIONS

EUROPEAN ECONOMIC COMMUNITY SINGLE EUROPEAN ACT. *Supra*, p. 232.

GENERAL AGREEMENT ON TARIFFS AND TRADE. *Supra*, p. 714.

CHAPTER 29
SPECIAL AREA MANAGEMENT

Editors' Introductory Note Regarding Special Area Management

It is increasingly common to impose additional restrictions on activities in particularly sensitive or important parts—sometimes referred to as "special areas"—of an area already covered by an international regime. For example, there are several instances of special area management regarding marine areas of recognized significance due to their biological, geological, cultural, or historical significance. Examples include Regulations 1 and 5 of Annex V to MARPOL 73/78 and article 211 of the Law of the Sea Convention.

LONDON INTERNATIONAL CONVENTION FOR THE PREVENTION OF POLLUTION FROM SHIPS, 1973, AS MODIFIED BY THE PROTOCOL OF 1978 RELATING THERETO (MARPOL 73/78), ANNEX V: REGULATIONS FOR THE PREVENTION OF POLLUTION BY GARBAGE FROM SHIPS. *Supra*, p. 327.

UNITED NATIONS CONVENTION ON THE LAW OF THE SEA. *Supra*, p. 332.

RAMSAR CONVENTION ON WETLANDS OF INTERNATIONAL IMPORTANCE ESPECIALLY AS WATERFOWL HABITAT. *Supra*, p. 497.

CANBERRA CONVENTION ON THE CONSERVATION OF ANTARCTIC MARINE LIVING RESOURCES. *Supra*, p. 520.

PROTOCOL ON ENVIRONMENTAL PROTECTION TO THE ANTARCTIC TREATY. *Supra*, p. 536.

UNITED NATIONS EDUCATIONAL, SCIENTIFIC AND CULTURAL ORGANIZATION CONVENTION FOR THE PROTECTION OF THE WORLD CULTURAL AND NATURAL HERITAGE. *Supra,* p. 554.

WASHINGTON CONVENTION ON NATURE PROTECTION AND WILDLIFE PRESERVATION IN THE WESTERN HEMISPHERE. *Supra,* p. 211.

GENEVA PROTOCOL CONCERNING MEDITERRANEAN SPECIALLY PROTECTED AREAS. *Supra,* p. 389.

CHAPTER 30
DEVELOPMENT ASSISTANCE

MULTILATERAL DEVELOPMENT BANKS DECLARATION ON ENVIRONMENTAL POLICIES AND PROCEDURES RELATING TO ECONOMIC DEVELOPMENT

Popular Name: MDB Declaration

Adopted at New York on 1 February 1980, *reprinted in* 19 ILM 524 (1980), IPE(2) I/B/01-02-80.

Language: English

Editors' Note

The principal multilateral development banks adopted the following declaration in response to public controversy about the role of such institutions in sponsoring projects that arguably had deleterious environmental impacts. Other international-assistance organizations, such as the United States Agency for International Development (AID), 22 C.F.R. § 216 (1990), and the Overseas Private Investment Corporation (OPIC), *see* Pub. L. No. 99-204 (1985), 22 U.S.C. § 239(g), now require environmental impact assessments before projects may be funded. The World Bank issued its first annual report on the environment—*The World Bank and the Environment*—in 1990.

DECLARATION OF ENVIRONMENTAL POLICIES AND PROCEDURES RELATING TO ECONOMIC DEVELOPMENT

WHEREAS, economic and social development is essential to the alleviation of major environmental problems by providing for an integral relationship between societies and their environment, realizing also that economic development and social goals should be pursued in such a manner as to avoid or minimize environmental problems peculiar to it,

RECOGNIZING THAT, the major environmental problems of the developing countries are not necessarily of the same nature as those of developed countries in that they are problems which often reflect the impacts of poverty which not only affects the quality of life but life itself,

CONVINCED, that in the long run environmental protection and economic and social development are not only compatible but interdependent and mutually reinforcing,

ACKNOWLEDGING, that the need for environmentally sensitive and responsible development has become more important and urgent in light of increasing population and concomitant pressures on the earth's resources and life-supporting ecological systems in some areas,

727

ACKNOWLEDGING, the sovereign right of governments to determine their own priorities and development patterns,

RECALLING, that the states which adopted the declaration of the United Nations Conference on the Human Environment (Stockholm, 1972) stated their common conviction (Principle 25) that they will ensure that the international organizations play a co-ordinated, efficient and dynamic role in the protection and improvement of the environment,

CONSIDERING, furthermore, that international development assistance institutions have, along with their member governments, a responsibility to ensure the sustainability of the economic development activities financed by them,

THEREFORE, the undersigned declared that they:

I. *REAFFIRM* their support for the principles and recommendations for action of the United Nations conference

II. *WILL*, to the best of their abilities, endeavour to:

1. *INSTITUTE* procedures for systematic examination of all development activities, including policies, programmes and projects, under consideration for financing to ensure that appropriate measures are proposed for compliance with Section I above;

2. *ENTER* into co-operative negotiations with governments and relevant international organizations and agencies, to ensure integration of appropriate environmental measures in the design and implementation of economic development activities;

3. *PROVIDE* technical assistance, including training, on environmental matters to developing countries, at their request, thus developing their indigenous capacity, and facilitating technical co-operation between developing countries;

4. *GIVE* active consideration and, if appropriate, support project proposals that are specially designed to protect, rehabilitate, manage or otherwise enhance the human environment, the quality of life, and resources thereto related;

5. *INITIATE* and/or otherwise co-operate in research and studies leading to improvement of project appraisal, implementation and evaluation methodologies, including cost-benefit analysis of environmental protection measures;

6. *SUPPORT* the training and informing of operational staff in the environmental dimension of economic development;

7. *PREPARE*, publish and disseminate documentation and audio-visual material providing guidance on the environmental dimension of economic development activities.

ADOPTED AT NEW YORK ON 1 FEBRUARY 1980

THE AFRICAN DEVELOPMENT BANK
* * *

THE ARAB BANK FOR ECONOMIC DEVELOPMENT IN AFRICA
* * *

THE ASIAN DEVELOPMENT BANK
* * *

THE CARIBBEAN DEVELOPMENT BANK
* * *

THE INTER-AMERICAN DEVELOPMENT BANK
* * *

THE WORLD BANK
* * *

THE COMMISSION OF THE EUROPEAN COMMUNITIES
* * *

THE ORGANIZATION OF AMERICAN STATES
* * *

THE UNITED NATIONS DEVELOPMENT PROGRAMME
* * *
THE UNITED NATIONS ENVIRONMENT PROGRAMME
* * *

CHAPTER 31
POLLUTION RESTRICTIONS

A. PROHIBITIONS

RESTATEMENT (THIRD) OF THE FOREIGN RELATIONS LAW OF THE UNITED STATES. *Supra*, p. 354.

TREATY BANNING NUCLEAR WEAPONS TESTS IN THE ATMOSPHERE, IN OUTER SPACE AND UNDER WATER. *Supra*, p. 632.

LONDON ADJUSTMENTS AND AMENDMENTS TO THE MONTREAL PROTOCOL ON SUBSTANCES THAT DEPLETE THE OZONE LAYER; AND NON-COMPLIANCE PROCEDURE. *Supra*, p. 298.

INTERNATIONAL MARITIME ORGANIZATION CONVENTION ON THE PREVENTION OF MARINE POLLUTION BY DUMPING OF WASTES AND OTHER MATTER. *Supra*, p. 318.

ANNEX V, REGULATIONS FOR THE PREVENTION OF POLLUTION BY GARBAGE FROM SHIPS. *Supra*, p. 327.

UNITED NATIONS CONVENTION ON THE LAW OF THE SEA. *Supra*, p. 332.

PARIS CONVENTION FOR THE PREVENTION OF MARINE POLLUTION FROM LAND-BASED SOURCES. *Supra*, p. 360.

Editors' Introductory Note Regarding the Mediterranean Sea. *Supra*, p. 370

BARCELONA CONVENTION FOR THE PROTECTION OF THE MEDITERRANEAN SEA AGAINST POLLUTION. *Supra*, p. 370.

BARCELONA PROTOCOL FOR THE PREVENTION OF POLLUTION OF THE MEDITERRANEAN SEA BY DUMPING FROM SHIPS AND AIRCRAFT. *Supra*, p. 377.

ATHENS PROTOCOL FOR THE PROTECTION OF THE MEDITERRANEAN SEA AGAINST POLLUTION FROM LAND-BASED SOURCES. *Supra*, p. 384.

Editors' Introductory Note Regarding the International Law Associations Helsinki and Seoul Rules. *Supra*, p. 395

INTERNATIONAL LAW ASSOCIATION HELSINKI RULES ON THE USES OF THE WATERS OF INTERNATIONAL RIVERS. *Supra*, p. 395.

INTERNATIONAL LAW ASSOCIATION SEOUL RULES ON INTERNATIONAL GROUNDWATERS. *Supra*, p. 403.

CANADA-UNITED STATES OF AMERICA: WASHINGTON TREATY RELATING TO BOUNDARY WATERS AND QUESTIONS ARISING ALONG THE BOUNDARY BETWEEN THE UNITED STATES AND CANADA. *Supra*, p. 412.

UNITED NATIONS INTERNATIONAL LAW COMMISSION DRAFT ARITICLES ON THE LAW OF THE NON-NAVIGATIONAL USES OF INTERNATIONAL WATERCOURSES. *Supra*, p. 404.

ECONOMIC COMMISSION FOR EUROPE DECLARATION OF POLICY ON PREVENTION AND CONTROL OF WATER POLLUTION, INCLUDING TRANSBOUNDARY POLLUTION. *Supra*, p. 433.

BONN CONVENTION FOR THE PROTECTION OF THE RHINE RIVER AGAINST CHEMICAL POLLUTION. *Supra*, p. 442.

CANADA-UNITED STATES OF AMERICA: GREAT LAKES WATER QUALITY AGREEMENT. *Supra*, p. 419.

B. LIMITATIONS

Editors' Introductory Note Regarding the 1979 Convention on Long-Range Transboundary Air Pollution and Related Instruments. *Supra*, p. 249.

ECONOMIC COMMISSION FOR EUROPE CONVENTION ON LONG-RANGE TRANSBOUNDARY AIR POLLUTION. *Supra*, p. 250.

HELSINKI PROTOCOL ON THE REDUCTION OF SULPHER EMISSIONS OR THEIR TRANSBOUNDARY FLUXES BY AT LEAST 30 PERCENT. *Supra*, p. 256.

SOFIA PROTOCOL CONCERNING THE CONTROL OF EMISSIONS OF NITROGEN OXIDES OR THEIR TRANSBOUNDARY FLUXES. *Supra*, p. 259.

Editors' Introductory Note Regarding Protection of the Ozone Layer. *Supra*, p. 274.

VIENNA CONVENTION FOR THE PROTECTION OF THE OZONE LAYER. *Supra*, p. 276.

MONTREAL PROTOCOL ON SUBSTANCES THAT DEPLETE THE OZONE LAYER. *Supra*, p. 289.

LONDON ADJUSTMENTS AND AMENDMENTS TO THE MONTREAL PROTOCOL ON SUBSTANCES THAT DEPLETE THE OZONE LAYER; AND NON-COMPLIANCE PROCEDURE. *Supra*, p. 298.

ANNEX V, REGULATIONS FOR THE PREVENTION OF POLLUTION BY GARBAGE FROM SHIPS. *Supra*, p. 327.

PARIS CONVENTION FOR THE PREVENTION OF MARINE POLLUTION FROM LAND-BASED SOURCES. *Supra*, p. 360.

BONN CONVENTION FOR THE PROTECTION OF THE RHINE RIVER AGAINST CHEMICAL POLLUTION. *Supra*, p. 442.

BONN CONVENTION FOR THE PROTECTION OF THE RHINE RIVER AGAINST POLLUTION BY CHLORIDES. *Supra*, p. 450.

CANADA-UNITED STATES OF AMERICA: GREAT LAKES WATER QUALITY AGREEMENT. *Supra*, p. 419.

CANADA-UNITED STATES OF AMERICA: OTTAWA AGREEMENT ON AIR QUALITY. *Supra*, p. 263.

CHAPTER 32
PENALTIES

A. CIVIL AND ADMINISTRATIVE

PARIS CONVENTION FOR THE PREVENTION OF MARINE POLLUTION FROM LAND-BASED SOURCES. *Supra*, p. 360.

B. CRIMINAL

PARIS CONVENTION FOR THE PREVENTION OF MARINE POLLUTION FROM LAND-BASED SOURCES. *Supra*, p. 669.

UNITED NATIONS INTERNATIONAL LAW COMMISSION DRAFT ARTICLES ON STATE RESPONSIBILITY. *Supra*, p. 202.

CHAPTER 33
EDUCATION

INDEX OF POPULAR NAMES

(Page references are to reproductions in this book. Page references are not provided to the list of References.)